Corrective Reading

Fifth Edition

Miles V. Zintz
University of New Mexico

Zelda R. Maggart
University of New Mexico

wcb
Wm. C. Brown Publishers
Dubuque, IA

Reviewers

Thompson Moffitt
Central Michigan University

J. Douglas Cawley
Metropolitan State College—Denver

Cover Photo: by Bob Coyle

Copyright © 1966, 1972, 1977, 1981, 1986 by Wm. C. Brown Company Publishers. All rights reserved

Library of Congress Catalog Card Number: 85–73052

ISBN 0–697–00774–X

Printed in the United States of America
10   9   8   7   6   5   4

*To Mary Hatley Zintz
and Harley B. Maggart*

Contents

Appendices   441

Preface

Reading is a major source of learning in today's society. Yet thousands of children are denied the opportunities to learn from print because they failed to master the process of reading. Instead they develop negative attitudes toward themselves and their own capabilities as well as toward books, teachers, reading, and schools. It is of critical importance that teachers learn as much about the teaching of reading as possible. It is equally important that they learn how to help those students who have yet to experience success with the task. No group of children is immune to reading difficulties, but children who are poor, hungry, neglected, or abused; children who speak little or no English; and children of the unemployed, the migrant workers, the isolated, rural communities, and shattered families are far more vulnerable to reading failure than others. It is toward helping teachers respond to both the cognitive and affective needs of their students, whomever they may be, that *Corrective Reading* is oriented.

Philosophical Orientation

Corrective Reading is organized to promote the diagnostic teaching of reading. Teachers are encouraged to view boys and girls realistically and to accept all their differences in outlook, achievement, interest, and ability. The text is oriented to the instructional model of preassessment, teaching, and postassessment for students at any achievement level.

The writers assume an awareness that reading is only one of the skills of communication and that oral language must be extended and enriched to make reading meaningful. The language-experience approach—"writing" books from the students' own verbalized stories—is a very logical way to move from the spoken to the written word. The first experiences with books may best come through wordless picture books; predictable books; and high-interest, low-vocabulary titles.

For many underachievers, writing is very difficult. To encourage them to write, teachers must look first at the story content and accept their work without criticism of misspellings, poor organization, and "bad" grammar. Teachers should also provide models for the children by being active writers and readers themselves. This text emphasizes such an approach.

Textbook Organization

The fifth edition of *Corrective Reading* has been prepared to address many of the problems teachers face in providing reading instruction for the poor readers in their classrooms. In Chapters 1 and 2 teachers will find a general overview of reading as one of the communication skills necessary for all children. Discussions of the nature of the reading process, methods of teaching reading, the humanistic side of learning, and mainstreaming to accommodate exceptional children in the classroom are included in these chapters. Regular classroom teachers can provide learning environments to accommodate in constructive ways all of the individual differences in the class—intellectual, linguistic, social, emotional, physical, and psychological.

Suggestions for working diagnostically with several of the better-known word lists and on the development of an understanding of print as a medium are provided in Chapter 3. The need of teachers to be able to diagnose their students' strengths and areas for growth in reading is addressed in Chapters 4, 5, and 6. The topic of Chapter 4 is the informal reading inventory, its construction, administration, scoring, and interpretation. Updated information about standardized tests, including a discussion of the terminology used in reporting student performance in a statistical frame of reference, is provided in Chapter 5. Teachers will find discussions and examples of a wide variety of informal ways to diagnose reading difficulties, including measuring intelligence; using interviews, inventories, and anecdotal records; obtaining oral language data; and working with sociograms and bibliotherapy, in Chapter 6.

Managing the classroom so that there is time for corrective reading instruction for those children who require it is addressed in Chapters 7 and 8. Detailed information about teaching word recognition and comprehension is given in Chapters 9 and 10. Chapter 11 on study skills and reading in the content fields has been added in this edition. Children who have reading difficulties must also study mathematics, social studies, and science; consult reference books; make use of libraries; and obtain and organize information. Chapter 11 is intended as a source of help for teachers as they work to improve the learning experiences of reading disabled children in these areas.

The frequently ignored topic of the attitudes teachers hold toward children who have difficulty in learning to read is discussed in Chapter 12. This important chapter should stand as a reminder that little will be gained cognitively in learning to read unless the affective domain is properly considered. Chapter 13 addresses the need for teachers and parents to work cooperatively. It is becoming increasingly clear that success in learning to read is influenced by the community and family in which the child lives. The greatest progress will occur when there is ongoing, two-way communication between teachers and parents about the successes and problems children experience in learning to read.

Chapter 14 explores the needs of the linguistically and culturally different children. New information about the limited English proficiency child is included in this chapter. Chapter 15 includes information from the previous edition on helping children with the most serious reading problems, while a variety of new methods and techniques for teaching these youngsters has been added.

This text includes six appendixes. Appendixes A and C are composed of lists of references and reading tests that teachers may find helpful. An extensive annotated bibliography of high-interest, low-vocabulary books for disabled readers is included in Appendix B. Details about teaching the directed reading lesson are given in Appendix D. A sample informal reading inventory (IRI) may be found in Appendix E. It is hoped that this sample will suggest ways for teachers to develop their own IRIs, uniquely suited to their students' interests and needs. A sample home information blank is given in Appendix F as a suggested means of gathering useful information about students who need corrective instruction.

Use of the Book

Corrective Reading is appropriate for undergraduate students. Many classroom teachers have recognized the practical nature of the text. Of course no teacher, unaided, can solve all the problems of reading failure, so one must always be aware of special resources when they are needed. Because the emphasis in this text is *corrective,* not clinical, it is not research oriented and does not ask teachers to administer tests that require technical skills that they do not possess.

Miles V. Zintz
Zelda R. Maggart

Corrective
Reading

1
An Overview of the Reading Process

Vocabulary

feedback
reading readiness
Predicting Reading Failure
Concepts about Print Test
method
approach
basal reader
phonics
skills
affective learning

Questions

1. How do *you* define reading? How does your definition compare with the definition and description of reading in the chapter?

2. Describe the three methods of teaching reading. What approaches are derived from these methods?

3. What is important about each of the four jobs of teaching reading?

4. Describe the stages in moving children to independence in reading.

5. What aspects of the affective side of learning are important in the teaching of reading?

6. What criteria would one look for to describe a good reading program?

What Is Reading?

Basically, reading is a thinking process. It requires some kind of response on the part of the reader. If people utilize the reading they do, they can make different generalizations, draw new inferences, and plan new next steps on the basis of it.

Reading can provide excellent vicarious experiences. Most teaching requires that teachers utilize vicarious experiences to open new vistas to children who cannot experience them firsthand. Contrariwise, reading depends on experience. Words are meaningful only as one comes to know them through experience. If a word is new or unknown, one must find synonyms, or associative words, to clarify meanings.

Gray identified four different steps in the reading act: *word perception, comprehension, reaction,* and *integration.* The first step is word recognition, including both the ability to pronounce the word and to attach meaning to it as a concept. The second step is the ability to make individual words construct useful ideas as they are read in context. The third step requires judgmental action—a feeling about what the author has said. The final step is the crucial one: the ability to assimilate this idea, concept, new reading, into the background of experience so that it becomes a part of the total experience of the individual. These steps are completely interdependent in the meaningful use of reading as a tool in the solutions of problems.[1]

Ernest Horn defined reading in this way:

. . . reading includes those processes that are involved in approaching, perfecting, and maintaining meaning through the use of the printed page. Since there are many such processes, and since each one varies in degree, the term must be elastic enough to apply to all the varieties and gradations of reading involved in the use of books.[2]

He further reminded us:

The author does not really convey ideas to the reader; he merely stimulates him to construct them out of his own experience. If the concept is already in the reader's mind, the task is relatively easy, but if, as is usually the case in school, it is new to the reader, its construction more nearly approaches problem solving than simple association.[3]

Smith described reading as "a matter of making sense of written language rather than of decoding print to sound" and as marked by four basic characteristics, "that it is *purposeful, selective, anticipatory,* and based on *comprehension.*"[4]

The Nature of the Reading Process

Reading is the process by which readers bring to lines of print the necessary understanding out of their background of experience so that they can construct new concepts, reinforce old concepts, or adjust previous thinking to fit a new idea. When readers combine what the eye fleetingly tells the brain with what the brain is already telling the eye, they construct meaning, wholly or partially, so that they can extend their previous intelligence. This becomes a kind of chain reaction, since with each new reading assignment readers add to their long-term memory storage something that they can bring to their next reading assignment.

For mature readers, reading is a pleasurable activity in which they rapidly absorb ideas with which to agree or to disagree, or new thoughts to ponder. For each reader, this is an individual, unique system. Readers may process information very rapidly, rapidly, or slowly. Many constitutional factors determine ease, speed, understanding, and degree of satisfaction involved in this process.

Reading for mature readers who have already habituated all the necessary skills is a far different process than is reading for beginners who must acquire mastery of the written form of the words already common in the speaking vocabulary. For the students learning the first necessary skills, however, reading must provide for the anticipation and acquisition of meaning in context with the very first lessons. This emphasis is based on the knowledge that children of six bring to school a fully developed language and possess all the skills of thinking, reasoning, and problem solving in oral communication. Instead of supposing that the children "don't know any words," teachers must recognize that they know thousands of words but have not met most of them in written form. By using the children's personal experiences, conversations, and explanations of events, teachers can write their language. Children can see their language preserved in written form, and eventually they understand that the written message is merely an extension of the oral language they have been using for some time. Thus the language-experience approach is a very logical way to extend children's listening and speaking skills to include reading and writing.

When children read from this frame of reference, they have *three* kinds of *feedback* to help them evaluate how accurately they are anticipating meaning in the context of the printed word. First, they must make the printed word correspond to an idea or concept they already know in the language. If they say it incorrectly, they should reject it as nonsense and arrive at a new response that makes sense. Second, they will know whether their pronunciation of a printed word fits the grammar of a sentence as correctly spoken in the vernacular. If they need a noun, but supply a verb or an adjective, they should reject it because the syntax is not sensible. Third, they should continually test the appropriateness of the meaning of the sentence the way they have read it, and in relation to the context of the passage, they should reject any words that do not make sense. So their knowledge of words, grammar, and of semantic correctness provides *both* feedback about the quality of reading *and* the anticipation, to a remarkable degree, of what they are going to read next. The process then necessitates, for the novice, mediated steps in knowing what the words are in the lines of print.

Pleasurable reading depends on one's having an automatic vocabulary to draw upon in any reading situation. Word knowledge is the basis of comprehension. Independence and versatility in recognizing and using words are paramount in facile reading. Readers

---

Making Connections 1.1: What Is Happening to School Children?

Children's ability to learn to read or to progress in reading is affected by many factors outside the classroom. In many instances what happens away from school is more powerful as a determiner of achievement than what happens in school.

Find two articles from newspapers and magazines that describe events and experiences occurring in the lives of children. You are sure to find articles about poverty, child abuse and neglect, latch-key children, Little League sports, recitals, and clothing bank drives, for example. Bring your articles to class at an agreed upon time. You will find that sharing the articles with class members will make everyone more aware of the real forces impinging on children's lives.

---

need many sight words in order to recode easily into thoughts—they need a vocabulary as rich and extensive as possible to extend meanings, promote further growth, and develop permanent reading interests. A wide vocabulary increases interest in reading. Words that are colorful, descriptive, discriminating, or expressive add enjoyment to reading. A good vocabulary decreases dependence on slow, anxiety-laden analyzing of words that have been anticipated. An extensive, lucid vocabulary augments the speed of comprehension of the phrase, the sentence, or the paragraph.

The Dimensions of Reading

1. Reading is *a social process.* It is augmented by self-reliance, social acceptance, and cooperation in a group. Attitudes affect reading: loyalties, prejudices, and conflicts. Negative factors affect reading: broken homes, second-language problems, and conflicting cultural values between home and school.
2. Reading is *a psychological process.* How one feels about oneself, how one feels about others, and how others feel about one, all affect the reading process. Emotional stability, balance between egocentrism and sociocentrism determine one's comfort in the reading situation. Defense mechanisms—rationalization, repression, inhibition, introjection, projection, aggression, compensation, and nervous mannerisms—are responses to anxiety in all types of situations.
3. Reading is *a physiological process.* One must be able to focus on a line of print and move along the line, to make return sweeps, to note likenesses and differences, to discriminate figure-ground relationships. One needs skills in auditory discrimination, verbal expression, syntactical maturity, eye-hand coordination, and motor skills to execute all the mechanical skills associated with reading.

4. Reading is *a perceptual process*. It utilizes perceptual clues: size, shape, combinations of letters and sounds, figure-ground relationships, relationships of the part to the whole, sequencing, ordering.
5. Reading is *a linguistic process*. It requires mastery of phoneme-grapheme relationships, understanding of intonation, stress, pauses, and tone sequence. Reading is dependent on context meanings—grasping the idea in whole thought units. Reading requires acceptance of social variations in language: nonstandard usage, figurative language, and slang.
6. Reading is *an intellectual process*. It is dependent on vocabulary, verbal reasoning, perceiving relationships, generalizing, memory, critical judgment, and accommodation to extreme individual differences.

Figure 1.1 defines graphically the complex process of reading. From the definition already given of the four-step process—perception, comprehension, reaction, integration—Robinson has circumscribed the process with the speed of comprehension or the facility in assimilating ideas through written language.[5] The necessary entry skills for success in learning to read—the cognitive factors in word recognition, sequencing, and sentence meaning described by Geyer;[6] the linguistic factors in decoding, associating, and encoding the significant meanings in the language used;[7] and the affective factors exhibited in the self-concept, one's perception of self, and attitudes toward reading[8]— have all been incorporated in the diagram.

Readiness for Reading

Because so many students do have problems with reading assignments in school, it behooves us to think briefly about the readiness of boys and girls when they enter school. Most people have known *one* child of age three or four, like Debbie described in the following example, who seemed to learn to read without *ever* being taught. And most people have known a few boys and girls whose reading ability remained almost *nil* even after years of tutoring. But we tend to categorize everyone as *either* successful *or* unsuccessful as if there were just *two* clearly defined groups. This is not true at all. The following paragraphs emphasize the great range of individual differences in interests, motivation, and achievement in students. In formal school programs with curricula that are *much too inflexible,* the system, that is, the school as an institution, *creates* the problems that this book has been written to help alleviate.

Occasionally children are fluent readers before they enter the first grade. Teachers have been known to make disparaging remarks about the parents of these children and to intimate that the children read only because parents "pushed" them. Terman, in *Genetic Studies of Genius,* found that about 50 of his 1,500 gifted children in California were reading when they were five years old.[9] One occasionally finds a four- or five-year-old child among the children of one's acquaintances who can do formal reading.

It is necessary to divide children who read early into *two* distinct categories. The first category includes those children who are placed in groups to be *taught* reading

Figure 1.1. The four parts of the circle show reading as a four-step thinking process: perception, comprehension, reaction, and integration. The cognitive process also includes interpretive or creative reading in a word recognition-sequencing process. The linguistic process includes the syntactic, semantic, and meaning (deep structure) in decoding-encoding print into meaningful concepts. The affective processes are interactions of self-concept, attitudes, and anxieties. All of these affect a reader's facility in assimilating ideas through written language—that is, the speed of comprehension in reading.

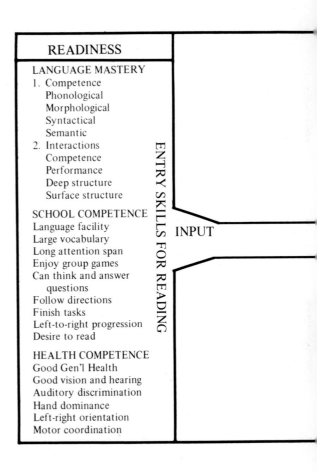

READINESS

LANGUAGE MASTERY
1. Competence
   Phonological
   Morphological
   Syntactical
   Semantic
2. Interactions
   Competence
   Performance
   Deep structure
   Surface structure

SCHOOL COMPETENCE
Language facility
Large vocabulary
Long attention span
Enjoy group games
Can think and answer
   questions
Follow directions
Finish tasks
Left-to-right progression
Desire to read

HEALTH COMPETENCE
Good Gen'l Health
Good vision and hearing
Auditory discrimination
Hand dominance
Left-right orientation
Motor coordination

ENTRY SKILLS FOR READING

INPUT

as a series of lessons to be learned. The lessons are presented and the children are expected to respond. In this frame of reference, many four-, five-, or six-year-olds are not motivated and may learn to avoid reading rather than to enjoy it. These children, literally, are being "pushed" into reading. Then there are those who learned to read entirely as a result of their own curiosity about words and who asked questions that were answered by sympathetic adults. The important point here is that the children learned to read on their initiative; the adult only followed the children's lead in helping them to identify word symbols. This kind of learning to read informally is a happy situation. Debbie was such a child.

Debbie was a very bright little girl who talked fluently in sentences when she was one year old. She listened for long periods of time to *Mother Goose* when she was eighteen months old. She could study magazine pictures and "tell" four- and five-sentence stories about them when she was two. One day when she was three years old, she was sitting in the car downtown with her mother. Without warning, she spelled the name of the department store across the street, "B-A-R-N-E-Y-S," and asked, "What does that spell, Mother?" When Debbie was three and one-half years old, she began

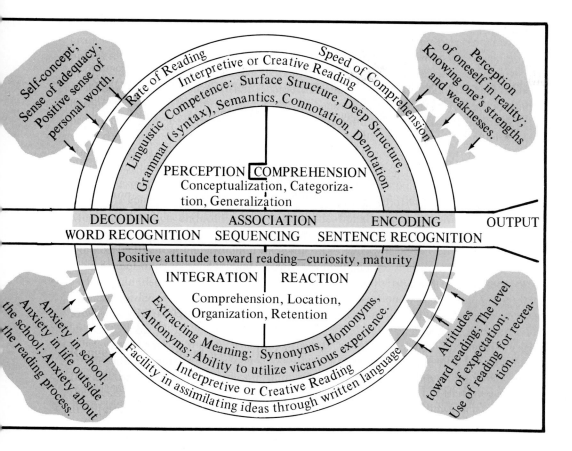

studying the comic strips in the newspaper and spelling out words for her mother to pronounce for her. When she had spelled out a series of words and waited each time for the pronunciation, she could, all by herself, keep in mind what the words were telling her, and at the end of the sentence, repeat the complete sentence. By the time Debbie was four, she was able to read sentences in a first reader without help. By the time she was five and one-half, she was able to pronounce all the 220 words in the Dolch Basic Sight Word List. The crux of the matter here is that Debbie *did not* learn to read because some adult decided to teach her to read and began flashing basic sight words for her to recognize; neither did she have to memorize the isolated sounds of all the initial consonants through monotonous, prolonged lessons.

The urgency to expose all children at age six to formal reading must be countered with the differences among the six-year-olds who enroll in school. Such writers as Huey, Dewey, and Glass assure us that some children could learn well through other avenues for some time.

Huey wrote in 1908:

Thus far I have said little about the child's use of *books,* because I think we should be in no hurry to have him use them. The age is over-bookish, and bright children, at least, are all too soon possessed with a notion which never leaves them that all knowledge lies within the covers of books. Reading, writing, drawing, may be learned and practiced in such ways as I have suggested and in others that will suggest themselves, and may supply all the child's needs for years, without the use of books. Languages, arithmetic, geography, nature may all be studied effectively, in the early stages, with no books other than such as the children and teacher may make for themselves. In the schools of the future books will surely be but little used before the child's eighth or ninth year. In the home at present the child should be taught to read them only as early and as fast as his spontaneous interest calls for them.[10]

Huey also cites Dewey as feeling that early emphasis on reading was fatiguing for young children, required too much drill on "form" that was monotonous, and made a mechanical tool of the process of learning to read.[11]

Gerald Glass asks why we should insist that everyone read so soon and suggests that we may not have put first things first, even for those who read successfully at age six. He writes that concepts can be developed solely through listening, speaking, feeling, seeing, and that the potential for extending the young child's intelligence and understanding of fairly technical concepts is great. Forcing all young children into the reading mold is apt to diminish the possibilities of creative thinking and problem solving.[12]

Enriching Oral Language Competence

One of the most important tasks of the teacher both at the stage of beginning reading and all through the primary grades is to provide many activities for the children to build their language competence. Some of these activities are:

1. Using the Bill Martin *Sounds of Language,*[13] Muriel Crosby *World of Language,*[14] the Hap Palmer *Learning Basic Skills Through Music,*[15] and any other tape-recorded materials that will give pleasure in assimilating the rhythm of the language.
2. Understanding words in different parts of speech, for example, "A feather is *light.*" and "Turn on the *light.*"
3. Rhyming words: Listening and repeating *Mother Goose,* listening to such poems as "I Know an Old Lady Who Swallowed a Fly,"[16] and "I Can't Said the Ant."[17]
4. Learning and repeating finger plays, tongue twisters, and childhood songs.
5. Telling riddles.
6. Writing with the teacher repetitious reading charts:
   What is Yellow?
   The sun is yellow.
   The baby duck is yellow.

The butter is yellow.
Our car is yellow.

7. Finishing sentences when the last word is left out.
8. Developing sensory awareness, for example, the different textures in the feeling box.
9. Organizing the daily events in the schedule.
10. Learning and repeating number rhymes and number concepts.
11. Hearing stories read and told; telling stories.
12. Discussing language of idioms, slang, and figures of speech.

Judging Readiness for Reading

Facility with language is imperative, since children are not going to learn how to read a language any better than they can understand it. The communication skills of listening, speaking, reading, and writing develop as a hierarchy of skills. Beginners must be able to understand and speak the language before they are ready to try to read it meaningfully.

So, the first-grade teachers must plan some kind of room organization for the class of beginners. Soon they begin classifying roughly which children

1. Talk easily and have big vocabularies when they talk.
2. Have long attention spans and can get engrossed in a task for long periods.
3. Become engrossed in activities based entirely on language.
4. Become engrossed in active games or exercises of a manual nature.
5. Can think and answer the teacher's questions easily.
6. Follow directions and finish the jobs they start.
7. See and hear likenesses and differences.
8. Demonstrate increasing knowledge of how print functions.
9. Have motor control in writing their names, following lines.
10. Recognize left-to-right progression for following print.
11. Indicate basic training in how to handle books with care.
12. Exhibit a desire to read.

Measuring Readiness for Formal Reading

First-grade teachers may find it important and reassuring to support their observations and judgments of children's readiness for formal reading with some types of testing. The 10 to 15 percent of six-year-olds who are apt *not* to retain basic sight words and to be required to repeat first grade, must be identified and given the kind of developmental program that will increase motor skills; visual, auditory, and tactile discrimination; verbal fluency, and knowledge of concepts. It is disastrous to the self-concept of the children to push them into formal reading programs and "punish" them for not learning in the initial stages of reading instruction when they lack the minimum skills for achievement.

There are a number of screening devices to help alert the first-grade teachers in their efforts to establish such readiness. De Hirsch, Jansky, and Langford described a series of tests that were found to predict to a very high degree reading failure of beginning first graders. They have described these tests, established critical scores for "passing," and over a period of time determined that one child can be tested individually on these measures in forty-five minutes. Such a use of time at the beginning of first grade may seem difficult to teachers, but it is sure to be a good investment if it helps them program wisely the work for that child for the first year of school.[18]

Zaeski reported a study in which he found the predictive index a very valuable tool in predicting potential failures.[19]

Weimer experimented with most of the tests used in *Predicting Reading Failure* on a group-administered basis and found some evidence that teachers can gain the necessary information on all of the tests but one (Wepman's test of auditory discrimination) by administering them to children in small groups.[20]

Clay developed the Concepts about Print[21] test, which has two forms, *Sand*[22] and *Stones*[23]. This instrument was designed to yield information about the child's understanding of print, book format, and the vocabulary used in reading instruction, such as "letter" and "word." Clay cited studies that suggest that children are slower than expected in developing these concepts. She stated that lack of knowledge in these areas contributes to many cases of reading failure.[24]

Sultman and Elkins tested 150 children at school entrance with a variety of measures and found that the *Sand* test correlated most highly with reading achievement when it was measured after a year in school.[25]

Methods of Teaching Reading

There are numerous approaches to the teaching of reading.[26] They can be grouped under three methods: the analytic, the eclectic, and the synthetic. It is helpful to know about the beliefs behind each method and the better-known approaches derived from them. Most children are taught from the basal reader, which is usually an example of the eclectic method. Frequently, teachers using basal readers also include aspects of other approaches. As a result, many children have reading experiences that derive from all three methods of teaching reading.

The Analytic Method

The analytic method is well characterized by the language experience approach to the teaching of reading. This approach is based on the belief that children read most easily those stories that use personally appropriate language to express familiar ideas. It is organized around children's writing and reading of their own stories. Allen wrote that children can talk about their own experiences and that their language can be written and later read.[27] The classroom in which the language experience approach happens is a busy place filled with interesting, stimulating materials ranging from shell collections to scrapbooks of picture postcards and travel brochures to easels and paints. It is a setting in which children are encouraged to talk, to ask questions, to role play, and to listen to and tell stories. The environment is rich with meaningful print. Experiences outside the classroom are frequent, but not necessarily elaborate, events. Children may have rich experiences studying ant hills and cloud patterns, as well as taking trips to zoos and museums.

Whatever experiences the children have should evoke much language. Some of it can be recorded on charts on in class books or on the display of the microcomputer to be read and reread. Teachers can find library books related to the children's experiences to share. Art, music, and drama lessons can extend the experiences. During all of these activities, teachers can be alert to opportunities to extend the children's knowledge of the reading process by studying current abilities and needs. Future lessons can be designed to meet the needs that have been identified.

The language experience approach starts with the meaningful language of the children. Smaller units of language are attended to as the teacher perceives the needs of individuals or small groups of children.

The Eclectic Method of Teaching

Most reading instruction today is eclectic, utilizing the desirable facets of all *different* methods. Emphasis is placed on the meaningful nature of reading at all times. Reading readiness continues when children begin a formal reading program. The children learn *initial sight vocabulary* by a *word* method. This is achieved through chart reading, experience stories, labels in the room, blackboard work, workbook lessons, and direct teaching on the part of the teacher of a specific list of words. Children read in selected series of basic readers to build systematically a larger and larger sight vocabulary, but simultaneously with building the sight vocabulary they learn many *word-attack skills.* Early in their reading, they begin a systematic approach to word-attack skills by learning initial consonant sounds, a few consonant blend sounds, and the structural elements *s, ed,* and *ing,* as well as some compound words. A free reading or supplementary reading program begins as soon as children have the vocabulary necessary to read other books at the level of difficulty they have finished in the instructional program.

Learning the Sight Vocabulary

Because most children were able to master a controlled sight vocabulary by reading these selected words in story context, all writers of beginning reading books followed the pattern of using fewer and fewer words in the first book, introducing only one or two new words on a page and repeating all words several times through successive pages.

It is logical to assume that children will be more strongly motivated to read stories with simple plots than to drill on structural and phonic elements in words for long periods of time.

Horace Mann recognized the advantages of the "whole word" approach, and recommended it as a method of teaching in 1838. He stated:

> Presenting the children with the alphabet is giving them what they never saw, heard, or thought before. . . . But the printed names of known things (dog, cat, doll) are the signs of sounds which their ears have been accustomed to hear, and their organs of speech to utter. Therefore, a child can learn to name 26 familiar *words* sooner than the unknown, unheard of and unthought of letters of the alphabet.[28]

While children are learning the first 50 sight words, they are concomitantly strengthening their phonics training in *hearing* words that begin the same and rhyme, and they put pictures of things that begin with the same sound together.

In summary, the eclectic method attempts the following:

1. Emphasis on the *meaningful nature* of reading is always primary.
2. Reading readiness is continued with children while they are learning a sight vocabulary.
3. The children learn their initial sight vocabulary by a *word* method. This will be achieved through chart reading, experience stories, labels in the room, blackboard work, workbook lessons, and direct teaching by the teacher of a specific list of words in their first reading books.
4. The children read a series of basic readers to build systematically a larger and larger sight vocabulary.
5. Simultaneously, children begin a systematic approach to word-attack skills by learning:
    a. most of the initial consonant sounds and a few consonant blend sounds in phonic analysis, and some suffixes in structural analysis.
    b. the consonant blends and some knowledge of long and short vowels, compound words, many suffixes, and a few prefixes. Also, they learn alphabetical order and elementary uses of alphabetical order.
    c. further work as needed in phonic and structural analysis, and beginning dictionary skills.
6. Their reading, from the very beginning of preprimers, is supplemented by experience stories, chart reading, labels, and reading to follow directions.
7. A "free reading" or supplementary reading program begins as soon as the children have the vocabulary necessary to read other books at the level of difficulty they have finished in their instructional program.
8. Thus, the reading program is:
    a. Developmental to teach "learn-to-read" skills.
    b. Functional, requiring application of all these skills in order to "read to learn."
    c. Recreational, encouraging wide reading according to the individual's background of interests and abilities.

Teaching with Basals

It is no news that many children are not learning to read as well as they should—this has always been true. The main reason there is greater and greater demand for remedial reading instruction is because as schools evolve additional ways to adapt the school program to helping individual children, they find increasing problems with which to deal. Teachers *and* parents are no longer willing to put young children in categories—*one can* learn to read, but *another cannot* as if that ended the situation.

Reading, as taught in most basal reading series, adheres to the following steps:

1. Children are taught to recognize words as whole units before they are asked to deal with letter components. The *word* is the smallest unit that the child needs to begin to read. As long as a student is learning a few elements so that she can read meaningful context, she can just as well memorize that "look" is the word *look* as she can learn that "l" is the letter *l*. McKee has illustrated how easily an adult can quickly learn a few "sight words" in a completely strange alphabet.[29]

2. Children are being taught a complete course of study in phonic and structural analysis in the process of learning to read. The series of readers available today provide, in teachers' manuals and in pupils' workbooks, exercises for the teaching and learning of all the phonic and structural analysis skills needed to become an independent reader.

3. The all-important *result* in reading is realizing that reading is a thinking process that necessitates comprehension and integration with one's experiential background. Overemphasis on phonic sounding or overanalysis of words into parts is apt to interfere with reading as a thought-getting process.

4. Books in series are developed from the preprimer level with a severely controlled vocabulary. It is often argued that the preprimer written with so few words (many have twenty or less) could not possibly be interesting. This may be true for an adult reader. Motivated children, however, show considerable interest and excitement in reading them. These children could not possibly read anything else in context, and these books provide them with a great deal of repetitive practice. Most children need this practice. One important question, of course, that teachers should ask their critics is, "What alternative do you propose?" Context taught by a "phonic method" will hardly be any more interesting. Note the reading lesson that could be introduced after the pupil has learned the short *a* and several consonants:

   The rat sat on a mat.

   The cat sat on a mat.

   A fat cat ran.

   A cat and a fat rat ran.

The directed reading lesson plan is described in detail and illustrated in Appendix D.

The Synthetic Method

The synthetic method of teaching reading is exemplified well by the phonics approach to reading instruction. Those teachers who use a phonics approach believe that the child learns most readily when sounds and letters are introduced before reading stories begins. Usually a small set of letters and the sounds they frequently represent are introduced. Stories composed of the words that can be made from various combinations of these sounds are then read. For example, if the sounds /f/, /k/, /r/, /t/, and /s/ are introduced along with the short sound of *a,* and *the* is introduced as a sight word, the child can read such sentences as "The fat cat sat. The fat rat sat." The sentences and stories will become more varied as more letters, corresponding sounds, and rules are introduced.

The phonics approach focuses on the smallest units of language first: the sounds and the letters that represent them. Gradually, the child builds toward whole words and finally whole sentences and stories. The concept that print is meaningful and relevant is delayed until the mastery of the many "pieces" of language is completed.

The Microcomputer

It is tempting to think of the microcomputer as a new method of teaching reading. However, this is *not* the case. The microcomputer is a *tool* for learning and thinking that can interface with any method of reading instruction if the right software, the actual instructional program, is chosen. If the teacher is working with the analytic method, there are several word processing programs for children that permit the writing and editing of stories and books.[30] Many programs are available to support the skills, both in word recognition and comprehension, that are congruent with the eclectic (basal) and synthetic methods.[31]

Much has been learned about how to prepare programs for children, but even more remains to be explored. It is critical that teachers study carefully the software that is available before making instructional choices. It is important to make sure that programs for the classroom represent the best possible knowledge concerning the reading process, the needs of boys and girls, the development of language abilities, instructional techniques, and the functions of computers in varied portions of society.

The teacher needs to arrange the classroom schedule so that *all* students have opportunities singly or in very small groups to work at a variety of tasks on the microcomputer—practice and tutorial exercises, simulation games, and word processing.[32] The teacher must also arrange space for one or more microcompuer units including keyboards, display screens, disk drives, and hopefully a printer. Related materials, such as bookmaking supplies, art materials, and a recordkeeping system should be convenient and inviting. Planning for the use of microcomputers in the classroom must also include arranging time to talk with children about what has been learned, since no

---

Making Connections 1.2: Methods of Teaching Reading

If you are a teacher in training, you should complete the first project in the following list. If you are a practicing teacher, complete the second activity.

1. If you are a teacher in training, interview two teachers in some detail about the reading programs in their schools. It would be helpful if two or three of your peers worked with you to develop a set of questions that would gather a large body of specific information about each teacher's reading program.

     When you have conducted your interviews, analyze the responses in terms of the reading methods being used. Does the teacher use a single method, or does the teacher use elements of more than one method? How successful does the teacher feel the reading program is?
2. If you are a practicing teacher, examine the teacher's manual you follow or the prescribed reading program of your school for your grade level. Does the material base its approach in only one method, or does it draw from several methods? If it uses several strategies, list the elements in the program that are derived from each of the various methods.

Class members developing one of the activities may find it useful to share their findings with persons completing the other activity.

---

matter how exotic the microcomputer may seem, it cannot perform this vital teacher function.

Characteristics of a Good Reading Program

Some basic principles that guide the overall reading program in the school must be established. A complete reading program is based upon these generalizations:

1. Learning to read is a developmental process. This means that each individual arrives at the maximum state of readiness for learning at an individual time and that readiness must be achieved in all areas of growth: intellectual, academic, social, physical, and emotional. It means, further, that the reading program will emphasize differences in individuals while it must, of necessity, also utilize the homogeneity of interests, knowledges, and skills of groups within a class.
2. Classroom teachers will need to find methods of teaching that will span the differences in a single classroom. This will always include some type of grouping for reading instruction.

3. The language arts—reading, writing, speaking, and listening—are not developed as four compartmentalized subjects in a school day. They are interrelated aspects of a communication process that goes on all day, every day. Every teacher teaches the language arts. Every teacher is a reading teacher, an English teacher, a speech teacher, and a spelling teacher. These communication arts are the medium of instruction in all subjects.

4. The teacher has excellent manuals to use as guides for efficient methods of teaching reading and adequate information about the nature of children.

   a. First, a basic vocabulary must be developed. This is controlled, but leads step by step to higher levels of reading.

   b. Second, word-attack skills that help children unlock new words are taught. These include picture or context clues, word form or configuration clues, phonic analysis, structural analysis, and the necessary dictionary skills to make that instrument useful and habitual with the student.

   c. The child reads *many* books at each level at all stages of reading. The school should provide many sets of readers within the school system and *many grade levels* of difficulty *within one* classroom.

   d. A variety of purposes for reading and varying methods of study to conform to these purposes are taught. As Francis Bacon has said:

   Read not to contradict and confute; nor to believe and take for granted; nor to find talk and discourse; but to weigh and consider. Some books are to be tasted, others to be swallowed, and some few to be chewed and digested; that is, some books are to be read only in parts; others to be read, but not curiously; and some few to be read wholly, and with diligence and attention. Some books also may be read by deputy, and extracts made of them by others; but that would be only in the less important arguments, and the meaner sort of books, else distilled books are like common distilled waters, flashy things. Reading maketh a full man; conference a ready man; and writing an exact man. And therefore, if a man write little, he had need have a great memory; if he confer little, he had need have a present wit; and if he read little, he had need have much cunning, to seem to know that he doth not. Histories make men wise; poets witty; the mathematics subtle; natural philosophy deep; moral grave; logic and rhetoric able to contend.[33]

   The teachers help the students appreciate various types of reading matter and evaluate their purpose in reading. Pupils adjust their speed in reading according to their purpose, select what is to be retained, and fix their sights on achieving a specific purpose so they will retain what is significant.

5. All students must be accepted and respected at the level at which they can perform successfully, and they should be helped to grow from that point in the developmental skills in reading.

The Four Jobs in Teaching Reading

There are four major jobs to do in the teaching of beginning reading: (1) develop a basic sight vocabulary; (2) teach word-attack skills (this has been called *phonics* or *self-help sounding* and is now popularly referred to as *decoding* or *breaking the code*); (3) teach that reading is always, and completely, a thinking process that requires understanding (far from being a word-calling process, reading is the interpretation of the ideas behind printed symbols); and (4) give every child a great deal of easy reading practice. Fluency is achieved through meaningful practice. Teachers should move children to the next higher level of reading difficulty *only* when they read comfortably and fluently at the lower level.

The Skills of Reading

Students must learn all the skills in word recognition and in comprehension so they will be able to gain meaning readily. They are aided in word recognition by using the context of the reading wisely, by studying the picture clues provided, and by using structural and phonic analysis. Students must master many skills to enable them to read with understanding and to be able to think about and use the material they have read.

1. a. Phonic analysis is the application of a knowledge of consonant and vowel sound clues to the pronunciation of a word
   b. Phonic elements: single consonant letters, consonant blends, consonant digraphs, single vowel letters, vowel digraphs, diphthongs
2. a. Structural analysis is the means by which the parts of the word that form meaning units or pronunciation units are identified
   b. Structural elements: root words, compound words, prefixes and suffixes
3. Vocabulary
4. Comprehending material is using content to predict meanings of words
   a. Understanding relevant and important details or facts
   b. Understanding the main idea or central thought
   c. Understanding the sequence of time, place, ideas, events, or steps
   d. Following directions
   e. Reading for implied meanings and drawing inferences
   f. Reading to understand characterization and setting
   g. Sensing relationships in time, place, cause and effect
   h. Reading to anticipate outcomes
   i. Recognizing author's mood, tone, intent
   j. Understanding and making comparisons
   k. Drawing conclusions and making generalizations
   l. Skimming as a form of partial reading

5. Study skills
   a. Location of information
   b. Organization of information
   c. Interpretation of visual aids to learning
   d. Presenting information
   e. Remembering
   f. Test taking
6. Oral reading skills

The Affective Side of Learning

The self-concept, attitudes toward learning, and the anxieties children face are affective processes that must interact positively with all the cognitive competence and language mastery the learner is trying to achieve. The affective features of the learning process are depicted in figure 1.1 as continuously affecting the language process.

Teaching in the elementary school requires that teachers respect children as people even though they are small. They have individual personalities to be nurtured, not thwarted. Valuing individual differences leads to the ultimate objective that children grow more different, not more alike, as they progress through the school.

Teaching is not at all synonymous with *telling*. Teaching is providing opportunities for learning; providing a rich environment for choices for children to explore; and providing guidance needed to solve problems. The physical environment for the children in school should be a safe, attractive place that invites the learners to use, to explore, and to feel good about the surroundings.

Because children are trying to "order" their worlds, they can make use of learning only as it meets their needs to further that "ordering." They are unique (unlike anybody else); they have their own individual learning styles; and they bring to school a complete set of cultural values learned at home. With respect to what they *will* learn, the relationship between the teacher and the children is more important than the intellectual content of the course of study.

Many teachers have never had any professional education to prepare them to interact with human feelings in the classroom. Neither have they had systematic feedback about responding to feelings expressed by others. Further, they may have an indefinite, undefined belief that feelings must be "left out" of the teaching process. With this point of view, teachers are sure to respond minimally to emotion and feeling in the classroom.

However, there is a positive and significant relationship between the teachers' level of empathy, congruence, and positive regard for the students they teach and the levels of cognitive gain made by those students as measured by standardized tests.[34] The classroom social-emotional setting directly affects what the pupils try to do and what they learn. Teachers who are skilled in listening to, accepting, and reflecting feelings as they hear students' cognitive responses use a great deal of praise and encouragement, let the students know that their feelings are accepted, and attempt to avoid criticism. These positive behaviors enable the students to perceive themselves in a wholesome manner and to respond more successfully. Looking for and reinforcing desirable behavior and ignoring all possible undesirable behavior is helpful. Accepting and reflecting feelings in a positive way helps students overcome frustration, hostility, indifference, and timidity.[35]

Nonverbal Communication

Teachers and students are communicating all through the school day with messages that are sent by means other than the use of words. Teachers "say" more to the students in their classrooms in nonverbal ways than they do in verbal ways. Generally speaking, the students in school are young, in need of adult support, and on the defensive when they have done something wrong, made a mistake, or feel inadequate. Recognizing these conditions, then, it is easy to understand the importance of a smile or withholding a smile; a pleasant voice or a stern unfriendly voice; a friendly, close proximity to the student or a distant, stand-offish nature; even the eye behavior of the middle-class Anglo requires that the interested person look directly into a person's eyes to communicate. Personal grooming, mode of dress, presence or absence of perfume, or even the contrast of stiff or relaxed posture—all of these things are communicating messages all day long. Many teachers need to recognize the great variety of ways in which approval or disapproval is expressed. Such behaviors as simply recognizing the child, giving attention to the child, being close to the child, gesturing, touching, or smiling may be the support the child needs. If the teacher says "I'm sure you did the best you could," but has a cold, rejecting manner, the child will attribute more value to the nonverbal behavior observed than to the verbal expression.

These humanistic processes help the student build awareness and acceptance of self. This awareness and acceptance will lead to positive self concept and increase each individual's level of trust. Quandt writes:

Acceptance is a value of oneself that enables that person to see himself as important and worthwhile. It develops when there is no threat that others will express judgments about the person. Acceptance leads to risk taking, an atmosphere in which an individual is willing to uncover and confront his or her own emotions, attitudes, and values. Risk taking leads to openness, a condition under which individuals share their emotions, attitudes, and values with others without fear of nonacceptance.[36]

Developing Independence in Reading Power

The developmental process through which children must grow has been divided into *five* stages. The labels may be helpful in understanding the children's gradual progress toward the level at which they can read independently and effectively.

The first stage is getting ready to be introduced to formal reading, that is, *initial reading readiness.* The need for a broad experience background, good language facility, auditory and visual discrimination, physical coordination, ability to attend for longer and longer periods of time, ability to follow instructions, and a genuine desire to read—all have already been discussed as facets of the readiness program.

The second stage is *beginning reading.* Reading in this stage provides the pupils with a growing stock of sight words. In addition to readers, they read charts, labels, and much teacher-prepared material.

The third stage is the period of *rapid progress.* This includes the normal instructional program of the second and third grade levels. While comprehension is emphasized, an extensive course of study in word recognition skills is taught to children reading at these levels. An abundance of reading materials is provided to give a great deal of easy, interesting practice.

The fourth stage is *wide reading,* generally designated as the fourth, fifth, and sixth grades. All the skills previously taught will be extended, and there will be much teaching of the work-type reading skills. Children should do more and more independent reading both in and out of school.

The fifth stage is *refinement of reading skills.* The student in junior and senior high school needs practice in making value judgments, outlining, summarizing, and generalizing.

The ability to "shift gears in reading," that is, to adjust the speed of reading to the level of difficulty or type of writing so that understanding will result, is one indication of mature reading ability.

Summary

Reading is a process by which the graphic symbols are translated into meaningful sound symbols in the reader's experience. Meaning is the key: learning to read necessitates mastery of all the linguistic cues that facilitate anticipation of meaning in a line of print.

Perhaps too much emphasis has been placed on the techniques of teaching reading and not enough on the peculiar nature of the children who do not learn what they are taught. The myriad of different abilities of children varies extremely so that teachers need to be continually evaluating the children as individuals in order to help them learn to read more effectively.

Learning to read is a developmental process and requires an extended period of time for most people to grow into mature readers. Reading is a part of the communication process and must be seen in the integrated hierarchy of listening with understanding, speaking, reading, and writing.

The four major jobs to do in reading are: (1) acquire a sight vocabulary of words; (2) learn word-attack skills for decoding strange words; (3) learn comprehension and study skills; and (4) provide for a great deal of meaningful practice. Eclectic methodology for helping students master these jobs to become good readers was discussed. The chapter concluded with a short list of the necessary skills of reading.

For Further Reading

Calfee, Robert C., and Drum, Priscilla A. *Teaching Reading in Compensatory Classes.* Newark, Del.: International Reading Association, 1979.

Holdaway, Don. *Stability and Change in Literacy Learning.* Exeter, N.H.: Heinemann Educational Books, 1984.

Martin, Mavis. *Valuing Reading.* Grand Forks: Center for Teaching and Learning, University of North Dakota, 1979.

Pearson, P. David, and Johnson, Dale D. *Teaching Reading Comprehension.* New York: Holt, Rinehart and Winston, 1978. Chapter 2, "Factors Influencing Reading Comprehension," pp. 7–22.

Smith, Frank. *Reading without Nonsense.* New York: Teachers College Press, 1979.

Smith, Frank. *Understanding Reading,* 3d. ed. New York: Holt, Rinehart and Winston, 1982.

Taylor, Denny, *Family Literacy: Young Children Learning to Read and Write.* Exeter, N.H.: Heinemann Educational Books, 1983.

Notes

1. William S. Gray, *On Their Own in Reading* (Chicago: Scott, Foresman, 1948), pp. 35–37.
2. Ernest Horn, *Methods of Instruction in the Social Studies* (New York: Charles Scribner's Sons, 1937), p. 152.
3. Ibid., p. 154.
4. Frank Smith, *Understanding Reading,* 3d ed. (New York: Holt, Rinehart and Winston, 1982), pp. 2–3.
5. Helen M. Robinson, "Major Aspects of Reading," in *Reading: Seventy-five Years of Progress,* edited by H. Alan Robinson (Chicago: University of Chicago Press, 1966), p. 28.
6. John J. Geyer, "Models of Perceptual Processes in Reading," in *Theoretical Models and Processes of Reading,* edited by Harry Singer and Robert B. Ruddell (Newark, Del.: International Reading Association, 1970), pp. 47–94.
7. Robert B. Ruddell, "Psycholinguistic Implications for a System of Communications Model," on *Theoretical Models,* pp. 239–58; Ronald Wardhaugh, *Reading: A Linguistic Perspective* (New York: Harcourt, Brace, 1969); and Miles V. Zintz and Zelda R. Maggart, *The Reading Process: The Teacher and the Learner,* 4th ed., (Dubuque, Ia.: Wm. C. Brown, 1984), pp. 64–88.

8. Irene Athey, "Reading Research in the Affective Domain," in *Theoretical Models,* pp. 352–80.

9. Lewis M. Terman, *Genetic Studies of Genius* (Stanford, Calif.: Stanford University Press, 1925, 1926), 1: 271–72; 2: 247–55.

10. Edmund Burke Huey, *The History and Pedagogy of Reading* (New York: Macmillan, 1918), p. 145. Reprinted by the Massachusetts Institute of Technology, 1968.

11. Ibid., p. 120.

12. Gerald G. Glass, "Let's Not Read So Soon: Even Those Who Can," in *Elementary Reading Instruction: Selected Materials,* 2d ed., edited by Althea Beery, Thomas C. Barrett, and William R. Powell (Boston: Allyn and Bacon, 1974), pp. 381–86.

13. Bill Martin, Jr., *The Sounds of Language* (New York: Holt, Rinehart and Winston, 1967).

14. Muriel Crosby, *The World of Language* (Chicago: Follett, 1970).

15. Hap Palmer, *Learning Basic Skills Through Music,* vols. I and II. Record or cassette. (Freeport, N.Y.: Educational Activities, Inc., 1980).

16. "I Know an Old Lady" in Tom Glazer, *Eye Winker, Tom Tinker, Chin Chopper, Fifty Musical Fingerplays* (New York: Doubleday, 1973).

17. Polly Cameron. *I Can't Said the Ant* (New York: Scholastic Book Services, 1961).

18. Katrina DeHirsch, Jeannette Jansky, and William S. Langford, *Predicting Reading Failure* (New York: Harper and Row, 1966).

19. Arnold Zaeski, "The Validity of Predictive Index Tests in Predicting Reading Failure at the End of Grade One," in *Reading Difficulties: Diagnosis, Correction and Remediation,* edited by William Durr (Newark, Del.: International Reading Association, 1970), pp. 28–33.

20. Wayne Weimer, "A Perceptuomotor and Oral Language Program for First Grade Children Identified as Potential Reading Failures Using the Predictive Reading Index" (Ph.D. dissertation, University of New Mexico Graduate School, Albuquerque, 1971).

21. Marie M. Clay, *The Early Detection of Reading Difficulties: A Diagnostic Survey with Recovery Procedures,* 2d ed. (Auckland, New Zealand: Heinemann, 1979).

22. Marie M. Clay. *Sand* (Auckland, New Zealand: Heinemann, 1972).

23. Marie M. Clay. *Stones* (Auckland, New Zealand: Heinemann, 1979).

24. Marie M. Clay, *Early Detection of Reading Difficulties,* p. 17, and Marie M. Clay, *Reading: The Patterning of Complex Behavior,* 2d ed. (Auckland, New Zealand: Heinemann, 1979).

25. William F. Sultmann and John Elkins, "Readiness Assessment and Early Reading: A Multiple Regression Analysis," *Reading Education* 7, no. 1 (Autumn 1982), pp. 25–31.

26. Robert C. Aukerman, *Approaches to Beginning Reading,* 2d ed. (New York: John Wiley and Sons, 1984).

27. Roach Van Allen, *Language Experiences in Communication,* (Boston: Houghton Mifflin, 1978), pp. 23–24.

28. Lillian Gray, *Teaching Children to Read,* 3d ed. (New York: Ronald Press, 1963), p. 47, citing Horace Mann's *Report to the Board of Education in Massachusetts in 1838.*

29. Paul McKee, *A Primer for Parents,* rev. ed. (Boston: Houghton Mifflin, 1975).

30. Colette Daiute, "Word Processing: Can It Make Even Good Writers Better?" *Electronic Learning* 1 (March/April 1982), pp. 29–31.

31. See the various volumes of *The Digest of Software Reviews, Education,* and *Computers, Reading and Languages Arts.* (Modern Learning Publishers, Inc., 1308 East 38th Street, Oakland, Calif.).

32. Gary G. Bitter and Ruth A. Camuse, *Using a Microcomputer in the Classroom* (Reston, Va.: Reston Computer Group Book, 1984). Chapter 3, "Computer-Assisted Instruction," pp. 39–70; Chapter 4, "The Computer as a Tool for Teachers and Students," pp. 71–107.

33. Francis Bacon, *Essays, Civil and Moral, and the New Atlantis,* vol. III of *The Five Foot Shelf of Books, The Harvard Classics,* edited by Charles W. Eliot, (New York: P. F. Collier and Son, 1909), pp. 128–29.

34. David Aspy, "The Humane Implications of a Humane Technology," *Peabody Journal of Education* 53: (October 1975), pp. 3–8.

35. David N. Aspy, E. N. Roebuck, M. A. Willson, and O. B. Adams, *Interpersonal Skills Training for Teachers,* NIH Research Grant PO 1MH19871 (Monroe, La.: National Consortium for Humanizing Education, Northeast Louisiana University, 1974).

36. Ivan J. Quandt, *Teaching Reading: A Human Process* (Chicago: Rand McNally, 1977), p. 31.

2
Getting Ready for Corrective Instruction

Vocabulary

mental age
chronological age
I.Q.
readiness
educational retardation
expected reader level
mental retardation
range of achievement
general reading immaturity
specific reading immaturity
limiting reading disability
complex reading disability
mainstreaming
individualized education
  program (IEP)
self concept
remedial reading
corrective reading

Questions

1. What are the major factors that contribute to success or failure in learning how to read?

2. What is the important issue that the phrase "Mental Retardation versus Educational Retardation" highlights?

3. What are two ways to identify the expected reader level?

4. Explain how it is that the differences in a group of children will increase as they progress through school, even with good teaching.

5. What are the requirements of PL 94–142 that every teacher should know?

6. What are some specific things to do to help children grow in positive feelings about themselves?

7. Distinguish between corrective and remedial reading.

According to Stephen D. Sugarman:

> Some schools do very bad things to some children. Too often, a teacher is unaware that a child does not possess the same basic skills as his or her classmates. Children who speak little or no English are taught only in English. Some nonlearners are identified, but then nothing is done to help them. School officials may attribute nonlearning to out-of-school factors but fail to inform the child's family of this diagnosis. They may try remedial programs that past experience has already demonstrated will not work.[1]

Background Knowledge

One of the first realities to be faced by the classroom teacher upon meeting the new class at the opening of the school term will be the range of differences among the individuals in the group. These differences will evidence themselves in physical appearance, in facial expression, in motivations to work with or against the teacher, in interests, aptitudes, and aspirations, and in ability to achieve in all of those academic skills commonly accepted as criteria of school success. The teacher may think of these behaviors, learned since infancy, as affective, cognitive, or psychomotor. The emphasis is, nevertheless, upon the range of differences. And since reading success or failure is an integral part of all these behaviors, *Corrective Reading* attempts to help classroom teachers organize what they already know cognitively; or to present ideas new to them, in effective classroom management, designed to enable each child to grow in the ability to read. Because reading is still the basic requirement for success in our schools as they are presently organized, classroom teachers have to assume a heavy responsibility for coping with the idiosyncratic behaviors of the students and meeting the needs of those students. Sugarman's comment about troubled children further accentuates the teacher's dilemma.

Anita Wants to Read and Write the Way Her Sisters Do

Anita is nineteen and has just graduated from high school. She has two sisters who are enrolled in college and are successful there. She has no particular desire to go to a liberal arts college, but she is deeply frustrated because she cannot read or write adequately for the pursuit of further education at any kind of school. She attended many schools in getting through the twelfth grade because her family moved from Michigan to Florida, and on to Okinawa, West Germany, and Alaska. Her mother had been a teacher in high school and thought Anita probably needed to be taught by a phonics method, but none of the schools had used that method as far as she knew. All Anita remembers now about her first years in school was that she never did "get the hang of reading" the way everybody else apparently did.

Figure 2.1 contains a paragraph written by Anita during the summer after she finished high school.

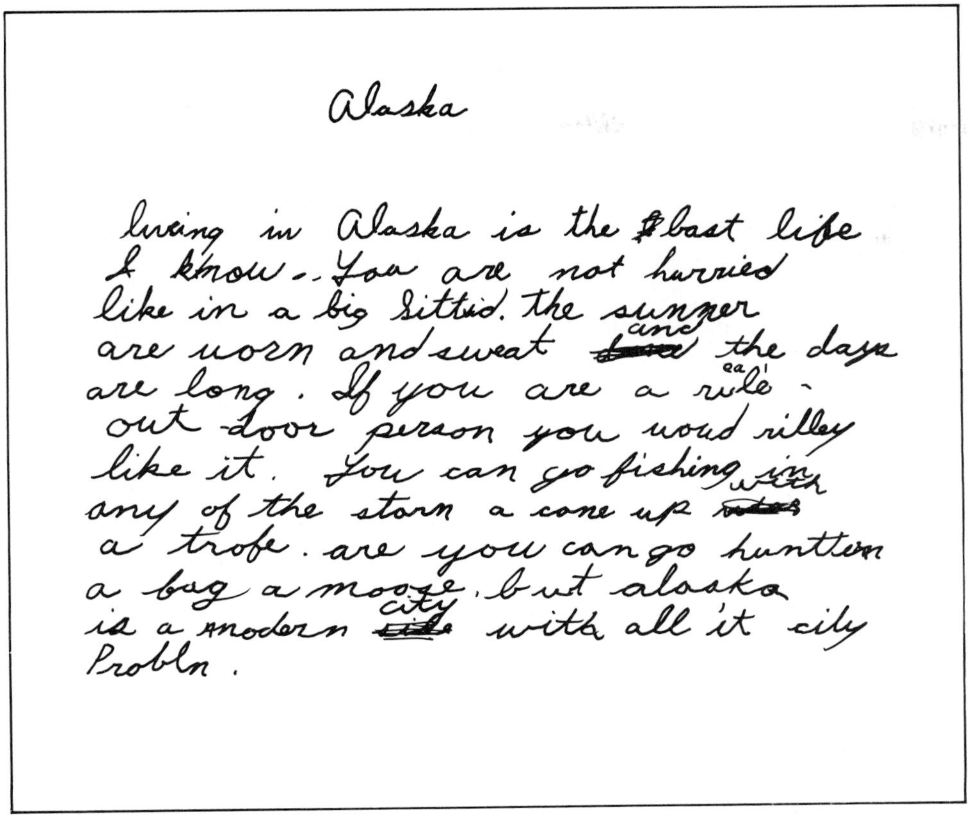
Alaska

living in Alaska is the bast life
I know.. You are not hurried
like in a big Sittid. the sunner
are worn and sweat and the days
are long. If you are a rile -
out door person you woud rilley
like it. You can go fishing in
any of the storm a cone up
a trofe. are you can go huntten
a bag a moose. but alaska
is a modern city with all it city
Probln.

Figure 2.1. A paragraph by Anita

Anita's paragraph reveals that she does not begin sentences with capital letters, *C* words can begin with *S*, *m's* and *n's* are alike, "real" and "really" must sound like "rile" and "rilley," and sometimes *W* is made correctly and sometimes it isn't. Perhaps the paragraph was intended to read:

> Living in Alaska is the best life I know. You are not hurried like in a big city. The summers are warm and sweaty and the days are long. If you are a real outdoor person you would really like it. You can go fishing in any of the streams and come up with a trophy. Or you can go hunting and bag a moose. But Anchorage is a modern city with all its city problems.

One cannot help but feel that if Anita's teachers of some ten or twelve years before had been sophisticated about the learning disabilities of many children, Anita might have had the kind of listening, reading, and writing instruction that would have made school work a much more successful adventure for her.

Factors Influencing Success

Chapter 1 indicated four major jobs to be done in teaching beginning reading: teach a basic sight vocabulary, teach word-attack skills, develop comprehension in reading, and give lots of easy reading practice. These tasks are specific and clear-cut. The problems arise, however, when the teacher attempts to perform these four major jobs with a class of, perhaps, thirty students. The technical difficulties are not apt to arise in the development of these reading techniques but in the differences within the heterogeneous group of *students who do not learn as the teacher teaches*. The causes of individual differences have been categorized by Monroe and Backus as constitutional, intellectual, environmental, emotional, and educational.[2] Pupils' learning at school is conditioned by these factors in their life experiences. An attempt has been made to show this diagrammatically in figure 2.2. Constitutional factors include chronological

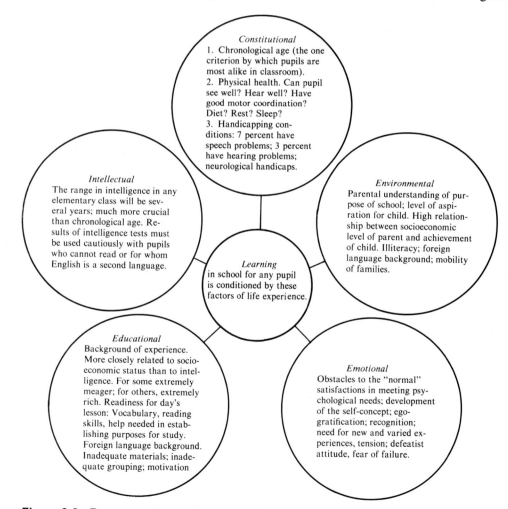

Figure 2.2. Factors explaining individual differences.

age, status of physical health, rest, and sleep, and the presence or absence of handi-capping conditions in speech, hearing, and coordination. Intellectual factors are closely related to general learning ability and the development of reading skills. The range of intelligence in any class will be several years unless students are specifically grouped on this basis. Environmental factors include the parental understanding of the school and its program, the socioeconomic levels of school patrons, mobility, and foreign language background.

Emotional factors relate to the psychological needs of children: development of the self-concept, recognition of the need for new and varied experiences, reduction of tensions, and fear of failure. Educational factors are those factors in experience background: understanding of concepts, understanding of the language of the school, having adequate materials, adequate subgroupings in the room, and motivation techniques that are rewarding.

Figure 2.3 emphasizes concisely the many factors upon which the pupil's learning depends. Chronological age is the most tangible factor now used to determine chil-

Figure 2.3. The child's learning depends on many factors.

dren's placement within the school. It is probably the least important of all the factors with respect to how successful children will be in learning. It is not unusual for the chronological age spread in a classroom to be only one year. In this respect, groups are extremely homogeneous.

The range in mental ages in any given classroom will be much greater, however. Six-year-olds in the first grade may have a mental age range from less than four years to more than nine years as measured by intelligence tests administered individually. To the teachers this range in general learning ability is much more significant than is the chronological age status of the pupils. In fact, it is easy to understand the theoretical ceiling on learning in children in terms of their intelligence, but it has been difficult to put this understanding into practice in everyday teaching. Figure 2.4 shows the range in mental ages of six-year-olds with intelligence quotients (I.Q.'s) from 50 to 150. It also shows that this range of six years has doubled by the time the pupils are twelve years old. If the I.Q. spread is as great as 50–150 in a large group of twelve-year-olds, the range of mental ages is from six to eighteen—a spread of twelve years.

In addition, the child with an I.Q. of 50 reaches a ceiling at adulthood of about seven years and six months mental age; the child with an I.Q. of 75 reaches a ceiling at adulthood of eleven years and three months. The normal adult mental age is fifteen years. As measured by tests currently in use, these are arbitrary differences that can never be reconciled. They will always exist. They arbitrarily fix limits on children's achievement.

Teachers must, however, always be realistic about the fallibility of test measurements. One must accept inflexible limitations cautiously and recognize that if cultural, social, or emotional difference exists, the "true" measure of potential has not been assessed.

Not all children will have had the same firsthand experiences before they come to school. By the time they are in first grade, many children have had a rich background of experience, while for others the background of experience has been extremely meager. Background of experience is not necessarily related to mental age, although the children with the higher mental age will be much better able to assimilate the experiences to which they are exposed and to understand and make use of them.

It is helpful if the teachers can in some way evaluate the children's work habits and their perseverance at a school task. Pupils of lesser ability but who work hard will probably get much more done than bright pupils who do not develop good work habits or "drive" for achievement.

In a follow-up study of one thousand "nonacademic" boys, McIntosh concluded that in the I.Q. range of 65–85, good work habits and perseverance were of more value in holding jobs than were twenty additional points on an individual intelligence test.[3]

Readiness is an important part of the learning tasks of the pupil all the way through school. The idea that teachers teach readiness for several weeks in first grade and then reading the rest of the year is a *false* concept. Readiness should technically be thought of as the "getting ready" period for studying *any* lesson one has to do. Reading readiness in its traditional sense should continue concurrently with the teaching of the initial

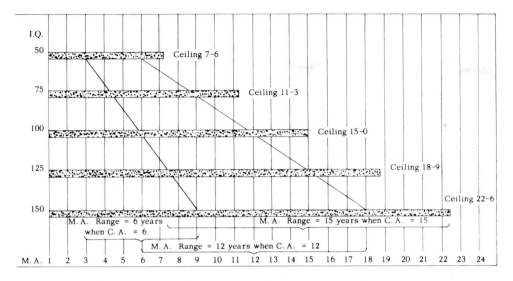

Figure 2.4. Ranges of mental development at ages six, twelve and fifteen for different I.Q. levels as measured by intelligence tests administered individually.

sight vocabulary in the primary school. Relating the new lesson to the previous experiences in the pupil's background includes considerable "readiness" all the way through school if learning is to be meaningful.

The health habits and possible handicapping conditions of a child have a direct bearing on his or her ability to make progress in school. When a child fails to progress, the classroom teacher should consult first with the school nurse. In the absence of a school nurse, the mother should be asked for a report of a general physical examination by the family physician or the child's pediatrician. If all these factors—impaired vision, hearing, or motor coordination; fatigue; malnourishment; and infections—can be ruled out, then the teacher must look to some other cause for the failure to progress. If these physical factors *do help to explain* the difficulty, *they should be corrected first.* In the event that they cannot be corrected, the best possible adjustment must be made to the handicap.

While defective *vision* is the first impairment usually considered, and one always to be checked by a vision specialist, there are other less obvious physical handicaps limiting many children's progress. Obese children referred to family physicians have been found to have conditions of underactive thyroid and/or very low basal metabolism (see Case II: Betty, in this chapter), which may explain lethargic behavior and complete lack of intrinsic motivation. Asthmatic conditions and allergies may handicap children's general well-being to the extent that they never "feel like" learning to read. Because of the extreme importance of learning auditory discrimination of sounds and developing acuity in this ability, hearing impairment must be evaluated as a possible contributing factor to failure to learn to read. A hearing disability may be of only a temporary nature, and a second-grade child who has a head cold for several weeks or

Making Connections 2.1: What Makes Successful Readers?

Reading teachers are encouraged to be aware of factors that frequently contribute to reading difficulties for certain children. It is hoped that knowledge of these factors may help teachers and parents to arrange positive experiences for students learning to read.

It is equally useful to find out what factors contribute to success in learning to read. Such insights can lead to community and school planning for optimum learning experiences. Plan to interview at least someone of high school age or older who see themselves as successful readers. Ask each to share with you what factors contributed to success in learning to read and enjoying reading.

When each class member has completed his or her interviews, prepare a composite list of factors contributing to success in reading. Did some factors appear more than once? Were some factors prevalent among particular subgroups of the total group that was interviewed? Do the identified factors fall into a few large categories? Perhaps you can prepare a statement that suggests what factors seem to contribute to success in learning to read.

an ear infection of some duration may have some temporary hearing impairment for many weeks and so "miss" much of the second grade course of study in phonic analysis.

Finally, the psychological needs of the child have significant ramifications in child behavior, but they may be the most difficult for the teacher to change or accommodate. If the children have group recognition and approval, feel that they really belong and are accepted in their groups, and are challenged by a variety of new experiences, their needs usually will be adequately met.

The home is the primary agent in determining whether a child's psychological needs are met. A great many parents are finding it very difficult to meet the overt behavior problems of their children.

The serious psychological problems of latch key children, malnourished children, or confused children derive from home and community rather than the schoolroom. The adults in the home establish the values the child holds for education. The purpose of learning, the importance of reading as a valuable activity, and the intrinsic motivation to learn are likely set by the time the child enters first grade.

Mental Retardation versus Educational Retardation

Problems also arise as a result of children being "labeled" as mentally retarded when they are not. Wide discrepancies sometimes exist between children's achievement levels and their tested intelligence. Occasionally pupils who manifest a "normal" I.Q. score when given an individual test fail completely to learn to read in the elementary school. When this problem is *not adequately faced* by those concerned—the parents, the school principal, the school psychologist, and the school social worker—such children occasionally get all the way into, or even through, the senior high school. They are usually

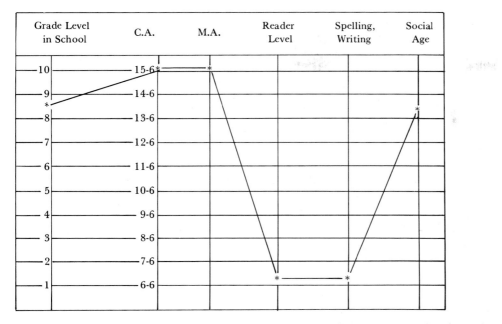

Figure 2.5. Jerry's profile of abilities. Jerry's individual intelligence test results showed normal intelligence. His behavior in social situations was judged to be "normal" for one in the eighth grade. He could not, however, read or write.

then given diplomas because they have good attendance records, are socially adjusted with their peers, and practice some of the social amenities. Frustrated teachers have not known what to do or where to turn for adequate help in specific situations, and so have passed the students through school. In spite of this inability to read, these students are not mentally retarded.

Jerry was referred for a reading analysis by his minister. The minister described him as a fifteen-year-old boy who *seemed* bright enough and who had excellent social behavior, but who could not read. An individual intelligence test indicated perfectly normal intelligence (Wechsler I.Q. 100). A speech check indicated such serious speech articulation difficulties as to render his speech almost unintelligible to many listeners. A reading test established his status as a nonreader. This profile of abilities is diagrammed in figure 2.5. Obviously, Jerry had tremendous potential for reading and language growth.

The case history provided by the family explained much of *why* the situation existed. Attendance in several schools in three states during the primary grades, concomitant with a serious asthmatic condition that was not arrested until he was ten years old, were given as causes of failure to learn to read.

Eighteen months after tutoring was started, Jerry was attending high school classes, reading fairly well at sixth- or seventh-grade level, had developed an easily understood speech pattern, played on the high school football team all fall, and had earned passing grades at the first reporting period in the senior high school. "He attended the high school prom after their homecoming football game and appeared on the dance floor completely indistinguishable from any of his football teammates," according to his school superintendent. Yet this boy and the many who have his school learning problems are often referred to as mentally retarded or as slow learners. It is obvious that these problems are correctable and any description alluding to mental deficiency does not apply here.

While a wide range of achievement is normally expected in a class, there is need for many of the poor achievers to have instruction in remedial reading. Pupils who need remedial reading in such a class are underachievers. Pupils whose capacity for learning is below the average of the class, but who are achieving as well as their ability permits, are not underachievers. The difference is estimated on the basis of an expected reader level.

Expected Reader Level

If teachers had accurate measures of mental ages of their pupils (group intelligence tests have no value in assessing the abilities of poor readers), they could get a *rough estimate* of expected reader level by *subtracting five and one-half years* from the mental age, since six and one-half is the average age of beginning first graders. Formulae have been derived for more accurately estimating this expected reader level. Bond and Tinker found that using a formula of *years in school times I.Q. plus 1.0* gave a practical estimate of grade achievement expectancy.[4] Thus a child in the middle of fourth grade with an I.Q. of 120 has a reading expectancy of 3.5 times 1.20 plus 1.0, or 5.2.

The amount of educational retardation for seven students, based on Bond and Tinker's formula for estimating expected reader level, is illustrated in table 2.1.

Betty is underachieving by five years, educationally speaking; George, eight years; Bill, three and one-half years; and Tom, three years. The expected reading level column in the table shows the level at which each child would be achieving if he or she were performing at his or her so-called capacity level. Sally, Mary, and Jim, on the basis of mental age given in table 2.1, are achieving at approximately capacity level. They are not educationally retarded.

When children who are underachievers enter the intermediate school at fourth grade, and the junior high school at seventh, they face a crucial test. A great deal of pressure is exerted to make sure the school teaches them what it has in mind for them to learn, but it often does not vary the assignments to give them a chance to learn what they are ready to learn.

To clarify further the distinction between mental retardation and educational retardation, three brief illustrative cases are presented. The first is a mentally retarded boy for whom the school should provide an adjusted program. This boy is *not a remedial case*. The other two cases are students with "normal" ability who need remedial teaching of basic reading skills.

Table 2.1 Educational Retardation is the Difference Between Expected and Present Reading Levels

Name	C.A.	M.A.	I.Q.	Years in School	Expected Reading Grade Bond-Tinker	Present Reading Level	Educational Retardation Bond-Tinker
Betty	12–6	13–4	108	6	7.48	Second Grade	About 5 years
George	14–11	14–9	99	8	8.9	First Grade	About 8 years
Bill	9–8	9–11	102	3.5	4.5	First Grade	About 3½ years
Tom	9–0	13–6	150	4.0	7.0	Fourth Grade	About 3 years
Mary	7–6	6–6	87	1.5	2.3	Beginning Reader	None
Jim	12–8	10–0	79	6.0	5.7	Easy fifth	None
Sally	12–0	9–0	75	4.0	4.0	Hard third	None

Case I: Ronald

Ronald was thirteen and in the sixth grade. The results of the Stanford-Binet Intelligence Scale, Form L, showed his I.Q. to be 68. He was referred for testing so that some evidence could be obtained to determine whether he was mentally retarded and the extent to which his reading retardation might be explained by low intelligence.

The intelligence test indicated that Ronald's mental age was about nine years and that the things expected of him in his schoolwork ought to be no more difficult than would be expected of a nine-year-old child.

Technically, a diagnosis of mental retardation is never made on the basis of the administration of the Stanford-Binet Test alone. A complete case study of a child (see chapter 7) necessitates medical examinations, a psychological evaluation of many behaviors, a social case history, and a consideration of life values, motivations, and aspirations. From the point of view of the classroom teacher, however, this test of intelligence has revealed extremely valuable information about Ronald's present ability to function. It may perhaps be all the information immediately available to the teacher, and the *teacher must plan something* for Ronald *now*.

The teacher's major problem is to help Ronald make a contribution to the group and to help the group understand and appreciate him. His classmates need to learn to recognize his limitations and his contributions, and to be helpful. Ronald will be accepted by many as a friend; by many he will often be ignored.

Ronald can make a satisfactory adjustment as an adult if he is supervised and taught some personal, social, and occupational skills as he grows older (if he is retarded as this test result indicated).

Ronald's teacher, who is one of the primary factors in his success, must maintain for Ronald standards that will result in success rather than failure. The teacher must remember always to start *where Ronald is* and to move slowly from one step in learning to another. *Sixth-grade standards have no place* in the teacher's approach with him.

Since Ronald can now read at third-grade level, he is not seriously retarded in reading if the intelligence test score is reliable. During the class period when the other children work on skills, the teacher should make sure that Ronald gets adequate instruction and practice using work-type reading skills of third-grade level. Because his teacher teaches social studies and science by the unit method and provides reading materials in the classroom covering a range of several years of reading difficulty, Ronald will be able to participate in the class as well as others with poor reading skills. In addition to his efforts in the three R's, his teacher will utilize whatever talents he may have in drawing or illustrating, mounting pictures, making bulletin boards, or making models to clarify concepts.

Case II: Betty

Betty was referred to the educational clinic in May, at the end of her sixth-grade school year. The sixth-grade teacher had decided to move Betty to *special education* in the elementary building for next year's assignment, because she could not read, had no aptitude for school work, seemed tired all day, and responded to no type of motivation. Her referral to the clinic was made through the school psychologist, who found that Betty's I.Q. score on the Stanford-Binet test was 114. The psychologist could not approve Betty's transfer to the room for educable mentally retarded and made the referral for an analysis of reading ability.

The reading analysis showed Betty's reading abilities were somewhat as follows:

Reader level as found in a series of readers	Second grade, first semester (2^1)
Grade placement on Gates Basic Reading Tests	3.2
Reading to appreciate general significance	3.0
Reading to note details	3.4
Spelling grade placement	Third grade
Word-attack skills	End of grade 2
Dolch Basic Sight Vocabulary of 220 service words	Score of 192—second-grade level (See table 3.3)

Betty's chief-expressed interest was horses. This interest was utilized in giving her many stories about horses and employing her talents in drawing and writing about them.

It was concluded that if Betty were to be helped, her remedial program should begin with all the developmental skills at second-grade level.

Her mother and father accompanied her for the analysis and were much interested in the results. They were determined that she should not be transferred to the class for retarded children. The father expressed the greater interest in having Betty achieve success in reading. Betty's vision and hearing had been checked at the teacher's suggestion during the school year. Since Betty was much overweight, this physical condition was discussed with her parents. They indicated that Betty was sixty pounds too heavy; they had tried to keep her from eating sweets until she felt that they nagged at her about eating anything; and they recognized that she seemed tired a great deal.

Her mother insisted that Betty got sufficient sleep, as much as ten hours a night. She had taken Betty to the doctor, who found Betty to have a very low metabolism rate and had prescribed medication. Betty's mother expected Betty to accept the responsibility for taking the medicine, however, and had not supervised it. No one in the family seemed to recognize the seriousness of this and the interrelationship between Betty's lethargy, her excess weight, and her lack of motivation. It was suggested that the parents have Betty again visit the doctor, and that they follow through carefully on any advice for Betty's taking medication regularly.

The first step in remedial teaching was to assure Betty that she was a bright girl, that she could learn to read, and that if she were willing to work at it, she would be able to catch up with her class and eventually be able to read and write as well as they could. Since Betty was now ready to transfer to the junior high school and the challenge of going on made a considerable impression, it was not difficult to convince her that her situation could be remedied.

Betty attended the reading clinic during the eight-week summer school. In the fall, she attended the clinic two hours each day and went to the junior high school at 11:00 A.M. This program continued until the following May when, in one calendar year, Betty's reader level had progressed to sixth-grade level. Her last tests in the clinic revealed the following scores:

Reading Vocabulary	7.2
Paragraph Meaning	6.4
Total	6.8

Conferences with her mother indicated that her parents had not given Betty much encouragement and praise for the rather remarkable growth she had effected during seventh grade. They were counseled to give her encouragement, to spend time with her, and to appreciate her as a person. The parents were encouraged to help her appreciate her physical problem, since she was still much overweight. They were counseled that while she did not read at what might be considered eighth-grade level, she would be able to read competently enough to complete eighth-grade work, and that in her free reading she would be able to find plenty of reading material at her reading level.

The clinic program for Betty had been primarily one of:

1. Starting where she was and building security and confidence.
2. Following the same steps that are necessary in good first teaching of reading.
3. Building attitudes toward reading that helped her accept herself, her school work, and encouraged personal reading outside of the schoolwork.

In Betty's case, the program included giving attention to health problems that would make her feel like working and encouraging the parents to be more interested in and to give greater acceptance to her school effort. Not the least task, by any means, was convincing Betty that she was a bright girl who would meet expectations.

Case III: George

George was 14–11 (C.A.) and in the seventh grade in a three-teacher rural school when he was identified on a reading screening test as a nonreader. On the Gates Basic Reading Tests given to all the children in grades three through eight, George attempted only a few answers and missed so many of those that one could only conclude that he was guessing. An individual reading inventory disclosed that his reader level was primer. His sight vocabulary was limited (120 words on the Dolch Basic Sight Word Test), and he had little knowledge of phonics.

George was quiet; however, his conversation with the psychologist suggested that he was not mentally retarded. On the Stanford-Binet, George earned an I.Q. score of 99. His performance in problem solving, immediate recall, and memory for digits was good; his scores on vocabulary and items requiring much use of the language were more limiting.

George's school record showed that he had been promoted each year through the fourth grade. At that point, the fourth-grade teacher found that George could not read and put him back into the second grade. He had since been promoted regularly and was now in the seventh grade. His family history showed that his father had died when George was six, and that at the age of twelve George had acquired a stepfather.

George's present teacher had never considered the possibility of teaching him *how to read*. She read a lot of his subject matter to him and hoped that he would be allowed to graduate from the eighth grade!

In a conference with the teacher, it was decided that George could be excused from regular seventh-grade spelling, language arts, and reading. In their place he could learn to spell the basic words he would need in stories that he wrote. At first, he would dictate stories to a retiree from the community who helped in the class twice weekly. Later, he would be encouraged to write his own stories, seeking help with words and the organization of sentences as needed. It was planned that he would have many chances to read his stories to the teacher, the helper, to younger boys and girls, and to the principal who was in charge of three schools and worked in George's school two days a week.

When several stories had been written, George was encouraged to bind them into a book just as other class members bound their writings. The teacher planned that the community helper would take time to read to George each day that he was in the classroom. He also helped George find interesting books in the small library for the boy to read to him.

By the end of the year George had heard a dozen trade books read to him. He had written eight books and had himself read nineteen library books. At first the books had been comparable to a primer level of difficulty. By the end of the year George was able to read a library book on his favorite subject, horses, that was approximately of fourth-grade difficulty. While his reading still lacked fluency, George was pleased with his progress and anxious to continue reading during the summer months and in eighth grade.

The point to recognize is that George read many interesting books at increasingly harder levels. By using library materials and books that George had written, the teacher provided lots of easy practice with materials that did not look like primers. He experienced writing, spelling, and word-identification skills at the level at which he was able to work at any given time.

Discussion

Mentally retarded children may also be educationally retarded. Mentally retarded children who have a capacity to achieve higher than their achievement level will profit from corrective reading, although their rate of growth will be slower, corresponding to their rate of mental development.

It should also be stressed that if children are mentally retarded, they need to work at *their reader levels,* and the teacher should conscientiously remember to "go back to where they are" just as if the children were not mentally retarded.

Range in Achievement within the Class

In view of recognized principles of human growth and development, one must accept the thesis that not only do boys and girls grow at different rates, but that they all arrive at different destinations in varying lengths of time. It logically follows that all children *will not* learn the *same* lessons in the *same* amount of time with the *same* amount of practice. A most important concept for teachers follows: *The range of differences in a given class will increase through the year and from year to year* as the class progresses through school. If the range of reading ability in second grade is *four years* on standardized reading tests, it is to be expected that, with good teaching this range will, by the eighth grade, be about *ten years.* Teachers who feel a strong compulsion to work especially hard with the slowest group in the class, hoping to get them to achieve at grade level, are not only attempting the impossible, but may be neglecting the other groups who have greater capacity.

The reading level of the class may be defined as that level at which the "middle child" reads. Measured by a standardized test, it is the level above which and below which half of the class reads. The scores on the Nelson Reading Test, Form A, administered to a fifth grade at the end of the school year, presented in table 2.2 show the class median to be 6.5 (fifth month of sixth grade) while the grade norm is 5.9 (the last month of the fifth-grade year). The class, as a group, is performing above grade level. The scores on the California Reading Test, Form W, administered to a sixth grade at the beginning of the school year, presented in table 2.3, show the class median to be 5.0 (beginning fifth grade) while the grade norm is 6.0 (beginning sixth grade). The class, as a group, is performing one year below grade level expectancy. The reader

TABLE 2.2. Range of Reading Ability in a Fifth Grade: The Nelson Reading Test for Grades 3 to 9* Revised Edition, Form A

May 10, 19 _____

Grade Norm: 5.9
Class Median: 6.5

Student		Raw Score	Grade Equivalent	Student		Raw Score	Grade Equivalent
F	— 1	133	10.5	M	— 7	81	6.5
M	— 1	125	10.5	M	— 8	80	6.4
F	— 2	122	10.4	F	— 10	80	6.4
F	— 3	111	9.4	M	— 9	77	6.2
M	— 2	107	9.1	M	— 10	73	6.0
F	— 4	106	9.0	F	— 11	67	5.7
F	— 5	105	9.0	M	— 11	67	5.7
M	— 3	100	8.6	F	— 12	67	5.7
M	— 4	98	8.3	M	— 12	65	5.6
F	— 6	95	7.9	F	— 13	55	5.0
M	— 5	95	7.9	F	— 14	55	5.0
M	— 6	92	7.5	F	— 15	49	4.6
F	— 7	91	6.7	F	— 16	47	4.4
F	— 8	81	6.5	F	— 17	40	3.9
F	— 9	81	6.5				

*M. J. Nelson, *The Nelson Reading Test* (Boston: Houghton Mifflin Co., 1962).

will note that the range of differences in the fifth-grade performance on the Nelson Reading Test is 6.6 (six years, six months) while the range of the sixth grade on the California Reading Test is only 4.6 (four years, six months). The greater range is the more desirable, since it indicates that the more able students are more appropriately challenged to achieve at higher levels.

Teachers must not permit children with special learning problems to go beyond the primary school without bringing to light the nature of their problems in reading, and finding out which specialized techniques need to be used. Such a procedure will preclude students "going through" the grades with their age mates without learning reading skills.

Probably the best way to help children with reading is to combine the teaching of "how to read" with counseling for whatever social or emotional problem exists concurrently with the reading failure. This attacks the so-called blocks to learning that may lie behind the inability to learn, and as children's minds become "free" to learn, they are successfully retaught "how to read." The problems of cause and effect go together and are often inseparable. Sometimes it is not possible, and perhaps not necessary, to say that the poor reading resulted in delinquent or disturbed behavior or that the delinquent or disturbed behavior caused the poor reading. The classroom teacher can assess where children are in the reading process and try to alleviate both the bad behavior and poor reading by giving those children success experiences, building up their feelings of importance, and adding to their security in the classroom and to their feelings of belonging and contributing something worthwhile to the group.

The aim of the diagnosis is not so much to be able to say that one particular factor (for example, poor teaching, poor vision, poor home environment, or lack of motivation

TABLE 2.3. Range of Reading Ability in a Sixth Grade: The California Reading Test, Intermediate, Form W*

September 12, 19 _____						Grade Norm: 6.0	
						Class Median: 5.0	
		Grade Equivalent				Grade Equivalent	
Student	Vocab.	Comp.	Total	Student	Vocab.	Comp.	Total
No. 1	8.4	7.0	7.7	No. 17	5.3	4.7	5.0
No. 2	6.8	7.7	7.3	No. 18	4.2	5.5	4.9
No. 3	7.1	7.2	7.2	No. 19	4.2	5.5	4.9
No. 4	7.5	6.6	7.1	No. 20	4.9	4.6	4.8
No. 5	7.3	5.7	6.5	No. 21	5.0	4.4	4.7
No. 6	5.8	7.1	6.5	No. 22	4.3	4.8	4.6
No. 7	5.9	6.9	6.4	No. 23	4.5	4.6	4.6
No. 8	5.4	7.1	6.3	No. 24	4.3	4.9	4.6
No. 9	5.9	6.0	6.0	No. 25	3.8	4.9	4.4
No. 10	6.7	5.2	6.0	No. 26	4.5	3.8	4.2
No. 11	5.0	6.7	5.9	No. 27	4.5	3.8	4.2
No. 12	5.9	5.6	5.8	No. 28	4.1	4.0	4.1
No. 13	6.2	4.9	5.6	No. 29	3.8	4.0	3.9
No. 14	4.7	6.5	5.6	No. 30	3.0	4.7	3.9
No. 15	4.9	5.2	5.1	No. 31	4.1	2.8	3.5
No. 16	4.7	5.3	5.0	No. 32	3.3	2.8	3.1

*California Test Bureau, Del Monte Research Park, Monterey, Calif., a Division of McGraw-Hill Publishing Company.

to learn) is the cause of failure, but to learn as much as possible about all the causal factors and correct as many contributing conditions as possible.

Psychological, physical, and sociological factors that explain individual differences in learning need to be explored. *The fact is* that these disabled readers are with us in almost every classroom, and their presence must be acknowledged by every competent classroom teacher. The regular teacher is the key person who must accept the responsibility for identifying the child who is not making satisfactory progress.

Characteristics of Poor Readers

Generally, poor readers are those boys and girls who are not able to function as well in reading ability as their general learning ability would indicate that they should. If they have "normal" intelligence, they should, other things being equal, progress "normally" in acquiring the developmental skills of reading. Students may have problems with reading if most of their skills in this area are adequate but they are deficient in a few specific skills. Many children are crippled all the way through the elementary school because they do not learn how to "attack" polysyllabic words. They may do well enough with sight vocabulary but cannot attack longer words because they do not know what a syllable is or how to divide words into *parts*.

Poor readers include the boys and girls who have either emotional problems that overlay their ability to attend and prevent their learning what the teacher teaches, or have organic problems currently labeled neurological, minimum brain dysfunction, or a number of others.

Bond *et al.* classify poor readers according to:

1. *General Reading Immaturity* Simple retardation suggests general immaturity in reading. Fourth graders who have average general learning ability, but whose profiles of skills consistently indicate an ability to use second grade material, are an example. They just need to be motivated to learn all the developmental skills they have missed.

2. *Specific Reading Immaturity* Specific reading immaturity is used to describe the student whose general profile shows one or two serious deficiencies but who otherwise performs normally. Such deficiencies might be (1) the inability to sense and use syllabication; (2) the inability to read and follow directions; or (3) the inability to organize and remember material read.

3. *Limiting Reading Disability* The term *limiting reading disability* is used to describe the student who shows "gaps" in skill learning or who is seriously deficient in school learning. An example is the student whose word recognition and general vocabulary are adequate for grade level but whose ability to understand and remember ideas in content reading is inadequate. Such a student who has average learning ability can be taught the missing skills. Such a student who lacks basic skills in comprehension will need to be taught all the skills basic to analysis, synthesis, and evaluation of paragraph units.

4. *Complex Reading Disability* Complex reading disabilities are those cases whose limiting disabilities are further complicated by negative attitudes, poor self-concepts, or sensory or other handicaps. Limiting disability cases should be identified, diagnosed, and rehabilitated *before* they become complex.[5]

Dechant describes poor readers as slow learners, reluctant, disadvantaged, and retarded readers.[6] The slow learners are limited by general learning ability; the reluctant readers lack the desire to read; the disadvantaged readers may fail to see the relevance of the school to their personal lives, and they may need to learn "how to learn"; the retarded readers include all those who are performing in reading considerably below their potential level of performance.

The implication that remedial reading practices are something technical or beyond the preparation of the regular classroom teacher should be modified. If classroom teachers do not meet the reading needs of most children, there is not the slightest hope that those needs will be met at all.

Teachers justifiably raise questions about overcrowded classrooms; three, four, or more reading groups; lack of materials for instruction; individual differences to be met in all the subjects in addition to reading; and considerable pressure to complete the course of study.

Under some pressure about her responsibility to children who have reading problems, one fifth-grade teacher said:

I think of a teacher as being all day in the classroom with thirty-five or even forty children. Perhaps one-fourth need individual conferences, extra time, parent conferences, and some need remedial tutoring. Not always can I refer a child to the school's centralized guidance services and have any results of diagnosis from the psychologist in time to help me during the school term.

The comments of this teacher are directly related to the philosophy of this book. The existence of the problem is not new; *a great deal of awareness of it may be new.* The solution, to a considerable degree, is dependent upon classroom teachers.

Mainstreaming and the Education of All Handicapped Children Act of 1975

Public Law 94–142, the Education of All Handicapped Children Act of 1975, reflects a present day concern that all handicapped learners have optimum educational opportunity. This requires that all people be educated in the least restrictive environment in which they can function.

The classification of children by "labels" has produced problems. Assigning labels has created stereotyped behavioral expectations for many who can modify their behavior. Decisions for placing children in any situation should be made cooperatively with the parents and after learning as much as possible about all aspects of the individuals' lives. Certainty that language facility, cultural heritage, and experience background will not discriminate against the children is needed in testing and evaluation. The school can no longer use such arguments as: the children cannot learn; their handicaps are too severe; or a program for these children does not exist. The 1975 law requires constructive, individual programs. Individualized educational programs (IEP's) must be provided for all children based on a thorough evaluation of the children's strengths and weaknesses.

The major requirements of PL 94–142 include:

1. Extensive child identification procedures.
2. Assurance of full service with a projected timetable.
3. Guarantee of *due process* procedures.
4. Regular parent or guardian consultation.
5. Comprehensive personnel development (in-service training).
6. Full service in the least restrictive environment.
7. Nondiscriminatory testing and evaluation.
8. Guarantee to protect the confidentiality of data.
9. Maintenance of an IEP for all handicapped children.
10. Guarantee of appropriate, public education at no cost.
11. Assurance of a responsible adult to act in lieu of parents when parents are unknown or unavailable.

Federal law required that all eleven of these provisions be in effect as of September 1, 1978. The implications of this law are profound. All children must be provided with an opportunity to learn since it is now accepted that all children can learn something. The law also has provisions for parents who do not feel that the program of the school is adequate to receive independent evaluations of their children or report to regional federal offices their dissatisfaction.

This major change in education specifies that education will take place in the least restrictive environment. School administrators, generally, accept some form of mainstreaming as the least restrictive. Mainstreaming provides that all children who can profit from doing so must be accommodated in a regular classroom for some part of each school day. Thus, mainstreaming serves major purposes in the social, psychological, and environmental aspects of the development of the handicapped children.

Public Law 94–142, Section 612, 5B provides:

> To the maximum extent appropriate, handicapped children, . . . are educated with children who are not handicapped, and special classes, separate schooling, or other removal of handicapped children from the regular education environment occurs only when the nature or severity of the handicap is such that education in regular classes with the use of supplementary aids and services cannot be achieved satisfactorily.[7]

The emphasis throughout is that all decisions must be made on an individual basis. All students must be given the education that is appropriate to their individual needs. This law, in its broadest application, relates also to those children who may be taught in remedial reading centers in local schools or sent to special reading clinics in city schools. The children may be helped more in their total development if their remedial programs can be worked out within the classroom. Such programs could include: specific help to the teacher from the reading specialist or supervisor, provisions for an itinerant teacher to work in the classroom during the school day, provision for peer tutoring or cross-age grouping, and specific lessons designed to teach students the developmental skills they need to learn. With respect to the child who may have been labeled as dyslexic, Simpson says:

> It is not the specific difficulty with words that makes the dyslexic's problem so serious. It is the massive, relentless pressure brought to bear on him through the anxiety of parents and the demands of the school.[8]

Classroom Teachers and Individualized Education Programs (IEP)

Classroom teachers should be aware that special programs for individual special education students have been used for some years now, and individual teachers are, in some measure, accountable for the part of an individualized education program that should transpire in the regular classroom. The National Association for Children with Learning Disabilities has pointed out that misunderstandings may be avoided when school systems:

1. Follow carefully the guidelines disseminated at the federal level. Parents must be notified about any meeting concerning their child and parent participation is extremely important. Evaluations must be complete and up to date. Such meetings must not become lax and disorganized.
2. Make sure that the personnel who work directly with the student are at the meetings with the parents. Classroom teachers, rather than supervisors who consult occasionally with teachers, should discuss the children's behavior with the parents.

Making Connections 2.2: Utilizing Support Personnel

The roots of difficulties in learning to read have already been identified in this text as being extremely complex. Frequently, the classroom teacher is not able to deal effectively with the problems, since they reside in the conditions of the family or the community.

Support personnel within the school system can often be effective in helping the teacher resolve some problems so that the child can get on with the business of learning. The principal, the nurse, the speech therapist, the psychologist, the counselor, the special education teacher, the librarian, the physical education teacher, and the home-school liaison person are examples of professional people who can help.

Make arrangements to interview at least two support persons in a school concerning *specific* ways in which they can help the classroom teacher with children who are having unsuccessful experiences in learning to read. You will want to find out how teachers can make arrangements to work with the support personnel and how communication will be maintained.

Bring notes from your interviews to share with your class when all members have completed the assignment. In addition to comparing services of persons in different jobs, also note what different people holding the same job see as possible ways they can help.

3. Set up evaluation conferences to respond to the concerns of the parents, the teachers, the therapists, and any others who may work with the child. Evaluations must be kept "open" and broad. The school needs to understand the student's *abilities, disabilities,* and *possibilities.* Good evaluations are multidisciplinary. Also, if parents bring independent evaluations, schools are required by federal guidelines to study them carefully.

4. State IEP's clearly, so that parents can understand the specific objectives the student will work on during the time period.

5. Include in IEP's all the needed related services such as physical therapy, occupational therapy, and speech therapy.

6. Do not "mainstream" students into regular classrooms with vague objectives that do not meet the social adjustment needs of a student. What is available may not be what the individual student needs! The school is required by law first to accurately diagnose the student's need and then to provide the service that meets that need.

7. Make sure that the IEP for any student is properly communicated to each regular classroom teacher who will teach him or her. There have been instances in which classroom teachers have never seen the IEP for students who have spent parts of their school days in their rooms for long periods of time.

8. The student's program is worked out and mutually discussed by the parents and everyone who will work with the student. It is most unfortunate if school officials convey to the parents that the school system is doing the parents a great favor by accommodating their child.

It will be well for classroom teachers to cultivate the best skills possible in their public relations with patrons of the community.

Appraising Problems

Now that some background knowledge about the student and the expectations for his or her success in school have been presented, we will look at three important affective aspects of a school program to meet the needs of the one who has difficulties in reading and writing. These affective aspects are: (1) the self-concept: success and failure; (2) corrective versus regular reading programs; and (3) emotional problems and reading.

The Self-Concept: Success and Failure

Attitudes toward education as a process, the immediacy with which the learner perceives the *need* for what he or she is learning, the way the teacher feels about the child and the child feels about the teacher, the techniques of rewards and punishments, the application of the pain-pleasure principle and many other facets determine the learner's attitude—how he or she participates—toward the learning process.[9]

Henry cites a number of specific situations in which values being taught in the classroom are at considerable odds with those expected as a result of the philosophy of the school. If children are destructively critical of others, have feelings of vulnerability, fear of internal hostility, engage in evil deeds, and are bored in the classroom, these are the values they are learning. Henry also observed that docility in children, both in conforming to external pressures from the group and in submitting to teacher authority, was strongly rewarded in school behavior although docility is never stated as an intended value in objectives of education. Henry concluded that teachers, like parents, are gratifying their own unconscious needs in their overt responses to children. The constructive approach to this dilemma is not to condemn teachers but to give them insight into how they project their personal problems into the classroom situation.[10]

Schools are organized to accommodate groups. Many times they are not as well organized to meet the needs of the individual. This organization places all the values and rewards on conformity and achievement. In this pattern:

1. Children are lumped together in large groups.
2. Children are given identical assignments with the expectation that everyone will complete them and hand them in.
3. Teachers are apt to express, overtly or covertly, some displeasure at poor, incomplete work.

4. Teachers are apt to unconsciously think "he can't," "he's dull," "he won't get far," "he should have had help before," or "he's inadequate."

Teachers need to be admonished *not to rationalize* the problems of the underachiever: (1) that the classes are too large to give such a student help; (2) that there is too little time in the school day (the student will be here six hours and needs to fill all that time with constructive work); (3) that there are not any materials to work with (the student cannot help this either); or (4) that underachievers have developed negative behaviors and do not want to try.

Many people begin their efforts with much zeal and are sincere in their desire to be helpful to children, but when children do not respond to the methods of teaching, teachers allow their zest to cool and begin saying, "Yes, but."

Don'ts That May Encourage the Teacher

The following *don'ts* may be helpful:

1. Don't have any preconceived notions of quick success. You may have it and that will be fine, but you should not anticipate it.
2. Don't feel "guilty" because you have a pupil in your room who cannot read. All teachers have had seriously underachieving pupils, and many are alert to the existing needs.
3. Don't feel expected to "get them up to grade level."
4. Don't blame former teachers for lack of success.
5. Don't lose patience and say sarcastic things to the child.
6. Don't feel that everybody expects you to know how to teach every child how to read. If they do, they shouldn't.
7. Don't decide that the student is stupid just because you do not make progress. There are probably lots of specialized techniques that you have not tried. Rather, if you feel that you have failed up to now, try to think of the child as your challenge and begin looking for new ideas to try . . . or other people to ask.

A negative self-concept, which may be the consequence of poor achievement in school, may be irreversible in our present-day schools by the time the student reaches the sixth grade. Dealing with aggression in ways to make follow-up positive instead of negative is very difficult for many teachers. Confluent education emphasizes that there are two components in learning: the affective and the cognitive. Rogers writes: "The facilitation of significant learning rests upon certain attitudinal factors that exist in the personal relationships between the facilitator and the learner."[11] All the variables—interest, anxiety, appreciation, values, motivation, self-concept, and self-acceptance—are part of the affective domain of the student.

Rucker mentions such words as *lonely, hunger, want of love, poor self-concept, confusion*—but these are some of her direct quotes from different Johnnies:

"You've got to let me cover the other words in the row or I can't read."
"Readin ain't real. Real is outside that window."

"Every time you have that readin class, I have to go to the john."
"Them kids won't sit beside me cause they say I stink. I smell all right to me."
"Mom says I'll end up in the pen like my dad."
"You don't say 'good' when I read, teacher."[12]

Sparks describes the student that gets sent to the office: downcast, general air of detachment, defensive, seems to neither know nor care what is going to happen next. Sparks suggests this student is too often an unwanted child, may be the victim of multiple divorce and remarriage, may be ethnically different, may be the child of over-zealous, struggling middle-class parents, or there may be many other causes for the behaviors he or she has learned.[13]

Attitudes toward Success

Sociologists have defined for teachers the narrow scope of life experience that the curriculum of the school encompasses. A rather narrow, inflexible set of values aptly describes the behavioral pattern of teachers in their overt judgmental reactions to students. This set of values places strong rewards on succeeding, working hard, doing good, being right, saving, planning for a bigger and better future, climbing the ladder of success, and individuals shaping their future destinies.

Many teachers have internalized these values and have perpetuated the narrow channeling of acceptable behavior. In their implementation of the curriculum, they cause a great deal of frustration because of unreconciled conflict in purposes between the teacher and the student. Students who are of lower-class socioeconomic status do not have the same values as their teachers. Those American Indians not acculturated to a middle-class life-style and the many Spanish-speaking children throughout the country who come from homes where language, culture, and experience have not prepared them for the ideology that the teacher takes for granted will find difficulty. The Protestant ethic, to which teachers universally subscribe, refers to the complex of ideas that includes the notion of personal responsibility, personal obligation, the desirability of hard work, thrift, and accumulation of wealth. Allison Davis chides us:

> The present curricula are stereotyped and arbitrary selections from a narrow area of middle-class culture. Academic culture is one of the most conservative and ritualized aspects of human culture. . . . For untold generations, we have been unable to think of anything to put into the curriculum which will be more helpful in guiding the basic mental development of children than vocabulary building, reading, spelling, and routine arithmetical memorizing.[14]

Corrective versus Regular Reading Programs

Corrective reading is for people whose functioning level in reading is below their capacity level for reading. In other words, in terms of individuals' abilities as they are assessed, they should be able to read better than they are now reading. Instruction that will narrow the gap between their present functioning and their potential for performing is corrective or *remedial reading* instruction. If this work is done in the classroom by the regular teacher, it is usually designated as *corrective reading* in contrast to the remedial instruction that takes place under "special" arrangements outside the usual class procedure.

Corrective reading instruction is exactly the same process as good teaching of developmental reading, except that it is planned in a very different setting and is directed toward some additional and difficult goals. In the *first* place, the student has experienced failure which, in our culture, is often a traumatic experience. Depending on the nature and extent of this failure, reading instruction will now need varying degrees of adjustment. In the *second* place, remedial instruction is usually done in very small groups or with individual students. Of course, if original instruction could have been individual or nearly so for many of these cases, the instruction might have been effective the first time. The fact that remedial work is highly individualized makes it much different from regular teaching. In the *third* place, it is expected that the children will learn to read, beginning at some level of difficulty below their grade placements. If their regular day-by-day work had been so adjusted, they might have made desired progress without "special" help. When the work is *labeled* corrective or remedial, it is apparently easier to *accept* the below-grade performance and thus reduce the tensions under which the children may feel placed otherwise. In the more permissive atmosphere, the students are allowed to reestablish some confidence, rebuild their egos, learn at their rates, compete only with their own past records, and accept their performances as adequate for them. After these criteria are met, most disabled readers can learn to read. In the *fourth* place, the search for causes of lack of success is continued. Reference will be made frequently to continuing diagnosis. The reading teachers search for causes of nonachieving while they teach the reading skills that the students lack.

One does need to *know more* to deal successfully with the student who has failed. There are additional problems in motivation, in reward, in conferring with a troubled parent, and in adequately planning a learning program *for all day* with the underachiever. But these are not strange and mysterious tasks. These must be incorporated in the "standard" operating procedure of the conscientious teacher.

Corrective reading should be aimed at any individual who is missing any skills that have already been taught. Primary grade children are usually not referred to clinics for special tutoring because two years of retardation is sometimes used as a guide for teachers making referrals. But many who are two years behind can be helped adequately in classroom programs, and many that are less than two years behind should have help early so they will not continue to get farther behind. The only valid criterion for the teacher is to help any children who are not achieving their potentials.

The person who teaches corrective reading needs to know more than just the basic reading skills to be taught. Nevertheless, the best teaching practices are the best remedial practices. The prerequisites to success are patience, understanding, optimism, and ingenuity. It is the classroom teacher's task to determine where the children lost their way, to get them back to their point of departure, and to help them move forward.

Emotional Problems in Reading

Emotional disturbance is evidenced in the behavior of students by mannerisms such as nail biting, stuttering, extremely short attention span, defiant behavior, and daydreaming. Other manifestations may be the haggard, tired-out expression; inhibited, withdrawn behavior; hyperactivity and the inability to sit still; or aggression. In deciding what to do about these behaviors, the teacher must be cognizant of the fact that the emotional disturbances may be the cause of poor reading habits, the result of poor reading, or the two behaviors may not have a direct cause-effect relationship. The teacher must attempt, however, to improve reading ability and to adjust the behavior as much as possible.

First of all, the teacher can obtain additional information about the pupils through careful observation of their total behavior throughout the school day—their play activities, the way they come to and leave the school ground, their comments in casual conversation, their responses as the teacher subtly pursues their interests, their attitudes, and their aspirations. If the teacher can, through the remedial reading effort, meet the pupils' needs sufficiently to rebuild the students' egos and attain greater emotional stability, they may need no further psychological help. In most cases, however, it would be desirable for the teacher to request special help for these pupils.

The second step is to request the school psychologist to obtain further data concerning the pupil's total behavior pattern by using projective tests of a structured and/or an unstructured nature. The interpretation of the results of such tests requires the skills of a specialist.

A third step in preparing to help most of these remedial cases is contact with the parents of the pupil. This will best be done by the school social worker, who is in a position to help the parents analyze their problems in relation to their child and to plan some kind of rehabilitation of a parent-child relationship that may be the major cause of the difficulty. In the absence of the school social worker, it is imperative that the teacher visit the parents, report observations of the child, and ask the parents for their evaluation. The important point is, however, that the child's reading difficulty may not be the basic problem in failure to learn at school. The nature of family problems, the techniques for helping parents analyze their difficulties, and the techniques for helping them solve their problems and work out constructive solutions and put them into practice—these skills are not within the scope of classroom teachers, but are the basic techniques used in social casework. The reconstruction of the family pattern of living is often basic to a satisfactory solution of the child's school learning problems. Louttit says:

> Therefore, a child with a reading disability who exhibits emotional or personality problems should be considered as needing attention beyond remedial reading. This is usually the responsibility of a specialist in psychology or psychiatry, and such special service should be sought.[15]

Ephron aptly describes the frustration many teachers feel when adolescents they try to teach fail to learn. Note the way she entreats teachers never to use words for labels that do not explain:

> Johnny is not responding to our tutoring him. I have a feeling he is resisting. His parents always put too much pressure on him, and now he is resisting them. He wants to defeat them. He is being contrary, defiant, uncooperative. But he's so foolish to cut off his nose to spite his face. Doesn't he realize it's his own life that's at stake? Defeating his parents won't help him any, nor do him any good.
>
> The adolescent boy is being "negative." Why does he cling so stubbornly to his "negativism"? If our understanding of the boy stops here, we are indeed defeated, and so is the boy.
>
> The words "resistance," "negativism," "defiance," "stubbornness," "spite"— all these words (like "lazy") are pawns being pushed back and forth across the chessboard. They are busy words, much in use, which explore no depth and explain nothing.[16]

Ephron further points out, following one of her interviews with Donald, that teachers need to be aware of the inflexible situations within which many schools operate, and that life experiences are not always "either-or" situations. "Either-or-ness" forces people into anxiety states when they cannot always succeed.

> [Donald's] statement, "You either know or you don't," is an interesting reflection of education's emphasis on absolute accuracy. Education impresses upon children the *need to be right,* and they grow up under the tyranny of immediacy and unrelenting accuracy. There is desperation in rushing to be right, with the accompanying fear of being hurled down the abyss of rejection if one is *wrong* instead of *right.* Therefore, Donald feels that one either knows or does not know, almost by magic, and without the trust in his own good mind to stay with a problem and reason it out.[17]

A Case Study: Fred

Fred (an emotionally disturbed boy to whom psychotherapy and remedial reading instruction were given concurrently) was ten years old and was tested in March of his fourth-grade year.

Fred attended an elementary school where he had a succession of excellent classroom teachers. When he was in the fourth grade, he was referred to the psychoeducational clinic for tutoring in remedial reading.

A reading analysis was made and tutoring began at the preprimer level. While Fred had an individual intelligence test score of 122, and appeared to be interested and cooperative with his clinician, he was no more ready to move into more difficult material at the end of twelve weeks of tutoring than he had been at the beginning.

An analysis of his relationship with his mother did suggest to the remedial reading supervisor that Fred was overdependent and was having some difficulty growing up. Fred had two older sisters who were already married and had children of their own. His interests and abilities in play were with younger children, and he often engaged in solitary play much more characteristic of much younger boys.

It was suggested to the mother that, since the remedial reading clinic did not seem to be helping and there was a child guidance clinic in the community, she and Fred visit the child guidance clinic. It was explained that the clinic would expect her also to appear for interviews and some counseling. Fred's mother accepted this willingly, and the two entered therapy sessions in June after school closed in May. The following fall, Fred came to the reading clinic four days a week and attended the guidance clinic the fifth day for the hour. He began making progress in his remedial reading instruction, and at the end of his fifth grade in the elementary school he was able to read successfully for instructional purposes at the third-grade level.

The "apron strings" should be severed gradually, but they must be severed. A child who has not learned to be responsible for his own actions may not feel the importance of learning to read. The responsibility for effecting such changes in children's behavior may require special services outside the classroom, as indicated in Fred's case.

Most parents want to cooperate with school personnel when they recommend examinations of hearing, vision, or psychological factors. They also want a clear explanation of the problem and some interpretation of the results of testing. Parents of children with reading problems indicate almost unanimously that the schools should provide guidance services in the lower grades of the elementary school to prevent as many of these problems as possible.[18]

It is true that with determination and persistence the reading clinician might have measured some success in Fred's reading, but the primary problem was apparently psychological, and Fred needed the clinical psychologist to help him find himself, to strengthen his ego, to make a person of him "in his own right," and to free him of his dependence on his mother.

The Relationship between Reading Disability and Emotional Disturbance

There are three possible ways in which remedial reading and emotional disturbances may be related:

1. Some children are emotionally disturbed before they try to learn to read, and fail.
2. Some children fail in reading and become emotionally disturbed as a result of reading failure.
3. Some children experience emotional problems and reading failure as a concomitant experience.

Harris indicates that all of the children with reading disability seen in the Queens College Educational Clinic show maladjustment of some kind. He states further that the emotional difficulties are thought to be the cause of the reading difficulty in more than 50 percent of the cases.[19]

Arthur I. Gates, in a summary of his studies of emotional and personality problems in relation to reading disability, stated that emotional instability was found in about 75 percent of retarded readers but that in only about 19 percent of these cases was it found to be the specific cause of the reading disability. It was a contributing, but not necessarily the primary cause.[20]

Grace Fernald reported that, of seventy-eight cases of extreme reading disability treated in her clinic, only four entered with no history of emotional maladjustment. The extreme emotional reaction did not take place until after the child had experienced repeated difficulty and lack of success. This condition produces a deep-seated sense of inferiority in many children and kills any incentive to try to learn. Sometimes an aggressive, irritable personality develops, and the child tries to compensate for his or her inability to learn by the extra attention received from teachers and parents, who recognize this child as different from other children.[21]

The Educational Clinic of Boston University reported that "39% . . . [of the cases analyzed] showed an emotional disturbance of some kind."[22] In these cases, discouragement, nervousness, and family trouble were the three causes mentioned most frequently.

Bond and Tinker state that in the great majority of cases teaching the child adequate reading skills reduces the anxiety and alleviates the emotional problem.[23]

The writer's experience provides evidence in agreement with Bond and Tinker. Most of the pupils referred to clinics for reading analyses exhibit anxiety and nervous mannerisms. However, when reading clinicians demonstrate that they are really "being accepted as they are," their tensions are reduced quickly. Further, as children observe others working at instructional levels far below assigned grade levels, they are willing to "begin at any level" if they can successfully learn to read.

According to Sires:

> Many children in analyzing their own problems say, "I got lost in the first grade." How much would be gained if each child spent enough time on the primer level, for example, to become a fluent and thoughtful reader before moving on to first-reader materials! This plan does not involve a non-promotion policy but simply that the teachers become less conscious of grade lines and accept children as they are. If we did this in the primary grades, our middle grade "remedial reading problems" would decrease.[24]

Louttit tells us:

> The remedial teacher has the task of helping the child with his disability. He cannot hope to affect parental rejection or inconsistency. He cannot undertake psychotherapy with the child. But he can accept the child as he is, give him support and security, appreciate and encourage him in his positive characteristics, and in this way afford a more wholesome atmosphere in which the child can attack his specific problem.[25]

Even when an emotional problem has been identified and is apparently causing the reading difficulty, one must remember that there are other children with similar emotional problems who learn to read without difficulty. Often, there is a concomitant factor such as an unidentified vision problem, directional confusion, a temporary hearing loss due to head colds, or poor teaching.[26]

> If his problem has been carefully diagnosed, and if effective and varied remedial techniques are used, evidences of success will appear early and the child's confidence will begin to be restored. If the child's emotional tensions are not relieved by the gradual improvement of his learning problem, outside technical help may be necessary. This child might then be referred to a Bureau of Child Guidance or a psychiatrist for further study and recommendations.[27]

The types of problems that children have are sometimes difficult to define, and teachers many times must work with very little information. When children are assigned to classes, teachers should hope that they will respond and progress normally. When emotional distress is evident, teachers must proceed as if these children will be able to learn through group teaching and give as much individual help as possible.

When emotional factors are the primary cause of reading disability, classroom teachers should attempt the following:

1. Become the child's friend (first and most important).
2. Study the child's past history and gain understanding of his or her emotional make-up.
3. Help the child to talk freely about likes and dislikes, fears and hopes, hobbies and interests, friends, and family. With this information, teachers will try to discover causes for emotional states and take steps to help each child to adjust. Be sympathetic listeners.
4. Try to determine if the child failed to read because of emotional instability or if emotional instability caused the failure to learn. Are reports available from a mental health center or a child guidance clinic?
5. If the child is not seriously disturbed, give reassurance of the ability to read, and motivate and encourage with a good corrective reading program.
6. If there is evidence of a severe emotional disturbance, refer the child for a psychological evaluation before undertaking remedial work.
7. Maintain a classroom atmosphere that has maximum permissiveness.

Summary

In this chapter, the problems of the students who do not make adequate progress in reading were discussed. Studies suggest that these children are, on the average, from the dull normal and normal ranges of intelligence.

Factors influencing learning are constitutional (physical), intellectual, environmental, educational, and emotional. How much pupils learn depends upon their mental ages, experience background, linguistic differences, general health, work habits, physical handicaps, and psychological needs; and the degree to which the conditions surrounding these factors can be improved to accommodate the learners.

Case studies were cited to distinguish educational retardation, mental retardation, and mental *and* educational retardation. The problem of educational retardation was further illustrated by the contrast between expected reader levels and present reading levels of students selected by classroom teachers for work in corrective reading.

Causes of reading failure are rooted in the fact that individuals are different from each other, that they learn at extremely different rates, and that motivation and drive have much to do with their enthusiasm for learning. Causes of reading failure are sometimes persistent and long-suffering. Failure may be rooted in the cultural difference between the middle-class life-style of the school and the home background, the mobility of much of our present-day population, the almost universal acceptance of automatic (social) promotion *without its concomitant need* for adequate study of why the child failed, and the greater holding power of the school, so that more children with all levels of ability remain in classrooms longer.

For Further Reading

Bond, Guy L.; Tinker, Miles A.; Wasson, Barbara B.; and Wasson, John B. *Reading Difficulties, Their Diagnosis and Correction,* 5th ed. Englewood Cliffs, N.J.: Prentice-Hall, Inc., 1984, Chapter 3: "Description of Disabled Readers," pp. 35–50; Chapter 7, "Basic Considerations in Diagnosing Reading Difficulties," pp. 97–122.

Burmeister, Lou E. *Reading Strategies for Secondary School Teachers,* 2d. ed. Reading, Mass.: Addison Wesley, 1978. Chapter 1, "Understanding How Well Students Read," pp. 3–28.

Dallmann, Martha; Rouch, Roger L.; Char, Lynette Y. C., and DeBoer, John J. *The Teaching of Reading,* 6th. ed. New York: Holt, Rinehart and Winston, 1982, Chapter 12: "Classroom Diagnosis of Reading Ability," pp. 337–55.

Griffin, Peg. "How and When Does Reading Occur in the Classroom?" *Theory into Practice* 16 (December 1977), pp. 376–83.

Heath, Shirley B. *Ways with Words: Language, Life and Work in Communities and Classrooms.* Cambridge: Cambridge University Press, 1983.

Harris, Albert J., and Sipay, E. R. *How to Increase Reading Ability,* 7th ed. New York: Longman, 1980, Chapter 5, "Differentiated Reading Instruction I," and Chapter 6, "Differentiated Reading Instruction II," pp. 93–133.

Kabler, Michael L., and Carlton, Glenn R. "Educating Exceptional Students: A Comprehensive Team Approach." *Theory into Practice* 21 (Spring 1982), pp. 88–96.

Lambie, Rosemary A., and Brittain, Mary M. "Adaptive Reading Instruction: A Three Pronged Approach." *The Reading Teacher* 37 (December 1983), pp. 243–48.

Notes

1. "If Johnnie Can't Read—Get Yourself a Lawyer," *Learning* 2 (April 1974), p. 29.
2. Marion Monroe and Bertie Backus, *Remedial Reading* (Boston: Houghton Mifflin, 1937), pp. 17–33.
3. W. J. McIntosh, "Follow-Up Study of One Thousand Non-Academic Boys," *The Journal of Exceptional Children* 15 (1949), pp. 166–70.
4. Guy L. Bond, Miles A. Tinker, and Barbara B. Wasson, *Reading Difficulties, Their Diagnosis and Correction,* 4th. ed. (Englewood Cliffs, N.J.: Prentice-Hall, 1979), p. 62.
5. Guy L. Bond, Miles A. Tinker, Barbara B. Wasson, and John B. Wasson, *Reading Difficulties, Their Diagnosis and Correction,* 5th. ed. (Englewood Cliffs, N.J.: Prentice-Hall, 1984), pp. 45–47.
6. Emerald V. Dechant, *Improving The Teaching of Reading,* 2d. ed. (Englewood Cliffs, N.J.: Prentice-Hall, 1970), p. 455.
7. Cited by Alan Abeson and Jeffrey Zettel in "The End of the Quiet Revolution: The Education of All Handicapped Children Act of 1975," *Exceptional Children* 44 (October 1977), p. 125.
8. Olive C. Simpson, "Fifty Years of Dyslexia: A Review of the Literature, 1925–1975, II Practice," *Research in Education,* no. 15 (May 1976).
9. Jules Henry, "A Cross-Cultural Outline of Education," *Current Anthropology* 1 (July 1960), pp. 267–305.
10. Jules Henry, "Attitude Organization in Elementary School Classrooms," *American Journal of Orthopsychiatry* 27 (January 1957), pp. 117–33.
11. Carl A. Rogers, *Freedom to Learn,* (Columbus, Ohio: Merrill, 1969), p. 106.
12. Helen Rucker, "Why Can't You Read, Johnny?" *Instructor* 83 (March 1974), p. 14.
13. Richard Sparks, "The Walking Wounded in Our Schools," *Instructor* 83 (June/July 1974), p. 12.
14. Allison Davis, *Social Class Influences upon Learning,* (Cambridge: Harvard University Press, 1952), pp. 97–98.
15. C. M. Louttit, "Emotional Factors and Reading Disabilities," *Elementary School Journal* 56 (October 1955), p. 72.
16. Beulah Kanter Ephron, *Emotional Difficulties in Reading* (New York: The Julian Press, 1953), p. 13.
17. Ibid., p. 98.
18. E. A. Tufvander and Miles V. Zintz, "Follow-up Study of Pupils with Reading Difficulties," *Elementary School Journal* 58 (December 1957), p. 156.
19. A. J. Harris and E. R. Sipay, *How to Increase Reading Ability,* 7th ed. (New York: Longman, 1980), p. 316.
20. Helena H. Zolkos, "What Research Says about Emotional Factors in Retardation in Reading," *Elementary School Journal* 52 (May 1951), p. 516.
21. Ibid., p. 515.
22. Ibid., p. 514.
23. Guy L. Bond and Miles A. Tinker, *Reading Difficulties, Their Diagnosis and Correction,* (New York: Appleton-Century-Crofts, 1967), p. 109.

24. Louise Sires, *Newsletter* (New York: The Macmillan Co., 1950).

25. Louttit, "Emotional Factors and Reading Disabilities," p. 72.

26. A useful list of forty behaviors to watch for is given by Robert F. Topp, "Pre-adolescent Behavior Patterns Suggestive of Emotional Malfunctioning," *Elementary School Journal* 52 (February 1952), pp. 341–43.

27. Leo J. Brueckner and Guy L. Bond, *The Diagnosis and Treatment of Learning Difficulties,* (New York: Appleton-Century-Crofts, 1955), p. 83.

3
Evaluating Word Recognition Abilities

Vocabulary

Trying the book on for size
miscue
"running words"
service words
basic sight vocabulary
reader level
phonics
reversal
VAKT
letter confusion
compound word
concepts about print
environmental print

Questions

1. Why would word lists such as the ones described in this chapter be important in the analysis of reading strengths and areas for growth?

2. What is important about the fact that different word lists identify the same words as being the most frequent in the language?

3. Why should a teacher know the content of phonics very well?

4. What are the different forms you may expect reversals to take? What can you do about reversals?

5. How are reversals distinguished from confusions?

6. Why should the reading teacher be concerned about the child's spelling ability?

7. What concepts should the reader have about the nature of print?

Making a Quick Class Survey

The classroom teacher inventories the oral reading abilities of the students at the beginning of the school year. This can be done, superficially but quickly, by asking individuals to read parts of a story that has been selected and reviewed for them. Preferably the teacher will be able to assemble the students in subgroups of six or eight. The teacher asks the students to read aloud in turn. The pupils who read fluently and keep the attention of the audience may read longer passages. The pupils who show immediate signs of difficulty may read only one sentence. The students who experience considerable difficulty are the ones about whom the teacher needs more information quickly.

With some practice, the teacher learns to "try on the book for size" very quickly by asking students to read a passage they have not previously seen to find out if they make more than one miscue in twenty consecutive words. This meets the criterion for instructional level of reading, which will be defined later in the text. Reading orally as described here is sight reading, without previous practice, because this constitutes a "test" situation for the teacher to learn about the students' word recognition abilities.

Another "rule of thumb" that many teachers give students is this: "Select a page in a book you'd like to read. Begin reading and turn down a finger when you come to a word you do not know. If you turn down all the fingers on one hand before you finish reading the page, this is a strong indication that this book is too difficult for you to read. Put it back and select an easier one."

Much of the reading for the quick class survey will be done from the commercially published basal readers on classroom teachers' bookshelves. Because this is true, attention is now directed to those basal readers with severely controlled vocabularies and the need for teachers to be aware of some of the abbreviated word lists.

In the basal reading series published during the past four decades, the general practice has been to introduce up to 30 words in the first book, and an additional 15 or 20 in each of two succeeding books (designated as the preprimers). The preprimers taught from 60 to 100 words before the child was introduced to the first hardbound reader in the individual reading series.

Before 1935, many teachers introduced children to reading through the writing of dictated stories of common interest to the group. During the years of the basal reader, many competent first-grade teachers have consistently introduced reading to children through what is now commonly called the language-experience approach. This approach applied to reading has many advantages because it makes use of the child's language, it uses the experiences of the child for its story content, and the children use it when they are writing their own books of stories.

One can readily see strong psychological advantages to this method for all children. In corrective reading particularly, after the students have had unsatisfactory reading encounters, it is even more important that they learn that reading is one facet of communication, that they can begin with what they want to read about, and that they can compose their own stories, which can be preserved in their own books.

One of the problems that arose when preprimers were more in vogue was to determine which words should be taught first. What are the most important words to be used, overlearned, and made a part of the instant recognition vocabulary?

Abbreviated Word Lists

Several reading researchers have demonstrated that a relatively small nucleus of words exists that boys and girls must learn as quickly as possible in order to progress in beginning reading from the task of mediating what words are, to reading ideas rapidly. The study of Durr showed that only 188 different words constituted 68.41 percent of all the *running* words in 80 trade books selected by elementary school students for their free reading.[1]

Ten words that appeared most frequently in Durr's study—*the, to, and, he, a, I, you, it, of, in*—occurred a total of 25,010 times in a total word count of 105,280 in the 80 trade books. These 10 little words represented 23.76 percent of all the *running* words in the study. When 15 more words are added—*was, said, his, that, she, for, on, they, but, had, at, him, with, up, all*—the 25 most frequently used words constituted 35 percent of the *running* words tabulated. This finding suggests that teachers need to teach these most common words early in the reading program and that teachers must provide sufficient relevant practice to ensure permanent learning of these words.

McNally and Murray found that the twelve most frequently used words were *a, and, he, I, in, is, it, of, that, the, to,* and *was.* They stated that these words accounted for about 25 percent of the running words in their print sample.[2] All of their words except *is,* appeared in Durr's high-frequency list of twenty-five words; nine of McNally and Murray's twelve words were in Durr's first ten. The essence of the word count data is that a very few words account for a high percentage of the running words in print. It is essential that these words be known well to achieve fluent reading. The best way for most children to learn these words is to engage in lots of meaningful reading and writing, since these high-utility service words are bound to appear again and again.

Some of the useful abbreviated word lists teachers may wish to use include:

1. Edward W. Dolch, *The Basic Sight Word Test: Parts I and II* (Champaign, Ill.: The Garrard Publishing Co., 1955).
2. Eldon E. Ekwall, "300 Sight Words, Graded in Levels from Pre-Primer to Third Grade," *Diagnosis and Remediation of the Disabled Reader* (Boston: Allyn and Bacon, 1976), pp. 69–71. This list contains all of the Dolch 220 sight words and the first 200 of the Fry list.
3. Peter Edwards, "The 100 Most Frequent Words," and "The Edwards List of 800 Easy Words," *Reading Problems, Identification and Treatment* (London: Heinemann, 1978), pp. 77–80.
4. Edward B. Fry, "The Instant Words" (a 600-word basic vocabulary, graded according to frequency and approximate grade level of difficulty), *Elementary Reading Instruction* (New York: McGraw-Hill Book Company, 1977), pp. 73–74.

5. Albert J. Harris and Milton D. Jacobson, *Basic Reading Vocabularies,* (New York: Macmillan Publishing Co., 1982). Words common to four or more series of basals are given in order of frequency, in alphabetical order, and in order of teaching.
6. Robert L. Hillerich, "Word Lists—Getting It All Together," *The Reading Teacher* 27 (January, 1974), pp. 353–60. (A list of 240 starter words is compared to the Dolch 220-word list in figure 3.2 in this chapter).
7. J. McNally and W. Murray, *Key Words to Literacy* (London: Schoolmaster Publishing Co., Ltd., 1968), p. 1.
8. Wayne Otto and Robert Chester, "Sight Words for Beginning Readers," *Journal of Educational Research* 65 (July/August 1972), pp. 435–43.
9. Lillie Pope, "Sight Words for the Seventies," *Academic Therapy* 10 (Spring 1975), pp. 285–89.
10. Clarence R. Stone, "One Hundred Important Words for Prebook, Preprimer, and Early Primer Reading," *Progress in Primary Reading* (New York: McGraw-Hill, 1950).

Word Recognition Tests

The tests discussed in this section are the San Diego Quick Assessment, The Slosson Oral Reading Test, The Wide Range Achievement, and the Dolch Basic Sight Word Test. The San Diego Quick Assessment includes instructions for administering and interpreting the results. The Slosson Oral Reading Test's discussion involves the test's interpretation, while the consideration of the Wide Range Achievement deals with both administration and interpretation. The discussion of the Dolch Basic Sight Word Test includes a methodology for analyzing students' errors and estimating a grade equivalent based on number of words recognized at sight.

The San Diego Quick Assessment

The San Diego Quick Assessment is a word recognition test that provides 10 words at each grade level, beginning with preprimer level and continuing through grade eleven.[3] The instructions suggest giving the student the 10 words for one level typed on an index card. For primary grades it will be well to use a primary-type typewriter. By starting two grades below the students' grade levels, most students will be able to begin successfully. This test is easy to administer and requires very little time. Teachers report a high degree of agreement between the performance on this test and the Informal Reading Inventory (IRI). Teachers should use this test before administering an IRI to determine the appropriate grade level for the student to begin in the series of passages of the IRI. The San Diego Quick Assessment, the suggestions for the teacher, and the directions for administering are presented in figure 3.1.

Suggestions to the Teacher

1. Have the students read lists until they miss three words in one list.

2. The list in which students miss no more than one of the ten words is the level at which they can read independently. Two errors indicate their instructional level. Three or more words identify the level at which reading material will be too difficult.

3. Be sure to analyze the errors.

4. Observe behaviors that accompany the reading.

Administration

1. Type out each list of ten words on index cards, one list to a card. If available, type the first three or four lists with primary type.

2. Begin with a card that is at least two years below the students' grade level assignments.

3. Do not put the reading level on the cards where the students can read it. Do your coding on the back of the card.

4. Ask the students to read the words aloud to you. If they misread any on the list, drop to easier lists until they make no errors. This indicates the base level.

5. Write down all incorrect responses or write them on the copy of the test.

6. Encourage the students to read words they do not know so that you can identify the techniques they use for word identification.

7. Keep reading lists until they miss three words on any one list or all lists are exhausted.

PP	*Primer*	*1*	*2*
see	you	road	our
play	come	live	please
me	not	thank	myself
at	with	when	town
run	jump	bigger	early
go	help	how	send
and	is	always	wide
lock	work	night	believe
can	are	spring	quietly
here	this	today	carefully

Figure 3.1. San Diego Quick Assessment (From Margaret La Pray and Ramon Ross, "The Graded Word List: Quick Gauge of Reading Ability," *Journal of Reading* 12 [January 1969], pp. 305–7.)

3	4	5	6
city	decided	scanty	bridge
middle	served	certainly	commercial
moment	amazed	develop	abolish
frightened	silent	considered	trucker
exclaimed	wrecked	discussed	apparatus
several	improved	behaved	elementary
lonely	certainly	splendid	comment
drew	entered	acquainted	necessity
since	realized	escaped	gallery
straight	interrupted	grim	relativity

7	8	9	10
amber	capacious	conscientious	zany
dominion	limitation	isolation	jerkin
sundry	pretext	molecule	nausea
capillary	intrigue	ritual	gratuitous
impetuous	delusion	momentous	linear
blight	immaculate	vulnerable	inept
wrest	ascent	kinship	legality
enumerate	acrid	conservatism	aspen
daunted	binocular	jaunty	amnesty
condescend	embankment	inventive	barometer

11	
galore	exonerate
rotunda	superannuate
capitalism	luxuriate
prevaricate	piebald
risible	crunch

Figure 3.1.—*Continued.*

The Slosson Oral Reading Test

The Slosson Oral Reading Test (SORT) measures the ability to pronounce words at different levels of difficulty.[4] The words, in lists of 20, by level of difficulty, range from preprimer level to high school level. The entire test contains 200 words. The students should pronounce first the list of 20 words that the teachers estimate the students will be able to get right. Then they pronounce words that are progressively more difficult until they indicate that they know no more of the words. Their raw scores are the number of words pronounced correctly, and if they did not begin with the easiest words, they get credit for having pronounced all of those also. Their raw scores convert to grade placement scores. Teachers generally have reported that the Slosson test assigns a grade placement value about one year above the instructional level determined by the IRI. Knowing that it may not be completely accurate, the teachers can adjust the reading levels determined for the children. It needs to be emphasized that this is only a word recognition test. It is not a reading test, as the title indicates, because it does not test comprehension.

The Wide Range Achievement Test

The Wide Range Achievement Test (WRAT) is a standardized test that measures ability in reading (word recognition), spelling ability, and arithmetic computation.[5] Its administration is divided into two levels: Level I for children between the ages of five and twelve, and Level II for persons twelve years through adulthood. The reading subtest has some utility for Level II because the people taking the test are asked to pronounce a relatively long list of words (75) that become progressively more difficult. Some of the word lists are too easy to test the adult level. The test can be administered in about ten minutes and gives a rough estimate of word recognition ability. The raw score earned can be converted to a grade placement score. It must be emphasized that, while it is labeled as a reading test, it is only a test of word recognition ability. It is not a test of reading ability, since it does not test comprehension.

For students in corrective reading, the spelling subtest of the WRAT will also be useful. The examiner dictates from a list of 45 words ranging from very easy to quite difficult, and the raw score can be converted to a grade placement value. As a screening test, it will alert the teachers to the kind of writing to expect from the students when corrective reading classes begin.

The Dolch Basic Sight Word Test

Dolch wanted a list of words that would be utilitarian for the classroom teacher, especially in the primary grades. In the mid–1930s he selected three word lists, arranged them in dictionary order in juxtaposition, and chose the words common to these three lists as the most needed service words.[6] The first list was published by the Child Study Committee of the International Kindergarten Union.[7] It is a study of the vocabulary of children before they entered first grade. The list was based on detailed observation in the kindergarten classroom. It contained 2,596 words. Only those with a frequency of 100 or more on this list were selected, making a list of 510 words often spoken in the kindergarten.

The second list used was the first 500 of the Gates List, which has been used as a basis of many studies in reading vocabulary. It is recognized as containing words of first importance in children's reading.[8]

The third list was that compiled by Wheeler and Howell, consisting of 453 words found in ten primers and ten first readers published between 1922 and 1929.[9] This list represents the actual reading vocabulary used in grade one, and therefore the vocabulary upon which all later reading was built in those series of readers.

TABLE 3.1. Origin of the Dolch List

List	Source	Number of Words
I.K.U.	Spoken Vocabulary (5 year old s)	510
Gates	Reading Vocabulary (Primary Grades)	500
Wheeler and Howell	Ten Primers and Ten First Readers	453
Common to all three lists		193
Common to two lists (selected)		27
Total		220

From E. W. Dolch, *Teaching Primary Reading* (Champaign, Ill.: The Garrard Press, 1941). By permission.

When the words common to all three lists were identified, they totaled 193 words. Dolch then arbitrarily selected 27 words common to two of the lists that he felt "rounded out" the list. The 27 words that appeared on only two of the three lists were included since they "seemed to belong"—*which* with *who* and *that; done* and *does* with *did* and *do; start* with *stop* and *write* with *read.* The number words (six, seven) under ten not included were added, since some of them were in the list.

The origin of the Dolch Service Words is summarized in table 3.1.

The Dolch Basic Sight Words are, as the name implies, a short list of words that children should recognize "at sight"; that is, they should not expect to "sound out" or otherwise hesitate on these crucial service words. The 220 words of The Dolch Word List are *service* words, and "service" in this frame of reference means that these are the most common words used in all reading and writing—making up over half of all the running words children read in their elementary textbooks. No nouns are included in the service words, since they change with the subject matter and, for young children, are often identifiable from the illustrations on the pages of the reading material.

The Dolch Basic Sight Word List becomes an extremely valuable list of words in classroom work—if used appropriately. Suggestions for its use as a teaching aid are given later in this chapter.

The greatest value of the list of 220 words is to emphasize the importance of a few service words *in all reading.* The complete Basic Sight Word List itself is presented in figure 3.2.

Based on a 1,000-word sampling of each book, Dolch determined what percentage of all the running words in textbooks used in the elementary school were sight words. Sampling of four first readers showed that 70 percent of the running words were on the service list; for the four second readers, 66 percent were service words; of four sixth-grade readers, 59 percent were service words. This emphasizes the extreme importance, for every child, of having complete mastery of these words. These percentages, and those for word counts in arithmetic, geography, and history textbooks, are given in table 3.2.

TABLE 3.2. Percentage of the Basic Sight Vocabulary in Running Words in School Textbooks

Textbook	Number of Series	Grade					
		1	2	3	4	5	6
Reading	4	70	66	65	61	59	59
Arithmetic	2			62	63	57	57
Geography	2				60	59	54
History	2				57	53	52

From E. W. Dolch, *Teaching Primary Reading* (Champaign, Ill.: The Garrard Press, 1941), p. 208. By permission.

1. by	at	a	it	sit	me	to	the
2. in	I	be	big	not	of	we	so
3. did	good	do	go	red	too	seven	walk
4. all	are	any	an	six	start	show	stop
5. had	have	him	drink	put	round	right	pull
6. its	is	into	if	no	on	or	old
7. ask	may	as	am	yellow	you	your	yes
8. many	cut	keep	know	please	pick	play	pretty
9. does	goes	going	and	take	ten	they	today
10. has	he	his	far	my	much	must	together
11. but	jump	just	buy	own	under	off	over
12. black	kind	blue	find	out	new	now	our
13. fast	first	ate	eat	open	one	only	once
14. help	hot	both	hold	try	myself	never	two
15. brown	grow	bring	green	us	up	upon	use
16. four	every	found	eight	with	white	was	wash
17. from	make	for	made	shall	she	sleep	small
18. around	funny	always	because	who	write	would	why
19. long	let	little	look	some	very	sing	soon
20. away	again	after	about	wish	well	work	will
21. cold	can	could	clean	ran	read	run	ride
22. full	fall	five	fly	then	tell	their	them
23. before	best	better	been	see	saw	say	said
24. live	like	laugh	light	that	there	these	three
25. her	here	how	hurt	when	which	where	what
26. down	done	draw	don't	thank	those	this	think
27. give	get	gave	got	want	went	were	warm
28. came	carry	call	come				

Figure 3.2. Dolch Basic Sight Word List (From E. W. Dolch, *Dolch Basic Sight Word Test*. Copyright 1942 by Garrard Publishing Company, Champaign, IL.)

Finding the Children's Instructional Levels Using the Test

Two methods of testing knowledge of basic sight vocabulary are presented here. The basic sight word test can be administered either as a recognition test or as a recall test. The differences seem significant. A recognition test is one in which the teacher reads one word in each row of four words and asks the children to find and circle it. This is the method suggested for classroom teachers to use when packages of the Basic Sight Word Tests are used with groups. However, a recall test is one that requires the child, without any stimulus, to say each word. The teacher has a better measure of how many sight words the child knows if the teacher asks the children to pronounce each word in each row, progressing down the page. This is a recall test.

A Scale for Determining Reader Level

The 220 words in the Dolch Basic Sight Word List constitute more than 60 percent of all the running words in primary grade reading materials and about 50 percent of all the running words in intermediate grade reading materials. This emphasizes their importance as *service words* in all children's reading. If children recognize these at sight, they will be less handicapped if they must hesitate to figure out other words in general elementary reading. These should not be analyzed phonically, but learned as purely "automatic" sight words. All children reading at third-grade level need to know all 220 of these words as sight words. *A Scale for Determining a Child's Reader Level* has been prepared for testing the children's knowledge of these words and then estimating their reader levels on the basis of the number of these words they can recognize.[10]

In establishing the scale, each child was asked to pronounce the words as a recall test. The words were presented from flashcards,[11] one at a time, or in groups arranged on the children's desks; or the teacher used the Dolch Basic Sight Word Test, Parts I and II.[12] The children, supplied with a three-by-five inch index card or similar marker, were asked to pronounce all four words in each line across the page. Sliding the marker down one line at a time, they proceeded in this fashion down the page.

The test can usually be completed in one sitting. If the children make many errors, there may be no value in continuing. If the children know very few of the words at the top of Test I, they need not continue. Younger children, or less successful ones who work slowly, may complete successive parts of the 220-word test over more than one work period, or identify the words on flashcards presented a few at a time.

The following criteria serve as a basis for computing the children's scores on the test.[13]

1. The child should respond within a few seconds (ten or less); if not, encourage the child to go on to the next word.
2. The teacher may indicate children's responses in the following way:
    a. If the word is called properly, draw a line through it.
    b. If the word is miscalled, and then corrected before going on, write above the word what the child said and then indicate with a *C* in front of the word that it was corrected.

    c. If the word is miscalled but not corrected, write the children's pronunciation above the word.

    d. If the child is willing to skip a word or move on without identifying it in any way, do not mark it.

    e. If the child makes several guesses and seems to get the word right only by guessing, write down the mispronunciation but do not draw a line through the word.

    f. The child's score on the total test is the number of words lined through.

    g. If the child makes pertinent comments about words, it is wise to jot them down on the margin of the page, for example:

        (1) Spelling out each word: "c-a-n, that's can."

        (2) "Oh, I know it but I just can't say it."

        (3) "I had that word in spelling just this week."

        (4) "It's 'on' or 'no' but I don't know which."

        (5) "Am I doing all right? Is this good?"

3. The scale for determining reader level on the basis of this score devised by McBroom, Sparrow, and Eckstein[14] is shown in table 3.3.

Standards[15] used in giving the Dolch Basic Sight Word Test individually were developed by Sparrow and Eckstein and included the following:

1. The criteria upon which children were given credit for knowing a word were:
   a. If they could pronounce it at sight;
   b. If they could sound it out and then pronounce it on first trial;
   c. If they corrected themselves immediately after miscalling it and then pronounced it correctly.

2. In no case were children given credit for knowing a word if any of the following occurred:
   a. If they miscalled it and then (after correctly pronouncing one or several others in the list) came back to that word and pronounced it correctly.
   b. If they took more than one trial of sounding to get it.
   c. If they miscalled it and gave more than one original mistaken word before finally getting the right one. Example: If for the word *could* children said *called, cold,* and then *could,* they were given no credit.
   d. If they omitted the word and then later came back and gave it correctly.
   e. If they hesitated longer than fifteen seconds before giving the word.[16]

TABLE 3.3. Approximate Reader Levels Based on the Dolch Basic Sight Word Recall Test

Dolch Words Known	*Equivalent Reader Levels*
0–75	Preprimer
76–120	Primer
121–170	First Reader
171–210	Second Reader or Above
Above 210	Third Reader or Above

The scale is useful in selecting an appropriate beginning level for the informal reading inventory, but the San Diego Quick Assessment is quite accurate, requires much less time, and allows the teacher to assess students reading at even high school levels.

Administering the Basic Sight Word Test and Analyzing the Errors Made

Part I of the Dolch Basic Sight Word Test was administered to a sixth-grade boy enrolled in a reading clinic. The scoring of the test is reproduced in figure 3.3. Because he made many errors and omissions, he was not given the second half of the test. It was possible to estimate subjectively a score on the total test to compare with the scale of known Dolch words in figure 3.3 by multiplying his score on Part I by two.

Name of Student: _George_   Date: _March 3, 19– –_

				down brown	*good* grow	*drink* bring	green
by	at	a	it	*four*	*it* every	found	eight
in	I	be	big	*if* from	make	for	made
did	good	*don't* do	go	around	funny	*away* always	because
all	are	any	*and* an	*he* have	*very* had	him	*did* drink
long	let	little	look				
set its	is	into	if	away	*into* again	after	about
as ask	*my* may	as	am	cold	*an* can	could	clean
many	*cat* cut	*be* keep	know	full	fall	five	fly
don't does	*go* goes	going	and	before	best	*butter* better	been
has	his	he	far	live	like	laugh	light
but	jump	just	buy	*he* her	*has* here	how	hurt
back black	kind	blue	find	down	*down* done	draw	*didn't* don't
fast	first	*eat* ate	*ate* eat	give	get	*good* gave	got
help	hot	both	hold	*come* came	*call* carry	*all* call	*came* come

Score _47_

Errors and Omissions _65_

Figure 3.3. The Dolch Basic Sight Word Test: Part I (From E. W. Dolch, *Dolch Basic Sight Word Test.* Copyright 1942 by Garrard Publishing Company, Champaign, IL.)

Since the words are to be recognized *at sight,* children are *not* taught to use word analysis techniques in identifying them unless a severe perceptual or neurological condition exists.

It is now possible to make a detailed analysis of the errors made on this recall test. The miscues can be grouped as wrong beginnings, wrong middles, wrong endings, reversals, wrong several parts, miscellaneous, and omissions (words failed to pronounce). A sheet of paper divided into spaces for recording miscues with these suggested headings is shown in figure 3.4. Figure 3.4 shows an analysis of George's errors recorded in figure 3.3. Other headings may be indicated, but these will contain most of the errors.

If George performs equally well on Part II, his total score will be 94. He will need to read from primer (or easy first grade) reader level. The analysis shows that he makes all types of miscues. Probably the teacher will concentrate first on correcting wrong beginnings. This individual makes only a few miscues on beginning sounds. Omissions—failing to attempt the word—account for his greatest number of miscues.

Wrong Beginnings	Wrong Middles	Wrong Endings	Reversals	Wrong Several Parts	Omissions		Miscellaneous
black-back	may-my	do-don't	its-sit	drink-did	any	full	had-very
					long	fall	
can-an	cut-cat	an-and	eat-ate	have-he	as	best	keep-be*
					am	been	
down-brown	always-away	ask-as	ate-eat	grow-good	many	how	
call-all	better-butter	does-don't	from-if	bring-drink	his	light	
					has	hurt	
	don't-didn't	goes-go	again-into	every-it	far	draw	
					just	got	
	came-come	done-down		gave-good	buy	get	
	come-came	carry-call			kind	give	
					find		
		her-he			fast		
					first		
		here-has			hot		
					both		
					found		
					let		
					about		
					could		
					clean		

Figure 3.4. Analysis of errors made on Dolch Basic Sight Word Test: Part I (See fig. 3.3 for errors. *May be a reversal of *p* and *b*.)

One objective in teaching reading is to build up the stock of basic sight words quickly. However, there are some cautions and suggestions to be pointed out in teaching the Dolch Sight Word List to a child.

1. Since uninteresting, unmotivated, meaningless drill on word pronunciation of the list is apt to intensify dislike for reading, offer the needed practice through personalized, relevant reading and writing activities. The Dolch words will likely constitute at least half of the words children read and write.
2. Since words in a list are devoid of contextual clues to meaning and pronunciation, be sure that practice activities and games provide contexts to aid the reader. This is the normal way that word identification is accomplished, and the children should learn to employ a variety of clues to identification.
3. When new words are added too fast, the usual result is confusion and frustration. Let children have many chances to read and reread stories containing new words. Reading experiences may be planned with basals, trade books, or stories the children themselves have written. Children can also get meaningful word recognition experience with signs, labels, announcements, and directions posted in the classroom and changed frequently.
4. Children are likely to have trouble spelling words that they do not read. They should have a variety of meaningful opportunities to use the words that they meet in their reading. Developing personal dictionaries or card files may be helpful.

Is the Dolch Basic Sight Word List Still Satisfactory?

Because the Dolch Word List is based on word counts made in the 1920s, several writers have questioned whether the list is still sufficiently relevant to the reading of six-year-olds today. Haven't television, home computers, space travel, and the continuous influx of new technologies outmoded most of the life of the twenties?

Hillerich has summarized the results of fourteen different studies and arrived at some very significant conclusions: (1) The recency of a list is no assurance of its importance; (2) the language base of the word count may be more important than the date it was compiled; (3) even though language is continually changing, the *structure* words tend to remain constant; and (4) while the Rinsland list contains some rural and childlike words little used today, the Dolch list does not seem particularly outmoded.[17]

The Hillerich list of 240 words that were drawn from the composite certainly contains no words that young children will not soon need to recognize.[18] However, he included 40 nouns that Dolch deliberately omitted. Dolch believed that nouns would be dependent upon context and many times included in illustrations. Disregarding the nouns, however, Hillerich includes 42 words not selected by Dolch, while Dolch included 62 words not selected by Hillerich. Be that as it may, they are all common sight words, common enough that children must readily master all the words on both lists.

Do word lists as basic as that containing the Dolch words become outdated in the course of a few decades? It is true that language is constantly changing because of the infusion of new concepts and changing societal behaviors. However, the converse, that language changes very slowly, is just as true. Further, the most basic words, such as those in the Stone list of 100 most common words,[19] *and, at, big, for, go, on, said, she, the, to,* and *up* have been basic for a long time, and we may expect them to remain so for some time to come. Skim through Shakespeare's famous lines about the seven ages of man written more than 350 years ago and notice that about 50 percent of the total running words appear as service words on the Dolch List.

The words that are used in "The Seven Ages of Man" (Act II, Scene VII) in Shakespeare's *As You Like It* are underlined to point out that approximately half of these words are found on the *Dolch Basic Sight Word List.*

Jaques:
All the world's a stage,
And all the men and women merely players:
They have their exits and their entrances;
And one man in his time plays many parts,
His acts being seven ages. At first the infant,
Mewling and puking in the nurse's arms.
And then the whining school-boy, with his satchel
And shining morning face, creeping like snail
Unwillingly to school. And then the lover,
Sighing like furnace, with a woeful ballad
Made to his mistress' eyebrow. Then a soldier
Full of strange oaths and bearded like the pard,
Jealous in honor, sudden and quick in quarrel,
Seeking the bubble reputation
Even in the cannon's mouth. And then the justice,
In fair round belly with good capon lined,
With eyes severe and beard of formal cut,
Full of wise saws and modern instances;
And so he plays his part.[20]

In the first 141 words of this passage, 73 are sight words on the Dolch list. The three forms of "play" are also used and if also counted, make 76/141 words, or 54 percent of the total.

A chart that compares the composite Hillerich list of service words with the Dolch list is in figure 3.5. The 40 nouns of the Hillerich list are presented at the far left. The 158 words common to the two lists are presented as the *common list;* the words on the Dolch list not in the Hillerich are listed in the column *Dolch List;* and the words on the Hillerich list not in the Dolch are listed in the column *Hillerich list.*

The important principle to guide the teacher is that any of these abbreviated lists can serve as a guide to common words. It is more important that the students use *their* words in the beginning reading situation, and after they have learned perhaps 100 words through their language experience stories, they are ready to broaden their base of word recognition by reading meaningful ideas in context, using phonic and structural skills, and remembering sight words.

Hillerich Nouns	Dolch List	Common List	Hillerich List	Dolch List	Common List	Hillerich List	Dolch List	Common List	Hillerich List	Dolch List	Common List	Hillerich List
air		a		fall	for	few		me			them	
back		about		far	found			much	might		then	
book		after		fast	four			must	more		there	
boy		again		fly	from			my	most		these	
car		all		full	gave		myself	never			they	
			almost	funny					need			
			also						next	those		
children		always			get			new			think	
city		am			give			no			this	
day		an		goes	go	gone		not			three	
door		and	another	going	good	great		now		try	to	told
end		any	anything	green	got			of			today	took
				grow							together	
family		are			had			off			too	
father		around			has	half		old			two	
fire		as			have	hard		on			under	
girl		ask			he			once				
head		at			help	heard		one		upon	up	until
	ate					high					us	
home		away			her			only			use	
house		be			here			open				
land		because			him		own	or	other	walk	very	
life		been		hold	his			our		warm	want	way
man		before		hot	how			out		wash		
		best		hurt						wish		
men		better		I		I'm	pick	over		write	we	
money		big		if			please	play			well	
morning				in			pretty	put			went	
mother	blue	black		into			pull	red			were	
Mr.	bring	both		is			ran	right			what	
	brown		brought	it			read					
Mrs.	buy	but		jump	its		round	said	same		when	
name	call	by			just		ride	saw			where	
night		came			keep		run	say			which	
part	carry	can			kind	knew	seven	see			white	while
people	clean	come			know		shall	she			who	
	cold											
place	cut	could		laugh		last	sing	show	should		why	
room		did	didn't	live	let	left	sit	small	something		will	
school	does	do	different		like		six	so	still		with	
table		done			light		sleep	some	sure		work	
thing		don't			little			soon			would	
side					long		start					
time	draw				look		stop	take		yellow		
town	drink	down	each		made			tell	than	yes	you	
water	eat	every	enough		make			the	thought		your	
world	every	find	even		many		ten	that	through			
year		first	ever		may		thank	they				
		five						their				

Figure 3.5. Chart comparing the Composite Hillerich list with the Dolch list of service words. A comparison of the 240 starter words: A basic reading/writing vocabulary, by Robert L. Hillerich, and the Dolch Basic Sight Words, showing the 158 words common to both lists. Forty-one Hillerich words (excluding nouns) are not on the Dolch List; 62 Dolch words are not on the Hillerich list. (From Robert L. Hillerich, "Word Lists—Getting It All Together," *Reading Teacher* 27 (January 1974): 357. Reprinted with permission of Robert L. Hillerich and the International Reading Association.)

Making Connections 3.1: How Many Sight Words Do You Find?

Select a piece of printed material about 200 words in length. It might be from the newspaper, from this textbook, from a basal reader, or from a story written by a child.

Complete an analysis of the passage in terms of the number of Dolch words included in the running words. Simply slash out each word that is on the Dolch List. After you have marked through all the words that appear on the list, figure the percentage of Dolch words in the running words in the passage by dividing the number of words with the slash marks by the total number of words in the passage. You will obtain a decimal for your answer; the decimal may then be changed to a percent.

This activity will be particularly useful if several people evaluate different kinds of materials judged to be at a variety of levels of difficulty. The shared findings will undoubtedly suggest the value of readers knowing well a small, but high-utility, collection of sight words.

Other Methods of Testing for Reader Level

Other methods for finding the reader level are summarized here.

1. The teacher can estimate children's abilities to read new books by:
   a. Selecting passages near the beginning of the books and asking the child to read aloud. If more than 5 errors in 100 words are made, an easier book to improve context reading is indicated.
   b. Pronouncing words here and there on selected pages and asking the pupil to point to them.
2. A selection of 25 or 50 words can be compiled by choosing every fourth or fifth word from the vocabulary list of a given book. If there is no such list, the teacher may then pick words at random. Ask the child to pronounce each word and give the meaning. This may be done by using the word in a sentence. If the child can pronounce and know the meaning of 20 of the 25 words in the test, or 40 of the 50-word test, the child probably can read adequately from that book. This is the procedure:
   a. Turn to the total list of words in the back of the book.
   b. Select 25 or 50 words by some method, such as choosing every fourth or fifth word.
   c. Make two copies of these words, one for yourself and one for the child. Use manuscript writing if the child cannot read cursive writing.
   d. Ask the child to pronounce the word as you point to it.
   e. Record on one sheet the errors made.

f. Next, ask the child for the meaning of each word. The word may be used in a sentence.

g. The child should be able to pronounce 20 of 25 or 40 of 50 words, without much hesitancy, and know the meanings.

Inventorying Phonic and Structural Skills

The teachers cannot assume that all students know the names or the sounds of all the letters of the alphabet, and some students may not know how to write them. It is a simple task to:

1. Show the students a card with the letters in mixed-up order:

c	i	d	f	m	g	k	x
a	l	b	h	p	r	y	e
j	n	s	o	v	t	w	u

   Then point to some of the letters and ask the students to name them. If the teachers circle only those the students do not know, the teachers have a written record to show which ones the students have been able to identify.
2. Ask the students to write all of the letters of the alphabet in their alphabetical order. It will be apparent which ones they omit, which ones they confuse, and which ones they reverse.
3. Provide the students with a piece of paper. Then direct them to write the letters that you name and say some of the names of the letters above.
4. Be sensitive to the fact that the children may never have been taught how to make the letters properly. Or, they may make the letters with "upside-down movements" that will make rapid writing during the school day very difficult. Patiently teach the students how to form the letters they cannot make properly.
5. It is easy to sample the knowledge of the sounds of the most used consonants by asking the child to tell the first letter in the word. Give a short list orally: *bear, cow, dog, fox, kitten, top, milk, lion, pony, rooster.*

Pictures like those found in figure 3.6 can be used to elicit beginning or ending sounds.

All of the phonic elements are presented in figure 3.7. Most students learn the consonants and consonant combinations with a minimum of oral practice. For some students, practice lessons in hearing minimal pairs may be helpful. Minimal pairs of words are those that sound exactly alike except for one phonemic difference. For example, in *big* and *pig* the words are the same except for the phonemes *b* and *p*.

Also, the chart of phonic elements makes clear that there are not a great many sounds to be distinguished and remembered. More importantly, the sounds need to be presented or taught only when they are being used as sounds in words that distinguish meaning. Thus, *one* sequence for teaching a series of sounds is not necessary since teachers who use a great deal of language experience work should teach those sounds needed to discriminate the sounds in the words the boys and girls use in their stories. Also, if children can hear sounds clearly and can decode words, they have no need for further lessons in phonics as far as reading is concerned. If difficulties arise in spelling, that problem needs to be seen as a spelling problem.

Hearing Beginning Sounds. Tell me the name of each picture. What is the letter each picture begins with?

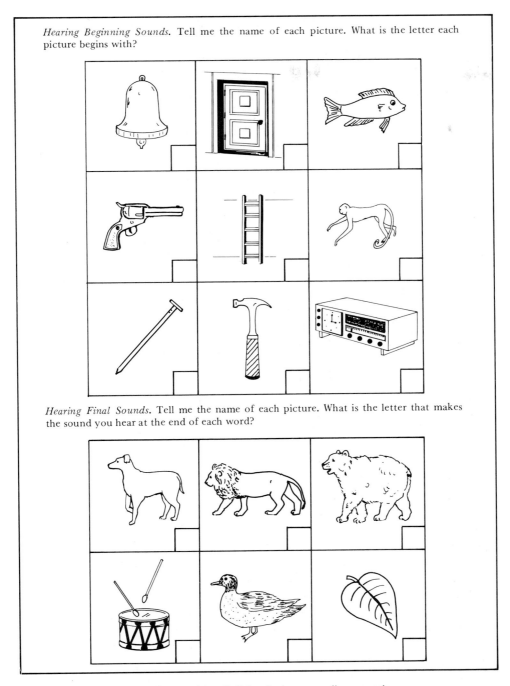

Hearing Final Sounds. Tell me the name of each picture. What is the letter that makes the sound you hear at the end of each word?

Figure 3.6. Pictures can be used to elicit beginning or ending sounds.

The Phonic Elements

CONSONANTS		VOWELS			
Single Consonants	Consonant Combinations	Single Vowels	Vowel Combinations	Vowel-Consonant Combinations	The Schwa
Single consonants (one phoneme):	Consonant blends:	Single vowels (May be long or short):	Vowel digraphs:	Vowels A followed by "l" or "w":	(ə)
b d f h	bl br sc tw		ai in sail		pencil
i k l m	cl cr sk scr	a e i	ay day	"aw" in bawl	about
n w y z	fl dr sm spr	o u	ea beat	"al" in wall	beckon
	gl fr sn str	y (sometimes)	ea head		latent
			ea tea		
Single consonants with two or more common sounds:	pl gr sp shr		ee sleep	Vowels followed by "r":	
	sl pr st spl		ei receive		
	dw tr sw sch		ie believe	a in arm	
"c" as "k"	wr thr		ey key	e fern	
"c" as "s"			ey they	i dirt	
			oa boat	o word	
"g" as "g"	Consonant digraphs:		oe toe	u hurt	
"g" as "j"	One sound:		ow show	y martyr	
			ou though		
"s" in hiss	gh, ph, sh, ck,			q and u	
rose	ng, nk		Vowel blends (diphthongs):		
sugar				qu in quick	
	Two or more sounds:		oi in soil	squ squirrel	
"x" in six			oy boy		
xylophone	th: this, thin		ue true		
exact	wh: what, who				
	ch: chin,		ew in new		
	chalet		ow now		
	choir		ou though		
			oa goal		

Figure 3.7. The phonic elements

It is important that teachers have a strong knowledge of phonics themselves before they attempt to test that knowledge in children or before they teach students the use of phonics as a word identification tool. A knowledge of phonics will help teachers avoid spending a lot of time testing students' phonic knowledge, since they will be more able to observe students' reading behaviors and detect specific needs for information or practice that are phonic in nature.

Teachers often feel that they know no phonics and state that "it wasn't taught when I was in school." Others may not realize the range of information about letters and sounds that collectively is called phonics. Making Connections 3.2 is a phonics test for teachers. It may be useful to take the test to demonstrate how much you do know already, to discover the range of information that is designated as phonics, or to learn some of the phonics rules if you have not worked with them before. (The reader is referred to p. 16 for a discussion of the synthetic method of teaching reading).

Making Connections 3.2: A Phonics Test for Teachers

Why a phonics test for teachers? We know that phonics is just one tool to aid in word identification, so why give it so much time? The answer may be helpful. If the teacher has extensive knowledge of the subject, he or she can recognize when the student needs information in the area of phonics and can give it accurately and economically. When the teacher does not have a thorough knowledge of the subject, he or she will usually find it necessary to follow one of two approaches:

1. Skip the subject altogether (which is not helpful).
2. Teach everything in the teacher's manual (which is also not helpful).

Knowledge of the subject will allow the teacher to make professional decisions about what, how much, and when phonics will be taught.

Now try your hand at these questions:

1. Underline seven words in this sentence starting with a single consonant sound.
2. Circle the words below that contain consonant blends:
   Irish   trigger   flag   clip   bland   picture   blot
3. Two three-letter blends are _____ and _____ .
4. What is a consonant digraph? _____
   _____
5. The word *diphthong* contains three consonant digraphs. They are _____ ,
   _____ , and _____ .
6. Six words that might help a child decide how to pronounce words with hard "g" are _____ , _____ , _____ , _____ , _____ ,
   _____ .
7. A "soft" *g* is in the word: got   ghost   frog   wage.

8. After each of these nonsense words, write *H* if the *c* is "hard" or *S* if the *c* is "soft."
   calum _____ cebut _____ cinky _____ cottle _____ cuve _____ cybers _____ .

9. "Th" is *unvoiced* in: them thimble thistle thin they

10. Following are four nonsense words containing various sounds *y* often represents. Match them with words that contain the same sounds usually represented by *y*.
    deyorg syntax tyth twenty gry yellow perry my

11. The letter *x* stands for three sounds. Write a word to represent each of these three sounds: _____ , _____ , _____ .

12. The letter *q* stands for two sounds. Words that contain examples of each of these are _____ and _____ .

13. On words ending in *s*, you may hear either an *s* or a *z* sound. Write *s* or *z* after each word, indicating which sound you hear at the end: hands _____ baths _____ bathes _____ hats _____ .

14. There is a silent consonant in each of these words. Circle each silent consonant: comb wren talk knew listen often.

15. Write an L or an S after each of these words depending on whether the word contains a long or a short vowel sound. Write *X* if the word contains neither.
    pipe _____ ways _____ sounds _____ salve _____ which _____ use _____
    fold _____ have _____ leek _____ word _____ tint _____

16. In the nonsense word *dode*, the letter *o* would probably represent the sound that the *o* represents in: on out comb hotter brown.

17. In the nonsense word *oap*, the letter *o* would probably represent the sound that the *o* represents in: rot round fox Rome.

18. A vowel digraph is in the word: slam goat bugle couch funnel.

19. A diphthong is _____ .
    Circle all the diphthongs in these words: couch boy through oil now known.

20. The *schwa* sound is represented in the dictionary by a _____ .

21. Circle the vowel in each word below that represents the *schwa* sound:
    balloon eaten ago golden beautify silent button circus consistent modify second

22. Circle all of the following nonsense words that are correctly divided into syllables: ham/ner de/fort/ly deg/or mec/hor

23. The word *polysyllabic* contains _____ syllables.

24. Write *O* or *C* after each word to show whether the syllable is open or closed: like _____ no _____ tend _____ thee _____ ban _____ it _____ .

25. A grapheme is _____ .

26. A phoneme is _____ .

Answer Key to a Phonics Test for Teachers

1. seven, words, sentence, with, single, consonant, sound
2. trigger, flag, clip, bland, blot
3. for example *spl, spr, str* (*thr* is a digraph plus *r*)
4. (something like this): two letters that represent a sound different than the individual sounds represented by each letter
5. *ph, th, ng*
6. get, got, gum, gave, game, goose, geese, gush are examples
7. wage
8. calum H, cebut S, cinky S, cottle H, cuve H, cybers S
9. thimble, thistle, thin
10. deyorg—yellow; tyth—syntax; gry—my; perry—twenty.
11. *z*—xylophone; *ks*—box; *gs*—exaggerate
12. *kw*—queen; *k*—antique. These are examples
13. hands—z; baths—s; bathes—z; hats—s
14. com*b* *w*ren ta*l*k *k*new lis*t*en of*t*en
15. pipe—L; ways—L; sounds—X; salve—S; which—S; use—L; fold—L; have—S; leek—L; word—X; tint—S
16. comb
17. Rome
18. goat
19. Two vowels that both affect pronunciation—there is a change in mouth position in the production of the new sound. c*ou*ch, b*oy,* thr*ou*gh (*ou* is not a diphthong here), *oi*l, n*ow*, kn*ow*n (*ow* is not a diphthong here)
20. ∂
21. b*a*lloon, eat*e*n, *a*go, gold*e*n, beaut*i*fy, sil*e*nt, butt*o*n, circ*u*s, c*o*nsistent, mod*i*fy, sec*o*nd
22. ham/ner, de/fort/ly
23. five
24. like—C; no—O; tend—C; thee—O; ban—C; it—C
25. A written form
26. A smallest unit of sound

Phonics Tests

Several useful phonics tests are:

1. The Sipay Word Analysis Tests (SWAT), a series of sixteen individually administered subtests, provide the teacher a great deal of information. (Edward R. Sipay, Cambridge, Massachusetts: Educators Publishing Service, Inc., 1974.)
2. The Corrective Reading System measures the child's achievement on a wide range of word-recognition skills. It could be administered in sections over a period of

time to give the teacher a greater understanding of the child's strengths and weaknesses in word recognition. (Eldon E. Ekwall, Glenview, Illinois: Pyrotechnics, Inc., 1975.)

3. The Phonics Inventory Tests: Tests 1, 2, and 3 (Boston: Houghton-Mifflin, 1972) for use with readers functioning at roughly first-, second-, and third-reader levels. Each test is divided into parts that test specific aspects of phonics deemed important at the particular reader level.

4. The Word Attack Test of the Woodcock Reading Mastery Tests. (Circle Pines, Minn.: American Guidance Service, 1973.) This test requires the reader to demonstrate knowledge of phonic elements by reading nonsense words that demonstrate important rules governing English words.

5. Wilma H. Miller, in the *Reading Diagnosis Kit,* 2d. ed. (West Nyack, N.Y.: The Center for Applied Research in Education, 1978) presents some useful phonics tests on pages 230 through 233. They are meant for readers who are at or beyond the upper-primary reading level.

6. Margaret LaPray, in *On the Spot Reading Diagnosis File* (West Nyack, N.Y.: The Center for Applied Research in Education, 1978) includes a test on applied phonics on pages 75 through 79. Phonics knowledge ranging from initial consonants to syllabication rules is included.

Reversals and Confusions

In making an informal reading analysis, one should be observant of any errors the students make that may relate to directional orientation on the page. Do they say "was" for *saw,* "day" for *bay,* or "form" for *from?* Kennedy concluded that while a high percentage of reversal tendencies exists in kindergarten, they tend to practically disappear by the third grade.[21] On one form of her test, internal interchanging of letters, for example, *from* to *form,* decreased from 38.5 percent in low kindergarten to 11.5 percent in high grade two. Also, such reversals as *b* for *d* or *p* and *n* for *u* decreased from 22.1 percent in low kindergarten to 3.07 percent in high second grade when both groups were tested in multiple choice selection in isolation.

Awareness of the reversal problem and having a few constructive techniques to help the children habituate left to right progression in word identification will help the teachers provide the correct practice for the children.

Reversals and confusions may be:

1. Reversing whole words:
   "was" for *saw;* "on" for *no;* "pot" for *top;* "rats" for *star*
2. Rearranging letters within words:
   "paly" for *play;* "how" for *who;* "spot" for *stop*
3. Confusing word configuration:
   "and" for *said;* "when" for *then;* "there" for *three;* "for" for *from*
4. Rearranging whole phrases:
   "once there was" for *there once was;*
   the boy saw the dog read as "the dog was a big"

5. Interchanging letters:

"b" for *d* or *p;* "m" for *w;* making the slant line in *N* or *z* backwards

Monroe gives the following examples of rearranging whole phrases:[22]

A boy saw a dog on the street read as "A doy was a god no the treest"
The boy saw the dog read as "The boy was good"
He felt sad read as "He left home"
The boys had no caps read as "The boys had on caps"

One fifteen-year-old girl *wrote* these sentences early in her remedial program in a clinic situation:

For:	She wrote:
I can work and play.	I cna wrck adn paly.
Who did it?	How idd ti?
The old crow sat on its perch.	The eld corw saw no sit perch.

Overcoming Reversals

Specific teaching suggestions for children who lack directional sense include the following:

1. Underline the first letter in each of the words confused. This directs the children to the beginning of the word.
2. In making lists of words for children to read, begin at a "starting line" or margin that is identifiable as the beginning point. For example, if you put words on the blackboard, make the list at the extreme left side of the board. Help the children see the starting place.
3. Over and over, uncover words from left to right.
4. Make the first letter with a different color.
5. Use medium-grained sandpaper and cut out letters in either cursive or manuscript. The letters should be two-to-three inches high. The children should trace over them with the middle and index fingers of the hand with which they normally write. This is one more way to emphasize the kinesthetic-tactile dimension in the VAKT (visual-auditory-kinesthetic-tactile) method of overcoming reversals or confusions.
6. For individual letters, figure out any mnemonic device that works and let the children use it as a crutch until their habit pattern accommodates the correct response. For example, one teacher found that one child could remember to distinguish *b* from *d* by thinking that *c* had to come before *d* in the alphabet, and in writing he could not make a *d* unless he made a *c* first. As long as his *c* was correct, he could use this device. The converse, that he could not make *c* before *b,* was a part of the device.
7. With a great deal of high motivation, purposefully write the words being learned. If the children are old enough to do cursive writing instead of manuscript, it may

help to use cursive writing because all letters are joined and reversing is less plausible. Some children find writing words on the typewriter useful.

The teacher must recognize reversals when they appear in the spelling papers of pupils at any grade level, but especially at the primary level. The spelling paper (figure 3.8) that was written by a second-grade boy was returned by his classroom teacher with the following notation across the top: "Too many mistakes." Actually both letter reversals and confusion of order of letters appear several times in this paper. If this happened to be the first paper the teacher saw that had been written by this child the teacher should immediately be alerted to watching carefully to see if this error persists in the child's work. If it does, tracing, copying, comparing two words often confused, and filling blanks especially prepared to distinguish between two often confused words in context are all possible methods the teacher can use to help the pupil establish the proper habits of left-to-right orientation on the page. If the *habit* of reversing or of being utterly confused has persisted through several years, it will be necessary first to erase the old habits and then to form new ones.

A fifth-grade boy was once asked to write on the blackboard the word *shade*. He thought a minute and then wrote: *shade* . When the examiner asked him whether the letter was a *b* or a *d* in the word, the boy said that when he wrote it that way, the teacher counted it right if it was a *b* and right if it was a *d!* Another boy in the sixth grade was asked to pronounce *dab* and *bad* when they were written on the blackboard. He said, "One of them is *bad,* but I don't know which one."

Specific exercises need to be provided to help those having difficulty with letters or words that cause confusion, for example:

was–*saw* confusion	*how–who* confusion
He *was* here.	*Who* came in?
I *saw* the boy.	I see *how* to do it.
It *was* my pet.	He saw *who* I was.
The dog *saw* the rabbit.	*How* did he do that?

Sentences in which the pupil selects the appropriate one of a pair of confused words have been found helpful. It may be best to work on only *one* word first, then the second word of the pair before using sentences such as the following:

Choose *on* or *no:*

1. My birthday is _____ the first of May.
2. Mrs. Hill said, "_____ , thank you."
3. The street was empty. There were _____ people there.
4. He is sitting _____ a bench in the park.

Choose *where* or *there:*

1. How long will it take to get _____ ?
2. _____ is a glass on the table.
3. _____ are you going?
4. I don't know _____ the boys went.

Spelling test

1. dog
2. by   bird
3. ball
4. sgg   eggs*
5. Look
6. bte   pet*
7. rabben   rabbit
8. N   was
9. Mother
10. dig   pig*
11. off
12. Father

13. flying
14. my
15. cat
16. is
17. the
18. Mat   am*
19. doy   boy*
20. Kitten
21. We   nest*
22. bed
23. get   girl
24. nude   under*

Name: **Joe**   Date: **Mar. 2, 19--.**

* *either reversals or transposing of letters in words.*

Figure 3.8. Spelling test discloses letter reversals and confusion of letter sequence.

Other Word Recognition Abilities

1. Knowledge of compound words. The teacher wishes to know whether or not the children see quickly how to divide compound words into two parts. A list of compound words from three representative second readers appears in figure 3.9. Until the children do pronounce these words easily, they will not profit from instruction in syllabication of words.

2. Ability to pronounce pairs of often-confused words. If the children have completed the other word-attack tests somewhat successfully, ask them to pronounce the forty words in either of the two lists of paired words often confused, found in figures 3.10 and 3.11. The teacher can use such exercises as "bolt-blot" flash card drill or completion sentences to help children who make such errors. If the more difficult words, figure 3.11 present many problems in pronunciation, ask the pupils to pronounce the more elementary list figure 3.10.

somebody	something	tonight
daytime	peanut	workbag
another	grandmother	farmhouses
birthday	lonesome	anyone
himself	everywhere	haystack
firemen	schoolhouse	boxcar
railroad	package	waterfall
runway	lemonade	maybe
downtown	popcorn	blueberries
watchman	policeman	watchdog
postman	sandwiches	tablecloth
whoever	campfire	bedroom
popover	sometimes	housekeeper
schoolbook	grandfather	without
snowbank	everything	indeed
schoolroom	pullman	fireplace
gatepost	jackknife	anything
buttermilk	scarecrow	whatever
blackboard	Thanksgiving	somewhere
airplane	grandma	grandchildren

Figure 3.9. Compound words found in representative second-grade readers.

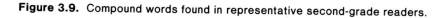

stop	pots	tops
who	how	now
and	said	new
star	rats	tars
was	saw	on
no	not	ton
or	our	off
for	of	from
tap	pat	apt
tub	but	put
team	meat	yes
eyes	say	net
dab	bad	add
pal	lap	alp
god	dog	nap

Figure 3.10. Words often confused in primary reading.

left	very	even
tired	freight	tried
pitcher	angle	fright
spilt	verse	felt
scared	quit	ever
broad	spotted	nowhere
trial	trail	blot
serve	through	fight
angel	board	picture
form	quiet	from
quite	weather	stopped
though	every	sacred
whether	thought	
bolt	split	

Figure 3.11. Paired words often confused—second list.

Spelling Ability

When considering the ability of given students to spell words correctly, teachers need to remember:

1. Children should not be trying to learn to spell words that they cannot pronounce.
2. Children should not be trying to learn to spell words if they do not understand their meanings.
3. Children do not need to learn to spell words that will not be used in writing. *It is a waste of time for both the children and the teacher for the pupils to study spelling words at the fifth-grade level if they are reading at the second-grade level.*

The correlation between reading and spelling abilities is a high positive one. This fact would suggest that children who have reading difficulties might profit from work on spelling, especially work that emphasizes auditory discrimination and special attention to the order of letters in words. Writing practice directed toward habituating the spelling of most common service words is recommended. This writing practice must be motivated and purposeful, with adequate rewards provided when the work is done well.

When an informal reading inventory is being completed, the teacher should measure the student's ability to spell words correctly. This is true because one of the ways the teacher must work with the students within the classroom is to assign different types of work that require some writing. Many of these boys and girls are very reluctant to write because they know they do not have adequate spelling skill. One of the best ways to improve spelling ability is for the students to write about topics of interest to them and to have the opportunity to talk about the types of errors they can correct.

There are several ways the teacher can sample the students' abilities to spell:

1. The 220 Dolch Basic Sight Words or the first 300 of the Fry Instant Words are good lists to use for spelling. They contain the words used most often.
2. A list of spelling words from a graded speller can serve adequately. The students need to begin with a list which they can write about 60 percent correctly after pronouncing them with the teacher but before study. For example, fifth-grade students might be able to write correctly before study 12 of the 20 words in a third-grade list. If so, this is 60 percent correct and they could begin working with words for writing at this level.
3. The Spelling Subtest of the Gates Diagnostic Reading Test. Arthur I. Gates and Anne McKillop, *Gates-McKillop Reading Diagnostic Tests* (New York: Teachers College Press, 1962).
4. Spelling Test for Grades Two and Three; Spelling Test for Grade Four and Above, *Durrell Analysis of Reading Difficulty.* Donald D. Durrell, *Durrell Analysis of Reading Difficulty, Manual of Directions* (New York: Psychological Corporation, 1937, 1955, 1980).

Huelsman developed a word discrimination test to study the ability of the reader to select the correct spelling of a word when it appears with four foils in a line of print.[23]

There are a few students who need "extra" help with the order of letters in words and in the quick perception of the configuration of common words.

Sample items from the Huelsman test include:

1. eht tle the thc lhe
2. hittle ilttle fittle lihhle little
3. yonp pouy pony ponv pnoy

Concepts about Print

Clay[24] has made teachers aware of the need to consider more than word recognition in helping children gain an understanding of the nature of print. She found that readers frequently experienced reading problems, not because they were having trouble memorizing sight words, but because they did not have adequate concepts about letters, words, sounds, directionality of print, the role of pictures in books, and the organization of books. Without these and other related concepts, children experience confusion when teachers give directions or talk to them about the reading process. Clay has developed two tests, *Sand*[25] and *Stones*,[26] which appear to be simple story books, but can yield important information about the child's understanding of the vocabulary used in reading instruction and in discussing the reading process. Clay intended that one of these tests would be used in conjunction with a large collection of tests aimed at giving a comprehensive picture of the child's reading status.

Several researchers have reported that young children usually become aware of print in the environment (such words as "Coke," "Stop," and "Safeway.") and that these observations contribute to the growing concepts about words and reading. It may be useful to develop a collection of common environmental signs—both words and phrases—to show to children for identification. The teacher can observe the children's responses and infer the attention that is being paid to environmental print, the growing understanding of the meaningfulness of print, and the children's curiosity about these print examples.[27] It is encouraging to children to see in school the print they have seen away from school and to have a sense that they actually "can read"; this knowledge may be very useful as the child confronts the more common print forms of the classroom.

Summary

This chapter presented suggestions for evaluating word recognition abilities, awareness of problems of reversals and confusions, and sensitivity to the child's need to understand important concepts about print and reading. As soon as the classroom teachers have summarized the results of these tests, they are ready to select materials at the students' instructional levels of reading and to begin teaching at that level *while* searching for further information about the students and the causes of the disability.

For Further Reading

Bond, Guy L.; Tinker, Miles A.; Wasson, Barbara B.; and Wasson, John B. *Reading Difficulties, Their Diagnosis and Correction,* 5th ed. Englewood Cliffs, N.J.: Prentice-Hall, 1984, Chapter 10; "Correcting Deficiencies in Meaning Clues to Word Recognition," pp. 173–194; Chapter 11, "Correcting Faulty Perceptual and Decoding Skills in Word Recognition," pp. 195–223.

Clay, Marie M. *Reading, the Patterning of Complex Behavior,* 2d. ed. Auckland, New Zealand: Heinemann, 1979: Chapter 13, "The Visual Perception of Print," pp. 216–43.

Ekwall, Eldon E. *Diagnosis and Remediation of the Disabled Reader.* Boston: Allyn and Bacon, 1983: Chapter 4, "Letter Knowledge and Sight Words," pp. 80–117; Chapter 5, "Word Analysis Skills," pp. 118–88.

Fry, Edward B. *The Reading Teacher's Book of Lists.* (Englewood Cliffs, N.J.: Prentice-Hall, 1984).

Harris, Albert J., and Jacobson, Milton D. *Basic Reading Vocabularies.* New York: Macmillan, 1982.

Harris, Albert J. and Sipay, E. R. *How to Increase Reading Ability,* 7th ed. New York: Longman, 1980: Chapter 8, "Assessing Reading Performance I"; Chapter 9, "Assessing Reading Performance II," pp. 163–250.

Sakiey, Elizabeth and Fry, Edward. *3000 Instant Words.* Highland Park, N.J.: Drier Educational Systems, 1979.

Notes

1. William Durr, "Computer Study of High Frequency Words in Popular Trade Juveniles," *The Reading Teacher* 27 (October 1973), pp. 37–42.
2. J. McNally and W. Murray, *Key Words to Literacy* (London: Schoolmaster Publishing Co., Ltd., 1968), p. 1.
3. Margaret LaPray and Ramon Ross, "The Graded Word List: Quick Gauge of Reading Ability," *Journal of Reading* 12 (January 1969), pp. 305–7.
4. Richard L. Slosson, *The Slosson Oral Reading Test* (140 Pine St., East Aurora, New York: Slosson Educational Publications, Inc., 1963).
5. J. F. Jastak and S. R. Jastak, *The Wide Range Achievement Test* (1526 Gilpin Avenue, Wilmington, Del.: Guidance Associates of Delaware, Inc., 1965).
6. E. W. Dolch, *Teaching Primary Reading* (Champaign, Ill.: The Garrard Press, 1941), pp. 196–215.
7. Child Study Committee of the International Kindergarten Union, *A Study of the Vocabulary of Children Before Entering First Grade* (Washington, D.C.: The International Kindergarten Union, 1928).
8. Arthur I. Gates, *A Reading Vocabulary for the Primary Grades* (New York: Teachers College, Columbia University, 1926).
9. H. E. Wheeler and Emma A. Howell, "A First Grade Vocabulary Study," *Elementary School Journal* 31 (September 1930), pp. 52–60.
10. Maude McBroom, Julia Sparrow, and Catherine Eckstein, *A Scale for Determining a Child's Reader Level* (Iowa City: Bureau of Publications, Extension Division, State University of Iowa, 1944).

11. *The Popper Words,* Dolch Basic Sight Word Cards (Champaign, Ill.: The Garrard Press, 1942).

12. *The Dolch Basic Sight Word Test* (Champaign, Ill.: The Garrard Press, 1942).

13. McBroom, Sparrow, and Eckstein, *A Scale,* pp. 9–10.

14. Ibid., p. 11.

15. These standards, as well as the limits for the scale, were summarized from the two following studies: Catherine Eckstein, *Use of the Dolch Basic Sight Word List as a Measure to Determine Reader Level* (Master's Thesis, State University of Iowa, 1944); and Julia Sparrow, *Accomplishment on the Dolch Basic Sight Word List as a Measure of Reader Level* (Master's Thesis, State University of Iowa, 1944).

16. Ibid., p. 10.

17. Robert L. Hillerich, "Word Lists—Getting It All Together," *The Reading Teacher* 27 (January 1974), pp. 353–60.

18. Ibid., p. 357.

19. Clarence R. Stone, *Progress in Primary Reading* (New York: McGraw-Hill, Inc., 1950).

20. William Shakespeare, *The Plays and Sonnets of William Shakespeare,* vol. I, edited by William George Clarke and William Aldis Wright. *Great Books of the Western World,* vol. 26 (Chicago: Encyclopedia Britannica, 1952), p. 608.

21. Eloise Kennedy, "Reversals, Reversals, Reversals!" *Journal of Experimental Education* 23 (December 1954), pp. 161–70.

22. Marion Monroe, *Children Who Cannot Read* (Chicago: University of Chicago Press, 1932), pp. 127–28.

23. Charles B. Huelsman, *The Huelsman Word Discrimination Test,* Forms A and B (Oxford, Ohio: Miami University, 1958).

24. Marie M. Clay, *The Early Detection of Reading Difficulties: A Diagnostic Survey with Recovery Procedures,* 2d ed., (Auckland, New Zealand: Heinemann, 1979).

25. Marie M. Clay, *Sand* (Auckland, New Zealand: Heinemann, 1972).

26. Marie M. Clay, *Stones* (Auckland, New Zealand: Heinemann, 1979).

27. Kenneth Goodman and Yetta Goodman, "Learning to Read is Natural," in Lauren Resnick and Phyllis Weaver, eds., *Theory and Practice in Early Reading,* vol. I (Hillsdale, N.J.: Lawrence Erlbaum Associates, 1979); Elfrieda Hiebert, "Developmental Patterns and Interrelationships of Preschool Children's Print Awareness," *Reading Research Quarterly* 16, no. 2 (1981), pp. 236–60. and Frank Smith, "Learning to Read by Reading," *Language Arts* 53 (March 1976), pp. 297–99.

4
The Informal Reading Inventory

Vocabulary

informal reading inventory
  (IRI)
independent level
instructional level
frustration level
capacity level
miscue
substitution
mispronunciation
hesitation
repetition
omission
insertion
comprehension
sight reading

Questions

1. What do you see as the advantages of and the importance of the informal reading inventory?

2. Define the criteria for each of the four reading levels—independent, instructional, frustration, and capacity.

3. In the word recognition portion of the IRI, what are the reading behaviors that are counted as kinds of miscues?

4. What behaviors should be noted but will not be counted as miscues?

5. How would you go about making an informal reading inventory for your classroom?

6. What are the steps in administering and scoring an informal reading inventory?

Introduction

One of the most serious problems in elementary school classrooms today is the very large percentage of children who are kept reading at their *frustration* level. If a book is too difficult, if too many new concepts appear and are not repeated several times, and if the decoding process of unlocking new words has not been learned, boys and girls spend much time in school trying to gain information that is beyond their grasp. At the same time, when teachers look at standardized test results and arbitrarily assign all the children in their rooms to three reading groups, they may be asking some children to stay frustrated all day long. Learning does not progress when children work at the frustration level.

While standardized reading achievement tests have a very important place in assessing the total school reading program, and they provide teachers with a distribution of their students from best to poorest performer, they do not provide the teachers an adequate measure of what book is the appropriate one for children to read at their *instructional* levels. The standardized test is a power test, and may more nearly measure children's frustration levels of reading when they read for a short period of time.[1]

Standardized test scores may yield grade placement equivalents one or more years higher than children can actually read with understanding.

Wheeler and Smith found that the grade placement scores on standardized reading tests in the primary grades often have little relationship to the children's actual instructional reading levels.

The teachers cannot meet all children at their levels of functioning and provide instruction from which they can profit unless the teachers can somehow determine with a fair degree of accuracy what those functioning levels are. An informal reading inventory (IRI) will provide the classroom teachers with this fundamental information.

The advantages of the IRI for finding where to begin to instruct the children are:[2]

1. The teachers use the materials they have at hand; there is little cost.
2. With direct and rapid administration, the teachers get some needed answers quickly.
3. In terms of textbook reading the children will do, the IRI is more valid than other tests.
4. IRIs can be either group or individual for appropriate purposes.
5. The students can be made aware of how well they read.
6. The students can be made aware of progress as they achieve it.
7. As achievement is appraised, specific needs are revealed.
8. Interesting materials can be selected to use in the inventory.
9. Readability of materials can be checked in series of texts.
10. The test situation can be a valuable instructional situation also.

What Is the Informal Reading Inventory?

The IRI is an individual test in which the child reads both orally and silently from increasingly difficult material until the material becomes frustrating either in terms of accuracy of pronunciation or understanding of ideas in the content. The informal reading test is diagnostic in that it reveals many specific areas of difficulty in reading for the observant teachers. Clearly, the values derived from administering the IRI depend entirely upon the competence of the teacher, who must make judgments as the child reads. An informal reading inventory should provide a selection of reading at each level from preprimer through the sixth grade for both oral and silent reading. Comprehension questions must be provided to obtain a measure of the child's understanding of what is read.

The child should read from the book while the teacher has a reproduced copy for marking errors, making notes, and evaluating. At the level at which the child makes too many errors for the instructional level, either in comprehension or pronunciation, the teacher begins reading one passage orally at each reading level and asking the prepared questions to measure the child's capacity for understanding ideas heard when listening to someone else read the material. This is referred to as the *capacity level, listening level,* or *hearing comprehension level.*

The Four Reading Levels to Be Defined

The IRI will enable the teacher to establish an independent level of reading for the student; the instructional level of reading; the frustration level; and the capacity level. These are defined below.

The *independent* level of reading is the *highest* level at which the child can read fluently and with personal satisfaction without help. In independent reading, the child encounters practically no mechanical difficulties with the words and no problems with understanding the concepts in the context. The level is generally defined as that level where the child makes no more than 1 miscue in 100 words in the mechanics of reading and where there are no difficulties in comprehension. Much of the material the child selects for free reading from the library should be at this level, as well as some of the collateral reading for unit work in social studies and science.

The *instructional* level of reading is the teaching level. This is defined as the *highest* level at which the child makes no more than 5 uncorrected miscues in reading 100 running words with at least 75 percent comprehension of the ideas in the text. Such materials are difficult enough to be challenging but sufficiently easy that the student can do independent seatwork with only the usual readiness help from the teacher when assignments are made. The most important task of the elementary teacher is to establish for all children their instructional levels of functioning in reading and provide them with work at those levels. Instructional reading material should be read silently before it is read orally. Then no difficulties with phrasing, punctuation, finger-pointing, or tension will arise. Many children are not given the opportunity to read at this level at school. The instructional level is reached when the child uses a conversational tone, without noticeable tension, with satisfactory rhythm, and with suitable phrasing, making proper use of word recognition clues and techniques.

The *frustration* level is the *lowest* level at which obvious difficulties cause confusion, frustration, and tension in the reading situation. Betts lists inability to anticipate meanings, head movements, finger pointing, tension, slow word-by-word reading, vocalization, and too many substitutions, omissions, repetitions, and insertions as evidences of frustration.[3]

There is not always a clear line of separation between what is instructional level and what is frustration. The teacher's purpose is to keep the child on the growing edge of learning without pushing along too fast. The teacher will do well to choose the lower of two possible reader levels when there is a question about which is appropriate for given individuals. It is preferable to let students have more practice at easier levels and strengthen their abilities and skills than to move them into material that is too difficult and stop their progress.

The capacity level for reading is the *highest* level at which the child can understand the ideas and concepts in informational material that is read aloud. The teacher begins reading to the student at the level of difficulty at which oral or silent reading stopped because of reaching the frustration level. The questions prepared to ask if the child had read the material are now also appropriate to ask after the teacher reads the material. The standard expected for instructional level, 75 percent comprehension, is an adequate measure of establishing capacity for understanding reading.

The capacity level measures the level at which the readers would function if they were able to use all their innate abilities for reading. So, if their instructional level is third grade, but their capacity level (listening or understanding level) is fifth grade, they should be able to profit from remedial instruction and raise their reading levels two years.

Importance of the Informal Reading Inventory

Practice by any classroom teacher will provide a great deal of confidence in use of the IRI and demonstrate its absolute necessity. It is the most accurate test measure that can be provided to evaluate the child's ability to use textbooks for instructional purposes. The reading inventory should be the very core of the teacher's whole reading work-program for the year. The teacher can learn to prepare a reading inventory and use it to study the abilities and disabilities of the boys and girls in the classroom with respect to developmental reading.

Since the child is reading only brief passages and the test situation represents only one small sample of the child's total behavior, it is easily possible that there are facets of reading not adequately assessed. It is also possible that on another day or at another time, the same individual might perform somewhat differently.

The individual texts in the reading series may not be accurately graded so that a readability formula may need to be applied to determine the level of difficulty. Fry's Readability Graph (see figure 8.2) may be used for this purpose. A passage needs to be sufficiently long to check adequately comprehension of ideas.[4]

It is the classroom teachers who, in the final analysis, *must make all the decisions* about the child's reading ability in day-to-day work. The teachers must *unavoidably* select their reading materials in language arts, social studies, arithmetic, science, and literature.

An excellent way for a teacher to get initial skill in administering an informal reading inventory is to record the children's oral reading on the tape recorder so that it can be played back a number of times. Most clinicians are apt to hear a few miscues the second time that they missed completely the first time. Without a specific plan of what to listen for, the listener is probably not able to make any kind of objective summary of the results of the oral reading.

Construction of the Informal Reading Inventory

The first step in preparing the inventory is the selection of a series of books, probably a series of readers. Preferably, a series of readers not already familiar to the children being tested should be used. While there are many words *not common* to two series of readers, the controlled vocabularies, the picture clues, and the context clues all help the children anticipate meanings and most of the words are already in the children's speaking vocabularies.

Selections from preprimers, primers, and first and second readers, need to contain 60 to 125 words and to be sufficiently informational in nature that questions can be asked to measure understanding of the ideas about what is read. For grades three to six, passages need to be somewhat longer, perhaps 100 to 200 words in length.

One selection must be identified to be read orally and one to be read silently. The selection from each book should be taken at the end of about the first one-third of the book. This follows the first few stories containing mostly review words from previous books in the series.

When the children read, they must be given an introduction to the story and a motivation question to set a purpose for reading. It is wise to select the silent reading selection immediately following the oral reading selection so the children can continue reading without teacher explanation and, thus, save time.

The comprehension questions should be carefully thought out so that they measure understanding as completely as possible. Levels of questioning are pertinent: factual or memory items; inferential items requiring reading between the lines; vocabulary items to test concepts; and items to test ability to interpret and evaluate. Authors need to provide meaningful concepts for new or difficult vocabulary items: "Erosion, which is the washing or blowing away of the soil, is therefore a serious problem."[5] The careful reader can now answer the question: "What is erosion?" "The stumpage, or timber in standing trees, is sold to lumbermen, who come in and cut the timber which is marked by the rangers for cutting."[6] The careful reader can now answer the question: "What is stumpage?"

When choosing selections for the informal reading inventory, teachers should consider the nature of the context material. Can good comprehension questions be derived

---

Making Connections 4.1: Creating an IRI Passage

One skill that each reading teacher needs is the ability to create an informal reading inventory. For this Making Connections, the task will be to create just one oral and one silent reading passage. The following steps will be helpful.

1. Select a basal reader designated for a particular reading level. (In a later chapter, you will be given information about how to estimate reading levels independent of the publishers' stated levels.)
2. Identify a passage long enough to be divided into oral and silent parts. Each part should be of suitable length for the estimated reading level.
3. Develop questions to accompany your two reading passages. Follow the guidelines given in the chapter for comprehension questions.
4. Type the two passages, the accompanying questions, the number of words in each passage, and the motivating statements. Using the IRI in the Appendix E as a guide, prepare the chart for showing percentages correct for word recognition and comprehension.
5. Type the pupil's copies of the two passages; remember the pupil's copy has nothing on the pages except the stories.

Bring your work to class to share with others. Each student should receive feedback from peers so that the best possible IRIs can be produced.

---

from the story? Vocabulary, sentence structure, human interest, and the number and complexity of the ideas dealt with influence the comprehension level of the material. In preparing the questions, the teachers should use questions that can be answered from the reading material, not from what the children already know. Also, they should ask questions requiring recall, rather than those requiring only yes or no. For example, ask, "What color was the hound?" *not,* "Was the hound in the story red?"

Administering the Informal Reading Inventory

Before the teacher can decide what selection to give the child to read, some idea of the child's functioning level is needed. There are several ways to get information for making this decision:

1. One way to decide at what grade level to begin the IRI with given students is to ask them to pronounce the words on the San Diego Quick Assessment. If nine out of ten words are correct at grade three but several are missed at grade four, the reader begins the IRI at grade three.
2. In September, the teachers can check the cumulative records from the previous year and see in which books the children were reading when the last school year ended. Of course, there will be errors in such a listing, but if the selection is too difficult, the teachers will move to easier material.

3. The teacher may be able to assemble subgroups of children in a reading circle very early in the year, and ask them to "read around the circle" sampling a story for which the teacher has developed readiness. For those who have difficulty, only one sentence is sufficient. For those who read well, a much longer passage is fine.[7]

4. If the teacher estimates that a book at second level, first grade is appropriate, a sampling of words can be made from the list in the back of the book to make a word recognition test of 20 words. The sample will be obtained by dividing the total number of words in the list by 20 and selecting words from the list at intervals of that quotient. For example, if there are 200 words in the list, 200 divided by 20 is 10, so the teachers will select every tenth word through the list. If the child knows at least 80 percent of these words at sight, this book may be at his or her instructional level of reading.

The following list of twenty words has been selected from the word list in the back of the basal, *People Need People,* a 2^1 reader[8] (a first semester, second reader), by selecting every 27th word from a total list of 548 new words. (When the 27th word in the list was *Marie* Antoinette, that word was skipped over and the next word taken.)

or	dance	thing	set
straw	round	policeman	nearby
squirrels	potter's	climbing	shades
Mrs. Greenhouse	hatbox	lake	pulled
wind	marry	class	papers

If a child can read 16 or more of these words at sight, this would be an appropriate book to sample for the instructional level of reading.

The easiest way to establish rapport with the child is to explain exactly what it is that you are doing and why determining the instructional level of reading is so important. If the child is interested, discuss the changing sizes of print in more difficult books, the amount of reading on a page, and the decrease in the use of pictures. The child must not be made to feel that the test is a "threat" to acceptance, and if the child continually asks for reassurance ("Am I doin' good?"), the teacher needs to be completely reassuring.

If the child makes more than five uncorrected miscues in reading the first selection attempted, the teacher may select an easier one and continue reading until a satisfactory instructional level is found. It is occasionally true, that the child makes more miscues on the first passage than on the next, more difficult one, so the teacher has to be alert for any psychological factors that may cause this to happen and be sure to find the highest level at which the student meets the criterion for instructional level.

While the pupil is reading, the teacher will record all word substitutions, hesitations, words not pronounced, repetitions, omissions, and insertions. It will be most helpful to the busy teacher to record the pupil's reading on the tape recorder so that the teacher can replay it when the child is gone and can give more concentrated attention to the reading. It is possible that the teacher can arrange the work of the rest of the class in independent activities, so that fifteen or twenty minutes may be used in one corner of the room where the child can complete the inventory. The relatively uninterrupted environment is necessary. Some teachers arrange to test one child each day during a recess period or during the special music or physical education period. A properly conducted informal reading inventory is the best instrument the classroom teachers have to determine most adequately what the child can and cannot do in formal reading.

Method of Marking Miscues

The miscues to be noted include substitutions, omissions, insertions, hesitations, words pronounced by the examiner, and repetitions. The important point for teachers is to have a definite, well-learned system of marking that will be meaningful. By such a method, a child may read a passage of 300 words, for example, on which twenty miscues are made in the mechanics of reading. If three months later, the same passage is read with only five miscues in mechanics, the teacher has a very favorable measure of the student's growth. However, the use of the system of recording miscues must be consistent if the pre/post-test record is to have value.

The system used here is borrowed from the manual of directions of the Gilmore Oral Reading Test.[9] The use of that test will be discussed later in the continuing diagnosis of the students' problems. The teachers should become habituated to one marking system and use it in all the individual testing that they do. Other detailed marking systems also work well. Marking of miscues is explained in table 4.1.

With only a minimum amount of practice, groups of experienced teachers find they mark children's oral reading with a very high percent of agreement. So, even though the administration of the IRI has subjective qualities, and many judgments must be made informally by the teacher very quickly, with some practice the results become quite objective for the competent teacher.

Analyzing the Oral Reading.

The following types of oral reading miscues constitute most of the children's difficulties (see table 4.1):

1. Hesitation: Mark after two seconds of hesitation with a (✓). Proper nouns are given to the child as needed and are not scored as miscues unless the proper noun is a word that most children would know. Examples: Big, Brown.
2. Word pronounced for the child: If the pupil hesitates for approximately five seconds on a difficult word, pronounce it and make a second check mark (✓✓) above it.
3. Mispronunciation: This results in a nonsense word that may be produced by: (1) false accentuation, (2) wrong pronunciation of vowels or consonants, or (3) the omission, addition, or insertion of one or more letters, without creating a real or new word. Example: *cret ik* for *critic*. Write the child's pronunciation above phonetically. Notice word-attack methods and enunciation. If miscues come too rapidly for recording, draw a line through mispronounced words. Do not count foreign accent or regional speech mannerisms.

TABLE 4.1. Recording Miscues in Oral Reading*

Type of Miscue	Rule for Marking	Example
1. Substitutions.	Write in the substituted word.	*black* The boy is back of . . .
2. Mispronunciation.	Write in the word phonetically or draw a line through the word.	~~symbolic~~ or / sim bŏl ĭk
3. Hesitations. A pause of two seconds or more.	Make one check above the word on which the hesitation occurs. (Two seconds or more.)	It is a ✓fascinating
4. Word pronounced by teacher. Word on which child hesitates more than five seconds.	Make two checks above the word pronounced. (Five seconds or more.)	It is a ✓✓fascinating story.
5. Repetitions.	Draw a wavy line beneath word or words repeated.	He thought he saw a whale.
6. Omissions.	Encircle the word or punctuation omitted.	It is the largest (living) animal. It is a whale
7. Insertions.	Use caret and write in inserted words or punctuation.	*is a* This big fellow from the jungles of Africa,

*John V. Gilmore and Eunice C. Gilmore, *Gilmore Oral Reading Test, Manual of Directions* (Harcourt, Brace, & World, Inc. 1968), general directions modified by the writer. With permission.

4. Omissions: Encircle the omitted word, syllable, letter sound, or endings. Count as one miscue the omission of more than one word of consecutive print.
5. Substitutions: This occurs when one sensible or real word is put in the place of the word in print. Write the substituted word directly above the word presented in print. Note if it makes sense or if it is irrelevant to the context.
6. Insertions: These are words that do not appear in the printed material. Place a caret (∧), and write the added word or words. Count as one miscue the insertion of two or more words consecutively.
7. Repetitions: A word, part of a word, or groups of words that are repeated; this may indicate that the child is having trouble understanding what he or she reads. Draw a wavy line under the repeated words.

If the teacher adopts a consistent pattern of marking the pupils' miscues in oral reading, the marked copy becomes an important part of each child's record. For example, if the teacher marks twelve uncorrected miscues in a passage at the initial testing and only three uncorrected miscues at a second testing at the same level of difficulty, this is an encouraging measure of progress.

One uncorrected miscue in 20 consecutive words is often interpreted as one mispronounced word or one not-known word. In this text, hesitations, repetitions, insertions, and omissions are also considered; however, many repetitions are made only to

David Woodward

Completing an informal reading inventory provides the teacher with critical information needed for planning a successful reading program for a child.

correct a substitution miscue. The subjective judgment therefore must be made in each case whether two or three recorded miscues represent only one miscue in reading in terms of accuracy in mechanics.

For example:

. . . one . . . after another . . . one after another . . .

The reader fails to pronounce "after." After reading falteringly through "one . . . after . . . another" with help, it is repeated to regain the thought, perhaps, before continuing. This is recorded in the tabulation of miscues as one word *failed to pronounce,* and not as a repetition. However, if the reader reads:

. . . one . . . after another . . . one after another . . .

this repetition is a miscue counted in the tabulation, because the mere fact that the phrase is repeated indicates the reader is having difficulty for some unknown reason. Often, by reducing the level of difficulty of material, pupils who do much repeating will no longer need to do so. The teacher needs a series of readers from which pupils can read. In order to establish a satisfactorily easy level for some, a complete series beginning with the preprimer or primer and continuing through the sixth-grade level will be needed.

The child begins reading selections and continues to read until the frustration level is reached. Then the teacher reads one selection at each level beyond that to the child and checks the comprehension score. This will provide a measure of the *understanding* of context material read aloud, or the capacity level of reading.

Marking Oral Reading Miscues in Informal Reading

Figure 4.1 (p. 106) is an illustration of the marking of oral reading done by Mary, a seventh grade student. The method of marking miscues is that found in Table 4.1. The reader is reminded that proper nouns are not counted and that if a word is pronounced more than once for the student it is counted as only one miscue. Questions for checking comprehension are given below the reading (70 or 75 percent is a minimum level of acceptable comprehension), and a list of oral reading miscues is given so that the total miscues with the mechanics of reading can be computed. The story is part of an unpublished informal reading inventory prepared in a class at the University of New Mexico under the direction of Dr. Robert White.

With respect to comprehension, Mary answered three questions correctly, as indicated by the three pluses, and missed two questions, as indicated by the two minuses. One cannot judge from only one sample such as this, but 60 percent suggests frustration level. Fourteen or fifteen uncorrected miscues in oral reading is nearer to one miscue in twelve running words than it is to one miscue in twenty words. Mary needs to read other passages, but this exercise suggests a frustration level of reading.

Marking and Scoring the IRI

The examiner must record these reading behaviors:

1. Corrections: Write a C by the mistake when the child corrects the miscue.
2. Phrasing: Use a diagonal mark to indicate undue pauses or incorrect phrasing.
3. Punctuation: Put an X on punctuation marks that the child ignores or passes over.
4. Rate: As difficulty increases, the child may read "slowly" and/or "haltingly." Indicate this. One must record reading time in seconds for each selection in order to determine words per minute.

In scoring the oral reading inventory, it seems logical to:

1. Count only one miscue at any place in the reading. If the child repeats a phrase to correct a word substitution, the important miscue is that of sight word substitution.

A Hunting Guide

When Robert Gonzales ✓✓ was 18, he signed up as an ✓✓ apprentice mountain porter and hunting guide. As an ✓✓ apprentice, he helped the other ✓✓ guides when extra men were needed on the climbing rope or on a pack trip.

After a year as a porter, Robert was ready for the test to become a guide. This tricky test lasted three days. It was given by the "guide chief" appointed by (the) Park Service.

starting
Many of the test questions stressed the safety rules a guide must follow. Part of the test was taken right on the mountains. Robert had to show that he could do all the work *for* of a guide—from getting a man out of trouble to giving first aid.

taking
At the end of three days, Robert was taken on a climb by the guide chief. Robert led (on) *waited for* *short* the rope, while the chief watched every move he made. The climb called for every sort (of) *
a *bal* *slabs* climbing technique: step-cutting in snow and ice, "~~balance~~ climbing" on smooth slabs, and many knots of the rope.

Level of difficulty of this passage: fifth grade on Fry Readability graph. Mary is in the seventh grade.

Total words in passage: 169. Maximum permissible miscues for the instructional level of reading: 8 or 9.

Questions to check comprehension:	*Scoring the oral reading:*	
+ 1. How old was Robert when he signed up as a guide? (18)	Substitutions	6
	Mispronunciations	1
− 2. How long did he work as a guide? (one year)	Hesitations- Words pronounced	
− 3. What was a guide supposed to do? (Make dangerous climbs safely.)	by examiner	3 **
	Repetitions	
+ 4. What did Robert have to do to pass his test? (Know safety rules and go on a climb)	Omissions	3/4
	Insertions	1
	TOTAL ERRORS	14/15
+ 5. Would you trust Robert if he passed the test? Why? (Yes, he'd have the skills)		

Omitting "of" makes sense; doesn't need "of" with short.
**Do not count proper names (Gonzales) "apprentice" is counted only once.*

Figure 4.1. An illustration of marking oral reading miscues

2. If a phrase of two or three words is omitted, count as only one miscue.
3. If a phrase of two or three words is inserted, count as only one miscue.
4. If the child makes one substitution miscue and then in the same sentence makes a second miscue to get proper grammatical structure with verbs or pronouns, count this as only one miscue.
5. If the proper names are unusual or difficult, do not include them in the miscue count. If they are common names like *Brown, Green,* or *Smith,* they should be counted as miscues. If the proper names are miscalled several times in one passage, the teacher must decide whether to count this as only one miscue. For example, the children may have read regularly about Tom and Betty previously; then in the IRI consistently pronounce Fred as Tom. This should be counted as only one miscue.
6. In basic sight word substitutions, the miscue should be counted each time it occurs. If the reader says "then" for "when" three times, this is three miscues.

Method of Recording Oral and Silent Reading Comprehension

The teacher must record the child's responses to the comprehension questions as they are given so an accurate measure will result. When the child's comprehension falls below 70–75 percent, there is no need to continue the reading even if the child has few mechanical difficulties.

The teacher needs to think about the conditions under which the child will be asked to respond to comprehension questions. The usual practice has been to expect the child to answer the questions without referring back to the passage that has just been read. That practice confuses memory for what has been read with comprehension of the material. In order to determine comprehension alone, it may be appropriate to allow the reader to look back if needed. Kender and Rubenstein found that children could not look back and find answers if they did not comprehend the material.[10] It would seem that comprehension scores will not be significantly inflated if children are allowed to keep the material they have just read and look back as needed.

Interpreting the IRI

The teacher will be able to summarize the results of the reading of the IRI in a chart, as in figure 4.2.

General Reading Habits

Nervous mannerisms such as fidgeting, twisting hair, picking nose, drawing a heavy sigh, or exhibiting undue restlessness indicate discomfort and frustration. These should be noted on the child's test. Also, teachers should notice such difficulties as losing the place in the story, holding the book close to the face, pointing with the fingers, or moving the head.

In silent reading, the child may vocalize everything read, read very slowly, or need encouragement to keep on reading.

ORAL					
Level of Book	Total Words	Total Miscues	Percent of Miscues	Percent Accuracy	Suitability of Level of Difficulty
_____	_____	_____	_____	_____	_____
_____	_____	_____	_____	_____	_____
_____	_____	_____	_____	_____	_____

SILENT					
Level of Book	Total Words	Time in Seconds	Rate per Minute	Percent of Comprehension	Suitability of Level of Difficulty
_____	_____	_____	_____	_____	_____
_____	_____	_____	_____	_____	_____
_____	_____	_____	_____	_____	_____

Figure 4.2. Chart for summary of IRI reading

Observations about Reading Performance

In determining the child's instructional level of reading from a series of readers, the following points are made:

1. This is "sight reading." That is, the material is read orally without first *studying* it silently. This is a test situation; in everyday work, children should have opportunity to read silently any material they will be expected to read well orally. Here the teacher is trying to find out what the child *can* read.
2. The first concern in this basic step in establishing corrective instruction is to measure the ability to pronounce the words. However, understanding of the content read is basic and must be measured also.

3. All the miscues that the child corrects immediately without help are deducted in arriving at a figure to compute percentage of error or percentage of accuracy. If the child makes two miscues in the same place in reading, this will usually be counted as one miscue. For example, repeating a phrase where a word has been omitted so the reading can be corrected constitutes an *omission*.

4. The instructional level sought is the *highest level* at which the child reads orally with 95 percent accuracy in the mechanics and has at least 75 percent comprehension.

5. One of the common defects in oral reading is nonfluency or word-by-word reading. The word caller plods along slowly, tending to make a noticeable pause after each word. Word callers may not phrase adequately; they may not group words together; and they may disregard and misuse punctuation marks. Keeping the place with the finger is common. Getting the sense of what they read is hard for students who struggle to get the words pronounced.

6. In evaluating the oral reading sample, the teachers should identify the "context reader." They may read rapidly enough, but quite inaccurately. They may skip over words or add words, but their most usual miscue is in substituting freely what they think the story will say. Below are three textbook sentences with children's context reading of them:

The story reads:	*The child says:*
"The little rabbit went down the road."	"The small bunny hopped down the lane." (The picture at the top of the page gave the idea clearly.)
"Come out of the back door."	"Come out on the back porch."
"Behind the band came a man on a big elephant."	"After the band wagon went, a man came by on an elephant."

Organizing and Reporting Test Information

After several tests have been given to a child and information from other sources has been gathered, the teacher must find a way to arrange all of the data for use in planning the reading program. An easy way to accomplish this task is to devise a sheet such as the one in figure 4.3. All of the test scores are recorded in one place, along with summaries of inventories and previous records. At the bottom of the sheet space should be provided for a brief plan for meeting the needs of the student. It is most important that such a summary sheet be dated if it is to have usefulness at some later time.

Commercial Informal Reading Inventories

Within recent years, a number of Informal Reading Inventories, as such, have been published in formats that make them appear to be formal. With an increase in the extent to which rigid steps are outlined for their administration and technical skills

A Quick Screening Report about the disabled reader in your room.

Name _____ Grade _____ Age _____ School _____

Date Collected   *Comments:*

1. Last year's report in
   cumulative folder: _____

2. Informal Reading Inventory:

   Independent Level: _____

   Instructional Level: _____

3. San Diego Quick Assessment: Raw Score _____

   Grade Level _____

4. Spelling Test: (Source of word list) _____

5. Writing sample: (Specific types of problems) _____

   _____

6. Keystone Visual Survey Test: (Need for referral)   Yes _____ No _____

7. Interest Inventory: _____

8. Interview about reading: _____

   _____

9. Parent Interview: _____

   _____

10. Vocabulary measure; _____

11. Wepman Auditory Discrimination Test: (Need for referral)

    Yes _____ No _____   (This test is discussed in Chapter 6)

12. Status summary: What can you do in the immediate future to make constructive use of
    the student's time? Who is available in your school to help you get further information?

Figure 4.3. A Quick Screening Report

required for the interpretation of their results, they have tended to lose their "infor-mality." However, they are labeled as informal inventories when they are designed to help the teacher estimate rather quickly *instructional* levels of reading (both oral and silent), the *frustration* level where difficulties show up, and (if the teacher then reads to the student) the understanding or *capacity* level of the student.

Inventories currently in use include:

1. Lois A. Bader, *Reading and Language Inventory* (New York: Macmillan Publishing Co., 1983).
2. Morton Botel, *Botel Reading Inventory* (Chicago: Follett Publishing Co., 1970).
3. Paul C. Burns and Betty D. Roe, *Informal Reading Assessment* (Chicago: Rand McNally College Publishing Co., 1980).
4. Eldon E. Ekwall, *Ekwall Reading Inventory* (Boston: Allyn and Bacon, 1979).

Making Connections 4.2: Administering the IRI

Each teacher needs to be able to administer an IRI quickly and effectively. Only practice will aid the teacher in achieving this goal.

Plan to do one of these two activities:

1. Administer the IRI passages that you prepared in Making Connections 4.1 to three children who should be able to read them. Tape record each child's reading and score the word recognition and comprehension tasks carefully. Compare the performances of the three readers. Plan to share your results with other class members.
2. Administer the informal reading inventory found in Appendix E to one child. Tape record and then evaluate carefully the child's reading. Were you able to find any of the reading levels of your reader with this abbreviated IRI? Prepare a description of the many observed reading behaviors of the child you tested. Plan to share your findings with peers.

---

5. Edward B. Fry, *Reading Diagnosis, Informal Reading Inventories* (Providence, R.I.: Jamestown Publishers, 1981).
6. Jerry L. Johns, *Basic Reading Inventory: Preprimer–Grade 8,* 2d ed. (Dubuque, Ia.: Kendall/Hunt Publishing Co., 1981).
7. Margaret LaPray, *On the Spot, Reading Diagnosis File* (New York: Center for Applied Research in Education, 1978).
8. Wilma Miller, *Reading Diagnosis Kit* (New York: Center for Applied Research in Education, 1978).
9. Nicholas J. Silvaroli, *Classroom Reading Inventory,* 4th ed., (Dubuque, Ia.: Wm. C. Brown, 1982).
10. George D. Spache, *Diagnostic Reading Scales* (Monterrey, Calif.: California Test Bureau/McGraw-Hill, 1972).
11. Floyd Sucher and Ruel A. Allred, *Reading Placement Inventory* (Oklahoma City: The Economy Company, 1973).

Summary

Classroom teachers have no alternative to administering of informal inventories to students in their classes. There is no other way to help students find the books that they can read adequately for study. If teachers are not in complete agreement, each one's consistent judgment may be more important. But they must make the decisions. The informal reading inventories that have been made available commercially are not as useful to the competent teachers as their own abilities to take a book off the shelf and ask the students to "try it on for size." Of course the published inventories give teachers valuable pre- and post-test results and are easily available for use with many students. But the teacher needs to be able to try the geography text, the science text, or any other to determine level of difficulty for any one student.

As Powell has very aptly concluded:

> The strength of the IRI is not as a test instrument but as a strategy for studying the behavior of the learner in a reading situation and as a basis for instant diagnosis in the teaching environment.[11]

For Further Reading

Betts, Emmett A. *Foundations of Reading Instruction.* New York: American Book Co., 1946.

Ekwall, E. E. *Diagnosis and Remediation of the Disabled Reader.* Boston: Allyn and Bacon, 1983: Chapter 11, "Using Informal Reading Inventories, the Cloze Procedure, and the Analysis of Reading Scores," pp. 366–411.

Fuchs, Lynn S.; Fuchs, Douglas; and Deno, Stanley L. "Reliability and Validity of Curriculum-Based Informal Reading Inventories." *Reading Research Quarterly* 18, no. 1 (1982), pp. 6–26.

McCracken, Robert A. "Using an Informal Reading Inventory to Affect Instruction." In Albert J. Harris and Edward R. Sipay, eds., *Readings on Reading Instruction,* 3d ed. New York: Longman Inc., 1984, pp. 156–59.

McGinnis, Dorothy J. and Smith, Dorothy E. *Analyzing and Treating Reading Problems.* New York: Macmillan Publishing Co., 1982: Chapter 6, "Informal Assessment of Reading Performance," pp. 63–75.

McKenna, Michael C. "Informal Reading Inventories: A Review of the Issues." *The Reading Teacher* 36 (March 1983), pp. 670–77.

Schell, Leo M., and Hanna, Gerald S. "Can Informal Reading Inventories Reveal Strengths and Weaknesses in Comprehension Subskills?" *The Reading Teacher* 35 (December 1981), pp. 263–68.

Velmont, William J. "Creating Questions for Informal Reading Inventories." *The Reading Teacher* 25 (March 1972), pp. 509–12.

Notes

1. Page Simpson Bristow, John J. Pikulski, and Peter L. Pelosi, "A Comparison of Five Estimates of Reading Instructional Level," *The Reading Teacher* 37 (December 1983), pp. 273–79. and Lester R. Wheeler and Edwin H. Smith, "A Modification of the Informal Reading Inventory," *Elementary English* 34 (April 1967), p. 224.
2. Emmett A. Betts, *Foundations of Reading Instruction* (New York: American Book Company, 1950), pp. 478–79.
3. Ibid., p. 448.
4. Roger Farr and Nancy Roser, *Teaching a Child to Read* (New York: Harcourt, Brace, 1979), pp. 42–43; Margaret A. Richek, Lynne K. List, and Janet W. Lerner, *Reading Problems, Diagnosis and Remediation* (Englewood Cliffs, N.J.: Prentice-Hall, 1983), p. 131; and George D. Spache, *Reading in the Elementary School* (Boston: Allyn and Bacon, 1964), p. 245.

5. Ernest Horn et al., Progress in Reading Series, *Reaching Our Goals* (Boston: Ginn, 1940), p. 138.
6. Ibid., p. 145.
7. E. W. Dolch, "How to Diagnose Children's Reading Difficulties by Informal Classroom Techniques," *The Reading Teacher* 6 (January 1953), pp. 10–14.
8. Bernard J. Weiss et. al., *People Need People,* Level 9 (New York: Holt, Rinehart and Winston, 1983).
9. John V. Gilmore, *Manual of Directions, Gilmore Oral Reading Test* (New York: Harcourt, Brace 1968).
10. Joseph Kender and Herbert Rubenstein, "Recall Versus Reinspection in IRI Comprehension Tests," *The Reading Teacher* 30: (April 1977), pp. 776–79.
11. William R. Powell, "The Validity of the Instructional Reading Level," in Althea Beery, Thomas C. Barrett, and William R. Powell, eds., *Elementary Reading Instruction: Selected Materials,* 2d ed., (Boston: Allyn and Bacon, 1974), pp. 89–96; and Everett Davis and Eldon E. Ekwall, "Mode of Perception and Frustration in Reading," *Journal of Learning Disabilities* 9 (August/September, 1976), pp. 448–54.

5
Standardized Tests and Records of Progress

Vocabulary

standardized tests
validity
reliability
norms
grade equivalent score
percentile
stanines
norm-referenced tests
criterion-referenced tests
silent reading test
lines of importance
group test
profile
miscue analysis

Questions

1. Compare the terms *validity* and *reliability*.

2. What problems can you see in using grade equivalent scores? Percentiles? Stanines? Which would you prefer to use? Why?

3. What differences characterize norm-referenced and criterion-referenced tests?

4. What are the primary limitations of standardized tests?

5. Describe any one of the reading tests discussed in some detail in this chapter.

6. What is meant by miscue analysis? How is the *Reading Miscue Inventory* different from the other reading tests in this chapter?

Introduction

Early in the school year, teachers will complete several informal measures of reading abilities in an attempt to get the necessary information to assign work individually, to small groups, and to the whole class. Some informal reading inventories provide a great deal of information about students. The students' abilities to write paragraphs, to complete seatwork assignments, and to successfully complete spelling exercises will help the teacher understand better the range of abilities in the class.

Beyond these measures, a few students may need referrals to other specialists for hearing, vision, or personality tests.

Some few students need referral to the reading diagnostician for further testing in reading. Thus, teachers must have some understanding of the terminology used in interpreting standardized tests used with their students.

Terminology Used to Interpret Standardized Tests

In order for teachers to use and understand information about standardized tests, they should have some knowledge of the terms used in statistical measurement. Also a clear distinction needs to be made between norm-referenced and criterion-referenced tests.

Validity

The *validity* of a test is a measure of the extent to which the test measures what it was designed to measure. For example, a test that is labeled an "intelligence" test will be valid to the extent that it is, in reality, a true measure of global intelligence. Since intelligence is a very complex set of factors, it is doubtful whether any one test can be a valid measure of all the facets of intelligence.

As another example, teachers may set teaching a specific list of vocabulary words as their objective. They can prepare a valid test of their success by testing to see if their students know the meanings of the words they proposed to teach. It would be valid to the extent that the word meanings tested and the answers acceptable were those that the students were supposed to learn.

Reliability

The *reliability* of a test is a measure of the extent to which it measures consistently over time whatever it is designed to measure. If people complete a test today and then complete the same test (or an equivalent form) six weeks from today and earn approximately the same score, the test is apparently reliably measuring their ability to perform on those test questions. With respect to the intelligence test just referred to, it would have *little* validity if it did not really sample global intelligence; however the test could consistently yield the same results and, therefore, have high reliability.

Intelligence tests that are heavily loaded with vocabulary items, testing the students' extent of word meanings, may be extremely reliable when administered to large groups of students. What this tells us is that some students always get high scores on vocabulary tests and others always get low scores. However, in the frame of reference that global intelligence is one's ability to cope with new situations and solve problems, a vocabulary test is not a valid test of general ability.

Norms

Norms provide information about the typical performance for students for whom a test has been constructed. To determine the "typical performance" it is necessary to give the test when it is constructed to a large number of students representative of the population for whom the test is intended. Norms are intended to facilitate evaluation of pupil progress through time and are expressed in such units as grade placements, percentiles, and stanines. These are illustrated in table 5.1. Norms on tests provide a basis for comparing a given individual's performance with the standard reference group.

Table 5.1 shows us that John Doe earned a grade-placement score of 4.5, which ranked him at the fiftieth percentile and at the fifth stanine. If John Doe is in the fourth grade, this test would indicate that he is performing normally in the "middle" of the distribution for his class. Bill, with a grade-placement of 8.2, performs much better than the average of his class if he is in the fourth grade, and Tom is achieving below grade level if he is also in grade four.

Grade Equivalent Scores.

Grade equivalent scores are usually provided by test publishers so that teachers can easily translate raw scores into ratings easily understood as school achievement. If John's grade placement is 4.5, the four represents the school grade (fourth) and the second number represents the month of the school year (fifth), he is performing at the norm for one who is now half through the fourth grade. The grade equivalents for the fourth grade are 4.1 to 4.9. Since there is a tenth of a point to be accounted for so that the first month of fifth grade can be represented by 5.1, the scoring allows one month of growth for the summer vacation period. This accommodates to an easy plan for assigning ten "parts" to the year of growth.

It is important to point out that John's score of 4.5 may be an "average" score at midyear in fourth grade, *but* this is telling us, statistically, that half of his group tested

TABLE 5.1. Norms for Text Evaluation

Student	Raw Score	Grade Placement	Percentile	Stanine
John Doe	42	4.5	50	5
Bill Doe	72	8.2	97	9
Tom Doe	21	2.8	07	2

above this score and half tested below it. *Average,* equivalent to the fiftieth percentile, means that half of the students must be either above or below this level of achievement.

Grade equivalents encompass the grade range of the public school, from 1.0 to 12.9. One limitation of this range of scores is that the teachers will understand that the *sizes* of units of learning representing what constitutes grade 1, or 4, or 8, or 11 are not necessarily equal units. It is difficult to say, for example, whether growth from 7.1 to 8.0 in reading is equivalent to all the rapid growth a child may make in reading from 2.1 to 3.0.

Teachers need also to recognize that while achievement at 5.0 means beginning fifth grade *for fifth graders,* achievement of an 8.0 on a test for fifth graders means they are achieving extremely well, but they may not be able to perform as beginning eighth graders. The only standard to which the fifth graders are being compared is the range of performance of all of the fifth graders.

Percentiles.

A *percentile rank* is a point on a distribution that defines the relative position of one individual with respect to the total group. Expressed in terms of 100 percent, it has an absolute value that is independent of the number of cases with which it is being compared and it is clearly understandable. For example, a percentile rank of 58 means that 42 percent of all those tested performed better and 58 percent performed less well. Percentile ranks afford a direct and ready means for interpreting an individual performance in comparison with the whole group. Students who rank at the seventy-fifth percentile have done very well; they have exceeded the performances of 75 percent of their peers. The students who rank at the tenth percentile have exceeded the performance of only 10 percent of their group or of only 10 in 100 of their peers.

Because percentiles are easy to compute, interpret, and understand, they are frequently used for local norms in a school district. Publishers almost always provide percentile norms with their test data. However, percentile norms are meaningful only in terms of a specific test administered to a particular group at a given time. And local percentile norms may be different from the national norms.

Percentiles are not based on a scale of equal units of difference. For example, the raw score difference between the ninetieth and the ninety-fifth percentiles may not be the same number of raw score points between the forty-fifth and the fiftieth percentiles. Raw scores tend to cluster around the mean of the distribution so that many scores will be the same or nearly the same at the middle, or fiftieth percentile.

Stanines.

The *stanine* is a norming term expressed in the numbers from one to nine. The distribution of raw scores is divided into nine parts. The fifth stanine accounts for all the students whose raw scores cluster at the middle of the distribution. A stanine of nine is the highest level and a stanine of one is the lowest level. The same caution that was

TABLE 5.2. Distribution of Stanine Levels

Percent of cases:	4%	7%	12%	17%	20%	17%	12%	7%	4%
Stanines:	1	2	3	4	5	6	7	8	9

earlier stated for percentiles applies to stanines; stanines are not of equal value in the range of raw scores. Stanines tell us that the fifth stanine is the performance of the large group in the middle (20 percent of the total population); the fourth and sixth stanines are those below and above average (each stanine accommodates 17 percent of the total population); stanines three and seven include those students farther above and farther below average. The lowest achievers are in stanines one and two and the highest achievers are in stanines eight and nine. The distribution of the percentages of the test population is shown in table 5.2.

If teachers keep in mind that 54 percent of a distribution falls in stanines four, five, and six, they will know that stanines one, two, and three account for the bottom 23 percent of the distribution and stanines seven, eight, and nine account for the 23 percent at the top of the distribution.

In summary, norms are a more consistent way of talking about and making evaluations of achievement from one test to another. Norms, as grade equivalents, express average performance of students at various grade levels. Norms, as percentiles, describe students' places in a distribution in terms of the percent of students who scored lower and higher. Stanines indicate how far above or below the average given students are in the norming group.

Interpretations of test results, however, require more information than just knowledge of norms. One must know what the test is measuring, the language and cultural background of the students being tested, and the kind of motivation for school success learned at home.

Norm-Referenced Tests and Criterion-Referenced Tests

The norms discussed earlier have traditionally been applied to tests standardized on one large population and then administered to any selected group. These tests are norm-referenced and provide comparisons of a specific group with the population on which the test was normed. Competitive scholarship exams, for example, are norm-referenced and then all students, without regard to their specific status, compete to see if they can out-perform everyone else who takes the test.

Criterion-referenced tests are those developed in response to criteria specified in the objectives teachers develop. They set out to teach a specific body of subject matter, or a set of principles, agreed upon before the teaching starts. Then they can design a test that measures whether students learned what they were taught. Criterion-referenced tests are tailored to more individual purposes.

Making Connections 5.1: Exploring Test References

It is important for teachers to have access to organized and objective reports about current standardized tests. *Tests in Print III* from the Buros Institute of Mental Measurements is undoubtedly the best reference available.* From time to time newer editions are prepared.

Most of the standardized tests mentioned in this chapter are listed and described in this reference. You will also find extensive bibliographies of articles and reports in which each particular test has been reviewed or employed in research.

Look up at least three of the tests given in this chapter. Obtain as much information as possible about the forms of the test and the grades for which various forms are intended, the author(s), publisher and publication dates, previous editions, and so on. Also, locate and read at least one of the references cited for each test.

Bring all this information to class for sharing. Your group may decide to "pool" the information collected into a useful handbook for class members.
*James V. Mitchell Jr., ed. *Tests in Print* (Lincoln, Nebraska: University of Nebraska, Lincoln, 1983).

Limitations of Standardized Tests

Silent reading tests are useful for surveying the general abilities of students. Such tests measure vocabulary ability and the ability to associate ideas in print. The clinician can identify some strengths or weaknesses of given students by comparing their performances with the performances of a large number of their peers on whom the test was normed.

Silent reading group tests are *not* diagnostic and have limitations with respect to testing any specific comprehension or study skills. It is possible that if students have any knowledge of a subject, they may be able to answer literal level questions for a paragraph as well *without* reading it as after reading it. The purpose of the silent reading test will be to measure the level at which given students perform when they are compared with a large number of their peers.

Since most silent reading tests measure vocabulary, literal comprehension, and possibly relationships such as cause and effect, clearly they are severely limited in helping teachers find strengths and weaknesses in students' abilities to use discrete comprehension or study skills. Therefore, the teacher will do well to evaluate the grade placement score achieved by the student and teach many of the skills included in the outline in the chapter on comprehension.

Reading Tests

A discussion of several well-known reading tests follows. The tests are grouped under the headings of oral and silent reading tests, diagnostic reading tests, criterion-referenced tests, reading tests accompanying basal readers, and the Reading Miscue Inventory. Additional information about a selected group of tests is included in Appendix C.

Oral Reading Tests

The oral reading test is a well-known form of standardized reading tests. It resembles the informal reading inventory because it includes paragraphs for the child to read orally; a marking code for the teacher to use to record word-recognition problems; comprehension questions to be asked for each oral passage; and a table for converting errors, time required for reading, and accuracy of comprehension into a reading score. This type of reading test requires that the teacher or diagnostician have approximately half an hour of uninterrupted time to administer the test.

Gilmore Oral Reading Test

The Gilmore Oral Reading Test[1] analyzes *oral* reading abilities at grade levels one through eight. The test provides grade placement scores for accuracy of oral reading, comprehension of material read, and rate of oral reading. *A* and *B* and *C* and *D* forms provide equivalent tests for use at the beginning and ending of a learning period. About twelve to fifteen minutes are required for administration of the test to an individual; a few cases may take up to twenty minutes.

The manual provides for a system of recording errors as the pupils read. The errors, to be recorded as the pupils read, include substitutions, mispronunciations, words pronounced by the teacher, hesitations, repetitions, insertions, omissions, and disregard of punctuation. The recording of errors in informal reading made use of this system (see chapter 4); thus, the teacher has already learned the method for administering this test. In scoring the test, the result will be in *grade placement scores,* rather than in the percentage of accuracy in mechanics and comprehension.

On the Gilmore Test, the individuals establish a beginning level with the paragraph in which they make no more than *two* errors in mechanics of reading. They read until they make ten or more errors in a paragraph. Their accuracy determines the level at which they stop reading. However, their comprehension score is computed by tapering their paragraph comprehension scores successively by one point less for each level more difficult than the first paragraph where they made ten or more errors. This "compensation" in computing the comprehension score helps in some cases to approximate more closely the expected level of comprehension for the disabled readers. Total raw scores are converted to grade equivalent scores and ratings by use of tables in the manual of directions. See test summary for Paula in figure 5.1.

NAME *Paula*

TEST SUMMARY   Form C

PARA-GRAPH	ACCURACY		COMPREHENSION	RATE	
	ERRORS	10 MINUS NO. ERRORS	NO. RIGHT (OR CREDITED)	WORDS IN ¶	TIME IN SEC.
1	0	10	5	24	18
2	3	7	5	45	32
3	8	2	5	50	62
4	11	0	4	73	80
5			3	103	
6			2	117	
7			1	127	
8			0	161	
9				181	
10				253	
	ACC. SCORE (TOT. "10 MINUS NO. ER-RORS" COLUMN) 19		COMP. SCORE (TOT. NO. RIGHT OR CREDITED) 25	(1) NO. WORDS READ* 95	
				(2) TIME IN SEC.* 94	
STANINE	3		7	(1) ÷ (2)	X 60
GRADE EQUIV.	2.8		5.1	RATE SCORE (WPM)	60
RATING	Below Ave.		Above Ave.	Slow	

Basal (aligned with paragraph 1)
Ceiling (aligned with paragraph 3)

*Do **not** count "ceiling" paragraph or paragraphs below "basal."

COMMENTS: Paula is finishing third grade, has a W.I.S.C. Iq. of 120, and would be an excellent student if she could master quick word-recognition skills.

Figure 5.1. Gilmore Oral Reading Test Summary for Paula (Reproduced from John C. Gilmore and Eunice C. Gilmore, *Gilmore Oral Reading Test,* copyright 1968 by Psychological Corporation. Reproduced by special permission.)

TABLE 5.3. Improvement in Gilmore Test Performance for Martha (High Average I.Q.)

Date	Form	Accuracy	Grade Equivalents Comprehension	Speed Rating
February 26, 1975	B	4.4	9.8 +	Very slow
July 28, 1975	A	5.9	9.8 +	Slow
July 16, 1976	B	8.6	9.8 +	Slow
Improvement		4.2		

Improving oral reading with remedial reading cases should decrease errors in silent reading, improve auditory abilities in discriminating similar sounds, and build the individual's confidence.

Martha was fourteen and in the ninth grade when she was given the Gilmore Oral Reading Test. She made many substitutions of easy words, many repetitions of words and phrases, and hesitated too long on many polysyllabic words. Her accuracy score was 4.4. Her ability to answer the comprehension questions was good, even when she made more than the maximum of ten errors. Martha attended a reading clinic during an eight-week summer school session where she did a great deal of easy oral reading, speed of comprehension exercises, and worked on roots, prefixes, and suffixes. At the end of the tutoring program, she was again given the Gilmore Test, and earned an accuracy score of 5.9. She was given the Gilmore Test, Form B, one year later as a follow-up. This time her accuracy score was 8.6. The small amount of individual tutoring she had apparently helped a great deal. These three administrations of the test are summarized in table 5.3.

The Gray Oral Reading Test

The Gray Oral Reading Test[2] is another useful instrument that any classroom teacher can use. While its rationale is somewhat different, the score is based on errors in the mechanics of reading and the time required for reading. While the comprehension score is not used directly in arriving at a reading level, the test provides the teacher with a careful check on comprehension of ideas within the content read. The cover page of the Gray Oral Reading Test is presented in figure 5.2, giving the summary and the types of reading errors made by a fourth-grade child who functions at first-grade reading level.

Silent Reading Tests

Silent reading tests are designed to be used with more than one child at a time. In fact, large numbers of children frequently take these tests simultaneously in school settings. These tests are designed to provide school personnel with scores expressed in stanines, percentiles, and grade scores. They provide little useful diagnostic information. Computer printouts of pupils' responses on individual test items may suggest a greater degree of diagnostic usefulness than is justified. The teacher must also be careful not to

EXAMINER'S RECORD BOOKLET

for the

GRAY ORAL READING TEST

FORM A

Name *Audrey Jackson*   Grade *4*   Age *10-3*
School *Washington Elementary*   Teacher *Smith*   Sex *F*
City _____   State _____
Examiner *Mrs. Maggart*   Date *July 24, ___*

SUMMARY

Pas-sage Number	No. of Errors	Time (in Seconds)	Pas-sage Scores	Compre-hension
1.	3	13	6	3½
2.	4	23	3	3
3.	6	52	0	4
4.	8	55	0	3
5.				
6.				
7.				
8.				
9.				
10.				
11.				
12.				
13.				
Total Passage Scores		9		
Grade Equivalent		1.6		

TYPES OF ERRORS

1.	Aid	1
2.	Gross Mispronunciation	
3.	Partial Mispronunciation	
4.	Omission	
5.	Insertion	2
6.	Substitution	12
7.	Repetition	4
8.	Inversion	2
		21

OBSERVATIONS
(Check statement and circle each part)

_____ Word-by-word reading
✔ Poor phrasing
_____ Lack of expression
_____ Monotonous tone
_____ Pitch too high or low; voice too loud, too soft, or strained
✔ Poor enunciation
✔ Disregard of punctuation
✔ Overuse of phonics
✔ Little or no method of word analysis
partial Unawareness of errors
_____ Head movement
_____ Finger pointing
_____ Loss of place

COMMENTS: *Little awareness of the end of a sentence. Nearly all errors begin the same as the correct word.*

THE **BOBBS-MERRILL** COMPANY, INC.
A SUBSIDIARY OF HOWARD W. SAMS & CO., INC.
Publishers • INDIANAPOLIS • NEW YORK

Copyright © 1963, The Bobbs-Merrill Co., Inc. Indianapolis 6, Indiana

Figure 5.2. Audrey takes the Gray Oral Reading Test. (Reproduced from Examiner's Record Booklet, *Gray Oral Reading Test,* Form A. Copyright 1967 by Psychological Corporation. Reproduced by permission.)

make inferences about the child's oral reading skills based on information obtained from silent reading tests. Research has yet to confirm that oral and silent reading are similar enough to enable the teacher to evaluate only one.

Group Standardized Silent Reading Tests

1. *Gates-MacGinitie Reading Tests,* 2d ed. (Riverside Publ. Co., 1978). This series of tests measures vocabulary, comprehension, speed, and accuracy. The levels are Primary A (grade 1); Primary B (grade 2); Primary C (grade 3); Survey D (grades 4–6); Survey E (grades 7–9); and Survey F (grades 10–12).
2. *Nelson Reading Skills Test,* revised by Gerald Hanna, Leo M. Schell, and Robert L. Schreiner, (Nelson, Riverside Publ. Co., 1977). Comes in three levels: A (3.0–4.5), B. (4.6–6.9), and C (7.0–9.9). Tests vocabulary and comprehension. Optional tests are word parts and rate tests. Grades 3 to 9. The time required is thirty minutes for vocabulary and comprehension.
3. *Stanford Reading Tests* (New York: The Psychological Corp., 1974). Tests vocabulary, reading comprehension, word-study skills, and listening comprehension. Primary levels I, II, and III, and Intermediate levels I and II.
4. *California Achievement Tests: Reading* (Monterey, California: California Test Bureau/McGraw-Hill, 1970). Tests vocabulary and comprehension. Level 1, grades 1 and 2; Level 2, grades 2–4; Level 3, grades 4–6; Level 4, grades 6–9; and Level 5, grades 9–12. Forms C and D (1977).
5. *New Developmental Reading Tests* (New York: Rand McNally, 1968). Primary levels test word recognition, comprehending significant ideas, and comprehending specific instructions. Lower primary, grades 1.0–2.5; upper primary grades 2.5–3.9. Intermediate levels, grades 4–6, measure reading vocabulary, reading for information, relationships, and interpretation.

Diagnostic Reading Tests

There are many diagnostic reading tests among which teachers and school diagnosticians may choose. A diagnostic reading test is usually designed for a particular group of children's reading levels and skills. The reading teacher should become familiar with several of these tests so that one can be selected that fits best the child who will take it. Diagnostic tests tend to be exhaustive in their coverage of reading skills and to require over an hour of working time with a child. A child may take only certain subtests, because in many cases the responses on these subtests will provide sufficient information to guide decisions about the child's reading problems.

Durrell Analysis of Reading Difficulty

This test is an individually administered test that yields a profile of grade equivalent scores ranging from low-first to high-sixth grade.[3] The abilities tested are oral reading, silent reading, listening (a kind of capacity test), flash-word recognition, word analysis, spelling, and handwriting. The test can be administered in about thirty minutes. It provides one subtest in word association for the nonreader.

Speed of reading is the determining factor in finding the pupil's reading grade level in the Durrell Analysis. Scoring is detailed for the teachers in the manual of directions. Figure 5.3 shows errors marked and scored for the third paragraph for both the oral and silent reading subtests.

Figure 5.4 shows the recording of errors and scoring of one pupil's performance on the word recognition and word analysis subtests. Teachers using the test will do well to learn to use such devices for quick scoring as *NR* for "No response," *C* for "correct" when they get something right after failing to respond or after responding incorrectly, and *dk* for "don't know" when they say they don't know. Further, teachers can record on the margins of test pages useful information about types of responses children make or fail to make.

Examples of notes made by the teacher when testing word recognition are:

> Harold was unable to pronounce *away* but knew *way* when I covered the *a*. Even after pronouncing *way*, he was unable to add the vowel and pronounce *away*.
>
> Harold may be "reversing" in *near* for *rain* and in *feel* for *leaf*.

Tom's profile on the Durrell Analysis is presented in figure 5.5. Tom was a very bright boy (WISC IQ 125) who needed tutorial help to make reading make sense for him.

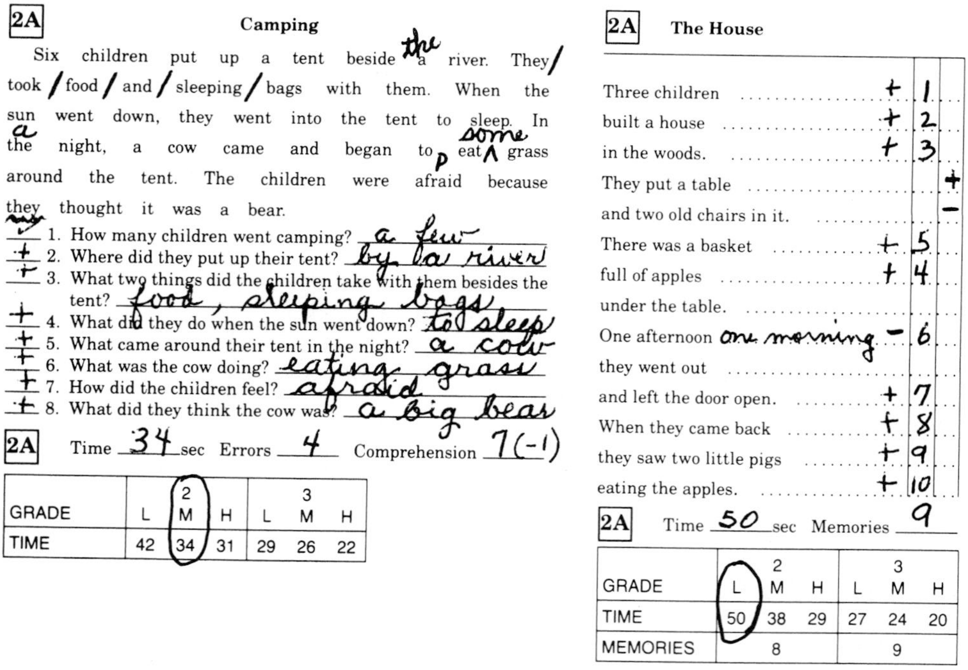

2A **Camping**

Six children put up a tent beside a river. They took food and sleeping bags with them. When the sun went down, they went into the tent to sleep. In the night, a cow came and began to eat grass around the tent. The children were afraid because they thought it was a bear.

1. How many children went camping? *a few*
2. Where did they put up their tent? *by la river*
3. What two things did the children take with them besides the tent? *food, sleeping bags*
4. What did they do when the sun went down? *to sleep*
5. What came around their tent in the night? *a cow*
6. What was the cow doing? *eating grass*
7. How did the children feel? *afraid*
8. What did they think the cow was? *a big bear*

2A Time *34* sec Errors *4* Comprehension *7(-1)*

GRADE	2 L	2 M	2 H	3 L	3 M	3 H
TIME	42	34	31	29	26	22

2A **The House**

Three children	+	1
built a house	+	2
in the woods.	+	3
They put a table		+
and two old chairs in it.		−
There was a basket	+	5
full of apples	+	4
under the table.		
One afternoon *one morning*	−	6
they went out		
and left the door open.	+	7
When they came back	+	8
they saw two little pigs	+	9
eating the apples.	+	10

2A Time *50* sec Memories *9*

GRADE	2 L	2 M	2 H	3 L	3 M	3 H
TIME	50	38	29	27	24	20
MEMORIES		8			9	

Figure 5.3. Marking errors and scoring oral and silent reading in the *Durrell Analysis of Reading Difficulty*, 3d ed. (Reproduced by permission from *Durrell Analysis of Reading Difficulty*: Third Edition. Copyright © 1980, by Harcourt Brace Jovanovich, Inc. All rights reserved.)

Word Recognition/Word Analysis

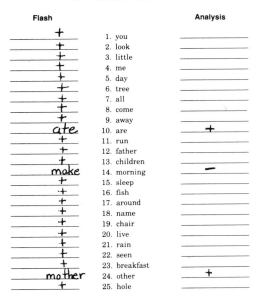

LIST A—GRADE 1 READING LEVEL

Flash		Analysis
+	1. you	
+	2. look	
+	3. little	
+	4. me	
+	5. day	
+	6. tree	
+	7. all	
+	8. come	
+	9. away	
ate	10. are	+
+	11. run	
+	12. father	
+	13. children	
make	14. morning	−
+	15. sleep	
+	16. fish	
+	17. around	
+	18. name	
+	19. chair	
+	20. live	
+	21. rain	
+	22. seen	
+	23. breakfast	
mother	24. other	+
+	25. hole	

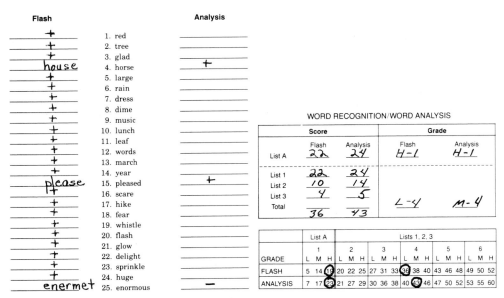

LIST 1—ABOVE GRADE 1 READING LEVEL

Flash		Analysis
+	1. red	
+	2. tree	
+	3. glad	
house	4. horse	+
+	5. large	
+	6. rain	
+	7. dress	
+	8. dime	
+	9. music	
+	10. lunch	
+	11. leaf	
+	12. words	
+	13. march	
+	14. year	
please	15. pleased	+
+	16. scare	
+	17. hike	
+	18. fear	
+	19. whistle	
+	20. flash	
+	21. glow	
+	22. delight	
+	23. sprinkle	
+	24. huge	
enermet	25. enormous	−

WORD RECOGNITION/WORD ANALYSIS

	Score		Grade	
	Flash	Analysis	Flash	Analysis
List A	22	24	H-1	H-1
List 1	22	24		
List 2	10	14		
List 3	4	5		
Total			L-4	M-4
	36	43		

	List A		Lists 1, 2, 3														
	1		2			3			4			5			6		
GRADE	L	M H	L	M	H	L	M	H	L	M	H	L	M	H	L	M	H
FLASH	5	14 (19)	20	22	25	27	31	33 (36)	38	40		43	46	48	49	50	52
ANALYSIS	7	17 (23)	21	27	29	30	36	38	40 (43)	46		47	50	52	53	55	60

Figure 5.4. Marking errors and scoring word-recognition and word-analysis in the *Durrell Analysis of Reading Difficulty,* 3d ed., Grade 1 reading level. (Reproduced by permission from *Durrell Analysis of Reading Difficulty*: Third Edition. Copyright © 1980, by Harcourt Brace Jovanovich, Inc. All rights reserved.)

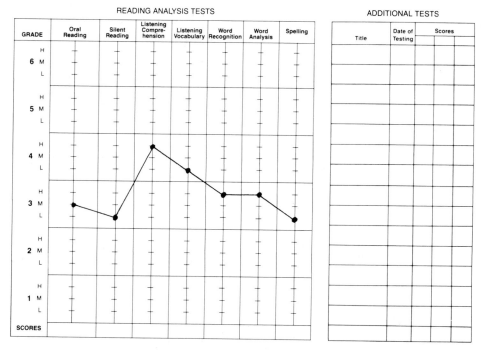

Durrell Analysis of Reading Difficulty
THIRD EDITION

INDIVIDUAL RECORD BOOKLET

Donald D. Durrell and Jane H. Catterson
Professor Emeritus, Boston University   Professor of Education, University of British Columbia

NAME **Bobby G.**

SCHOOL **Hill Top Elem.**

PHONE

AGE **11** GRADE **5**

DATE OF BIRTH **4/2/7—**
Mo/Day/Yr

DATE **9/17/8—**
Mo/Day/Yr

EXAMINER **Carol James**

REPORT TO

ADDRESS

PHONE

Profile Chart

READING ANALYSIS TESTS

ADDITIONAL TESTS

THE PSYCHOLOGICAL CORPORATION
A Subsidiary of Harcourt Brace Jovanovich, Inc.

Figure 5.5. Cover page of the *Durrell Analysis of Reading Difficulty* used for Tom's reading. (Reproduced by permission from *Durrell Analysis of Reading Difficulty*: Third Edition. Copyright © 1980, by Harcourt Brace Jovanovich, Inc. All rights reserved.)

Silent Reading Diagnostic Test

The Silent Reading Diagnostic Test can be administered to all the pupils in a reading group at the same time. Separate subtests can be given at work periods so that the teacher can fit the test to the time available. This test is effective with children whose reading abilities range from grade two to grade six. It provides an adequate check on needed word perception skills in silent reading. The profile contains eight subtests:

1. Words in isolation
2. Words in context
3. Visual-structural analysis
4. Syllabication
5. Word synthesis
6. Beginning sounds
7. Ending sounds
8. Vowel and consonant sounds[4]

A profile is made on the test cover to show graphically the results of all the subtests. Raw scores convert to grade placement scores. The teacher's manual explains clearly the methods to be followed.

Interpreting the Results It is necessary to draw *lines of importance* on the profile to determine those subtests on which the pupil's performance indicates need for remedial teaching. Bond and Tinker suggest limitations for lines of importance—one-half year on either side of the student's reading level.[5]

Those subtests on which scores fall below the left line of importance indicate need for reteaching of specific word perception skills. Appropriate use of this test by classroom teachers, and corrective teaching as a result, could help to eliminate many of the difficulties of retarded readers in the schools.

In summary, then, this test measures vocabulary, word recognition, visual and auditory abilities in word forms, and word synthesis. It differs from the other tests in that it is a *group* test and measures abilities involved in silent reading.

Doren Diagnostic Reading Test

The Doren Diagnostic Reading Test is designed to measure the degree to which students have mastered the word recognition skills in primary reading.[6] The students who have mastered all the skills through the third grade will have a very high profile on this test. The administration of the test to a subgroup in a class will reveal to the teacher which skills need reteaching.

The Doren Diagnostic Reading Test offers a profile comparable to the Silent Reading Diagnostic Test previously described. While it requires nearly three hours to administer, it can be useful to the teacher in locating those pupils who need reteaching of specific skills. It can be administered over a period of time by completing one or two subtests each day.

This type of diagnostic test serves a very useful purpose in familiarizing the teacher with the specific skills to be checked in clarifying where the weaknesses of the disabled readers may be. The test has value in that it enables the teacher to be more alert to gaps in the pupil's learning in the reading process.

The Stanford Diagnostic Reading Test

The Stanford Diagnostic Reading Test is available in three forms at primary and intermediate levels.[7] It assesses literal and inferential comprehension, vocabulary and syllabication, sound discrimination, and blending. It also measures rate of reading. Figure 5.6 presents a profile of Thomas's abilities. The profile suggests that mechanics of reading, syllabication, and blending are his greatest weaknesses.

Basic Achievement Skills Individual Screener

The Basic Achievement Skills Individual Screener (BASIS)[8] is a useful test for examining not only reading abilities, but also mathematics and spelling skills. The test is designed for levels from primer through grade eight. All of the reading paragraphs, from grade one through grade eight, require students to fill in cloze exercises. The cover sheet for the BASIS is shown in figure 5.7.

Making Connections 5.2: Administering a Standardized Reading Test

Work with your instructor to select a standardized reading test for you to administer. Plan to work on this project with a peer. Once the test has been identified, study the manual well so that you know as much about the test and its administration as possible.

The next step is to identify a child whose age and reading ability appear suitable for the test in question. Then make plans for appropriate space and time for administering the test. If permission to test is required, be sure you obtain the necessary approval. As you administer the test, take turns with the various subtests or parts. During the time that each of you is the observer, take detailed notes of the language and nonlanguage behaviors observed. It will also be helpful to tape record the entire session.

After the testing session is completed, work on three analyses:

1. Analyze the child's performance on the test and prepare appropriate recommendations about the instruction of this reader.
2. Analyze the test administration techniques of you and your partner. One of the best ways to grow professionally is to observe and be observed and then to engage in analysis sessions afterwards.
3. Analyze the particular test in terms of the information you were able to obtain, its appropriateness for the child you tested, the ease with which the test may be given, and the way(s) in which raw scores are converted to some kind of standard scores.

Prepare a joint report to your instructor, providing information about the three analyses completed after the test was administered.

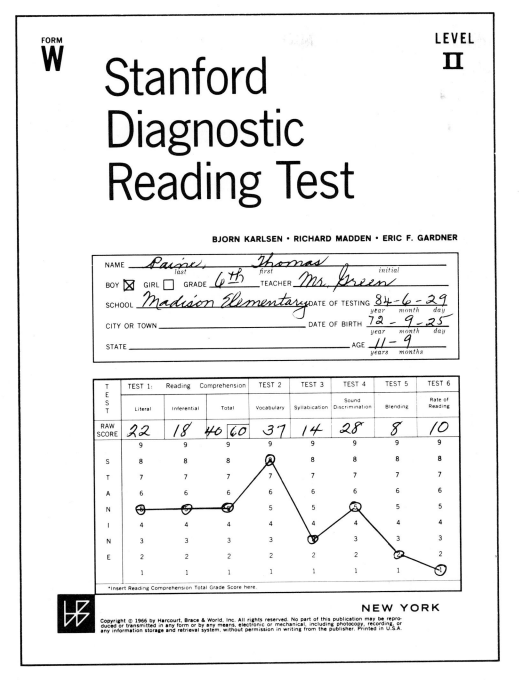

Figure 5.6. Thomas's diagnostic reading test (Reproduced from Bjorn Karlsen, Richard Madden, and Eric F. Gardner, *Stanford Diagnostic Reading Test,* Level II, Form W. Copyright 1966. Psychological Corporation. Reproduced by special permission.) (A 1976 revision of this test is available. See list of tests in Appendix C.)

	Grade Scores					Age Scores				Grade-Referenced Placement	Writing Sample Used: Grade____
	Total Raw Score	PR	S	GE	SS	Total Raw Score	PR	S	AE	SS	
MATHEMATICS												
READING	50	42	5	4.8 97		50	32	4	10.3 93			Below Average / Average / Above Average (circle one)
SPELLING												

MATHEMATICS TALLY

Cluster Grade	No. Right	Base Score
Readiness		0
1		6
2		14
3		22
4		30
5		38
6		46
7		54
8		62
Total No. Right	+	
TOTAL RAW SCORE		

READING TALLY

Cluster Grade	No. Right	Base Score
READINESS		
Letter Ident.		0
Visual Disc.		
BEGINNING READING		
Word Rdg.		8
Sentence Rdg.		
PASSAGES		
P-1		16
P-2		
P-3		
(1-1)	3	(22)
1-2	2	
2	5	28
3	5	34
4	4	40
5	5	46
6	3	52
7		58
8		64
Total No. Right	27 + 22	
TOTAL RAW SCORE	50	

SPELLING TALLY

Cluster Grade	No. Right	Base Score
1		0
2		6
3		12
4		18
5		24
6		30
7		36
8		42
Total No. Right	+	
TOTAL RAW SCORE		

DIRECTIONS FOR TALLYING AND SCORING

Read these instructions before completing the above Tally charts and the box for Summary Scores. More detailed instructions can be found in the Manual.

1. Follow carefully the scoring directions for each test as described in the Manual, and indicate on each item in the Record Form whether it is correct or incorrect.

2. For each test, determine the *lowest* grade-referenced cluster administered. Circle this Cluster Grade on the Tally charts.

3. Circle the Base Score in the same row as the circled Cluster Grade. Record this Base Score at the bottom of the "Base Score" column to the right of the "+".

Directions Continued

4. For each grade-referenced cluster administered, count the number of items the student answered correctly, obtaining this information from the appropriate Record Form page. Then, opposite the appropriate cluster in the Tally chart, enter each count in the "No. Right" column.

5. Add the entries in the "No. Right" column and enter the sum at the bottom of the column in the "Total No. Right" row (to the left of the "+"). Add this number to the Base Score and write the sum in the "Total Raw Score" line. Copy this Total Raw Score into the appropriate "Total Raw Score" column of the "Summary Scores" above.

6. See the Manual for converting Total Raw Scores into Grade or Age Scores.

12

Figure 5.7. Cover page from the *Basic Achievement Skills Individual Screener.* (Reproduced by permission from *Basic Achievement Skills Individual Screener.* Copyright © 1983 by Harcourt Brace Jovanovich, Inc. All rights reserved.)

Criterion-Referenced Tests

Criterion-referenced tests are part of an instructional testing system. Instructional objectives written in behavioral terms are prepared for individual children. Sometimes the objectives are prepared by the publishers of systems approaches to reading; in other situations, the child's teacher may prepare the objectives. Then materials are identified that will help the child meet each individual objective. After the child has done the required reading, skills work, and other related activities required to meet a particular objective or small group of objectives, the child takes the criterion-referenced test for those objectives. If the child answers the questions to the level of accuracy stated in the behavioral objectives, then work is begun on a new set of objectives. If the child fails to meet the stated criterion, then more work must be done on those particular objectives, and the test must be taken again.

1. *Prescriptive Reading Inventory* (PRI) (Monterey, Calif.: California Test Bureau/ McGraw-Hill, 1977). Criterion-referenced tests that assess many different reading skills taught in the elementary school are: Red book, grades 1.5–2.5; green book, grades 2.0–3.5; blue book, grades 3.0–4.5; and orange book, grades 4–6. The inventory includes ninety objectives.
2. *Wisconsin Tests of Reading Skill Development* (Monterey, Calif.: California Test Bureau/McGraw-Hill, 1972). See pp. 213–215 for an expanded description.
3. *Comprehensive Tests of Basic Skills: Reading* (Monterey, Calif.: California Test Bureau/McGraw-Hill, 1976). This test is identified as a criterion-referenced test and is designed for grades K–12. It has two forms. Word attack, vocabulary, and comprehension are tested. The CTBS can be considered as a criterion-referenced test, since computer scoring and analysis provide teachers with item analyses from which instructional objectives and plans may be developed.
4. *Distar Mastery Tests: Reading 1 and 2* (Chicago: Science Research Associates, 1978). Designed to be used from preschool to grade 3. Tests letter recognition, phonics, vocabulary, and comprehension.
5. *Sipay Word Analysis Tests* (Cambridge, Mass.: Educators Publishing Service, 1974). Begins with grade one and extends to the adult level. Seventeen tests covering many aspects of phonics and contractions.

Normed Tests Accompanying Basals and Children's Newspapers

Basal readers provide tests to be administered to students after they finish either sections of the book and workbook or after they complete the entire book. These tests measure the degree to which students have mastered the skills taught in that reading series. Teachers who have access to such tests will do well to use them regularly for their diagnostic value.

Also, the current events newspapers issued weekly often provide tests of comprehension skills in reading with normed scores for the grade for which the test is intended. These tests also help teachers identify strengths and weaknesses of students.

Reading Miscue Inventory

The Reading Miscue Inventory is a measure of the accuracy with which students read a passage orally.[9] The examiners will study the "mismatch" between the exact wording of the passage and language used by readers in reproducing the text. *Miscue* is the term used to describe the oral response that differs from the word in the text. The inventory allows teachers to make a clear distinction between reading miscues that preserve meaning and may be overlooked and reading miscues that represent the traditional "inability to read well" to which so much attention is given in the informal reading inventory.

Goodman and Watson write:

> The Reading Miscue Inventory provides a view of a student's reading performance that is very different from the ones provided by the traditional standardized reading tests or by informal reading inventories. During the oral reading, the student receives no external help; he must rely on his own strategies. His miscues are evaluated to see if he makes appropriate use of syntactic and semantic information. The results of the inventory register the reader's strengths and give information about ineffective and inefficient uses of strategies. It also provides the teacher with information about causes and quality of miscues.[10]

The Reading Miscue Inventory provides for the examiners to analyze grammatical function, semantic acceptability, intonation patterns, and dialect differences. The rationale and interpretation of the inventory is valid when the students are reading narrative passages to which they should be able to relate. However in subject matter where terminology may be unfamiliar, the students will have to rely on phonic or structure clues for word recognition. Karlin's summary seems appropriate:

> The Reading Miscue Inventory provides a qualitative and quantitative analysis of reading proficiency based on psycholinguistic theory. It is a tool for matching materials to readers, for analyzing the reading strategies students use, and for planning lessons. Its use by classroom teachers will be limited by the extent to which they can become familiar with its rather complicated procedures. Until those procedures are simplified, the inventory will probably be used mainly by reading specialists.[11]

Hood has raised the question of whether or not the analysis of the Reading Miscue Inventory is a practical exercise for the busy classroom teacher. What do the classroom teachers need to know in order to find the proper book for each child in the class? It is clear that miscue research has much value for the clinician and the researcher. It has value for the classroom teacher, too, if enough practice in analysis of miscues is done so that in the classroom the teacher will use this knowledge in making many of the on-the-spot decisions that need to be made every day.[12]

Classroom teachers *do* need to decide whether reading miscues are of an "acceptable" or "excusable" variety or if they are "wrong" in the sense that meaning will be lost if they are not corrected. If the students read "frightened" for "afraid" or "put the tent up" for "put up the tent" these are obviously acceptable miscues since no meaning is lost.[13] However, if the readers read "The message was brought by the teacher to the children" instead of "The message was brought to the teacher by the children," the meaning is lost and the miscue needs to be corrected for meaning. Some experience with the Reading Miscue Inventory will develop teacher sensitivity to the types of miscues that students make in oral reading. This achievement will be useful to the teachers every day. However, Hood concludes that the classroom teachers can continue to select reading material for the students by means of total miscue scores.[14]

Children's performances on the Reading Miscue Inventory can now be scored and analyzed using the computer. Such a program makes it more possible for the teacher to consider the type of data that can be obtained from the inventory in planning children's reading experiences.

Summary

This chapter has contained information about testing: norms, grade placement scores, percentiles, stanines, and differences between norm-referenced and criterion-referenced tests. Silent reading standardized tests have cumulative value in measuring gains in achievement, although their limitations in measuring different comprehension skills has been explained. There are also basal reader tests and such reading tests as supplied by *My Weekly Reader* that also have value for the teacher.

As the teachers continue to teach corrective reading to pupils in the class, formal tests are needed to help them evaluate the pupils' progress and to show tangible evidence of success. While many tests and rating scales are available, the Gilmore Oral Reading Test, the Gray Oral Reading Test, the Silent Reading Diagnostic Test, the Durrell Analysis of Reading Difficulty, The Stanford Diagnostic Reading Test, the Doren Diagnostic Reading Test, and The Basic Achievement Skills Individual Screener (BASIS) have been described here. In addition, the basic reading tests for graded readers were discussed. Ability to perform well on these tests is a good indication that the students are ready to progress to the next higher level of reading. The Reading Miscue Inventory has also been described as a means of evaluating a child's reading.

For Further Reading

Baumann, James F., and Stevenson, Jennifer A. "Understanding Standardized Reading Achievement Test Scores," *The Reading Teacher* 35 (March 1982), pp. 648–54.
———. "Using Scores from Standardized Reading Achievement Tests," *The Reading Teacher* 35 (February 1982), pp. 528–32.
Ekwall, Eldon E., and Shanker, James L. *Diagnosis and Remediation of the Disabled Reader,* 2d ed. Boston: Allyn and Bacon, 1983: Chapter 17, "Interpreting Test and Research Results in Reading," pp. 579–95.

Richek, Margaret A.; List, Lynn K.; and Lerner, Janet W. *Reading Problems, Diagnosis and Evaluation* (Englewood Cliffs, N.J.: Prentice-Hall, 1983: Chapter 5, "Assessing Reading Achievement I: Formal Methods," pp. 87–111.

Smith, Lawrence L. et al., "Using Grade Level vs. Out-of-level Reading Tests with Remedial Students," *The Reading Teacher* 36 (February 1983), pp. 550–53.

Stewart, Oran, and Green, Dan S. "Test-taking Skills for Standardized Tests of Reading," *The Reading Teacher* 36 (March 1983), pp. 634–38.

Notes

1. John V. Gilmore and Eunice C. Gilmore, *Gilmore Oral Reading Test* (New York: Psychological Corp., 1968).
2. William S. Gray, *Gray Oral Reading Test* (New York: Psychological Corp., 1967).
3. Donald D. Durrell and Jane H. Catterson, *Durrell Analysis of Reading Difficulty,* 3d ed. (New York: Psychological Corp., 1980).
4. Guy L. Bond, B. Balow, and C. J. Hoyt, *Silent Reading Diagnostic Test,* rev. ed. (Chicago: Rand McNally, 1970).
5. Guy L. Bond, Miles Tinker, Barbara Wasson, and John Wasson, *Reading Difficulties: Their Diagnosis and Correction,* 5th ed. (Englewood Cliffs, N.J.: Prentice-Hall, 1984), p. 219.
6. Margaret Doren, *Doren Diagnostic Reading Test of Word Recognition Skills* (Circle Pines, Minn.: American Guidance Services, 1973).
7. Bjorn Karlsen, Richard Madden, and Eric F. Gardner, *Stanford Diagnostic Reading Test* (New York: Psychological Corp., 1976).
8. *Basic Achievement Skills Individual Screener, BASIS* (New York: Psychological Corp., 1982).
9. Yetta Goodman and Carolyn Burke, *Reading Miscue Inventory: Procedure for Diagnosis and Evaluation* (New York: Macmillan, 1972).
10. Yetta Goodman and Dorothy J. Watson, "A Reading Program to Live with: Focus on Comprehension," *Language Arts* 54 (November/December 1977), pp. 868–79.
11. Robert Karlin, *Teaching Elementary Reading: Principles and Strategies,* 2d ed. (New York: Harcourt Brace Jovanovich, 1975), p. 82.
12. Joyce Hood, "Is Miscue Analysis Practical for Teachers?" *The Reading Teacher* 32 (December 1978); pp. 260–66; reprinted in *Readings on Reading Instruction,* 3d ed., A. J. Harris and E. R. Sipay, eds. (New York: Longman, Inc., 1984), pp. 170–76.
13. Ibid., p. 262.
14. Ibid., p. 266.

6
Additional Data Needed for Further Diagnosis

138

Vocabulary

diagnosis
intelligence test
individual intelligence test
reading potential
auditory discrimination
audiogram
refractionist
otologist
color blindness
allergy
interest inventory
Incomplete Sentences Blank
parent interview
sociogram
bibliotherapy
emotional disturbance
cloze test
anecdotal record

Questions

1. Outline the steps the teacher should take in gathering data about the reading abilities of a child.

2. What relationships do there appear to be between intelligence and reading? What cautions should one observe in assessing the intelligence of a disabled reader?

3. List the major points you think a teacher should remember about vision and hearing difficulties of children.

4. Make a list of health problems that may be factors in reading programs.

5. Why should a teacher want to find out about interests of children in the classroom?

6. How might personality data be useful in planning reading instruction?

7. What kinds of information might one expect to obtain from the varied kinds of interviews and observation strategies?

8. What is bibliotherapy, and how might it be used in the classroom?

9. How could assessments such as storytelling, the writing sample, a cloze test, and the Peabody Picture Vocabulary Test provide important information to the reading teacher?

Introduction

In order to plan more efficiently with the pupils those study jobs that will help them most quickly to learn to read, the teacher must obtain further information in order to round out as complete a case history as possible. Hopefully, there will be specialists in the school system from whom information relating to intelligence factors, physical factors, and social and emotional factors can be obtained. However, because many of the learning problems of children cannot be resolved without the close cooperation of the parents, chapter thirteen will be devoted to this tremendously important factor.

Steps in Diagnosis

The first characteristic of a sound reading program for a school system is a well-worked-out statement of purpose in developing language arts skills from kindergarten through the senior high school. It will not be possible to attain maximum efficiency in reading in this program unless adequate diagnostic facilities are provided for students with learning difficulties.

Since 1945, mental health centers have been established across our country. Generally they have been staffed by clinical psychologists, psychiatric social workers, and a psychiatrist who serves as the director. The schools have now had a long experience in the employment of school social workers to work with school psychologists.

The teachers need available counsel about the nature of children's problems and the types of assessments that are available. Table 6.1 lists several areas of health, behavior, language development, general learning ability, and neurology in which special services are needed for children with reading difficulties in regular classrooms. Once these areas have been considered, the next step is to press for a formal diagnosis.

The school social worker and the school psychologist are key personnel in providing teachers with needed information about the students in their classrooms. The school social worker will obtain the intake history with the parents and analyze those problems that deter learning in school. These problems may be interpersonal conflicts within the family or they may be primarily economic. Social workers may need to make repeated home visits to resolve difficulties before teaching the student can be effective. The school psychologist is prepared to obtain intelligence test data, school achievement data, and limited information relative to personality problems the pupils may face.

Figure 6.1 diagrams the process for obtaining and channeling to principals and teachers necessary information that will enable them to plan constructively for goals through which the individual will more nearly achieve self-realization.

TABLE 6.1 Special Services Needed for Children with Reading Problems

Areas where possible causes may exist	Professional people who offer help in this area	Adjustments that may be necessary on the part of the classroom teacher
1. General health	The family doctor needs to give a general medical examination.	Special needs in response to physical health and general growth and development.
2. Behavior of the student in the classroom.	The school counselor can discuss with the teacher current report card data: uses self-control; accepts guidance; is courteous; works and plays well with others; uses good judgment; is cooperative; contributes to activities of group; assumes responsibility. The counselor may administer the Vineland Social Maturity Scale.[1]	Six-year-olds generally are: active, curious, eager to explore the environment; like to manipulate things, need time to work in groups but time to work alone also; not very responsible for finishing tasks; not very understanding of rigid time sequences.
3. Thinking processes	The school psychologist can test convergent and divergent thinking, putting things in categories, acquisition meaning, classifying, creative/innovative thinking, cognitive levels as defined by Piaget.[2]	Activiites can be provided for: putting things in categories: colors, names, days of the week, domestic animals; interpreting pictures, creating stories; classifying; working in art, carpentry, block, housekeeping centers.
4. Use of language	The language specialist can observe oral language use, auditory discrimination and awareness, ability to retell a story. Administer the Illinois Test of Psycholinguistic Abilities.[3]	Encourage: verbal expression, adequate English syntax, auditory decoding, auditory association, listening, concept development through oral language, listening to and telling stories.
5. Psychological examinations	The school psychologist can administer the Wechsler Preschool and Primary Scale,[4] the Wechsler Intelligence Scale for Children,[5] the Wechsler Adult Intelligence Scale.[6] Other tests or observations.	The open classroom concept accommodates the wide range of differences in many abilities. Teachers can plan for a wide range of achievement in a class; learning centers may be an option.
6. Neurological factors: (Perceptual skills)	The psychologist or the reading specialist may administer: The Developmental Test of Visual Perception,[7] Visual Motor Gestalt,[8] Purdue Perceptual Motor Survey,[9] Identifying Children with Specific Learning Disabilities.[10]	Activities can be provided to teach motor coordination, directional sense, visual-motor coordination; language and concept development; space relationships; perceptual constancy.

1. S. Sparrow, D. Balla, and D. Cicchetti, *Vineland Adaptive Behavior Scales* (Circle Pines, Minn.: American Guidance Service, 1984). Formerly called the Vineland Social Maturity Scale. This scale requires an indepth interview with a parent or parent substitute and measures social development based on observation and information about the client's habits and practices.
2. John L. Phillips, Jr., *The Origins of Intellect: Piaget's Theory,* 2d ed. (San Francisco: Will Freeman and Co., 1975).
3. S. A. Kirk, J. J. McCarthy, and W. D. Kirk, *The Illinois Test of Psycholinguistic Abilities,* ITPA, revised edition (Urbana: Univ. of Illinois Press, 1968). This test measures the child's language

reception, word association, and ability to give information through language. The test is composed of ten subtests.

4. *Wechsler Pre-School and Primary Scale of Intelligence.* WPPSI (New York: The Psychological Corporation, 1967). This is an individually administered general intelligence test with norms for young children ages 4.0–6.5.
5. *Wechsler Intelligence Scale for Children,* revised edition, WISC-R (New York: The Psychological Corporation, 1974). This scale measures general intelligence for ages 6–16.
6. *Wechsler Adult Intelligence Scale,* WAIS (New York: The Psychological Corporation, 1955). This scale is for ages 15-adult. The Weschler tests provide verbal, performance, and full scale scores (intelligence quotients) and is to be used only by qualified psychologists.
7. Marianne Frostig, *The Developmental Test of Visual Perception* (Chicago: Follett, 1966).
8. Lauretta Bender, *The Bender Visual Motor Gestalt Test* (New York: The Psychological Corporation, 1938).
9. E. G. Roach and N. C. Kephart, *Purdue Perceptual Motor Survey,* (Columbus: Chas. Merrill, 1966).
10. Beth Slingerland, *Identifying Children with Specific Learning Disabilities* (Cambridge, Mass.: Educators Publishers Service, 1974).

A program of diagnosis must include the following steps:

1. Provide a means for the initial referral of cases.
2. Gather together all pertinent data needed for building a case history.
3. Evaluate the effects of observed conditions upon the pupil's behavior.
4. Make suggestions for remedial measures to improve the pupil's adjustment.
5. Reevaluate the case at intervals to see if the progress has been satisfactory.

As diagrammed, five types of information are needed about the pupils in preparing their case studies. These involve:

1. A case history interview that provides family background, general significance of reading success in the family, and reasons given by the parents for pupils' reading failure.
2. A medical examination that evaluates visual and hearing acuity and general physical development. Especially important are referrals by the family doctor to various specialists for further study of possible neurological problems, problems of basal metabolism, or convulsive disorders.
3. A psychological evaluation that may include both tests of general intelligence and structured or unstructured tests of personality. Further testing by clinical psychologists—with such tests as the Rorschach or referral to a consulting psychiatrist—may be indicated.
4. A summary of the student's school history that reveals such evidence as grades repeated in school, attendance in kindergarten prior to encountering formal reading, persistence of learning problems through the years' membership in special education classes, and teachers' evaluations of work habits.
5. Guidance information revealing motivations, aptitudes, and levels of aspiration. This information helps to show how the students view themselves in their world, how they view others, and how they view their worlds around them.

A great deal of a pupil's social and emotional adjustment may be revealed by honest answers to three questions.[1] (1) Do people like me? (2) Do I like people? and (3) Do I like myself?

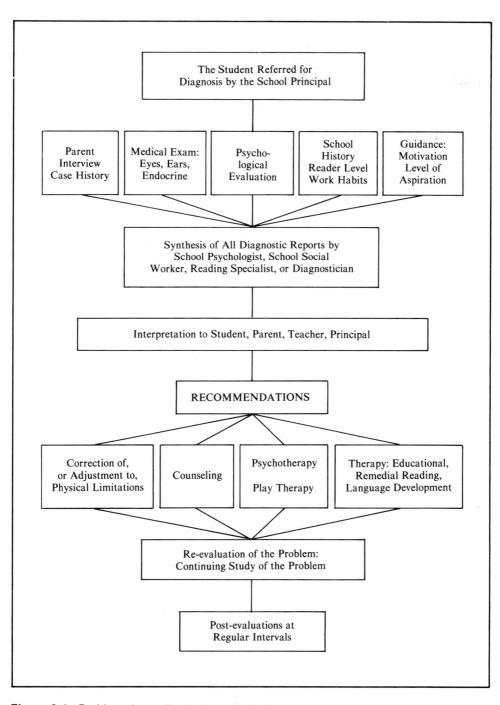

Figure 6.1. Problems in reading in the school: diagnosing and planning

This body of information must be synthesized by a guidance counselor, school psychologist, school social worker, the diagnostician, or the reading specialist; then it must, in turn, be interpreted to the pupil, the parents, and the pupil's teachers and principal.

A plan of action to correct or alleviate the situation must be worked out. For some pupils there are medical problems for which there may be correction or to which they must make an adjustment. For example, some pupils with visual limitations cannot have their vision improved, but there are many ways the school program can be adapted to serve them. A change in seating within the classroom, use of sight-saving print, early use of the typewriter for completing assignments, counseling, and in more disturbed cases, psychotherapy may make regular class attendance possible.

In many instances the major problem lies in adapting the teaching to the individual, that is, remedial procedures. The teacher needs to understand what can and cannot change. The schoolwork must be geared to the pupil rather than the pupil to the schoolwork. The teacher should be an expediter of growth. To be such an expediter, the teacher must start where the pupil is and use knowledge of the growth and development of children.

Finally, after the pupil's problem has been studied and remedial programs effected, the case must be reevaluated and subsequent evaluations made on a continuing basis. Whatever the initial prognoses may have been, continuing evaluations are necessary for the purpose of adjusting the recommendations to ensure maximum learning opportunities for the pupils.

It may be well that the recommendations resulting from the case studies are all related to language development and *intensive* reading instruction. This is the challenge to the teacher—supported by the school social worker and the school psychologist—to find adequate teaching techniques for diminishing the gap between the pupils' functional levels in reading and their grade placement.

If the teachers refer only severely disabled readers for case study, however, it is almost certain that there will be concomitant problems that need to be met through medical or psychological therapies.

If professional help is not available in the school, if the services of school social workers or school psychologists are nonexistent in a school system, this only means that greater responsibility rests with the principal and the teachers. The problems exist whether or not the specialists are there to help. With the help of the teachers, principals must follow as systematic a program as possible for gathering information for diagnosing problems. They can obtain information about the child's family from the parents, about the child's problems at school from previous teachers, from standardized test results, and from available medical reports. On the basis of the information secured, they must plan the best possible program for the pupil.

To illustrate, the classroom teachers, without benefit of the services of a school social worker or psychologist, are applying this procedure in its most common form when they encounter pupils who cannot read, and act upon the situation promptly. If they talk with the pupil's parents about the problem; if they make the best possible subjective judgments about behavior and performance at various tasks and decide that the pupil probably has "normal" intelligence; if they test present specific abilities in reading;

if they interpret to the child and the parents the nature of the reading problem as they see it; and if they make time during the school day for the pupil to learn how to read by the same methods used in good first teaching of reading, then the teachers have applied these principles in the solution of the problem.

As a specific example, we illustrate how Victor and his fourth-grade teacher met the problem together without the help of others.

Miss Jones, fourth-grade teacher in a small midwestern town, placed Victor's name on the list to be tested by the visiting school psychologist because Victor was unable to read. Victor appeared with a well-scrubbed look, wearing faded jeans. He seemed to be a very normal, alert nine-year-old. The I.Q. score earned on the Stanford-Binet, Form L, was 97 (C.A. 9–10, M.A. 9–7). The psychologist wrote the following statement:

> This report is of necessity a superficial one. Its accuracy needs to be tested further by the teacher's observations. Victor gives evidence of being a child with very limited first-hand experiences. He has recently moved from an extremely isolated area in a neighboring state. He apparently got off to a bad start in beginning reading. His reader level in context is first grade. He recognized only 182 of the 220 sight words of the Dolch Basic Word Test. Since the school nurse found nothing wrong with his vision or hearing, he needs to begin with easy first-grade reading, including stories he has written, and learn all the developmental skills in both phonic and structural analysis and comprehension and move as rapidly as possible to catch up to his present grade placement.

The fourth-grade teacher asked for and was given permission to discuss retention with the parents, and, with their consent, retained the boy in her fourth-grade room the following year.

The next spring when the visiting school psychologist called at the school, he asked the fourth-grade teacher about Victor. She seemed surprised that there would be any question about Victor until the psychologist showed her the results of the previous year's testing. She reported that he was doing good work in her middle group in fourth grade. Then she told the psychologist that Victor himself had been very pleased to stay with her when she had convinced him that she could teach him, and that occasionally she had talked with his mother, who had been much relieved to see Victor's progress.

Other teachers had shared worksheets on needed skills that were appropriate for a ten-year-old working at primary level. Victor's teacher had arranged for a retired man in the community to come three times weekly to read to Victor, to listen to Victor read, and to help him write stories.

Inventorying Abilities at the Beginning of the Year

While teachers need to make more detailed studies of pupils who present learning difficulties, cumulative folders in most schools do provide accumulated information about all pupils as they progress through the grades. During the first few weeks of the school year, the teachers collect, coordinate, and study all the information they have available on their pupils. This information will be found in:

1. Cumulative folders. All pupils should have cumulative folders in which are included each year data concerning physical health, school achievement, standardized test results, and other pertinent information.
2. Health records. School nurses often have valuable information about vision, hearing, or special physical handicapping conditions.
3. Anecdotal records of behavior. Notes written by previous teachers may reveal persistent problems such as concern with reading, continual absences from school, reports from social agencies or private clinics.

Using such information, the teachers can:

1. Compare mental test results with reading test results to see that reading capacity and achievement correspond.
2. Evaluate previous indications of a reading problem identified by previous teachers, or by the parent, or in unusual attitudes of the pupil.

In addition to the reading tests discussed in Chapters 4 and 5, the teacher should obtain data on intelligence, health status, interests and attitudes toward reading, social and psychological information, and language and special reading abilities. Additional information may be obtained by the use of anecdotal records and ongoing teacher observation.

Measuring Intelligence

Intelligence is probably the one most important factor in the determination of how well pupils can be expected to read. Test scores for pupils with learning disabilities are often invalid, however, and need careful interpretation. For instance, in many public schools there are records giving the results of group intelligence tests on all students in designated grades in the school. Group intelligence tests are the only instruments available to most classroom teachers for assessing general learning ability. Because the majority of students perform rather consistently over the years on these tests, it may be said that these tests are statistically reliable in situations where large groups are screened. The pupils who have reading problems will be handicapped, however, if given a group intelligence test in which they are expected to do reading and writing. Because reading is required for the completion of most group intelligence tests, Strang has written that they should not be used to predict growth in reading for poor readers.[2]

Farr writes specifically and pertinently about the limitation of tests involving reading skill as measures of student *ability:*

> . . . a student's score on any reading skill test represents *one* sampling of behavior, on *one* operational definition of that skill, under *one* specific set of conditions, at *one* particular point in a student's development: . . . what is really needed for valid and reliable evaluation is the sampling of *many* sets of conditions, at *many* points in a student's development.[3]

Clymer concluded that certain group intelligence tests were of *no* value in testing general mental ability of fifth-grade pupils who tested in the lowest 40 percent in reading ability.[4] This is to say that for practically all those pupils under consideration in corrective reading programs, because they would test in reading in the lower two-fifths of their classes, the group intelligence test results are of no value to the teachers. Any time pupils with reading disabilities are being tested to assess their learning potentials, they should be given the advantage of individual intelligence tests.

There are two such individual intelligence tests in common use by psychologists and psychometrists. They are the Stanford-Binet Intelligence Scale and the Weschler Intelligence Scale.[5]

A few years ago, a fifteen-year-old boy in the seventh grade was given the California Test of Mental Maturity in a group. His I.Q. score was computed as 76. A few weeks later he was given the Stanford-Binet, Form L, and his I.Q. score was computed as 99. He proved to be a lad of perfectly normal intelligence who had a serious reading disability. His reader level, when tested, was primer level. To have classified this boy as mentally retarded on the basis of the group test would have been entirely unjustified.

Another test is the Peabody Picture Vocabulary Test.[6] This consists of 150 plates arranged in order of difficulty designed to test an age range of eighteen months to eighteen years. One stimulus word is illustrated on each plate. Mental ages and percentile norms are provided, based on a population of 4,000 persons.

School psychologists will have other individual tests in their repertoire and, at times, will need to administer one or more to an individual. Teachers need to study carefully the interpretations of the test results, written by the psychologist who administers the test, because individual intelligence tests also have their limitations. This is evidenced by the comments on the Wechsler Intelligence Scale—Revised (WISC—R) test profile for José, who has both a learning disability and second-language interference (See figure 6.2).

Estimating General Alertness and Ability for School Tasks When Individual Intelligence Test Results Are Not Available

The teachers have some means at their commands to judge general intelligence even when there are no standardized tests of any kind on record, as, for example:

1. The teachers should observe leadership qualities both on the playground and in the room, mechanical aptitude, ingenuity in problem solving, and maturity in interpersonal behavior.
2. After selecting a story from a graded book (such as fourth, eighth, or ninth grade level), the teacher should prepare a list of questions to test comprehension of ideas, then read a selected passage from the story aloud, telling the student beforehand that he or she will be asked questions. If the student answers more than 75 percent of the questions correctly, it can be assumed that the student has the *capacity* for understanding reading material at that level. To establish any ceiling for the student's capacity, however, it is necessary to sample the *most difficult* level from which the student can grasp 75 percent of the ideas. Obtaining the capacity level on the informal reading inventory provides this information.

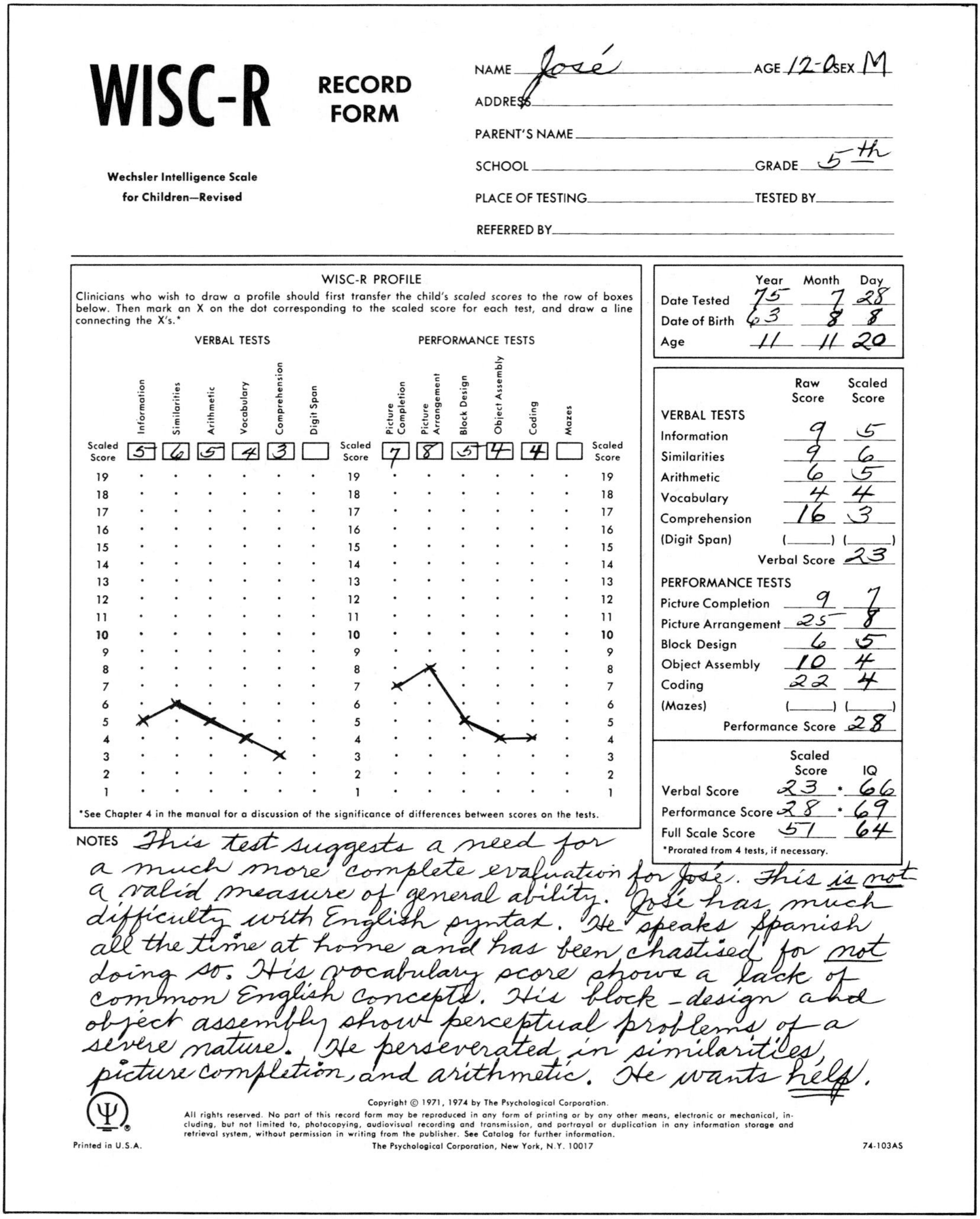

WISC-R **RECORD FORM**

Wechsler Intelligence Scale for Children—Revised

NAME José AGE 12-0 SEX M
ADDRESS
PARENT'S NAME
SCHOOL GRADE 5th
PLACE OF TESTING TESTED BY
REFERRED BY

WISC-R PROFILE

Clinicians who wish to draw a profile should first transfer the child's *scaled scores* to the row of boxes below. Then mark an X on the dot corresponding to the scaled score for each test, and draw a line connecting the X's.*

	VERBAL TESTS						PERFORMANCE TESTS					
	Information	Similarities	Arithmetic	Vocabulary	Comprehension	Digit Span	Picture Completion	Picture Arrangement	Block Design	Object Assembly	Coding	Mazes
Scaled Score	5	6	5	4	3		7	8	5	4	4	

*See Chapter 4 in the manual for a discussion of the significance of differences between scores on the tests.

	Year	Month	Day
Date Tested	75	7	28
Date of Birth	63	8	8
Age	11	11	20

	Raw Score	Scaled Score
VERBAL TESTS		
Information	9	5
Similarities	9	6
Arithmetic	6	5
Vocabulary	4	4
Comprehension	16	3
(Digit Span)	( )	( )
Verbal Score		23
PERFORMANCE TESTS		
Picture Completion	9	7
Picture Arrangement	25	8
Block Design	6	5
Object Assembly	10	4
Coding	22	4
(Mazes)	( )	( )
Performance Score		28

	Scaled Score	IQ
Verbal Score	23	66
Performance Score	28	69
Full Scale Score	57	64

*Prorated from 4 tests, if necessary.

NOTES This test suggests a need for a much more complete evaluation for José. This is not a valid measure of general ability. José has much difficulty with English syntax. He speaks Spanish all the time at home and has been chastised for not doing so. His vocabulary score shows a lack of common English concepts. His block-design and object assembly show perceptual problems of a severe nature. He perseverated in similarities, picture completion, and arithmetic. He wants help.

Figure 6.2. The WISC-R Test profile record for José (From the Record Form of the *Wechsler Intelligence Scale for Children—Revised.* Copyright 1971, 1974, by the Psychological Corporation, New York, N.Y. Used by permission.)

3. The teacher can administer a commercially prepared picture vocabulary test for which there are norms in terms of grades and ages. Two such tests are:

   a. The Durrell Listening-Reading Series of Tests. Donald D. Durrell and Mary T. Hayes, *Durrell Listening-Reading Series: Primary Level, Intermediate Level,* and *Advanced Level.* (New York: Harcourt Brace, 1969). This is a group test designed specifically to measure reading *potential* through measuring listening comprehension—without requiring the students to read context. The test is done by classifying or categorizing vocabulary words, sentences, or ideas from paragraphs read to the students. Raw scores are converted into grade-placement or percentile values. Pupils who are reading at the second-grade level but show listening ability at the fourth-grade level may be considered to be two years retarded in reading ability. These tests replace the 1937 edition of the Durrell-Sullivan Reading Capacity and Achievement Tests. If the children come from homes where a language other than English is spoken, the Listening Test will reveal their present functioning level or could measure their progress in understanding the English language.

   b. *The Ammons Full Range Picture Vocabulary Test* (Louisville: Department of Psychology, Southern University Press). On this test, all the pupil is expected to do is identify one of four pictures containing the stimulus word. For example, on card 1 the student is asked to point to *pie, window, seed, sill, transparent, rectangular, sector, illumination, culinary,* and *egress.* The student need only to point to the correct one of the four pictures containing the meaning of the word pronounced. A vocabulary score that is translated into a mental age is assigned from the raw score. This type of test can serve as a language test for students who have poor linguistic abilities or severe physical limitations.

4. The teacher can administer an oral vocabulary test. The oral vocabulary subtest of the *Gates-McKillop-Horowitz Reading Diagnostic Tests* (New York: Teachers College Press, 1981) is an example. The examiner reads to the students the stem of a question and four possible answers and asks the students to select the correct one:

   "A *head* is a part of a *coat saw man box.*"

   "*Gaudy* means *certainly wealthy beautiful showy.*"

   The raw score on the vocabulary test has a grade placement equivalent.

5. Bond and Brueckner suggest that teachers observe the extensiveness of the pupils' vocabularies, achievement in other subjects such as arithmetic, their abilities to apply school learning to solve problems, the knowledge they have been able to gain from radio and television, and the contributions to discussions they make from their firsthand experiences.[7] They also remind teachers that the aggressive or talkative students, the popular, quiet ones, and the overaverage ones are likely to be overestimated; the unattractive, shy, or rejected students are likely to be underestimated.

These measures for the classroom teachers to use to estimate subjectively what can be expected of pupils are not intended to substitute for more accurate testing by a counselor or school psychologist. The classroom teachers must make use of as many ways as possible to assess the potential of the students they teach, but it should be clearly understood that these supplement, but do not substitute for, examinations by a counselor or school psychologist.

Health Status

All available evidence points toward positive relationships between success in school and good general health. It is reasonable to expect that children free from illnesses, children who have abundant energy, who see and hear adequately, and who get sufficient rest and nourishment, and children who are free of handicapping conditions are far more likely to devote attention to learning in school than children who have one or more of these problems.

Vision and Hearing

The teacher should be alert to any symptoms suggesting that students who have difficulty learning how to read may have vision or hearing problems. Nurses usually give vision tests, and either nurses or speech and hearing therapists give hearing tests. All pupils who fail to pass screening tests should be referred to the vision specialist or to the otologist. Teachers should discuss in personal conferences with parents any problems in the area of health that may explain learning difficulty. Parents are usually anxious to take their child for a physical examination when the teacher has evidence that such is indicated. Public health nurses or social workers can often obtain services for children whose parents are not financially able to pay for them. The teacher should be alert to the techniques for helping the pupil with limited vision or impaired hearing to make the best use of his or her abilities.

All pupils with school learning problems should be referred routinely for hearing and vision tests. The Auditory Discrimination Test (figure 6.3) can serve as a basis for referral for further hearing evaluation. According to the Manual of Administration, Scoring, and Interpretation for the Auditory Discrimination Test, Revised, scoring is arrived at as follows:

Directions: Do the pairs of words sound alike or different? If the children make a score of less than 10 (out of 30 items) in the *different* column or less than 7 (out of 10) in the *same* column, the test should be considered invalid . . . and other means of assessing hearing discrimination be found. Only the *different* column counts in scoring:

Threshold accuracy for

age	5	6	7	8+
is	18	20	24	25

The median scores earned by large numbers of children were:

age 5	median	23.8
age 6	median	24.6
age 7	median	26.3
age 8+	median	27.3

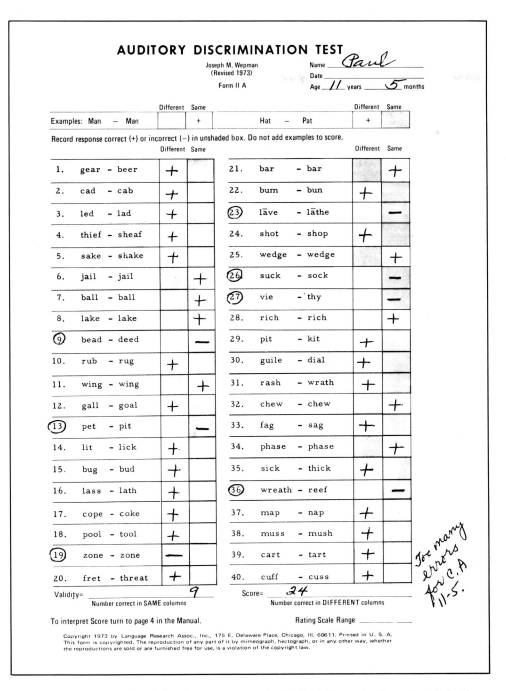

AUDITORY DISCRIMINATION TEST

Joseph M. Wepman
(Revised 1973)

Form II A

Name *Paul*

Date _____

Age __11__ years ____5____ months

	Different	Same			Different	Same
Examples: Man — Man		+	Hat — Pat	+		

Record response correct (+) or incorrect (−) in unshaded box. Do not add examples to score.

#	Word Pair	Different	Same	#	Word Pair	Different	Same
1.	gear - beer	+		21.	bar - bar		+
2.	cad - cab	+		22.	bum - bun	+	
3.	led - lad	+		㉓	lāve - lāthe		−
4.	thief - sheaf	+		24.	shot - shop	+	
5.	sake - shake	+		25.	wedge - wedge		+
6.	jail - jail		+	㉖	suck - sock		−
7.	ball - ball		+	㉗	vie - thy		−
8.	lake - lake		+	28.	rich - rich		+
⑨	bead - deed		−	29.	pit - kit	+	
10.	rub - rug	+		30.	guile - dial	+	
11.	wing - wing		+	31.	rash - wrath	+	
12.	gall - goal	+		32.	chew - chew		+
⑬	pet - pit		−	33.	fag - sag	+	
14.	lit - lick	+		34.	phase - phase		+
15.	bug - bud	+		35.	sick - thick	+	
16.	lass - lath	+		㊱	wreath - reef		−
17.	cope - coke	+		37.	map - nap	+	
18.	pool - tool	+		38.	muss - mush	+	
⑲	zone - zone	−		39.	cart - tart	+	
20.	fret - threat	+		40.	cuff - cuss	+	

Validity= _____ **9**

Number correct in SAME columns

Score= **24**

Number correct in DIFFERENT columns

Too many errors for C.A. 11-5.

To interpret Score turn to page 4 in the Manual.

Rating Scale Range _____ _____

Copyright 1973 by Language Research Assoc., Inc., 175 E. Delaware Place, Chicago, Ill. 60611. Printed in U. S. A.
This form is copyrighted. The reproduction of any part of it by mimeograph, hectograph, or in any other way, whether
the reproductions are sold or are furnished free for use, is a violation of the copyright law.

Figure 6.3. Auditory discrimination test as used with Paul (From *Auditory Discrimination Test, Revised* by Joseph M. Wepman. Copyright 1973 by Language Research Associates, Inc., 175 E. Delaware Place, Chicago 60611. Used with permission.)

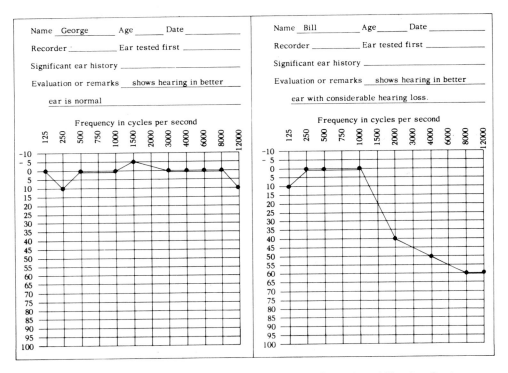

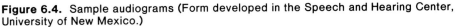

Figure 6.4. Sample audiograms (Form developed in the Speech and Hearing Center, University of New Mexico.)

In figure 6.4 the audiogram on the right shows the results of a severe hearing loss in both ears, although the student insisted that his hearing was perfectly normal. The audiogram on the left shows normal hearing.

It is generally accepted that information revealed by the Snellen Chart and the AMA Visual Survey Chart is very limited. There are many types of visual difficulties not revealed by these tests. The *Keystone Telebinocular Visual Survey*[8] and The *Orthorater*[9] are instruments used for screening and for referral to vision specialists for diagnosis of eye difficulties. The *Eames Eye Test*[10] is an inexpensive visual survey that possesses many of the qualities of more expensive tests. A *Keystone Visual Survey Test* for José, an apparent visual problem, appears in figure 6.5.

A competent refractionist can determine whether or not visual defects contribute to the reading difficulty; an otologist can assess hearing problems that may prevent learning by usual auditory methods.

Possible Symptoms of a Hearing Loss

1. Fails to talk in appropriate tones (speech too loud).
2. Ignores comments (either negative or positive).
3. Constantly asks teachers or classmates to repeat.
4. Has difficulty learning and retaining (word sounds or spelling words).

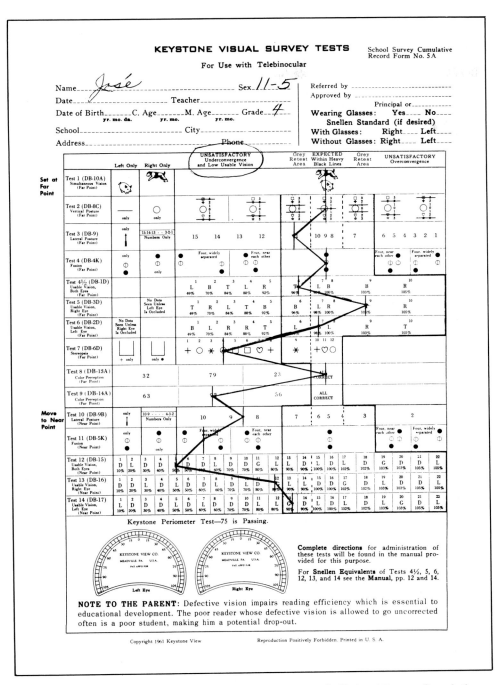

Figure 6.5. *Keystone Visual Survey Test*—marked by José. (School Survey Cumulative Record Form No. 5A. Copyright 1961 Keystone View Division. Mast Development Co., Davenport, Iowa. Used by permission.)

5. Frequently picks or probes the ear.
6. Strains to hear: tilts the head, cups hand behind ear, leans toward speaker, stiff or restrained posture while listening.
7. Enunciates poorly.
8. Scores low on auditory discrimination or auditory memory tests.
9. Misses or misinterprets details in oral directions. Responds to written instructions better than to oral instructions.
10. Has physical evidence of ear problem: discharge, ringing sound.
11. Shows low attention span while oral activities are going on.
12. Has colds frequently; history of ear infections.
13. Tends to withdraw from peers and to play alone.
14. Tends to avoid listening-center activities.
15. Is easily distracted.
16. Complains of noise. Cannot concentrate in a noisy environment because of the confusion of many sounds.
17. Opens mouth while listening.
18. Watches the speaker closely as if lip-reading.

Possible Symptoms of a Visual Problem

1. Rubs eyes when reading.
2. Needs to hold the book very close to eyes to read.
3. Squints.
4. Has difficulty copying from the blackboard. Makes lots of mistakes when copying.
5. Skips lines when reading. Unable to keep or find place.
6. Turns head at unusual angle to try to see better.
7. Has frequent headaches.
8. Holds hand over one eye to block it out.
9. Has watery, bloodshot eyes.
10. Is unable to continue reading very long.
11. Points to words while reading.
12. Has prescription glasses but never wears them.
13. Prefers to sit very close to TV screen.
14. Is inattentive when activity involves reading.
15. Has difficulty in tracing.

Color Blindness

There is a relationship between color blindness and reading success in first grade. In most of the printed materials currently used for teaching children in kindergarten and first grade, extensive use is made of color. Reading readiness work teaches color words early; seatwork involves use of the major colors; and teachers use colored chalk to give emphasis or differentiate. Children's books are filled with highly colored illustrations. Picture interpretation is extended by discussions of colors used; pictures are completed

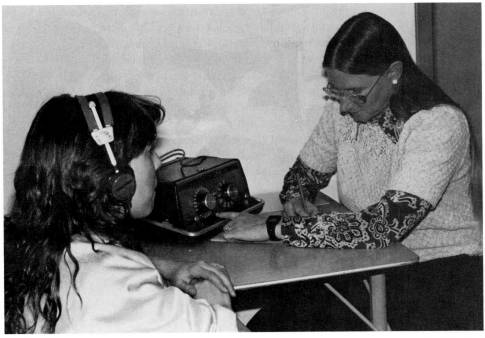

David Woodward

Since the teacher needs to know about any hearing problems that the child might have before reading instruction is begun, an examination with the audiometer is important.

by coloring according to printed directions; and games are devised using color identification. Many first-grade teachers have been observed dismissing children with such commands as, "Now, all who have on something *blue* may go next." In safety, *red, green,* and *yellow* are of primary importance; yet, to the color-blind child, all three of these colors may appear only as varying degrees of the same color. Older boys often have trouble with colors on maps, colors of game pieces, and printed descriptions of colors in scenes.

With approximately five percent of the boys in the schools color blind, should there be some special precaution taken to ensure their school success in the first grade? With this question in mind, Olson administered the AO H-R-R Pseudo-Isochromatic Plates individually to 275 boys in twenty-three first-grade classrooms in five randomly selected elementary schools.[11] Twelve boys were found to be color blind. They were matched with twelve color-vision children based on Goodenough Intelligence Scale I.Q. scores and chronological ages. These twelve pairs were given the California Reading Achievement Test, Lower Primary, Form W, in the last month of their first-grade school year. On the vocabulary subsection, the t-test value of the difference in performance was significant at the .005 level of confidence in favor of the color-vision boys; on the comprehension subsection of the reading test, the t-test value of the difference in performance was significant at the .05 level of confidence in favor of the color-vision boys; and the value of the difference on the total test was significant at the .01 level of confidence.[12]

Olson found the incidence of color blindness to be 4.3 percent.[13] Since only a few minutes are required to test each pupil, it seems very important that teachers screen their classes to identify those who have some optical color defect. The implications of reading retardation and the concomitant feelings of failure seem to signal the need to give some consideration to the child who is color blind and can easily be identified before he experiences such frustration. Primary teachers certainly should not overlook this additional possibility in eliminating all the factors that may be causing learning difficulties.

Schiffman has reported that when teachers are informed that boys in their rooms are color blind, those boys do statistically better in first-grade reading than color-blind boys in other first-grade rooms where the teachers have not been given this information.[14] This finding emphasizes the importance of teacher knowledge of color blindness to use as a guide for appropriate instruction on behalf of color-blind pupils.

Two tests for color blindness are:

(1) Dvorine Pseudo-Isochromatic Plates, Second Edition
    Scientific Publishing Company
    2328 Entaw Place
    Baltimore 17, Maryland
(2) AO H-R-R Pseudoisochromatic Plates, Second Edition
    American Optical Company
    Vision Park
    Southbridge, Massachusetts 01550

Because teachers can test a whole class very quickly with either set of plates (twenty-five or thirty students in thirty to forty minutes), teachers should realize that it is very important that all children be screened in the primary grades. The tests are valid, reliable, and easy to administer and interpret.

The color-blind children need to be identified. If the color plates are not immediately available, teachers can confirm their first judgments about children's understanding of color by asking them to do color matching, color naming, color sorting, or object arrangement by color patterns. This can be done quickly and informally.

If students are color blind, they need to be given special consideration in any work that calls for identifying, naming, or using colors. Teachers can offer subtle kinds of help in finding the right crayons, such as teaching the child to read color names on the crayon wrappers; they may compensate somewhat for such students by emphasizing auditory avenues to learning. The teachers' greatest need for the color-blind children is the *awareness* that they are color blind, an understanding of what being color blind means, and a few coping skills to enable the children to complete their reading tasks confidently without frustration caused by their inabilities to identify colors.

Other Health Problems

Endocrine disturbances, especially thyroid problems, have in many cases been found to bear directly on difficulties in learning to read. Hypothyroidism manifests itself in such overt behavior as lack of effort, fatigue, and nonlearning. The detection of thyroid deficiency or any other medical problem is not within the province of the educator; neither is its treatment. Without help from the medical specialist, however, the teacher's effort to teach reading is apt to be unsuccessful.

To illustrate, Gerald was doing very poor work in the fourth grade when he was given a thorough physical examination. A basal metabolism test revealed an extremely underactive thyroid. He was given heavy dosage of thyroid extract and tested for enrollment in an eight-week remedial reading clinic. His reading skills were fairly evenly developed at easy second-grade level. His instruction during the eight-week summer school included thirty-seven two-hour sessions. He was taught all the developmental reading skills in second-grade teacher's manuals for the school readers, and he began reading well from an easy third-grade book before the close of summer school.

Gerald's fifth-grade teacher the following year was an excellent, permissive, experienced teacher who used the detailed summer report as a basis for planning his reading in her room. He adjusted well and made further progress.

In a follow-up study five years later, Gerald's parents reported that in tenth grade he had no reading problems, and that they were pleased with his progress in senior high school. He took thyroid extract for about three years, after which the family doctor had determined that it was no longer needed. He had been a member of the varsity football squad in his high school, and his physical stamina was assessed as "good, now."

Joseph is another example of a child who had a variety of health problems. Joseph was in the second grade in a large city school. He was a small child for his seven years. He walked haltingly because of a congenital hip deformity. He had few friends. He was uninterested in his school work, even though his teacher made her lessons interesting and varied. At home he was not interested in active play and preferred to sit watching television both before and after school. His parents met with the teacher and principal about his failing school grades. They decided stricter demands should be placed on Joseph, both at home and at school. The stricter demands made no difference; the child's work became steadily worse. Finally, one day during recess, the teacher on duty found Joseph asleep behind one of the portable classrooms. This event caused the teacher and parents to decide that some action should be taken. A check-up by the family doctor revealed two serious problems—an abnormal thyroid that led to extreme lethargy and a low blood sugar condition that left the child continually tired and bothered by headaches. The label of "lazy" was quickly forgotten, a strict diet and medication for the thyroid condition were begun, and a careful schedule of play, work, and rest was established. Within weeks, Joseph was performing at grade level in his reading class and showed no further problems with school. He found several new friends and became a happy, active child at school and at home. After high school he entered college to study electrical engineering. He must still follow a strict diet and take certain medications, but he is a successful student who expects a satisfying career as an engineer.

Chemical imbalance, low vitality, metabolism, and vitamin deficiency may affect reading as well as motor and speech activities. Slight, unrecognized birth injuries may account for a number of cases of undiagnosed reading difficulty.

Allergies

An allergic reaction is the body's adverse response to alien substances in the environment. Hay fever, some forms of hives, and asthma are common forms of allergies. Visible effects of allergic attacks include itching eyes and nose, runny nose, hives, sneezing, or throat constriction. Difficulty in breathing is usually the result of muscle spasms in bronchial walls that constrict the passages. Inhaling particles of plant pollen, animal dander, or dust causes such discomfort. Specific foods, tense situations, or house dust may generate hives, eczema, or gastrointestinal allergies. Sensitization that results from having been administered drugs for illnesses can cause individuals to become allergic to miracle drugs.

Children whose allergies are chronic but not treated may find concentration on school work impossible. Outward signs of breathing discomfort, hearing loss, and general distress need to be understood by the children's teachers. Teachers must understand that these children need help, not admonishment. Some children's allergies may be seasonal with the presence of pollens, animal dander, or dust. Other children who are chronically affected have no seasonal respite.

Inventories and Interviews

An Interest Inventory

By talking privately with any pupil, the teacher can gain a great deal of personal information that can be useful when any question about the pupil's school success arises. In other words, the more one knows about a person, the more apt one is to be able to understand the person's behavior.

For the student who has difficulties with reading, the teacher may wish to conduct a more systematic inventory of the student's background and interests. The following sugggestions are made for obtaining this type of information.

The teacher can complete part of an interest inventory on the basis of information he or she has already obtained from formal records and informal visits. When asking the pupil questions, the teacher should use short periods of time when both teacher and pupil can talk freely. If nothing particularly worthwhile is revealed, it may not be of special use to the teacher in planning the remedial program. On the other hand, some information may be very helpful. For instance what the pupil does after school, in the evening, and on weekends; the relationship with siblings and the kind of fun shared with the family; whether or not a great deal of time is spent with friends; special hobbies being developed; private lessons outside of school, such as tennis, art, piano; whether the pupil has collections or pets—all of these may reveal needed information. Habits of rest, sleep, play, and diet need to be investigated. Places where the pupil has been—a long train trip, a trip by airplane or by bus, or a visit to an art museum—give facts about the background of experience. Experience stories can be dictated by the pupil and typewritten by the teacher for reading practice. A collection of original stories based on these experiences may be very important to the pupil and provide meaningful reading practice.

The pupil's knowledge of radio, television, and movie entertainment may add to the ability to write experience stories that will provide practice in reading. Interest in school, in the library, in what he or she wants to be when grown up, and other factors will be useful in extending reading skills.

The types of information to be sought out in the compilation of an interest inventory include the answers to such questions as are suggested in figure 6.6.

Obviously each teacher can obtain pertinent information from the pupils without a formal questionnaire, but he or she should write this information down while it is fresh in mind. Items revealed in such an interview may be useful in planning future remedial work in reading and writing.

Personality Data

Incomplete Sentences Blank The Incomplete Sentences Blank, College Form,[15] has been used as a measure of individuals' reactions and feelings about situations in everyday life. The instructions for this test read: "Complete these sentences to express *your real feelings*. Try to do every one. Be sure to make a complete sentence."[16]

Two purposes can be achieved in using this form with disabled readers. First, the blanks will reveal some of their feelings about the reading situation, and second, they may reveal other areas in which there are psychological problems affecting reading success.

The test is reproduced here with answers given by a sixteen-year-old girl who had not learned to read. She had been attending a reading clinic, and her clinician had established sufficient rapport to believe the answers were reliable. Because she could not read, the stems were read to her; she responded orally, and her answers were written for her. The sentences with her endings are:

1. I like . . . Max.
2. The happiest time . . . March 10—ten minutes to nine.
3. I want to know . . . if I ever can learn to read.
4. Back home . . . friends.
5. I regret . . . not learning to read.
6. At bedtime . . . I hit the hay.
7. Boys . . . fun!
8. The best . . . what can I do best? don't know.
9. What annoys me . . . a lot of things.
10. People . . . friends.
11. A mother . . . is a person that looks after you.
12. I feel . . . good.
13. My greatest fear . . . never learning to read.
14. In high school . . . fun.
15. I can't . . . read.
16. Sports . . . horseback riding, swimming.
17. When I was a child . . . had fun.

Name _____　Age _____ Grade _____ Date _____

Date _____　Parents name and address: _____

I. About *you*:

What do you usually do after school? In your spare time? In the evening? On Saturday? On Sunday?

What do you like best to do at home?

How many brothers and sisters do you have? How old are they? Do you play games with them? What are some of your favorite games?

Does your father or mother ever spend time with you? What do you do together?

II. About *your friends*:

Do your friends come to your house to see you? Would you rather go to their houses?

What do you play? Do you usually play whatever games they want to play?

Do you belong to any clubs?

III. About *your hobbies*:

Do you have a hobby? Tell me about it. What kinds of things do you like to make? Do you have a collection of any kind?

IV. More things about *you*:

Do you take any kind of special lessons outside of school? What kind? Would you rather take something else?

Do you have a pet? What is it? Tell me about feeding and caring for your _____?

What time do you usually go to bed at night?
What are you afraid of?
What time do you usually get up in the morning?

Do you like milk to drink?

Are there any things you don't like to eat? (Especially that your mother wants you *to eat*.)

V. Places *you* have been:

Have you ever been to a circus? Zoo? Farm? Ball game? Picnic? Concert? Camp? Museum?

Have you taken a boat trip?

Have you taken a train trip?

Have you taken an airplane trip?

Tell me about some trip you have taken.

VI. Ways *you* learn new things:

Do you have a transistor?
What do you listen to most?
What do you watch on television?

Do you go to movies? What movies have you seen lately? Tell me about one you liked.

Who do you go to movies with? Do you have a favorite movie actor or actress?

Do you like to read?
Do you ever read out loud to anyone? To whom?

Do you like to go to school?
What is your favorite subject? What subject do you like least?

Do you have a library card?
Do you go to the library?
What are some books you have read recently?

Do you read the comics? What is your favorite comic strip? Do you see cartoons on TV on Saturday mornings?

What do you want to be when you grow up? Do you know what your parents want you to be when you grow up?

Figure 6.6. An interest inventory

18. My nerves . . . ha! why?
19. Other people . . . just people.
20. I suffer . . . a lot on account of I can't read.
21. I failed . . . reading.
22. Reading . . . I wish I could.
23. My mind . . . Oh, Gad! nothing comes, I don't think.
24. The future . . . work.
25. I need . . . friends.
26. Marriage . . . fun.
27. I am best when . . . happy.
28. Sometimes . . . what do you mean? happy.
29. What pains me . . . a lot of things irritate me.
30. I hate . . . I don't know.
31. This school . . . isn't bad.
32. I am very . . . happy.
33. The only trouble . . . reading.
34. I wish . . . I could read.
35. My father . . . is a carpenter.
36. I secretly . . . nothing.
37. I . . . swim.
38. Dancing . . . some clubs where you can dance, dancing is fun.
39. My greatest worry is . . . Ha! one is reading; I want a letter from someone.
40. Most girls . . . like me.

Those answers that might have revealed some conflict with other people—items 7, 10, 11, 14, 19, 35, and 40—do not indicate any problem for this student. However, the answers to items 3, 5, 13, 15, 20, 21, 22, 33, 34, and 39 all relate to the reading failure. Certainly this shows genuine anxiety on the student's part about the failure in learning how to read. Alleviating such an anxiety might make for possible faster progress in reading in the future.

Larry's Responses to the Incomplete Sentences Following is another observation of reading difficulties amid emotional problems. Larry was in the fourth grade. His reading ability was limited to easy second-grade level, although he had a Stanford-Binet I.Q. of 102. During a semester of individual tutoring in reading, the reading clinician obtained the following information.

About the Parents. Larry lived in a strict authoritarian household. His parents were trying very hard to teach him to be honest, fair, and just. They constantly applied excessive pressure to get what they considered to be acceptable behavior. Larry's father seemed to have a need to realize through his son what he, himself, wanted to do in life. Larry's psychological needs were not met at home because his father had such rigid notions of what Larry should do and be.

About the Five-Year-Old Brother. Larry expressed considerable hostility and jealousy toward his brother.

Making Connections 6.1: Using the Interest Inventory

Locate a child who would be willing to complete an interest inventory with you. You may wish to use the sample inventory shown in figure 6.6. You may find that you want to add certain questions or perhaps delete some, depending on the age of the child or circumstances unique to that particular youngster.

Complete the interview with the child. You may wish to take detailed notes, or you may find it more appropriate to record the session and transcribe the tape later.

When your information is ready for sharing, bring the record of your interview to class. In small groups, share your experience and the resulting data with others. Be sure to discuss how this information could be used in planning a reading program for the particular child.

About the Teacher at School. The child had been referred to the school's child guidance department, and a written report was in the school file. The teacher had not read this report! While she expressed concern about the problem, she was doing nothing observable to solve it. Larry was often scolded in the classroom and was once required to write two hundred times, "I will respect my teacher." As soon as Larry's teacher saw evidence of his growth in reading with the reading tutor, she moved him up to the middle reading group and eliminated the lower reading group entirely.

From the Reading Tutor. Larry did make progress during the semester and gained a great deal of self-confidence. His sight vocabulary and his word analysis skills improved, although he needed outside help with his psychological problems and further help with reading. One day Larry completed eight sentences of the incomplete sentences variety:

1. When I was little . . . I was bad.
2. Grownups think . . . right.
3. I hardly ever . . . am bad.
4. My father . . . is very good to me.
5. I am . . . a bad boy.
6. I used to . . . be bad but you are now.
7. When I get big . . . I will be a big man.
8. My mother . . . is a good cook.

The four items about himself all emphasize Larry's inadequacy. The answers about grownups make one think that these were learned responses that one must make! Grownups must think right, and one must say of one's father that he is very good.

When Larry was asked to draw a picture in which he put a house, a tree, and a person, he drew a very small girl in his house instead of a boy. Does this suggest that he feels he needs to be a girl so that he won't be so displeasing to his father? Is the diminutive size of the person (see drawing in fig. 6.7) indicative of his feelings of insignificance and inadequacy?

Figure 6.7. Larry's drawing in the house-tree-person test

The Interview about the Reading Process

When the teacher begins to gather information about the child's reading status, it may be useful to find out what is understood about the reading process and about the vocabulary used in reading instruction. The teacher may discover that the child has views about reading that contribute to poor learning and negative attitudes. Some children may view reading as a decoding act and focus almost entirely on naming words accurately. These readers may complain that reading is boring and no fun. They may well be right if they have never learned to see reading as a meaningful activity. Some children, when asked who they know is a good reader, will select someone who is bigger, who "knows all the words," or who reads fast. Often such children have not learned what makes reading effective or what characteristics accurately describe the "good" reader. Other questions in a reading interview may focus on the child's knowledge of such terms as *syllable, word, sentence, line, sound, first,* and *last.* Failure to recognize the meanings of these and other words used by teachers in reading instruction may further confuse the child who is already having reading problems. The teacher may put together a list of questions that will yield information about the child's concepts of the reading process, or he or she may use prepared lists of questions developed explicitly for this purpose.[17]

Parent Interviews

When parents and teachers work together for the educational well-being of children, the greatest possible academic gains can be expected. One way in which the significant adults in the lives of children can work together is through conferences or interviews.[18] If the teacher plans to conference with or interview parents, careful planning must precede the meeting. The teacher must prepare classroom information, work samples from the child, and reports from other school personnel to share with the parents. In addition, thoughtful questions must be prepared that will let the parents know what kinds of information will be most valuable in contributing to the solution of the child's reading problems. Parents can be helped to plan their part of a conference or interview through suggestions about the kinds of records and information they may need to share during the meeting.

After all information from school and home has been collected, the parents and teacher have the task of using that information to make plans for the child's learning. The teacher should be prepared to take the lead in this final phase of the conference or interview, but it is important that the ideas of the parents, who probably know the child best, be respected and incorporated into any plan of action that is prepared.

An example of a form a teacher might use as a guide for a parent interview may be found in Appendix F.

Strategies that Yield Social and Psychological Data

A variety of techniques can help teachers to assess the social situations of children in their classrooms. The sociogram is one common, practical technique for obtaining information about interpersonal relationships among students. Bibliotherapy may be used as a technique to work toward more favorable social settings. It may also be used to help provide insights for children as they deal with a wide variety of difficult life situations.

The Sociogram

A *sociogram* is a chart showing the social interaction among the members of a group at a given time. Many teachers construct sociograms based on children's friendships so that they can take an objective look at the social status of all pupils. The popular students, the two who are always together but with no one else, the pupils who have no friends, and the one most children reject—are delineated for the teachers when the sociogram is finished.

There are several logical facts to be emphasized about the sociogram. It will, of course, not be shown or discussed with the students. Teachers never indicate to children who is the isolate or the reject, or naively urge popular children to be "nice" to unchosen ones. While the chart shows stars, isolates, and rejects, it does not in any way show what to do about them! If the teachers are apprised of some techniques to change the behavioral pattern, it can be a very valuable device. Naturally, choices made by children may be superficial, temporary, or fickle. A sociogram made in October may not tell the story in February. Nevertheless, as one index of pupil interaction, it is well worth the work involved in its construction. The following steps may help you in making a sociogram:

1. The students express two or three choices of friends or partners among their classmates. These choices will be most valid if there is some real purpose for making them. Sometimes the question the child will answer is simply, "Who do you consider to be your three best friends in this room?" or "Who do you want to have sit near you when a new seating chart is made?" After some discussion of the question that is to be answered and the uses to be made of their choices, all pupils may be asked to write their names on one side of a three-by-five card and their three choices of classmates on the other side. The teachers need to make clear that they will make use of their preferences *as much as they can,* if this is to precede a new seating arrangement, for example. Sometimes a class activity is being planned in which committees will do projects or write research reports, or the teachers may plan small group work in arithmetic. The teachers must also make clear that *no one* but them will see the cards with the choices on them.

2. If thirty children make three choices each, it is apparent that there is considerable tabulating to be done. The choices can be tabulated on a large sheet of paper so that the total number of times each child has been chosen can easily be seen. Such a tabulation pattern is suggested in figure 6.8. The names of all the children are to be listed both horizontally and vertically, and lines drawn so that the necessary squares for recording choices are provided. The totals at the bottom of each column become the data for making the sociogram. In most cases, if three choices are plotted, no distinction needs to be made between first, second, or third choice. However, only *first* choices should be plotted on a separate chart.

3. It may be necessary to begin more than one plotting of the sociogram. It will help if some large concentric circles are drawn first on the large sheet of paper and the "children" placed outward from the center on the basis of number of choices. It may also be helpful to cut out small circles on which the girls' names are written and small hexagons on which the boys' names are written. These circles and hexagons can then be moved around on the master plan until their locations make possible the clearest drawing of lines. Careful study often helps in the discovery of small isolated groups, presence of cliques, and sometimes divisions strictly on ethnic group lines (see figure 6.9).

Chooser \ Chosen	Jack	Roger	Mary	David	Joan	Rose	Betty	Jane	Greg	Sara	Dan	Jean	Doris	Carol	Barbara	Grace	Jim	Laura	Andy	Anita	Larry	Dean	Bruce	Patsy	Donny	Ray	Kay	Glenn	Bill	John	Bobby
Jack									3																			2	1		
Roger																			2		1					3					
Mary				1					2																			3			
David									2																3	1					
Joan									1									2						3							
Rose							3							1										2							
Betty		3							1				2																		
Jane				1									3											2							
Greg										2						3														1	
Sara			3		1								2																		
Dan			1											2										3							
Jean	2					3							1																		
Doris													1		3										2						
Carol						3	1																		2						
Barbara		3															1								2						
Grace				3									2											1							
Jim									3																1						2
Laura													2	1													3				
Andy		2							3												1										
Anita														1											2		3				
Larry		2						1														3									
Dean																							2	3		1					
Bruce					3	2																	1								
Patsy				2	3									1																	
Donny													2				1				3										
Ray			1					3																	2						
Kay								2				1													3						
Glenn		3																				2			1						
Bill	1	2										3																			
John									1	3																			2		
Bobby (Absent on day of vote)																															
Totals	2	5	1	3	2	4	7	2	4	4	0	5	2	3	7	1	2	2	2	0	4	2	1	6	8	4	2	1	2	1	1

Figure 6.8. Sociogram tabulation: "Three Best Friends"

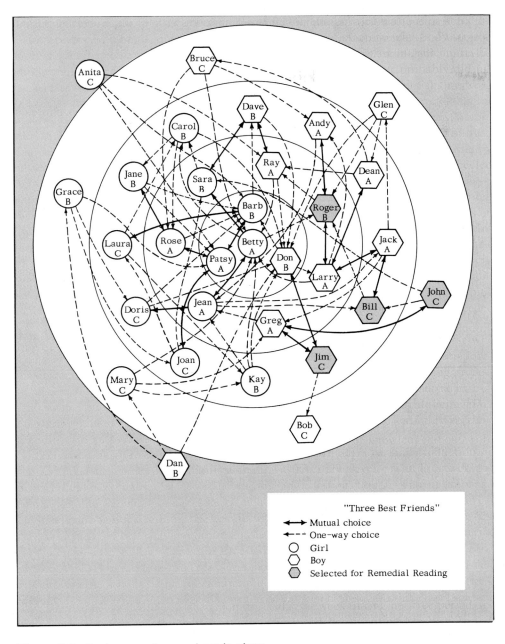

Figure 6.9. Sociogram of second grade class

4. After the sociogram is completed, consider how by assignment to working pairs, small group projects, or by seating in quartets or at tables, a child who is an isolate might be grouped with one who might become friendly if he knew him better. Think of positive ways to give recognition to the shy, withdrawn, or silent child. Think of reasons for the rejection of the disliked child. Strickland sugggests:

Many times the evidence points to the fact that the isolate has become lost because of his inability to communicate with other children because he has a speech defect, comes from a foreign background, or uses speech in a manner different from that of other children. A child may be excluded by the children because he is "bossy" and over-aggressive in his use of language, because he is inept in making contacts with people, or because he cannot fit into a group as a cooperative, participating member.[19]

A second-grade teacher made a sociogram of her thirty-one students based on the question, "Who do you consider to be your three best friends in the room?" Figure 6.8 shows the tabulation of their choices and figure 6.9 is the completed sociogram based on this tabulation. The letter *A, B,* or *C* under each child's name indicates the reading group to which each was assigned at the time the chart was drawn. Roger, Jim, Bill, and John were designated by the teacher as the least successful in the reading program.

If children who are failing in reading are chosen by their peers, then this is one indication that their reading failure is not affecting their social interaction in the group. If they are on the fringe, are isolates, or rejects, the teachers may need to consider how a better interaction with the group might be achieved. In the sociogram, Roger was chosen five times, Bill three times, Jim twice, and John once.

Bibliotherapy

Shrodes defines bibliotherapy as "a process of interaction between the personality of the reader and imaginative literature which may engage his emotions and free them for conscious and productive use.[20]

Tews states: "Bibliotherapy is a program of selected activity involving reading materials, planned, conducted, and controlled as treatment under the guidance of the physician for emotional and other problems.[21]

Literally, bibliotherapy is "treatment through books" or "healing through books." Books, that is, print materials, have different values for different people. If the right book can be selected at the right time, books may, for some people, provide the language and the ideas to clarify their personal problems.

If teachers were to entertain notions of recommending books for therapeutic purposes for their students, they should abide by these cautions:

1. Students *must* have freedom of choice in what they read.
2. Students should have *no* pressure to show results, such as book reports.
3. Teachers should proceed with caution.

Bibliotherapy is affected through the personality mechanisms of (1) identification, (2) catharsis, and (3) insights. Identification, catharsis, and insight must be present for a dynamic interaction between the reader and the books. First, the reader must identify with character elements of the story; share some characteristics such as age, sex, hopes, fears, problems. If the reader can identify with and admire the character, the reader can build self-image and increase the feeling of belonging. Sometimes when this personal identification is not possible, these positive effects can occur through hero-worship. *Identification,* then, is the recognition of commonalities between reader and characters.

Second, *catharsis* is the sharing of motivations, conflicts, and emotions of a character in a book. It is an active release of emotions, experienced either first hand or vicariously. It goes beyond the simple recognition of commonalities and involves empathy (feeling as the character does). The readers relive *their* own past experiences. The generation of empathy is basic to catharsis.

Third, *insight* requires that after people see themselves in the behavior of the characters in the book, they get an awareness of their own motivations, needs, and problems. People need to see similarities and differences between themselves and fictional characters. Now, the reader considers a course of action to try to solve (overcome) the problem. This step requires the taking of some action to meet a need.

Personality changes occur through response to emotional experience, not through teaching and learning. Intellect is not a key factor in the therapeutic process. The personality change in bibliotherapy requires identification, catharsis, and insight. People overcome feelings of guilt, inadequacy, or inferiority by identifying these in characters, generalizing or seeing these traits as universals in human behavior; then, the catharsis is the ability to express "bad" feelings and understand them. In adults this is likely achieved through talking; in children it is achieved through action (this is often play therapy). This must lead to *insight* in order for the reader to grow through to emotional maturity.

Roswell and Natchez have reported the case of Claude, age twelve, seventh grade, who felt that he was a failure and resorted to being a nuisance in class. His reading achievement was at least two years below grade level although he had normal intelligence. After reading Hans Christian Andersen's life in *Stories to Remember, Classmate Edition* (high fourth-grade level);[22] Thomas Edison's Life story in *Teen Age Tales,* Book 1 (fifth-grade level);[23] Dr. Fleming's strugggle to discover penicillin, and Madame Curie's life story, both in *Doorways to Discovery* (seventh-grade level);[24] observable behavioral changes did take place.

Learning that Hans Christian Andersen was *the* Ugly Duckling; that Edison was considered dull and stupid by his classmates; that Dr. Fleming had the patience to wait nearly two decades for personal recognition for having discovered penicillin; and that Madame Curie's discovery of radium was a long and tedious process caused Claude to realize that perseverance won in the face of failure and he might really change his life. He did, according to his case file, make a three-year reading growth during one year, and when followed up in tenth grade was still achieving well.

Not all students will respond to these same stories, nor is it expected that all teachers will be sufficiently analytically oriented to guide all students in this way. However, if a key is found that helps students unlock the world to them, they should be encouraged to take advantage of it.[25]

Making Connections 6.2: Identifying Books for Use in Bibliotherapy

Bibliotherapy is a useful strategy to help a child understand a problem and develop valid ways of dealing with it. It is important for teachers to know books well enough that they can make suitable choices to recommend to children for specific purposes.

Identify some problem or situation that might confront a child who has a reading problem. Then, build a bibliography of books that might be used with such a child to understand the situation better. Besides the usual bibliographic information on each book, include a sentence or two summarizing the book and its potential for bibliotherapy.

If class members prepare sufficient copies of their bibliographies, sharing will permit each person to have the beginning of an extensive collection of books suitable for use in bibliotherapy.

Recognizing cultural values, meeting and solving personal and human relations problems, and understanding people with physical limitations, all subjects to be found and discussed in good literature suitable for children, may help pupils develop wholesome attitudes toward all kinds of differences when they become adults. Teachers will find further suggestions in such books as *Reading Ladders to Human Relations*[26] and *Facilitating Human Development through Reading*.[27]

Other Language and Reading Assessments

Storytelling

Teachers may ask children to tell or retell stories in order to obtain more information about the students' understanding of stories. Relationships between children's understanding of the structure of stories, the goals, motivations, and feelings of the characters, and overall comprehension abilities are becoming clearly established. When building a collection of data sbout a child's reading status, the teacher may ask the child to tell a story based on a picture or a wordless picture book and to retell a story that has been read. These tellings should be taped and transcribed for analysis. The teacher may look to see if the child includes all of the parts of a story in the telling. Evidence of the child's perception of the goals of the characters may be noted. Words that indicate the child's understanding of the feelings of the characters should be identified; it should also be noted when the child seems to take no note of goals and feelings. Children who have trouble with these tasks may well be failing to comprehend relationships within the stories, even though they may be able to answer simple recall questions.

David Woodward

The child may be asked to create a story about an intriguing picture, and the tape recorded story can be transcribed and evaluated later.

The Writing Sample

The teacher may find it useful to ask children to prepare a writing sample as a part of the collection of information about language and reading development. The children may be asked to write on a teacher-identified topic, to tell or retell a story, or to write on a subject of their own choosing. The teacher will be able to observe how well the child has mastered the mechanics of writing and spelling. The child's ability to tell a story in writing may be evaluated and compared with oral storytelling capabilities.

Peabody Picture Vocabulary Test

The Peabody Picture Vocabulary Test is designed to assess oral receptive language. Plates of four pictures are presented to the child, who is required to select one picture that best fits the stimulus word. The test can be administered in a short time period and provides the teacher with an estimate of the child's ability to understand words that are heard. Scores in stanines may be helpful to the teacher as decisions are made about the child's oral language status. One cannot expect the child to read with understanding vocabulary that is not understood orally.

Cloze Procedure

The term *cloze* from the word *clozure* explains the tendency of a thinking individual to anticipate the completion of a not-quite-finished pattern. Clozure, as an idea, is a term used by Gestalt psychologists.

Clozure is the ability of the readers—or the listeners for that matter—to determine by anticipating contextually, the word or concept that is needed immediately.

Weaver and Kingston found that the ability of students to write in every "nth" word in a passage correlated significantly with vocabulary and comprehension sections of the *Diagnostic Reading Test.*[28]

The cloze procedure does not require special expertise in test construction. It merely presents the readers with a series of contextually interrelated blanks in a passage. A passage is prepared with every "nth" word missing with a blank of standard length substituted. Students read the passage and write in the missing words. It follows that the better the passage is understood by the readers, the more likely they can guess what words are missing. Schneyer found that cloze tests have adequate validity for evaluating reading comprehension for most general uses.[29]

Research to date suggests that the most valid and reliable cloze test for measuring passage difficulty is one in which:

1. An every "nth" mechanical mutilation system is used.
2. Not more than 20 words out of every 100 are deleted.
3. Passage length is at least 250 words.
4. Deletion ratios of 1:10 and 1:12 in longer passages may be valid for certain purposes.
5. At least 50 words are deleted in order to insure adequate sampling of passages.
6. The exact word deleted is indicated as the most useful and efficient scoring criteria.
7. Other scoring systems (synonym, form class) provide less interscorer reliability and require substantially more time.
8. The separate scoring of form classes or content and function words may provide specific information for specialized purposes.[30]

Taylor believed that cloze procedure was a very useful tool in measuring general understanding of written material. Factors that affect comprehension—general language facility, specific knowledge, native ability to learn, specialized vocabulary, motivation, and ability to attend—are all being evaluated by cloze tests in which all types of words are deleted.[31]

Bormuth found cloze tests to be valid, reliable, and flexible measures of the comprehension of the passage being read.[32]

Tonjes found that the cloze procedure, using lexical deletions of nouns and verbs, and synonym scoring criteria, was a valid way to measure factual comprehension of an entire story. She recommended that the cloze procedure be used to supplement standardized tests of comprehension.[33]

Potter used Osgood's (1962) concept of cloze for expressing and receiving verbal interchanges.[34]

Some of the principal intervening variables relating to the cloze procedure have come from Osgood's (1962) concept "total language context." These include verbal factors such as grammatical skills, the effective use of multitudes of symbols, and non-verbal cues such as past experience and intelligence.

Osgood's theory of communication suggests that redundancies and transitional probabilities lead to the development of dispositional mechanisms that play a large part in transmitting and receiving messages.

A. The first-grade teachers can provide their reading groups a kind of comprehension test in the cloze procedure by duplicating a story like the one following:

Directions: Read the sentences, decide which word is missing, and write it on the blank space.

Mother said, "Dick, will you go to the store for me?"

"Yes, _____ ," said _____ , "What do you want me to _____ ?"

"I need a loaf of _____ ," _____ Mother.

_____ ran to the store.

He got a loaf of _____ .

Dick was soon _____ .

Mother said, "Thank you, _____ . You are a good _____ ."

Dick went out to _____ .

B. The following exercise is of seventh grade difficulty:

Directions: In this exercise you will use context clues to think accurately and to supply the missing word to give the meaning. Read the selection all the way through before filling in the blanks. You will need only *one* word for each blank.

FROM THE CLUTCHES OF DEATH

In France, about seventy-five years ago, a desperate woman brought her young (1) _____ into the laboratory of Louis Pasteur. The boy (2) _____ been badly bitten by a mad dog, and a terrible death from (3) _____ was certain to follow.

Pasteur was a (4) _____ . He had saved the silk industry of France from (5) _____ by working out a method for prevention of two diseases of (6) _____ . He had invented a process for preserving (7) _____ by killing the bacteria contained in it and chilling it. And he (8) _____ discovered a vaccine which protected chickens against virulent (9) _____ of chicken cholera, and another which protected both animals and men from the feared (10) _____ of anthrax. Pasteur had also developed a (11) _____ which would usually prevent rabies in animals (12) _____ by mad dogs. But the vaccine had never been (13) _____ on man. It would be a daring experiment, but the (14) _____ had been bitten so badly that he would surely (15) _____ unless quick action were taken. Pasteur (16) _____ the risk. He tried his vaccine on a human being for the first (17) _____ . The boy lived! Thus, a rabies vaccine was (18) _____ to the world.

Today, Louis Pasteur (19) _____ considered one of the greatest scientists of all time. Some of his (20) _____ made possible the control of diseases that (21) _____ cost millions of lives.

Key: (Grade level 7.0)

1. *son,* boy, child
2. *had*
3. *rabies*
4. *scientist,* doctor
5. *ruin,* destruction, disaster, bankruptcy, failure, extinction
6. *silkworms*
7. *food,* milk
8. *had,* also, then, alone
9. *attacks,* cases
10. *disease,* sickness
11. *vaccine,* serum
12. *bitten*
13. *tried,* used, tested
14. *boy,* child, patient
15. *die,* perish
16. *took*
17. *time*
18. *given,* known, introduced, presented, shown
19. *is*
20. *experiments,* works, vaccines, discoveries
21. *had,* would('ve), might, could('ve), once, normally[35]

Anecdotal Records

A most useful teaching technique for gathering data about a reader over a period of time is the keeping of anecdotal records. The teacher should keep a note pad available to make notes about reading behaviors that are observed. Care must be taken to make records of actual events and behaviors and to avoid recording opinions and conclusions. If anecdotal records are kept faithfully over a period of time, growth can be identified, patterns of behaviors can be detected, the child's responses to various kinds of materials and techniques can be clarified, and language samples can be preserved for later study. These kinds of information can add information to the study of a reader's problems that formal testing cannot be expected to contribute or can serve to clarify responses given during testing that are puzzling to the teacher.

When anecdotal records are kept, it is important to date each notation and, to the extent possible, to note the conditions under which the observation was made. In the busy life of the classroom, the teacher cannot trust that each incident and its surrounding circumstances will be clearly remembered.

Observation

Classroom life is immensely complex. The teacher is constantly responding to demands from many sources. It is a rare luxury to have time to observe carefully a single child over a period of several minutes. However, if such observation time can be planned and the teacher can be free to record exactly what a child does over time, especially as it relates to reading and writing activities, much useful information can be obtained providing new insights into a child's difficulties, learning patterns, and avoidance strategies.[36]

The daily schedule will need to be examined in order to find short periods of time when the teacher may be an observer. Perhaps, if self-selection is a part of the daily schedule, the teacher can be freed to watch and make notes. Another possibility is to observe while someone else is working with the children, or to ask another person to be the observer while the teacher continues with the usual class schedule. However the time for observation may be arranged, the teacher will want to make sure that the information recorded is the actual behavior of the child, not an interpretation or an opinion.

Reading Problems in Special Education

Figure 6.10 is a summary chart that may be useful in helping the teachers to recognize that some of the students with problems in reading in the regular classroom have concomitant problems that can be analyzed and perhaps alleviated by the department of special education.

Special Education	The "in-between area" of reading problems that are problems in special education	Remedial Reading
Areas of exceptionality	Reading problems in special education	Programs in remedial and corrective reading

The mentally retarded
The intellectually gifted
The physically handi-
  capped
  Hearing handicapped
  Visually handicapped
  Crippled
  Convulsive disorders
  Speech problems
  Heart conditions
Emotionally disturbed
Brain damaged
Neurologically handicapped
	Teaching reading to the
	  brain-injured child
	Teaching reading using
	  sight-saving materials
	  with visually handicapped
	Neurological problems
	  Strephosymbolia
	  Hyperactivity
	Motor handicapped
	  Cerebral palsied
	  Congenital anomalies
	
	Lacking abilities in
	  <u>selected</u> primary
	  mental abilities, i.e.,
	  the child with very
	  low scores on block
	  design and object as-
	  sembly on WISC[a]
	Convulsive disorders:
	  Petit mal seizures may
	  prevent consistent, se-
	  quential learning in
	  regular classroom
		Ten to 15 per cent of the
		  school population exhibit
		  reading problems in var-
		  ious forms from mild to
		  severe.
		Two-thirds to three-fourths
		  of all these cases can be
		  provided for in regular
		  classes and are not legiti-
		  mately called SPECIAL
		  EDUCATION.
		Many of the remaining one-
		  fourth to one-third are
		  included in the "in-
		  between area" as out-
		  lined.

a. A child may earn scaled scores on all other subtests indicating normal or above general intelligence and still earn only very low scores on using blocks to build designs from models or in putting puzzles together.

Figure 6.10. When is a reading problem a problem for the Department of Special Education?

Summary

The classroom teacher makes ongoing efforts to obtain information about the pupils with reading difficulties. This information could be categorized as pertaining to intelligence, health, information about interests and concepts about reading, social and psychological status, other language and reading data, and general information obtained through anecdotal records and observation of behavior. When causal factors are identified, the teacher should have the opportunity to discuss their ramifications with the school psychologist or school social worker.

Teachers in public schools will find psychologists willing to assist in bringing psychological services to children. The classroom teachers must insist upon outside help for all problems that do not resolve themselves in the group teaching situation.

It may summarily be pointed out that the children, after receiving psychological help, still need to be taught the missing reading skills. Psychological services for the children who are emotionally disturbed in no way eliminate the need for the reading teachers, but can make their work much easier and ensure greater success. Conversely, without the psychological services for disturbed children, the remedial teachers may work very hard with little success.

For Further Reading

Bond, G. L., Tinker, M. A.; Wasson, B. B.; and Wasson, J. B. *Reading Difficulties, Their Diagnosis and Correction,* 5th ed. Englewood Cliffs, N.J.: Prentice-Hall, 1984: Chapter 4, "Causes of Reading Disability: Physical Factors," pp. 51–67; Chapter 5, "Causes of Reading Disability: Cognitive and Language Factors," pp. 69–77; Chapter 6, "Causes of Reading Disability: Emotional, Environmental and Educational Factors," pp. 79–95.

Fredericks, Anthony et al. "How to Talk to Parents and Get the Message Home." *The Instructor* 93 (November/December, 1983), pp. 64–69.

Harris, Albert J., and Sipay, Edward R. *How to Increase Reading Ability,* 7th ed. New York: Longman, 1980: Chapter 10: "Correlates of Reading Disability, I: Cognitive Factors," pp. 251–79; Chapter 11, "Correlates of Reading Disability, II: Physical and Psychological Factors," pp. 280–307.

Jalongo, Mary Renck. "Bibliotherapy: Literature to Promote Socioemotional Growth." *The Reading Teacher* 26: (April 1983), pp. 796–803.

Marshall, Nancy. "Using Story Grammar to Assess Reading Comprehension." *The Reading Teacher* 36 (March 1983), pp. 616–20.

Pertz, Doris L., and Putnam, Lillian R. "An Examination of the Relationship between Nutrition and Learning." *The Reading Teacher* 35 (March 1982), pp. 702–6.

Richek, Margaret Ann; List, Lynne K.; and Lerner, Janet W. *Reading Problems, Diagnosis and Remediation* Englewood Cliffs, N.J.: Prentice-Hall, 1983: Chapter 3, "Correlates of Reading Disability I: Ecological, Emotional and Physical Factors," pp. 27–54; Chapter 4, "Correlates of Reading Disability II: Intellectual Potential and Language Development," pp. 55–86.

Searls, Evelyn F. *How to Use WISC Scores in Reading Diagnosis.* Newark, Del.: International Reading Association, 1975.

Westby, Carol E.; Maggart, Zelda; and Van Dongen, Richard, "Language Prerequisites for Literacy." Paper presented at the Third International Congress for the Study of Child Language, Austin, Texas, July 1984.

Notes

1. Herbert A. Carroll, *Mental Hygiene, The Dynamics of Adjustment,* 4th ed. (New York: Prentice-Hall, 1964), pp. 11–12.
2. Ruth Strang, Constance McCullough, and Arthur E. Traxler, *The Improvement of Reading,* 4th ed. (New York: McGraw-Hill, 1967), p. 19.
3. Roger Farr, "Reading Tests and Teachers, Use of Tests in Evaluation," in *Reading Diagnosis and Evaluation,* edited by Dorothy L. DeBoer (Newark, Del.: International Reading Association, 1970), p. 52.
4. Guy L. Bond, et al., *Reading Difficulties, Their Diagnosis and Correction,* 5th ed. (New York: Prentice-Hall, 1984), p. 41.
5. Louis M. Terman and Maude Merrill, *Stanford-Binet Scales,* rev. form (Boston: Houghton Mifflin, 1960); David Wechsler, *Wechsler-Bellevue Intelligence Scale for Children,* (New York: Psychological Corp., 1974).
6. Lloyd M. Dunn and Randall K. Hartley, "Comparability of Peabody, Ammons, Van Alstyne, and Columbia," *Exceptional Children* 26 (October 1959), pp. 70–74.
7. Guy L. Bond and Leo J. Brueckner, *The Diagnosis and Treatment of Learning Difficulties* (New York: Appleton-Century-Crofts, 1955), p. 34.
8. *Keystone Telebinocular Visual Survey* (Keystone View Division, Mast Development Company, 2210 East 12th Street, Davenport, Iowa).
9. *The Orthorater* (Rochester, N.Y.: Bausch and Lomb Optical Co.).
10. T. H. Eames, *Eames Eye Test* (Yonkers, N.Y.: World Book Co., 1941).
11. Arleen L. Olson, "An Experimental Study of the Relationship Between Color Blindness and Reading Achievement in the First Grade," (Master's Thesis, University of New Mexico, 1963).
12. Ibid., pp. 68–69.
13. Ibid., p. 58.
14. G. B. Schiffman, *The Effect of Color Blindness upon Achievement of Elementary School Males,* Experimental Research Series Report No. 106 (Towson, Md.: Board of Education, 1963).
15. Julian B. Potter, *Incomplete Sentences Blank, College Form.* Copyright 1950, The Psychological Corporation, New York. All Rights Reserved. Reproduced by Permission.
16. Ibid., p. 1.
17. Marie Clay, *The Early Detection of Reading Difficulties: A Diagnostic Survey with Recovery Procedures,* 2d ed. (Auckland, New Zealand: Heinemann, 1979); Bess Altwerger and Yetta Goodman, "Print Awareness in Preschool Children: A Working Paper," A study of the development of literacy in preschool children. (University of Arizona: Program in Language and Literacy, Arizona Center for Research and Development, June 1981).
18. Eldon E. Ekwall and James L. Shanker, *Diagnosis and Remediation of the Disabled Reader,* 2d ed. Boston: Allyn and Bacon, 1983): Chapter 12, "Diagnosis and Remediation through the Use of Interviews," pp. 412–42.
19. Ruth Strickland, *Language Arts in the Elementary School* (Boston: D.C. Heath, 1957), p. 136.

20. Caroline Schrodes, "Bibliotherapy: An Application of Psychoanalytic Theory," *American Imago* 17 (Fall 1960), pp. 311–19.
21. R. M. Tews, "Introduction," *Library Trends* 11 (October 1962), pp. 97–105.
22. Margaret Keating, "The Boy of Odense," in *Stories to Remember, Classmate Edition,* edited by Guy L. Bond and Marie C. Cuddy (Chicago: Lyons and Carnahan, 1953), pp. 37–55.
23. Joseph George Cohen and Will Scarlet, "The Wizard of Menlo Park," in *Teen Age Tales,* Book 1, 3d ed., edited by Ruth Strang and Ralph Roberts (Boston: D.C. Heath, 1966), pp. 93–102.
24. Irmengarde Eberle, "Penicillin—the Life Saver," in *Doorways to Discovery,* edited by David Russell and Mabel Snedaker (Boston: Ginn and Co., 1956), pp. 340–48; *idem.,* "Marie Curie," Ibid., pp. 167–73.
25. Florence G. Roswell and Gladys Natchez, *Reading Disability, A Human Approach to Learning,* 3d ed. (New York: Basic Books, 1977), pp. 68–76.
26. Virginia Reid, ed., *Reading Ladders to Human Relations,* 5th ed. (Washington, D.C.: American Council on Education, 1972).
27. Joseph S. Zaccaria and Harold A. Moses, *Facilitating Human Development through Reading* (Champaign, Ill.: Stipes Publishers, 1968).
28. W. W. Weaver and A. J. Kingston, "A Factor Analysis of Cloze Procedure and Other Measures of Reading and Language Ability," *Journal of Communication* 13 (1963), p. 253.
29. Wesley J. Schneyer, "Use of the Cloze Procedure for Improving Reading Comprehension," *The Reading Teacher* 19 (December 1965), p. 174.
30. Thomas C. Potter, *A Taxonomy of Cloze Research: Part I: Readability and Reading Comprehension* (Englewood, Calif.: Southwest Regional Laboratory for Educational Research and Development, 1968), pp. 39–40.
31. Wilson L. Taylor, "Cloze Readability Scores as Indices of Individual Differences in Comprehension and Aptitude," *Journal of Applied Psychology* 16 (February 1957), p. 19.
32. John Bormuth, "Cloze as a Measure of Readability," in *Reading as an Intellectual Activity,* IRA Conference Report No. 8 (1963), p. 134.
33. Marian Tonjes, "Evaluation of Comprehension and Vocabulary Gains of Tenth Grade Students Enrolled in a Developmental Reading Program" (Master's Thesis, University of New Mexico, 1969), pp. 30–40.
34. Potter, *Taxonomy of Cloze Research,* pp. 2–3.
35. Tonjes, "Evaluation of Comprehension," pp. 61, 68.
36. Courtney B. Cazden, "Contexts for Literacy: In the Mind and in the Classroom," *Journal of Reading Behavior* 14, no. 4 (1982) pp. 413–28.

7
Scheduling Time for Corrective Reading

Vocabulary

course of study
unit method
webbing
theme
learning laboratory
planning time
learning materials center
seatwork
developmental skills
skills application
reading groups
committee structure
enrichment
time blocks
bilingual-nonlingual

Questions

1. What are the instructional planning resources that teachers frequently have available for teaching? How should these resources be used?

2. What are some criteria for seatwork (individual instructional materials)?

3. What should be included in the organizational plan for the school day?

4. What are the similarities in the case studies of the three students? The differences?

If the school as an institution really exists for the education of all children and youth, then the students who need corrective reading must be given time *during the school day* for this purpose. They deserve their fair share of the teacher's direct attention for instruction from which they can profit.

Even those children who receive reading instruction from special education teachers and special reading instructors must have help with reading in the regular classroom as a part of the ongoing instructional program. These special programs are designed to supplement and support—but never to replace—the regular instructional program.

Instructional Resources for the Classroom Teacher

Finding time and keeping a positive, constructive attitude require a common sense evaluation of instructional resources for the classroom teacher: (1) the place of the course of study in teaching; (2) the unit method or problem approach to teaching in the content fields; (3) the classroom, very flexibly controlled, as a learning laboratory; (4) the development of a center for instructional materials in the school; (5) suggestions for "making time" for corrective reading; and (6) organizing the elementary school day in large blocks of time.

Following this discussion, case studies are presented of three students, in fourth, eighth, and twelfth grades, respectively, who were helped throughout the school day to improve their developmental reading skills.

The Course of Study/Curriculum Guide

An often heard but *misleading idea* voiced in teachers' groups is that teaching has to follow a rather rigid, inflexible pattern outlined in the state course of study or the school curriculum guide. Too many times this apparently generates a slavish endeavor to force all students through precisely cut and well-established patterns as they progress through any particular grade in school. Obviously, the disabled readers will be unable to perform satisfactorily if held to such an inflexible standard.

A course of study or curriculum guide is a very valuable document. It makes possible some kind of standard for judging the achievement of the "average" children in a given grade. It permits teachers to arrive at some judgment about what is adequate achievement for children who are six, eight, or ten years old. This comparative expectation of children at various ages is worthwhile and important. *But,* teachers must recognize the course of study or curriculum guide for exactly what it is: an outline of materials that the *average* students may logically be expected to utilize. *Average,* in this frame of reference, is that statistically hypothetical median performance above and below which half of any unselected class of students will probably perform. When given an achievement test battery, only a relatively small percentage of children in any given class actually perform *at the grade level* to which they are assigned.

Beyond this philosophical basis, the course of study is only as useful or as meaningful as the classroom teachers can make it. One of the basic purposes of formal education is the transmission of the cultural heritage. In this respect, the course of study and curriculum guide provide more or less generally uniform education for students as they progress through school. It makes possible more satisfactory school adjustment when students transfer from one school to another or from one part of the country to another.

Adaptations for poor readers must be made all day long when the class is working in reading and writing activities. The children must learn reading as a developmental process, beginning each succeeding year where they left off the previous year. Where the children are should be established in terms of an informal diagnosis of abilities, completely without regard to any arbitrary standard set forth in a formal outline by either the state course of study or the teacher.

No single textbook can ever accommodate the range of reading abilities in a class. The teachers must be continuously alert for new and additional ways to plan learning experiences that are not dependent upon the single textbook in any content area.

The *unit method* of teaching, the theme or problem approach lends itself to this purpose. The *learning materials center* in the school provides a great variety of materials the teachers need to manage their classrooms as *learning laboratories* where many activities go on simultaneously and many levels of achievement are accommodated.

The Unit Method of Teaching

The *unit method* is the curricular organization of subject matter material into problems to be solved or projects to be developed. Developing a unit is an evolving process by which a series of learning experiences that interrelate are taught. The purpose of the unit method is to integrate the learning experiences around a central theme. This is to be contrasted with the teaching of a "separate subjects" curriculum, where the learning may be compartmentalized and unrelated.

The unit develops through five stages: first, the orientation to, or introduction of, the unit; second, the teacher-pupil planning, which may develop out of a webbing experience[1] (See Figure 7.1); third, obtaining information; fourth, sharing information; and fifth, the culminating activity.

Since reading is likely to be the key activity in obtaining information as outlined in the third stage, it becomes important to plan for many levels of reading maturity. If the teachers have skillfully directed the teacher-pupil planning periods so that a comprehensive list of questions and tasks has been formulated, reading material must be made available so that all pupils can read something, answer some of the questions, and carry out a variety of activities. For units of work in both social studies and science, teachers need to find reading material that typically encompasses a range in achievement from three levels below the grade being taught to three levels above it. This is a difficult task for many units of work and must be systematically and jointly worked on over long periods of time by school faculties. It should be the goal of every school to house its own library in the learning materials center. The resources of state traveling libraries and public libraries should also be explored. Many children can bring many worthwhile books and references from home to contribute to the unit under study.

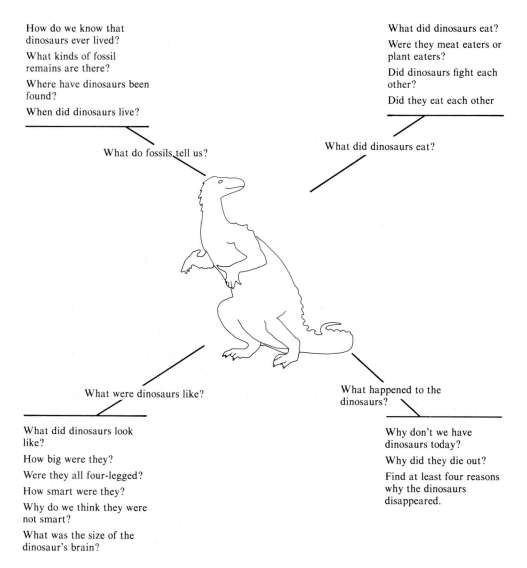

How do we know that
dinosaurs ever lived?

What kinds of fossil
remains are there?

Where have dinosaurs been
found?

When did dinosaurs live?

What do fossils tell us?

What did dinosaurs eat?

Were they meat eaters or
plant eaters?

Did dinosaurs fight each
other?

Did they eat each other

What did dinosaurs eat?

What were dinosaurs like?

What did dinosaurs look
like?

How big were they?

Were they all four-legged?

How smart were they?

Why do we think they were
not smart?

What was the size of the
dinosaur's brain?

What happened to the
dinosaurs?

Why don't we have
dinosaurs today?

Why did they die out?

Find at least four reasons
why the dinosaurs
disappeared.

Figure 7.1. A web for a dinosaur unit

The Classroom as a Learning Laboratory

The classroom must become a learning laboratory where students can experiment with
a wide variety of learning aids that will lead them to make discoveries of meanings
and ideas, to work out solutions, and to gain insights. Adequate equipment and materials must be provided if the classroom is to become a learning laboratory.

In a learning laboratory there are jobs to do for which pupils see real purposes; there
are tasks that will satisfy some fairly immediate need in solving other problems so that
a kind of chain reaction to the solving of problems evolves; jobs that are easy and jobs

David Woodward

When the teacher and child develop a web around a theme, they identify many topics to explore that will encourage meaningful reading and writing activities.

that are difficult; tasks that individuals can do, as well as those that groups of pupils work together to complete; jobs demanding cooperation, sharing, and planning, as well as jobs of reading, writing, and answering teachers' questions.

In a learning laboratory, where students are actively participating in the learning process, there will be a great deal of oral communication—listening to explanations, giving instructions, asking questions to clarify instructions, reporting, conversing, and discussing. A clear understanding of a purpose, before starting work, can prevent the waste of unlimited amounts of time after beginning.

Planning time is an activity that needs a generally increased emphasis in the classroom. A detailed, well-structured planning period early in the day should give each pupil a feeling of definite tasks to be accomplished throughout the day. Planning also needs to be done during the day with individuals and small groups as needs emerge. The teacher usually will conduct the planning session, but the objectives for getting work done must be defined in terms of the abilities of the pupils.

Planning requires a great deal of time and conversation. Then, pupils need to express clearly in their own words what their personal objectives are.

Informal room arrangement is essential in creating an atmosphere of a working, active laboratory. Movable desks, separation into small groups, interest centers, ongoing projects, interesting things to catch one's eye and to be observed, and freedom to talk in connection with one's work—all are an integral part of the learning laboratory.

The learning laboratory has another basic criterion. There is no minimum or maximum level of performance set as a standard for the whole group for the year. In this classroom where learning is an active, participating process, problem solving, creative thinking, memory work, and drill can be engaged in at all levels, from that of readiness for reading to generally mature reading habits with the discussion of problems of interest far above the traditional grade placement where the student is enrolled. Teachers must keep in mind that some students may be much farther advanced academically at the beginning of the year than others in the same class will be at the end of the year.

The Learning Materials Center

The solution to the problem of providing a variety of materials of instruction in the school seems to be most attainable through the learning materials center. A learning materials center housed in one central place within each separate building is a functional unit of the larger curriculum laboratory of the whole school system. A learning materials center should house the following: a good, well-stocked library; extensive audiovisual aids, maps, globes, and charts for social science and science teaching; all of the apparatus needed for extensive teaching of general science throughout the elementary or junior high school; art and industrial art materials and equipment to be drawn on loan by classrooms; music listening rooms with audio equipment; film and filmstrip viewing rooms; committee and conference rooms; and three-dimensional materials for making arithmetic meaningful.

It must be emphasized that schools without libraries place teachers in the same position as that in which any tradesperson would be without tools. There is no way to learn to read except by reading; reading can be made pleasurable to the pupils only when the choice of material fits their needs, interests, and levels of reading abilities. The school library should contain a minimum total number of volumes equal to ten times the student enrollment.

Scheduling Time for Corrective Reading

When will time be found for doing the corrective or remedial teaching with the students? The most important thing, probably, is that the teachers will save the students' time by not having them do tasks at which they will not be successful. In other words, the students will save time by not trying to do something that they cannot do anyway, thus leaving them free to do things that they can do. If they work on spelling words that are too difficult and memorize a list of words all week so that they can write them on Friday but forget them by Monday, if they sit frustrated while others complete textbook assignments, or if they sit looking at the workbook without knowing what to write on the blanks in the sentences, they are using time that they could spend doing their special assignments. In other words, if the teachers would stop the students from doing the frustrating things, that time would be saved for tasks at which they could succeed.

Very short periods should be used all day long. The teacher may take three minutes in going from one activity to another with other groups to go over a page of seatwork covering a reading lesson with an individual reader, or may save three minutes before dismissal for a brief period to summarize something, or to drill on word recognition, word attack, or vocabulary. The teacher should find five minutes to listen to the pupil read the beginning of a story orally. This will help the child become interested in the content of the story so that he or she will want to finish reading it silently. The student's assignment needs to be very specific and of the type that can be checked quickly and easily. The student should be praised for successful efforts. Peer teachers can do reading exercises with the one who needs help.

Teachers need to build, in succeeding years, an ever-greater repertoire of *creative opportunities for learning* that can be planned quickly with individuals either on the chalkboard or at their seats.

Examples of creative seatwork are:

1. "A Butchering"—(teacher to child) "You told me that your father and your uncles were going to butcher a hog last Saturday and that you were going to help. Could you write me a story that would tell me what happened? I'm sure you began early in the morning. Did it take a long time? How did you and your brother help? If you will begin writing, I'll help you put all your ideas into a good story."
2. You know that the opposite of "up" is "down." "In" is the opposite of "out." Make two columns on your paper and write all the pairs of words you can think of that are opposites. You may use the wall dictionary for spelling or ask a friend.
3. Make a seek-and-find puzzle. Put all the words for the colors in it.

The teachers will use some commercially prepared seatwork for the very disabled individuals and the very small groups that are doing corrective reading. Then, of course, they will confer with specialists whenever possible for additional suggestions.

One of the activities badly needed by most retarded readers is a great deal of *easy oral reading practice*. (Appendix B is a bibliography of appropriate books.) Listening to the children read aloud is something that other adults can do if they know the story being read and if they have empathy with the children. The listener must be genuinely interested in the content being read and must discuss it carefully with the reader. Aides, volunteer mothers, interested senior high school students, members of grandparent clubs, and the student's own peers will all be effectively used in classrooms when differentiated staffing is more clearly understood.

Good readers within the classroom can act as "helping teachers" by listening to oral reading practice of individuals or small groups. The teacher needs to exercise judgment in providing capable pupil-teachers and adequate working space so that other children's work is not disrupted.

Such a program in the regular classroom has many advantages:

1. The regular teacher, if alert, can spot problems that can be prevented or corrected at their inception. Most children whose retardation in reading stems from absence

from school, change of school, or interim environmental problems can be helped through intelligent classroom procedure. Helping the children before their difficulties become too acute can do much to lessen the number and the seriousness of the reading problems with which schools are faced today.

2. The regular teacher can plan a better balanced "all day program" to enable the students to spend more time on reading if indicated, but reading fitted to their levels of attainment.

3. The regular teacher, having an awareness of the pupils' new achievements in gaining reading power, can plan opportunities for the pupils to put their reading to use throughout the day.

4. The regular teacher is in a position to plan for some prevention and correction for all those who are working below their capacity. Many borderline or "fairly good" readers who could not be included in a special teacher's case load have minor difficulties or "gaps" in learning.

5. The regular classroom teacher can plan for children to work independently in available periods during the day. Children can also work together or help each other. Games, devices, and seatwork exercises can be used.

6. The regular classroom teacher, having considerable opportunity to know the children, their interests, aptitudes, abilities, and limitations, and to find their needs, has an opportunity to utilize the children's other abilities throughout the day, which may provide the needed stimulus, the ego satisfaction, or source material for reading lessons to raise their reader levels.

7. The regular teacher can use an abundance of vocabulary-controlled reading material in other subject areas so that the individual's reading assignments all day long fit the instructional level of reading. It is vitally important that reading be integrated with the total school curriculum. Reading is not a subject to be taught as such, but as a necessary tool to be used constantly in the learning process.

8. A contract plan between teacher and students making explicit the students' objectives for the day in behavioral terms may be useful with several members of the class or with all members for certain subjects or assignments.

9. Fifth- or sixth-grade students can be brought in to teach first-, second-, or third-grade students, under the watchful eye of the regular teachers. Some schools have arranged such opportunities on schedules like twenty minutes three times a week. The older children can listen to the younger ones practice oral reading, they can read to the younger children, or they can do word recognition exercises if the teachers are careful to make sure the words are in the younger children's sight vocabularies. Volunteer mothers, teacher aides, or high school or college students can be valuable support to teachers with large numbers of children. Classroom teachers do not have enough time to provide a sufficient amount of easy oral reading practice for the bottom 40 percent of the class. (The staggered day is another way for primary teachers to get more individual time with children. Half of the class report from 8:30 until 2:30 and the other half report from 9:30 until 3:30. Much more individualizing can go on with twelve to fifteen youngsters the first and last hour than can go on with up to thirty youngsters the remainder of the day.)

Adequate reading instruction in the schools necessitates both special teachers for clinical cases and good corrective teaching for those who will respond to proper practices in classroom remedial teaching. Attention is focused here only on specific suggestions for the classroom teachers, relative to finding time in the school day for remedial teaching.

1. Allow the children to work independently of usual reading groups for skills work in reading, spelling, and language. Excuse the children from academic assignments too difficult for them and extend their time for completing work at their own levels.
2. Start the remedial teaching at a level that is sufficiently easy to give confidence and ensure success. It is better to select material a half-year easier than necessary and build confidence than to select material above the instructional levels.
3. Make use of very short periods of time. Stop at a child's desk for two- or three-minute periods when you may be able to encourage him or her to keep on working or to see that what is being done is correct.
4. Include commercially prepared materials for worthwhile seatwork to keep the learner profitably employed while the rest of the class does something else. Some of the pupil's time should be spent in writing stories, being read to, preparing personal dictionaries or word files, illustrating stories, and working at listening-reading centers.
5. Select books with controlled vocabulary easy enough to be "fun reading" for all the children and have them read aloud to other children. If there are two or three children all reading at about the same level, they can have shared oral reading. Be sure that these books are easy enough. (See Appendix B for a list of books with controlled vocabularies.)
6. Work on the attitudes of the students and others with whom they associate to get more understanding of the problem and the need for working constructively to solve it. These may be termed psychological aspects of the problem that the teachers work on during the day as an integral part of helping all children grow and develop:
   a. Help the child to accept his or her situation.
   b. Help the child's parents to understand the situation and accept it (see chapter 13).
   c. Help the entire class to understand the many individual differences in people.
   d. Keep trying to locate causes of the difficulty and be sure to get results of vision, hearing, and physical examinations.
   e. Assume that what you try will work and then be willing to discontinue it if it does not work.

Tables 7.1 and 7.2 may be helpful in pointing up alternative ways of organizing instructional time for reading instruction. Table 7.1 suggests a plan in which the students in the class may be divided into three reading groups. Each group will spend about forty minutes in independent constructive activities so the teacher needs to plan several learning experiences that can be completed during that time. The teacher will spend the time working with each of the three groups in turn in directed reading lessons.

TABLE 7.1. Division of Time for Directed Reading Lessons in Three Reading Groups

Time Period	Group I	Group II	Group III
9:00–9:20	Exercises related to directed reading: 1. Workbooks 2. Questions on board to answer 3. Mimeographed seatwork 4. Practice reading orally in pairs or small groups 5. Draw original pictures	Free time reading activity: 1. Games 2. Seatwork exercises 3. Dramatizations 4. Library books 5. Work related to other subjects	Reading group with teacher
9:20–9:40	Free time reading activity: 1. Games 2. Seatwork exercises 3. Dramatizations 4. Library books 5. Work related to other subjects	Reading group with teacher	Exercises related to directed reading: 1. Workbooks 2. Questions on board to answer 3. Mimeographed seatwork 4. Practice reading orally in pairs or small groups 5. Draw original pictures
9:40–10:00	Reading group with teacher	Exercises related to directed reading: 1. Workbooks 2. Questions on board to answer 3. Mimeographed seatwork 4. Practice reading orally in pairs or small groups 5. Draw original pictures	Free time reading activity: 1. Games 2. Seatwork exercises 3. Dramatizations 4. Library books 5. Work related to other subjects

Table 7.2 suggests the use of small groups or committees as learning groups. These small groups may be formed on the basis of interests or other needs. The teacher will spend time with one group each day, but will also find time to observe and interact with other groups and individuals. Dated records will be made of the observations; in the records the teacher may include verbatim use of language, notations about the needs of learners, and observations of what children have learned. The record may also contain suggestions about needed changes in the learning environment, requests from children, and materials and supplies needed for the next day.

TABLE 7.2. Time Organization for Reading/Language Arts Using a Committee Structure

Time Period 9:15–10:15

Committee I	Children in this committee will be sharing stories they have read silently. The theme will have been identified earlier as "dogs." The children, of varying reading abilities, will read the stories they have chosen orally. The last twenty minutes of the committee time will be spent illustrating the stories with chalk and paper and writing a brief summary of the day's work for the teacher.
Committee II	This group of children, of varying reading abilities, will spend time with the teacher learning encyclopedia reference skills that will be needed in two weeks for a unit to be initiated in social studies. The teacher will provide a variety of experiences both in learning the new skills and in practicing them.
Committee III	These children will have a bookmaking experience. Each child, prior to this committee cycle, will have written a book to be bound. A parent, who has book binding knowledge and has planned with the teacher, will be the resource person for this group. The children will display their books at the end of the day as their "report" of the group's work.
Committee IV	This group of children will be spending their committee time in the school's microcomputer lab playing a variety of reading games. The teacher has reserved the lab for the same time each day this week so that a different group may work with the lab director on the games. The last ten minutes will be saved for the children to write a brief report about their experiences and their reaction to them. The report will be posted in their classroom.
Committee V	This group will spend their committee time reading a story and preparing to role play it later in the day for the rest of the class. A sixth-grade student will serve as the resource person for this group. As each group works on this task, the teacher will provide a different story to be prepared for presentation.
Note:	The rotations through the various committee tasks are planned to last for a week. In the beginning, to ensure success of committee work, the committees might meet for only twenty minutes. Or, the teacher may focus on one committee per day and still allow time to observe the students, to talk with individuals, and to gather data for planning future committee cycles. Each child is able to do all of the activities each week; at the end of each activity each child has some responsibility for helping the group think through and summarize the completed learning experience.

Organizing the School Day

The elementary school teachers should see the school day in terms of three types of teaching: (1) time to teach developmental skills in the three R's; (2) time for the functional application of the skills needed in unit or problem teaching in social studies, science, and health; and (3) time for the enrichment activities experienced through music, art, physical education, and literature.

Table 7.3 graphically presents such organization of time in the school day.

Using Blocks of Time

Many teachers find that breaking the school day into a few large blocks of time allows for more integration of subject matter and for more efficient use of time. One time block early in the day needs to be set aside for group planning. During this class meeting

TABLE 7.3. I. Organizing the School Day: The Elementary School Day Divides Itself into Three Main Types of Activities

Learning the Developmental *Skills: "how-to-do" skills*	*Applying* Functional *Skills: "putting skills to work" part of the school day*	*Enrichment and Appreciations*
Since tests indicate that by the time students reach fourth grade the teacher must expect the class to have a spread of abilities in reading of at least six or seven years, all teaching must be done in subgroups within the class.	This will be accomplished through the unit or problems approach in (1) social studies, and (2) science and health. With adequate materials, the teacher develops the Unit through *five* steps:	In this area, everyone participates within a heterogeneous group according to his individual skills.
Grouping will vary from one class to another, but teachers may expect to have from two to ten small groups of students occupied at developmental skills according to their present functional level of reading.	1. Orientation 2. Teacher-pupil planning 3. Gathering information 4. Sharing information 5. Culminating activity	Art and Industrial Arts Music—Theory and Applied Physical Education Literature
This block of time includes: 1. Developmental reading skills 2. Sequential development of arithmetic skills 3. Ability to spell 4. Oral and written English	A shelf of books of all levels of difficulty about the unit topic is available. Teacher-prepared study guides give students direction in learning to do research to find answers. Everyone looks for answers to questions in different sources. *No two* students need to read the same book or answer the same questions. Materials other than print will be plentiful and recognized as valid sources of learning experiences.	Reading ability is useful, but most of the teaching utilizes other avenues to learning. Or, conversely, those with little reading ability can participate effectively.
(This kind of teaching is analogous to the traditional one-teacher school that housed all eight grades of elementary school.)	Discussion, sharing ideas, and questioning will correct erroneous ideas, as well as stimulate creative thinking.	
	Making murals, viewing educational motion pictures, and summarizing will each aid learning.	

the plans for the day are developed and perhaps recorded on a chart so that they can be referred to when needed. Other, shorter planning times may be needed, but the morning planning time must not be missed. Teachers may count on the planning session as a time for the application of language skills as students listen to the teacher and one another, as they agree on a workable plan for the day, and as they record it and read it together.

The teacher may designate a large block of time in the morning for language arts. During this time, all aspects of language development—reading, writing, spelling, and

---

**Making Connections 7.1: Finding Out about
Classroom Organization for Reading**

Achieving a satisfactory organizational plan for reading in the classroom is one of the most demanding tasks for the teacher. Good plans do not *just* happen. They are planned thoughtfully and are adjusted as children's needs change.

Plan to do one of the following activities, depending on whether you are now teaching.

1. If you have not taught, gain permission from at least three teachers to interview them concerning their plans for managing reading instruction. Take rather complete notes on their responses. If you feel comfortable enough to do so, you might ask what they see as strengths of their system. You might also ask if they are thinking of possible changes, and why these changes seem important.

   Bring all your information to class to share with other class members. You should have quite a range of possible plans of organization, as well as strengths and weaknesses of them.

2. If you are teaching or have taught, write out your organizational plan for reading instruction. Pay particular attention to that part of the plan that addresses the needs of the poorer readers in the room. Ask another teacher in your building, who is willing to share with you, what his or her plan for reading instruction is like. Compare your two plans. Try to critique both plans in terms of their strengths and weaknesses.

   Plan to share the plans and your critique with class members. The group should produce quite a variety of plans, along with their accompanying critiques.

---

oral language—will receive attention. No effort is made to compartmentalize the different forms of language; instead, they are used as tools as children explore stories, write and tell their own tales, engage in drama experiences, consult references on topics of interest or ones that have been assigned, practice skills that are timely, and share experiences with one another.

Other large blocks of time may be devoted to math and science and to social studies. Some teachers design even larger time blocks in which the distinctions between these content areas and the language arts tend to blur. Such time periods are usually organized around large units designed to permit students to explore the theme at appropriate levels of difficulty without concern for information that is usually associated with particular content areas. When learning opportunities occur at many levels, the teacher has opportunities to help children with a variety of needs—those who are capable of functioning well beyond the level of most of their classmates, the bilingual and bidialectal children, those who have learning difficulties, and those with physical problems such as vision or hearing.

At the end of the day the teacher allows another time block during which children can reflect on the learning experiences that have occurred, can evaluate the plans made that morning, and can look forward to tomorrow.

Case Studies

The following three case studies are examples of how classroom teachers at different grade levels have attempted to effect a corrective reading program for students in (1) the fourth grade, (2) the eighth grade, and (3) the twelfth grade. These case descriptions show, further, that the program was made effective throughout much of the school day.

Planning Work All Day for Jimmy in the Fourth Grade

Jimmy was a nonreader at the beginning of his fourth-grade year. He could not read the arithmetic problems, do research in social studies or science, spell or write anything that could be read, or read in the lowest reading group. It was no wonder that he was a behavior problem, causing general annoyances all day long by shooting pins, throwing spitballs, and kicking girls! It was no wonder that he sat staring out the window and never seemed to be aware when the class changed from one subject to another. The reader may wonder how Jimmy passed the first three grades with this condition. The cumulative record did not show that any diagnostic reading tests had ever been administered.

There was no doubt in the fourth-grade teacher's mind that Jimmy needed attention, and although he was low in all subjects and seldom said anything, his California Test of Mental Maturity results of the year before had shown him to have normal intelligence—an I.Q. of 92.[2]

The teacher concluded that he must be able to learn to read, and she was challenged to find a way to do it. She began by observing him throughout the day. The observation showed the following: He did nothing constructive, but just sat during all activities, even art. An interest in learning anything seemed to be nonexistent. He appeared to be very uninterested in his teacher also. He never paid any attention to her directions or suggestions even when given to him individually. It was evident that his past failures had grown into a pattern of failure acceptance.

Had this child no ambition for himself? He did not seem particularly unhappy. In his home personal development and ambition were apparently not greatly stimulated. His father was a laborer; a brother who recently graduated from high school was staying at home and was unemployed. Jimmy had one school friend, a very poor student in another fourth grade in the school. When together, they were constantly in mischief.

At the beginning of the fourth-grade year, Jimmy's teacher gave several informal reading tests to determine Jimmy's reading level—what he knew, what his difficulties were, and where to begin his instruction. He knew thirty-six Dolch Basic Sight Words. He failed to identify some of the initial consonant sounds and knew only a few blends. He had not learned hard and soft sounds of *c* and *g*. He could not write in cursive writing or spell. This evidence indicated definitely that any scores recorded on standardized reading tests were meaningless. To determine what reader he could read as his instructional level (that is, with 95 percent accuracy in mechanics and 75 percent comprehension as determined by answers to questions asked by the teacher), he attempted a preprimer. He made too many errors. The instructional level at which he would progress best in learning to read would be at the beginning of a reading series—a first preprimer.

His capacity level for reading, determined by the Bond-Tinker formula (number of years in school $\times$ I.Q. $+ 1.0$),[3] was the seventh month of third grade (3.7) [(3 $\times$ .92 $+ 1.0 = 3.76$)].

In summary, the fourth-grade teacher was faced with a nonreader, with normal intelligence, no foreign language handicap, a potential behavior problem, and a very passive attitude toward reading.

Accepting this challenging problem, the teacher:

1. Went back willingly and ungrudgingly to this child's level. She found very easy library books, since Jimmy resented the idea of reading preprimers.
2. Removed *competition* with other fourth graders and initiated a system of rewards for improvements he made on his past records.
3. Removed all pressure of trying to get "grade-level work" out of the child at any time during the day.
4. Initiated and taught an individualized program in "how-to-read."
5. Provided kinds of activities the child could do throughout the entire day.
6. Located a great variety of materials that would interest the child and that could be completed and checked while the room activity continued for the thirty-three other youngsters.
7. Continued looking for *reasons why* the child failed in reading, but began reteaching without wasting any time, making sure that the child's reading was successful this time.

The teacher began by trying to do all these things. In the beginning, she gained his confidence and cooperation, found it quite easy to find two or three minutes at different times during the day to stop by his desk to see if his worksheets, writing exercises, or matching games were being done correctly.

The teacher's day was so organized that she had a thirty-minute work period for the class during the morning that all children used for "catch-up" time, free reading, or study. Jimmy could always be checked on during this period. This time period also provided a much-needed opportunity for the teacher to conference with any of her thirty-four students, to check on knowledge of basic sight words, to sample a new book where the level of difficulty was questionable, or to discuss other little problems that arose.

Jimmy's day was organized, eventually, to follow a schedule somewhat like this: He arrived at school with his morning studies already planned the previous afternoon; he read orally to another fourth-grade child for twenty minutes; he reviewed his growing file of sight vocabulary cards; he did seatwork exercises related to the oral reading he had just completed and to his word file; he wrote simple sentences and stories and on occasion a simple "book." Then he worked on the classroom microcomputer using the Houghton Mifflin Microcourse, "A Comprehensive Skills Program—Reading.[4] Initially, he worked with the software on word attack skills. He became the classroom *expert* on the operation of the microcomputer; he was able to help other students "boot it up" and could explain how to handle the floppy discs so they would not become damaged. Occasionally, he completed some of the Hegge-Kirk-Kirk *Remedial Reading Drills.*[5] Jimmy had been doing a great deal of sound-tracing, based on what his teacher had read about the Fernald Method[6] and the Harris Visual-Motor Method.[7]

In arithmetic, where Jimmy was also achieving at a very low level, he was in a group of six children who constituted a separate class within the room.

Social studies was more difficult to encompass. He saw movies, went on a field trip, and was included in the total group during the teacher-pupil planning sessions. He drew a fairly detailed map (from copy) that was used on the bulletin board; he collected pictures (from copies of *Saturday Evening Post, Look, Life, National Geographic, Time,* and *Newsweek* magazines provided by the teacher); he made a scrapbook, and the teacher wrote brief explanations for him to read from context. On two occasions, a capable fourth-grade girl wrote summaries that were typed by the teacher and given to Jimmy for reading material. When studying about Mexico, Jimmy read an easy picture book to a reading partner after he had sampled it with the teacher.

Science is possible for fourth-grade children without relying primarily on reading. Jimmy gathered lists of needed equipment for science experiments. He did an experiment with an empty tin can with a screw-type lid that was placed on a hot plate with some water in it. The following story of what happened was carefully planned with Jimmy and made possible his reading about the experiment. He carefully typed the story using the word processing program on the classroom microcomputer.

Air Pressure

Here is a can.
We put water in the can.
Then we put the can on the stove.
The water boiled.
Steam came out.
Steam pushed some of the air out.
We put the lid on the can.
Then we took the can off the stove.
The can cooled.
Now, there is little air inside the can.
The can collapses.
The air outside pushes in the sides of the can.

Jimmy
November 6, 19. . . .

Jimmy's teacher made him feel that he was a needed and wanted member of the class and, at the same time, provided activities for him that were instructional and interesting.

There are many games and devices that the teacher can have available. As time permits, one child who knows a game well can play it with one or more other children who need the practice. Jimmy learned to play *Take*,[8] matching *initial* sounds. He learned to play both *Go-Fish,* beginning sounds, and *Go-Fish,* blends.[9] He learned to play *Phonetic Quizmo*,[10] *Bingo*[11] using Dolch Basic Sight Words, and *Bingo*[12] using phrase cards based on phrases he learned to recognize quickly. He used short flashcard drills on words the teacher was anxious to habituate in game situations with another child.

Reading games, as such, are of value only if they are teaching children a skill or ability. Lots of easy reading practice is of more value if the child is interested in reading independently as quickly as possible. By the time the fourth-grade year was half over, Jimmy had read twenty easy, predictable books to another child or to someone in the family. He then was quite proud of himself because his teacher entered the title of each book on the class's reading chart showing the number of books read. His twenty books showed his rocket approaching the moon far ahead of many other children in the room (see figure 7.2).

The teacher recognized the importance of Jimmy's learning as quickly as possible the 220 Dolch Basic Sight Word List so that he would know the commonest service words in children's reading. During the semester, he improved in his ability to recall these. In September, he knew 36; on November 1, he knew 60; on January 15, he knew 85; and in February, 110. His graph of progress continued throughout the year. Jimmy's teacher reinforced his progress by using visuals such as bar graphs.

The teacher gained confidence in her ability to keep Jimmy progressing. She felt that her entire array of teaching skills was improving by experimenting with new ways of meeting individual needs. Jimmy was doing well at primer level by midyear. His attitudes had improved to the point where he did his work without prompting; he gained confidence in his teacher's interest in helping him. He seemed to feel that he had become a genuine working member of the class and worked and played better with the other children.

The teacher found that Jimmy's mother was most willing to listen to him read at home those things that he had already read at school. In a home visit, the teacher explained to the mother that Jimmy did have normal intelligence (a happy relief for parents, always), but that he could not read and would need to start from the beginning in the reading process. The mother volunteered that perhaps Jimmy needed a physical examination to see if there were any reasons why he was somewhat listless and indifferent. The teacher emphasized the need for such an examination and encouraged the mother to make an appointment right away. The teacher took time to send the mother short informal notes to tell her when Jimmy had done something especially well on a given day. The mother needed this encouragement as much as Jimmy did.

Peter, an Eighth Grader

Pete was an easy-going fifteen-year-old in the eighth grade. He got along smoothly and graciously with his peers.

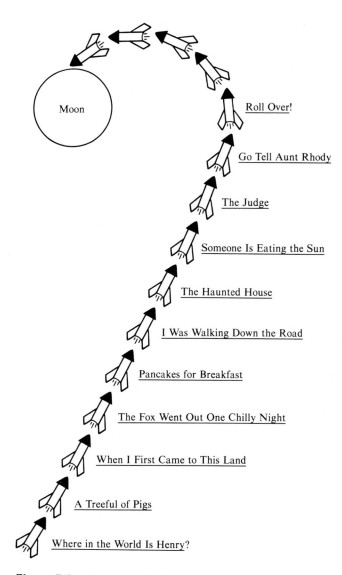

Moon

Roll Over!

Go Tell Aunt Rhody

The Judge

Someone Is Eating the Sun

The Haunted House

I Was Walking Down the Road

Pancakes for Breakfast

The Fox Went Out One Chilly Night

When I First Came to This Land

A Treeful of Pigs

Where in the World Is Henry?

Figure 7.2. Jimmy's rocket moves closer to the moon by using predictable books.

Pete's cumulative folder indicated that most of his previous teachers had labeled him as a "lazy" boy who took no interest in his work. (The reading teacher knew that there is no such thing as a "lazy" boy, but boys who, for reasons that need investigation, act in such a way that teachers call them "lazy.")

Pete had repeated two grades, the third and the fifth, and seemed to be getting nowhere after he entered junior high school. Several other boys had dropped out of school as soon as they had become sixteen, so the fact that Pete was interested in learning, attended school regularly, and responded intelligently in his general behavior prompted his reading teacher to offer needed extra help.

Pete was *bilingual.* He spoke Spanish a great deal outside of school. Because his parents relied almost entirely on Spanish for communication, Peter probably did his thinking in Spanish. Because he had never learned to read and write Spanish, however, he was severely limited in the amount of Spanish he knew. His Spanish vocabulary was limited to meeting the needs of satisfying casual conversation and understanding work assignments around the house. Because Pete never learned to read English well and had little comprehension of what he did in English, he might be thought of more correctly as *nonlingual* than bilingual in terms of the language performance expected by the school.

Pete's intelligence had been tested with a group intelligence test and was recorded in his cumulative folder as an I.Q. of 82. But the teacher had read that I.Q. scores on a group intelligence test earned by the bottom 40 percent of the class are entirely unreliable.[13] In addition, Pete had a language handicap, so the I.Q. score was of little help in his case.

Pete was able to pronounce many words if given enough time to analyze them, but he could not supply meanings for them. When the teacher showed interest in helping Pete, he asked for almost constant help, and the short assignments or instructions needed to be repeated many times.

When a hearing problem was suspected, Pete was referred to the school nurse who said that, even though she found a very slight loss in one ear, it was not to be considered serious enough to affect his school work.

When the teacher tested from a series of readers for Pete's instructional level of reading, he read the words well enough at the fifth-grade level, but he could not answer questions to indicate comprehension of ideas until he read from the second level, third reader.

Pete knew all the 220 Dolch Basic Sight Words, although he made half a dozen substitutions, which he corrected himself. He was given the Inventory of Phonic Skills, Level 3, and had no difficulty except for a few vowel errors.

The reading teacher was also Pete's general science teacher for one period every day. In eighth-grade reading class, SRA Laboratories were used three days a week, and the teacher was able to call Pete to her classroom when she had her "free" period on some days. In addition, by talking with several of his teachers and the school principal, she was able to exercise considerable influence over much of Pete's school day. His program evolved in a pattern somewhat as follows:

1. The teacher called Pete to her room three days a week during her free period and used this time for administering tests—the Woodcock Reading Mastery Tests,[14] vocabulary tests she designed for measuring his ability with multiple meanings of common words, synonyms, homonyms, antonyms, prepositions, and oral reading abilities. Much of the need here proved to be that of teaching a much broader knowledge of English as a second language.
2. The reading teacher arranged for Pete to use the *Reading for Understanding, SRA Laboratory,*[15] rather than the graded series of laboratories. He needed to start with

the lowest level to be sure that he could read and could always get meaning in context. The record of his SRA work was kept on graphs in his Student Record Book.

3. The teacher planned carefully for Pete to do work closely related to each chapter in the eighth grade science book which was her guide for subject matter material to be covered. The teacher found reading materials in third-, fourth-, and fifth-grade science books related to the topics being discussed in class. She then prepared questions, always easy at first, such as filling in blanks, matching words with definitions, making lists of terms, giving reasons "why" when clearly stated in easy books. She made sure Pete had opportunities for first-hand experiences with concepts that seemed unfamiliar to him. In this way, Pete was able to answer seatwork exercises just like the other students in the class.

4. Since Pete needed help primarily with story problems in arithmetic, the mathematics teacher was willing, *after he was alerted,* to assign Pete to work with a cooperative partner when such problems were to be read and worked, either as silent seatwork or as a group work assignment in class.

   The history teacher learned that the *Children's Catalog*[16] and the *Standard Catalog for High School Libraries*[17] were invaluable for searching out books on specific topics related to all the units in American history. A few books and many stories in readers or in nonfiction collections were available on a third-to-fourth-grade reader level.

5. The first book that Pete read for "fun reading" was *Secret Island,*[18] followed by *Rescue*[19] and *Flying to the Moon.*[20] Each was read with the teacher. Pete particularly liked the books because they contained many suggestions of related activities that extended the ideas and made words more meaningful. He then read *2-B and the Rock 'n Roll Band,*[21] which he enjoyed so much that he obtained permission to read it to both the second- and third-grade boys. Reading *The Missing Aircraft*[22] was a more difficult task, since the reading level was higher and the ideas were more complex. He persisted, however, and his reading improved noticeably as he read through the book.

George, a Twelfth Grader

George, nineteen years old, lived with his mother and three brothers and was a senior in high school. In spite of a severe reading disability all through school, he had expressed an ambition to go to college, to major in physical education, and to become an athletic trainer. Cultural deprivation offers at least a partial explanation for George's meager vocabulary and limited experience. His physical examination revealed no visual, auditory, or neurological handicapping conditions.

George asked for remedial instruction in reading when he learned that one of his teachers was enrolled in a corrective reading class and needed a "case" to work with for a semester.

George had been given an intelligence test, but because it had been a group intelligence test involving reading, the teacher suspected that the recorded IQ score of 82 was entirely unreliable.

When the 220 Dolch Basic Sight Word Test was administered as a recall test, George made thirty-three mistakes, many of which were middle-vowel substitutions. George was given the Inventory of Phonic Skills, Level Three[23] and he made many errors in Subsection D, Vowels. He was not aware of roots, prefixes, and suffixes as clues to word pronunciations, and he did not know their separate meanings. He placed fifth-grade level in the placement test of the Reading for Understanding, SRA Laboratory.

As a measure of George's capacity level for reading, the teacher found that he understood the material in the twelfth-grade textbooks quite well when the teacher read it aloud to him.

Early in the semester, George was selected to complete a special short training course as the athletic trainer to help the high school coach. He completed the course and demonstrated aptitude for successfully carrying out this assignment. The teacher found a book called *Treatment and Prevention of Athletic Injuries,*[24] which contained many illustrations and elementary reading. With some help, George succeeded in reading this book. He was highly motivated, and he reread and explained the text to the remedial reading teacher. George then read *Baseball Bonus Kid*[25] in the *Signal Book Series* independently. He also enjoyed books from the *Sportellers Series,* especially *Strike Two*[26] and *Foul Play.*[27]

The high school teaching staff gave its complete cooperation to help George successfully carry out his remedial program. When staff personnel who were George's teachers were informed about his reading problems and his level of aspiration, they were very willing to use suggestions for carrying out helpful lessons in their respective subjects. George's first period in the day was spent in supervised study. His remedial teacher kept this study hall so the period was utilized in checking on the worksheets done the previous day in all classes, and in making plans about what George would do that day. He usually read orally fifteen minutes of this first period from one of the *Teen-Age Tales* books.[28] Special arrangements were made for George during his English period. He did exercises with such useful materials as *Vocabulary Building Exercises for the Young Adult*[29] and the *TR Reading Comprehension Series.*[30]

The reading teacher recognized the great need for expanding George's English vocabulary, and she prepared many exercises involving idiomatic and slang expressions, multiple meanings of common words, synonyms, homonyms, antonyms, fifty common prepositions in the English language, and figures of speech.

Summary

In this chapter an attempt has been made to alleviate any anxiety the teachers may feel about permitting the students to do the work they can do rather than forcing them to continue with work that is too difficult. The teachers must understand the place of the course of study in teaching and must have adequate materials available in order to convert the classroom into a learning laboratory. Reports of classroom teachers demonstrate that by faculty cooperation it is possible to help students at elementary, middle school, and senior high school levels begin to overcome their reading disabilities.

Making Connections 7.2: Making a Case Study of a Poor Reader

After your instructor has identified some classrooms in which active plans are made and carried out for the poorer readers, arrange with one of the teachers to complete a case study on a student using the case studies in this chapter as models. Try to focus on how instruction is being individualized or modified, what materials and instructional strategies are being used, test results that suggest the need for the plan and its effectiveness, and any other aspects of the school experience that relate directly to the efforts to improve the student's reading.

When the case studies are finished, your instructor may arrange an opportunity for class members to share their findings.

Note: It is important to preserve the privacy of the student. Real names and other identifying information should be altered to protect the student.

For Further Reading

Dechant, Emerald. *Teacher's Directory of Reading Skill Aids and Materials.* West Nyack N.Y.: Parker Publishing Co., 1981.

Gamby, Gert. "Talking Books and Taped Books: Materials for Instruction." *The Reading Teacher* 36 (January 1983), pp. 366–69.

Griffin, Peg. "How and When Does Reading Occur in the Classroom?" *Theory into Practice* 16 (December 1977), pp. 376–83.

Lapp, Diane, and Flood, James. *Teaching Reading to Every Child,* 2d ed. New York: Macmillan, 1983: Chapter 13, "Developing and Managing Your Reading Program," pp. 461–86.

Loughlin, Catherine, and Suina, Joseph. *The Learning Environment: An Instructional Strategy* New York: Teachers College, Columbia University, 1982.

Nevi, Charles N. "Cross-age Tutoring: Why Does It Help the Tutors?" *The Reading Teacher* 36 (May 1983), pp. 892–98.

Tompkins, Gail E., and Webeler, Mary Beth. "What Will Happen Next? Using Predictable Books with Young Children." *The Reading Teacher* 36 (February 1983), pp. 498–501.

Rubin, Dorothy. *A Practical Approach to Teaching Reading.* New York: Holt, Rinehart and Winston, 1982: Chapter 13: "Organizing for Reading in the Classroom," pp. 319–41.

Notes

1. The center pages of any issue of *The Web* published by the Ohio State University Press provide examples of webs organized around themes and emphasizing the use of children's books.
2. Vision and hearing checks were normal.

3. Guy L. Bond, Miles A. Tinker, Barbara B. Wasson, and John B. Wasson, *Reading Difficulties: Their Diagnosis and Correction,* 5th ed. (Englewood Cliffs, N.J.: Prentice-Hall, 1984), p. 43.

4. Houghton Mifflin Minicourse, *A Comprehensive Skills Program—Reading* (Hanover, N.H.: Houghton Mifflin, 1984).

5. T. Hegge, S. Kirk, and W. Kirk, *Remedial Reading Drills* (Ann Arbor, Mich.: George Wahr Publishers, 1955).

6. Grace Fernald, *Remedial Techniques in Basic School Subjects* (New York: McGraw-Hill, 1971), pp. 21–82.

7. Albert J. Harris and Edward R. Sipay, *How to Increase Reading Ability,* 7th ed. (New York: Longman, 1980), pp. 409–11.

8. *Take* (Champaign, Ill.: The Garrard Press).

9. *Go-Fish* (Washington, D.C.: Remedial Education Center).

10. *Phonetic Quizmo* (Springfield, Mass.: Milton Bradley Co.).

11. *Group Word Teaching Game* (Champaign, Ill.: The Garrard Press).

12. Modeled after *Group Word Teaching Game.*

13. Bond, Tinker, Wasson, and Wasson, *Reading Difficulties,* p. 41.

14. R. Woodcock, *Woodcock Reading Mastery Tests* (Circle Pines, Minn.: American Guidance Service, 1973).

15. *Reading for Understanding, SRA Laboratory* (Chicago: Science Research Associates, Inc.).

16. *Children's Catalog,* 14th ed. (New York: H. W. Wilson Co., 1981).

17. *Standard Catalog for High School Libraries,* 11th ed. (New York: H. W. Wilson Co., 1977).

18. Edward Ramsbottom and Joan Redmayne, *Secret Island* (Cleveland: Modern Curriculum Press, 1983).

19. ———, *Rescue* (Cleveland: Modern Curriculum Press, 1983).

20. Edward Ramsbottom and Joan Redmayne, *Flying to the Moon* (Cleveland: Modern Curriculum Press, 1983).

21. Sherry Paul and Bob Miller, *2-B and the Rock 'n Roll Band* (Cleveland: Modern Curriculum Press, 1981).

22. Ben Butterworth and Bill Stockdale, *The Missing Aircraft* (Belmont, Calif.: Pitman Learning, 1977). A book from the Jim Hunter Series.

23. *The Inventories of Phonic Skills,* Levels One, Two, and Three (Boston: Houghton Mifflin, 1972).

24. Joseph P. Dolan, *Treatment and Prevention of Athletic Injuries* (Danville, Ill.: The Interstate, 1955).

25. Steve Gelman, *Baseball Bonus Kid* (Garden City, N.Y.: Doubleday, 1961).

26. George Shea, *Strike Two* (Belmont, Calif.: Pitman Learning, 1981).

27. Dick O'Connor, *Foul Play* (Belmont, Calif.: Pitman Learning, 1981).

28. *Teen-Age Tales,* Levels A, B, 1–6 (Boston: D. C. Heath).

29. Dorothy McCarr, *Vocabulary Building Exercises for the Young Adult* (Beaverton, Oreg.: Dormac, Inc., 1983).

30. *TR Reading Comprehension Series* (Hingham, Mass.: Teaching Resources, 1983).

8
Planning Work with the Underachieving Student

Vocabulary

corrective instruction
drill
graded readers
high-interest, low-
    vocabulary books
trade books
predictable books
systems approaches
readability graph
behavioral objective
lesson plan
summary report
simultaneous oral spelling

Questions

1. What are the important guidelines to remember about the use of drill?

2. How might high-interest, low-vocabulary books and trade books be used successfully with disabled readers?

3. What are some important criteria for the successful use of the microcomputer in the classroom?

4. Describe how Fry's Readability Graph works as a predictor of reading difficulty.

5. What criteria distinguish behavioral objectives from nonbehavioral ones?

6. Why are lesson planning and recordkeeping so important to the instruction of disabled readers?

7. What are the important guidelines for planning the student's time at school?

If the teachers administer informal tests as presented in chapters 3 and 4, they will have determined the present functional level of reading of the disabled readers. The first cardinal principle in helping these students is to go back to where they are in learning sequential, developmental skills in reading. This must be a sufficiently easy level in order to establish security and to build confidence. The students' instructional work for the entire day must be planned at this level.

Three aspects of the problem of working with the poor reader will be discussed. They are: (1) managing the corrective instruction from the teacher's point of view; (2) materials of instruction for accomplishing these reading activities; and (3) planning with the disabled reader to use the time wisely throughout the school day.

Managing Corrective Instruction

Managing corrective instruction in the classroom is dependent primarily upon the teacher's abilities and willingness to convince the students that the work they are going to do together is important, worthwhile, and well regarded. This, of course, includes convincing the student that the teacher can successfully teach him or her how to read.

In planning time for instruction, the corrective reading class *must* be a part of the regular school day, just as all other reading instruction is given during the regular working day. It should not embarrass the child or substitute for enjoyable activities like recess and physical education. On the other hand, it should be done in such a way as to alleviate anxiety and should not be hurried or seem to be "just squeezed into" the day's work. It will be apparent that the attitude of the teacher and the total climate of the classroom are basic ingredients in managing this learning situation effectively. The child must sense that *it is all right to be different.* This is not because one or two children in the room are "special," but because every individual is different. Many interesting activities and individual assignments *must* teach the child that all the children in one classroom do not do the *same* things in the *same* amount of time with the *same* amount of practice.

If the basic principles of corrective instruction are followed, the great majority of underachievers will improve in reading ability under the tutelage of the classroom teacher.

Use of Drill

Some teachers who have tried to do corrective reading with children have assumed that *what the children needed was drill and more drill.* They have used the same general method and have employed the same materials and have aimed at the same goal as in their regular class teaching. The results of relying upon more drill and nothing but more drill have usually been disappointing. This is not to say that there in no place for drill, but *effective drill is never mere repetition;* drill is effective only when there is *understanding* of what is being drilled and where the *learners see need and purpose for the drill.*

Effective drill is repetition where the conditions of learning have been considered and are appropriate. Some of these conditions of learning are:

1. Practice periods should be short and spirited.
2. Drill should be individualized and *at the point of error*. This means that the drill for children who cannot succeed very well is different from that for children who succeed very well, and the topic that they drill on is that which they missed.
3. Drill should involve the use of ideas and, in reading, should use context. The first grade teacher teaching the sight word *said* calls attention to the word in meaningful context in the sentences of a dictated story. Each sentence changes only slightly from the sentences just preceding it. By turns, several children read the story of their recent cooking experience.

    Rubin *said,* "Put in the flour."
    Jean *said,* "Put in the salt."
    Jamie *said,* "Put in the baking powder."
    Coleen *said,* "Now, put in the shortening."
    Everybody *said,* "Yum, yum, good!"

    The drill is in context with respect to the word *said,* and the pupils should be thinking as they read.
4. Practice must be motivated. Too many motives in school are artificial. Learners work for grades. Reading teachers are competing for the pupils' interest, which may be centered in many other activities at school. For young children, immediate goals are much better than distant goals. They need to experience success. Marks that signify *hope* rather than *despair* ought to be given, especially to the poorest in the class. If the children are to keep on working, they must feel that they are successful; otherwise they have no reason to continue to work.
5. Knowledge of results helps the students to define *success and failure for them*. Immediate knowledge of results will help them to know whether they are succeeding. Success is rewarding. Success brings personal satisfaction; with failure, the mere fact of having failed is in itself a form of punishment.

Drill, based on these criteria, will be very useful in corrective reading.

Use of Games and Devices

If children are going to play games, there are three criteria to keep in mind:

1. The primary emphasis must be on *learning a skill* needed in reading. In the case of *vowel domino,* every time the child plays a domino, a decision identifying the short vowel sound is made.[1]
2. The *mechanics of the game* must not be such that little time is spent on learning the skill needed in reading. In other words, if the child bounces a ball each time he or she says a word and gets much more interested in bouncing the ball than in saying the word, perhaps that game should be discarded.

3. The *fun of the game should center around the reading skill* rather than being something that the child enjoys apart from reading. In other words, the thing rewarded must be the learning of a reading skill. In playing *Go-Fish,* winning the largest number of books so as to win the game is the reward. In order to win each book of three cards alike, however, the child is practicing "hearing" the initial sound.[2]

Commercially prepared devices, homemade games, and work exercises that can be prepared by the teachers to be used over and over and that meet these criteria should be collected and filed in materials centers of all elementary schools.

Many games are available commercially through textbook publishing companies, variety stores, department stores, and drug stores. Some are more useful than others, although all teachers must make their evaluations and try to build up a stock of games that can be used by small groups or individuals during unsupervised work periods within the school day. The following list is only illustrative of those known to the authors.

1. *Alphabet Acrobatics* (Sullivan Associates, Palo Alto, Calif., 1972). The kit provides a big book showing children how to make their bodies look like letter shapes. It emphasizes the role of motor learning in learning to read.
2. E. W. Dolch, *Word Learning Games* (Champaign, Ill.: The Garrard Publishing Co.). Games available include: *Phonic Lotto, Group Word Teaching Game, Group Sounding Game, Take, The Syllable Game,* and *What the Letters Say.* Two consumable booklets are available in which children can practice recognizing the Dolch words in short sentences. The booklets may be cut up, laminated, and used in learning centers as permanent learning materials.
3. *Gold Cup Games* (Bomar, 622 Rodier Drive, Glendale, Calif. 91201, 1972). The games are independent activities in which up to six children can participate at one time. The purpose is to reinforce reading and language skills. Individual games are entitled *Horse Trail Ride, Bicycle Rally, Motor Cycle Motocross,* and *Dune Buggy Rally.*
4. Lift-up puzzle games (The Child's World, Elgin, Ill., 1972). These little puzzle booklets are in three series: *Guess Who, What and Where,* and *What and Which.* The individual puzzle booklets in the *What and Where* series are *What Belongs Where, What's Part of What, What Goes with What,* and *Going Through the Tunnel.*
5. *Little Brown Bear* (Learning Associates, Inc., P.O. Box 561167, Miami, Florida 33156). Publishes a variety of games aimed at improving decoding skills. One of the games is *Tick-Tack-Go,* a vowel game. Some games give practice with the skills taught in related books.
6. Milton Bradley Company, 43 Cross Street, Springfield, Mass. 01103. Games include *Picture Word Builder, Sentence Builder, Phonic Drill Cards, Phonetic Quizmo, Dial 'n Spell, Concentration,* and *Vowel Wheels.*
7. *Monster Hunt* (Allied Educational Council, Distribution Center, Box 78, Galien, Mich. 49113). *Monster Hunt* assesses ten levels of phonic or structural abilities: beginning consonants, short vowels, consonant clusters, long vowels and final *e,*

long vowel digraphs, reinfluenced vowels, irregular double vowels and diphthongs, syllabication, prefixes, suffixes, and affixes.

8. *The New Phonics We Use Learning Games Kits* (Chicago: Rand McNally). Kit one—ten supplementary, small-group learning games—primary grades; kit two—ten supplementary games adding some more difficult phonic skills—intermediate grades. The kits must be purchased in their entirety, which makes them very expensive. If the kit can be housed in the school learning center and made available to many teachers, the purchase may be worthwhile.

9. Parker and Sons Publishing Co., 241 E. Fourth St., Los Angeles, Calif. 90013. Games include: *Spill 'n Spell,* and *Play 'n Talk.*

10. *Reading Laboratory 1: Word Games* (Chicago: Science Research Associates, Inc.). Contains 44 word games, a Phonics Survey Test, a pupil's workbook, teacher's guide, and progress tests.

11. *Reading Wheel: Consonants and Vowels* (Teaching Resources Corp., Boston, Mass., 1974). An attractive version of the phonics wheel using pictures and individual words provides an activity for one or two children at a time with each wheel.

12. The Remedial Education Press (Kingsbury Center, 2138 Bancroft Place, N.W., Washington, D.C. 20008). The games are: *Go-Fish, Series 1* and *Go-Fish, Series 2, Vowel Dominoes, Build It,* and *Affixo.*

13. *Sullivan Reading Games* (Palo Alto, California: Behavioral Research Laboratories). The games reinforce the decoding concepts taught in the Sullivan Reading Program. The ten games are available only as a set. Again, if the box is housed in the school learning center where it is available to many teachers, the purchase may be worthwhile.

14. Teach Key Reading and Spelling (Box 9905, St. Paul, Minn.) *Teach Key:* four volumes, each containing twenty-four colorful word and picture cards.

Use of Graded Series of Readers with Teacher's Manuals and Workbooks

These readers should be a series not used in any previous grade for regular group instruction. In some cases, the underachieving reader has experienced failure with the usual texts to the point where he or she can no longer be motivated to want to read them. In such instances, other approaches should be used. For the majority, however, the graded series of readers provides the teacher with well-planned, sequentially developed materials for building all the missing word recognition skills. If the teacher's demeanor has been persuasive and optimistic, and the child is convinced that he or she is going to learn to read, beginning at the instructional level in a series of readers and making progress as fast as possible may be the most satisfactory way for the busy classroom teacher to proceed. Much excellent, usable material is available to the teacher in the teacher's manuals and the workbooks that accompany the readers.

Teachers are constantly needing sources of reading material with a controlled vocabulary load and of interest to older children. With these sources, when motivation based on interest is present, limited reading power will not preclude getting the material read. Appendix B wil be useful for finding materials.

Publishing companies make detailed teacher's manuals available for their texts. These manuals should be studied carefully when the corresponding reader is being taught. Teacher's manuals are as completely detailed as manuals of directions that explain how to put a toy together or how to do a do-it-yourself job. While teacher's manuals need not be adhered to inflexibly, they contain a myriad of suggestions for teaching the directed reading lesson with all its follow-up. These manuals contain a great deal of information for the teacher about the philosophy of the reading series—the "why" of the methodology employed. They provide many suggestions to the teacher for taking care of individual differences within groups and for extra teaching of any missing skills. Building concepts is provided for in the sequential development of sight vocabulary, and through suggestions for teaching what a particular word means in a stated context.

Use of Reading Materials with a High Interest Level but Low Vocabulary Level

Many series of readers that are not prepared as basic readers are now on the market. The severely controlled vocabularies of these books make them much more usable with underachievers than many books one might choose from library shelves to fit children's reading abilities. A detailed bibliography of such series of specially prepared materials will be found by individual titles in Appendix B.

Use of Trade Books

A careful inspection of the school's library shelves will reveal a collection of books that have been written with young readers or disabled readers in mind. Some of these books are in series and are identified as the "easy" books about various topics. The vocabulary is usually kept simple, and the sentences are short. Frequently, good pictures instead of new or difficult vocabulary serve to clarify concepts the authors want to introduce.

Teachers will find that a growing number of trade books are now sold along with taped readings of the stories. Sometimes four or more copies of the book are packaged with the tape. Children may listen to the tape of a story and follow in the book. After hearing the tape several times, they may be able to read along with the tape. Teachers may use listening centers for this activity; the children wear head sets and listen to the story without disturbing the rest of the class.

Predictable books[3] are a special group of trade books that are easy to read because the structure of the text makes the words highly predictable. Careful examination of a variety of trade books will yield quite a collection of predictable books. Once such a book has been read with the child, it is likely that the child can then read the book alone. A few predictable books are listed here. Others can be identified by the school librarian.

Cameron, Polly. *I Can't Said the Ant*. Coward, McCann and Geoghegan, 1961.
Emberly, Barbara, and Emberly, Ed. *One Wide River to Cross*. Scholastic Press, 1966.
Gàg, Wanda. *Millions of Cats*. Coward, 1928.

Making Connections 8.1: Getting Children and Trade Books Together

Teachers are finding more and more ways to use trade books (library books) in their reading programs. Two particularly useful categories of trade books for children with reading problems are the high-interest, low-vocabulary books and the predictable books. Work with your instructor in planning to carry out one of the experiences described below.

1. Using references in this chapter and in Appendix B or suggestions from your instructor, identify and locate at least three high-interest, low-vocabulary books. Evaluate the books carefully. Check to see how all are alike and how they differ. Make a list of what you see as strengths and weaknesses of each book. Then select one that you can share with a child. You may take turns reading the book, the child may do all the reading, or you may do most of the reading. What you do will depend largely on the reading ability of the child with whom you work. You may find that the child's comments and questions, if carefully recorded, will provide you with special insights. Share your evaluations of the high-interest, low-vocabulary books you examined. Also plan to share with peers your experience in reading one book with a child.

2. This chapter lists some predictable books. Your instructor or a librarian can help you identify many more titles. Examine several of these books to draw your own conclusions about their predictable language. Plan to share the books and your conclusions with class members. Before the time set for sharing, read one of the books with a child. Note carefully how or if the child identifies the predictable nature of the language. Observe what happens when you read the story together. Does the child then try to read the book alone? Does the child preserve the meaning (if not the actual language) of the author? During the time you share this experience with your class, discuss the experience of reading a predictable book with a child, as well as your observations of several predictable books.

Higgins, Don. *Papa's Going to Buy Me a Mockingbird.* Seabury Press, 1968.
Joslin, Sesyle. *What Did You Say Dear?* Scholastic Press, 1958.
Martin, Bill. *Brown Bear, Brown Bear, What Do You See?* Holt, Rinehart and Winston, 1967.
Martin, Bill, *Instant Readers.* Holt, Rinehart and Winston, 1970. (Series)
Martin, Bill. *Sounds of Language.* Holt, Rinehart and Winston, 1966. (Series)

Use of Microcomputers

As the teacher organizes the classroom, plans must be developed for the use of the recent teaching tool, the microcomputer. Hopefully, the daily schedule will be developed in such a way that every child will have opportunities to have experiences with

David Woodward

Teachers who are concerned about providing children with more opportunities for book experiences than the teacher can manage welcome community persons who volunteer to read to children.

a variety of programs. Much computer time should be spent with simulation and word processing programs. However, the teacher may find that some "skill and drill" programs may be helpful.[4]

A careful evaluation of any microcomputer program should be made before it is introduced into the classroom. The teacher may find that not all programs are suitable for all students. Some of the criteria that might be used to evaluate programs are:

1. Is this the most effective way to teach this particular skill or concept?
2. Does the program encourage a variety of responses?
3. How much teaching is required before the child can work independently?
4. How legible and readable is the print on the screen?
5. Does the computer experience encourage the child to continue learning about the subject in other ways?
6. Is there a recordkeeping system so that the teacher knows what the child has accomplished?[5]

Use of Systems Approaches to Teach Reading Subskills

Checklists of reading skills to be mastered to ensure that all students develop mature reading habits became commonplace during the 1970s. Administrators sometimes hold high hopes that if teachers teach and test all the skills sufficiently, their school reading deficiencies will somehow be removed. Because of this, long lists of skills, outlined in minutely detailed subskills, are prepared so that teachers can complete checklists of all the skills mastered, taught but not mastered, and not yet learned. There are many educators who would question whether we have a sequenced hierarchy of skills that can be defended as the one most likely to produce successful readers. And there are even more educators who seriously question the value of placing relentless effort on mastering subskills at the expense of many other facets of the total reading program. For these reasons, there may be some doubt as to the value of identifying 275 skills or 435 skills that must be taught to complete a commercial reading system.

Diagnostic prescriptive reading programs designed to teach the necessary skills for competent reading appeared in some profusion on the market in the 1960s and 70s. They provided preassessment tests and lessons to teach to all student's weaknesses, as well as post-tests. These tests were criterion-referenced since they were specifically designed to measure the success of teaching specific subject matter.

It is apparent that fairly detailed recordkeeping will be necessary if students are to progress through series of exercises at individual rates. Some of the programs available to teach skills include:

1. *Criterion Reading* (New York: Random House). This program develops competency in many reading skills.
2. *Fountain Valley Teacher Support System in Reading* (Huntington Beach, Calif.: Richard L. Zweig Associates). This program has 77 tests on tapes and measures 277 skills.
3. *Prescriptive Reading Inventory* (Monterey, Calif.: CTB/McGraw-Hill). This program develops competency in 150 reading skills.
4. *Wisconsin Design for Reading Skill Development* (Minneapolis, Minn.: Interpretive Scoring Systems).

Wisconsin Design for Reading Skill Development states as its purposes: (1) to identify and describe behaviorally the skills which appear to be essential to competence in reading; (2) to assess individual pupil's skill development status; (3) to manage instruction of children with different skill development needs; and (4) to monitor each pupil's progress. The program goes on to say that teachers must have an organized approach to teaching if they are to effectively guide children's development of reading skills. The program provides "a skill-centered base for an elementary school reading program, means for focusing on individual's skill development, and a management system for both pupils and instructional materials."[6]

The four major components of the *Wisconsin Design* are: (1) word attack; (2) comprehension; (3) study skills; and (4) self-directed, interpretive, and creative reading. The six steps in its use are outlined for teachers as: (1) prepare, (2) pretest,

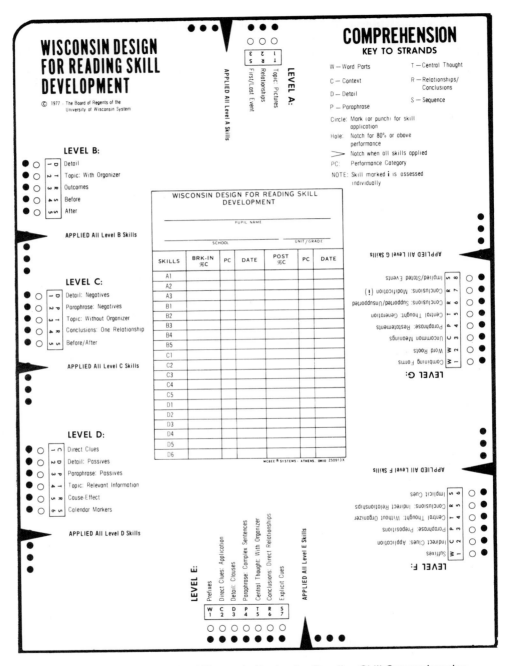

Figure 8.1. Record card for the *Wisconsin Design for Reading Skill Comprehension*

(3) record, (4) instruct, (5) post-test, and (6) report/reward. The record card for the comprehension skills for all levels A through G is reproduced in figure 8.1. While the record card reproduced shows spaces for scoring exercises A1 through D6, the reverse side of the card provides scoring space for E1 through G8.

Use of Readability Graphs

Fry's Readability Graph

By applying the easy-to-use formula in figure 8.2 to any book, teachers can find its level of difficulty, and thus not be limited to those books listed in Appendix B.

In using Fry's graph (figure 8.2) for *estimating* readability, one need only count the total number of syllables in 100 running words in each of three passages. Then count the number of sentences in the same passages and compute the average for the three. The average number of syllables in 100 words and the average number of sentences in 100 words provides the necessary information for an entry from the *x* and the *y* axes to find a point located in one of the grade-level areas. This is an estimate of the reader level or level of difficulty of that particular book.

If the point obtained falls in the gray area on the graph, the level of difficulty of that specific passage is probably not measured by this graph.

Following are examples of the use of the graph.

Book Title	Syllables per 100 Words	Sentences per 100 Words	Reader Level
Squanto and the Pilgrims	125	15	
	116	13	
	137	13	
AVERAGE	126	13.5	Second Grade
Danger Below	124	11	
(Deep Sea Adventures Series)	127	8	
	121	8	
AVERAGE	124	9	Fourth Grade
The Mystery of Morgan Castle	124	12	
	132	14	
	133	11	
AVERAGE	130	12	Third Grade

This method of finding readability is easily applied and should be very helpful to teachers who do not have at hand the information they need about level of difficulty of available books.

Raygor Readability Estimator

Raygor devised a readability estimate using a graph like the Fry Readability Graph, but substituting the number of words of six or more letters (long words) instead of the number of syllables.[7]

FRY'S READABILITY GRAPH

EXTENDED THRU PREPRIMER LEVEL

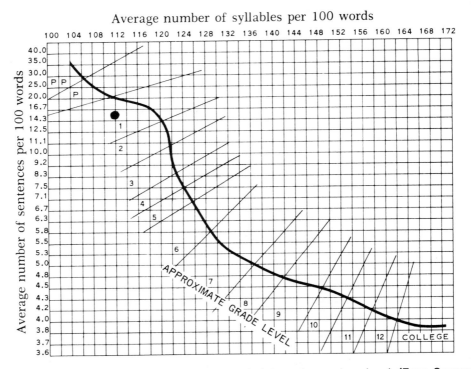

Average number of syllables per 100 words

Figure 8.2. Fry's Readability Graph extended through preprimer level. (From George Maginnis, "The Reading Graph and Informal Reading Inventories." *The Reading Teacher* 22 [March 1969], p. 518)

The directions for the use of the Raygor estimator are:

1. Use three 100-word passages.
2. Count the number of sentences in each passage, estimating to the nearest tenth.
3. Count the words of six or more letters in each passage.
4. Find the arithmetic average of the three counts for both number of sentences and number of long words.
5. Plot the point on the graph.

Baldwin and Kaufman have reproduced the graph in the *Journal of Reading* in their article reporting on the validity of the Raygor Estimator.[8]

A slide rule type of estimate maker is available for quickly assessing reading grade levels. It is available from Twin Oaks Publishing Co., Inc., 134 Mason Street, Rehoboth, Massachusetts 02769.

Classroom Management

It is easy to concentrate so much on finding suitable learning materials after initial testing of problem readers that the effect of classroom management on children's progress is forgotten. As teachers plan for instruction they should think about organizing their classrooms physically so that all children have opportunities to learn. They should also consider planning the instructional day to allow for *all* children to be taught during regular school hours. In addition, systems must be devised for establishing objectives, planning lessons, and keeping records that are efficient time-wise, but provide a comprehensive record of the lessons that have been taught and the learning experiences that have been provided.

Behavioral Objectives

Each lesson to be taught needs to have clearly stated objectives. That is, the lesson needs to state what it is the student will do and the level of performance the teacher will expect as a measure of achievement or mastery of the objective. Such objectives that are measurable in terms of student behavior are called *behavioral objectives*. If Joe is going to read a story about "Balloons in Albuquerque," he might be expected afterward to explain three reasons why Albuquerque is now called "The Balloon Capital of the World." If he can explain three reasons, he meets the objective although in this objective there are no specific criteria required in evaluating his reasons.

A behavioral objective meets three criteria: (1) it indicates what the learner will do; (2) it states how the achievement of the objective will be measured; and (3) it establishes the minimum level of acceptable performance. Contrast the following nonbehavioral objectives with behavioral ones:

Nonbehavioral Objectives

1. Make a list of several pairs of words usually associated together: cowcalf; cup-saucer; shirt-tie.

2. Arrange the list of given events in the sequence in which they appeared in the story.

Behavioral Objectives

1. When the teacher gives one of a pair of associated words, the student will be able to respond *every time* with the other word of the pair: knife-fork.

2. After the story has been read, the five events will be presented to the students in a mixed up order, and each student will number them in the correct order in which they appeared in the story.

Lesson Plans

A satisfactory format for lesson plans is presented in table 8.1. Within this format, behavioral objectives are stated, materials are identified, and activities and evaluations

TABLE 8.1. Lesson Plan Format

Target Behavior (Objective)	Name of Material	Describe Activities	Evaluation of self, client, material
When Fred finishes the story he is writing, he will proofread it for spelling errors and find 90% of them.	An original story based on fact being written by Fred.	Fred is writing a paragraph about "Learning to Ski in the Sandias."	Fred found most of his spelling errors except he missed some of the "easy" words. When I'd point one out, he'd say "Oh, yeah!" I don't think he was putting in much effort today.
After reading various "cures" for cramps, freckles, headaches, hiccups, etc., Fred will be able to discuss these cures and other "old wives tales" he has heard.	Ohlssom, Emrich, *The Hodge-Podge Book: An Almanac of American Folklore.*	Fred will listen to several "far-out" cures for various ailments, and he will discuss these and others he knows about.	We had a good discussion over these "cures," and Fred contributed some of the remedies he has heard; for instance, to cure hiccups, hold your breath for fifteen seconds.
After a brief discussion, George will read with clarity seven pages from *Huck Finn* with 85% accuracy.	*Huckleberry Finn,* Pendulum Press, 1973. (rdg. level: 4.9)	We read it orally as character parts in a play.	George read all his parts on pages 6–13 with 83% accuracy. He made mistakes with *ed* and *ing* endings.
After reviewing 15 spelling words, Tom will write at least 12 correctly.	The dictionary. Spelling list.	Tom reviewed words from previous lessons and three new words from his current writing.	Tom was able to write 12 of the 15 words correctly. Then he looked up the correct spelling for the three words he had missed.

are given. The lesson plan must be prepared for a group of children with similar needs or for individual children. The sample lesson plan in table 8.1 was designed to provide different learning experiences for several children. The teacher may prepare more than one objective and activity for each child if the child will have the time and support to accomplish them.

Teachers should recognize that there are many different lesson plan formats. Each teacher should select or develop a format that suits the needs of teacher and students. Some school systems will provide a standard lesson plan form for all teachers in the system. Whatever the format, the critical idea to remember is that the lesson plan is simply a tool to facilitate the planning of the school day and is of value only as it helps the teacher accomplish needed planning and organization.

The daily lesson plan may include:

1. An objective of the lesson, stated behaviorally.
2. Directed reading (instructional level); exact title of book and pages read (materials).
3. Workbook, seatwork, or special word-attack exercises (materials).
4. Word study, if separate from item 2.
5. Writing experience stories or unit work; spelling, dictation (activities).
6. Fun reading (independent reading level); exact title of book and pages read.
7. Anecdotes relative to children's behavior, if unusual (evaluation).
8. Evaluation of the success of the lesson.

Recordkeeping

Although recordkeeping should be reduced to a minimum, it is very necessary to keep records of past performances as a standard of comparison for future performance. In addition, the teacher needs samples of the pupil's work and other information for parent conferences or in planning new ventures in reading.

Keeping anecdotes as the events happen is possible if the teachers write notes to themselves in the margins of the daily assignment book, the class schedule book, or in a loose-leaf notebook. Later, these anecdotes should be placed in the pupil's cumulative folder as a part of a running record of what the teacher knows about the child.

The teacher should start a simple one-page record of each disabled reader. Interest inventories, sociograms and test results, and grade cards become part of the file of useful information from which pertinent data can be extracted.

Pretesting, teaching, and post-testing afford excellent opportunities for small assignments to become tangible measures of progress. The important consideration here is that progress at the first-grade reader level is commendable even if the student is in junior high school. The measure of progress is the important thing.

A concise record of pertinent information can be summarized on a single page, such as illustrated in figure 8.3. Using all the information gained through interest inventories, personality inventories, health data, family data, school history, and methods of evaluating intelligence, the teacher will be able to organize a summary. By accommodating new information as it is obtained through the school year, the teacher is enabled to adjust the pupil's reading program as often as necessary.

If the students are beginning corrective instruction, the teacher should be observant while working with them, making mental notes of conversation, behavior, and reactions to all subjects discussed. These should be recorded briefly in a daily log. They usually should not be recorded in the presence of the pupils. Having this kind of information will help the teacher guide daily conversation, obtain further information, and utilize interests of the pupils. A diary record of the materials used in corrective reading, including pages covered and books used, should also be kept.

Name of Pupil_____ Date_____

READING TESTS RESULTS

Oral Reading Test   Grade Placement   Grade Placement
                         Accuracy_____   Comprehension_____

Silent Reading (Skills needing reteaching): _____

_____

Other diagnostic tests_____

_____

Status of informal reading from series of readers: (Instructional levels)

    First test date_____ Book used_____ Result_____

    Second test date_____ Book used_____ Result_____

    Third test date _____ Book used_____ Result_____

ADDITIONAL CASE HISTORY INFORMATION

Intelligence: _____   Interest Inventory (Special Interests):

_____   _____

_____   _____

Health Factors: Personality Data:_____
    Vision_____ _____
    Hearing_____ _____
    Neurological_____ _____
    Endocrine_____ _____
School Factors: _____   Parent Contact Dates:

_____   _____

_____   _____

RECOMMENDATIONS OR COMMENTS:

_____

_____

Figure 8.3. Report of progress

Preparing the Summary Report with Recommendations

If the teacher has kept a daily log of the work completed and new case history information acquired, the completion of a summary report can be condensed from this information. A form for reporting testing is shown in figure 8.3. An outline for the summary report appears in figure 8.4.

Writing a Summary Report for a Student Who Has Had Special Instruction

I. *Personal data*

Student _____   Date _____

Grade in school _____   Parents _____

Age _____   Address _____

Present Reading level _____   Dates of lessons ____

School semester _____   Number of lessons ___

II. *Introductory statement.* Summarize generally the child's background reading experiences. First recognition of problem, first diagnosis, first remedial instruction, improvement or lack of it. Affective factors related to attendance, punctuality, general disposition, moods, personal evaluation of self as expressed in conversation.

III. *Personality data.* Describe personality factors pertinent to the reading or attendance at lessons. Omit superficial comments like "He's a nice boy."

IV. *Reading Progress.* The arrangement of topics should be adapted to the work you did with your client.

1. Writing experiences completed.
2. Books, pamphlets, magazines, or newspaper articles read.
3. Vocabulary skills. If you followed a commerically prepared set of lessons, give specific bibliographical information. If you planned your own, outline in detail.
4. Phonic and Structural Skills. Be specific about which skills were practiced.
5. Other kinds of language experiences.
6. Summary of progress.

V. Recommendations. What will be most helpful to the child in ensuing semesters?

VI. Your report needs to be signed and should generally be countersigned by your supervisor.

_____   _____
Date   Reading Clinician

_____   _____
Date   Reading Supervisor

Figure 8.4. Suggested outline for a summary report

Making Connections 8.2: Teachers' Record Keeping Systems

It is important to be aware of a variety of means for lesson planning and classroom recordkeeping. There are almost as many ways of doing these tasks as there are teachers! Each teacher needs to develop an effective system that is comfortable and practical.

Interview a classroom teacher to find out how lesson plans are developed and classroom records maintained. Perhaps the teacher will be able to let you bring blank forms back to your class to share with other students. Ask to see not only the unused forms but also plan books and records that have actually been written and used.

If each class member brings back information as well as actual lesson plans and record systems, the class should have a collective store of practical information to help in thinking about classroom organization and management.

Minimum testing for underachievers includes:

1. An informal reading inventory, including oral and silent reading passages.
   a. Assessment of word identification abilities.
   b. Assessment of comprehension by questions developed at different cognitive levels.
2. A test of sight word knowledge (May be one of the following)
   a. San Diego Quick Assessment
   b. Dolch Basic Sight Words
   c. Wide Range Achievement Test—Reading
   d. The Slosson Oral Reading Test
3. A sample of the student's writing
4. A test of phonic and structural ability
5. A spelling test
6. A measure of oral language vocabulary (Possibly *The Peabody Picture Vocabulary Test*)[9]

Second level of testing to be requested:

1. The Keystone Telebinocular Test of Vision
2. An individually administered intelligence test
3. Comprehension skill in silent reading includes evaluation at the different cognitive levels:
   a. recall
   b. interpretation
   c. application
   d. analysis
   e. synthesis
   f. evaluation

4. Personality evaluation
   a. Teachers may do:
      (1) The three wishes test
      (2) Incomplete sentences blank
      (3) Interest inventories
   b. The psychologist or diagnostician may select special tests according to the student's needs.

Teacher Resources

Today's boys and girls and their teachers are fortunate to have so many different learning materials available to them. The teachers must make responsible choices of materials so that the most appropriate ones are chosen for the varied needs in their classrooms. An annotated list of some of the remedial reading resources that may be used to help children develop better word recognition and comprehension abilities are provided in Appendix G: Instructional Materials for Word Identification and Comprehension.

Reading Material of Elementary Level of Difficulty for the Middle School Content Program

Middle School general science teachers need to be alert for materials that can be read and studied by students who function on only a third- or fourth-grade reading level. One recent set of texts is *Ideas and Investigations in Science:*

1. Harry Wong, Leonard Bernstein, and Edward Shevick, *Ideas and Investigations in Science: Life Science* (Englewood Cliffs, N.J.: Prentice-Hall, 1978).
2. Malvin Dolmatz and Harry Wong, *Ideas and Investigations in Science: Physical Science,* 2nd. ed. (Englewood Cliffs, N.J.: Prentice-Hall, 1977).
3. Leonard Bernstein and Harry Wong, *Ideas and Investigations in Science: Earth Science,* 2nd. ed. (Englewood Cliffs, N.J.: Prentice-Hall, 1979).

These materials are available in separate unit booklets or in combined textbooks with laboratory data books and teacher's manuals. Each investigation is carefully sequenced and the directions are very easy to follow.

Examples of other useful materials are:

1. John F. Mongillo et al., *Reading About Science* (New York: McGraw-Hill, 1981). Many science articles are presented in short articles with comprehension questions. Levels A–G cover difficulty levels 2.5 to 6.6.
2. Nila B. Smith, *Be A Better Reader,* 5th ed. (Englewood Cliffs, N.J.: Prentice-Hall). Reading skills in social studies, science, mathematics, and literature are covered. Grades 4–12.
3. Larry Berliner and Susan Berliner, *Reading Skills for Standardized Testing* (Maplewood, N.J.: Hammond, Inc., 1983). These materials (Levels A–E) are designed to help older students learn test-taking skills.

Handbooks of Word-Recognition Skills for Teachers

These commercially prepared handbooks will be useful:

1. Lou A. Burmeister, *Words—From Print to Meaning: Classroom Activities for Building Sight Vocabulary, for Using Context Clues, Morphology, and Phonics* (Reading, Mass.: Addison Wesley, 1975).
2. Paul C. Burns and Betty D. Roe, *Reading Activities for Today's Schools* (Chicago: Rand McNally, 1979).
3. Dolores Durkin, *Strategies for Identifying Words* (Boston: Allyn and Bacon, 1976).
4. Peter Edwards, *Reading Problems, Identification and Treatment* (London: Heinemann, 1978).
5. Eldon E. Ekwall, *Locating and Correcting Reading Difficulties,* 4th ed. (Columbus: Merrill, 1985).
6. Arthur Heilman, *Phonics in Proper Perspective,* 4th ed. (Columbus: Merrill, 1981).
7. Selma E. Herr, *Learning Activities for Reading,* 4th ed. (Dubuque, Iowa: Wm. C. Brown Company Publishers, 1982).
8. Josephine Ives, Laura Bursuk, and Sumner Ives, *Word Identification Techniques* (Chicago: Rand McNally, 1979).
9. Dale D. Johnson and P. David Pearson, *Teaching Reading Vocabulary* (New York: Holt, Rinehart and Winston, 1978).
10. Mary E. Platts, Sister Rose Marguerite, and Esther Shumaker, *SPICE, Suggested Activities to Motivate the Teaching of the Language Arts in the Elementary School* (Stevensville, Mich.: Educational Services, Inc. 1960).
11. Mary E. Platts, *Anchor: A Handbook of Vocabulary Discovery Techniques for the Classroom Teacher* (Stevensville, Mich.: Educational Services, Inc., 1970).
12. Lee Ann Rinsky and Barbara Griffith, *Teaching Word Attack Skills* (Dubuque, Iowa: Gorsuch Scarsbrick, 1978).
13. David H. Russell and Elizabeth F. Russell, *Listening Aids Through the Grades,* 2d ed., edited by Dorothy Grant Hennings (New York: Teachers College Press, 1979).
14. David H. Russell, Etta Karp, and Anne Marie Mueser, *Reading Aids Through the Grades,* 4th ed. (New York: Teachers College Press, 1981).
15. Delwyn G. Schubert and Theodore Torgerson, *Improving the Reading Program,* 4th ed. (Dubuque, Iowa: Wm. C. Brown Company Publishers, 1976).
16. Carl B. Smith and Peggy G. Elliott, *Reading Activities for Middle and Secondary Schools, A Handbook for Teachers* (New York: Holt, Rinehart and Winston, 1979).
17. Evelyn B. Spache, *Reading Activities for Child Improvement,* 3d ed. (Boston: Allyn and Bacon, 1981).
18. Jeannette Veatch et al., *Key Words to Reading: The Language Experience Approach Begins,* 2d ed. (Columbus: Merrill, 1979).

Focusing on the Learner

Planning Use of the Student's Time

Teachers must take advantage of every opportunity to check the progress of the students, to encourage them in their efforts, and to make sure that they understand what they are expected to do before they begin work.

In contrast with the usual procedure of having directed silent reading before oral reading, these students may need to read orally much of the story material they use for independent seatwork later.

Underachievers need to do a great deal of oral reading. Part of this can be done with a student-tutor if this can be arranged in the classroom, but the teacher needs to hear enough of this oral practice to note difficulties and to plan the seatwork and other learning experiences to overcome obstacles to progress. It is especially important to listen with undivided attention while the student reads so that teacher and student can enjoy the story together. The student may read into a cassette or tape recorder and the teacher can listen later.

Also in oral reading, the teacher can be alert to the need for sharing the oral reading by taking turns by pages, for example, or by interjecting questions to keep interest up when the reading may seem difficult to the students.

The students should read the directions for their work to the teacher before they begin to work alone. They should have a list of tasks in mind that they can do as time permits so that they need not wait for further instructions. *The work should be corrected as quickly as possible after it is finished.* Types of exercises for which a glance down the page will reveal mistakes or shortcomings should be used.

Checking-up time for all children just before recess or dismissal should be routine, and thus certain children are not singled out as the only ones who have need for this. If several children have assignments to be checked at times such as this, attention is not directed to the underachievers.

These pupils must have time to read aloud to the teacher. If it is not feasible to do this as a "reading group" in the daily schedule, it must be arranged at some other time. While not the most desirable plan, asking the children to come fifteen minutes earlier in the morning or to stay a few minutes after school may work out smoothly if the teacher makes the period a happy, optimistic one. The independent work period for all students in the room (recommended in chapter 7) may provide an opportunity to do some planning with the underachievers.

Planning is very important. Setting up realistic goals is a must, and deliberately making time to check regularly with the underachievers throughout the day will be rewarding over a period of time.

If the teachers look upon their classrooms as laboratories where few children need to do exactly the same things, and where the underachievers need do nothing as outlined in the proposed state course of study, there will be time to do many things from which they can profit.

Writing and Spelling the Basic Sight Vocabulary

Brenda was in the fourth grade but was reading at first-grade reader level. Her teacher discovered that Brenda could work independently using the *My First Picture Dictionary.*[10] Her assignment was to use five of the words on one page in sentences. With some imagination, Brenda thought out a connected story in which the five words used were related. She needed help from a student-teacher on spelling many of the other words she wrote, but she was able to write some excellent paragraphs using this little picture dictionary. This was helpful in her total language improvement program. An example of her work is shown in figure 8.5.

For children with specific reading and writing disability, simultaneous oral spelling when attempting to write exercises is a good idea. This simultaneous oral spelling is described by Gillingham and Stillman[11] and declared by them to be a must. If the

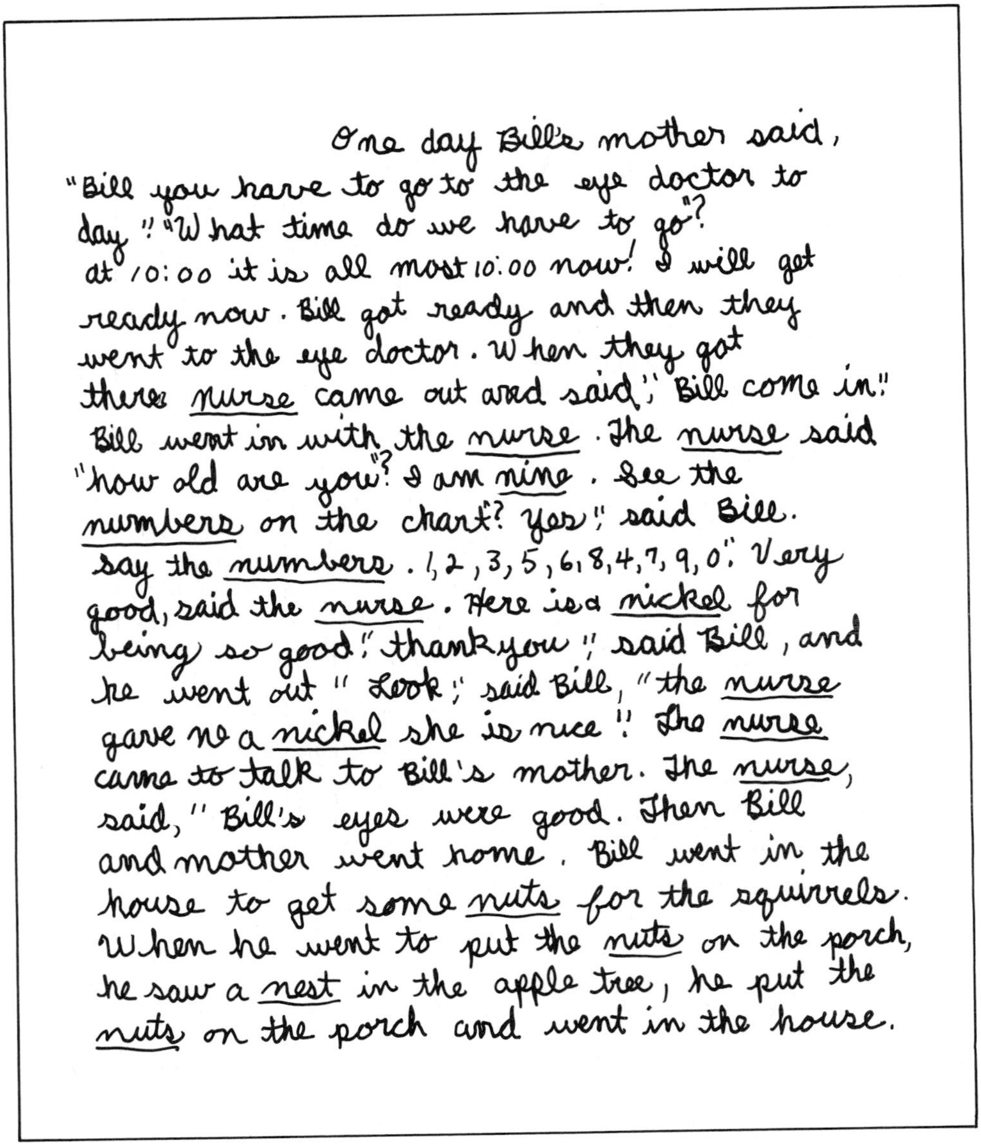

One day Bill's mother said, "Bill you have to go to the eye doctor to day"! "What time do we have to go"? at 10:00 it is all most 10:00 now! I will get ready now. Bill got ready and then they went to the eye doctor. When they got there nurse came out and said," Bill come in." Bill went in with the nurse. The nurse said "how old are you"? I am nine. See the numbers on the chart? Yes," said Bill. say the numbers. 1, 2, 3, 5, 6, 8, 4, 7, 9, 0". Very good, said the nurse. Here is a nickel for being so good." thank you," said Bill, and he went out " Look," said Bill, "the nurse gave me a nickel she is nice"! The nurse came to talk to Bill's mother. The nurse, said," Bill's eyes were good. Then Bill and mother went home. Bill went in the house to get some nuts for the squirrels. When he went to put the nuts on the porch, he saw a nest in the apple tree, he put the nuts on the porch and went in the house.

Figure 8.5. Brenda's story

students are writing the word *work,* they say the word to themselves; they hear the word; then they spell it aloud as they write or if they are uncertain, they spell it aloud before they write. They should spell the word so that their teacher knows what they are thinking and so that they themselves know what they are writing. They should spell the word so that when they write it, it will be correct and not in mixed-up order. Each time they write the word incorrectly, and it is not immediately corrected, they have once more practiced a bad or incorrect habit response, and this makes their habitual confused response become even more fixed and thus more difficult to correct. To prevent fixing a bad habit more strongly, they should do *right* those things that they do. Simultaneous oral spelling may slow people down. In these individuals' cases, that is not a negative factor. The problem is to overcome confusions and reversals and to fix the habit of hearing what the language says. It is probably a choice between developing *slow* readers or *no* readers, and here the ability to read slowly seems highly preferable. The teachers must remember that these disabled readers have had years of frustration and failure experience, and that they have been unable to achieve successfully with other students by the predominately visual techniques used in group teaching.

What Should We Teach?

Don't teach what can't or won't be learned.

A junior high boy came to his counselor almost in tears. "I have an exam tomorrow in English," he said, "and we will be asked to define and give an example of seven kinds of pronouns. I don't even understand the explanations in the textbook." The kinds of pronouns are relative, demonstrative, possessive, indefinite, personal, intensive, and reflexive. Since most of you would flunk the test, why inflict it on a 12-year-old boy?[12]

"I don't see why my Audrey doesn't get the special help she needs in reading."

Figure 8.6. Miss Emmy (Reprinted by permission of *The Oklahoma Teacher.*)

Certainly teachers can change priorities. First things can be put first instead of being second, third, or fourth or twentieth. But what priorities?

1. If you are doing some old things that don't work, discard those and try something new.
2. Try some things that may not work, a necessary condition for any innovative program.
3. Study what works and what doesn't work.

Summary

This chapter has discussed the many problems the classroom teachers face when they disregard the "grade-level" number on their classroom doors and allow students to work all day at many levels of achievement.

Making use of drill periods; acquiring and using an adequate assortment of easy books, games and devices, and work-type reading materials; and emphasizing spelling and writing the basic reading vocabulary: all combine to make for many diversified activities in busy classrooms. A significant number of professional books that contain many helpful suggestions for quiet seatwork for students and that are available for classroom teachers have been listed.

Teachers need to remember that materials of instruction do *not* instruct. They provide the basis and possible stimuli for instruction. Learners' responses to materials of instruction can be limited, cursory, or very fruitful. One can skim over the surface or one can study in depth. Trying to "cover the ground" is usually not helpful. Many a child has gone through a book without much of the book going through the child. One can read the lines, read between the lines, or read beyond the lines.

For Further Reading

Balajthy, Ernest. "Reinforcement and Drill by Microcomputer." *The Reading Teacher* 37 (February 1984), pp. 490–94.

Dickerson, Dolores Pauley. "A Study of the Use of Games to Reinforce Sight Vocabulary." *The Reading Teacher* 36 (October 1982), pp. 46–49.

Ekwall, Eldon E., and Shanker, James L. *Diagnosis and Remediation of the Disabled Reader,* 2d. ed. Boston: Allyn and Bacon, 1983: Chapter 15, "Relaying Information, Record Keeping, and Writing Case Reports in Remedial Reading," pp. 516–45.

Gamby, Gert. "Talking Books and Taped Books: Materials for Instruction." *The Reading Teacher* 36 (January 1983), pp. 366–69.

Harris, Albert J., and Sipay, E. R. *How to Increase Reading Ability,* 7th ed. New York: Longman, 1980: "Principles of Effective Motivation," pp. 334–52; "Materials for Improving Word-Recognition and Decoding Skills," pp. 434–46.

Lee, Dorris M., and Rubin, Joseph B. *Children and Language.* Belmont, Calif.: Wadsworth Publishing Co., 1979: Chapter 12, "Putting It All Together," pp. 318–34.

Richek, Margaret Ann; List, Lynne K.; and Lerner, Janet W. *Reading Problems, Diagnosis and Remediation.* Englewood Cliffs, N.J.: Prentice-Hall, 1983: Chapter 15, "Reports and Records," pp. 311–32.

Notes

1. *Vowel Domino* (Washington, D.C.: The Remedial Education Press).
2. *Go-Fish* (Washington, D.C.: The Remedial Education Press).
3. Connie A. Bridge, Peter N. Winograd, and Darlene Haley, "Using Predictable Materials vs. Preprimers to Teach Beginning Sight Words," *The Reading Teacher* 36 (May 1983), pp. 884–91.
4. Ernest Balajthy, "Reinforcement and Drill by Microcomputer," *The Reading Teacher* 37: (February 1984) pp. 490–94; John O. Green, "Computers, Kids, and Writing: An Interview with Donald Graves," *Classroom Computer Learning* 4 (March 1984), pp. 20–24.
5. I. C. H. Smith, *Microcomputers in Education* (New York: John Wiley and Sons, 1982), p. 28; Marc Tucker, "Computer in Schools: A Plan in Time Saves Nine," *Theory into Practice* 22 (Autumn 1983) pp. 313–20.
6. *The Wisconsin Design for Reading Skill Development:* Overview (Minneapolis: National Computer Systems, Inc., 1977).
7. Alton L. Raygor, "The Raygor Readability Estimate: A Quick and Easy Way to Determine Difficulty," in *Reading: Theory, Research and Practice,* edited by P. David Pearson, Twenty-Sixth Yearbook of the National Reading Conference (Clemson, S.C.: National Reading Conference, 1977), pp. 259–63.
8. R. Scott Baldwin and Rhonda Kaufman, "A Concurrent Validity Study of the Raygor Readability Estimate," *Journal of Reading* 23 (November 1979), pp. 148–53.
9. Lloyd M. Dunn and Leota M. Dunn, *Peabody Picture Vocabulary Test,* rev. ed. (Circle Pines, Minn.: American Guidance Services, 1981).
10. William A. Jenkins and Andrew Schiller, *My First Picture Dictionary* (Glenview, Ill.: Scott, Foresman, 1975).
11. Anna Gillingham and Bessie W. Stillman, *Remedial Training for Children with Specific Disability in Reading, Spelling and Penmanship,* Parts I and II (distributed by Anna Gillingham, 25 Parkview Ave., Bronxville, New York.)
12. Edgar Dale, "How Do We Provide Access to Excellence?" *Apropos,* a publication of the Center on Educational Media and Materials for the Handicapped (Summer 1974).

9
Teaching Word-Recognition Skills

Vocabulary

rapid word recognition
mediated word recognition
environmental print
dictated story
language experience
   approach
Dolch Basic Sight Words
Stone's Word List
Fry Basic Word List
rebus
wordless picture books
predictable books
taped books
context clues
picture clues
structured analysis
affix
prefix
suffix
combining forms
compound word
contraction
CVC-CVCe
homonym
synonym
antonym
consonant substitution
silent letter
blend
location skill
alphabetical order
pronunciation skills
meaning skills

Questions

1. Why is it important for the reader to learn a stock of sight words as quickly as possible?

2. Name and describe as many ways as you can to help children acquire a collection of words recognized at sight.

3. What is meant by the term *context clues*? Why is it important for children to become skilled in the use of context clues?

4. What word-recognition skills are classified as structural analysis skills? Describe what is meant by each of the structural analysis skills.

5. How are structural analysis and phonics skills different? What kinds of knowledge about word recognition are classified as phonics?

6. What is important to teach a child about using the dictionary for word identification?

7. What are the advantages and disadvantages of using the microcomputer for helping the child grow in word-recognition abilities?

Introduction

Word-recognition skills are all those skills and abilities the students need in order to unlock words independently and rapidly as they read. The mechanical aspect of *rapid word identification* in reading separates the beginning reader from the mature reader. The mature readers go directly from print to meaning, and they make the visual process a small part of the task in comparison with the manipulation of ideas, which is the reason for reading. However, the beginning readers must mediate what words are. This is a process that requires time, effort, and much practice.

The beginning readers must memorize a bank of sight words as rapidly as possible. The more words the readers have in their banks, the more readily they can move from print to meaning in reading. One of the teacher's first tasks is to help the children acquire a small vocabulary of sight words.

While memorizing a stock of sight words to begin reading is satisfactory, the students must acquire many additional skills if they are to grow in the ability to read independently. Picture clues are useful as long as the students are reading well-illustrated materials. When there are no illustrations to carry a story theme, the students must rely on other skills. Five of these skills are:

1. Learning a basic sight vocabulary.
2. Using meaning or context clues contained in the reading.
3. Using structural analysis clues: looking at word parts.
4. Using phonic clues: breaking the word into parts for sounding.
5. Using the dictionary.

Learning a Stock of Sight Words

An early task in learning to read or overcoming reading difficulties is developing a stock of sight words. Fortunately, the teacher has many means for helping children learn the needed sight words. The teacher will need to make some decisions about which strategies and materials to use to accomplish this necessary task.

Environmental Print

When children enter school, they usually come with some concepts about print and its meaning. Frequently, they can read signs such as "Stop," "Railroad Crossing," names of food products purchased in stores, names of favorite fast food outlets, service station signs, and labels on T-shirts and other clothing items. The teacher needs to acknowledge this recognition of labels and signs. Children may begin the year by making books of labels from cans, boxes, fast food containers, greeting cards, and other such sources of environmental print. The teacher may indicate that the children are going to learn more about reading, thus validating that what the children already know is a legitimate form of reading.

In the classroom environment the teacher will find many functional uses for print. There will be frequently changed "bubbles" containing records of children's talk in the classroom, signs providing needed information, requests for help, notes to children, task cards for small group work, records of small-group activities prepared by children, dictated stories to be read and reread, and labels indicating where classroom materials may be found and where they are to be stored. The important message is that print in the environment works for the children and can provide information, directions, enjoyment, and records for their use.

As children grow in their ability to understand environmental print, whether in the classroom or in the larger community, they grow in the confidence that they need to deal successfully with print in other settings. They also develop an increasing number of sight words and high-frequency words that will serve them well in other settings.

Moving from Speech to Print

As children associate spoken words with written words, they learn to recognize their own names and the names of classmates and names on labels in the room; in general they become word conscious. Such sentences expressed orally as "Howarya?" become "How are you?" as three separate words. The fisherman's question, "Ketchuninny?" becomes in its deep structure: "Are you catching any fish?" Beginning readers have to learn how spoken sounds are divided up into words—where a word begins and where it ends.

Dictated Stories

Most children begin to add to their first sight vocabulary by reading language experience stories that they have dictated. The teacher needs to spend sufficient time discussing orally an experience or topic familiar to and interesting for the children. Then the teacher writes the sentences the students dictate to tell the story in sequence.

If teachers are *aware* of the children's environments and life experiences, they can build stories using whatever language the children bring to school. If the first stories can be *personal* to the children, so much the better. An example is illustrated in figure 9.1.

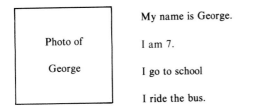

My name is George.

I am 7.

I go to school

I ride the bus.

Figure 9.1. Sample of children's personal stories

In this story, five high-frequency words, *is, I, go, to,* and *the,* appear. Since all the nouns will be familiar to George, he will probably read this story with ease.

If George is in a subgroup of four or five youngsters, they can collaborate on longer stories that provide much repetition of vocabulary.

Our names are
Mary, Grace, Bill and George.
Mary is 6.
George and Grace are 7.
Bill is 8.
Mary goes to school.
Grace goes to school.
Bill and George go to school.
We go to school every day.
We ride in a big yellow bus.
We like to go to school.

The teacher can keep a record of sight words introduced and make sure the children have opportunities to practice reading them in context. Short periods of flash card drill will be appropriate *later* but not at this time.

Language Experiences

This text emphasizes the language-experience approach, which permits students to write their own books of stories. And even though these stories may sound a bit like primerese to the adult, if they are the students' own books, they may be strongly motivating to them. The teacher needs some system for filing new words and reviewing them if they reappear in stories.

Language experience requires that the teacher and child or small group first discuss *orally* a topic of common interest. The children must verbalize sufficiently to demonstrate familiarity with the concepts and the language to talk about them. Then the teacher should accept the dictation of the children for "their" sentences.

The Balloons
We went to see the balloons.
They were very big.
They were red and yellow.
They were blue and green.
One looked like a big fish.
They went up in the sky.
We liked to see the balloons go up.

The language-experience approach to reading is a methodology in which the learners dictate personal experiences to be recorded and prepared for them to read later. This is a meaningful approach to beginning reading in which the children's own experiences and the children's personal language become the vehicles in learning to read. Hopefully, in this approach, meaning is the starting place, the emphasis, and the result of reading the prepared story. Instead of choosing characters in beginning reading books, children learn to read words that they've used in retelling their own personal experiences. This causes the content and choice of words to be unique to the children's cultural and experience background. It is believed that this approach to reading the written word relates spoken language more closely to written language. Children can learn several dozen sight words by this method if the teachers are careful to provide repetition on commonly used words and to use a "selecting out" process that causes children to center attention on words to be remembered.

The very high frequency of a few basic words indicates a need to help children learn these words as early as possible in their reading program. In the language-experience approach, these words can be taught in context with nouns and verbs familiar in the experiences of the learners so that reading can always be meaningful and purposeful. It must be emphasized that children should not be presented words in isolation and expected to retain them. The words need to be used orally in meaningful ways and then the oral form translated to writing.

Sight Word Lists

When teachers encourage children to dictate or write their own stories to be placed on charts or bound into books for reading and rereading, it may be helpful to have one or more basic sight word lists available. Teachers may consult these lists to find the words the children have written that have particularly high utility. They may also use the lists to make choices of words to include in stories and other chart materials.

There are several lists that teachers might use as guides to the most important words to be learned first as sight words. Among them is Stone's list, which appears in Figure 9.2. Other lists are the 220 words in the Dolch Basic Sight Word Test[1] (given in chapter 5) and the first 300 of the Fry Basic Word List.[2]

Other Ways to Develop Sight Vocabulary

The teacher needs a variety of means to help children develop rapid recognition of sight vocabulary. Young readers may lose motivation to continue learning if practice activities are limited in variety. The teacher should encourage the use of rebuses and games as well as a variety of activities with books.

Rebus Reading

Rebuses are symbols, usually pictures, that represent words. Road signs, when the words are not used and symbols replace them, are rebuses. While rebuses may be geometric or abstract, only the pictorial rebus will be discussed.

o	dog	I	not	the
after	doll	in	now	then
am	down	into	oh	they
and	father	is	on	this
are	find	it	one	three
of	for	jump	out	to
away	fun	kitten	play	too
baby	funny	laughed	rabbit	two
ball	get	like	ran	up
big	girl	little	red	want
blue	go	look	ride	was
bow-wow	good	make	run	we
boy	good-bye	may	said	went
came	had	me	saw	what
can	have	milk	school	where
car	he	morning	see	who
cat	help	mother	she	will
color	here	my	some	with
come	home	new	something	yes
did	house	no	stop	you

Figure 9.2. One hundred important words for pre-book, pre-primer, and early primer reading (Clarence R. Stone, *Progress in Primary Reading,* Manchester, Mo.: Webster Publishing Company, 1950).

The rebus technique used in *Mother Goose in Hieroglyphics*[3] probably has serious limitations in teaching. The use of "eye" for "i" and "corn" (an ear of corn) + "er" to replace "corner" serves only a novelty effect.

O'Donnell used the rebus in the pre-primers of the Harper and Row reading series. She justified it in this way:

The rebus may be used to represent words that have high interest value; so, without imposing upon the pupil the task of learning to read those words, the author is able to write interesting stories of high quality. . . . The use of rebuses makes possible a wider use of the child's speaking vocabulary.[4]

Woodcock taught five children to read twenty rebuses and compared the results with teaching the corresponding twenty words to five comparable children. His results were strongly in favor of introducing reading through the use of the rebus.[5]

With the rebus, the child can: (1) give more attention to the meaning of the passage; (2) avoid some of the frustration of abstract symbols in lines of print; (3) bypass part of the traditional readiness programs; and (4) give more attention to left-to-right direction and visual motor perceptual training that may be helpful. Figure 9.3 is a story about the cat and her kittens told by using a rebus.

Wordless Picture Books

During the past decade a number of illustrated books without words have appeared. *A Boy, A Dog, and A Frog* should elicit a good conversation from most any nonreader if the teacher provides the setting and takes the time to enjoy the story. Hopefully, it may stimulate original stories that the students will want to read because they will be their own. *Go Tell Aunt Rhody* can provide both conversation and the opportunity to sing the song they have heard and to create new verses to add to it.

Larrick has written about the wordless picture books and the teaching of reading to young children.[6]

A few examples from the many dozens of available wordless picture books are:

Aliki, *Go Tell Aunt Rhody* (New York: Macmillan, 1974).
Anno, Mitsumasa, *Anno's Journey* (New York: Collins-World, 1978).
dePaola, Tomie, *The Hunter and the Animals* (New York: Holiday House, 1981).
Krahn, Fernando, *The Great Ape* (New York: Viking Press, 1978).
Mayer, Mercer, *A Boy, A Dog, and A Frog* (New York: Dial Press, 1967).
Mayer, Mercer, *One Frog Too Many* (New York: Dial Press, 1975).
Spier, Peter, *Noah's Ark* (New York: Doubleday, 1977).
Van Soelen, Philip, *A Cricket in the Grass* (New York: Scribners, 1981).

The reading teacher can use this concept by encouraging the students to draw a series of pictures to tell a story and then asking them to dictate the sentences that the story tells. The teacher can write these sentences in manuscript below the picture, and then the children will have their own stories, which they can read, reread, or share with others.

The teacher can focus the children's attention on meaning, sequencing, prediction, and seeing relationships, since the problem of word recognition is avoided.[7] For children who have focused heavily on word naming, wordless picture books may be especially useful, since the reader must attend to meaning to make sense.

Predictable Books

In Chapter 8, predictable books were discussed as material that quickly allows a child to read independently. Predictable books are written so that the words are likely to be identified from the repetitive patterns, the sentence meanings, and the pictures. Once the children have heard the story, it is likely that they will be able to read it over and over to themselves. In fact, they will probably find enjoyment in doing so. If the teach-

Figure 9.3. Rebus example prepared by Jean Martin, graduate student, University of New Mexico, Albuquerque, 1979.

Making Connections 9.1: Using Wordless Picture Books

Teachers are beginning to appreciate the value of wordless picture books in helping children learn to read or improve their reading. These books may be used to help children learn to sequence events, to find the parts of a story (beginning, problem, resolution, end); to study the goals, plans, feelings of characters; to encourage the dictation or writing of stories; and to stimulate the desire to read again and again the stories that have been dictated or written.

A few wordless picture books are mentioned in this chapter. If you work with a librarian, you can learn the names of many more books of this type.

Select a wordless picture book that you especially enjoy. Share it with at least two children in separate sessions. After discussing the pictures in the book, have each child either write or dictate a story based on the pictures. You will probably get the most complete story if the child dictates or if you record the story on tape and transcribe it later.

After the stories have been written, dictated, or transcribed, have the children read their own and perhaps the story written by the other child. Make this an enjoyable experience, encouraging the children to feel proud of their efforts at authorship.

You will want to examine the children's stories to see if they maintained understandable story lines, if the important parts of a story were present, if the children kept the characters clearly identified through the use of pronouns, and if they made their stories fit the pictured situation. You may see clear differences in the abilities of the two children.

Bring the book, the stories, and your analyses to class to share with others. Discuss how these stories could help children practice basic sight vocabulary as well as learn more about the structure of stories.

er's goal is to promote the rapid recognition of sight words, the many rereadings of predictable books will surely help. Word-recognition practice will be associated with positive feelings about reading and with comprehension of a familiar story. The school librarian can supply a list of predictable books to help teachers build classroom collections.

Taped Books

A growing number of books are now published with accompanying records or cassette tapes of the story being read clearly and interestingly. Frequently, multiple copies of the book in paperback form with the tape or record come in a kit. As many as six to ten children may hear the book read, or a single child may enjoy the story alone. If a listening center equipped with earphones is available, the listeners may enjoy the reading of the story while the rest of the students go about their tasks undisturbed.

Listening to tapes or records of books while following along gives children an excellent way to practice word recognition in a meaningful setting. Since the children may listen again and again, the needed repetition of sight words is gained with enjoyment.

Bookmaking

When children make books, they have real and personally interesting reasons for learning words. They have many ideas to express, and the words they need to express them are frequently the words the teacher is anxious for them to learn. The teacher needs to keep a constant supply of various materials that may be used in making and binding books. The children should be encouraged to experiment with different materials and with different ways to produce both the contents of the book and its binding. It is helpful if a typewriter is available to the children as well as all sorts of pens, pencils, and markers. Some classrooms may be fortunate enough to have a microcomputer with a printer. With these tools children can write their stories and immediately have attractive printed copies to read and bind into books. Paper, glue, cardboard, laminating materials, fabrics, and sewing supplies should be readily available for binding.

Children may write books together, telling the story of a group experience. Groups of children may have experiences such as cooking, making birdhouses, or sailing boats, but each child will write an individual book. Some children want to write alone, basing their stories on what is important to them. Teachers should also write and bind books. They are powerful models for young writers.

In classrooms where book writing and binding are ongoing activities, children's own books are very popular during quiet reading times. Students read their own books and books made by their classmates. A large amount of enjoyable practice on basic sight words is gained, since the children use these words over and over in their writing.

Games

Teachers often think of games as a means to practice sight words. Studies have shown that games do indeed help children learn or retain vocabulary. Games in which children are active may be particularly helpful.[8] Teachers should study games carefully to make sure they provide for as much practice as possible and that the words are presented in meaningful settings. It is important to make sure the words in the games chosen for the class are words the children need to learn. Games that allow children to use words creatively are to be preferred over those in which players must follow set rules.

Many games are available, and more are being produced each year. A few games were suggested in Chapter 8. Teachers may also find it useful to ask children to make games for the class. One group of teachers gave each student a piece of cardboard two feet square at the beginning of the year. The first homework assignment was to develop a reading game for the classroom. As children brought in their completed games, each game was laminated. The classrooms had a generous supply of games for the year, and the children had the satisfaction of having made a useful contribution.

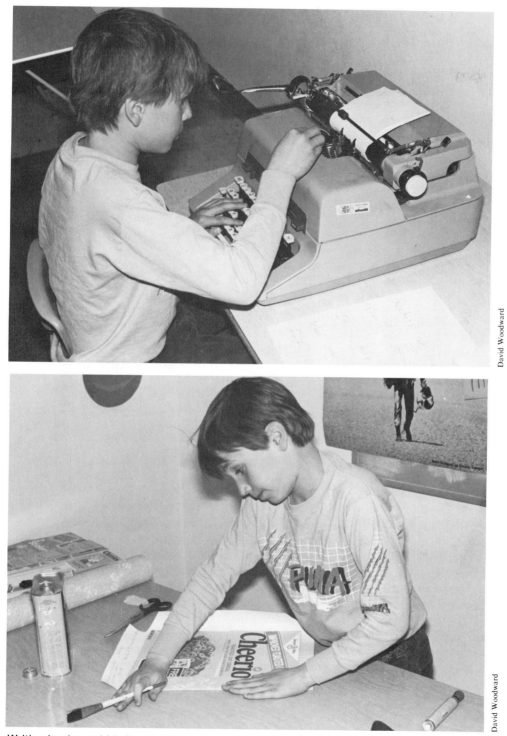

David Woodward

David Woodward

Writing books and binding them are recognized as important aspects of literacy development.

David Woodward

And when the book is finished, there is great satisfaction in sharing it with one's mother when she visits school.

Context Clues: Anticipation and Reconstruction of Meaning

The reader's ability to derive meaning from written language is primarily dependent upon how rich an experiential or conceptual background the reader brings to the passages being read. The reader should be predicting what is going to happen next, continually testing hypotheses to see if his or her predictions were correct, and confirming or rejecting the ideas by the concepts that they reveal. Just as the young children expand their oral language syntax and vocabulary by repeated cycles of sampling, hypothesis-testing, receiving immediate feedback kinds of reinforcement, and recycling new hypotheses about language usage, so the ones who are ready and have need to do so will exercise the same cycle of activity in learning to read print.

Children need guidance in:

1. anticipating what a word is from the meaning of the phrase or sentence containing the word;
2. anticipating the meaning of a sentence as a whole to help arrive at a meaning of a new word;
3. learning techniques of minimizing alternatives in word identification to transfer from the spoken language to the reading setting.

Picture clues may be profitably used by children as they read. They may tell what the whole sentence says. Pictures at the top of the page may give a clue to the new words in the reading material and may help evaluate the accuracy of the other word-recognition practices being used.

Context clues may help the reader derive the meaning of the word from the setting in which it is used. Meaning is so dependent upon context that all new words should be presented in meaningful context. Use of context to confirm meaning is an excellent check on the accuracy of all the other word recognition techniques.

The children's abilities to use picture clues effectively, their abilities to decipher context clues, and their abilities to anticipate what will come next—all three are dependent upon the storehouse of known concepts they already have. Their total backgrounds of experience make them able to cope with these clues as they appear. For those with limited conceptual backgrounds, the teachers will be most helpful by finding as many concrete ways as possible to help them expand their stock of word meanings.

The ability to predict what is coming next in the line of print can be taught. In children's context reading, the word, or even the entire next sentence, can be predicted many times from the reading already done. This partially explains the success of the cloze procedure in measuring comprehension in silent reading. When every nth word is deleted, the use of redundant words and syntax, the repetition of the same idea in different ways, and the restatement of fact make it possible for children to supply the missing word with considerable accuracy if they are attending to the thought as they move through the lines of print. Smith points out that the context itself is redundant. That is, it contains "prior knowledge, which reduces the alternative number of possibilities that a . . . word can be."[9]

Several types of context clues can be directly taught to children. They will be remembered and used if they are pointed out in meaningful lessons the students are doing.

Direct Explanation

The new word or concept is explained in a sentence:

1. A *chauffeur* is a man or woman who drives an automobile for a living.
2. A nest of young pheasants is called a *nide*.
3. The action of manufacturing food in the leaves of green plants is called *photosynthesis*.

Background of Experience

The meaning of the unknown word can be deduced from the students' backgrounds of experience:

1. Mother said that the old man with a hump on his back who lived down the street had *kyphosis.*
2. While a large number of cattle driven together is called a herd, a large number of whales is called a *pod,* and a large number of lions is called a *pride.*

Comparison and Contrast

Relating the meaning of a new word to an old word opposite in meaning may clarify a concept:

1. Sheep and deer are small animals, but the whale, the largest living mammal, is *enormous.*
2. Gayle was shy and retiring but her sister Helen was *effervescent* and *gregarious.*

The Synonym Clue

The new concept may be followed by a synonym or restatement of meaning:

1. The *cacique,* the person of highest authority in the village, asked all the men to come to the kiva.
2. We stayed in the *lobby,* a small waiting room in front of the doctor's office.

A Summary Clue

This is the use of a general term to encompass the description given:

1. His eyes were dull, his feet were sore, and his back ached; he was *exhausted.*
2. A child diagnosed as *dyslexic* probably has failed in school, lacks adequate oral language achievement, demonstrates persistent failure, and oftentimes has other family members with the same symptoms.

Previous Experience Clue

This clue is dependent upon the student's use of previous knowledge to transfer:

1. The *zebra* looks very much like a horse except he is covered with black and white stripes.
2. The station attendant said to stay on the *main artery* and they knew he meant that was the principal route.

Reflection of a Mood

The "tone" of the general situation provides a clue:

1. When the football team won a 7–0 victory, the *exuberance* of the crowd was uncontrollable.
2. We watched the *anguished* expressions on the people's faces as they saw the burning house collapse.

Recognizing Antecedents

Readers must recognize the antecedents of pronouns as they read;

1. Jane put the *scrapbook* on the top shelf so that *it* would not be lost.
2. The *dog that* caught and killed the rat was very valuable.

Directional (Structure) Words

There are words that indicate continuing, concluding, reversing, or illustrating action in the sentence:

1. I can't go skating with you today. *Moreover,* the ice is too thin. (continuing)
2. *As a result* of this study, we will shorten the lunch period by ten minutes. (concluding)
3. He was very tired; *nevertheless* he kept on working for several hours. (reversing)
4. Tom's doctor told him *specifically* that he must leave eggs and butter out of his diet. (illustrating)

These examples illustrate several types of clues students need to be aware of. They will be able to find others as they read critically in their texts. When *no clues* to meaning are given, students must be encouraged to use the dictionary.

Cloze Procedure

The cloze procedure is usually associated with the testing or teaching of comprehension skills. However, it can be used to facilitate word recognition, through the use of context clues. The teacher can develop cloze sheets in which words that the children need to learn are omitted. Passages can be prepared that contain words the children need to learn or need to practice in context. It may be useful to develop cloze passages in which certain kinds of words—prepositions, adjectives, verbs, and so on—are deleted. The children may find it helpful to attend to several prepositions, for instance, that have been especially troublesome.

At least initially, the teacher may find it useful to use highly predictable materials for creating cloze lessons. Well-known jingles and rhymes, material from predictable books, and stories written by the children are readily available sources that will provide enjoyable opportunities for word-recognition practice.

Using Structural Analysis Clues: Looking at Word Parts

Structural analysis of words includes the study of derived and inflected forms and compound words. Students need a knowledge of root words and affixes so they will be able to understand the changes in word forms, sound, accent, and spelling. Knowing what a syllable is and some generalizations about syllables in words will be useful.

The Syllable

A *syllable* is a word or part of a word that has only *one* vowel sound. A one-syllable word may have two vowels, but only one vowel is sounded. A polysyllabic word has as many syllables as it has separate vowel sounds. Teachers can help children hear how many sounds (syllables) there are in a word by counting (pen–1; cil–2); or by clapping as the teacher pronounces by syllables; or by saying the word in separated sections. Thus, by listening and counting, the teachers and the learners can tell how many syllables there are in words such as these: bookcase, countryside, paper, rule, notebook, pen, blackboard.

Syllabication

Following are some generalizations about dividing words into syllables. They need to be stated cautiously to keep students aware of exceptions.

1. In a polysyllabic word where there are two consonants between two vowels, the syllables will usually divide between the two consonants, unless the first vowel has a long sound. (If the readers are already aware that the vowel will have a long sound, they can probably pronounce the word and so do not need to worry about the generalization.) VCCV indicates letter order—vowel-consonant-consonant-vowel:

   VCCV words: mon key   ob ject   per fect   mis take
   VCCV words with the first vowel sound long: *se* cret   *mi* crobe
   "Twin consonants" between the separated vowels are also a part of this generalization: but ter   cab bage   lad der   cot tage
   skim ming   bal loon   com mon   cop per.

2. When there is one consonant between two vowels, in a polysyllabic word, the consonant usually goes with the second vowel if the preceding vowel has a long sound, and with the first vowel if the first vowel has a short sound. If the consonant between the two vowels is either *x* or *v,* this letter usually remains with the preceding vowel to form the syllable. VCV indicates letter order—vowel-consonant-vowel—in table 9.1.

3. Syllables are classified as open or closed. Open syllables are those that end with a vowel sound; closed syllables are those that end with a consonant sound:

   Open syllables: *se* cret   *po* nies   *ti* ger   *sto* ries   *fa* mous
   Closed syllables: *sun* set   *mon* key   *but* ter   *rab* bit   *cir* cle

4. Prefixes and suffixes are usually separate syllables:

   un fair   *re* paid   *dis* play   *mis* take   *in* active
   hope *less*   pay *ment*   like *ly*   work *ing*   mo *tion*

5. Usually *ed* added to a word does not constitute a separate syllable. However, when *ed* is added to a word that ends with a *t* or a *d,* the *ed* constitutes a separate syllable:

   bolt *ed*   bud *ded*   mend *ed*   plant *ed*   hint *ed*   need *ed*

6. Polysyllabic words ending in a consonant and "le" usually form the final syllable with the consonant + le. For example:

   an *kle*   ap *ple*   arti *cle*   bat *tle*   cir *cle*   bee *tle*   Bi *ble*
   nes *tle*   no *ble*   tan *gle*   sta *ble*   tri *ple*   sam *ple*   ket *tle*

TABLE 9.1. Syllabication of VCV Words

VCV words in which the consonant begins the second syllable			VCV words in which the consonant remains with the preceding syllable		
fa *tal*	be *gin*	to *tal*	*shiv* er	*tax* i	*rap* id
pa *per*	sa *ble*	a *muse*	*nov* el	*ex* ert	*trav* el
de *lay*	ti *ger*	po *lite*	*com* et	*per* il	*mon* ey
e *ver*	gro *cer*	a *corn*	*sol* id	*rob* in	*mim* ic

7. When a word is composed of two complete words, that is, a compound word, it is divided between the two words that make up the compound. For example:

    some where   bird house   school yard   air plane   cow boy   milk man

8. Syllables usually do not break between consonant blend letters or special two-letter combinations:

    lea *ther*,   bro *ther*,   chil *dren*,   an *gry*

9. When each of two adjacent vowels in a word forms a separate syllable, the word divides between the two vowels:

    gi *ant*,   cre *ate*,   li *ons*,   fi *at*,   Su *ez*

It is expected that the students will derive these generalizations after seeing them applied in a large number of words they are reading.

Affixes

Affixes added to root words may be either prefixes or suffixes. A syllable at the beginning of a word that modifies its meaning is a *prefix*. A *suffix* is a letter or a syllable added to the end of a word to modify its meaning. Some common prefixes and suffixes are defined and illustrated in table 9.2 and table 9.3.

Ten of the most frequently occurring prefixes with their meanings and examples are given in table 9.2.

Suffixes may be either inflected forms or derived forms. The inflected forms are the word endings needed because of grammatical changes such as number, case, gender, or tense: examples, dog-dogs, work-worked, it-its. Derived forms are syllables added to give the root word a new meaning: brave-bravery, amuse-amusement, trick-trickster. The commonest inflectional endings are *s, ed, ing, er, est*. Suffixes that are derived forms may have more than one meaning, and learners must be aware of this. Some of the common ones are given in table 9.3.

Combining Forms

Combining forms are those linguistic entities that occur in compound words and are distinguished from affixes by their ability to be the root of a word when used with an affix: *cephal* meaning "head," and *cephalic* meaning "of or relating to the head." Combining forms are generally derived from Greek or Latin. Each comes to us *with* and

TABLE 9.2. Common Prefixes

Prefix	Meaning	Examples
un	*not*	unassuming, uncertain, unlimited, unconscious
mis	*badly/wrongly*	misbehave, misconduct, mismanage, misjudge
fore	*before*	forehead, forethought, forecast, foremost
co, com, con	*together*	cooperate, compact, consolidate, coeducate
dis	*not*	disagreeable, disobey, disorganize, discolor
re	*again*	react, rearrange, rebuilt, redistribute
sub	*under*	submarine, submerge, subdivide, subterranean
trans	*across*	transgress, transport, transact, transatlantic
im	*not*	improper, impossible, imperfect, improbable
in	*not*	inadequate, infinite, insignificant, incomplete

TABLE 9.3. Common Suffixes

Suffix	Meaning	Examples
ful	*filled with*	wonderful, thoughtful
ness	*state of being*	sickness, weariness
less	*without*	doubtless, tasteless
ly	*like*	laughingly, curiously
er, ist	*one who performs*	builder, flier, geologist, druggist

retains its meaning. Knowing the meanings of these combining forms will help students to gather meaning from context efficiently. (See table 9.4)

Compound Words

Early in their reading experiences, children begin to meet compound words. English abounds in compound words, and new words entering the language are likely to be compounds. Rinsky and Griffith state that 60 percent of the new words are compounds.[10]

Children usually read compound words easily if they know the two root words from which the compound is made. However, the teacher must not assume that the child knows the meaning of the compound because the meanings of the roots are known. The new word may have a slightly different meaning, such as *doghouse* made from *dog* and *house,* or a very different meaning from the roots, such as *overdrawn,* made from *over* and *drawn.* The teacher should take time to talk about how the compound

TABLE 9.4. Combined Words

Word	Word Parts	Meaning	Literal Meaning
biology	bio	*life*	study of living things
	logy	*study*	
zoology	zoo	*animals*	study of animal life
	logy	*study*	
biography	bio	*life*	write about life
	graph(y)	*write*	
geography	geo	*earth*	write about the earth
	graph(y)	*write*	
photograph	photo	*light*	write in the light
	graph	*write*	
thermometer	therm(o)	*heat*	measure the heat
	meter	*measure*	
pentagon	penta	*five*	having five angles (sides)
	gon	*angle*	
polygon	poly	*many*	having many sides
	gon	*angle*	
synonym	syn(o)	*equal*	an equal name
	nym	*name*	
telephone	tele	*far*	sound from far away
	phone	*sound*	
diameter	dia	*through*	to measure through
	meter	*measure*	

words the children meet are formed, what the meanings of the roots are, and what the compound word itself means.

Children may be interested in making collections of compound words they find in their reading. They may cut compound words from magazines and newspapers. They may design their own games in which the object is to form pairs of words that become compound words.

Contractions

English uses many contractions. It appears that the numbers of contractions are growing. Children are exposed to many oral contractions that may be confusing when reading begins. Children are surprised and confused to find that *gonna* and *hafta* are not words, since they hear them spoken frequently. Teachers and children need to take time to talk about these oral forms that do not appear in print except as individual words.

Children need help in dealing with standard contracted forms. One cannot assume that because the child can read *can* and *not* that *can't* will be readily known. The child needs to see the teacher remove the letters that are to be dropped out and then see them replaced by the apostrophe. Sentences containing the full and contracted forms should be compared.

> John *did not* go to town.
> John *didn't* go to town.

Some contractions look quite different from the words they replace. For example, *I'd* may be a replacement for *I would* and *I had*. These contractions that bear little resemblance to the full forms need to be discussed and used in a variety of sentences until the children become familiar with them. Children need to practice changing contractions into the full forms. They also need to change pairs of words into contractions.

Word Analysis Practice

Word Analysis Practice through Phonics and Meaning includes three levels, or sets, of thirty cards each in the Intermediate Series:[11]

Level A: 720 words of low fourth-grade reading and spelling ability.
Level B: 1,200 words of high fourth- and low fifth-grade reading and spelling ability.
Level C: 1,200 words of high fifth- and low sixth-grade reading and spelling ability.

Every word is analyzed (if necessary), pronounced, classified by meaning under one of three categories, written, read, and spelled by the pupils. On one side of each card, students are directed to prepare their paper and write the words under the correct topics. Then, on the reverse side of the card, the words are correctly listed in the three categories. See figure 9.4 for an example of one of these cards, showing both the front and reverse sides.

Sample Lessons

CVC-CVCe Contrasts

The student should pronounce, use in sentences, and learn to spell words like the following:

hop	strip	can	tap
hopping	stripping	canning	tapping
hope	stripe	cane	tape
hoping	striping	caning	taping
star	pin	plan	mat
starring	pinning	planning	matting
stare	pine	plane	mate
staring	pining	planing	mating

(front side)

indoors	entire	underneath	bunch	future
eve	until	April	factory	downtown
border	caboose	loaf	daily	bale
afterwards	ounce	gymnasium	center	desert
less	season	gallon	last	autumn
clump	ever	there	mine	weight
schoolroom	double	handful	Sunday	Tuesday
ton	everyday	canyon	pint	playground

Write the topics on your paper. Put the words under the right topics.

Where   When   How Much

(reverse side)

Where	When	How Much
indoors	eve	less
border	afterwards	clump
schoolroom	until	ton
caboose	season	entire
underneath	ever	ounce
gymnasium	everyday	double
there	April	loaf
canyon	daily	gallon
factory	last	handful
center	Sunday	bunch
mine	future	pint
downtown	autumn	bale
desert	Tuesday	weight
playground		

Figure 9.4. Word-analysis practice card No. 16 (From *WORD-ANALYSIS PRACTICE, LEVEL B*, by Donald D. Durrell et al., © 1960 by Harcourt Brace Jovanovich, Inc. and reprinted with permission).

Homonyms

Common homonyms are used for spelling and writing in sentences to check meanings.

aisle-isle	great-grate	profit-prophet
ant-aunt	groan-grown	rein-rain-reign
beach-beech	heal-heel	sew-sow-so
meat-meet	cereal-serial	cite-sight-site
dear-deer	dew-due	vain-vane-vein
mail-male	shone-shown	pear-pare-pair
knew-new	in-inn	cent-scent-sent
hour-our	pain-pane	right-write-rite
fair-fare	foul-fowl	road-rowed-rode

Synonyms

Thinking of synonyms or finding them in the dictionary or thesaurus is good small group practice.

ghost: apparition, phantom, spirit, spook

anticipate: expect, surmise, contemplate, predict, forewarn

cry: weep, sob, whimper, shed tears

complain: mutter, grumble, growl, grunt

direct: manage, govern, conduct, order, prescribe, head

Antonyms

Practice may be given in naming antonyms and writing and spelling selected ones.

hard-easy	small-large	buy-sell
full-empty	tall-short	early-late
fast-slow	shut-open	summer-winter
noisy-quiet	sunny-cloudy	before-afterwards
bold-timid	halt-advance	capture-free
vacant-occupied	accept-reject	customary-unusual

Using Phonic Clues

The use of phonics to decode words is a *last resort*. The student should have learned to look carefully at the word to see if he or she understands its meaning in the rest of the sentence, if he or she can identify parts of the word and put the parts together to arrive at a meaning, or discover the meaning in an illustration on the page. Then, if these efforts have failed, the learner must use phonics to pronounce the word.

The phonic elements are single consonants, consonant combinations, single vowels, vowel combinations, vowel-consonant combinations, and the schwa. The phonic elements may provide the key to pronunciation so the readers can get quickly to meaning. The only purpose phonics serves in *reading* is to help the readers go from print to meaning immediately. A breakdown of all the phonic elements in English is presented in chapter 3. If teachers are confident about supplying the phonic elements when the learners need them, there will be no specific order in which these need to be taught. It is more appropriate to help the readers understand how the phoneme is *sounded* in a given context.

There are those who are over concerned with the matter of teaching the phonic skills so children can "break down and pronounce" words. The emphasis should be much more on reading and approximating what the authors had in mind when they put the ideas on paper.

Some steps for teaching consonant and consonant blend sounds are given in table 9.5. Most children will hear and remember the phonic elements easily if teachers have pictures and provide oral language lessons.

Young children will enjoy practice in using and hearing repetition of different consonant sounds:

C	*c:*	The cat, the cow, and the camel can come in.
Ch	*ch:*	The charming children chased the chickens.
D	*d:*	Daisy did the dirty dishes.
E	*e:*	Elsie the elephant eats everything.
F	*f:*	Funny Phillip fell over the footstool.
G	*g:*	There goes the girl with her gaggle of geese.
H	*h:*	Harry hung his hat on a hook in the hall.
J	*j:*	Jack and Jill enjoyed the jar of jam.
K	*k:*	The kangaroo kicked the copper kettle.
L	*l:*	Louise liked the lovely lemonade.
M	*m:*	The monkeys made more money than the men.
N	*n:*	The nine noisy nestlings never nestled in the nest.
P	*p:*	Pat put the pony in the pasture.
R	*r:*	Ruth and Robert ran around the red roses.
S	*s:*	Sally sells sea shells by the seashore.
Sh	*sh:*	Sharon shouted as she sheared the sheep.
T	*t:*	Tom took the toys to the table.
Th	*th:*	Thelma thinks that they're thin things.
V	*v:*	Verna arranged a vase of violets.
W	*w:*	Willie works in the west wing of the warehouse.
Wh	*wh:*	What a whale of a whistle!

TABLE 9.5. Steps in Teaching a Consonant or Consonant Blend Sound

Steps	*For the letter b*		*For the blend fl*	
1. Provide realia or pictures that are nouns beginning with the sound. Elicit from the learner that the nouns all begin with the same sound.	ball, box, boy, bear, bicycle, balloon		flag, fly, flower, flute, flame	
2. Ask the learner to think of words that begin with the same sound.	basket, baby, buffalo, banana, butterfly, bird		flat, flash, fleet, float, flock	
3. Ask the learner to look at a short list of words and underline all the words that begin with the designated sound.	ball dog boy pig	balloon baby cowboy box	flag play flash trip	drown flame flock fly
4. Say several words and ask the learner to indicate which ones begin with the designated sound.	boy, toy, pig, big, box, pack, back, bell, fell, banana, baby		flash, trash, flock, grass, float, flick, flag, clash	
5. Give the learner a list of words to be changed to new words beginning with the designated sound.	change: at to bat ox to box all to ball ill to bill and to band		change: ash to flash oat to float at to flat lame to flame lock to flock	
6. Ask the learner to identify the ending sound of the word.	cab, mob, rib, hub		does not apply to the consonant blend sounds; however, it does apply to the consonant digraphs: ch, ck, gh, ng, nk, ph, sh, th	
7. Ask the learner to use the new sound in figuring out new words in context.	*Bill* came *back* to the *bank.* The *beds* were *built* of *boxes.*		The *flag* is *flying.* The *flower* was on the *floor.* The *fly flitted* away.	

Teaching New Words Through Consonant Substitution

Initial Consonant Substitution

In primary reading, children have much opportunity to discover new words for themselves after they have already learned the necessary skills to do so.

The language which follows gives children practice in initial consonant substitution:

"Take <u>b</u> away from boy; put in <u>t</u> and you have <u>toy</u>."
"Take <u>s</u> away from sing; put in <u>fl</u> and you have <u>fling</u>."
"Take <u>t</u> away from tore; put in <u>sh</u> and you have <u>shore</u>."

With this skill, using sight words the children already know, they can:

Take <u>t</u> from <u>Tom</u> and <u>oy</u> from boy and discover <u>toy</u>.
Take <u>fl</u> from <u>fly</u> and <u>ing</u> from <u>sing</u> and discover <u>fling</u>.
Take <u>sh</u> from <u>show</u> and <u>ore</u> from <u>tore</u> and discover <u>shore</u>.
Take <u>ch</u> from <u>children</u> and <u>ance</u> from <u>dance</u> and discover <u>chance</u>.

Final Consonant Substitution

In the same way, children practice the same substitution exercise with final sounds:

from	boy	from	sun	from	cap	from	fit	from	pet
to	bo<u>x</u>	to	su<u>p</u>	to	ca<u>n</u>	to	fi<u>x</u>	to	pe<u>n</u>
to	bo<u>g</u>	to	su<u>b</u>	to	ca<u>t</u>	to	fi<u>n</u>	to	pe<u>g</u>
to	Bo<u>b</u>	to	su<u>m</u>	to	ca<u>b</u>	to	fi<u>ll</u>	to	pe<u>p</u>

Medial Letter Substitutions

Vowel substitutions in one-syllable words constitute the same type of practice:

from	pit	from	fill	from	pin	from	peg	from	pop
to	p<u>e</u>t	to	f<u>e</u>ll	to	p<u>e</u>n	to	p<u>i</u>g	to	p<u>u</u>p
to	p<u>u</u>t	to	f<u>a</u>ll	to	p<u>a</u>n	to	p<u>u</u>g	to	p<u>e</u>p
to	p<u>o</u>t	to	f<u>u</u>ll	to	p<u>u</u>n			to	p<u>i</u>p
to	p<u>a</u>t								

Initial Consonant Additions

Consonants or consonant blends can be affixed to phonograms:

ill	and	end
will	band	mend
hill	hand	bend
spill	stand	blend
still		spend
shrill		

Final Consonant Additions

Affixes can be added to change endings:

for	see	go	she
ford	seed	gob	shed
form	seek	God	shep
fort	seem	got	sheep
	seep		

Hearing Sounds

The letter *g* has two sounds. The hard sound of *g* is heard in *go* and *game*, the soft, or *j*, sound is heard in *gem* and *giant*. More words used in beginning reading instruction begin with the hard sound of *g*. In consonant blend sounds, the *g* has the hard sound. Two groups of words are given below: words in which *g* is followed by *e, i,* or *y,* and words in which *g* is followed by any other letter.

Words in which *g* sounds like *j:*

giant	generous	judge
giraffe	George	cabbage
germ	gentle	orange
gypsy	general	large

Words in which *g* has the hard sound:

game	gallon	glass
program	good	gold
gas	goose	gutter
grit	green	glad

The letter *c* has two sounds. The letter *c* has the *k* sound in words like *cat, cold, cut,* and when it is used in consonant blends, such as *clean, cream,* and *crumb.* The letter *c* has the *s* sound in *cent, cider,* and *cycle.* Two groups of words follow: words in which *c* is followed by *e, i,* or *y,* and words in which *c* is followed by other letters.

Words in which *c* sounds like *s:*

cent	city	circle
cedar	cycle	bicycle
ceiling	decide	celery
mice	cigar	cymbal

Words in which *c* has the *k* sound:

call	come	color
coat	catch	crow
client	cuff	crocodile
acre	alcohol	dedicate

Teachers need to be aware that the commonly made *ul* sound is not a representation of the *l* sound at the beginning of a word. They also need to be aware that the *l* on word beginnings is not exactly the same as the *l* on word endings:

little   lake   laugh   wall   bill   cupful

When *r* appears in words, it, too, has a different sound at the end of a word than it had at the beginning. *R* also produces different sounds when combined with vowels.

Making Connections 9.2: Structural Analysis Skills in Basal Readers—Scope and Sequence

It is useful to know what structural analysis skills are being presented in basal readers. It may be helpful to know which ones are presented in the primary grades and which are usually reserved for the upper elementary grades or even the middle school years.

The members of your class should divide themselves so that one or more persons can work with the teacher's manuals at the various grade levels from preprimer through eighth reader. Select one or more series, as your instructor directs, to study thoroughly.

Make a list of the structural analysis skills taught at your particular level. If you are evaluating more than one series, you will probably want to keep the two lists separate. Look to see not only what skills are taught but also how many lessons are suggested for each skill. Study the lessons to see how the textbook authors expect the teacher to develop the skills.

When all class members have their analyses prepared, the class should be able to develop a scope and sequence chart for structural analysis for one or more series of readers. A scope and sequence chart shows all the skills that are to be taught and the grades at which they are to be taught or reviewed.

Can you see some advantages or strengths of a scope and sequence chart? What are some of its disadvantages or weaknesses? What can you say about the structural analysis skills expected to be taught across a complete basal reader series?

Silent Letters

1. The letter *g* is silent before *m* and *n:* gnat, gnu, sign, diaphragm.
2. The letter *h* may be silent before any vowel or when preceded by *r:* rhyme, rhinoceros, honest, herb.
3. The letters *gh* are silent after *a, i,* or *o:* high, eight, bought, caught.
4. The letter *k* is silent before *n:* knock, know, knife, knee.
5. The letter *l* is silent before *k, d,* or *m:* talk, would, calm, salmon.
6. The letter *p* is silent before *s, t,* or *n:* psalm, pneumonia, ptomaine.
7. The letter *t* is silent following *s* or *f:* listen, often, thistle, soften.
8. The letter *w* is silent before *r:* wrist, write, wren, wrong.

Teaching Blends

Techniques for teaching the *cl* blend (see table 9.5) include:

1. Hold up such articles as *clothespin, cloth, clay, clown, clock, clip.* Elicit from the children that they all begin with the sound *cl.*

2. Underline the *cl* blend in a series of words (words in the child's reading vocabulary): *clean, climb, clothes, clap, clown, clock.*
3. Say a list of words and ask the children to raise their hands when the word begins with *cl.*
4. Give the children a list of words to be changed to *cl* words:

lip	clip	flash	clash
lean	clean	rub	club
bean	clean	slap	clap

5. Use the blend sound that is known to figure out new words:

clean——→	clog——→	climb
flash——→	flap——→	flask
bland——→	blush——→	blunder

The objectives of the child in mastering blends are: (1) to hear clearly the blended sound of the two or more consonants, and (2) to distinguish the different blended sounds from single consonant sounds in phonograms.

A consonant digraph is a combination of two letters which result in a new (single) speech sound. The new sound is not the separated consonants blended together but is a new sound.

The consonant digraphs are: *th* in *this* and *th* in *thimble, sh, ch* in *choir, chef,* and *chicken, ph, gh, ng, nk.*

Using the Dictionary

For purposes of finding words needed, determining proper pronunciation of words being used, and establishing meanings appropriate to the context in which the word is being used, all children must achieve proficiency in the effective use of the dictionary. Second-grade students who read at or above grade level should be developing many of the dictionary skills outlined in this section. Much time will be devoted to teaching dictionary skills in both fourth and fifth grade because children will not all acquire the skills when they are taught and the teachers must provide for much reteaching and review.

The teachers will need to provide for teaching and reteaching these skills in the third, fourth, and fifth grades because *all* children need the opportunity to learn a skill when it is useful, meaningful, and relevant to their needs. Presentation of new skills to small groups has a place in present classroom organization, but the teachers must have some way of measuring *all* children's success in learning and *using* skills.

There should be an effectively programmed, self-motivating set of exercises that could be completed individually by students whenever they are ready to learn these dictionary skills. Then such a program could be completed by any student, whether seven or seventeen years old, when knowing dictionary skills would be meaningful and relevant to him or her:

Three such programs are:

1. *David Discovers the Dictionary,* Programmed materials to teach dictionary skills, Coronet Learning Programs, Coronet Building, Chicago, Illinois 60601.

2. *Lessons for Self-Instruction.* Programmed materials to teach dictionary skills, California Test Bureau, 5916 Hollywood Blvd., Los Angeles, California, 90029.
3. The Macmillan *Beginning Dictionary* is accompanied by the *School Dictionary Practice Book.*[12]

A number of dictionaries are available for students in the elementary school, and classrooms should be provided with sufficient copies of a variety of dictionaries so that all children can have easy access to them. The dictionaries should span the range of reading levels in the classroom. This is necessary in order to make dictionary use possible for all the children and to develop the dictionary habit.

A few of the elementary school dictionaries are:

My First Dictionary, An American Heritage Dictionary (Boston: Houghton Mifflin, 1980).
The Golden Picture Dictionary, A Beginning Dictionary of More Than 2500 Words, Lucille Ogle and Tina Thorn, editors (New York: Western Publishing Co., 1976).
Children's Dictionary, An American Heritage Dictionary, Fernando de Mello Vianna, editorial director (Boston: Houghton Mifflin, 1979).
Scott Foresman Beginning Dictionary, Clarence Barnhart and E. L. Thorndike, editors (Glenview, Ill.: Scott Foresman, 1979).
Scott Foresman Intermediate Dictionary, Clarence Barnhart, editor (Glenview, Ill.: Scott, Foresman, 1979).
Webster's New World Dictionary for Young Readers, David B. Guralnik, editor (Cleveland: Collins, 1979).
The World Book Dictionary, 2 vols. Clarence L. Barnhart, editor-in-chief (Chicago: Field Enterprises Educational Corporation).

The skills needed for dictionary usage have been classified as location, pronunciation, and meaning skills, and are outlined here. This chapter includes some additional exercises and some important techniques to help children with comprehension in reading.

Location Skills

In order to find words quickly in the dictionary, children need to know how entries are made and how many forms of a word are included in the dictionary. If the children are looking for *reporting* and there is no entry for this word, they must know that *reporting* is derived from *report* and that they must look for the *report* entry. Six needed location skills are:

1. Ability to arrange words in alphabetical order: by initial letter, by second letter, and by third and fourth letters.
2. Ability to find words quickly in an alphabetical list.
3. Ability to open the dictionary quickly to the section in which the word is to be found; to the proper third or fourth of the book.
4. Ability to use the two guide words at the top of the page.
5. Ability to think of the names of letters immediately preceding and immediately following the letter being located.
6. Ability to use special pronunciation-meaning sections of the dictionary; for example, medical terms, slang expressions, musical terms, and foreign words and phrases.

Exercises to Learn Alphabetical Order

To fix alphabetical order, the teachers may use a number of different exercises, according to the needs of the children.

1. Alphabetical order may begin with only part of the alphabet.
   a. Put these words in alphabetical order:
      face, green, dog, cow, elephant, box, apple
      1. _____ 2. _____ 3. _____ 4. _____
      5. _____ 6. _____ 7. _____
   b. Write these words in alphabetical order:
      story, yellow, banana, pear, fruit, cat
   c. Write in the missing words in alphabetical order. Choose one from the box for each line:

      1. animal,   2. _____ , 3. fox,   4. _____

      5. milk,   6. _____ , 7. _____

      | boy |
      | study |
      | penny |
      | hill |

   d. Arrange all the words in the box in alphabetical order:

      1.
      2.
      3.
      4.
      5.
      6.
      7.
      8.

      | store |
      | house |
      | city |
      | boxes |
      | zoo |
      | yesterday |
      | puppy |
      | friend |

2. Alphabetical order can later include all the alphabet.
   a. Some words below appear in alphabetical order. Choose from the words in the box, the necessary words to complete a list of twenty-six words in alphabetical order:

1. after	10. _____	19. straw	zest	donkey
2. baby	11. kind	20. turkey	camel	Indian
3. _____	12. _____	21. _____	lake	uncle
4. _____	13. mouse	22. _____	orange	pony
5. _____	14. nest	23. _____	rabbit	water
6. friends	15. _____	24. xylophone	yesterday	jello
7. goats	16. _____	25. _____	hill	vest
8. _____	17. quickly	26. _____	evergreen	
9. _____	18. _____			

   b. The teachers can provide the students lists of twenty-six words and ask them to arrange the list in alphabetical order.
   c. Students can arrange all the first names or the surnames of the class members in alphabetical order.

3. Arranging alphabetical lists by second letters in words:

a. _____ must		a. _____ saying	
b. _____ mask		b. _____ sum	
c. _____ mend		c. _____ send	
d. _____ mint		d. _____ sold	
e. _____ mold		e. _____ sick	

4. Guide words

First part of the dictionary is A–G.

Second part of the dictionary is H–P.

Third part of the dictionary is Q–Z.

In which part will you find:

a. mathematics   c. favorite   e. question

b. weather   d. arithmetic   f. mood

5. Guide words

The guide words on one page of the dictionary are *storehouse-strain*.

Do these words come (1) before this page; (2) on this page, or (3) after this page?

a. _____ stony   c. _____ strike   e. _____ stork

b. _____ straight   d. _____ stub   f. _____ spy

Pronunciation Skills

Twelve skills in pronunciation are detailed below:

1. Ability to use the pronunciation key at the bottom of each page.
2. Ability to use the full pronunciation key in the front of the dictionary.
3. Ability to use and interpret accent marks, both primary and secondary.
4. Ability to select the proper heteronyms; for example, rec'ord or re cord', ob'ject or ob ject'.
5. Ability to identify silent letters in words pronounced.
6. Ability to recognize differences between spelling and pronunciation (lack of phoneme-grapheme relationship).
7. Ability to use phonetic spelling for pronunciation.
8. Ability to discriminate vowel sounds.
9. Ability to use diacritical marks as an aid in pronunciation.
10. Understanding of the way syllables are marked in dictionaries.
11. Ability to identify unstressed syllables in words.
12. Arriving at pronunciation and recognizing it as correct.

Exercises to Learn the Pronunciation Skills

1. The pronunciation key can provide for the comparison of sounds. If the teachers give the stimulus word *role,* the children can respond with $\bar{o}$ as in *go* and *open.* The children will use the pronunciation key in their dictionaries. If the teachers say *much-mush,* the children can respond with "*much* ends with the *ch;* mush ends with *sh.*"

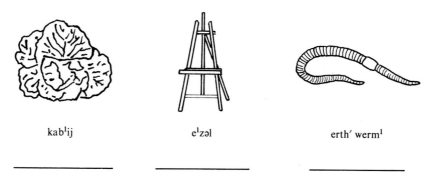

kab'ij   e'zəl   erth' werm[1]

_____   _____   _____

Figure 9.5. Exercises in pronunciation skills

If the teachers say "long *a*" or "short *e*," the children can give the appropriate words in the key or others.

2. After some familiarity with the key, pupils may be challenged by this exercise. Look at the picture and the phonetic spelling, then spell the word correctly. If the children are in doubt, encourage them to use the dictionary. They should avoid misspelling if possible. (See figure 9.5.)

Meaning Skills

Ten meaning skills in using the dictionary are:

1. Learning meanings of new words by reading simple definitions.
2. Using pictures and meanings in the dictionary to arrive at meanings.
3. Using an illustrative sentence to arrive at meanings.
4. Using two different meanings for the same word.
5. Approximating real-life sizes by using dictionary pictures and explanatory clues.
6. Selecting the specific meaning for a given context.
7. Understanding special meanings: idioms, slang expressions, and other figures of speech.
8. Using the concept of root word.
9. Interpreting multiple meanings of words.
10. Knowing when meaning has been satisfied through dictionary usage.

Some Dictionary Exercises

Syllabication and Dictionary Respelling

The dictionary tells you three things about a word:

1. How to divide it in syllables
2. Which syllable to stress or accent
3. Pronunciation by respelling

Look up these words. Copy them in syllables and put in the accent. Copy the respelling to show the pronunciation.

Words	Syllables	Respelling with marks
1. separate	sep-a-rate	sep'ə rāt
2. examination	ex-am-i-na-tion	eg-zam' i nā'sh ən
3. refinement		
4. understanding		
5. appreciate		

Selecting the Best Definition

Word study through the use of the dictionary: a sample lesson. Using your dictionary, write the meaning of the word *play* as it is used in each of the following sentences.

1. Children like to *play* during recess.
   Definition of play: (fun, sport, action to amuse oneself)
2. She will *play* the piano at noon today.
   Definition of play: (have fun; do something in sport; perform)
3. He will *play* a leading part in the game.
   Definition of play: (to take part in)
4. The children gave a *play* at the end of the unit.
   Definition of play: (a story acted on a stage)
5. John's dog will *play* tricks.
   Definition of play: (act)
6. We watched the sunlight *play* on the leaves.
   Definition of play: (make light, quick movements)
7. Let's *play* that the big paper box is a boat.
   Definition of play: (make believe; pretend in fun)
8. Tom made the winning *play* in the checker game.
   Definition of play: (a turn, act, or move in a game)
9. Don't *play* with your pencils.
   Definition of play: (act carelessly; do foolish things)
10. Our team will *play* the other sixth grade.
    Definition of play: (compete against)

Using the Microcomputer As An Aid in Teaching Word-Recognition Skills

The microcomputer offers the teacher several possible ways to help students with word recognition. There are numerous "skill-drill" types of programs similar to pages found in many workbooks and ditto packages. The teacher must decide if such programs have utility for the children or whether students can gain as much from more conventional presentations if such practice is needed at all. An advantage of microcomputer programs is that they can be used as many times as the child wishes to run them and that they respond with no impatience to the child's efforts.

A variety of many new software games is available to help the child develop more adequate word recognition abilities. These may be quite attractive to the children. They should be evaluated by the same standards that are used to assess the quality of regular games. The teacher will need to decide if all the skills practiced in playing the available games are necessary to learn to read.[13] Games that emphasize thinking strategies in addition to the skills of reading may be the most desirable ones.

Finally, word processing programs that allow children to write their own stories and print them out with printers that produce hard copy for bookmaking may be the most useful tools for promoting word recognition. As with writing with more conventional tools, the child writes the words he or she needs in meaningful and personally relevant settings. If a microcomputer is available, the teacher should take full advantage of at least one word processing program for the young writers and readers.

Summary

Helps for teachers in teaching word recognition skills to students have been presented in this chapter. Learning a meaningful stock of sight words through the use of language experiences was discussed. Language experiences could include using environmental print, dictated stories, rebus, wordless picture books, predictable and taped books and book making. The use of context clues, both those derived from pictures and from print, was stressed as a meaningful approach to word recognition. Aspects of structural and phonic analysis were outlined for teachers. A section on the use of the dictionary was included. The chapter ended with a discussion of the use of the computer as an aid to word recognition. The use of word processing programs by children was identified as an important way to encourage word recognition.

For Further Reading

Bond, G. L.; Tinker, M. A.; Wasson, B. B.; and Wasson, J. B. *Reading Difficulties, Their Diagnosis and Correction,* 5th ed. Englewood Cliffs, N.J.: Prentice-Hall, 1984: Chapter 10, "Correcting Deficiencies in Meaning Clues to Word Recognition," pp. 173–94; Chapter 11, "Correcting Faulty Perceptual and Decoding Skills in Word Recognition," pp. 195–224.

Bridge, Connie A.; Winograd, Peter N.; and Haley, Darlene. "Using Predictable Materials vs. Pre-primers to Teach Beginning Sight Words." *The Reading Teacher* 36 (May 1983), pp. 884–91.

Burmeister, Lou E. *Words—From Print to Meaning.* (Classroom Activities for Building Sight Vocabulary, for Using Context Clues, Morphology, and Phonics). Reading, Mass.: Addison Wesley, 1975.

Ekwall, Eldon E. *Locating and Correcting Reading Difficulties,* 4th ed. Columbus, Ohio: Chas. E. Merrill, 1985.

Ellis, DiAnn W., and Preston, Fannie W. "Enhancing Beginning Reading Using Wordless Picture Books in a Cross-Age Tutoring Program." *The Reading Teacher* 37 (April 1984), pp. 692–98.

Gamby, Gert. "Talking Books and Taped Books: Materials for Instruction." *The Reading Teacher* 36 (January 1983), pp. 366–69.

Holdaway, Don. *The Foundations of Literacy.* Sidney, Australia: Ashton Scholastic, 1979: Chapter 6, "Teaching Basic Strategies," pp. 104–25.

Miller, Edith F. *"Stimulate Reading . . . with a Dictionary."* In A. J. Harris and E. R. Sipay, editors, *Readings on Reading Instruction,* 3d ed. New York: Longman, 1984.

Moon, Louise, and Scorpio, Carolyn M. "When Word Recognition is OK—Almost!" *The Reading Teacher* 37 (May 1984), pp. 825–27.

Park, Barbara. "The Big Book Trend—A Discussion with Don Holdaway." *Language Arts* 59 (November/December 1982), pp. 815–21.

Ringler, Lenore H., and Weber, Carol S. *A Language-Thinking Approach to Reading, Diagnosis and Teaching.* New York: Harcourt Brace, 1984: Chapter 6, "Language As a Base for Word Identification," pp. 119–41.

Smith, Frank. *Essays into Literacy, Selected Papers and Some Afterthoughts.* London: Heinemann, 1983: Chapter 3, "The Role of Prediction in Reading," pp. 26–34.

Veatch, Jeannette et al. *Key Words to Reading: The Language Experience Approach Begins,* 2d ed. Columbus, Ohio: Charles E. Merrill, 1979.

Notes

1. E. W. Dolch, *Dolch Basic Sight Word Test* (Champaign, Ill.: Garrard Publishing Co., 1942).
2. Edward Fry, "The Instant Words," a 600-word basic vocabulary, graded according to frequency and approximate grade level of difficulty. These are found in Fry's book *Elementary Reading Instruction,* (New York: McGraw-Hill, 1977), p. 73.
3. *Mother Goose in Hieroglyphics* (Boston: Houghton Mifflin, 1962).
4. Mabel O'Donnell, *Teacher's Manual for the Pre-primer Program, The Harper and Row Basic Reading Program* (New York: Harper and Row, 1966), p. 21.
5. Richard W. Woodcock, *Rebuses as a Medium in Beginning Reading Instruction* (Nashville, Tenn.: Institute on Mental Retardation and Intellectual Development, George Peabody College for Teachers, 1968). Supported by Grant HD 973 from the National Institute of Child Health and Human Development.
6. Nancy Larrick, "Wordless Picture Books and the Teaching of Reading," *The Reading Teacher* 29 (May 1976), pp. 743–46.
7. Sharon V. Arthur, "What Can You Do with a Book without Words?" *The Reading Teacher* 35 (March 1982), pp. 738–40.
8. Dolores P. Dickerson, "A Study of Use of Games to Reinforce Sight Vocabulary," *The Reading Teacher* 36 (October 1982), pp. 46–49.
9. Frank Smith, *Understanding Reading* (New York: Holt, Rinehart and Winston, 1971), p. 7.
10. Lee Ann Rinsky and Barbara Griffith, *Teaching Word Attack Skills* (Dubuque, Iowa: Gorsuch Scarisbrick, Publishers, 1978), p. 61.
11. Donald D. Durrell, Helen A. Murphy, Doris Spencer, and Jane H. Catterson, *Word Analysis Practice through Phonics and Meaning, Levels A, B, and C* (New York: Harcourt, Brace 1961).
12. William D. Halsey, *Beginning Dictionary* (New York: Macmillan, 1977).
13. Ernest Balajthy, "Reinforcement and Drill by Microcomputer," *The Reading Teacher* 37 (February 1984), pp. 490–94.

10
Teaching the Comprehension Skills of Reading

Chapter Outline

Vocabulary

comprehension
compare and contrast
sequence
antecedent
prediction
literal level
interpretive level
evaluative level
scaffolding
skimming
function words, structure
  words
cloze procedure
schema, schemata
levels of questioning
writing techniques
context
figurative language
basal reader
trade books

Questions

1. Write a set of statements that describe comprehension and emphasize its importance in reading.

2. What kinds of activities can teachers do with students to emphasize comprehension?

3. What are the skills of comprehension as described by Smith?

4. Why is the building of schemata so important to the reading process?

5. What are the levels at which questions should be asked? Give examples of questions at each of these levels.

6. Name some writing techniques that readers should recognize as aids to comprehension.

7. What is the critical nature of context as it relates to comprehension?

8. What is the purpose of scaffolding?

9. How is an understanding of function words and figurative language important to comprehension?

10. What is important about lots of easy reading practice?

11. What kinds of materials can be used to facilitate growth of reading comprehension?

A primary concern of teachers is helping students develop meaningful concepts as they read. Unless the pupils learn to synthesize meanings as they read through the lines of print, they are wasting their time. For most readers, there is a positive relationship between the ability to handle the mechanics of reading and the ability to understand and interpret the ideas they read. Some children pronounce words well and comprehend little, while others glean much from the print but have great difficulty with fluent pronunciation.

In this chapter, perspectives for understanding comprehension are presented along with a list of comprehension skills, strategies for teaching, and materials for helping children learn to comprehend print.

Comprehension in Reading

All teachers probably would agree that the primary reason for reading anything is to understand it. Without that purpose, there would be little reason for reading. Dictionary definitions of comprehension include: to grasp mentally, to understand, to take in, to discern, to know, to think about and arrive at a meaning, intelligence, and sense.[1] If comprehension includes all of those items, it is not surprising that reading specialists have not yet detailed any specific way to teach comprehension of reading material. However, teachers do have available to them knowledge about the process of comprehension and many strategies that have helped children improve their comprehension skills. Teachers have the dual professional responsibilities of carefully assessing children's needs and matching instructional strategies and children so that improvement in reading comprehension will occur.

Comprehension requires the application of many skills that have been learned already. First, accurate, rapid word recognition ability without much attention to the mechanics of reading will free the readers to think about what they are reading; second, a large store of vocabulary and concepts will enable children to read quickly with good understanding; third, the greater the background of information the reader has and applies to what is being read, the greater the comprehension. If students read about opening the gates to *irrigate* the fields but know nothing about how irrigation systems work, they may not understand the concepts. In the fourth place, the readers' abilities to use the organizational structure of the paragraph or to sense organizational patterns or sequences of events will also help determine the efficiency of their comprehension.[2]

This text has emphasized the importance of enriched oral language competence before reading. Horn cautioned us, decades ago, about the language needs of reading-disabled students:

> . . . with the exception of a few special types, most of the so-called reading disabilities may more properly be ascribed to disability in language. The full significance of this fact for the teaching of reading has not always been appreciated. As a result, the more technical and peripheral aspects of reading, such as phonics, eye movements, and mechanical drills, have loomed overlarge both in research and

in practice, as compared with the vastly greater importance of the central thought processes. Yet it is clear that very little improvement may be expected from formal drill in reading unless at the same time provision is made for the enrichment of experience, the development of language abilities, and the improvement of thinking.[3]

In 1984, Adams presented similar ideas. In an interview he stated:

I take the word *self* to mean a personal model of language. That is, the way children make sense of themselves and their place within their world by using language to express themselves and explore their own identity. . . . Expressive discourse differs from other kinds of discourse in that it is highly personal, particular to the person doing the speaking. . . . In making sense of new information, the expressive is fundamental to learners of any age. When I am trying to cope with concepts that are new to me, I have to explore them, come to terms with them, by talking about them in my own personal language, before I am ready to cope with them in the language of the . . . textbook. . . .[4]

Avenues to Comprehension

Comprehension involves several intellectual skills. Teachers can work orally with young children and, of course, must help older students acquire these skills if they do not already have them. Teachers who are skilled in questioning and responding with children can extend the abilities of the children to observe accurately, to judge size, shape, and distance, to compare, contrast, and categorize and sequence. The following items suggest some of the things teachers may do:

1. *Comparison and contrast.* Discuss likenesses and differences in slightly different sizes and colors; or two people dressed similarly but not alike.
2. *Classifying.* Match the workers to their jobs—a teacher *instructs,* a firefighter *rescues,* a swimmer *dives,* a grocer *sells,* a shoemaker *cobbles.* Put things in categories—*flowers,* peony, dahlia, tulip; *foods,* butter, salad, cauliflower; *domestic animals,* donkey, pig, sheep. Categorizing may help children build better ideas of what the world is like and how it is organized.
3. *Sequencing.* Retell stories with events in proper order; list directions in the order given; remember the steps to complete a task.
4. *Matching.* Match titles to pictures; statements to speakers; words to objects or pictures; for example, five $= 5 = \therefore$.
5. *Remembering.* What did John say he could do to help us? Why do we need to tell our parents first? Can you say the poem we read yesterday?
6. *Responding creatively to open-ended questions.* What should Robert have done? Why? How can Jack get back home now? What would you do?
7. *Antecedents.* Mary gave the teacher *her* book. To whom does *her* refer? Give it to John if *he* comes back. To whom does *he* refer?
8. *Asking and responding.* Who, which, what, when, where, or how?

9. *Sensory awareness.* Utilize the think box or the feel box. Ask: What is it? What could it be used for? Does almost everyone have one? Is it soft, hard, fuzzy, light, rough, or smooth?

10. *Predicting.* Children can be asked to predict what will happen next in stories they hear and read.

Skills of Comprehension

The exercises cited in this section will illustrate both *literal level skills* and those skills beyond the literal level that are *inferential* or *evaluative*.

The twelve types of exercises suggested by Smith are.[5]

1. Understanding and remembering details or facts. The ability to do this exercise has value, but it is probably overused in many classrooms.
2. Finding the main idea in the paragraph.
3. Understanding sequences of time, place, idea, or events.
4. Following directions.
5. Reading for implied meanings and drawing inferences.
6. Reading to understand characterization and setting.
7. Sensing relationships in time, place, cause and effect.
8. Reading to anticipate outcomes.
9. Recognizing the author's mood or tone.
10. Comparing and contrasting.
11. Forming generalizations.
12. Skimming.

Examples of many of these skills are provided here.

1. *Understanding and remembering details or facts.*
   The example in figure 10.1 asks the reader to note important details. The second example in figure 10.2 asks the reader to eliminate irrelevant details. The recent work of August, Flavell, and Clift suggests that poor readers have much greater difficulty in separating main ideas from details in paragraphs or stories.[6]
2. *The main idea in the paragraph.*
   Read the paragraphs in figure 10.3. Circle the letter in front of the sentence opposite each paragraph that gives the correct answer.
3. *Understanding sequences of time, place, ideas, or events.*
   Exercises appear in student workbooks requiring the students to arrange ideas in numerical order or to decide what happened first, second, third, and so on. In the exercise in figure 10.4, the reader must decide which of two *events* occurred first or last.
4. *Ability to follow directions.*

• Read the following paragraphs, and pay close attention. Below the paragraphs are some unfinished sentences with three possible endings. Print an X beside the best ending.

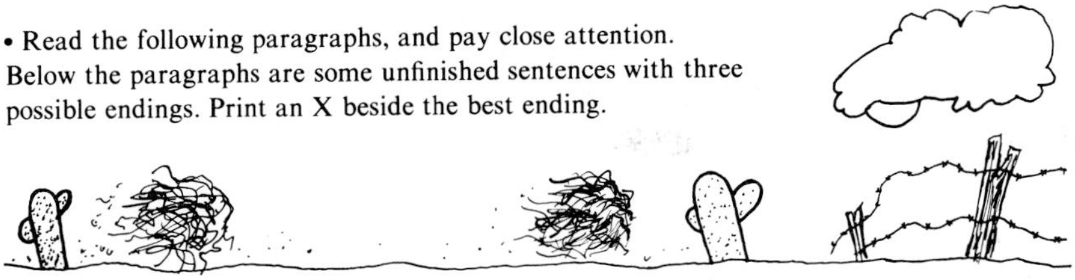

People in the western part of the United States are quite used to seeing large, dried bushes rolling along a plain or by the side of a road. These bushes are called *tumbleweeds*. The tumbleweed is a type of plant found on North American plains and prairies.

One of the best known tumbleweeds in the United States is called the Russian thistle. This spiny plant is round and bushy. It grows to be two feet high or more.

The main stem of the tumbleweed is pale green and has many white branches shooting out from it. On these branches are the tumbleweed's flat, egg-shaped leaves. In the fall, when the seeds of the tumbleweed are ripe, the leaves wither and the stem of the plant breaks off at ground level.

The dried plant is then carried along by the wind for many miles until it is stopped by a barbed-wire fence or until it falls into a gully. In this way, the tumbleweed is able to scatter its seeds over the plain.

1. The tumbleweed is a

_____ Russian weed.

_____ type of plant.

_____ prairie dog.

2. You would probably see tumbleweeds if you lived

_____ in a forest.

_____ on the western plains.

_____ near the ocean.

3. The tumbleweed's stem breaks off

_____ in the summer.

_____ in the spring.

_____ in the fall.

4. A tumbleweed dries up and is "tumbled" about by the wind to

_____ attract honeybees.

_____ scatter its seeds.

_____ fall into a gully.

Figure 10.1. Noting important details. (From William K. Durr, Jean M. LaPere, and Ruth H. Brown, *Practice Book for Passports* [Boston: Houghton Mifflin, 1976], p. 59.)

Read each paragraph. The first sentence in each paragraph tells the main idea. Draw a line through any other sentence that does not give details about the main idea. You will draw a line through two sentences in 2.

1. There was not enough light each day. This was because the sun ran too fast across the heavens. The people needed more light to finish their work. ~~The dogs were barking at the moon.~~ There was not enough light for plants to grow.

2. Maui's mother was a clever worker. The sun made the hills light and warm. His mother took bark from trees and made tapa cloth. She pounded the bark and made thin strips. Maui ran across the heavens. She pasted the strips together. They dried and became tapa cloth.

Figure 10.2. Finding irrelevant details. (Adapted from Theodore Clymer, Gloria Keil, and Robert B. Ruddell, *Skilpack for How It Is Nowadays,* Reading 720, Rainbow Edition [Lexington, Mass.: Ginn (Xerox Corporation), 1979, 1976], p. 137.)

Unit 3

1. Mushrooms don't grow on trees. If you see mushrooms stuck between the branches, you know they were put there. Most likely it was the work of a red squirrel. Red squirrels like mushrooms. They like to put them in trees. They they have food to eat in the winter.

2. Most dead birds are never found. Some may be covered by leaves or dirt. Others are eaten by animals. Still other dead birds may fall into the water or other places where they can't be found. We find only about two of every hundred dead birds.

3. Polar bears grow very big as they get old. When they are grown up, polar bears weigh about a thousand pounds. When polar bears are born, they weigh only one pound. Wouldn't it be something if older people weighed a thousand times more than they did at birth?

4. It's a salty world in which we live. There is salt in the ocean. There is salt in the earth. There is salt inside of you—in your blood, sweat, and even in your tears. It's a good thing too. Without salt you couldn't live.

5. How long can a cactus go without water? There is one type of cactus plant that lives for four years without water. When it finally rains, this plant makes up for lost time. It stores up to two tons of water!

Unit 3

1. The story mainly tells:

   (A) Why there are mushrooms in trees
   (B) Why squirrels like mushrooms
   (C) Where to grow mushrooms

2. The story mainly tells:

   (A) Why we don't see many dead birds
   (B) Why animals eat dead birds
   (C) Why birds die

3. The story mainly tells:

   (A) How big polar bears grow to be
   (B) How small polar bears are
   (C) How people are like polar bears

4. The story mainly tells:

   (A) How salty the world is
   (B) What salt is like
   (C) Why people use salt

5. The story mainly tells:

   (A) Where cactus plants live
   (B) How big cactus plants are
   (C) How long some cactuses go without water

Figure 10.3. (From Richard A. Boning, *Getting the Main Idea,* Book C, Unit 3. Copyright 1982 by Barnell Loft Ltd., 958 Church Street, Baldwin, Long Island, New York 11510. Used with permission.)

UNIT 9

Owney became the greatest dog traveler of all time. The dog was a pet of the post office. It went everywhere on the mail trains. After visiting post offices in America, it went across the sea. The Emperor of Japan gave the dog a medal. Owney finally returned to New York with more than 200 medals!

True or False

1. The scene above took place after Owney was allowed to travel on trains.

2. The ruler of Japan gave Owney a medal after the dog traveled across the sea.

Figure 10.4. (From Richard A. Boning, *Detecting the Sequence,* 3d. ed., Book D, Unit 9. Copyright 1982 by Barnell Loft Ltd., 958 Church Street, Baldwin, Long Island, New York 11510. Used with permission.)

MAKING A WORD GAME

Make this game. Then play the game.
1. Get some drawing paper. Cut out 22 cards of the same size.
2. Choose five different words you learned in *Images*. Write these words on a piece of paper.
3. Make five piles of four cards each. Write one of the words on each of the four cards in the first pile. Then write another word on each of the four cards in the next pile. Do this with all five words. Write TOO BAD on the two cards you have left.
4. Now you are ready to play. Get one or two others to play with you. Mix up all the cards. Spread them out on the table face down. Keep the list of words you wrote where everyone can see it.

5. Pick up one card. But before you look at the word, show it to the others. Try to guess what the word is. If you guess right, you can keep the card. If not, put it back in the same place you found it.

6. If you pick a TOO BAD card, you must return it to the table and mix it in with the others.

7. Each player picks a card in turn. The player who ends up with the most cards wins.[7]

5. *Reading for implied meanings and drawing inferences.*
Read the story.[8]

Old Ironsides has tall masts and many sails. A long time ago, it was used in a war at sea.

Old Ironsides was built at a *shipyard* in Boston in 1794. It is made of wood. But people called it "Old Ironsides" because its sides were very hard, like *iron*. Today, Old Ironsides is open to the *public*. All people can go on it and see what ships were like many years ago.

Circle the words that best complete each sentence.

Old Ironsides is a _____ .   *Iron* is a _____ .
building (ship) city   (metal) cloth color

A shipyard is _____ .
   a place where ships sail   a place to play games
       (a place where ships are built)

The *public* means _____ .
   (all people) sailors builders

6. *Reading to understand characterization and setting.*
Read each story. Then underline the two answers that tell what each story character is ilke.[9]

a. It had not rained for days. One hot day followed the next. "I must do something for my farm," thought the farmer. And she began to take water from the well to water her plants. Day after day she watered the plants wishing that it would rain on her farm.
   1. hard working   3. bossy   5. mean
   2. shy   4. hopeful   6. lazy

b. The bear was happy with the fish he had caught. "Look at all these fish," he tolds his friends. "I am a very good fisherman. I caught these fish all by myself. If you want some fish for supper, just help yourself. There is enough here for everyone."
   1. boastful   3. friendly   5. hopeful
   2. fearful   4. playful   6. brave

7. *Sensing relationships in time, place, cause, and effect.*

The sentences on the left tell what the children are doing. The sentences on the right tell what will happen because of their work. Match the sentences. Write each number on the line in front of the words that tell what will happen.[10]

1. The children are cleaning up the block.	**4** The children will have a nice picture to look at.
2. The children are planting seeds.	**5** There will be no broken glass on the street.
3. On one day a week, cars can not drive down the street.	**3** Children can play in the street.
4. The children are painting on the wall of one building.	**1** The block will look clean and nice.
5. The children are gathering bottles from all the people.	**2** Flowers will grow.

8. *Reading to anticipate outcomes.*

Read the story below. Then tell what will happen.[11]

Guess what happened to Sarah! Her baseball was caught in the tree branches. She tried throwing rocks into the tree. But she couldn't knock the ball down. She looked around the yard and saw the ladder. She leaned it against the tree and climbed up.

Dad came out of the house. "I'll need this ladder to put on the storm windows today," he said.

_____

_____

_____

9. *Recognizing the author's mood or tone.*

A good reader senses the author's mood or tone. This ability to respond to the writer's feelings is important to the reader. The author's purpose, mood, and general outlook need to be understood by the reader whether these are stated directly or subtly implied.

Tennyson reveals a great deal about how he feels about the brook as it "bubbles", "babbles", and "bickers" down the valley. The last four stanzas of Tennyson's poem "The Brook" follow:

I steal by lawns and grassy plots,
  I slide by hazel covers;
I move the sweet forget-me-nots
  That grow for happy lovers.

I slip, I slide, I gloom, I glance,
  Among my skimming swallows;
I make the netted sunbeams dance
  Against my sandy shallows.

I murmur under moon and stars
  In brambly wildernesses;
I linger by my shingly bars,
  I loiter round my cresses;

And out again I curve and flow
  To join the brimming river;
For men may come and men may go,
  But I go on forever.[12]

10. *Comparing and contrasting.*

GEESE AND AIRPLANES

Often fifty or sixty geese, hissing and honking in their excitement, fly southward together in the fall of the year. As they soar upward into the air, they gradually form a wedge, or huge "V" in the sky. Usually at the point of the wedge is a fearless old gander that leads the flight. Faithfully each year he pilots the flock to the South, where the geese spend the winter. Early in the spring, he brings them back to the northern wilderness. There, concealed by the tall reeds of a lake, the geese make their nests and raise their young.

During their long flight the geese must have places to rest and to recover their strength. Many little lakes hidden deep in the forest are used by the geese as resting and feeding stations. The pilot-gander always seems to know where each of the lakes is. He stops briefly so that his flock can rest and eat, just as the pilot of an airplane stops to rest and eat.

When pilots fly planes in a group, they form a wedge. The airplanes soar far upward into the sky and look much like silver geese flying fearlessly in calm or cloudy weather.

Flying in a V-shaped wedge helps the planes in many ways. The plane that flies ahead of the others leads the way safely. The pilot of each plane has a clear view before him. This would not be true if the planes flew in a straight line.

The strong wind made by the powerful thrust of the planes' jet engines stirs up waves in the air. By flying in a wedge, each plane can stay out of the strong wind that is stirred up by the airplanes ahead of it.

Put G before statements that are true about flying geese.
Put A before statements that are true about flying airplanes.
Put A and G before statements that are true of both geese and planes.

_____ They often fly in a wedge.
_____ In a wedge, each one is out of the wind wave made by the others.
_____ The one at the point of the wedge is the leader.
_____ They look like silver.

_____ The thrust of the jet engines stirs up a strong wind.
_____ While in a wedge, each one has a clear view.
_____ They stop for rest and food.
_____ They nest in northern lakes.[13]

11. *Formulating generalized statements.*

A generalization is a statement or principle that encompasses the common characteristics of a chain of ideas or individual statements. Generalizations can be developed with children through an inductive method of teaching. By analyzing their own experiences, and stating concepts that are meaningful and useful to them, they can organize the descriptive data they have to formulate generalized statements.

Very young children can discuss with the teachers the products provided for us to use by the cow. The cow gives milk; the cow provides butter and cheese; the cow provides meat; the cow gives us leather, tallow for candles, buttons, and even jello. From such a list, we can generalize that the cow is a very useful animal to people.

Teachers are asking their students to generalize when they use such informal questions as:

"How is this like what we did yesterday?"

"What would happen if . . . ?"

"Now do the experiment again and see if the same thing happens."

Successful people often seem to have similar qualities. Two of these qualities are *determination* and *courage*. Read the following article about Dr. Frederick Banting. Look for details in the article that demonstrate these qualities. Write the details under the headings below.

DR. FREDERICK BANTING

Dr. Frederick Banting was determined to help people suffering from diabetes. One day, while preparing for a lecture at his university, Dr. Banting thought of a new way to treat this disease. Although he was told that others had tried this method and failed, he was convinced that it could work. He continued to request help until he was given a laboratory in which he could prove his idea.

Later, he resigned his job at the university and gave up his medical career in order to give complete attention to his laboratory work. After eight months of steadfast labor, he discovered insulin. Insulin has helped to save the lives of many diabetics.[14]

1. Determination _____

_____

_____

_____

2. Courage _____

_____

_____

12. *Skimming.*

Skimming is a skill that can be developed to a high degree and used profitably in all kinds of reading. Skimming enables people to quickly select those items they are interested in reading and to reject those they are not. Most of us use skimming regularly in selecting those parts of the daily newspaper we want to read more closely. Teachers need to point out to students that skimming is only to grasp general significance and not to learn details or factual information. Skimming requires that the reader cover a large quantity of reading material without "reading the words"—perhaps moving down the middle of the column of print rather than following lines of print from left to right across the column.

Students are using skimming wisely when they can:

a. Look through a table of contents to see on what page a specific chapter begins.
b. Skim the article in the encyclopedia about Edna Ferber to see which of her novels was published in 1958.
c. Skim through the ending of the story to see if the lost puppy was rescued or came back home.
d. Skim through the story to find the part that describes what kind of person the old peddler was.

Strategies for Teaching Comprehension

Many students have an inadequate sense of organization; they are unable to make the parts of the lesson fit together or "fall into place" as key ideas, subordinate ideas, and details. Because they lack skill in synthesizing meanings as they read, they are unable to evaluate or interpret the content as they read.

Teachers may use many teaching strategies which help students with the problems of comprehension. Teachers should:

1. Plan to assign stories to be read that coincide with children's experiences. If stories must be read that contain ideas foreign to the experiences of the readers, then plan ways for the children to obtain the background information and language.
2. Use different levels of questioning to cause students to think about and use what they read: literal level, interpretive level, and applied or evaluative level.
3. Point out to students the techniques writers use to clarify meanings.
4. Encourage the students to use the context at the sentence and paragraph levels; they should also make use of the general context in which the material was written.[15]
5. Use scaffolding as a strategy in which the experienced language user (the teacher) guides the novice (the child) through unfamiliar language tasks.[16]

6. Point out those function words that signal meaning.
7. For all students, but especially those with either meager vocabularies or a foreign language background, spend considerable time with figurative language and the unusual facets of English.
8. Use the cloze procedure as a means to lead students to anticipate meanings and to think ahead about what the writers are thinking.
9. Plan time to have oral conference sessions in which the teacher can listen to the students and then question *how* they read to learn and why they make errors.
10. Since the only way students become competent readers is to *read, read,* and *read,* provide a great deal of meaningful, oral reading.
11. Make sure that students understand the close relationship between writing and reading.

Developing good comprehension skills is not a matter of a lesson or two or a single strategy. The teacher will need to utilize teaching techniques such as those in the list just given continuously if the goal of reading comprehension is to be met.

Encourage Experience and Language

It is generally accepted that children will write and read best about those topics with which they have the greatest familiarity. At least initially, children should have the opportunity to begin their literacy tasks dealing with familiar experiences, concepts, and language. Despite this general assumption, all too many children begin reading and writing dealing with books that contain words that represent concepts that are totally foreign to the beginners' experiences.

In recent years the word *schema* has become an increasingly common one in texts on the teaching of reading. A schema is an information structure believed to exist in the brain that contains knowledge about a particular concept and the ways that concept is related to other concepts.[17] Of course each person has many schemata, and the numbers continue to increase as long as the person has experiences. Anyone who knows about trees has a "tree" schema that relates all the parts of the "tree" concept. The schema for "tree" may also be related to the schema for "shoes," "closets," and "stores" if the person knows about *shoe trees* that are often kept in closets and that are usually bought in certain kinds of stores.

If world knowledge is organized through schemata, then this notion has serious consequences for reading instruction. If the student is asked to read material that demands that the reader have certain prior information (schemata), then that material will be utter nonsense, if the information is not available, even if all the words can be named.[18] If the material relates to the schemata of the child, then the understanding will be influenced by the child's concepts. For example, the child who has some concepts related to "ship" may be initially confused by the story of "ships of the desert" accompanied by pictures of camels plodding across sand dunes.

Making Connections 10.1: Developing Meaningful Experiences with Children

Select a story from a basal reader that contains a concept children might not understand. Make a careful plan about how you would introduce the concept to children through a concrete experience. Brainstorm a vocabulary list that you might use with the children during the activity. Decide how you would move from the activity to the story in the basal reader.

Prepare to share your proposed plans with others in your class. Ask for input from others on the value of the plan for developing the concept in question.

In order to encourage children to read for meaning, it is important for the teacher to begin with reading material that refers to familiar concepts; the children's own dictated stories and books will probably be the best materials. As the children move into prepared texts, the teacher must be alert to words and stories that deal with unfamiliar ideas and that require schemata children do not possess in order to provide even a chance of reading for meaning. If the teacher feels some stories containing strange concepts are necessary, it is important to build the required concepts before reading begins. Children should build these ideas through firsthand experiences with appropriate accompanying language when possible. Films, pictures, guest speakers, charts, and field trips are examples of possible substitutes, usually not as effective as building *real* experiences, but certainly better than no attempt to build background.

Actually making butter as butter was churned in the past is far more meaningful than seeing a movie about how it was done or hearing someone explain the process. Experiencing the tired arm muscles from turning the churn, watching the butter separate from the whey, squeezing the last drops of whey from the lump of soft butter with a wooden paddle, and spreading the smooth substance on slices of bread and eating them can never be equalled by words and pictures. As the children have such experiences, the teacher must be alert to provide the important language. In the butter-making experience, the teacher might introduce the words *churn, cream, butter, salted, paddle, whey, buttermilk,* and *fresh* in the context of the experience. Later the words could be included in stories the children write. These words should be meaningful now in a story about making butter.

Levels of Questioning

Bloom and others provide in their taxonomy a hierarchy of questioning.[19] He categorizes levels of operation from simplest to most complex: memory, comprehension (translation, interpretation), application, analysis, synthesis, and evaluation. Teachers need to challenge students with all levels of questions to keep them thinking, understanding cause and effect, and thinking beyond the convergent levels of right and wrong.

Of course, with students who have failed to learn to read in the usual progression, teachers may need to teach the students how to understand the simplest kinds of questions. The students must become adept at both reading the words and thinking what the words are saying to them.

Teachers can easily identify three levels of understanding—the literal, the interpretive, and the applied or evaluative one. Each builds on the previous level.

The *literal level* produces knowledge of what the authors said. However, it is quite possible for students to identify what the authors said, and even memorize and repeat it in class, without understanding what the authors meant when they wrote it.

The *interpretive level* is using what the authors said in order to derive meaning from the writing. The readers must find relationships among the statements in the material they have read. When they understand these relationships they can derive meanings.

The *applied level* is using what the authors said (literal) and what the authors meant to convey by what they said (interpretive) and applying it in some new situation to solve a problem.

Examples of the various levels include:

1. Recalling details in a narrative—requires literal meaning.
2. Predicting outcomes—requires some interpretation.
3. Associating personal experience with reading content—requires application or evaluative skill.

Questioning is an integral part of comprehension. Considerable time is devoted in reading methods courses and workshops on comprehension to the preparation of suitable questions to set the stage for reading, and to evaluate understanding of what is read. Questioning and answering strategies have other powerful uses. The careful selection of questions undergirds the correct use of scaffolding, the interpretation of figurative language, the use of the cloze procedure as a thinking activity, the interpretation of the writing techniques of authors, and the clarification for children of the relationships between reading and writing.

Specific Strategies for Improving Answers to Questions

Many poor readers have trouble answering questions that require inferencing abilities. Holmes wrote that answering inference questions requires strategies similar to problem solving, identifying the relevant problem, bringing to bear relative information in an active struggle for a solution, and carefully analyzing solutions until a satisfactory one is found.[20] Since so many poor readers have struggled with inference questions, she proposed the following steps that can be taught to children:

1. Read the material and the related inference question.
2. Develop tentative hypotheses as answers.
3. Identify important words that support or do not support the hypotheses.
4. Compare the student-generated hypotheses and the key words. The comparison can be done by answering yes/no questions.
5. Select the hypothesis that fits all the key words. This is the most likely answer.[21]

Cohen found that even primary-grade children could improve their ability to answer questions by learning to generate questions of their own.[22] Children seemed most able to generate literal-level questions, but it was not clear that they could improve in their ability to ask themselves higher level questions and transfer this ability to questions on worksheets and tests.

Writing Techniques Authors Use

Writers for children use techniques that will help children pick out meanings of new words within the context of what they are reading. Such techniques have been described by Artley and McCullough.[23] They include:

1. A brief explanation of the word can be given in parentheses or in a footnote: The *cacique* ordered an inquisition of the intruders who came into the village. (The *cacique* is the chief, or person of the highest authority in the village.)
2. A clause or phrase that explains the meaning of the word can be inserted in the sentence:
   a. At certain times during the year in the northern skies one can see the *aurora borealis,* a colorful display of flickering, shifting lights.
   b. Moss, grass, and flowers grow in the *tundra,* the treeless plains found in Arctic regions.
3. A synonym or substitute phrase is used to indicate the meaning:
   a. *shrimp,* a small shellfish
   b. *the lobby,* a small waiting room
   c. *the cacique,* the chief of the tribe
4. A new word is *emphasized* by using italics, quotation marks, or boldface type to call attention to it:
   a. The farmer uses a machine called a *combine* to harvest the wheat.
   b. Pioneer farmers used a "cradle," a scythe with a wooden frame attached, to harvest the grain.
   c. Farmers who shared their crops with the landowner were called **sharecroppers.**
5. A direct explanation of the word can be presented in a full sentence:
   a. In the hot desert, the man makes his garden in an oasis. An oasis is a green spot where there is a water supply.
   b. The nomads of the desert are coming to the trading center. Nomads are people who constantly move about and who have no settled home.

Using Context

It is important for teachers to encourage children to use the context of the sentence or paragraph to predict what unknown words might be. The teacher may ask questions such as, "What word would make sense there?" or "Read on to the end of the sentence. Now what should the word be?" If this prompting technique is used enough, children will begin to rely on the context on their own to make the text make sense.

Smith reminded teachers that children "just do not need so much visual information when a word is in context."[24] This is a strong argument for presenting words in sentences or other contextual settings. The context frequently gives meaning to the words, as in these sentences:

Jack played with the *top* on the floor.
His mother screwed the *top* on the jar.
Ralph said, "I will *top* off the tank at the filling station."

There are larger contexts than the sentence or the page to which the teacher and children must attend. The setting for reading provides a context, whether it is in the cozy reading corner of the classroom, in the supermarket, or in the doctor's office. Where we read dictates to some extent how we comprehend. Who the reader is and what the reader has experienced also provide a context that influences comprehension. Sometimes experiences support comprehension; other experiences may be the cause of misunderstanding if prior knowledge and the text are in disagreement.[25] Teachers need to be aware of these larger contexts and to use them when possible in designing effective opportunities for comprehension.

Scaffolding Techniques

When persons competent in some skill help novices acquire a skill with suggestions, supportive questions, or even a helping hand, the skilled person is providing *scaffolding* for the learner. When the young child tackles the problem of climbing a short ladder, the helpful adult makes suggestions about how to start the climb, holds the ladder steady for the child, and provides verbal feedback about each successful step. As the child starts to read, the adult may point to the left side of the page to suggest where to look, may provide cues or questions to encourage the child's word recognition, may even read the sentence with the proper inflection to help the child perceive the meaning, and may help the child connect the picture with the words.

Much scaffolding is done almost intuitively by adults who are interested in helping children master more difficult tasks than they might otherwise be able to learn. However, teachers may intentionally provide scaffolding for children through the lessons they plan and the questions and comments they design.[26] Teachers who deliberately use scaffolding techniques with disabled readers provide the students with strategies for asking questions to guide comprehension, for facilitating word recognition, and for using the cues in print such as punctuation marks. If these supports are given long enough and often enough, the child can learn to "talk" through many reading problems that are encountered. Teachers must remember that scaffolding is intended to help the learners accomplish their goals; it is not intended as a technique to enable adults to impose their purposes on the learners.[27]

Function Words That Signal Meaning

Words that have no referents are called *function* or *structure* words. It is estimated that there are no more than 300 such words in everyday English, but they comprise nearly half of all the words in elementary reading context. Because of this they need to be mastered as sight words as early as possible in the reading process. They are termed *markers* for the type of structural element they precede:

> Noun markers: *a, the, some, three*
> Verb markers: *am, are, is, had*
> Phase markers: *up, down, out, above*
>
> Clause markers: *if, until, because, how*
> Question markers: *who, why, how, when*

These structure, or service, words help the reader to anticipate meanings which nouns or verbs carry in a given sentence structure.

Some of these function words may also be key words appearing in content reading. In content reading these words alert the student to paragraph content and are helpful in the organization of the content being read. For instance, if in a long paragraph or in a series of short ones, the words or phrases *first, in the second place,* or *fourth and finally* appear, these are clues to items being listed that the reader should be able to sort out easily. If chronology is a key factor in the paragraph or essay, the words or phrases *in the first place, next, after a short while, then,* and, *in the end* are clues to the progress of movement of the writing. In other reading, emphasizing contrast with words, such as *both . . . and, neither . . . nor, on the one hand . . . on the other hand, nevertheless,* and *in spite of,* will be important.

Jenkinson suggests that the understanding of *function words* be developed systematically because in context they may carry the burden of precise interpretation. She lists function words that suggest:

1. cause and effect—*because, since, so that*
2. condition—*if, unless, although*
3. contrast—*whereas, while*
4. relationships—*as, before, when, after, during, while*
5. parallel ideas—*however, therefore, nevertheless, hence, accordingly*[28]

Figurative Language and Other Facets of English

In Jean Craighead George's *Julie of the Wolves*, there are sentences like the following:

> A flower twisted in the wind. (p. 8)
> The wolf groomed his chest with his tongue. (p. 10)
> The sun slid slowly down the sky, hung still for a moment, then started up again. It was midnight. (p. 43)
> Her eyes roamed the street. (p. 164)[29]

Louise Fitzhugh uses some expressions in her book *The Long Secret:*

> Beth Ellen was so overcome by shyness, a timidity so powerful it <u>turned her mind to dough</u>. (p. 33)

She felt <u>nailed to the floor</u>. (p. 54)
Mama Jenkins smiled a <u>beautiful hippo smile</u>. (p. 83)[30]

Figures of speech are used in writing to add beauty and color and to extend sensory images. Because most children hear these expressions all their lives, they begin using them in their own speech at an early age. They appear in all writing and must be understood by readers. Slang expressions, idioms, and unusual words can create problems for students with reading difficulties. Because understanding these facets of English presents problems for all students learning English as a second language, chapter 14 is devoted to teaching the linguistically and culturally different child.

Six useful articles in professional journals that contain suggestions for teachers are:

Leona M. Forrester, "Idiomagic!" *Elementary English* 51 (January 1974), pp. 125–27.
Linda G. Geller, "Exploring Metaphor in Language Development and Learning," *Language Arts* 61 (February 1984), pp. 151–61.
Estelle K. Lorenz, "Excuse Me, But Your Idiom Is Showing," *The Reading Teacher* 31 (October 1977), pp. 24–27.
John E. Readence, R. Scott Baldwin, and Robert J. Rickelman, "Instructional Insights Into Metaphors and Similes," *Journal of Reading* 27 (November 1983), pp. 109–12.
Joanne M. Rogacki, "Poetry in Motion," *Language Arts* 61 (March 1984), pp. 261–64.
Eleanore S. Tyson and Lee Mountain, "A Riddle or Pun Makes Learning Words Fun," *The Reading Teacher* 36 (November 1982), pp. 170–72.

Using the Cloze Procedure as a Teaching Technique

The cloze procedure as a *testing* technique was discussed in chapter 6. Many references to the cloze procedure describe it as a testing device. However, it may be used as a *teaching* technique. Sentences with blank spaces in which the children are asked to write the words that best complete the thought, or sentences in which the children think of a synonym for the underlined word, are types of exercises that develop skill in the use of the cloze technique. Sample cloze activities one might do with elementary school students follow.

Directions: Write the word that is missing in the following sentences:

1. He lives _____ the city.
2. Come to the party _____ me.
3. Sometimes on Sunday, we go _____ the zoo.

Or, complete the following sentences using words that describe:

1. The baby chickens were _____ and _____ .
2. The afternoon clouds were _____ and _____ .

Directions: Read the sentences all the way through. Decide what word is missing, and write it in the blank space.

The nest holds from three to six _____ . After the mother _____ has laid the eggs in the _____ , the father bird _____ sometimes take a turn sitting on _____ .

When the young _____ have hatched from the _____ , there is a noisy time. The _____ birds call for food, and _____ and father bird work hard filling the wide _____ of their young.

Catbirds are curious about people. Often they will _____ a man along a road just as if they _____ to find out where he is _____ .[31]

Even before children can read, teachers can read familiar rhymes and stories to them, leaving out endings or other known words. For instance, the teacher might say

Jack and Jill

Went up the _____

To get a pail of _____ .

Jack fell down

And broke his _____

And Jill came tumbling _____ .

When children are comfortable with such activities and they have begun to read, the teacher may print similar, known poems and rhymes for the children to read, filling in the blanks. Later, longer pieces of print may be presented on which children work together to fill in the blanks. They may even try to generate long lists of words that would make sense in the blanks. If the children used the sentence, "The boys walked silently to the _____ house," they would be able to fill in the blank with many different words that would help create entirely different pictures of the house—*tiny, haunted, tall, deserted, brick.* Children may enjoy drawing pictures to represent the houses they have described.

Helping Students Analyze Their Reading Situations

Strang suggests that teachers sit down with students individually and encourage them to *talk about* the miscues they have made, to tell why they chose the specific answers they did, and to analyze the students' thinking in arriving at the answers they chose.[32]

Standardized tests do not help to explain how the students read—how the process works for them—or what reading problems they have when reading tasks are presented. Two students may get exactly the same score on a standardized test but their levels of comprehension of the paragraph or their maturity in thinking about the reading material may not be at all equal. Strang suggests working individually with students in this way:

"Read the following paragraph aloud as you usually read orally. While the student reads, the teacher records errors by whatever method he usually uses. He also observes phrasing, intonation, stress, and pauses that indicate the student's understanding of the language structure of the selection. It is easy to detect word-by-word reading, mechanical division of sentences into parts of phrases and clauses and other evidence of failure to read in thought units. . . . Performance may cover a range from colorless monotone to the richness of feeling and significance that a great actor gives to every line.[33]

Making Connections 10.2: Locating Figurative Language

Figurative language occurs frequently in materials written for children. It may be helpful to survey some basal readers at different levels to see how much figurative language is actually being used.

Select basals at the first-, third-, and sixth-grade levels from a single publishing company. Examine at least four or five stories at each level, listing the figurative language. Then think about these points:

1. Compare the amount of figurative language you found in texts across the three grade levels.
2. Are different types of figurative language introduced at different levels?
3. Select three examples at each grade level. How would you plan to teach children the meanings of these examples?

In your class share your findings with your peers. It may be useful to compare your findings across different publishing companies.

The teacher can observe whether the student approaches reading with enjoyment, indifference, dislike, anxiety, resistance, or hostility.

Classroom teachers need to remember that formal diagnosis can be time consuming and is usually done by people other than those who expect to work daily with the students. Such formal diagnosis does, occasionally, overemphasize some single problem in learning to read when the real cause is a whole cluster of problems. Since the people who do the diagnosis may not communicate directly with the teachers who work with the students, the diagnosis itself will be inadequate unless the teachers make many astute observations about the students in the reading situations—judging their total *effect* in the reading situation and analyzing the nature of their successful and unsuccessful responses to questions for meaning.

Easy Oral Reading Practice

The way that all children become accomplished readers is by having hours and hours of reading practice. The way to learn to read is to *read, read, read!* Those students who do not have mastery over a large stock of sight words must read these common words over and over in interesting contexts until they have overlearned them. Because meaning is the center of all reading activity, reading context is much preferred over studying words in isolation, as in flash card drill.

While it is difficult for the teacher to find time, all children need as much oral reading practice as possible. However, when the children do read aloud, they must have an audience; this means that if the teacher asks them to read aloud, then the teacher must be prepared to give attention to the reading being done. Teachers may manage the classroom in many ways so that there is time for individual oral reading practice. Other children can be pupil-teachers if the regular teacher plans carefully with them how to read in pairs; older brothers and sisters who read well may be able to listen to children read; volunteer parents are one of the richest sources of interested adults who can give undivided attention to children for a few minutes two or three times a week; teacher aides, student teachers, and senior high school volunteers are other possible listeners. Placing a tape recorder in a quiet corner and stationing one student with it who can operate it makes it possible to ask children to record their oral reading exercise for the teacher to hear and evaluate at a later time.

Appendix B contains an extensive bibliography of books prepared to meet the teachers' needs for materials for easy oral reading materials for all students.

Uniting Reading and Writing

Children need to see the close relationships between reading and writing. There should be many opportunities to write stories and books and to read what has been written to teachers, other children, brothers and sisters, and parents. The children can learn that by writing they convey their meanings to the readers of their work. As readers they learn what writers must do to make their efforts understandable.

> Writing is the discovery process *a la* language. . . . Writers use language to unlock meaning. They do not follow a blueprint, but rather find their ideas developing as they express them. . . . Children learning the written form of language ought to be producing it as well as reading it. They should be reading *and* writing. They should be aware of someone reading their writing, and that what they are reading is someone's writing.[34]

Children need many concrete experiences demonstrating the relationships between reading and writing. It is important to stress that what has been read has obviously been written and that authors and readers are interacting in trying to share experiences and ideas. But children need to have experiences with these concepts. In Chapter IX, suggestions that would encourage understanding of the relationships between reading and writing included: (1) using dictated stories and language experiences, (2) writing rebus stories for others to read, (3) book making, (4) gathering and utilizing environmental print, and (5) using the computer to compose stories that will be printed for others to read. Chapter X provides other suggestions for integrating the related language behaviors of reading and writing. Teachers may encourage the study of authors' techniques, they may employ scaffolding strategies to help readers understand what they are trying to say, and they may teach children to be critical consumers of writing, whether it is found in basals, in trade books, or the books written by their peers.

Materials for Teaching Comprehension

The classroom teacher has access to many materials that can be used to teach comprehension. One of the most common is, of course, the *basal reader*. Much can be accomplished by using the basal to help children learn the varied skills of comprehension, including such diverse tasks as finding main ideas, reading to identify facts and opinions, sequencing parts of a story, and identifying cause and effect sequences. Teachers must be aware of the problems that may arise by following the basal without questioning the stories to be read or the questions and skill activities to be completed. Stories must be analyzed for their appropriateness for the children who will read them. Some selections simply will have no realistic connections with the lives of the children. These stories may well be omitted, or the teacher will need to prepare activities that will familiarize the children with the concepts and language to be introduced in the text. A careful analysis of the questions to be asked by the teacher may reveal that most of them are low-level, factual questions. The teacher may need to prepare new questions that require the children to think at higher levels and to exert more critical reading skills. The teacher may also need to develop careful plans to provide scaffolding for readers who are having difficulties with ideas or words.

Other Practice Materials

There are many commercial materials available to help children practice comprehension skills. Teachers need to study the materials carefully before they are given to the children to make sure the stories or articles are suitable for the readers' experiences, decoding abilities, and comprehension needs.

A few examples of materials prepared to promote growth of comprehension skills are given in Appendix G: Instructional Materials for Word Identification and Comprehension.

Trade Books

The teacher should have a rich variety of trade books, including wordless picture books, predictable books, picture story books, short books for reading in one sitting, and chapter books. As many topics as possible should be represented at a variety of levels of difficulty. The books should be attractively displayed; children are more likely to select books if the front covers are displayed than if they are shelved as in the library. Books should be included in interest and learning centers to provide opportunities for children to explore topics conveniently. Children who can select books on topics of interest at levels at which they can read comfortably will have few comprehension problems.

Books Written by Children

The trade book collection in the room needs to be supplemented by books that have been written by the children themselves (and their teachers). These may well be the most cherished books in the room. They are sure to be excellent means to promote comprehension, since they will be about known topics and reflect the interests of the children. If blank pages are included at the ends of the books, readers may be encouraged to write positive reactions and suggestions.

David Woodward

The intensity with which teachers and children work with the microcomputer may make the literacy aspects of the program even more valuable.

Microcomputer Programs

Various kinds of microcomputer programs may be used to further comprehension. Some are designed to give practice in specific skills very much as certain workbooks and practice sheets do. Simulation games may be useful in encouraging children to read critically, to follow directions, and to respond to sequences of events. They also encourage risk taking and making predictions which are critical to reading.[35] Word processing programs encourage writing, and when a printer is available, books may be produced from the children's efforts.

Some representative microcomputer programs are:

1. *The Bank Street Writer.* Broadway, New York 10003: Scholastic, Inc. This word processing program is suitable for young students as well as adults.
2. Edward Fry and Lawrence Carrillo, *Reading Comprehension Tutor Program* (Wilmington, Del.: BLS). This software is designed for reading levels 3–6.
3. *The Oregon Trail* (American Peripherals, 122 Bangor St., Lindenhurst, New York 11757), and *The Lemonade Stand,* (Minnesota Educational Computing Consortium—MECC, 3490 Lexington Avenue, St. Paul, Minnesota 55112). These are examples of simulation games that promote risk-taking, problem-solving, and alternative solutions, all critical to reading comprehension.
4. *Reading Comprehension* (Chatsworth, Calif.: Opportunities for Learning). There are ten programs for elementary levels and beyond.
5. *Reading: Tutorial Comprehension* (Westminster, Md. 21157: Random House). This tutorial program is suited to reading levels 2–4 and encompasses several of the subskills of reading comprehension.
6. *Story Tree* (Broadway, New York 10003: Scholastic, Inc.). Children at all levels can write and read their own stories.
7. *Trickster Coyote* (Pleasantville, New York 10570: Reader's Digest Services, Inc.). The two games are based on the coyote as the Native American Trickster. They are for ages eight and up.

Summary

This chapter has been organized around three aspects of teaching comprehension: an understanding of what is included in instruction in comprehension in reading, strategies for helping children learn to comprehend better, and suggestions about materials for the classroom that teacher and children can use to improve comprehension abilities.

The skills of comprehension as outlined by Smith were presented with explanation or illustration. At the literal level, this included remembering details, finding main ideas, understanding sequence, and following directions. Beyond the literal level, the list includes implied meanings, characterizing, sensing relationships, anticipating outcomes, recognizing author's intent, making comparisons and contrasts, drawing conclusions, and skimming for specific purposes.

Levels of questioning, writing techniques for aiding comprehension, awareness of signal words that control meanings, the cloze procedure, understanding figurative language, and provisions for easy reading practice are among the strategies teachers will find useful. Teachers who are familiar with these strategies will be able to draw upon them rather spontaneously throughout the day to help students develop skills for working independently.

For Further Reading

Ekwall, Eldon E., and Shanker, James L. *Diagnosis and Remediation of the Disabled Reader,* 2d ed. Boston: Allyn and Bacon, 1985: Chapter 6, "Diagnosis and Remediation of Educational Factors: Comprehension, Vocabulary Development and Study Skills," pp. 189–237.

Farrer, Mary Thomas. "Why Do We Ask Comprehension Questions? A New Conception of Comprehension Instruction." *The Reading Teacher* 37 (February 1984), pp. 452–56.

Goodman, Yetta M., and Burke, Carolyn. *Reading Strategies: Focus on Comprehension.* New York: Holt, Rinehart and Winston, 1980.

Harris, Albert J., and Sipay, Edward R. *How to Increase Reading Ability,* 7th ed. New York: Longman, 1980: Chapter 16, "Improving Reading Comprehension, I," pp. 447–78; Chapter 17, "Improving Reading Comprehension, II," pp. 479–514.

Johnston, Peter H. *Reading Comprehension Assessment: A Cognitive Basis.* Newark, Del.: International Reading Association, 1982.

Langer, Judith A., and Smith-Burke, M. Trika, eds. *Reader Meets Author/Bridging the Gap.* Newark, Del.: International Reading Association, 1982.

Lee, Dorris M. and Rubin, Joseph B. *Children and Language.* Belmont, Calif.: Wadsworth Publishing Co., 1979: Chapter 2, "Thinking: Its Development," pp. 31–56.

Wilson, Cathy Roller. "Teaching Reading Comprehension by Connecting the Known to the New." *The Reading Teacher* 36 (January 1983), pp. 382–90.

Notes

1. James Flood, ed., *Promoting Reading Comprehension* (Newark, Del.: International Reading Association, 1984).

2. "Teachers Ask, Researchers Listen," *Reporting on Reading, Right to Read* 5, no. 5 (August 1979), p. 7; Murriel K. Rand, "Story Schema: Theory, Research and Practice," *The Reading Teacher* 37 (January 1984), pp. 377–82; Ernest T. Goetz and Bonnie B. Armbruster, "Psychological Correlates of Text Structure," in *Theoretical Issues in Reading Comprehension,* edited by Rand J. Spiro, Bertram C. Bruce, and William F. Brewer (Hillsdale, N.J.: Lawrence Erlbaum Assoc., 1980), pp. 201–20.

3. Ernest Horn, *Methods of Instruction in the Social Studies* (New York: Charles Scribner's Sons, 1937), p. 156.

4. Anthony Adams, "Talk and Learning in the Classroom: An Interview with Anthony Adams," *Language Arts* 61 (February 1984), pp. 119–20.

5. Helen K. Smith, "Sequence in Comprehension," *Sequential Development of Reading Abilities,* Supplementary Monograph, no. 90, edited by Helen Robinson (Chicago: University of Chicago Press, 1960), pp. 51–56.

6. Diane L. August, John H. Flavell, and Renee Clift, "Comparison of Comprehension Monitoring of Skilled and Less Skilled Readers," *Reading Research Quarterly* 20 (Fall 1984), pp. 39–53.

7. Ellen Keller, *Skill Book for Images* (New York: American Book Co., 1977), p. 104.

8. Robert B. Ruddell, Anne L. Ryle, and Martha Shogren, *Workbook for Moon Magic* (Boston: Allyn and Bacon, 1978), p. 53.

9. Theodore Clymer, Gloria Keil, and Robert B. Ruddell, *Skilpak for How It Is Nowadays* (Lexington, Mass.: Ginn, Division of Xerox, 1979), p. 138.

10. Ruddell, Ryle, and Shogren, *Workbook for Moon Magic,* p. 11.

11. Robert B. Ruddell, Phyllis J. Adams, and Martha Shogren, *Workbook for Riding Rainbows* (Boston: Allyn and Bacon, 1978), p. 33.

12. Alfred Tennyson, "The Brook," in Clara Baker and Edna Baker, *Bobbs Merrill Readers, Fifth Reader* (Indianapolis, Ind.: Bobbs Merrill, 1924), pp. 426–27.

13. William S. Gray, Marion Monroe, and A. Sterl Artley, *Basic Reading Skills for Junior High School Use* (Glenview, Ill.: Scott, Foresman, 1957), p. 126.

14. Renni Fetterolf, Bernice Golden, and Ralph Weintraub, *Skillbook for Moments* (New York: American Book Co., 1977), p. 122. Litton Educational Publications, Inc., copyright.

15. Kathy Pezdek, "Arguments for a Constructive Approach to Comprehension and Memory," in Joseph Danks and Kathy Pezdek, eds., *Reading and Understanding* (Newark, Del.: International Reading Association, 1980), pp. 40–73; Argiro L. Morgan, "Context: the Web of Meaning," *Language Arts* 60 (March 1983), pp. 305–14.

16. Arthur N. Applebee and Judith A. Langer, "Instructional Scaffolding: Reading and Writing as Natural Language Activities," *Language Arts,* 60 (February 1983), p. 168.

17. David E. Rumelhart, "Schemata: The Building Blocks of Cognition," in *Theoretical Issues in Reading Comprehension,* Rand J. Spiro, Bertram C. Bruce, and William F. Brewer, eds. (Hillsdale, N.J.: Lawrence Erlbaum Assoc., 1980), pp. 33–34.

18. John D. McNeil, *Reading Comprehension, New Directions for Classroom Practice* (Glenview, Ill.: Scott, Foresman, 1984), pp. 8–9.

19. Benjamin S. Bloom et al., *Taxonomy of Educational Objectives, The Classification of Educational Goals, Handbook I: Cognitive Domain* (New York: David McKay Co., Inc., 1956).

20. Betty C. Holmes, "A Confirmation Strategy for Improving Poor Readers' Ability to Answer Inferential Questions," *The Reading Teacher* 37 (November 1983), pp. 144–45.

21. Ibid., pp. 145–46.

22. Ruth Cohen, "Self-Generated Questions as an Aid to Reading Comprehension," *The Reading Teacher* 36 (April 1983), pp. 770–75.

23. A. S. Artley, "Teaching Word Meaning Through Content," *Elementary English Review* 20 (1943), pp. 68–74; Constance M. McCullough, "The Recognition of Context Clues in Reading," *Elementary English Review* 22 (1945), pp. 1–5.

24. Frank Smith, *Reading Without Nonsense,* 2d ed. (New York: Teachers College Press, 1978), p. 30.

25. Marjorie Y. Lipson, "Some Unexpected Issues in Prior Knowledge and Comprehension," *The Reading Teacher* 37 (April 1984), pp. 760–64.

26. Applebee and Langer, "Instructional Scaffolding," pp. 168–75.

27. Dennis Searle, "Scaffolding: Who's Building Whose Building?" *Language Arts* 61 (September 1984), pp. 480–83.

28. Marion D. Jenkinson, "Increasing Reading Power in the Social Studies," *Corrective Reading in the High School Classroom,* eds. Alan Robinson and Sidney Rauch (Newark, Del.: International Reading Association, 1966), p. 76.

29. Jean Craighead George, *Julie of the Wolves* (New York: Harper and Row, 1972).

30. Louise Fitzhugh, *The Long Secret* (New York: Harper and Row, 1965).

31. Paul McKee, M. Lucille Harrison, Annie McCowen, and Elizabeth Lehr, *On We Go* (Boston: Houghton Mifflin, 1957), p. 233.

32. Ruth Strang, *Diagnostic Teaching of Reading* (New York: McGraw-Hill, 1964), p. 137.

33. Strang, *Diagnostic Teaching of Reading,* p. 66.

34. Suzanne L. Holt and JoAnne L. Vacca, "Reading with a Sense of Writer: Writing with a Sense of Reader," *Language Arts* 58 (November/December 1981), pp. 937–40.

35. Ernest Balajthy, "Computer Simulations and Reading," *The Reading Teacher* 37 (March 1984), pp. 590–93.

11
Study Skills and Content Fields Reading

Chapter Outline

Study Skills
  Locational Skills
    Using Reference Materials
    Using Book Parts
    Using the Library
    Using Tapes, Records, and
      Talking Books
    Finding Information Outside the
      Library
    Alphabetical Order
  Organizational Skills
    Outlining
    Note Taking
    Underlining
    Using Glosses, Advance
      Organizers, Structured
      Overviews, and Study Guides
    Summarizing
    Sequencing

  Interpretive Skills
  Skills in Presenting Information
  Following Directions
  Helping Students Remember
  Test Taking
Reading in the Content Fields
  General Skills in Content Fields
      Reading
    Narrative versus Expository Text
    Study Strategies
    Vocabulary
    Critical Reading
  Reading in Specific Content Areas
    Mathematics
    Social Studies
    Science
Summary

Vocabulary

study skills
locational skills
reference materials
card catalog
taped books
alphabetical order
organizational skills
interpretive skills
note taking
underlining
testing skills
general skills
expository text
specialized vocabulary
critical reading
gloss
advance organizer
structured overview
study guide
summarizing
sequencing
outlining
written report
oral report
directions
remembering
narrative
SQ3R
technical vocabulary

Questions

1. What are the locational skills that children need? How would you help a remedial reader acquire each?

2. Contrast glosses, advance organizers, structured overviews, and study guides.

3. What is included in interpretive skills?

4. How can a teacher help a child learn to present information?

5. What steps might be taken to teach a child to follow directions?

6. How can teachers make test taking a more positive experience for children?

7. Compare narrative and expository text.

8. What are the kinds of vocabulary that may be troublesome in content reading?

9. Describe ways to help a student read mathematics, social studies, and science texts.

Children who have reading problems frequently receive some form of special instruction. Some children attend Chapter I classes or are taught in a special education setting for a part of the day. A few have private tutoring or specialized instruction away from school. In the classroom, these children are allowed to read from readers at their instructional levels rather than being required to read grade-level texts.

The students who receive special attention for their reading programs are expected to study mathematics, social studies, science and other school subjects. They are usually given grade-level texts for these subjects, regardless of their actual reading abilities. Obviously, they experience difficulties in using the textbooks and often cease making any effort to complete assignments.

It is the responsibility of the classroom teacher to plan the student's *entire* instructional program so that success can be experienced. The teacher must plan not only for a reading program that will promote learning, but also for an adjusted academic curriculum that takes into account the student's reading strengths and problems. Texts and other materials must be available at several levels above and below the grade being taught because it is normal to have a range in reading abilities of several years in any classroom.

Study skills are not as much *something* to teach as they are a *way* to teach, if you accept the philosophy that the teaching of a particular subject is the teaching of the study of that subject so that we advance not only the students' knowledge of subject matter, but also their abilities to learn other subject matter independently whenever they wish to.[1]

Slow readers, disabled readers, and even nonreaders can achieve *something* in the content areas if the teachers are willing to set *different goals,* provide them with *different study guide sheets,* and a *different method of evaluation* at the end of the unit of work.

The teacher should be aware that content field texts pose some special problems for readers. The material is usually expository; basal readers contain mostly narratives. The vocabulary of social studies, mathematics, and science texts is studded with technical and specialized vocabulary items that often represent unfamiliar concepts. Specialized study skills are needed by the student, since content texts have different patterns of organization depending on the subject. All of these problems need careful attention for the student who may still be struggling with basic sight vocabulary.

This chapter is devoted to a discussion of study skills that need special attention if the disabled readers are to be successful and to the consideration of their problems in reading in the content fields. Methods for helping remedial readers with these difficulties will be suggested, along with the identification of suitable types of materials.

Study Skills

Study skills can be set apart from other skills by describing them as "deliberate procedures for retaining and applying what is read."[2] All children need at least some help as they learn desirable study skills. Even good readers need some guidance, but children with reading problems require careful, step-by-step teaching. The teacher should consider skills in locating information; organizing facts after they are found; interpreting visual information such as that found on maps, graphs, charts, and pictures; and applying what has been learned. The students should also have help with learning to follow written directions, to organize information so that it can be remembered, and to take tests successfully.

The assessment of a child's mastery of study skills can best be accomplished by observing the completion of a task requiring their application. When a child notes the copyright date or takes notes for a report, the teacher can infer mastery of that particular skill more surely than when the child completes a ditto sheet or workbook page on the skill. Rogers notes that many public schools have developed study skills lists that are often rigid and mechanical. It is important to remember that these behaviors are supposed to be secondary to pursuing a topic or activity or interest. They are simply a means to the end of increasing the efficiency with which students can learn from printed materials.[3]

Locational Skills

The effort that must go into teaching locational skills increases with time, for the sheer quantity of knowledge continues to grow amazingly, and the techniques for knowledge retrieval are becoming ever more sophisticated and complex. It is apparent that the students in today's schools will spend most of their adult lives in a world of electronic information retrieval; teachers must at least address simple forms of this system that are currently available, as well as teach more conventional skills such as dictionary use and making the most of an index.

Using Reference Materials

Social studies and science units are often planned to include the use of reference materials for locating information. Some typical references are encyclopedias, almanacs, dictionaries, nonfiction trade books, magazines, and newspapers. These materials may be much too difficult for remedial readers unless special care is taken. The school should make sure that sets of encyclopedias and other reference materials at different levels of difficulty are available to students. Some simple encyclopedias are written at the third- to fifth-reader levels of difficulty; their articles are richly illustrated. An example of a good encyclopedia for children is *World Book*.[4] The articles begin at the fourth-grade level and become more difficult after the first few paragraphs. These encyclopedias are more useful to struggling readers than are the more difficult sets. The children can be helped to locate information in an encyclopedia or other reference and read it by predicting what information is likely to be presented, by learning to study the pictures and captions carefully, and by reading headings and the beginning sentences of paragraphs.

Dictionaries are available from primary levels upward. Each class should have a variety of dictionaries at different levels. Of course, trade books range in difficulty from simple picture books to difficult references on most topics. Teachers can make sure magazines and newspapers at a variety of levels are available to children. Magazines and newspapers especially for school children represent the easier levels. Regular city newspapers and magazines such as *National Geographic* represent more difficult reading for elementary children.

Some teachers read parts of reference articles that will be needed in units on cassette tapes so that students who need the help can listen as well as attempt the reading. Other teachers mark the most critical information so that a child has a manageable reading task. Still others organize children in pairs that cross reading abilities so that one child in each group is able to read the reference materials to the other.

Children need help in selecting the right kind of reference book for a particular task. The teacher should examine the various reference materials with the class, discussing when one should refer to a dictionary, an encyclopedia, a trade book, an atlas, or other material. Particularly with struggling readers who have had fewer experiences with these materials than most children, the teacher should continue helping students decide which reference is suitable for what task.

Using Book Parts

Children must use book parts efficiently in order to make the best use of references. The parts of a book that children should learn about include:

1. Title page including author, publisher, copyright
2. Table of contents
3. Indexes
4. Chapter headings
5. Side headings
6. Footnotes, endnotes, sidenotes
7. References at ends of chapters
8. Glossaries
9. Questions

Children will grow in the knowledge of these aids if the teacher models their use and refers to them by their names and if meaningful activities are planned that emphasize their value. The teacher should label book parts accurately, saying, "Look in the index," and not "Look in the back of the book." Teachers should know their instructional materials well enough that they can point out book parts that are new or may cause confusion.

Using the Library

Children are feeling the effects of the information explosion when they go to their libraries in search of information. On most subjects they can choose from a wide variety of books. It is necessary even in an elementary school library to be able to locate entries in the card catalog or to use the computerized visual displays of library holdings that are rapidly replacing the catalog.

The student with reading problems will find either locational task difficult. The teacher or the librarian must assist in the reading task and then help the student locate the needed material. It may be helpful for the teacher to prepare large catalog cards for teaching the child what information is critical and what notations may be less vital in finding materials. Some of the words will need to be practiced enough times for the child to recall them. Beyond practice activities of these kinds, the child needs repeated opportunities to visit the library and find materials. Some teachers have paired good readers with poor readers to make library visits more successful.

Some collections in the library may be shelved or stored according to different schemes. For example, fiction is often alphabetized by authors' last names. Children will need alphabetizing skills to locate these books. Encyclopedias and similar references are usually housed separately near a study area. Newspapers and magazines have their own display systems; some libraries store back issues on microfiche. Many school librarians shelve paperbacks simply by authors' last names, regardless of whether they are fiction or nonfiction. Where materials are stored in the library, and how they are organized must be made clear to children or they will not elect to consult or select them.

Using Tapes, Records, and Talking Books

Many books are sold with accompanying tapes or records that permit children to hear the books read while following along. Frequently, the books are sold in sets so that several children can hear and read at once. The teacher may be able to find taped books that will fit units that are being taught. If reference materials that children will use to obtain information are not on tapes, the teacher or someone else who reads well may make tapes. These can be displayed with the matching books. By using tapes, poor readers can be exposed to content appropriate for their ages and grades rather than being forced to read overly simplified books that contribute little to the extension of their knowledge.

Talking books are becoming popular with good readers, both children and adults. They are readily available for times when one cannot conveniently read, as when driving a car. Many of these tapes will be equally valuable for students with reading problems.

Many books that are on tapes are also on records. Probably tapes are easier to use and cheaper to replace when damaged, but some schools are equipped only for records. Teachers will need to teach children how to care for records so that they will last as long as possible. Unless tapes and players are of very high quality, records may provide better reproductions of musical scores accompanying some story records.

Finding Information Outside the Library

The experience of finding information extends beyond the library. The child should view the environment as a potential source of important information. Slow readers can learn as much from the environment as good readers can. Concrete materials and first-hand experiences are rich sources of multisensory experiences that cannot be replicated with words. All readers can learn to ask thoughtful questions, make predictions, assume alternate viewpoints, and draw conclusions. Real experiences related to units being taught will provide valuable insights. The child who actually weaves a small mat can appreciate the work of a Navajo weaver or a pioneer mother in ways not possible if books are the only sources of information. The teacher may bring such experiences and reading together by having the child write about the experiences or by recording as the child dictates.

Reading skills will not limit the poor readers when interviews with knowledgeable persons are planned for gathering information. These children can ask good questions, tape record responses or take simple notes, and present what was learned orally to the class.

Alphabetical Order

The location of information is frequently dependent on the child's knowledge of alphabetical order. Since many slow readers have trouble remembering the order of letters long after their more successful peers have that information mastered, it will be helpful to have the alphabet displayed in order near encyclopedia sets and other references that are alphabetized. Children with reading problems may profit from alphabetizing activities such as getting in line based on first or last names, placing a collection of books in order based on authors' last names, or ordering collections of word cards alphabetically. They may enjoy trying to open the dictionary to a particular letter such as *S* or *M* without peeking.

Children may enjoy making a list of the ways alphabetical order is used in locating information. The list might include:

1. Words in the dictionary
2. Entries in encyclopedias
3. Cards in the card catalog
4. Volumes in the set of encyclopedias
5. Place names in the atlas index
6. Entries in an index
7. Arrangement of items in a glossary
8. Entries in a bibliography
9. Names in a telephone book

As the list grows, the children can begin to appreciate alphabetical order as a means of organizing information and the need to master the skills related to alphabetical order.

Ekwall and Shanker noted that a rather large number of upper-grade children are still confused about letter names and how to make or distinguish the letter forms.[5] Confusion about letters at this level almost always indicates a severe reading problem. While trying to remediate the problem these boys and girls are experiencing, the teacher may find it more supportive to help them locate information and participate in content classes through the use of taped books, films and film strips, records, pictures, and similar materials. These children may function as productive members of committees where locational tasks are divided up and their responsibility does not involve reading.

Organizational Skills

When children have located information, they then need organizational skills to make the data manageable. This group of skills includes outlining; note taking; underlining; using glosses, advance organizers, and study guides; summarizing; and sequencing. A number of these skills can be introduced in the primary grades, even kindergarten. Young children can work with simple materials including pictures to take notes, make outlines, and sequence events. Children who have had these experiences early often find the organizational skills required in later school years to be easier to master since they have already developed concepts about such tasks as outlining and are ready to refine them and develop appropriate mechanics and forms.

Slow readers need special support from teachers as they try to learn organizational skills. Some of the strategies that are used with younger children may be appropriate as long as the children do not view them as demeaning.

Outlining

Outlining instruction may begin as a modified sequencing activity. After a trip to the anthropology museum, the children might draw pictures and label their drawings. Then the teacher can caption a large paper with the title "The Trip to the Museum." The children begin to paste their pictures in order. When the record is finished, the teacher notes that the class has created a simple outline of the trip. The record is chronological. The children are helped to find that they could record the labels they wrote for the pictures, creating a sentence outline. If this kind of activity is carried out many times, the children will begin to gain a concept of what an outline is and how it is made. Only after they can complete the task easily is it necessary to include the mechanical aspects of the outline, the Roman numerals, capital letters, and numbers. Rubin suggests using the concept of sets to initiate outlining.[6] The teacher could suggest the term "animal" to the children. Then the children identify "wild" animals and "tame" animals. "Wild animals" are then divided into animals of each of the continents, or the children might decide to divide "wild animals" into "large" and "small" wild animals. Then each of the new subdivisions, whether it be by continents or by size, would be further subdivided. The children should be led to see that each new category becomes more specific. The teacher could then list all the information in outline form on the chalkboard. Dupuis and Askov remind teachers that skills like outlining *do have to be taught.*[7] On occasion a teacher will assign children to make outlines or take notes with no previous instruction. Unless the teacher checks the assignment carefully, it may not be known that the students had no idea of how to do the task.

Note Taking

A teacher took his first grade class on a trip to a ranch. Before they left the classroom, each child was equipped with a miniature, homemade clipboard with a pencil attached with a string. Each child was to take notes about what was seen and heard on the trip. Since it was early in the year, few of the children could write much, so most of them drew pictures of what they experienced. When the children returned to the room, they were able to talk at length about the experience from their "notes." The group had learned the value of note taking, even though few words had been written.

Children may want to know why they should take notes. Tonjes and Zintz suggest three purposes: (1) to organize information, (2) to hold the attention, and (3) to study material for exams.[8] It is important that the teacher emphasize that notes do serve these purposes by building into unit planning note taking experiences to meet each of the objectives.

The slow readers have at least three kinds of problems with which to cope when they attempt to take notes based on written materials. First, they may not be able to read the selection and may have the most trouble with the words that are critical in recalling the information. Technical and specialized vocabulary may prove the most difficult, yet the most important, to read. Because they are likely to spend so much time with the decoding problems, the slow readers may not know much about what they read. If comprehension has not occurred, then note taking will be useless, since the readers will not be able to identify what is important and worth remembering. Finally, the children will face all the problems of trying to write, framing ideas, organizing the page of notes, spelling words, and managing the necessary mechanics. Teachers can help these children by talking them through note-taking exercises many times. They can read with them, talk about how to make decisions about selecting facts and ideas to record, and guide the writing of the notes. When these children are asked to work independently, they should be able to read the material, they should be able to understand it well enough to identify the important points, and they should be able to record the ideas without frustration. Children can have successful experiences with note taking if instructional-level materials are chosen and if the task has been rehearsed with the teacher. The following points may also be useful to remember when working with slow readers who are learning to take notes:

1. It is the process and progress that are important.[9] The form chosen for the notes—words or phrases, whole sentences, outlining, paragraph—is important only in that it should match the writer's needs.
2. Notes are meant to remind the writer. They should not be graded or otherwise red-penciled.
3. Note taking should have genuine purposes; it should not be busy work and must not be used as a punishment.
4. Children should be encouraged to rely not only on print as a source of notes, but should also study pictures, graphs, charts, and other information sources in the selection to be read.

5. It may be helpful to prepare *with* the children a chart that will serve as a step-by-step guide for note taking and place it where the students are likely to be doing this kind of work.

Underlining

Underlining, marking the key ideas or sentences in a passage, is a valuable instructional tool for students of all ages and reading abilities. It may be even more valuable for slow readers, since they are relieved of the task of writing. Since students cannot mark in textbooks and references, it will be necessary for the teacher to duplicate the materials they will use. Even with this limitation, the activity is worthwhile, since it (1) presents important words and phrases in their original context; (2) highlights those key concepts in sequence; (3) forces the student to read a passage more than once; and (4) teaches selective comprehension.[10] Poostay suggests these steps for teaching underlining:

1. Select and pre-identify the key concepts, words, and phrases.
2. Make a copy of the material with your underlinings for each student.
3. Tell the students to point to your underlinings as you read only what is underlined aloud. Do not read the entire selection.
4. Discuss why each word or phrase was underlined.
5. Read the underlinings again, having the students predict the content from the underlinings.
6. Have the students read the original passage.
7. Have the students recall the material without the underlinings, then with the underlinings.
8. In later lessons, ask the children to do their own underlinings.[11]

With slow readers it is important to select material that is at the instructional level and to repeat the steps identified by Poostay several times.

Using Glosses, Advance Organizers, Structured Overviews, and Study Guides

The teachers of remedial readers should have available as many techniques as possible for helping children make sense of text. Glosses, advance organizers, structured overviews, study guides, and a variety of techniques of similar natures may be most useful. They help children know what is coming in the print they are reading, and they explain vocabulary or extend concepts.

"Gloss notations are marginal notes written to direct readers' attention while they read."[12] They may focus on either the content being read or on the process of reading. Glosses are written on strips of paper that are laid by the page of print. The usefulness of glosses for remedial readers lies in the ability of the teacher to make them fit the needs of individuals. The teacher can concentrate on vocabulary or skills known to be needed by the students.

Advance organizers, based on the theoretical work of Ausubel,[13] are passages prepared to introduce later material to be read. They prepare the reader by providing an organizing structure to aid in comprehension. The reader recalls better when there is a framework for remembering or for grouping ideas. Remembering is not as efficient when the reader tries to store lists of apparently unrelated ideas.

Making good advance organizers is difficult, especially when the reading abilities of the students are below grade level. The teacher must find simple ways to explain or call attention to sometimes complex ideas in the material to be read. It will be best if the teacher reads the advance organizer with the children to preclude reading problems. Tonjes and Zintz suggest the following steps for a teacher to follow in preparing advance organizers:

1. Read the chapter carefully, noticing the major ideas.
2. Reorder these ideas into a hierarchy that will show their relationship to each other or from superordinate (most general) to subordinate (most specific).
3. Write a 50 to 300-word passage showing this relationship or order, for the reader to understand while reading the chapter.
4. Go over the written organizer with the students before they read the chapter, making sure they understand the purpose and inter-relationships.[14]

Structured overviews, prepared *with* the children, and cognitive maps prepared by the teacher before meeting with the class, are diagrams that demonstrate the relationships that exist between related ideas. Also called *graphic organizers*[15] and *webs,* these graphic displays have appeal for remedial readers, since the amount of print on them is limited. A teacher developed the structured overview shown in figure 11.1 with three children who were interested in learning about the cat family. The relationships that were shown were used by the three children to develop their plans for dividing the tasks while they studied the cat family. (See figure 11.1.)

Study guides, called *guide-o-ramas* by Wood and Mateja,[16] are lists of questions, comments, and suggested tasks that provide a *written tutor* for readers. A study guide is more than just a list of questions to be answered. Its items should stimulate thinking through questions written at different levels, encourage conceptual thinking, and guide the student to see the relationships between ideas. The study guide is meant to be used during reading or as a follow-up lesson. Wood and Mateja suggest that the study guide be attractively designed to stimulate student interest.[17] Slow readers may find a study guide useful, since it will direct them to the most critical elements in the material they must read. The guide must be written in such a way that it does not add to the reading burden the children already carry.

Summarizing

Summaries become important in classrooms where children are expected to obtain ideas from several sources. Thoughtful, selective reading is necessary to write a summary. The assignment of summary writing will require reading comprehension. Harris and Sipay note that each language experience story that is written is a summary of an

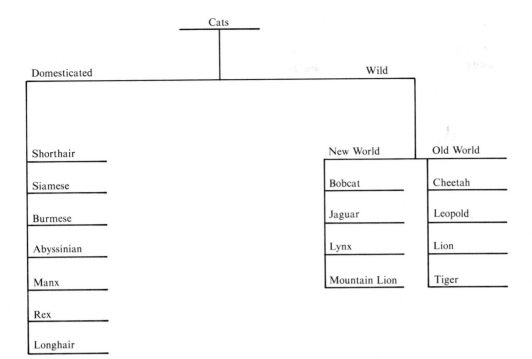

Figure 11.1. Structure overview to guide the study of the cat family

experience.[18] Children whose early school lessons have included the writing of many personal stories should be able to move easily into writing summaries of the experiences of others that they find in their reading. Some children will not have had the earlier opportunities to write about their own experiences. These children will require careful instruction, perhaps working first with note taking and underlining before attempting summarizing. Teachers whose students simply copy material from the reference books should examine the children's ability to identify critical ideas and compose summary paragraphs, not accuse them of copying. Copying can be the only strategy available to a child who must write a summary but does not know how. Remedial readers may be helped to concentrate on the ideas to be summarized by having the writing task delayed or eliminated. The child may do best at the task by dictating the summary and perhaps later copying it. If the child works in a group, the other members may find the poor readers' ideas to be valuable contributions to their summarizing task, but another group member will do the writing.

Taylor's investigations have led him to the belief that students generally do poorly at summarizing.[19] He indicates that there are three stages to summarizing—reading, analyzing, and writing. Poor readers tend to go directly from reading to writing. Good readers and trained persons insert the analyzing step, which may include second or third readings to make sure that the intent of the writer is captured. It would appear that teachers can promote summarizing skills by insisting that the middle step, analyzing, not be skipped. The second and third readings could be useful to slow readers not only for helping them become certain of the author's meaning but also to improve their fluency on a single passage.

Sequencing

Sequencing is closely related to outlining, but has broader implications. Very young children generally learn to think sequentially and to recall sequences of activities in their own lives. Children must be able to perform this metacognitive activity before they can understand sequences in the lives of others, in print, and in places and events long ago and far away. Sequence has a relationship to cause and effect thinking. This relationship is involved with understanding one's own plans and goals and, eventually, the plans and goals of others.[20] These understandings are essential to the understanding of characters in story and the actions of people recorded in subject-area texts.

Teachers should be sure to call children's attention to the sequence of events in material they read. For some children who find difficulty with this task, the teacher may need to help the child sequence the events in the classroom and in life outside the classroom on a daily basis. It may also help to talk about step-by-step directions for making a toy or constructing a gift. The child must learn that you can not put the pin through the pin wheel and into the stick until the paper has been folded, for example.

Interpretive Skills

Most school textbooks contain maps, charts, tables, pictures, graphs, and other types of visual aids. Each child needs to learn to make good use of these tools for learning. Learning how to use these visual aids should begin early in the elementary school years with children making them as summaries of their own experiences. Primary-grade children often graph the birthdays of classmates by months and their attendance daily as the teacher takes the role. Charts of schoolroom tasks and who will do them are typical in classrooms. Students may make tables that show the amount of candy that has been sold by class members or the weight of the various foods consumed by the hamster. Children enjoy drawing pictures. The teacher needs to be sure that each child explains about what has been drawn and points out important details to the observers. When the production of visual aids in the classroom is a normal part of the school day and they are discussed and referred to when needed, the same sorts of learning tools in published materials will be accepted positively.

The teacher needs to be aware that the visual aids in texts may be considerably more complex than those produced by children. Care must be taken to explain legends, to clarify meanings of symbols, and to discuss the information that can be obtained. When children do not understand and have not learned of their importance, the tendency is for the reader to glance briefly at visual aids and then skip them. With older boys and girls, reference to maps, charts, graphs, and other aids may be made in glosses and study guides that are prepared for reading chapters in texts. If slow readers are helped to understand these learning tools, they may find them inviting, since the amount of reading to be done is usually less than the explanations in the text.

Reading and *interpreting* cartoons and comic strips can keep students actively thinking and using the communication abilities they have, even though little reading may be necessary. The Small Society carries a message for the person who thinks about issues (figure 11.2); and Hi and Lois must evaluate important principles of child growth and development through briefly written anecdotes (figure 11.3). Key tells a story without words in the Hazel cartoon (figure 11.4).

Figure 11.2. *The Small Society* by Brickman (Used with the permission of the Washington Star Syndicate, Inc.)

Figure 11.3. Hi and Lois (Used with the permission of the King Features Syndicate.)

Figure 11.4. Hazel (Used with the permission of the King Features Syndicate.)

Skills in Presenting Information

It is not unusual for children to gather a lot of information on a topic, to take notes and make an outline, and then be unable to prepare a written or oral report that meets the teacher's expectations. Children need as much help at learning how to make reports and talks as they do with the information-gathering process. When children copy extensively from references, the teacher has a good indication that they do not know how to move from collections of information to putting ideas into their own words.

Some teachers will take a class through the entire process by having them gather data, organize notes and outlines, and dictate a report that will be written on the chalkboard. Class members experience the transition from gathering the ideas written by others to expressing those ideas as personal examples of understanding. Children see how major points on an outline become paragraphs fleshed out by the outline's supporting details. They learn how to prepare footnotes or other forms of citation. Together they experience creating an attractive opening paragraph and a summarizing closing one. The slow readers in the group may need extended help of this kind to grasp the necessary organization. It will probably be their reading and writing skills that will be troublesome; their ability to think about the task and to perform the cognitive tasks may be as strong as that of the rest of the class. For some students with severely impaired reading and writing skills, the tape recorder can be used. The report may be given orally and later be typed by the class "secretary."

Children also need practice in giving oral reports. Almost every adult can remember some unpleasant experience with an oral report in school—a time when you hoped the floor would swallow you or you felt sadness for another student's misery. These experiences need not happen if children from the first are encouraged to share experiences in front of their classmates. Later, children will begin to share the experiences of others based on their reading. Reports can be made more formal if, in the presentations of older students, the child works from an outline so that certain points that were preplanned can be made. The child can be given chances to rehearse with the teacher or a close friend. These efforts will not be "graded," since *grading* has a terrifying effect on many students. Children should be allowed to experiment with group presentations such as panel discussions, skits, and audiovisual productions. Slow readers may be quite successful at oral presentations, since the problems with recording print are removed. These children have an opportunity to achieve success in the same way as their classmates if the teacher makes sure they have prepared and rehearsed adequately.

Following Directions

Almost every teacher complains at one time or another about students who cannot follow directions. Harris and Sipay remind us:[21]

> In former times, children learned mainly by watching and imitating their elders. In modern life, people must rely more and more on printed directions and manuals of procedure. . . . Practice in reading and following directions is best pro-

vided in relation to activities that children wish to carry out or skills that they want to learn.

In a society in which being able to follow printed directions is essential, its children should have every possible chance to practice this skill. Teachers must take every classroom opportunity to have children follow directions. If a new piece of equipment is purchased, the children should help read the directions and assemble it. If a pet is purchased and a set of directions for its care comes along with the animal, the class should assume responsibility for reading and carrying out the directions. Sometimes teachers may need to contrive activities, even worksheets, for practicing following directions, but the best learning opportunities come out of real experiences. Following recipes in classroom cooking experiences, attending to construction steps in building some much-needed bookcases, and interpreting the guidelines in making a gift are all real reasons for reading and following directions.

For children who have problems, the teacher might:

1. Supplement the written directions with pictures or rebuses in place of some of the words.
2. Have the children read the directions, followed by an oral restatement of the steps to be taken.
3. Limit the number of steps in a set of directions and increase the number as the children's skills grow.
4. Play games and sing familiar songs that require following directions. Finger plays may be useful in this respect, too.
5. Work on varied sequencing activities; following directions is simply a specialized kind of sequence.
6. Encourage the child to work on the microcomputer. The microcomputer proceeds based on the directions the user gives it.
7. Rewrite complex directions using simpler words, smaller steps, and examples.

Helping Students Remember

One topic that is almost never dealt with in school is learning how to remember. Eventually, most people develop some personalized strategies that seem to work, but rarely are these shared with children. If one were to ask a group of adults how they would learn the names of the fifty states, the answers would include alphabetizing, associating the names with other ideas, learning groups of states located in the same geographical area, ordering the names from shortest to longest, listing them in the order the person has visited them, and saying them in random order as they were thought of. It would be helpful if the more useful remembering techniques were practiced in the classroom.

Children should see note taking and underlining as study strategies designed to help the person remember. They should learn that making a list reminds one to accomplish certain tasks. They should know that mnemonic devices (such as the famous string around the finger) are legitimate means of remembering.

In general ways, the teacher may take certain steps to make remembering more likely. Otto, McMenemy, and Smith made several suggestions:

1. Secure the learner's cooperation.
2. Offer material at the learner's level.
3. Reinforce success.
4. Keep tasks and materials meaningful.
5. Encourage pupils to discover relationships for themselves.
6. Provide spaced practice.[22]

Tonjes and Zintz offer these suggestions to teachers who want to help their students remember:

1. Teach students that they must always have a purpose for reading.
2. Students should work to grasp the author's organization. Outlining may help.
3. Make notes about important points. Students should know that writing facilitates memory.
4. Students should practice summarizing, including only important ideas.
5. Encourage students to discuss what has been read.
6. Students who apply what has been read will remember it better.[23]

Test Taking

Test taking is a challenge to almost all students. It is particularly burdensome for the slow readers in the class. The teacher may work to have these children excused from some testing, but inevitably they will have to participate. The tests they do take may be especially important to them, since they may be used to help determine special placements or eligibility for special services.

Children can be prepared to do their best on the tests they must take. Going into the testing session having studied and prepared to the best of one's ability offers reassurance. The teacher can describe to the children what to expect—the physical setting, how one will respond (essay, marking circles for machine scoring, and so forth), the time frame, how scores will be reported, and what the value of the test might be for the individual.

Rubin suggested the following test-taking principles:

1. Plan to do well; have a positive attitude.
2. Get enough rest before the test.
3. Be well prepared.
4. View a test as an opportunity to learn.
5. Look over the whole test before you begin.
6. Know how much time you have to work.
7. Concentrate on the test.
8. Read instructions carefully.
9. Begin with questions you are sure of.
10. If answers are not known, make intelligent guesses.

Making Connections 11.1: Finding Out What Children Know about Study Skills

Before you plan lessons to use with children, it is important to know what they already know. Over several months with a group of children, a teacher becomes very good at predicting the knowledge the children have.

It may be helpful to interview a group of three or four middle-grade students to gain a sense of what they know about study skills. Plan with a teacher, who will let you "borrow" some students, to include at least one or two children who are slow readers.

Develop a list of questions based on the outline of the study skills at the beginning of this chapter to find out what the children know and can do in relation to the various topics. Your questions might include:

1. If you needed to find out about a topic, perhaps locomotives, what kinds of references would you use? How would you find "locomotives" in the encyclopedia?
2. Have you ever made an outline? How did you do it?
3. Tell me how you go about taking notes. Do they help you remember what you have read? In what ways?
4. When you have to remember things that you have read, how do you do it?

You will want to develop questions in addition to these.

When you have conducted your interview, share your findings with peers who have also interviewed students. What conclusions can you draw from the collective information the children have given you?

---

11. After answering questions you are sure of, work on those items that count the most.
12. Go over all the answers before the time is up.
13. When (if) the test is returned, learn from the results.[24]

Reading in the Content Fields

When the teacher considers the responsibilities of instructing students in reading in the content fields, they fall into two categories: (1) general skills instruction and (2) instruction in specific content areas such as social studies or mathematics.

General Skills in Content Fields Reading

There are at least four areas of general skills that must be addressed by the classroom teacher. These areas are reading expository text as opposed to narrative text, using appropriate study strategies, learning a large amount of vocabulary, and employing critical reading skills. Each of these areas represents particular problems for the boys and girls with reading difficulties.

Narrative versus Expository Text

When children work in their basal readers, nearly all of the selections they read are narrative in nature. They are stories with beginnings, one or more problems that must be resolved, and endings. By the time the children have left the primary grades, they have heard or read hundreds of selections based on this organization.

When children begin to have reading assignments in content area textbooks, they meet a variety of other organizational patterns. Their history texts will usually be organized chronologically, their science books will have chapters devoted to concepts such as microscopic life or the solar system, and their mathematics books will use a particular quantitative concept as an organizer. The children who read their third-grade readers well may struggle with their third-grade textbooks. Children who have problems with reading narrative may be overwhelmed by their content area texts.

Part of the problem is the difference between narrative and expository text. The following lists provide a brief comparison of the two forms:

Narrative Text	*Expository Text*
Characters are central to story.	People are incidental to text.
Agent oriented.	Subject matter oriented.
Located in a time, indicated by verb tense.	Time is not focal.
Chronological ordering.	Logical ordering.
Strong story grammar.	Weak story grammar if at all.
Lower loading of content words.	Density of concepts.[25]

Alvermann and Boothby asked fourth graders to identify narrative and expository texts and found that children at that age could do so reliably.[26] The children were unable to say why they could tell the two types of text apart, but indicated that they thought expository text was harder to read, had harder words, and was less interesting than narrative.

It is important for the teacher to talk with children about the differences in the way print is organized in their various texts. The slow reader will be aided by any personalized help that can be given by a peer tutor; a parent or grandparent volunteer; the teacher during brief conferences; and well-planned, easy study guides and questions. The teacher may be able to find library books that will contain similar facts and ideas embedded in narrative forms. It may also be helpful to underline those parts of the child's text that contain the most significant information. The teacher may guide the child to read the first sentence of a paragraph or section and then predict the kind of information that is likely to be found in it. The follow-up reading will be for the purpose of confirming the prediction. This predicting/confirming strategy may help the child identify a structure in expository text that will make reading easier.

Study Strategies

The best known study strategy is surely SQ3R which was developed by Francis Robinson in 1941.[27] The SQ3R formula was designed to promote long-term memory of what has been studied and learned. The steps are S–survey, Q–question, R–read, R–recite, and R–review. The strategy was later revised to include a fourth R: reflect. A number of strategies, some suited to reading in particular content areas, have been developed from it. Variations include SQRQCQ for mathematics,[28] PQRST for science,[29] and REAP for processing information by reading, encoding, annotating and pondering.[30]

A consistent study strategy should be taught to remedial readers. To suggest a variety of strategies could well be confusing. The teacher should work with the child until the strategy is well learned. A card taped to the desk or other study site may serve as a reminder of the requisite steps. It is important to remember that the strategy will not work if the material to be read is too difficult. Successful study will depend on instructional level materials *and* a well-learned strategy such as SQ3R.

Vocabulary

Three kinds of vocabulary problems await the disabled reader when reading content field materials. The first is part of the general reading problem—lack of mastery of the basic sight vocabulary. Not only is the child troubled by the specialized words that abound in the text, but even *through, where,* and *tried* and other common words cause difficulty. The child with this level of difficulty will be much more successful with taped books, film strips, and greatly simplified texts while the mastery of basic sight words is attempted.

Many words that have common meanings are also used in specialized ways in content fields. These words may be particularly troublesome to remedial readers, who have basically one definition for each word.

An example of such a word is *bank*. The child has gone with Dad or Mom to the bank since infancy. In science class the teacher talks about water running down the *bank* washing away the soil. Then, in a story, the child reads that an airplane *banks* when it makes a wide turn. Another example might be the word *blocks*. They have been familiar toys for years. But the social studies book discusses city *blocks* and the physical education teacher says that Bill *blocks* the other players better than anyone else.

Teachers need to identify such words in texts and make sure that children apply the appropriate meaning. The words need to be discussed and written in sentences that will provide the needed contrasts in meanings. Children may enjoy selecting a word and making sentences using as many different meanings as possible.

Textbooks also have a variety of technical terms that children must learn to identify and relate to meanings. One third-grade social studies text that is representative of such materials contains the following sentences:

President Roosevelt knew that having more *national forests* was a good thing. But he thought it was an answer to only part of the problem of *conservation*. The

President asked the *governors* of the states to come to a meeting. . . . He wanted all the people to use *natural resources* with care.[31]

Children who read such passages with comprehension must have had some experiences with the concepts represented by the technical terms. If the teacher wishes all children to understand such material, it will be necessary to plan activities that allow children to conserve, to visit a national forest at least in a film, and to talk about our natural resources. Since many remedial readers are children who have had few experiences, building concepts related to technical terms is critical.

A student teacher planned a unit on the desert and its plants and animals. To his surprise, he found that the five children he was to teach had never been out of their city; two had never been farther than two miles from home. From the teacher's description of a desert, the children thought it was a bit like a nearby parking lot. The teacher made arrangements to take the children to an arid area about thirty miles from the school. The children were excited about the trip, but were able to control their enthusiasm to attend to what the teacher was telling them. He introduced several technical terms related to deserts. The children went on the trip prepared to see a sand dune, a blow-out, a blue-tailed lizard, and a dry wash. They returned able to talk knowingly about all these concepts and more. The unit proceeded successfully, with the children building a diorama of "their" desert. The student teacher knew that his unit would have been another unsuccessful experience for these unsuccessful students without this firsthand knowledge.

Critical Reading

Remedial readers tend to be very uncritical readers, because they are engrossed in the decoding task and hardly expect print to mean much. However, unless teachers make them aware of the fact that print is not always true, correct, or straightforward, they may become victims of the very skill they are trying so hard to master.

At the very least, teachers should help remedial readers understand that:

1. Untrue statements appear in print.
2. Writers can bias readers' attitudes and opinions.
3. *When* a text is written may have some bearing on its current accuracy.
4. Some texts make racist and sexist statements.
5. Advertising must be read with care to see what it is that the writer wants the reader to do.
6. Propaganda must be treated as an attempt to influence readers' thinking.
7. Some authors are more qualified to write on a particular subject than are others.

The teacher can prepare exercises or buy workbooks or spirit masters that can be used with children to give them practice with critical reading skills. However, the best materials are probably the children's textbooks and materials out of the environment, such as advertisements, slogans, biographies of authors, copyright dates, and propaganda materials. Some computer games will also encourage critical reading and thinking. The teacher should examine such software carefully to make sure the children will understand or even identify the point that is being made.

Reading in Specific Content Areas

Each of the elementary school subjects has textbooks that are organized to present its subject matter as authentically as possible. It is important for the teacher to examine these materials to see how they are written, where the organizational differences are and how these will affect the students, what aids for reading are present, and what concepts will have to be developed. Reading in subject-matter areas is generally more difficult than the reading done in organized reading classes. Such reading requires special vocabulary, comprehension of concepts, and organizing and evaluating. It also requires the ability to locate and read maps, graphs, and charts, and the ability to use their content in further reading of the text. Fay lists the following difficulties that students encounter reading in the content areas:

1. There is an unduly heavy load of facts and concepts.
2. The variations in typographical arrangement from one area to another may confuse the pupil.
3. All too frequently the materials are uninteresting to the pupils.
4. The ease of readability of materials is often considerably less than that of basic readers.
5. Many writers tend to assume greater background than pupils possess.
6. All this emphasizes the need for carefully fitting materials to pupils and for carefully organizing instruction for reading such materials.[32]

Mathematics

The difficulties of reading in mathematics are many. Nolan lists these potential sources of trouble:

1. The writing in mathematics books is terse, with a lack of redundancy.
2. Writing in mathematics texts is dense and requires slow, careful reading.
3. Mathematical symbols do not bear a grapheme-phoneme correspondence.
4. The student must employ left-right, right-left, up, down, and diagonal eye movements in reading and solving problems.
5. Mathematics has both a specialized and a technical vocabulary.[33]

Any one of these problems could seem grave for remedial readers. The teacher must spend much time helping these students learn to interpret the reading in mathematics. Talking children through pages in the text and being sure that needed vocabulary and symbols are thoroughly learned are two important techniques. Threadgill-Sowder et al. state that the solution of word problems is one of the most sophisticated of all mathematical tasks, because the solver must use so many reading skills.[34] They note that many children who can read well and can compute cannot solve story problems. Kresse supports their position noting that in a study of sixth graders, 95 percent could read the words in the problems, and 92 percent knew what the problem was asking them to find, but only 36 percent knew how to work the problem.[35]

Kresse proposed modeling the problem-solving task by talking the children through five steps: (1) surveying the task by reading the problem and making needed sketches; (2) asking the important questions related to "what it is that it wants me to find"; (3) reading pertinent parts of the problem again; (4) working the problem; and (5) checking your reasoning.[36] She proposed going through these steps so many times that they become automatic.

Aaron discusses the areas of difficulty in reading in mathematics: (1) vocabulary; (2) concepts necessary to understand mathematical ideas; (3) knowing *how to read* in mathematics with respect to speed of comprehending the problem; (4) ability to read the variety of types of mathematical stimuli, print, equations, charts, tables; and (5) interpreting appropriate symbols and abbreviations in mathematics.[37] Aaron also has suggestions for students about how to read problems in mathematics.

1. Read the problem quickly to get an overview.
2. Reread the problem, this time at a slower rate, to determine what facts are given.
3. Think of the specific question to be answered.
4. Think of the order in which the facts are to be used in answering the question raised in the problem.
5. Think of the operations required for solving the problem.
6. Estimate an answer that seems reasonable.
7. Work the problem by performing the appropriate operation.
8. Compare the answer with the estimated answer.
9. Go back to the first step if the answer seems unreasonable.[38]

Radebaugh suggests that children's literature can be the source of mathematics insights and problems.[39] She lists many books that could be used to develop counting, geometric knowledge, number concepts, addition, the history of our number system, money, large numbers, multiplication, and fractions. These materials could well be attractive to slow readers, much easier to read, and less likely to stimulate negative attitudes.

Social Studies

Blake suggested that the skills required to read the social studies texts fall into three categories—technical and specialized vocabulary development, comprehension skills, and study skills.[40] The major comprehension skills to be developed include cause and effect, comparison and contrast, sequence, fact versus opinion, and graphic patterns. The study skills include many already discussed, including establishing a purpose for reading, using the parts of the textbook, organizing information, note taking, and using the rate skills of skimming and scanning.

Children with poor reading skills will find many of the required skills listed in the previous paragraph very difficult to master. They may find more success in learning social studies content with trade books. The school librarian can help the classroom teacher identify a collection of books at varied reading levels on most social studies unit topics. The teacher may also send for the annual list "Notable Children's Trade Books in the Field of Social Studies" from the Children's Book Council, 67 Irving Place, New York, New York 10003.

Cunningham, Cunningham, and Arthur suggest additional ways to help slow readers with social studies reading tasks.[41] They suggest having children work in small groups with one child reading the text. The reading is stopped frequently, and all children engage in discussion to identify main ideas and supporting details. Poor readers can learn from listening in this setting. They also suggest that the teacher gather slower readers together and read the assignment to them. The children are then asked to translate what has been read, that is, to put it in their own words. Finally, they suggest that the elementary classroom emphasize nontext resources in the social studies; these resources would include many firsthand experiences.

Science

The final example of an elementary school content field that may pose serious reading problems for poor readers is science. Science texts are rich with technical and specialized vocabulary. It is important that students have as many real experiences as may be arranged to make these words and the concepts they represent come alive. If this is not done, children may have the feeling that they are trying to read a foreign language in their science texts. In addition to the complex vocabulary, Weidler notes that science books are characterized by cause and effect writing and causal chaining patterns in which one action causes another, which in turn causes another. The writing is filled with passive forms and embedded sentences that also contribute to increasing the difficulty of reading.[42]

Smith analyzed fifty-two science texts, sixty social studies texts, forty-nine mathematics texts, and forty-five literature texts to find out about the special writing patterns in the content fields.[43] From these she identified unique patterns of writing for which students can develop special reading skills and abilities. In science, students need to identify the following:

1. *The Classification Pattern.* A major heading, living things, will have two subheadings: plants and animals. Animals can be subdivided into vertebrates and invertebrates. Once the students are aware of the form (pattern) in which the content will be presented, they can adapt their reading style to that pattern.
2. *Explanation of a Technical Process.* The explanation of a process is usually accompanied by diagrams that must be read carefully and concomitantly with the text.
3. *Instructions for an Experiment.* This pattern usually requires the ability to follow precise directions. However, in order for the experiment to be successful, the readers must make all the correct observations and decisions at each step of the way.

4. *Detailed Statement-of-Fact Pattern.* This pattern requires "intensive" reading, sorting out numerous "facts," selecting the main idea, and relating the subordinate ideas.

5. *The Descriptive Problem-Solving Pattern.* This pattern requires that the students identify each successive problem and be sure they grasp its solution before going on to the next.

6. *Abbreviations and Equations.* Students need to recognize special symbols and abbreviations as they appear in context in addition to the word symbol—for example, the symbol for "degree" in Fahrenheit (F) and Centigrade (C) scales.

To help readers, Cunningham, Cunningham, and Arthur recommend walking children through the science lesson pointing out pictures, graphics, headings, and special vocabulary. The children are invited to make predictions and to read to confirm predictions.[44] This strategy gives even the poorest readers many clues as to what the reading is all about.

Smardo has developed a long list of trade books that children may read to help them develop or expand science concepts. The topics range from rainbows and insects to evaporation and seasons.[45] With the cooperation of the school librarian, it would seem that science reading could be done almost entirely with trade books. Since they are available at so many levels of difficulty, every reader should be able to find something to read.

Barrow, Kristo, and Andrew propose that science be carried out using the language-experience approach. Children in science classes have experiences of various kinds. These experiences would be followed by drawing and writing times. This approach allows even the slowest readers to have important science experiences and to process those experiences through talking, drawing, and writing.[46]

Making Connections 11.2: Examining Content Textbooks

Select one mathematics, one social studies, and one science textbook at a single grade level. Select just five pages from each text. They may be consecutive or widely separated pages. Study each of these pages in detail in order to make a list of reading difficulties a child might encounter. You will probably want to keep the problems you identify for each content area separate or code them for identification on a single list.

1. What problems seem to be common to all three texts?
2. What problems are unique to each subject area?
3. What did the authors do to try to make the reading tasks as easy as possible?
4. What would you do as the teacher to make reading these pages as worthwhile as possible for students?

You will want to share your findings and conclusion with others in your class who have also completed the assignment.

Summary

This chapter presented information on two closely related topics: study skills and reading in the content fields. Suggestions have been made for teaching study skills related to locating, organizing, interpreting, and presenting content. In addition, the specific topics of following directions, remembering, and test taking were discussed. When children prepare to read content texts they are faced with some general problems, including reading the less-familiar expository text form, employing study strategies such as SQ3R, learning specialized and technical vocabulary, and reading critically. Finally, there are problems unique to reading content in such areas as mathematics, social studies, and science. Suggestions were given for helping children do this type of reading more satisfactorily.

For Further Reading

Anderson, Thomas H. "Study Strategies and Adjunct Kids." In Rand J. Spiro, Bertram C. Bruce, and William F. Brewer, eds., *Theoretical Issues in Reading Comprehension.* Hillsdale, N.J.: Lawrence Erlbaum Associates, Publishers, 1980.

Boodt, Gloria M. "Critical Listeners Become Critical Readers in Remedial Reading Class." *The Reading Teacher* 37 (January 1984), pp. 390–94.

Dupuis, Mary M., ed. *Reading in the Content Areas: Research for Teachers.* Newark, Del.: International Reading Association, 1984.

Earle, Richard. *Teaching Reading and Mathematics.* Newark, Del.: International Reading Association, 1976.

Gentile, Lance M. *Using Sports and Physical Education to Strengthen Reading Skills.* Newark, Del.: International Reading Association, 1980.

Graham, Kenneth G., and Robinson, H. Alan. *Study Skills Handbook, A Guide for All Teachers.* Newark, Del.: International Reading Association, 1984.

Lunstrum, John P., and Taylor, Bob L. *Teaching Reading in the Social Studies.* Newark, Del.: International Reading Association, 1978.

Reutzel, D. Ray. "C⁶: A Reading Model for Teaching Arithmetic Story Problem-Solving." *The Reading Teacher* 37 (October 1983), pp. 28–34.

Thelen, Judith. *Improving Reading in Science,* 2d ed. Newark, Del.: International Reading Association, 1984.

Wade, Suzanne E. "A Synthesis of the Research for Improving Reading in the Social Studies." *Review of Educational Research* 53 (Winter 1983), pp. 461–97.

Notes

1. A. Sterl Artley, "Effective Study—Its Nature and Nurture," in *Elementary Reading Instruction: Selected Materials,* edited by Althea Beery, Thomas C. Barrett, and William R. Powell (Boston: Allyn and Bacon, 1969), p. 430.
2. Douglas B. Rogers, "Assessing Study Skills," *Journal of Reading* 27 (January 1984), p. 346.

3. Ibid., p. 352.
4. *The World Book Encyclopedia* (Chicago: Field Enterprises Educational Corp., 1984).
5. Eldon E. Ekwall and James L. Shanker, *Diagnosis and Remediation of the Disabled Reader,* 2d ed. (Boston: Allyn and Bacon, 1983), p. 81.
6. Dorothy Rubin, *Diagnosis and Correction in Reading Instruction* (New York: Holt, Rinehart and Winston, 1982), pp. 271–72.
7. Mary M. Dupuis and Eunice N. Askov, *Content Area Reading* (Englewood Cliffs, N.J.: Prentice-Hall, 1982), p. 229.
8. Marian J. Tonjes and Miles V. Zintz, *Teaching Reading/Thinking/Study Skills in Content Classrooms* (Dubuque, Iowa: Wm. C. Brown, 1981), p. 219.
9. James W. Cunningham, Patricia M. Cunningham, and Sharon V. Arthur, *Middle and Secondary School Reading* (New York: Longman, 1981), p. 64.
10. Edward J. Poostay, "Show Me Your Underlines: A Strategy to Teach Comprehension," *The Reading Teacher* 37 (May 1984), p. 829.
11. Ibid., pp. 828–29.
12. Donald J. Richgels and Ruth Hansen, "Gloss: Helping Students Apply Both Skills and Strategies in Reading Content Texts," *Journal of Reading* 27 (January 1984), p. 312.
13. David P. Ausubel, "Use of Advance Organizers in the Learning and Retention of Meaningful Verbal Material," *Journal of Educational Psychology* 51 (1960), pp. 267–72.
14. Tonjes and Zintz, *Teaching Reading/Thinking/Study Skills,* p. 286.
15. Richard A. Earle and Richard F. Barron, "An Approach to Teaching Vocabulary in Content Subjects," in *Research in Reading in the Content Areas: Second Year Report,* edited by Harold L. Herber and Richard F. Barron (Syracuse, N.Y.: Reading and Language Arts Center, Syracuse University, 1973).
16. Karen D. Wood and John A. Mateja, "Adapting Secondary Level Strategies for Use in Elementary Classrooms," *The Reading Teacher* 36 (February 1983), p. 494.
17. Ibid., p. 495.
18. Albert J. Harris and Edward R. Sipay, *How to Increase Reading Ability,* 7th ed. (New York: Longman, 1980), p. 498.
19. Karl K. Taylor, "Teaching Summarization Skills," *Journal of Reading* 27 (February 1984), p. 389.
20. Bertram C. Bruce, "Plans and Social Actions," in *Theoretical Issues in Reading Comprehension,* eds. Rand S. Spiro, Bertram C. Bruce, and William F. Brewer (Hillsdale, N.J.: Lawrence Erlbaum Assoc., 1980), pp. 367–84.
21. Harris and Sipay, *How to Increase Reading Ability,* p. 492.
22. Wayne Otto, Richard A. McMenemy, and Richard J. Smith, *Corrective and Remedial Teaching,* 2d ed. (Boston: Houghton Mifflin, 1973), pp. 56–58.
23. Tonjes and Zintz, *Teaching Reading/Thinking/Study Skills,* p. 242.
24. Rubin, *Diagnosis and Correction,* pp. 277–78.
25. Carolyn E. Kent, "A Linguist Compares Narrative and Expository Prose," *Journal of Reading* 28 (December 1984), pp. 232–36.
26. Donna E. Alvermann and Paula R. Boothby, "Text Differences: Children's Perceptions at the Transition Stage in Reading," *The Reading Teacher* 36 (December 1982), pp. 298–302.
27. Francis P. Robinson, *Effective Study* (New York: Harper and Row, 1946), pp. 28–33.
28. Leo Fay, "Reading Study Skills: Math and Science," in J. A. Figurel, ed., *Reading and Inquiry* (Newark, Del.: International Reading Association, 1965), p. 93.
29. George Spache, *Toward Better Reading* (Champaign, Ill.: Garrard Publishing Co., 1963), p. 94.

30. Marilyn Eanet and Anthony Manzo, "REAP, A Strategy for Improving Reading/Writing/ Study Skills," *Journal of Reading* 19 (May 1976), pp. 647–52.

31. V. Phillips Weaver, *People and Resources, Teacher's Edition* (Morristown, N.J.: Silver Burdett Co., 1979), pp. 98–99.

32. Leo C. Fay, "What Research Has to Say about Reading in the Content Areas," *The Reading Teacher* 8 (1954), pp. 68–72.

33. James F. Nolan, "Reading in the Content Areas in Mathematics," in *Reading in the Content Areas: Research for Teachers* (Newark, Del.: International Reading Association, 1984), pp. 28–29.

34. Judith Threadgill-Sowder et al., "A Case against Telegraphing Math Story Problems for Poor Readers," *The Reading Teacher* 37 (April 1984), p. 746.

35. Elaine C. Kresse, "Using Reading as a Thinking Process to Solve Math Story Problems," *Journal of Reading* 27 (April 1984), p. 598.

36. Ibid., pp. 599–600.

37. I. E. Aaron, "Reading in Mathematics," *Journal of Reading* 8 (May 1965), pp. 391–95, 401.

38. Ibid., p. 394.

39. Muriel R. Radebaugh, "Using Children's Literature to Teach Mathematics," *The Reading Teacher* 34 (May 1981), p. 902.

40. S. Blake, *Teaching Reading Skills through Social Studies and Science Materials* (Brooklyn: New York City Board of Education, Division of High Schools, 1975).

41. Cunningham, Cunningham, and Arthur, *Middle and Secondary School Reading*, pp. 86–87.

42. Sarah D. Weidler, "Reading in the Content Area of Science," in *Reading in the Content Areas: Research for Teachers* (Newark, Del.: International Reading Association, 1984), pp. 54–55.

43. Nila B. Smith, "Patterns of Writing in Different Subject Areas," in *Elementary Reading Instruction, Selected Materials,* 2d ed., edited by Althea Beery, Thomas C. Barrett, and Wm. R. Powell (Boston: Allyn and Bacon, 1974), pp. 460–71. Reprinted from *Journal of Reading* 8 (October and November 1964), pp. 31–36, 97–102.

44. Cunningham, Cunningham, and Arthur, *Middle and Secondary School Reading*, p. 82.

45. Frances A. Smardo, "Using Children's Literature to Clarify Science Concepts in Early Childhood Programs," *The Reading Teacher* 36 (December 1982), p. 267.

46. Lloyd H. Barrow, Janice V. Kristo, and Barbara Andrew, "Building Bridges Between Science and Reading," *The Reading Teacher* 38 (November 1984), pp. 188–92.

12
Attitudes of Teachers toward Students Who Fail

Vocabulary

acceptance
causal approach
achievement differences
middle class values
empathy
negative self-image

Questions

1. What does it mean to completely accept a child?

2. How does good teaching increase the range of differences in a class as the school year progresses?

3. In what ways may teachers have trouble with the idea of student failure?

4. What kind of things can a teacher do to prevent the growth of negative self-image?

5. Make a list of the ways adults may reward children for not learning.

6. After studying Axline's eight basic principles, make definite suggestions about carrying each out in the classroom.

A frequently observed attitude of teachers toward those students who are not successful in achieving the expected norms is that of blaming the students in negative ways for their lack of success. Perhaps this is the expected attitude, since the alternative would be for the teachers to question their own teaching abilities, which would, in turn, immediately cause them to be defensive about their own shortcomings. But if children present themselves at school for the purpose of learning and fail to meet the expectations of the adults around them, who is really accountable for the results?

If the professional staff of the school has failed to accommodate the individual differences in achievement that are *normally* found in large numbers of people, who, then, fails? The school system, the classroom teachers, or the children? Has the curriculum as outlined for the teachers prescribed teaching of subject matter to the exclusion of consideration for those individual students who need a special opportunity to learn? This chapter will direct the reader's thinking toward the attitude of the teachers toward the students, the learning process, and the reading standards of the schools.

Acceptance: Positive and Negative

The most important single step in working successfully with students who are underachieving is to create a feeling of complete acceptance by the teacher. The teacher's manner and speech must not betray superficial attempts at acceptance. For all students who enter the classroom, it is the teacher's first and foremost obligation to accept them, make them feel that they belong to the group, and give them opportunity to win socially approved status and recognition as members of that group. Occasionally students who cannot do any particular academic tasks or meet any prescribed academic standards will be assigned to an intermediate-grade classroom. In order for the students to feel that they are accepted by their teacher, the teacher must see that they are provided with tasks that they can usually do *successfully*. Specifically with respect to reading, this means that the teacher must make sure that the pupils have reading material that is *sufficiently easy for their instructional levels* and, if they have no instructional levels, to recognize that fact and meet it objectively in planning assignments for them. The students will sense the empathic response of their teacher most by what the teacher *does* in recognizing what the students can do. If the teacher really "accepts" the students and envisions their growth toward self-realization, the teacher will analyze the present reading status and plan specifically and sequentially to build better reading skills, make a concerted effort to develop a long-range plan, and keep honest and objective records of results.

If students in the intermediate or upper grades have little reading ability, the teacher may say, "Because I teach by the unit method, they get along very well. They work with others on committees, and they do good work in construction activities and drawing." The teacher should not feel secure in the belief that any students make their only contribution to the group by the use of their hands. It is probably unfair to label *any* student by such a narrow measure. The basic problem rests in seeking reasons why they find reading very difficult. This necessitates accurate testing of their learning abilities to determine the degree to which they are mentally retarded, candidates for remedial reading, or a composite of the two.

If students are not able to do *any* academic work or are seriously educationally retarded, it may be most *desirable* for them to have some tutoring outside the classroom. On the other hand, if they are *not* mentally retarded, they should *not* be put in a classroom of educable mentally retarded students. In actual practice, a much greater number of these reading disability cases are totally dependent upon regular classroom teachers than are provided for in other ways.

Suppose you are a fourth-grade teacher and a child who moves into your school district is assigned to your classroom. The first day you discover that the child is

1. Unable to spell any of the fourth grade words correctly on the pretest in spelling.
2. Unable to read orally from the story in the fourth grade reader unless you pronounce every third or fourth word (which he or she seems to expect).
3. Unable to complete any independent writing and spelling in the English lesson.

When and how will you proceed? A *causal approach* can accept any of these answers only as rationalizations:

1. "I'm too busy already. How can I do anything about this when I've got thirty others who can all do fourth-grade work?"
2. "I'll let him listen and pick up what he can from the others."
3. "Put her back into the third grade until she learns how to do the work that the fourth grade is doing."
4. "I'll make her take her books home and study at night; then I'll keep her in to finish her written work."
5. "Perhaps she will do especially well in arithmetic. Everyone is good at something."

None of these answers indicates that the teacher is attacking the *problem* in order to meet the student's learning needs. What the teacher must do is obvious: find out what the student can do, *start where he or she is,* and try to teach the student something.

Need for Empathy

Empathy means to genuinely "accept the child where he or she is" and to communicate a sincere feeling for the child. The child may have had daily experience of hostility, resignation, and despair, and may not believe that the teacher wants to be empathic.

Smith reported comments made by parents in reporting behaviors of teachers toward reading problems in their classrooms. Smith interviewed scores of parents concerning the history of their children's reading failure. Teachers were reported to have reacted as follows:

"She scolded him continuously because he was unable to read."
"Teacher screamed at him when he tried to read and couldn't."

"The teacher continuously subjected him to embarrassment before the other children by referring to his lack of ability to read."

"The teacher complained constantly because he didn't get busy and learn to read."

"The teacher kept him after school because he couldn't read."

"The teacher often made him stand in front of the class for long periods because he couldn't read."[1]

Preston reported an investigation in which she drew the conclusion that 78 percent of the teachers studied could not refrain from expressing their annoyance at slow, stumbling readers.[2]

After Tommy had come for a few remedial reading lessons, his clinician called his regular fourth-grade classroom teacher to discuss his developmental reading skills and to find out what the teacher felt would be helpful ways in which they might work together. The teacher said, "Of course, there really isn't much that I can teach them in reading. They've already had all the reading skills by the end of third grade. We just work on comprehension a little bit."

She did not offer to make any adjustments in Tommy's schedule at school, suggesting that she really planned for him to do what other children in the fourth grade did each day.

Sally completed books A, B, and C in SRA[3] during her first-grade school year. At the beginning of second grade, she appeared to have forgotten the content of the three books, demonstrating no phonics sense. In grade two, she did books A, B, C, and D and was working in book E at the end of the school year. Sally herself wanted to read desperately, but it was obvious even to her that she wasn't learning "any words to read with." Her mother arranged for summer tutoring. During one of her early lessons, Sally told her clinician, "I sure don't want to begin over again with book A next year." When tested in April, she was well informed about phonics, sounded each phoneme in isolation, and pronounced the word "time" as "Timmy"! During one of her early tutoring lessons in June, while playing *Go-Fish*, she said, "I'll have your "ju" as in *gate*."

Sally's avenue to learning is obviously not in the auditory channel. Two years there had netted practically nothing. She still did a little bit of reversing and could not tell the difference between *where, when, what, who, there, then, that, these,* and *three* as sight words. She sounded slowly through each word, wanted very much to read, and was so aware that she could only guess. Only seven years of age, she had started school *young* because she was given an individual intelligence test and was found to be a bright child.

When George got his report card at the end of the year, he read: "At the mother's insistence, he is being promoted on probation. I know that George is not ready for fifth grade, and George knows that he is not ready for fifth grade, but, at the mother's insistence, he is being promoted on probation." This was followed by other negative statements. Later, George told his father: "You know I'm smart, and mother knows I'm smart, and Mrs. Zintz thinks I am, but that's not what counts. You don't give me the grades."

Teachers should recognize and provide for achievement "differences" all through the students' school lives. Children see clearly that some run faster than others, some plan more wisely, some grow fatter or taller, and some *read better*. When they settle down to schoolwork they need purposes that are personal to them, and their efforts ought to be inner-directed to an increasing degree as they continue through school.[4] This is possible only if assignments are differentiated.

Differences Are Normal

The teachers who help students at various levels will understand that with good teaching the range of differences in their rooms increases as the year progresses. Hence, they *will not aim to make the group more alike,* but will welcome the natural development that makes them more different. They will not try to bring the poor ones up to grade level in academic achievement while they neglect the gifted; rather they will anticipate that the gifted will continue to learn rapidly at their capacity, the slow at their rate of development, and that the spread will increase as it properly should.

> Education within a democratic culture must provide for equality of individual opportunity in accord with inborn capacity so that an individual will not be deprived of educational advantages because of race, religion, age, geographical location, physical, social, or economic conditions, and the group will not be deprived of the possible services and contributions of any individual.[5]

Wang expressed similar ideas in 1980:

> When the instructional program is designed to accommodate the individual differences of all students in the class, differences in the placement and learning progress of individual students are expected and even assumed by the teacher, students, and parents. In such classes no special labeling is needed to differentiate one child from another, and momentary problems in learning are not viewed as failures, but as occasions for further teaching.[6]

The students who cannot read well will find themselves in many school situations attempting a fixed curriculum, forced to go to school in the first place, and then expected to conform to a pattern that defeats them. There is an old Greek legend concerning the bed of Procrustes that is analogous to the situation in which such children find themselves. According to the legend, Procrustes and his men were robbers who extracted a toll from all who wished to pass the fording place that they controlled. When a traveler was given lodging on one of Procrustes' famous beds, Procrustes had an ingenious way of fitting the bed to the sleeper. If the guest was too long, his legs were cut off to make him fit; if he was too short, ropes tied to his head and feet stretched him until he fit the bed.

The inflexible school program, too often observed, says that children should achieve a fixed standard—a standard set from outside the children that does not take into consideration what they are actually able to do. Such a fixed curriculum and social promotion practices place considerable pressure on the children who fail. This pressure is observed in the behavior of the peer group, the organization of the school, and the expectations of the parents and community that the child move along in a lock-step pattern through the traditional grades in the public school. The school is not making use of what it knows about child growth and development if more effort goes into forcing the students to fit the pattern than goes into tailoring the learning experiences to fit them. Much is said concerning the attainment of standards prescribed by a course of study. This, far too often, means that school authorities are conveying to the students that they disapprove of them because they do not measure up to what is wanted or what is considered adequate. Buckingham said:

> There are no misfit children. There are misfit textbooks, misfit teachers, and misfit courses of study. But by the very nature of things there can be no misfit children. The child is what education is for. One might as well say that a man does not fit his trousers as to say that a child does not fit the school.[7]

Teachers and parents need to understand and accept the rate of each child's ability to learn. If there is indication that what the child is doing is at the maximum rate of growth, it must be accepted and no more expected. Much difficulty comes from pressuring children to achieve beyond their ability. This pressure to achieve comes, of course, from both parents and teachers.

The concept of flexible standards of attainment for children is a most significant one, not only to believe and give lip-service to, but definitely to be internalized.

The Teacher's Attitudes toward Failure

As pointed out elsewhere, sociologists recognize three major socioeconomic strata or classes. These have been termed *upper, middle,* and *lower.* Each of these social classes has a way of life that is distinctly its own and is different from that of the other two. Children from the lower class have a value system that works best for them in their everyday life. Immediate rewards, low level of aspiration, live today and face tomorrow when it comes, earning money today is better than getting ready to earn more tomorrow—all are values adhered to by the lower class.

In middle-class life, education is very important. The lower middle class values education for the ways in which it encourages social mobility to the next social class. This social group sees its opportunity to improve its status and to acquire more and more of the artifacts and value patterns of the upper middle class through hard work, climbing the ladder of success, and acquiring higher education.

The major drives of the middle-class teachers are achievement and early success, work for "work's sake," getting education, being responsible, and shaping one's own destiny. There is nothing wrong if teachers hold these values for themselves if they represent a means for achieving their goals in life. It is extremely important, however, for them to see these values for what they are: those by which they live their own lives, not divinely mandated values that cover the ambitions of all the students they teach.

How aware are the teachers, for example, that the students may be expected to learn a completely different set of behaviors if they try to achieve these goals? How aware

are the teachers that many children have never been taught to value these goals? How aware are the teachers that children may originate in strangely different cultures where the teachers' values are in direct conflict with the harmonious life of their social group?

More pertinent to the present discussion, however, is how aware are the teachers of what attempting to achieve these values does to the children who cannot meet them? What about the children who face constant failure and whose egos are shattered until they have little feeling of personal worth?

Teachers have been conditioned to work in a social order where failure is unacceptable, where hard work brings rewards to most people, where "pollyanna-ish" promises are often given in the hope that, with this encouragement, success will come. A very high value has been placed on being able to conform. If teachers make single assignments to entire classes, they convey the notion that they think everyone should conform to an already fixed arbitrary standard. Not to conform is to be disapproved, rejected, inadequate, unacceptable.

What Is Success?

Unless people critically appraise their own systems of values, they are apt to think that success for each of the students they teach is the same level of achievement that was success for them. Furthermore, this level of achievement that they remember as success is only as they remember it now in retrospect after perhaps a decade.

An understanding of all the individual differences found among children forces school philosophy to accept the logical fact that success, per se, is different for different people. "Success" for the so-called normal children, cannot be narrowly defined as "success" for the bright children, and an entirely new concept of "success" is necessary for the slow learners. At the same time, the need for success is acknowledged by the mental hygienist as basic to good mental health.

Combs, Avila and Purkey wrote:

> With a positive view of self one can dare, be open to experience, confront the world openly and with certainty. Negative views of self may lock a person in a vicious circle in which efforts to deal with life are always too little, too late, or inappropriate.[8]

Deutsch investigated the existence of special problems in educating black children in a large urban area. He analyzed social and behavioral factors as they related to the perception of self, frustration, tolerance, group membership, and the rate of learning. The effect of social stress on motivation, personal aspiration, and the concept of self suggested an urgent need for understanding of the value conflicts between the middle-class teacher and the lower-class child. Before the children leave the elementary school, Deutsch reported, they have learned that the larger society views them as inferior and expects an inferior performance from them. A *negative self-image* relates strongly to the fact of being black. Observers keeping diaries during the study recorded that teachers often directed derogatory remarks toward individual children.

The most frequent such remark was to call a child "stupid," and as a result, the teacher, and through the teacher, the school played a role in reinforcing the negative self-image of the child, and contributed a negative reason for learning.[9]

Deutsch emphasizes over and over the role of the social scientist in the study of these racial-class problems: the social psychologist or the cultural anthropologist should study extensively the dynamic relationships between environmental and social circumstances and personality and intellectual performance.

An Ounce of Prevention

Teachers must approach their classroom at the beginning of the school year ready to ignore the grade numbers posted on the doors. They must accept all children in terms of their abilities to perform at that time. (If the principal assigns them to your room, they *belong,* whether or not they can read anything!) Teachers must carefully assess exactly where all children are in a developmental reading program and teach them at that level. They must insist on mastery, unit by unit, before putting the children in more advanced work. Teachers must overcome any "we-must-hurry-and-cover-the-ground" attitude.

The teachers must help the children face their problems squarely, set attainable goals, and keep tangible records of their progress. Tangible evidence rests in seeing a box of new words or phrases grow, an attractive bulletin board of books read, a graph of speed and comprehension scores, or a graph of sight words learned on different testing dates. The teachers should try to:

1. Help the children build a positive attitude toward themselves and toward reading. (If needed, toward adults, too.)
2. Reward them at each step of the way in the right direction.
3. Accept and appreciate them as people. Some teachers may think of slow learners as nuisances and would prefer to be rid of them. They take a fatalistic attitude toward retardation in reading.
4. Let them talk—encourage them to express themselves.
5. Help them see that reading must be fun. It cannot be fun if the books are all too hard.

Be Consistent Throughout the Day

Many teachers feel that there is much pressure to complete a prescribed course of study for their specific grade level. They recognize that it will not be possible to do the prescribed work with disabled readers. Yet, at the same time they do not completely accept the level of work that they could do successfully throughout the school day.

Mrs. Wall teaches third grade. Sandy came as a "repeater" from another third grade, yet he was unable to read beyond the preprimer level. Mrs. Wall recognized the need to "begin over again" in the reading process and arranged for Sandy to work both with three older boys who had reading difficulty, and entirely alone for as much time as she

Making Connections 12.1 What Does "Success" Mean?

Frequently, teachers and students are failing to communicate, yet neither know it. Because the communication breakdown is not identified, further misunderstandings result. It is most important that teachers and students listen carefully to each other to hear not just the words but what the actual meanings are that are being verbalized.

To get a feeling of the different perceptions that teachers and students have about success, and particularly success in becoming readers, talk with a teacher and a student about the meaning of the word success. You may want to ask a child questions similar to these:

1. Whom do you know who is a successful reader? What makes this person successful?
2. Are you a successful student? Reader? Why?
3. Do your parents and teacher think you are a successful reader? Why do you think so?
4. How do you know a successful reader/student from an unsuccessful one?
5. How do you think teachers feel about successful readers? Unsuccessful ones?
6. How important is it to be a successful reader?

You might ask a teacher questions similar to these:

1. How do you identify successful readers in your class?
2. What behaviors characterize unsuccessful readers?
3. Do you and your students always agree on what behaviors contribute to success in reading and in the classroom?
4. Who is the most successful reader in your class this year? What criteria did you use for making your choice?
5. How important is it for the child to be successful in reading?

After you have completed your conversations make lists of critical words and phrases each group used to identify success. In what ways did the two people agree? Disagree? What could a teacher do to understand these different perceptions and to talk about them with children? Could such a discussion become a valuable learning experience for all in the classroom? How?

When you share your lists, interpretations, and ideas in class with other students, you should become more sensitive to the ways in which teachers and students often fail to understand each other.

could devote to an extra reading group for just Sandy. She planned his seatwork carefully after analyzing his errors on the Dolch Basic Sight Words and on the Inventory of Phonetic Skills for Grade 1. Because Sandy had concomitant problems that might be physical, neurological, or psychological, Mrs. Wall referred him to the school's guidance clinic. In discussing Sandy's school work with her supervisor, however, Mrs. Wall showed the supervisor regular third-grade arithmetic papers, language papers, spelling papers, and penmanship practice lessons.

The point for emphasis is that children who cannot *read* a basic sight vocabulary certainly cannot write or spell it for any useful purpose. Neither can they perform "story" problems in arithmetic. It is pointless to "go only half way" in accepting the children at their levels in a reading group and then not give them opportunity during the rest of the school day to put to work the new skills they have learned.

Emphasis on Reading

Earp raises the question as to whether reading is *overemphasized* in the schools.[10] Certainly parents and teachers are apt to cite failure to learn to read as the school's number one problem. Title I Programs, The Right to Read Program, and special federal grant programs all emphasize the emotional climate attached to reading success in school. So the children who fail to acquire the needed skills learn to see themselves as failures, see leaving school as an escape, and reflect overt behavior that their parents and teachers are prone to evaluate negatively. Whole-group objectives—to have everyone read a certain book, know a standard vocabulary, turn in the expected assignment—are diametrically opposed to the individualized learning styles of the students in school. But if the pressures were removed, and if learning opportunities were available and their values understood, with great variations in terms of time for expected mastery, students themselves might find learning to read a desirable objective *from their own point of view* and the school might find its program much more successful. The teachers who worked with Michael (see chapter 15) during his first four years in the elementary school were able to demonstrate this possibility, at least in some measure.

Reward for Not Learning

Attitudes in children that cause them to accept an antisocial or negative reward for not learning may be generated through failure. If somebody usually nags or gets excited when the child does not learn, the child may value this as a reward for keeping right on not learning. If the child's inability to do the work forces an adult to give that child a great deal of attention, the child has a reward for not learning.

Jack was such a boy. He probably gained satisfaction from coming every morning to the reading clinic where he had the undivided attention of a reading clinician for a fifty-minute period. Back in his fourth-grade room, he was one of thirty-five children expected to read textbooks of fourth-grade difficulty. His reader level in the reading clinic had progressed over a period of one and a half years from preprimer to second

---

Making Connections 12.2: How Much Should Reading Be Emphasized?

Each class member should read the article by N. Wesley Earp, "Challenge to Schools: Reading Is Overemphasized," *The Reading Teacher* 27 (March 1974), pp. 562–65.

Plan a class discussion in which members are free to agree or disagree with the points the writer of the article presents. Perhaps, after the discussion, class members could divide into groups of four or five members. Each small group should then prepare a statement describing its position on the stress schools should place on reading instruction.

---

level, second grade. While Jack was in fourth grade, however, the reading in the clinic at hard second-grade level seemed to be on a plateau. When Jack's reading did not improve over a relatively long period of time, his clinician arranged a conference with the fourth-grade teacher. The clinician asked how the clinic might best help Jack so that he could make better progress in the fourth grade during the day. The fourth-grade teacher asked if the clinician might each day have Jack read the story in his fourth-grade reader that the rest of the children read while he was gone. She said that Jack was expected to do the pages in his workbook when he got to school, but he had not read the story. Since the exercises in the workbook were geared to a reader level two years beyond Jack, and since he was attempting to do the exercises without having read the related story in the reader, it is easy to understand why Jack found coming to the clinic a welcome escape from a rather impossible situation. If he did not learn to read, he could continue to attend the clinic and thus avoid a school situation with which he was unable to cope. He had a rather tangible reward in the enjoyment of his hour of clinical reading, and if he did not learn to read well it might go on indefinitely. This is a kind of negative reward that usually greatly puzzles the teachers. When children feel that they are not accepted as they are or when they feel that adults do not accept their inability to perform or that the performance of other children more nearly fits what adults had expected, the children may subconsciously refuse to learn.

Occasionally children in the primary grades find out that their slightly younger siblings can read better than they can or at least can read with greater confidence. They go to great lengths to think of all the reasons why they should not read; they think of many other things they prefer to do instead of reading; or they merely state objectively, "I can't read." They seek for themselves a multitude of pleasurable activities, none of which involves reading.

Concerning the idea that children learn "not to read" the same as they learn "to read," Stroud has this to say:

> It is understandable . . . if the pupil who puts in a year in not learning to read, and who to boot is the object of invidious comparisons or of guilt-producing behavior at home, does not show up next year filled with enthusiasm for his reading lesson. . . . Given more failure the second year, more trips to school by the mother

who "can't see why . . ." more "helps" from mother or father, and we can see how escape from reading actually becomes rewarding. As these avoiding reactions are rewarded we have exactly the conditions required for learning *not* to read . . . the task has been made needlessly hard. What he really needs by this time is a reconstruction of his personality.[11]

Bettelheim has written concisely and lucidly about the problem of children having motivation to fail instead of to succeed in an article "The Decision to Fail."[12]

One of the serious problems in school is that of allowing children to "sit through" weeks and weeks of school attendance without developmental learning taking place. Classroom teachers need to be more accepting of, and much less defensive about, this fact. When adequately accepting and less defensive, they will ask for and demand outside help for problems that are not amenable to the limited individual instruction they can provide. Such children, for whom the school is not offering successful instruction, *might be excluded* from the school. At least in this way their problem will not be "unrecognized," and once it is made clear that the child needs special help, most communities can provide it.

Terry is a case in point. Terry was referred to the educational clinic in the spring of his eighth grade year. His parents had been notified by the principal that the school would be glad to give him an eighth-grade diploma if the parents would promise *not* to enroll him in the ninth grade in high school. With this "threat," the parents could no longer remain complacent as they had up to this time. They took the problem to their minister who made inquiries and found a reading clinic for a diagnostic examination for the boy. The fact that special arrangements were made and the boy learned in fifteen months of tutoring to read well at the sixth-grade level indicates that the school would have done a big favor both to the boy and to his parents if they had excluded him five years earlier when he enrolled in fifth grade as a nonreader. As it was, the school allowed him to sit through one year each in fifth and sixth grades and two years each in seventh and eighth grades as a nonreader, and then asked that he not come back! Many referrals to reading clinics come from ministers, school nurses, and social workers instead of from classroom teachers themselves who should be calling for help with difficult problems.

Cultivating Positive Affective Responses

If teachers learn to put *feelings* first, they will try to be open, warm, nonthreatening, and nonpunitive partners in the learning process. They will perform in the role of facilitators of learning; not as authoritarians exacting work from others. Clarification of one's values in relation to the values of others becomes a primary problem in such a facilitating relationship. While the teachers may value punctuality, excellent grades, future rewards for hard work, and the nonwasting of time, the students in their classes may never have had these same values emphasized in their experiences of living. At least those values, or some of them, may not have been emphasized for the students by those for whom they care most.

In relation to this objective acceptance of all people in the teachers' classrooms as fully functioning, worthwhile individuals, there are some commonsense guidance principles that the classroom teachers should bear in mind and probably reread frequently until they feel that they practice them most of the time.

Basic Counseling Principles for Classroom Teachers

1. Confident teachers do not need to seem authoritative to children. Try to cultivate a more "we're equals" kind of atmosphere. Naturally if teachers are mature adults, the children are not going to take advantage of their kindnesses. If they do, then the teachers must help them achieve more mature behavior in an atmosphere of mutual respect.
2. Learn to listen. Learn when to allow periods of silence. Learn how to accept long pauses while children are thinking through something they can explain to you if you give them time. Some specifics might be:
   (a) Be sure you do not talk more than your half of the time;
   (b) Do *not* interrupt students even if you think they are off the subject.
   (c) Pause long enough before answering to see if the students will add anything else.
3. Watch for and try to interpret nonverbal clues. Are the students especially fidgety today? Are they acting inattentive most of the time? Could they be really worried about something else they face that day? Are they talking faster or in voices that are higher-pitched than usual—or are they unusually quiet today?
4. When they make a statement, whether you agree or not, learn to make neutral statements that reflect their feelings so that they can think through their thoughts and respond further. For example: "How did you feel when he said that?" "Is this really *your* idea?" "How do you feel when this happens?" "Do you care very much what he does?" "Were you really glad about that or didn't it make much difference?" Empathic expressions like these may help the students clarify and interpret their thinking.
5. Do not show rejection or negative feelings. Be patient, nonthreatening, and use *no* sarcasm.
6. Do not make false promises. What happens to students will result much more from their behavior than from yours.
7. Questions that can be answered "yes" or "no" may get little language out of the students. *What, how, why, which,* and words like these to start the question may get you much more information.
8. Make no moralistic admonishments. Things are *good* or *bad* in relative ways. The teachers must constantly be trying to think through "Why do they do this?" "Why have they failed?" "What did I do that turned them off that time?"

Axline outlined eight basic principles used by a psychotherapist and expressed the belief that teachers could become much more therapeutic in their relationships with children than they have been in the past. Worked at sincerely, consistently, and honestly, these principles have much to offer the teacher-student relationship:

1. The therapist must develop a warm, friendly relationship with the children.
2. The therapist accepts the child exactly as he or she is.
3. The therapist establishes an environment in which the child is free to express his or her feelings completely.
4. The therapist recognizes the child's feelings and *reflects* them back in such a way that the child gains insight into his or her behavior.
5. The therapist has a deep respect for the child's ability to solve his or her own problems if given the opportunity to do so.
6. The therapist remains largely nondirective—the child leading the way in discussing or acting out his or her difficulties.
7. The therapy is a gradual process and cannot be hurried.
8. The therapist establishes only those limitations that are necessary to anchor the therapy to the world of reality and to make the child aware of his or her responsibility in the relationship.[13]

Axline explains:

When a teacher respects the dignity of a child, whether the child is six or sixteen, and treats the child with understanding, kindliness, and constructive help, the teacher is developing in the student an ability to look within the self for the answers to his or her problems, and to become responsible as an independent individual in his or her own right.

It is the relationship that exists between the teacher and students that is the important thing. The teacher's responses must meet the real needs of the children and not just the material needs—reading, writing, and arithmetic.[14]

Bibliotherapy, using books to help persons cope with their problems, may be useful for some teachers in improving their affective responses to children. Rubin suggests using bibliotherapy in "preventive and ameliorative" ways.[15] She describes ways to link bibliotherapy with role playing, problem solving, drawing, and discussion.

Summary

Acceptance of the students has been described in this chapter as the genuine willingness of the teachers to analyze the levels at which the students can work and to *permit* them to grow from that level.

Empathy for children requires understanding of their frustrations about their failures, and an empathic response to the children includes alleviating anxiety and sequential development of missing skills.

Smith and Preston reported negative attitudes of teachers toward children who are unsuccessful in reading. Teachers need to re-evaluate their own attitudes toward success and failure—what is approved and what is disapproved—and to evaluate objectively the status of the underachievers.

Finally, it was pointed out that children can learn "not to learn" if their school situation offers more rewards for not progressing than for continuing to grow up. This is one of the areas where it is most necessary for teachers to be sensitive to the thinking, feeling, and behavior of children.

For Further Reading

Axline, Virginia Mae. *Play Therapy*. Boston: Houghton Mifflin, 1947, 1969.

Beane, James A. "Self-concept and Self-esteem as Curriculum Issues." *Educational Leadership* 39 (April 1982), pp. 504–6.

Combs, Arthur W.; Avila, Donald L.; and Purkey, William W. *Helping Relationships,* 2d ed. Boston: Allyn and Bacon, 1978.

Fredericks, Anthony D. "Developing Positive Reading Attitudes." *The Reading Teacher* 36 (October 1982), pp. 38–40.

Heathington, Betty S., and Alexander, J. Estill. "Do Classroom Teachers Emphasize Attitudes Toward Reading?" *The Reading Teacher* 37 (February 1984), pp. 484–88.

McDermott, R. P. "Achieving School Failure: An Anthropological Approach to Illiteracy and Social Stratification." In Harry Singer and Robert Ruddell, editors, *Theoretical Models and Processes of Reading,* 3d. Newark, Del.: International Reading Association, 1985, pp. 558–594.

Quandt, Ivan, and Selznick, Richard. *Self-Concept and Reading,* 2d ed. Newark, Del.: International Reading Association, 1984.

Simon, Sidney; Howe, L.; and Kirschenbaum, H. *Values Clarification: A Handbook of Practical Suggestions for Teachers and Students*. New York: Hart Publishing Co., 1972.

Notes

1. Nila B. Smith, "Teachers' Responsibility to Retarded Readers," *Education* 77 (May 1957), p. 548.
2. Ibid., citing Mary I. Preston, "Reading Failure and the Child's Security," *American Journal of Orthopsychiatry* 10 (April 1940), pp. 239–52.
3. Donald Rasmussen and Lynn Goldberg, *Basic Reading Series* (Chicago: Science Research Associates, 1965).
4. Alice R. Eldredge, "An Investigation to Determine the Relationships Among Self-Concept, Locus of Control, and Reading Achievement," *Reading World* 21 (October 1981), pp. 59–64.
5. Arthur B. Moehlman, *School Administration* (Chicago: Houghton Mifflin Co., 1940), p. 127.
6. Margaret C. Wang, "Adaptive Instruction: Building on Diversity," *Theory Into Practice* 19 (Spring 1980), p. 123.
7. B. R. Buckingham, *Research for Teachers* (Chicago: Silver Burdett and Co., 1926), p. 299.
8. Arthur Combs, Donald L. Avila, and William W. Purkey, *Helping Relationships,* 2d ed. (Boston: Allyn and Bacon, 1978), p. 85.

9. Martin Deutsch, *Minority Group and Class Status as Related to Social and Personality Factors in Scholastic Achievement,* Monograph No. 2 (Ithaca, N.Y.: The Society for Applied Anthropology, Cornell University, 1960).

10. N. Wesley Earp, "Challenge to Schools: Reading Is Overemphasized," *The Reading Teacher* 27 (March 1974), pp. 562–65.

11. James B. Stroud, *Psychology in Education,* (New York: Longmans, Green and Co., 1956), p. 127.

12. Bruno Bettelheim, "The Decision to Fail," in Nicholas Long, William C. Morse, and Ruth Newman, eds., *Conflict in the Classroom: The Education of Emotionally Disturbed Children* (Belmont, Calif.: Wadsworth Publishing Co., 1965), pp. 435–46.

13. Virginia Mae Axline, *Play Therapy* (Boston: Houghton Mifflin, 1947, 1969), pp. 75–76.

14. Ibid., pp. 156–57.

15. Dorothy Rubin, *Diagnosis and Correction in Reading Instruction,* (New York: Holt, Rinehart and Winston, 1982), p. 335.

13
Working Cooperatively with Parents

Vocabulary

mainstreaming
socioeconomic status
values
reading environment
parent conference
parent interview
Parent Advisory Council
home visit
advocacy

Questions

1. How would you describe the responsibility shared by parents and teachers for the education of children?

2. What are some valid reasons why parents should not *teach* their children to read?

3. What are important contributions parents should make in helping their children learn how to read?

4. Why should teachers be aware of the feelings that can become a factor in parent-teacher interactions?

5. Make a list of guidelines for successful parent conferences and interviews.

6. What roles might parents play in the classroom?

7. What does a parent do in the role of advocate?

Parents and Teachers Share a Responsibility

A great deal of the variation in student achievement scores is caused by family-related factors. Clearly, then, focusing only on the child at school overlooks a dynamic family interaction that supports or fails to support the school program. The development of children is dependent upon a process of parent-teacher sharing and interacting. When one stops to realize that a teacher can influence children for only one year while parents may have considerable influence for nearly twenty, one sees why parents must be made teaching partners.[1]

The need for school personnel to emphasize the relationship of parent and teacher as one of *equals* working together on mutual concerns is well-stated by Kelly:

> No matter what level of expertise I possess, you know your own child, his needs and feelings, his reactions to success and failure, his good and bad points, better than I ever will. In our own separate ways we are responsible for his social, emotional, and educational growth, interested in his welfare and his progress toward maturity. Let us, therefore, as equal partners in the instructional process, find ways that we can work together to help this child in both school and home contexts, to learn and enjoy learning to the best of his abilities.[2]

Mainstreaming, as a new thrust in education, demands the close cooperation of parents and the school in program planning for all children. The definition of mainstreaming by Houck and Sherman is pertinent here:

> Mainstreaming is the integration of eligible handicapped children and normal peers based upon individually determined educational needs which necessitates the shared responsibility for planning and programming by regular and special education administrative and instructional personnel. Key words are *eligible* and *shared responsibility*. The rationale for mainstreaming is praiseworthy. Handicapped children should not be isolated if they *need not* be. Integration provides better opportunity for acceptance and understanding. Mainstreaming deemphasizes the labeling of individuals. Legal mandates for equal protection support some mainstreaming. Perhaps mainstreaming will help insure that each child does have a well-worked out individualized plan for his education.[3]

When children have learning difficulties in school, the teacher must bear in mind that the parents play the most crucial role in the total life experience of their children. Reading success is dependent upon all the other facets of the children's lives: motivation, level of aspiration, values rooted in socioeconomic background, and the expressed attitudes children hear at home about the value of education.

For students from the lowest socioeconomic level or most culturally deprived homes, teachers are their greatest hope for achieving mature reading interests and habits as a basis for adding to their values and improving their economic status.

Specifically, for example, over half of the children come to the public schools from homes and neighborhoods of lower socioeconomic status, while teachers have universally internalized middle-class socioeconomic values. Some of the conflicts in these sets of values can be stated in this way:

Lower-class environment values	*Middle-class values*
Living in the present	Living for the future
Immediate rewards	Anticipating future rewards
Quit school and get work	Graduate and get a better job
Work today; get paid today; enjoy the reward now	Save for a rainy day
No expectation of rising in the class system	Upward mobility to climb the ladder of success

While teachers are certainly as tolerant as any group, they must recognize social stratification as it operates in American society.

Since mobility in the social classes requires drive and directed purpose as well as willingness to forego immediate pleasures for greater future gain, lower-lower-class members have values in conflict with striving, and few will be motivated to try. Many upper-lower-class members were not successful in such an attempt when they aspired to social mobility.

Middle-class parents may exert too much pressure for success. It is, perhaps, safe to generalize that parents from the middle class, socioeconomically speaking, *expect* success of all their children because they themselves were successful in school.[4]

The children who have parents who graduated from college will likely be expected to attend college. However, reading problems in school may set in motion a whole chain reaction of emotional responses rooted in child-parent conflicts, sibling jealousies, or sibling comparisons. Without remediation or counseling to restructure personalities, the conflicts may never be resolved.

Sally came for some remedial reading instruction the year she was in the sixth grade. She profited greatly from study of phonic analysis, structural analysis, word study, prefixes, roots, and suffixes, and speed of comprehension exercises. Recently, when her name appeared on the senior high school honor roll list, the clinician remarked to a teacher friend, "I'm delighted to see her name on the honor roll. I taught her remedial reading in sixth grade." The teacher, uninitiated in the nature of remedial reading, said, "Oh, no. You couldn't have. She has always been a very bright little girl." The clinician remembered the mother's anxiety six years before when she felt the child's reading difficulty might preclude effective use of her good intelligence.

Charlene came for some reading tests because her parents recognized her inability to read and the fact that her little sisters were reading better than she was. Charlene was in the sixth grade and told the reading tutor that she was reading the regular sixth-grade reader at school. After making an informal analysis, the tutor selected an easy second reader that Charlene could read adequately.

When her tutor established her capacity for reading achievement at or above her grade level, her tutor assured her that she was an intelligent girl. Charlene said, "You mean I'm not dumb?" Later she explained, "Wait till I can read! I'll show Mary. She said I was in the dumb group and that I was the dumbest one in it!" With help to achieve reading success, Charlene also may meet her parents' aspiration that she attend college successfully.

Working with parents necessitates an understanding of the way parents feel, how they think about schools and teachers, how completely they can be convinced that their children can profit by the school's program, and whether they feel that too much success in school will eventually mean less and less acceptance of the way of life at home by the children.

Parent-teacher conferences in an environment in which an unhurried, constructive exchange of views can take place, are necessary if the children's academic, social, and emotional growth is to be discussed and evaluated fairly. Parents may wonder about the extent to which they need to try to teach their children; they surely want to know in what ways they can contribute constructively to their children's greater success; they may sense rejection of their children by the teachers; and the parents may have rejected teachers because of their past experience. This chapter will discuss these problems and give suggestions for structuring parent interviews.

Ways Parents Help Their Children with Reading

Should Parents Try to Teach Reading?

Many parents wonder if they should teach their child to read. Sometimes they feel that they must supplement the teacher's work by helping their child do exercises at night. But *most teachers are agreed that, in general, parents should not try to teach their children to read.* Dolch explains that parents are also concerned with their children's development in areas other than reading and that "the learning of reading can hardly be the chief interest of parents if they think of all these activities."[5]

The teacher-pupil relationship is not as emotionally charged as the parent-child relationship. Wollner points out that it is much better for the child's morale if correcting is done by one who is not as emotionally involved as the parent. The children are able to progress best in an "atmosphere of friendly impersonality."[6] Wollner also points out that:

> Parents, when they try to be teachers, tend to focus their main attention on the outcome and to view the errors as stumbling blocks. Reading clinics focus their main attention on the learner and his individual way of learning; they view the errors as sign posts to help them to design correct instruction.[7]

It is only as the teachers become fully aware of the role parents play in their children's education that they are able to teach most effectively. This point deserves special emphasis, because it seems that too often teachers ignore parents, keep them away from the schools, or do not make an effort to cooperate or work with them. Of course this minimizes any parent-school relationship, and it is harmful to the children since the teacher-parent relationship is reflected in the child-parent relationship.

Keeping in mind the influence parents have on their children, one becomes aware of the myriad problems that can arise when the child does *not* make progress in learning to read. A very normal reaction of parents is "if the school won't do it, we will." That the teaching is more complicated and requires more skill than this has often been stated, and the only way this problem can be handled is by continuing contact between teachers and parents. This communication must involve more than progress reports on the children. It must also be an education program for the adults. This will require both time and effort on the part of classroom teachers.

Ways Parents Should Help

Be Sure Children Are in an Optimum State of Physical Health

Parents can cooperate with the school psychologist and the family doctor to make sure that the child is in an optimum state of physical health with respect to hearing, vision, and other physical or psychological factors. Parents can make sure that the child's physical needs are adequately taken care of. It may mean adequate rest for a child. It may mean prohibiting the watching of television until midnight. It is not hard to understand why a child's behavior at school is not conducive to learning if he or she has had insufficient sleep and rest. It may also mean planning a diet that provides adequate nutrition and stresses healthful foods.

Parents are usually anxious to cooperate with the school in obtaining hearing and vision screening examinations for their children. Teachers need to be aware of community social agencies that are available to provide these services for children from families in low socioeconomic groups. The teachers must feel responsible for discovering many of these problems and referring them to the principal, the school nurse, the school psychologist, or the school social worker.

Children Need to Feel Secure and Confident

Mental health, a basic need, is so important that it should be discussed separately. Of it, Potter says:

> Finally, all parents need to understand more fully the emotional dynamics of the child, the personality needs which require recognition and fulfillment if he is to be happy and successful. The father and the mother must see the relationship between mental health and reading achievement, and must realize that what happens in the family environment is likely to be the paramount factor in their child's emotional adjustment. Given the child who, in his home, knows affection, security, confidence, and cheerfulness, the school has a long start in the development of a successful reader.[8]

Wollner explains this by saying:

> Sensitive parents are torn between their desire to help children and their impatience to see them progress. We feel that whenever a parent attempts to teach in

a subject in which the child has chronic difficulty, there is great danger that the child will absorb the impatience of the parent, become impatient with himself, and lose all courage to proceed.[9]

Just as sometimes it is difficult for teachers to hide their anxiety, so parents who are even more emotionally involved with their own children would have an extremely hard time hiding their anxiety.

One of the principles that teachers and parents must be aware of is that just as children grow physically at their own paces, so they develop their reading skills at their own paces. This means that all children will not be ready to start reading at the same time, nor will they progress at the same speed. That this is a difficult concept for parents to grasp is not surprising, since teachers sometimes ignore it in their teaching. Parents need to realize that children's emotional and physical health affect their growth in reading.

Children Who Live in a Reading Environment Learn More Easily

Parents can surround children with books. Children should be surrounded with books at home as well as at school. School boards should spend a great deal of money on books for children. There is an economic factor for parents; they must learn how to purchase as many good books as their budget will allow, and then rely upon libraries to supply the rest. Parents can read to children. Children need to be read to even after they begin to read for themselves. Reading is a way of sharing experiences, and the things read can be talked about. This further enhances language skill. Reading to children gives adults mutual experiences with children, and this is desirable.

Parents need to be aware that they are powerful models for their children. They should not only encourage their children to read and to read with them. They should also be readers in their own right, letting their children see them reading and enjoying a variety of printed materials.

Parents can also point out other aspects of the environment where print is important. Letters that are sent and received, lists that are made and followed, directions that appear on cans and boxes of food products, and notes left for family members are all forms of print that can be significant in the lives of children. Print in the environment is now recognized as a significant factor in learning to read. Parents need to be apprised of its value.

Parents Need to Understand the Methods of Teaching That the Teacher Uses

It would help parents if they were aware of some of the different methods that are used in teaching reading today. Probably this knowledge would enable them to be more enthusiastic and less critical about the teaching of reading. They need to understand the "whole thought" method and the word-recognition techniques. Phonics is taught today, but it is taught differently. Oral reading is not synonymous with general reading skill, and it certainly should not be considered as the result. Today many different comprehension skills are taught to increase reading skill. Certainly drill in itself is not a way to increase reading skill.[10] The necessity for parents to obtain the correct information about the teaching and development of reading cannot be overemphasized.

Children Can Be Encouraged to Read Aloud to Parents

Finally, parents can encourage the child to read aloud to them. Teachers should ask children to take books home to read aloud to their parents. This should be done when the teachers are sure that the child will be able to read well; thus, reading to the parents will be rewarding. As a rule, it should be done in such a way that parents will listen to the child read, so that they will praise good reading, and so that they will not expect the child to sound out words. They will not expect to supplement the teaching of phonics, but will supply any words with which the child needs help. Their primary motive will be to enjoy the story with the child.

Developing Constructive Attitudes

Exerting undue pressure on the child who is having difficulty in reading is perhaps the cardinal mistake that parents make. Scolding him and telling him that he *must* learn to read may cause him to become so tense and worried that he will be unable to make use of learning in reading to which he has been exposed, and such a condition may even be so severe that it prevents new learning from taking place.[11]

Making Connections 13.1: Interviewing Teachers about Working with Parents

One way to help yourself feel confident about working with parents is to have as much information about successful parent-teacher interaction strategies as possible.

Arrange to interview at least two teachers about how they work with parents. Pay particular attention to the strengths they see in such cooperation, the varied strategies they use, and the problems that they have experienced. Make notes of the points that are made or gain permission and tape record the meetings.

Bring your information back to your class for a general discussion of strategies for working *with* parents. You should have a good list of practical suggestions at the end of the discussion.

Feelings Experienced by Parents, Children, and Teachers

Wollner states that "release from home pressures in the very same area that surrounds the subject of reading is one factor essential to the progress of each pupil."[12] She also points out one of the reasons why the release is so important, "Release from pressure is a protective measure; that is, it is intended to protect and preserve the essential qualities of the parent-child relationship."[13]

Removal of pressures is also emphasized by Bliesmer:

> If a child is having trouble a lot of his day is spent in frustration . . . he needs to be able to get away from this.
>
> If he's forced to spend hour after hour, at homework, the home is no longer the place of security which it should be for the child; and he has no opportunity to escape.[14]

Parents simply must realize what the frustrated children experience day after day at school and become cognizant that they must not put them through the same thing at home.

Lieben reported that in a graduate class of seventeen experienced teachers and five psychologists, all "clearly reflected hostile, negative attitudes toward the parents of the poor achievers."[15] She went on to say that "there was little recognition of the feelings that parents might be experiencing when children consistently perform below normal."[16] Lieben also reported that teachers often put too much stock in the adage "Find the disturbed child, and you find the disturbed parent." " 'Overanxious,' 'over-ambitious,' and 'rejection' are terms too loosely used to describe parents of children who are failing to progress academically in expected ways."[17] The relationships between parents, their children, and their children's school progress are far too complicated to make such generalizations.

When teachers have feelings about parents similar to those just discussed, the situation becomes worse, because whatever the teacher says to parents will be reflected in the child-parent relationship. Lieben says that the following happens:

> The mother knows something is wrong, but she has only vague generalizations about the causes and is told there's little which she can do. She then either gives up on the child or gets mad at him for not trying harder.[18]

Teachers must realize that most parents do the best they can for their children, and the mistakes which they make are not intentional.

> . . . the mother of a child delayed in reading does the very best she can within the limits of her understanding, capacities and the exigencies of the everyday living. Few parents fail their children willingly, and most parents suffer pangs of guilt over their real or imagined failures.[19]

Redl and Wattenberg describe the special roles in which teachers and parents cast each other that may prevent them from achieving cooperation and understanding.[20] For example, one such role is that in which the teachers feel that the parents should be called to school and told what to do. Another example of casting parents in special roles is where mothers' clubs are thought of and tolerated as necessary evils. In another the teachers think of the parents as powerful and punishing adults; probably this is the way they see their own parents. In this case, the teachers will be shy and timid and lack confidence, and they may feel persuaded to say what they think the parents would like to hear.

A fourth such special role is that in which parents are of a low or very different economic status or of a much different background of experience.[21] This often brings classroom teachers to such confusion in their own thinking that they wonder how to "handle" parents, how to "conquer and outwit the enemy." As long as the teacher must think in terms of *handling* parents, it is hardly possible to work with them confidently in solving mutual problems.

Parents also often cast teachers in specific roles. For example, parents think of Johnnie's teacher as the same old ogre who taught them a generation ago. A specific role is one in which parents resent and resist the authority of the school, and see in the teacher the symbol of school authority. These parents are apt to be defensive just because they come to the school.

Parents may be in awe of the school, accepting its decisions and mandates without question. Wolf wrote of such parents:[22]

> They would not have dreamed of questioning a decision made by their child's teacher. Public education was sacrosanct. They were so grateful for the opportunities their child had for formal education. They would not think of questioning any decision made by school people.

A specific role is one in which parents fear they will not measure up to the teachers' standards. They have an unrealistic set of arbitrary standards for themselves and their children. Fear of failure thus is a threat to their security.

Bringing Parents to the School

> Many parents have had a history of dehumanizing and disillusioning experiences with the school. Their feelings of alienation and powerlessness are reinforced by society, which blames the home and parents for the difficulties children experience.[23]

Ferreiro and Teberosky made it clear that normally there is no evil intent on the part of teachers. They wrote: "We are not referring to the conscious intentions of teachers as particular individuals but to the social role of the educational system."[24]

The school is fortunate if it has sufficient space for a room that can be set aside as an open room for parents to come at any time. If there is a coffee pot, some reading material, displays of children's work on the bulletin boards, and information about coming events, many parents who would like to talk about the education of their child are apt to find their way to such a room. Then, if teachers use their coffee-break time or arrange other special conference time, they may be able to listen to parents and learn a great deal about what they are thinking.

Suggestions for Parent-Teacher Cooperation

After teachers have begun to view parents as partners in the education of children, they must identify a variety of ways to make that partnership effective. Five suggestions to implement this cooperation are: (1) suggestions for the parent-teacher conference, (2) suggestions for working with parents in the interview situation, (3) using written materials with parents, (4) home visits, and (5) parents as resources in the classroom. Each of these suggestions will be discussed below.

Suggestions for Parent-Teacher Conferences

Keeping parents informed is essential to building positive, cooperative attitudes. Hastily written notes for children to carry home, phone calls at times convenient for the parent, and brief home visits are ways of keeping two-way lines of communication open. Some teachers find that weekly or monthly newsletters telling about class experiences, explaining teaching methods, and suggesting at-home learning activities are good communication tools.

The best practice in reporting children's progress to their parents must come through two-way communication. This is to say that there must be some time and some way that the teacher can discuss in a face-to-face situation with the parents the progress in academic work and social development the children are making, and the parents can say in that same face-to-face situation what they are thinking. Then, in this same conversational atmosphere, teachers and parents can work out any semantic differences and, while they may not agree, at least they have a greater degree of understanding of each other's opinions. Such a conversation can give them a great deal of mutual support in accomplishing their respective goals with the children. The semantic differences that may stem from the teachers' overuse of professional jargon that does not seem meaningful to the parents can be overcome if parents are sufficiently at ease to raise questions.[25]

One of the best ways to begin helping children who are having difficulty in reading is to have a parent-teacher conference. Here, if the parents seem uncooperative and resistant, the teacher must not take the behavior at face value, but determine *why* the parents are acting as they are. If the teacher can be honest and concerned about the problem, there should not be difficulty in working with the parents. The teacher should look upon the parents as people who can help in finding the answers to and correction of the child's reading difficulties. It is all right for the teacher not to have all the answers to the problem, but together the teacher and the parents should be able to work out possible solutions.

Suggestions for Working with Parents in the Interview Situation

Teachers may find that the interview is an effective technique for obtaining useful data for working with remedial readers. It will probably be necessary to be selective in choosing which parents to interview, since the process requires a significant amount of time to plan the interview, conduct it, and evaluate the information obtained.[26]

1. Meet the parents (both together, if at all possible) early in the school year to talk about their child.
2. Give the parents an opportunity to talk first. Inquire about their ideas concerning the cause of the child's difficulty.
3. Evaluate parents' comments during the interview and begin tactfully to:
   a. Restore their confidence in the child (if loss of confidence is indicated).
   b. Alleviate any indicated guilt feelings or concerns about mental deficiency.
   c. Reassure parents if they depreciate the current methods of teaching reading.
   d. Explain the harmful effects of comparing siblings, nagging, blaming, scolding, and applying other pressures, if any of these is indicated.
4. Give an honest, sincere appraisal of the remedial situation as you have found it up to the time of the interview.
5. Share with the parents all objective information you have.
   a. Samples of the child's school work.
   b. Standard test scores in achievement tests.
   c. Information of a meaningful nature concerning intelligence and achievement tests. Classification of test scores as high, above average, average, below average, dull normal, retarded are more accurate than exact I.Q. scores. Percentile ranks can be interpreted to parents in a very meaningful manner to give them an understanding of the child's rank in a group. The I.Q. score of 110, for example, can be understood if it is interpreted as a percentile of 73 if the parents understand that their child has done better on that specific test at that specific time than 73 out of 100 children of the same age in the general population who have taken the test. Teachers can clarify scores with parents.
   d. Anecdotal records that describe child behavior in specific situations.
6. Suggest, if it appears necessary, the parents' responsibilities to their children include:
   a. Providing for the child's psychological needs: love, security, belonging, recognition, response from others, and new experience.
   b. Providing for the child's physical needs: assurance of adequate sleep and rest, diet and exercise, vision, hearing, and coordination. If there are handicaps that cannot be corrected, the best possible adjustment to the limitation should be made.
   c. Developing individual responsibility, a healthy attitude toward growing up and achieving independence; and developing habit patterns commensurate with achieving these goals.
7. Emphasize that learning to read is a developmental process that requires a long time and much practice. *Never* promise that a remedial problem can be eliminated within a specified amount of time. Reading teachers do not work miracles. Growth in reading is usually not phenomenal. It is gradual and should be expected to show only step-by-step improvement through the school year. The teacher hopes this

improvement will be consistent, but can never be sure that there will not be long periods of plateaus showing little growth. The teacher must help the parents to understand that the children will *never* move to higher levels of reading until they register success at each level of difficulty preceding the next higher level.

Kroth has written very succinctly the nature of positive teacher-parent interaction:

1. The teacher obtains as much information from parents as is necessary to plan educational programs for the children;
2. The teacher provides the parents with the information they need to work cooperatively with the teacher toward common goals for the children; and
3. Cooperative planning between teachers and parents may prevent, alleviate, or solve many problems that arise during the school year.

Teachers and parents who recognize their roles as complementary and not supplementary, who approach their interactions enthusiastically and not apprehensively, and who view their relationship as a partnership will usually be rewarded with happy, achieving children and warm personal feelings of mutual respect.[27]

The greatest difficulty is in getting that first, positive contact between teachers and parents to take place. Since the school is the institution offering service to the parents, one might surmise that it is the responsibility of the teachers to initiate this contact. Many teachers either lack the confidence or are reluctant to give the time to take the first step.

Using Written Materials With Parents

When PL 94–142 and other similar legislation were enacted, it was specified that parents be involved in the education of their children. The Parent Advisory Council (PAC) that is part of Chapter I reading programs is an example of required parent involvement. Frequently, the parent must read and comprehend information about the diagnosis and placement of a child. Roit and Pfohl reported that much of this written material is difficult to read and is far above the reading capabilities of many parents.[28] It is important that teachers read over these materials *with* parents, clarifying terms and explaining what is happening to their children. Teachers must be astute in determining how much help parents may need. Too much help may be interpreted as patronizing; too little leaves parents confused, suspicious, and helpless.

Meetings with Parents

Plans for parents' involvement at school necessitate understanding of values in the home, cultural expectations, community mores, and special problems of working mothers with very young children.

When parents say to the teachers, "I think Bill is behind in his reading. Is there anything I can do at home to help him?" they would probably like to have some specific, helpful suggestions. Harrington feels that this question is important enough to warrant her teaching an evening course for parents, "Helping Children with Reading

---

Making Connections 13.2: Getting Ready for Parent Conferences

One of the important jobs of the teacher is conducting parent conferences. An effective parent conference does not "just happen." It requires careful planning and conscientious follow-up. In fact, there are at least three phases in a conference cycle. First, the teacher must gather together examples of the child's work and other materials or records to be shared with the parents. Careful notes need to be made concerning information to be discussed. A tentative agenda needs to be prepared. The second phase is the conference itself. The teacher is responsible for seeing that important topics are discussed, that the child's strengths along with areas for growth are identified, and that notes are made of the interaction. Finally, the teacher must follow up on suggestions or other agreements that were made at the conference.

One way to prepare to conduct a parent conference is to role play this teacher responsibility with a peer. Find another member of your class to team with you. Prepare a paragraph describing the child you will be discussing. Then after deciding who will be the "parent" and who the "teacher," role play the meeting. Ask your audience to critique your practice conference. You may want to carry out the task more than once, making use of the feedback from class members each time. You might also vary the routine by having both "parents" attend the conference with the "teacher."

---

in the Home." Such a course usually meets for two hours once a week, over a six-week period. She has also prepared a guide for parents *How to Help Your Child with Reading at Home.*[29]

Criscuolo also describes such a reading course for parents taught by two reading teachers in the New Haven public schools. Their course met twice a week for ten weeks in high school buildings.[30]

Hunter believes that it may be helpful for school faculties to use staff meeting time occasionally to role play parent conferences. Teachers might learn better to listen to the words and feelings of parents with an atypical problem. They might become more adept at reflecting feelings and probing for better explanations from parents: "Let me see if I understand you now, . . ." "Help me to understand what you meant when you said . . ." or any other forms of neutral responses.[31]

Suedmeyer reported the results of a remedial program for thirty-two fourth graders when the parents of the children were involved in programs to gain awareness and understanding of their children's problems. The parents were assigned to one of four subgroups: One group attended a weekly seminar for six weeks and was given supplemental instruction to enable group members to participate in the tutoring sessions; a second group was given the instruction for participating in tutoring but did not attend weekly seminars; a third group observed the tutoring of their children and participated in ways possible without instruction; and the fourth group did not participate and served as a control. Post-testing did not highlight any significant differences among the four groups. Suedmeyer suggests, however, that the understanding and the ability to verbalize their children's problems achieved by the first two groups would indicate that further investigation over a longer time period might be worthwhile. The overt indications of personal interest on the part of the parents and their suggesting to other parents that they inquire about the service also suggests that further evaluation of the procedure is warranted.[32]

Home Visits

Teachers need to approach home visits with an optimistic attitude. Such visits should be flexibly planned so that the time may be as short as is comfortable or extended if parents have interest or questions. Bringing samples of children's work is an excellent means of opening conversation. A major purpose of home visits is to get information *from* parents. Be sure they have ample opportunity to talk. Be a good listener.

David Woodward

When a teacher makes a home visit, insights into the life of the child are sure to be obtained. The child profits from being able to explain her work to both her parents and the teacher.

Parents as Resources in the Classroom

Some parents find satisfaction in working in the classroom as support to the teacher. They can be helpful in listening to children read and supplying words that are not known. Some parents may be able to make notes about the reading of individuals for the teacher's use. Other parents may prefer to work with small groups in various kinds of assignments and activities, from completing worksheets to bookmaking. Still others may enjoy making games and other instructional materials and learning how they will be used in the classroom. Parents who can type may take dictation as children write books.

If parents are to work with children who have learning difficulties, they must recognize the frustration-tolerance levels of their children and accept and respect them. *Some* parents are able to enjoy:

1. Listening to their children read. Tell them the words they may not be able to pronounce as they read;
2. Talking about a story read. (What was interesting, unusual, or different; if you liked it, why?)
3. Reading together, taking turns page by page.
4. Playing word games, for example, *Concentration,* with a pack of sight word cards.
5. Reading directions in a do-it-yourself kit and assembling something for the learners.

Fortunate are the teachers who learn early in the school year about any "special skills" some of the parents have. Anyone who makes really good *tortillas* will usually be flattered to be asked to come to school and show the children how *tortillas* are made, and then will enjoy watching the children enjoy eating them. Someone who knows how to do folkdances from other countries may be happy to demonstrate, and perhaps teach them to the children. Even a young father whose memories of his primary school years are not pleasant may be glad to come to school to repair the cage that holds small animals when they are brought in.

Some parents will have traveled, bringing back interesting objects and materials that could make far away places more real to schoolbound children. Some will have hobbies ranging from rock collecting to knitting and candle making. Such activities will prove to be learning opportunities for children. Other parents may be fine story readers or tellers who can hold children spellbound. It may be possible for some parents to take small groups of children to their homes to cook, build birdhouses, or practice fly casting. Whatever talents parents and other community members may have, teachers should be aware of these and plan ways to use them in the instructional program.

The Advocacy Role

Advocacy means that parents will have strong support and encouragement in asking for optimum education for their children. The conceptual bases for parent advocacy lie in (1) the legal aspect as provided in PL 94–142 and supporting court cases; (2) the

TABLE 13.1 Professional Responses to Disagreements with Parents

Advocate Behavior	*Nonadvocate Behavior*
1. Stays with parents and encourages them not to give up. Keeps trying to communicate.	1. Basically tells parents that they are on their own.
2. Does not take criticisms or rejections of recommendations as personal affronts.	2. Turns red, loses composure, talks loudly and in an angry tone.
3. Continues to suggest and explore alternatives with parents.	3. Gets defensive and slows down the communication process. Gets fidgety and shows impatience.
4. Continues to clarify committee recommendations and provides as much information as possible.	4. Quotes regulations or school policies in attempts to intimidate parents and solve the problem to the satisfaction of self.
5. Stays cool and calm while working on the problem.	

James A. McLoughlin, Robert McLoughlin, and William Stewart, "Advocacy for Parents of the Handicapped: A Professional Responsibility and Challenge," *Learning Disability Quarterly,* 2: 55 (Summer 1979).

logical theoretical concept that parents have always been team members at any level or in any phase of their child's program; (3) the research aspect, which shows that parental activity in such areas as motor skills, language development, academic progress, and social skills yield favorable results; and (4) the moral and ethical responsibility to support parents' rights for optimal educational facility for all children. This advocacy approach is a continuing interaction between parents and teachers as partners in assuring appropriate services for handicapped students.[33] Wolf wrote that advocacy groups should be in contact with one another, as well as with school boards, legislators, and school personnel.[34]

McLoughlin, McLoughlin, and Stewart have summarized the positive and negative behaviors concerning advocacy in the interaction of professionals and parents. They further detail some of the professional responses to disagreements with parents. Examples of these responses are in table 13.1. Parents must be communicated with frequently, actively involved in the educational process of their children, and continually guided in their search for their legal, moral, and ethical rights.

Summary

In discussing children's work with parents, teachers should accept in principle that the parents will have considerable and unique information to share. In the areas of behavior, physical health, and possible handicapping conditions, the teachers and parents can share information and exchange opinions about working with the children. There is one area of operation in which the teachers should express themselves clearly, however; they should be able to help the parents to understand the nature of the learning process with respect, specifically, to the teaching of reading. In this particular area—reading in the primary grades, when to teach phonics, how much phonics to teach, size

of the child's basic sight vocabulary, present reader level in a reading book—the classroom teacher should have a background of knowledge and approach to the teaching
of reading so the parents can expect whatever adjustments are necessary in accommodating their children in the classroom.

It is important that teachers see children's problems objectively and not become
defensive about not having all the answers. If the teacher has assigned Charlene, described earlier in this chapter, to a sixth-grade reading book, he has made a mistake
that must be faced realistically, and corrected. Teachers need *never* answer parents'
comments about their children's failures with superficial responses: "He's doing quite
well lately," or "Don't be worried; he's getting along all right." If the parents say that
the child needs easier material and the teacher has not checked to find out, an informal
reading inventory is indicated to find out about missing skills.

There are ways that parents can and must help their children including participating in the school program; but these do not include the teaching of the "how-to-
read" skills. Suggestions for conducting profitable parent-teacher conferences and interviews about the child's reading have been detailed.

For Further Reading

Butler, Dorothy, and Clay, Marie. *Reading Begins at Home.* Exeter, N.H.: Heinemann Educational Books, 1982.

Fredericks, Anthony et al. "How to Talk to Parents and Get the Message Home," *The Instructor*
93 (November/December, 1983), pp. 64–69.

Heath, Shirley Brice. *Ways with Words, Language, Life, and Work in Communities and Classrooms.* Cambridge: Cambridge University Press, 1983.

Kroth, Roger, and Simpson, Richard. *Parent Conferences as a Teaching Strategy.* Denver: Love
Publishing Co., 1977.

Sittig, Linda H. "Involving Parents and Children in Reading for Fun." *The Reading Teacher*
36 (November 1982), pp. 166–68.

Swibold, Gretchen V. "Bringing Adults to Children's Books: A Case Study." *The Reading Teacher*
35 (January 1982), pp. 460–63.

Taylor, Denny. *Family Literacy, Young Children Learning to Read and Write.* Exeter, N.H.:
Heinemann Educational Books, 1983.

Vukelich, Carol. "Parents' Role in the Reading Process: A Review of Practical Suggestions and
Ways to Communicate with Parents." *The Reading Teacher* 37 (February 1984), pp. 472–77.

Notes

1. Ira J. Gordon, "The Effects of Parent Involvement on Schooling," in Ronald S. Brandt, ed.,
Partners: Parents and Schools (Alexandria, Va.: Association for Supervision and Curriculum Development, 1979), pp. 4–5.

2. Edward J. Kelly, *Parent-Teacher Interaction* (Seattle, Wash.: Special Child Publications,
Bernie Straub Publishing Company, 1974), p. 143.

3. Cherry Houck and Ann Sherman, "The Mainstreaming Current Flows Two Ways," *Academic Therapy* 15 (November 1979), pp. 133–40.

4. Dorothy J. McGinnis and Dorothy E. Smith, *Analyzing and Treating Reading Problems* (New York: Macmillan, 1982), p. 163.

5. E. W. Dolch, "If Parents Help With Reading," *Elementary English* 32 (March 1955), pp. 143–46.

6. Mary Wollner, "Should Parents Coddle Their Retarded Readers?" *Education* 80 (March 1960), p. 431.

7. Ibid., p. 432.

8. Willis Potter, "The Role of the Parent in Relation to Pupils' Reading Progress," *California Journal of Elementary Education* 18 (February 1950), p. 140.

9. Wollner, "Should Parents Coddle Their Retarded Readers?" p. 430.

10. Robert M. Wilson and Craig J. Cleland, *Diagnostic and Remedial Reading for Classroom and Clinic,* 5th ed. (Columbus: Charles Merrill, 1985), p. 376.

11. Guy L. Bond, Miles A. Tinker, Barbara B. Wasson and John B. Wasson, *Reading Difficulties, Their Diagnosis and Correction,* 5th ed. (Englewood Cliffs, N.J.: Prentice-Hall, 1984), p. 84.

12. Wollner, "Should Parents Coddle Their Retarded Readers?" p. 430.

13. Ibid.

14. Emery Bliesmer, "Some Notes on Helping Children with Reading Difficulties," *Education* 77 (May 1957), pp. 551–54.

15. Beatrice Lieben, "Attitudes, Platitudes, and Conferences in Teacher-Parent Relations Involving the Child with a Reading Problem," *Elementary School Journal* 58 (February 1958), pp. 279–86.

16. Ibid., p. 280.

17. Ibid., p. 281.

18. Ibid., p. 280.

19. Ibid., p. 282.

20. Fritz Redl and William W. Wattenberg, *Mental Hygiene in Teaching,* 2d. ed. (New York: Harcourt, Brace, 1959), pp. 452–76.

21. McGinnis and Smith, *Analyzing and Treating Reading Problems,* p. 163.

22. Joan S. Wolf, "Parents as Partners in Exceptional Education," *Theory into Practice* 21 (Spring 1982), p. 77.

23. Shirley C. Samuels, "Johnny's Mother Isn't Interested," *Today's Education* 62 (February 1973), p. 37.

24. Emilia Ferreiro and Ana Teberosky, *Literacy Before Schooling,* (Exeter, N.H.: Heinemann Educational Books, 1982), p. 4.

25. Wilson and Cleland, *Diagnostic and Remedial Reading,* pp. 372–73.

26. Eldon K. Ekwall and James L. Shanker, *Diagnosis and Remediation of the Disabled Reader,* 2d. ed. (Boston: Allyn and Bacon, 1983), pp. 412–13.

27. Roger Kroth, *Communicating with Parents of Exceptional Children* (Denver: Love Publishing Co., 1973), pp. 9–10.

28. Marsha L. Roit and William Pfohl, "The Readability of PL 94–142 Parent Materials: Are Parents Truly Informed?" *Exceptional Children* 50 (April 1984), p. 504.

29. Alma Harrington, Professor of Education, State University of New York, Buffalo.

30. Nicholas Criscuolo, "Reaching Unreachable Parents," *Journal of Reading* 17 (January 1974), pp. 285–87.

31. Madeline Hunter, "Staff Meeting: Madeline Hunter Discusses Parent Conferences," *The Instructor* 83 (February 1974), p. 18.

32. Joan Ann Suedmeyer, "Reading Remediation, Parent Group Meetings and Reading Performance of Fourth Grade Children," *Dissertation Abstracts International,* vol. 32 (Ann Arbor, Mich.: Xerox, University Microfilms, 1972), pp. 4256A–57A.

33. James A. McLoughlin, Robert McLoughlin and William Stewart, "Advocacy for Parents of the Handicapped: A Professional Responsibility and Challenge," *Learning Disability Quarterly* 2 (Summer 1979), pp. 51–57; 52.

34. Wolf, "Parents as Partners," p. 78.

14
Teaching the Linguistically and Culturally Different Child

Vocabulary

second language
limited English proficiency
cultural values
cultural differences
narrative
middle-class values
Standard English
nonstandard speaker
BICS
CALP
dialectology
bidialectal
phonology
morphology
syntax
semantics
discourse analysis
cohesion
inference
idiom
figurative language
multiple meanings
metaphor

Questions

1. Who are the children who may be linguistically and culturally different?

2. Describe some important relationships between language and culture.

3. What factors facilitate or inhibit the learning of a second language?

4. What are the problems of the child who speaks a nonstandard dialect? How can the school help such a child?

5. Name and explain the major ways to describe language.

6. What are some particular aspects of school language that bilingual and bidialectal children will need to learn?

Reading success is closely related to children's abilities to use the language they are learning to read. Teachers who have observed children closely will be able to illustrate this point easily.

A four-year-old boy in a bookstore was browsing among some rather difficult books, looking at their titles. The clerk approached him and said, "If you can read any one of those books, I'll give it to you." The child again perused the titles for a minute, selected one, removed it from the shelf, opened it and read aloud, without error, a sizable paragraph. The astonished clerk could only say, "The book is yours."[1]

A girl of three-and-one-half attended Sunday school and made paper boats that were floated on a pan of water. At home that afternoon, after floating her paper boat for a while, she came to her mother and said, "My boat's disintegrated in the water."

These examples can be contrasted with the fourteen-year-old ninth-grade girl who had great difficulty when trying to give "opposites" as words were read to her. She was unable to respond to *full* with *empty* or to *sunny* with *cloudy*.

A nine-year-old fourth-grade boy held up his hand and asked the teacher how to spell *if*. When the teacher bent over his desk and said *"i-f,"* the boy looked surprised and said, "Oh, I thought it was a four-letter word."

Psychological research data that has been accumulating for decades points up the English language deprivation of culturally different children, the children from the lower socioeconomic groups, and those living in isolated geographical areas. Tests have further indicated that I.Q. scores diminish as these children from meager language backgrounds progress through the school. While their innate capacity for learning did not decrease, their verbal abilities to respond, in comparison with other children of their age group, did decrease. In the greater American society, 25 percent of the population belongs to the lower-lower socioeconomic class. This indicates, immediately, serious handicaps for one child in four in the public school, having a bearing on such factors as (1) motivation to succeed in school, (2) setting a high level of aspiration, (3) desire to remain in school longer with children from higher social classes, and (4) selection of college preparatory courses. The subtle discrimination in school has a punishing effect, which decreases the students' self-respect, causes them to do poorly, and eventually makes them want to quit.

The migrant workers represent another group of children lacking language competence. The insecure pattern of living in the family, the irregular attendance at school, and the low educational achievement of the parents cause serious educational retardation among this large school population in the United States.

Marco, a Spanish-American twenty-year-old who was enrolled in Job Corps, came to a university reading clinic. Though he wanted to learn to read very much, the best efforts of his tutor produced few results. After four weeks he could write his name and recognize a few words, such as *stop*, from the environment. An interview was part of an effort to get to the heart of his problem. He was the son of a migrant worker in the Texas-Oklahoma-Kansas corridor. He remembered first grade, his kind teacher, and a book about a family that he learned to read. But his own family soon moved on, and he remembered no other kindly teachers or books he could read. He dropped out of school in sixth grade and drifted until he enrolled in Job Corps at nineteen. The interviewer questioned him about the book he had learned to read and, on a chance, showed him an old copy of *We Look and See*,[2] the first of the Dick and Jane preprimers. His eyes lit up, and he took the book, thumbing through its pages fondly. A few of the words were identified for him, and he proceeded to piece together several of the simple stories. He was given the book and he took it with him as though it were a treasure. Such an irrelevant book for this man, but it represented his own brief period of success in school!

The discussion presented here is based on research conducted among second-language children in the Southwest. The basic problems of language competence are, however, completely analogous to those of culturally different children or those from families of limited education.

The Child for Whom English is a Second Language

The public school pupils in the United States are taught by English-speaking people who value the ability to speak English as a basic requirement for success in today's world. Wherever large groups of children for whom English is a second language have attended public schools, they have, on the average, been educationally retarded to a severe degree. This has been especially true in the Southwest where large groups of Indian children, Spanish-American children, and Mexican children have been absorbed in public school populations. It is true also where other groups of foreign-born people have settled in the United States.

With the advent of intelligence tests in the 1920s, there were many studies completed that demonstrated that these children lacked intelligence when compared with unilingual, middle-class white children. Standardized reading tests demonstrated that as these children progressed through the grades, they fell farther and farther behind their unilingual companions. Tests comparing performances of urban and rural children gave an advantage to the wealth of experiences and sophistication of the typical, urban English-speaking children. Further, those from urban areas who lacked English were apt to have come from the lower socioeconomic classes, and thus lacked the experiences that would make school learning meaningful. Cultural differences were recognized as having a profound effect on the life values of the children and what their parents expected the school to do for them.

The Child with Limited English Proficiency

The 1980 census shows that 4,500,000 school age children, almost all with varying degrees of limited English proficiency, came to the United States in the decade of the 1970s. Four and one-half million children represent 10 percent of all the school age children in the country.[3]

The Natural Approach to Language Learning

One method widely accepted by the English as a second language specialist for teaching English as a second language is called the Natural Approach to Language Learning. The Natural Approach encompasses three major facets:

(1) A point of view about how language is acquired.
(2) A provision of maximum input of learning stimuli to the learners that is *always comprehensible* to them.
(3) A low-anxiety environment in which the children's *affect* is always positive and they feel that they will be successful at whatever they attempt.[4]

According to Terrell, *language acquisition* may be defined as the unconscious absorption of general principles of grammar through real experiences of communication using the second language. This absorption of grammatical principles is the basis for most first-language ability and in terms of the second language is commonly known as "picking up the language."[5]

Brian Gray helps teachers develop and expand concentrated encounters with children. The *concentrated encounter* is any meaningful situation in which language context is developed, expanded, and shared by the teacher and children. Probing and modeling strategies enable teachers to maximize language development. Gray gives "Saddling a Horse" and "Making Toast" as two examples of context in the real life experiences of the boys and girls with whom he works.[6] Gray suggests that we start with the children and find out what content is important, interesting, or necessary to them and encourage them to talk about it. Children will talk when or because they want to talk. In this way, children negotiate their own language development. Then the only methodology the teacher needs is that of facilitating effective interaction to get language out of the children that can be used for talking, writing, and reading. Concentrated encounters become significant when the teacher finds out what language, in the child's current circumstances, is important to him or her and serves a need. Once the teacher finds this out, he or she can then negotiate topics of conversation of intrinsic interest to the students.

Asher, using a strategy called Total Physical Response, has contributed two significant ideas to the teaching of English as a second language. These two concepts— (1) that we should give the learner ample time to get ready to speak the language before demanding oral responses, and (2) that when first learning a new language, the learner responds through physical activity to the language stimulus of the teacher to show understanding of the language—contribute significantly to the natural approach to language learning.[7]

The elementary classroom teacher must help the second-language learner develop enough sophistication to succeed in the regular classroom and to achieve on a par with his or her agemates. Cummins has explained the two aspects of the language program that help ensure this success. First, there are the skills termed *basic interpersonal communicative skills (BICSs)*, which includes all the language required for the interpersonal communication during the day. Greetings, talk about the weather, personal questions teachers must ask to complete their records, following directions, and responding to general command constitute basic interpersonal communicative skills. BICSs require knowing the most common expressions: What's your name?; How old are you?; What grade are you in?; What is your father's name? Drill books for teaching English as a second language include much practice on these common expressions.

But another corpus of language needed to ensure success in academic subjects is *cognitive/academic language proficiency (CALP)*. Cognitive/academic language proficiency is the dimension of language related to achievement in school. Understanding concepts of time, measurement and distance in mathematics; understanding metaphor, simile, and idiom in literature; and knowing the meanings of such concepts as latitude, altitude, the equator, and the life zones of the earth are all examples of this cognitive/academic language.[8]

We may suppose that it will take more time in school to master the CALP skills in English than to master the BICSs. Transition programs, then, must not move boys and girls back to the mainstreamed classroom without further special help, until they are ready. Chamot, writing for the National Clearing House for Bilingual Education, states:

> "Recent Canadian research shows that whereas the limited English proficient child requires only about *two* years to reach native speaker proficiency in BICS, it takes *five* to *seven* years to reach a CALP level comparable to the native speaker."[9]

Methodology

The literature in educational journals contains many suggestions that teachers can adapt to their own needs. Only a few are listed here.

1. Phillip Gonzales, in a recent issue of *Language Arts*, gives specific suggestions for teaching English to young non-English-speaking children.[10]
2. Eustolia Perez, in *The Reading Teacher*, reports a small study that improved very significantly the oral language competence of Mexican American third graders.[11]
3. Martin and Zintz have illustrated the schema concept through webbing to show language learners the multiple meanings and the interrelationships that many common words have. The word *blue* may be a color (navy, turquoise, robin's egg), used in an idiom (blue sky, blue collar, blue blood), used in a name of food (blueberries, blue cheese) and as part of an animal's name (blue jay, blue bird, blue whale). The writers' objective was to encourage teachers to start with as few meanings as the children have and build on that until there are many.[12]
4. Harris, in talks to teachers of aborigine children, discusses informal methods that have been working: the lap method of reading, the shared book experience as elaborated by Don Holdaway,[13] the use of stories with many repetitive lines, listening posts with cassettes, and the impress method in which adult and child read together.[14]
5. Elley and Mangubhai developed an experimental reading program for teaching English as a second language to Fiji Island children.[15] They used high-interest

illustrated storybooks written in English instead of the formal ESL drills used in the schools. The authors felt that the traditional drill work did not represent genuine communication, the repetitions were contrived and often monotonous, the exposure was minimal and carefully controlled, and many of the teachers themselves were teaching in their *second* language. These authors selected a sample of 380 boys and girls in classes four and five in eight Fijian rural schools and provided in each classroom 250 high-interest, low-vocabulary storybooks in English. (The titles are comparable to those found in Appendix B.) Generally, these classrooms had very few books for student selection for reading. The sixteen participating teachers used either a usual SSR program or a shared book experience approach. A control group of 234 boys and girls continued the traditional program of oral English drills. The control group put little emphasis on reading.

Post-tests after eight months showed that students exposed to many stories progressed in reading and listening comprehension at twice the normal rate. At the end of the following year, the gains had increased further and spread to related language skills.

. . the critical factors which brought about the substantial improvements were related to greater and repeated exposure to print in high-interest contexts, in conditions where pupils were striving for meaning, and receiving sufficient support to achieve it regularly. These features were common in the experimental groups and absent in the controls.[16]

This study strongly supports the provision of a wide range of suitable, well-illustrated, high-interest story books for children with limited English proficiency and planning for scheduled time to ensure that students read them.

Assessing Intelligence of Bilingual Children

Being born as poor whites, blacks, Indians, or Spanish-speaking children means that the children will learn about the world whatever it is that their indigenous culture teaches them. They will learn to feel in certain ways about people, about events, about themselves. They will learn food preferences, preferences in personal living habits, customs and mores of their own social groups, and specific ways of behaving in all the situations of daily living. They will acquire specific attitudes toward sex, sin, death, illness, even arrogant middle-class adults. It is their responses to all the specific practices in behavior in the basic social institutions of their groups that cause them to behave like *blacks, Mexicans, Indians*—not like the typical middle-class people that their teachers may be expecting them to imitate or emulate. "Learning" a culture, as the children do growing up in it, has not only cognitive elements but also affective elements. The socialization process is heavily laden with emotional overlay—the individuals have "emotional sets" about their ways of life and the way all adults respond to it.

The individuals from a minority group perceive and attend to the values of the dominant group in a manner quite different from that in which they are perceived and attended to by one born in this dominant culture.

Havighurst wrote in 1957:

The conclusion which is drawn by most social scientists from the data on Indian cultures and Indian intelligence is that the American Indians of today have about the same innate equipment for learning as have the white children of America. But in those Indian tribes which have preserved their traditional cultures to some extent, there is a limited motivation of children for a high level performance in schools and colleges.[17]

As the above paragraphs make clear, assessing intelligence of children is a complex, abstract process. We have no tests that are not culturally biased since test builders function through their own cultural milieu. Tests designed for children whose first, or only, language is English will be unfair measures for children who are learning to use English as a second language. Cultural values and personal experiences of children that differ from the typical middle class values and experiences of the school will also create conflicts in functioning in the expected school behavior.

Use of Language and the Cultural Difference

Language and culture are interdependent. Culture is the accumulated experience of a social group throughout time. The only way accumulated experience can be recreated or interpreted is through language. Without language, there would be no way of reviewing past experiences and communicating them to others. People transmit their cultural heritage through their language.

It is believed by many that since thought itself requires some kind of symbolization, thinking is, in a sense, a way of talking things over with oneself. The cumulative aspect of culture, which clearly and completely differentiates people from lower animals, is made possible by language.

This is expressed succinctly by Strickland:

Communication through spoken and written language belongs to people and to them alone. It is the most important influence in their upward climb through the centuries. This ability to communicate has permitted each generation to rise on the shoulders of the thinkers and achievers who have gone before, to profit from their gains, to avoid their mistakes, and to pursue their dreams and aspirations and make some of them realities.[18]

It is of concern to teachers that the transmission of the cultural heritage is made through language.

The complete vocabulary of a language may indeed be looked upon as a complex inventory of all the ideas, interests and occupations that take up the attention of a community, and were such a complete thesaurus of the language of a given tribe at our disposal, we might to a large extent infer the character of the physical environment and the characteristics of the culture of the people making use of it.[19]

Concepts are represented by verbal symbols, *but* the verbal symbols are conditioned by the culture. In English, the clock *runs;* in Spanish, it *walks.* In English, people say they missed the bus; in Spanish, they say the bus left them. If dishes break by falling away from people, and objects lose themselves, the way language says something may reveal the way people in a culture evaluate their personal responsibilities.

Special problems arise in learning a new set of language patterns when native language habits are in conflict. One of the chief difficulties is that children have learned not only to attend to certain stimuli but also to ignore all those features that do not have a function in their own language. These blind spots may be exactly those features that do have signaling value in the second language.[20]

Researchers and educators have become aware of aspects of language beyond the word and the sentence that may be troublesome to children. It has been found that different cultures and different language groups employ varying implicit rules to shape oral discourse. Ainsworth pointed out, for example, that the typical classroom discussion cycle is strictly a verbal process, but that "Indian learning traditionally begins silently and continues with a low level of verbal interaction. . . . The CDC (classroom discussion cycle) calls for spontaneous unrehearsed performance, before an audience, whereas the Indian system calls for practice away from the spotlight."[21]

Narratives, which make up much of the reading material of the classroom, have been found to vary in their structure from culture to culture. Tafoya contrasted the typical mainstream narrative organization which is in threes (Three Bears, Three Billy Goats, three wishes, and so on) with the Native American story organization in sets of fours.[22] Both Cronin[23] who worked with Crow and Metis children and Brown[24] in Australia confirmed Tafoya's conclusion that the story structure from another culture may cause confusion as children try to read or listen to narratives, at least in the early years of school.

Most teachers have middle-class values. This means that teachers come from homes where the drive for achievement and success causes parents to "push" their children to climb the ladder of success, where "work for work's sake" is important, and where everyone is oriented to future-time values. To teach the children successfully, the teachers must recognize that the children may come to school with a radically divergent set of values and the teachers must try to understand, not disparage, these values.

Some contrasting values of the school teachers and the traditional values of the Pueblo Indian children are cited here. The children's values and those of the teachers may be generalized to a considerable degree as following the pattern of:

1. *Harmony with* nature as juxtaposed with *mastery over* nature.
2. *Present time* orientation rather than *future time* orientation.
3. Inclusion of mythology, fear of the supernatural, and sorcery rather than a total commitment to a scientific explanation of all natural phenomena.
4. A level of aspiration to follow in the ways of the old people, to cooperate and maintain the status quo rather than to develop a keen sense of competition and climb the ladder of success.

5. To value anonymity and submissiveness rather than individuality and aggression.
6. To work to satisfy present needs and to be willing to share rather than always working to "get ahead" and save for the future.

It is necessary at this point to recognize that Indians as individuals do not all conform to generalized patterns. Acculturation takes place on a long continuum of behaviors—all the way from those who still very completely fit the traditional patterns to those whose life-style is completely middle-class, or has become bicultural. The serious problems lie in the twilight zones of social disorganization.

Factors Influencing the Learning of a Second Language

Fries notes:

> Our language is an essential part of every portion of our experiences; it gets all its meaning from our experience, and it is in turn our tool to grasp and realize experience. Every language is thus inextricably bound up with the whole life experience of the native users of that language. The linguistic forms of my language "mean" the situations in which I use them. For me to be thoroughly understood, therefore, the hearer must in some way grasp completely the "situations" as they stimulate my utterances.[25]

In order for foreign-language children to succeed in the public schools, they must develop competence in English as the language of the school. Many factors influence the children's learning of English as a second language:

1. The children must want to learn.
2. Their families, as well as the leadership of their minority group, must accept such learning as a valuable goal. To acquire formal education in the public schools, they must use English well.
3. The amount of time spent on the second language, both in and out of school, will affect the quality of the learning. If the children think in another language from the time they leave school in the afternoon until they return the next morning, they will be very slow to learn to think in English and will rely on translating the teachers' questions, thinking out answers, and translating them into the teachers' language to answer.
4. The presence or absence of education adjuncts such as TV, newspapers, radio, or books in the home will influence learning.
5. Elements that the first and second languages have in common—phonology, structure, and sentence patterning—will facilitate the learning of the second language.
6. Reward for learning needs to be positive and immediate.
7. The congruence of the school's instructional practices with cultural perspectives on language use and learning is important.[26]

Children coming into the English-speaking schools from a minority group find a world alien in language and in meaningful concepts, a world geared to values of which they may be totally ignorant, and moreover, a world that is often not only ignorant but heedless of those values inherent in their way of life. An understanding of their culture by the teachers could facilitate their progress in learning both the culture and the language of the teachers. It must be appreciated that language and culture are mutually reinforcing and must be utilized jointly in teaching minority groups advantageously.

Dialectology: Language Problems of Bidialectal Children

Many black children feel that our society has rejected them. Many feel it has rejected them because they are black. Black children soon acquire a poor self-concept. They interpret blackness, poor self-concept, and so forth as inferiority.

Many black children speak a nonstandard dialect of English that differs, in varying degrees among blacks, from Standard English. For six-year-olds in school, nonstandard English sets up the same types of interference that a second language does to learning to read in Standard English and to obtaining cognitive learning in Standard English. Many teachers believe that the language spoken by these children is inferior and lacks complete grammatical construction and lexical form. This is not true. The morphology and verb structure constitute a complete grammar. The black children may have a very great number of words in their speech that substitute for words ordinarily used in Standard English. If the teachers are aware—know about the substitution of words or phrases for words commonly used in their own speech—no serious language problems need exist between the teachers and children. One language is not inferior, another superior; the two dialects of the language are just different.

When the teachers reject the children's language as "careless"—that is, "bad"—the children will likely feel that they are being rejected as people. In rejecting them, the teachers must also be rejecting those who mean the most to them, their immediate family. If the teachers continually say, "Don't say it like that, say it like this," the children interpret this as a rejection of them through their ways of behaving.

The black children, especially of the inner-city poor, have a number of reasons other than language, to believe that the teachers' values and life-style have little in common with theirs.

The absence of a father in many black families has a debilitating effect on boys. Aggressiveness is likely to be valued more than intellectualism. The readiness of these children for beginning school is different. Ghetto elementary schools need more black male teachers.

Labov says:

> One of the most extraordinary failures in the history of American Education is the failure of the public school system to teach black children in the urban ghettos to read. The fact of reading failure is so general, and so widespread, that no one school system, no one method, and no one teacher can be considered responsible.[27]

Labov illustrates the phonological problems of the "r-lessness," the "l-lessness," the difficulties with consonant clusters, and the weak final consonants. The r is absent in pronouncing *guard* as *god;* or *nor* more like *gnaw.* Without *l, toll* becomes *toe; help* becomes *hep;* and *tool* becomes *too.* Words ending with *st, ft, nt,* or *ld* usually lose the last consonant: *fast* becomes *fas; don't* becomes *don.* Weakened final consonants cause *seat* or *seed* to become *see; poor, poke,* or *pope,* to become *poo'.*

Labov suggests that teachers:

1. Distinguish carefully between dialectic differences in pronunciation and errors in reading.
2. It may help to spend more time on the grammar of the language to help some children understand the two ways in which the language is spoken.
3. Extra auditory perception instruction may be helpful in teaching children to hear and make distinctions in Standard and nonstandard speech.
4. Work on the premise that children can learn to read Standard English texts in a nonstandard pronunciation. The teachers need to know the language of the children—both its lexical and grammatical forms—as well as Standard English . . . and the differences between the two.
5. The teachers need to determine that the children "know" both differences in *meaning* and in *sound* if they think *cold* and *coal* are both *col.*[28]

Stewart reminds us that the black children may be able to set up their own sound-spelling correspondences—a system different from that of the speakers of Standard English—but that allows them effective word identification. For example, they will likely substitute *f* and *v* for two sounds of *th,* so that they learn to use *f* or *v* for *th* when *th* appears other than at the beginning of the word. Thus, they are able to read *bref* for *breath* and *brev* for *breathe.*[29]

Since language is primarily oral, and spoken language takes precedence over written, it is logical to suppose that children might profit from seeing their personal dialect of English in written form before they see Standard English (if they are not familiar with it). It should be easier for children to move into the very complicated process of formal reading if they adjusted first to the reading of the language that is personal and meaningful to them—and then, later, learned to read the Standard English, which, of course, they also need. Stewart has produced two little books for beginning reading in the vernacular of black children in one area of the United States. Four sample pages of one story written in black vernacular and in standard English follow.

Ollie and his sisters and brothers, they all live with Momma and Big Momma.	Ollie and his brothers and sisters live with their mother and their grandmother.
Momma she go to work. Big Momma she take care of Ollie and his sisters and brothers.	Mother goes to work. Grandmother takes care of Ollie and his brothers and sisters.
Here go Leroy. Leroy and Ollie playing together. They playing in front of the house.	This is Leroy. Leroy and Ollie were playing together in front of their house.
Ollie tell Leroy, he say, "I want some soda." And Leroy he say, "I want some soda, too."	Ollie said to Leroy, "I want some soda." Leroy said, "I want some soda, too."[30]

Wolfram and Fasold have rewritten the story of a little girl who is with her mother and brother when she looks at her reflection in a puddle of water. Her dog, Wiggles, is with her. The two versions of the story follow.

SEE A GIRL
[*Black English Version*]
Susan say, "Hey you-all, look down here.
I can see a girl in here.
The girl, she look like me.
Come here and look, David.
Could you see the girl?"
David, he say, "Here I come.
Let me see the girl."
David say, "I don't see no girl.
Ain't no girl in there.
I see me and my ball."
Susan, she say, "Momma, look in here.
David don't see no girl, and I do.
You see a girl in there?"
Momma say, "Look down there, David.
That little girl Susan.
And there go David."
Susan say, "Momma! Momma! Momma!

We can see David and me.
We can see Wiggles and a big girl.
You that big girl."

SEE A GIRL
[*Standard English Version*]
"Look down here," said Suzy.
"I can see a girl in here.
That girl looks like me.
Come here and look, David.
Can you see that girl?"
"Here I come," said David.
"I want to see the girl."
David said, "I do not see a girl.
A girl is not in here, Suzy.
I see me and my ball."
Suzy said, "Look in here, Mother.
David cannot see a girl.
And I can.
Can you see a girl in here?"
"Look down, Suzy," said Mother.
"Look down here, David.
That little girl is my Suzy.
And here is David."
"Mother! Mother!" said Suzy.
"We can see David and me.
We can see Wiggles and a big girl.
That big girl is you."[31]

Educators have often been blinded by their ethnocentric and egocentric ways of viewing education problems. Thus, when large numbers of speakers of nonstandard English failed to learn to read, our immediate assumption was "faulty language." We might more logically have blamed instructional methods and materials. Myers cautioned about the need to respect cognitive styles and learning preferences.

> The holistic world view of African culture has special significance . . . affective/ cognitive separations are artificial for them . . . intellectual stimulation, teacher/ student rapport, and personal, physical and environmental well-being all come together as mandatory concerns for the best learning situation.[32]

The teachers must believe that, for certain dialect speakers, the sentence "The dog, he look funny," is an accurate and meaningful translation of the printed words "The dog looks funny." This is a meaningful realization of a Standard English sentence for a nonstandard speaker. The insertion of "he" and the omission of "s" from "looks" have traditionally been considered word-recognition errors. We now know they are not reading errors for certain dialect speakers. The teachers must believe they are not errors.[33]

The bidialectal children must be permitted to read standard material in their own dialects. Likewise, they will learn to read more readily if their first language experience stories are written in the dialect of the language they speak. Cramer writes:

> The language experience approach is predicated upon the notion that reading can be most meaningfully taught when the reading materials accurately reflect the child's own experience as described by his language. The language of instruction then must be that which proceeds from the wealth of linguistic, conceptual and perceptual experience of the child.
>
> The language experience approach is an ideal means of overcoming the instructional problem created for the divergent speaker (the bidialectal child) by the mismatch between his language and the language of beginning reading materials. The language experience reading avoids the necessity of writing reading textbooks in dialect; it asserts that the child's nonstandard dialect is ideal for initiating him into the mysteries of reading written language.[34]

Making Connections 14.1: Experiencing Another Language

Though we may verbalize how we would function in a setting in which we do not know the language, many teachers have had few such firsthand experiences. In completing this assignment, you will have an opportunity to experience some of the feelings that accompany such an experience.

Arrange with your instructor to spend at least an hour and preferably longer in a setting where the language in use is unknown to you. It will be a better experience if you are not able to be a passive observer, but must actually try to communicate and to understand the meanings of others. You may need to be creative to find a setting. A few suggestions are: an ethnic club such as a German Club in a community, a meeting of a specific group of foreign students at your college or university, perhaps a family that will enjoy helping you with the experience, a classroom conducted in another language, or a preschool where small children are speaking another language.

After your experience, come to class prepared to talk about what you learned and how you felt during the visit. Share the strategies you used to communicate when language was denied to you. Then apply what you learned during this experience to the life of children in the classroom who speak little or no English. You should be a more sensitive teacher because of this experience.

The Structure of the English Language

Goodman summarizes five principles from linguistics that teachers should know and use.

1. By the time they come to school, children have already achieved virtual mastery over the oral language of their community. In the language-experience approaches, new emphasis must be given to preserving the *real* language of the child—his or her grammar, phrasing, vocabulary—instead of the teacher's style of language or that of the preprimer he is trying to learn to read.
2. Language is systematic. Words have to be arranged in an acceptable pattern within a language system in order to carry meaning. The system of language is its grammar.

   (Word lists, flash cards, and phonic charts isolate elements from their meaningful grammatical contexts.)

   The child senses, deep within the self, the grammar of his or her language—that is, understanding of the ideas expressed in sentences in that language.
3. A language is a family of mutually understood dialects. Each speaker of a language speaks one or more of these dialects. Dialects can and do differ in sounds (phonemes), inflections (word endings), grammar, intonation, vocabulary, and idioms.
4. Language is constantly changing. The child with a dialect has the same kind of language resource as any other child. The teacher should not confuse this student by correcting him or her when what the student has read is consonant with his or her own dialect.
5. Though English uses an alphabetic writing system, the oral and written systems have considerable irregularity in phoneme-grapheme correspondence. The reading program must be personalized to make it relevant to the learner or groups of learners.[35]

Ways to Describe Language

Language has phonology, morphology, syntax, and semantics. *Phonology* is the study of the distinct sounds of the language. The alphabet is an imperfect representation of the English phonemes. So, we have forty-four phonemes represented by twenty-six letters. Phonemes combine into meaningful sound units called *morphemes,* which may be words or parts of words. Morphology is the study of these smallest meaningful units of language. The morphemes that are especially important in elementary school are compound words, inflectional endings, prefixes, and suffixes, and Greek and Latin combining forms. *Syntax* is often thought of as the grammar of the language. More precisely, it is the set of rules governing how morphemes are combined into sentences. *Semantics* is the study of meanings communicated through language. Table 14.1 is a diagram that details these four facets of language.

TABLE 14.1 The Structure of Language

Phonology	Morphology	Syntax	Semantics
Phonology is the study of the distinctive sounds of language.	Morphology is the study of the smallest meaningful units of language, called *morphemes,* which are mainly words or parts of words. Morphemes especially important in elementary school teaching are:	Syntax is often thought of as the grammar of a language. More precisely, it is the set of rules governing how morphemes are combined into sentences.	Semantics is the study of the meanings communicated through language.
1. There are 44 distinctive sounds, called *phonemes,* in the English language. (Sources differ: 40, 44, 45, 47.) The alphabet is an imperfect representation of those sounds.	1. Compound words. 2. Inflectional endings *er, est, ed, ing, s, es.* 3. Prefixes and suffixes. 4. The common Greek and Latin combining forms	1. Word order, an important distinctive feature of English, is an aspect of syntax (a *pocket watch* is not the same as a *watch pocket*).	1. English is a language with a rich vocabulary, or lexicon, which has many words borrowed from other languages.

2. Phonemes combine into distinctive meaningful units, called *morphemes,* which are words or parts of words.		2. Basic ("kernel") sentence patterns:
		    1. Noun—transitive verb—object
		    b. Noun—linking verb—predicate noun or adjective
		    c. Noun—verb—prepositional phrase
			2. The listener or the reader must rely on context clues; meanings depend upon context.

3. Minimal pairs are two words with only one phonemic difference, which changes meaning (pick-pig, map-mat, big-pig, big-bag).		3. Transformations:
		    a. Negative statements
		    b. *Or* changes
		    c. Expansions
		    d. *There* changes
		    e. Question changes
		    f. Passive changes
		    g. Combined kernel sentences
		    h. *Until, if, because* changes
		    i. Tense changes
			3. The language contains many figures of speech, idiomatic expressions, and slang expressions.

4. Stress and juncture (called *suprasegmentals*) are also distinctive features of English, comparable to phonemes, which change meaning. (*You* bought that. You *bought* that. You bought *that.* A blue bird is not necessarily a bluebird.)			4. The vocabulary contains antonyms, heteronyms, homographs, homonyms, synonyms.
5. The phoneme-grapheme relationships are often confusing in English because the same sound may have many variant spellings, and different sounds may have the same spellings.			5. Suprasegmentals, which are phonemic because they change meanings, are also semantic in communicating meaning changes.

Miles V. Zintz and Zelda R. Maggart, *The Teacher and the Learner,* 4th ed. (Dubuque, Iowa: Wm. C. Brown, 1984), p. 71.

Phonology

The phonology (sound) of words includes the following features.

1. There are forty-four separate phonemes in English but only twenty-six letters in the alphabet.
2. Many times we rely on context to determine which meaning of a word is being used. The part of speech of the word may tell us what meaning to attach.
3. One phonemic difference can completely change the meaning in a pair of words. When two words have only one phonemic difference, they are said to be a minimal pair. Teachers have traditionally taught children a great deal of "phonics" distinguishing minimal pairs: for example, the final sounds: pic*k*-pi*g,* ma*p*-ma*t.*
4. Accent patterns change meanings phonemically. A *black bird* is not necessarily a *blackbird;* nor is the *green house* necessarily a *greenhouse.*
5. The phoneme-grapheme relationships are confusing in English, because some consonants have more than one sound and the five vowel letters have many sounds.
6. The suprasegmentals of stress, pitch, and juncture convey phonemic differences:
      Did you buy the *book?*
      Did you *buy* the book?
      Did *you* buy the book?
      Was that the *greenhouse?*
      Was that the *Green* house?
      Was that the *green* house?

Morphology

The morphology (structure) of words includes the following features.

1. Teaching of compound words.
2. Teaching inflectional endings *er, est, ed, ing, s, es.*
3. Teaching prefixes and suffixes.
4. Teaching contractions.
5. Teaching the common Greek and Latin combining forms.
6. Teaching the dictionary skills for reading and writing.

Syntax

Syntax is the grammar of the language. Grammar is the set of rules governing the use of the language so that people can communicate meaningfully with each other.

1. Generally, native speakers have no difficulty mastering language syntax that they hear from their models as they grow up. If they hear nonstandard English, they will learn to speak nonstandard English.
2. The language is quite arbitrary in following a specific, prescribed structure. One can say "The pencil is brown," but one cannot say "The is pencil brown."

3. The basic sentence patterns of children are:
   a. Noun-transitive verb-object
   b. Noun-linking verb-predicate noun or adjective
   c. Noun-verb-prepositional phrase
4. There are ways by which sentences can be *transformed* to discuss an idea in different ways. Meanings become more complicated when passive voice is used instead of active voice.

Semantics

Semantic difficulties in reading have been explored in earlier parts of this chapter. Teachers must build on *the oral language base* that the children have. Yet, ways are not available to determine that base for all children. The children may know the meaning of the sentence when you say, "The boy cries." But if you change *cries* to a noun in "The cries of the boy were heard," do they know? They may understand, "We are going to the *circus*." But, that is not the same *circus* in "We saw the *circus* clown." They may understand, "Put it on the *table*." But not, "*Table* the motion," or "Look in the *table* of numbers." The readers bring preconceived predictions to the reading; they read by following what they see and what they expect to see.

The beginning readers learn to zero in on the most helpful clue, which is usually the initial consonant. The reading process may then break down into three steps:

1. Predict,
2. Sample and select, and
3. Test it out.

In decoding the word *lead,* for example, when the linguistic form carries the information, "it is a noun and refers to a metal," the word is pronounced *led;* when it conveys the information, "it is a verb and refers to guiding or direction," *l-e-a-d* is pronounced *leed*—but *lead* and *lead* are spelled alike. Consider the linguistic forms of *mist* and *missed.* I *missed* the exit and could not get off the expressway. Or, the dense morning *mist* hid the house from view.[36]

Transformational grammar has two *levels* of syntactical structure: a surface level and a deep structure level. The *surface* level is that which is directly observed in the words themselves—"on the surface," so to speak. *Deep structure* is the meaning, or interpretation, level. It is the deep structure level of language that must be developed if students are to use language accurately and wisely.

Bowen's example of two sentences with the same *pattern* on the surface, clearly requires two very different interpretations:

Mary is *anxious* to paint.
Mary is *difficult* to paint.

In one case, Mary wants to do the painting herself; in the other, Mary is the subject of someone else's painting.[37]

Rutherford also illustrates the differences in meaning in many pairs of sentences that look on the surface to follow the same pattern:

1. a. What he wants is *more* of your business.
   b. What he wants is *none* of your business.
2. a. It was a moving *train.*
   b. It was a moving *experience.*
3. a. Who's the person you want to (want ta) call? (You make the call.)
   b. Who's the person you want to (wanna) call? (The person calls you.)[38]

The sentence, "I had Mary for lunch and made sandwiches," is clear in its deep structure. If one judged only on the surface language, it suggests the speaker is a cannibal.[39]

Goldfield makes some significant statements about "reading for meaning" and its dependence on semantics:

. . . Strictly speaking, one doesn't "get" meaning from print. Rather, he "gives" or "produces" a meaning. For example, ask students to explain "The chicken is too hot to eat." Responses could vary: too stove-hot to eat; too spicy to eat; a stolen chicken; a sexy chicken; or even a chicken who is too overcome by the sun to eat its feed.[40]

Efficient readers realize that words are not things they point to—the menu is not the meal. They understand that there are not written facts, only statements about facts. With this in mind, the able reader will not react to words as though they were, indeed, life-facts.[41]

. . . semantic awareness alerts the student that there is no one, exact meaning to words or phrases. It compels the reader to define terms with specific examples, and repeatedly demonstrates that most of the meaning is not in words but in people.[42]

Discourse Analysis

Another way to study language is to attend to units larger than words or sentences. This study, discourse analysis, provides the means for analysis of both oral and written texts and the settings in which they are produced.[43]

Because the analyst is investigating the use of language in context by a speaker/writer, he is more concerned with the relationship between the speaker and the utterance, on the particular occasion of use, than with the potential relationship of one sentence to another, regardless of their use.[44]

Two important characteristics of discourse or text as related to reading are:

1. Cohesion—those strategies that speakers have to bind parts of texts together. The interpretation of some element in the discourse is dependent on that of another.[45]

Elements that are cohesive include substitution, ellipsis, pronominalization, conjunctions, and lexical cohesion.[46]

Substitution	This copy is blurred. I need a clear *one.*
Ellipsis	This is a tasty pie. I've never *tasted better.*
Pronominalization	Bill chose Sue to work, and *he* put *her* to work stapling booklets.
Conjunctions	Sam wanted a winesap apple *because* he remembered the ones from his parents' tree on the farm.
Lexical cohesion	The *Coral Sea* is one of this country's older carriers.

2. Inference—the process which the reader (hearer) must go through to get from the literal meaning of what is written (or said) to what the writer (speaker) intended to convey.[47] The reader or listener must fill in one or more gaps to arrive at the intended meaning.

> The children swished down the hill on their sleds.
> They picked up speed as they went over the frozen snow.

The reader must infer that sleds are used for traveling over snow and that speed is related to going downhill and to slick surfaces. Poor readers are frequently troubled by the need to make inferences as they read. Teachers need to help children identify texts that require readers to infer meaning and to talk through the steps in thinking that may be required to make sense of the material.

Measuring Knowledge of English Usage

Measuring instruments for determining children's understanding of verbal concepts in English will be useful to the classroom teachers for both second-language and culturally different students.

Vocabulary Development

> One of the most fundamental problems relates to the matter of vocabulary. . . .
> This relates to the inability to distinguish between shades of meaning as expressed by words.[48]

Because reading is the ability to bring meaning to the printed symbols out of the background of experience, vocabulary growth is dependent upon real and vicarious experiences of the children.

The greatest single barrier to understanding is language.[49] The policy in American schools has been to censor rather ruthlessly any language other than English. The children must speak English on the playground and on the street, and they must read English books. This insistence on English usage may cause the children to think of their own parents as inferior, disapproved of, and old-fashioned. The social customs of their parents—in the preferred foods in their diet, their style of dress, their leisure-time activities, and certain deep-seated religious practices—add to the children's great inner conflict when they are forced to choose between the strongly motivated goals of the school and their desire to defend and uphold their parents' tradition.[50]

It would be helpful if the teachers:

1. Knew something of the language of the child's parents.
2. Knew something of the cultural practices and cultural contributions of the foreign culture.
3. Had tact, common sense, and sympathetic understanding.
4. Would visit the home not once, but many times.
5. Would explain the basic purposes of the school and clarify erroneous ideas brought home by the child.
6. Would show genuine appreciation for the worthwhile values of the culture of the parents.[51]

Understanding of English as the Language of the School

The teaching of English as a second language encompasses these three facets: (1) the memorization of, and drill on, the common speech utterances of the second language; (2) the extension of vocabulary in the second language beyond the initial levels required in such common utterances; and (3) the reading and writing of the second language.

Teachers can measure the extension of vocabulary in the language by investigating semantic difficulties as found in common idiomatic expressions, multiple meanings of common words, simple analogies, and opposites. Test exercises measuring these abilities indicated that Indian and Spanish-American children were significantly handicapped in comparison with Anglo children with whom their performances were compared. Fourth grade Anglo children with unilingual backgrounds performed significantly better statistically on all these tests than did Indian and Spanish-speaking sixth grade children enrolled in public school classes.

1. Understanding the idiom in the English language. Idioms found in context in the school readers:
    a. Mother will *piece out* the supper.
    b. Tom knew he was *saved by a hair.*
    c. His plan *fell through.*
    d. "O.K.," he retorted, *"Don't bite my head off."*
    e. He won't be *worth his salt* for a long time to come.
    f. Mr. Bird chuckled, "Now I've *let the cat out of the bag."*

    Student workbooks contain exercises to give some practice in identifying proper meanings for idiomatic expressions (see figure 14.1).

Foerster has suggested using idioms as motivation to get students interested in their language. Because idioms carry a meaning other than the literal one, when taken literally the meaning can be good humor. She illustrates with "I'd like to

33 **Comprehend phrase and sentence meaning; interpret figurative language.** First, pupils are to read the directions for marking each box. Then in each box pupils are to read the sentence and notice the underlined words. They are to think about the meaning of these words and put an x beside one of the three phrases below the sentence that has the same meaning. COPYRIGHT © 1968 BY SCOTT, FORESMAN AND COMPANY

What do the underlined words in the sentence mean? Put an x beside the answer.

Mr. Wills was a good neighbor and always ready to give a hand.

☐ shake hands

☐ hand out his autograph

☐ be helpful

Steve said, "I'll tell you a secret, Dick, but keep it under your hat."

☐ don't tell it to anyone

☐ don't believe it

☐ don't take off your hat

"I'll look after the baby so Mother can have a bit of rest," thought Mary.

☐ follow behind

☐ not look in front of

☐ take care of

The boys were all ears when their parents talked about a camping trip.

☐ covered their eyes

☐ listened carefully

☐ were covered with ears

"I live a stone's throw from a big park," said Nancy.

☐ a very short way

☐ a bumpy ride

☐ a walk on a rocky road

"Please drop me a line while you're on your trip, Jeff," said Roger.

☐ lower a rope to me

☐ catch a fish for me

☐ send me a letter

Jack said, "I'm going to round up some of the boys for a game."

☐ drive away

☐ gather together

☐ run rings around

Suddenly Ann left the room, and her sister wondered what she was up to.

☐ about to do

☐ reaching up for

☐ climbing on

Pat was all in at the end of the day.

☐ sleeping soundly

☐ very tired

☐ inside the house

Beth and the puppy sat side by side.

☐ across from each other

☐ in two seats

☐ beside one another

SET 7, BOOK 3 · PART 1

Figure 14.1. Exercises give practice in identifying proper meanings for idiomatic expressions. (Helen M. Robinson et al. From *Roads to Follow*, Duplicating Masters. Copyright © 1968 by Scott, Foresman. Reprinted by permission of the publisher.)

have you for dinner," or "Mother told you to get off the phone."[52] Foerster suggests:

a. drawing pictures to illustrate an idiom and then letting the class guess which idiom it is, using such idioms as "He's a big wheel," "He flew off the handle," or "It was a hair-raising experience."

b. pantomiming idioms, playing a charades-like game using such idioms as "You turn me on," "He kicked the bucket," or "He's got a chip on his shoulder."

c. classifying idioms:
   (1) idioms that involve color: "I'm in the red," "He's awfully blue."
   (2) idioms that include parts of the body: "Lend me your ear," "She has a sharp tongue," or "He has a nose for news."
   (3) idioms dealing with animals: "He's a fat cat," "She's no spring chicken," or "Quit horsing around."
   (4) idioms relating to food: "He's the salt of the earth," "She's in a pickle," or "I'm in a stew."

Edwards tested the relative level of difficulty of reading material containing idiomatic expressions and the same material rewritten with literal meanings. He was concerned only with those idioms that are common, widely-used, accepted Standard English, such as "fly in the ointment," "crow about something," or "steal the show." He found that the group reading passages rewritten in literal English performed significantly better than the group reading passages that contained idiomatic language. Edwards emphasizes the need for finding appropriate ways to develop better understanding of idiomatic language for all junior high school students, but especially for those from minority groups who lack knowledge about the cultural background in the books they are expected to read.[53]

2. Understanding commonly used slang expressions in the English language.
   a. Mr. Jones really *cramps my style.*
   b. When everyone else quit, I was *stuck with the job.*
   c. He is great for *talking through his hat.*
   d. It's about time to quit fooling around and *talk turkey.*
   e. Tom likes to *pull your leg* every chance he gets.

These slang expressions will surely be baffling if translated in a completely literal way. Figure 14.2 is a lesson developing understanding of slang expressions.

3. Understanding multiple meanings of the same English word. The word *run,* for example, has some seventy-five uses in the elementary school dictionary, such as:[54]
   a. The boy will *run* a race.
   b. The disease has *run* its course.
   c. The fence *runs* east and west.
   d. The man *runs* a garage.
   e. The boy has *run* a splinter in his finger.
   f. She will *run* out of money.
   g. He will *run* up a bill.

LANGUAGE ACTIVITY

Specific Objective

Language expression: Understanding the use of slang expressions

Part I

Directions: Read the sentences below. Then match each numbered sentence with the lettered sentence in Part II that means the same thing by writing the correct letter in the blank.

1. __b__ Let us know how those rich cats make out.
2. __g__ We'll be waiting to hear, our tongues hanging out.
3. __e__ Cut it out.
4. __h__ "Stay cool, stay cool," I kept saying to myself.
5. __c__ I spotted Larry with a group of older guys.
6. __a__ Are you just going to rake in all they give you over there because they feel sorry for you?
7. __f__ A bunch of guys were kidding them.
8. __d__ A few guys started to horse around.

Part II

a. Are you simply going to take all the things they give you because they feel sorry for you?
b. Tell us how the wealthy people behave.
c. I saw Larry with a group of older boys.
d. A few boys started misbehaving.
e. Stop that.
f. Several boys were teasing them.
g. We'll be eagerly waiting to hear.
h. "Stay calm, stay calm," I kept saying to myself.

Part III

Directions: Choose two more examples of slang expressions from the story, "The Long Ride." Then translate them into Standard English.

Figure 14.2. Understanding slang expressions (level 12, p. 79). (From *Teacher's Edition, On the Edge,* by Theodore Clymer and Constance M. McCullough, of the *Reading 360* series, Copyright © 1970, by Ginn [Xerox Corporation]. Used with permission.)

h. She may *run* across an old friend.
i. He can knock a home *run.*
j. There was a *run* on the bank.
k. She is not the common *run* of persons.

Directions: This is a test to find out if you know the right meanings of the underlined word in each sentence. Look at the groups of words above the sentences. These words tell the meanings of the underlined words. Read the sentences and decide which of the meanings is the best to use for each of the underlined words. Place the letter of that meaning beside the sentence in which the underlined word has that meaning.

1.   a. symbols   b. scratches   c. grades   d. targets   e. buffalo

——— 1.   Paul's boots made <u>marks</u> on the floor.

——— 2.   Eddie's <u>marks</u> in school are always high.

——— 3.   There are question <u>marks</u> after the words.

——— 4.   The men shot their rifles but missed the <u>marks</u> completely.

2.   a. tool   b. row   c. class   d. folder   e. lay away orderly

——— 1.   He kept a <u>file</u> of his best work.

——— 2.   <u>File</u> the pictures so they may be used next year.

——— 3.   Mary used a <u>file</u> to shape her fingernails.

——— 4.   The pupils followed the teacher in single <u>file</u>.

3.   a. most unlikely   b. lowest   c. most recent   d. endure   e. first

——— 1.   This paint will <u>last</u> forever.

——— 2.   John was the <u>last</u> person I expected to win.

——— 3.   Have you read Augusta Stevenson's <u>last</u> book?

——— 4.   He won the <u>last</u> prize.

4.   a. defeat   b. struck   c. throb   d. flee   e. sound

——— 1.   The angry man <u>beat</u> the dog.

——— 2.   His heart <u>beat</u> is regular and normal.

——— 3.   The <u>beat</u> of the drum could be heard in the distance.

——— 4.   Do you think their team will <u>beat</u> our team?

5.   a. class   b. room   c. mark   d. hill   e. level

——— 1.   The car went up a steep <u>grade</u>.

——— 2.   What <u>grade</u> are you in this year?

——— 3.   I will <u>grade</u> your paper now.

——— 4.   The workmen will need to <u>grade</u> the road after this rain.

Figure 14.3. Sampling of items used in a multiple meanings test. (From Clara Jett Cox, "An Experiment in the Teaching of Certain Facets of the English Language to Navajo Pupils in the Sixth Grade." Unpublished paper, University of New Mexico, 1963.)

4. Testing multiple meanings of common words. Most children for whom English is a foreign language have difficulty with multiple meanings of the same word. Figure 14.3 presents sample items from tests that measure understanding of multiple meanings. See also figures 14.7 and 14.8.
5. Lack of adequate word meanings for words heard. Children often misunderstand words completely when they attempt to use them orally in sentences.[55]

a.	*blot*	Where blood comes. (*clot*)
b.	*spool*	A place where there is water. (*pool*)
c.	*habit*	We habit be quiet. (*had better*)
d.	*rack*	When we go fast we rack the car. (*wreck*)
e.	*won*	The Indians have a wigwon. (*wigwam*)
f.	*tasks*	They cut the tasks of the elephant. (*tusks*)
g.	*bushel*	The name of a big bush.
h.	*climate*	The natives climate the trees to get coconuts. (*climbed up*)
i.	*oyster*	A kind of bird in the zoo. (*ostrich*)

6. Understanding simple analogies. Some simple analogies readily understood by Anglo fourth graders may give much difficulty to all those for whom English is a second language.
   a. Water is to drink as bread is to *eat*.
   b. Cowboy is to horse as pilot is to *plane*.
   c. Tree is to trunk as flower is to *stem*.

Figure 14.4 is an exercise from a student's workbook teaching analogous relationships.

7. Understanding antonyms.
8. Understanding figurative language.
   The simile expresses a comparison between two persons or things. It uses *like* or *as* to make the comparison. For people for whom English is the vernacular, these comparisons become everyday expressions through usage. For the children learning English as a second language, however, such expressions need to be specifically taught. "Brave as a lion," "cross as a bear," "sharp as a tack," or "clean as a whistle" are common expressions.
   Other examples include:
   a. The bad old shoemaker was *as sly as a fox.*
   b. A fox hid behind a log and kept *as still as a mouse.*
   c. The dog scampered off *as quick as a wink.*
   d. In her new dress, Judy looked *as pretty as a picture.*
   e. The cook's roast lamb was *tough as shoe leather.*

Figure 14.5 is a lesson to develop awareness of metaphors.

VOCABULARY ACTIVITY

Specific Objective

Word associations: Understanding analogous relationships

To help pupils see relationships between pairs of words, distribute the following exercise:

Part I

Directions: Read the example below.

A <u>bird</u> builds a <u>nest</u>, but a <u>man</u> builds a <u>house</u>.

A <u>bird sings</u>, but a <u>dog</u> _____ .

Did you think <u>barks</u> would fit in the blank? Finish the other sentences below in the same way.

1. In the <u>mountains</u> there are <u>passes</u>, but in <u>cities</u> there are <u>streets</u>.
2. A <u>waterfall</u> drops <u>water</u>, but a <u>landslide</u> drops <u>soil</u>.
3. When you <u>clamber</u> you go <u>up</u>, but when you <u>descend</u> you go <u>down</u>.
4. The <u>torches</u> light the <u>cave</u>, but <u>lightning</u> lights the <u>sky</u>.
5. A <u>mammoth</u> had <u>tusks</u>, but a <u>deer</u> has <u>antlers</u>.
6. In <u>summer</u> the stream is a <u>trickle</u>, but in <u>spring</u> it is a <u>torrent</u>.
7. <u>Lances pierce</u>, but <u>fire burns</u>.
8. <u>Running water</u> can dig a <u>gully</u>, but a <u>falling boulder</u> can dig a <u>pit</u>.

Part II

Directions: Another way of saying the example in Part I is like this:

<u>Bird</u> is to <u>nest</u> as <u>man</u> is to <u>house</u>.

<u>Sing</u> is to <u>bird</u> as <u>bark</u> is to _____ .

Did you think <u>dog</u> would fit in the blank? Finish the other sentences below in the same way.

1. <u>Streets</u> are to <u>cities</u> as <u>passes</u> are to <u>mountains</u>.
2. <u>Antlers</u> are to a <u>deer</u> as <u>tusks</u> are to <u>mammoth</u>.
3. <u>Burn</u> is to <u>fire</u> as <u>pierce</u> is to <u>lance</u>.
4. <u>Soil</u> is to <u>landslide</u> as <u>water</u> is to <u>waterfall</u>.

NOTE: Allow reasonable substitutions. For example, since many animals have tusks, the answer to number two above need not be <u>mammoth</u>.

Figure 14.4. Understanding analogous relationships (level 11, p. 287). (From *Teachers' Edition, The Sun That Warms,* by Theodore Clymer and Constance M. McCullough, of the *Reading 360* series. Copyright © 1970, by Ginn [Xerox Corporation]. Used with permission.)

LITERATURE ACTIVITY

Specific Objective

Writer's craft: Developing awareness of the use of metaphoric expressions

To reinforce the pupils' awareness of metaphoric expressions, ask them how an author makes comparisons without the use of words such as <u>like</u> or <u>as</u>. Lead the pupils to recall that such comparisons are called <u>metaphors</u>. Have them give examples, such as "the waves ran trembling into one another's arms."

Then distribute the following exercise for independent work:

Part I

Directions: Look at the underlined words. Use your imagination to think of an object the underlined words suggest to you. Write the answer in the blank following each sentence. The first one is done for you.

1. great <u>tongues</u> of ice _____ a giant anteater _____
2. driven by <u>howling</u> winds _____
3. winds <u>sweeping</u> across it _____
4. ice would <u>swallow</u> the land _____
5. had <u>carved out</u> valleys _____
6. ice <u>crept</u> forward _____
7. the <u>flow</u> of ice _____
8. <u>ground up</u> rock _____
9. <u>dug</u> great hollows _____
10. <u>scooped up</u> dirt _____

Part II

Directions: Write sentences of your own using comparisons the way the author did.

1. Make the ice seem like a monster.

_____

_____

2. Make the ice seem like a tool.

_____

_____

3. Make the ice seem like a machine.

_____

_____

Figure 14.5. Understanding and using metaphoric expressions (level 11, p. 298). (From *Teachers' Edition, The Sun That Warms* by Theodore Clymer and Constance M. McCullough of the *Reading 360* series. Copyright © 1970 by Ginn [Xerox Corporation]. Used with permission.)

9. Compound words.

The following exercise was designed to help children put two words together to build a compound word.[56] The students are to identify the root words in compounds as meaning units by putting together the two italicized words:

Father said, "I can't *work* in any *room* in this house. I need a _____ of my own."

The *bed* was *spread* with a fine old woolen cover. "I'm proud of this _____ ," said Mrs. Page.

The *side* of the *hill* was covered with beautiful purple flowers. They made the whole _____ look blue.

"A *crow* eats my seeds when I'm not around to *scare* it off," said Woody. "I'll make a _____ ."

An exercise from a child's workbook appears in figure 14.6, giving practice in recognizing and using compound words.

Teaching the Facets of English

By providing a special language program designed to improve vocabularies of bilingual and culturally different children in his sixth-grade class, Gallegos showed one year's growth in reading on the California Reading Test between the last week in September and the last week in February of one school year—a period of five months.[57] Of thirty-five children in his class, eighteen were culturally deprived English-speaking children and seventeen were children from Spanish-speaking homes. The mean scores obtained by each group on the vocabulary part, the comprehension part, and the total of the California Reading Test are given in table 14.2.

TABLE 14.2 Class Reading Achievement Scores Earned on the California Reading Test, Form W*

	Mean Scores		Mean Growth
	September 1962	February 1963	
Vocabulary Section			
English-Speaking	5.41	6.85	1.44
Spanish-Speaking	4.95	6.08	1.13
Comprehension Section			
English-Speaking	5.77	6.81	1.04
Spanish-Speaking	4.77	5.44	0.67
Total Test			
English-Speaking	5.68	6.85	1.17
Spanish-Speaking	4.90	5.83	0.93

English-Speaking children: N = 18
Spanish-Speaking children: N = 17

*Robert Gallegos, "A Report of a Language Program Designed to Improve Vocabularies of Bilingual and Culturally Deprived Children" (unpublished paper, University of New Mexico, 1963), p. 22.

2. **Understand language growth and change; use context and structural analysis to identify unfamiliar printed words.** Boys and girls are to read and follow the directions for marking the page.

Many words that have come into the English language are compound words, made when two old words were combined to make a new word. Which one of these compound words is missing in each sentence? Write the word on the blank at the right.

bathrobe	chatterbox	globetrotter	searchlight	toadstool
bulldozer	dragonfly	oatmeal	sportswriter	whitecap

The empty life raft was washed to shore on the bubbling crest of a huge _____.   _____

Mr. Lane was both a _____ for the newspaper and a sports broadcaster for the TV station.   _____

Martha looked down at the _____ and said, "I wonder if this mushroom is poisonous."   _____

The _____ roared up the hillside, pushing a pile of rocks and dirt with its wide steel blade.   _____

Henry was startled when the beam of a _____ flashed in his face.   _____

Miss Davidson was quite a _____, having gone around the world on sightseeing trips many times.   _____

Margaret talked so much that she was known as the _____ of her family.   _____

As Thomas sat down for breakfast, his mother asked, "Would you like a bowl of _____?"   _____

After Mr. Bell was awakened by Red's barking, he put on his _____ and stepped out on the porch.   _____

SET 10, BOOK 5

Figure 14.6. Exercises in recognizing and using compound words (Helen M. Robinson et al. From *Vistas,* Duplicating Masters. Copyright © 1970 by Scott, Foresman. Reprinted by permission of the publisher.)

Making Connections 14.2: Examining Instructional Materials

Some instructional materials are prepared specifically for children who speak another language and are learning English. These are often referred to as ESL (English as a second language) materials. Other materials are prepared in the first language of the children.

Locate a collection of these materials, whether in the public schools or in your university or college library. Select three books or other instructional items that particularly interest you. Examine them carefully, paying attention to the language used, the content, and the illustrations.

After you have studied the materials and evaluated them, bring them and your ideas to share with your class. This activity should allow students to see quite a variety of instructional materials and hear them discussed. Students should become aware of the commercial materials that are available for working with bilingual and ESL children.

Gallegos stated that his procedure for helping his students understand the English language had three facets: (1) using exercises taken from reading workbooks; (2) drawing illustrations to depict meanings of common multiple-meaning words selected from the *Thorndike Barnhart Junior Dictionary*—completed both as individual and committee assignments and shown to the whole class using an opaque projector, with discussion of sentences explaining specific meanings; and (3) using slang, idiomatic expressions, common proverbs, similes, and metaphors in sentences, dramatized, pantomimed, or flashed on a motion-picture screen through the use of an opaque projector, for discussion, correction, or amplification.[58]

The titles of specific exercises taken from children's workbooks included:

Using Different Meanings; Differentiating Various Meanings of Words; Opposite Meaning Words; Using Related Words; Selecting the Correct Definition; Homonyms; Context Clues; Cause and Effect; Matching Definitions; Word Perception; Selecting Appropriate Meanings; Categorizing Words; Synonyms; Figurative Language; Interpreting Figurative Language; Perceiving Part-Whole Relationships; Comprehending Sentence Meaning; Paraphrasing; Forming Sensory Images; Emotional Reactions; Matching Morals and Fables; Simple Analogies; Connotations; Comparing and Contrasting; Generalizing; Understanding Idioms; and Sensory Impressions.

Reading workbooks available for use were published by Scott, Foresman; Lyons & Carnahan; Macmillan; Houghton Mifflin; and Row Peterson.

The illustrations in figures 14.7 and 14.8 typify the drawing of students in Mr. Gallegos's sixth-grade class.

Lap

Baby sat in mother's <u>lap</u>.

The waves <u>lap</u> against the shore.

The dog will <u>lap</u> up all the milk in the pan.

The track men ran another <u>lap</u> around the track.

Figure 14.7. Multiple meanings for the word *lap*

Figure 14.8. Multiple meanings for the word *light*

Summary

Language and culture create barriers to understanding concepts taught in the school. Teachers are cautioned *not* to confuse language differences or cultural barriers with lack of innate intelligence. Many bright children fail because of lack of facility with English or because of meager backgrounds of experience.

Many types of exercises are available to teachers for developing better understanding of the facets of English—idioms, figures of speech, opposites, synonyms, homonyms, and prepositions. It is recommended that teachers search for specific helps in the commercially prepared workbooks for students and that they develop new materials experimentally and compile varieties of helpful exercises that prove successful.

1. Second-language children need nursery school and kindergarten experience with the English language.
2. Second-language children need to experience interaction in informal play situations with English-speaking children from an early age.
3. The use of the first language should *not* be discouraged. It should be directed.
4. The first reading lessons for second-language children should be experience stories using well-understood, firsthand knowledge from the children's backgrounds.
5. With older children, listening, speaking, reading, and writing may be developed simultaneously, providing the order in the hierarchy is not violated.
6. Teachers should help bilingual children write their *own* books of reading.
    a. Take the suggestion of Sylvia Ashton-Warner in *Teacher*[59] and write for the children the word they *want* to learn.
    b. Use pictures from newspapers and magazines, mount on writing paper, and write simple news stories.
    c. Ask the children to *do* an activity that they can then help write a paragraph to explain. Find topics of interest to the group. Such topics might be:
       (1) How to wrap a package.
       (2) Fire must have oxygen to burn.
       (3) Making tortillas.
       Individual, or small groups, may:
       (1) Draw a series of pictures to tell a story and write simple captions. Make it into a box movie.
       (2) Demonstrate first aid, draw pictures, label.
7. Teachers should study and utilize aspects of linguistic approaches. They can provide oral-aural English pattern practice where it is needed and use the language experience approach to teach reading.

For Further Reading

Bromley, Karen D'Angelo. "Teaching Idioms." *The Reading Teacher* 38 (December 1984), pp. 272–76.

Ching, Doris C. *Reading and the Bilingual Child*. Reading Aids Series. Newark, Delaware: International Reading Association, 1976.

DeStefano, Johanna S. "Learning to Communicate in the Classroom." In Anthony Pellegrini and Thomas Yawkey, eds., *The Development of Oral and Written Language in Social Contexts*. Norwood, N.J.: Ablex Publishing Corporation, 1984, pp. 155–65.

Feeley, Joan T. "Help for the Reading Teacher: Dealing with the Limited English Proficient (LEP) Child in the Elementary Classroom." *The Reading Teacher* 36 (March 1983), p. 650–55.

Hester, Hilary. "Peer Interaction in Learning English as a Second Language." *Theory into Practice* 23 (Summer 1984), pp. 208–17.

Manning, Maryann M. and Manning, Gary L. "Early Readers and Nonreaders from Low Socioeconomic Environments: What Their Parents Report." *The Reading Teacher* 38 (October 1984), pp. 32–34.

Shuy, Roger, ed. *Linguistic Theory: What Can It Say About Reading?* Newark, Del.: International Reading Association, 1977.

Stodolsky, Susan S., and Lesser, Gerald. "Learning Patterns in the Disadvantaged." *Harvard Educational Review*, Reprint Series No. 5, 1975.

Smith, Frank. *Reading without Nonsense*. New York: Teachers College Press, Columbia University, 1979.

Spolsky, Bernard; Engelbrecht, Guillermina; and Ortiz, Leroy. *The Sociolinguistics of Literacy: An Historical and Comparative Study of Five Cases*. A study supported with a grant from the National Institute of Education.

Theory into Practice 20 (Winter 1981). The whole issue is devoted to the study of ten cultural groups in the schools.

Notes

1. Harvey Zorbaugh, Rhea Kay Boardman, and Paul Sheldon, "Some Observations of Highly Gifted Children," in *The Gifted Child*, Paul Witty, ed. (Boston: D. C. Heath, 1951), p. 88.
2. William S. Gray et al., *The New We Look and See* (Atlanta: Scott, Foresman, 1956).
3. "Portrait of America," *Newsweek*, January 17, 1983.
4. Stephen D. Krashen and Tracy D. Terrell, *The Natural Approach: Language Acquisition in the Classroom* (San Francisco: Alemany Press, 1983).
5. Tracy D. Terrell, "A Natural Approach to Second Language Acquisition and Learning," *Modern Language Journal* 61 (November 1977), pp. 325–37.
6. Brian Gray, "Helping Children to Become Language Learners in the Classroom," Brisbane, Australia: Meanjin Reading Council, 1983.
7. James J. Asher, "The Total Physical Response Approach to Second Language Learning," *Modern Language Journal* 53 (January 1969), pp. 3–17.
8. Jim Cummins, "The Entrance and Exit Fallacy in Bilingual Education," *NABE Journal* 4 (Spring 1980), pp. 25–59.
9. Anna Uhl Chamot, "Applications of Second Language Acquisition Research to the Bilingual Classroom," *National Clearing House for Bilingual Education*, no. 8 (September 1981), p. 6.
10. Phillip C. Gonzales, "How to Begin Language Instruction for Non-English Speaking Students," *Language Arts* 58 (February 1981), pp. 175–80.

11. Eustolia Perez, "Oral Language Competence Improves Reading Skills of Mexican American Third Graders," *The Reading Teacher* 35 (October 1981), pp. 24–27.

12. Mavis Martin and Miles V. Zintz, "Concerns about Comprehension of Children with Limited English Proficiency," *The New Mexico Journal of Reading* (Vol. 5, No. 1, Fall, 1984, pp. 6–11.)

13. Don Holdaway, *Foundations of Literacy* (Sidney, Australia: Ashton Scholastic, 1979).

14. Stephen Harris, "Toward a Sociology of Aboriginal Literacy," A plenary address at the Sixth Australian Reading Conference, Canberra, August 1980.

15. Warwick B. Elley and Francis Mangubhai, "The Impact of Reading on Second Language Learning," *Reading Research Quarterly* 19, no. 1, (Fall 1983), pp. 53–67.

16. Ibid., p. 66.

17. Robert J. Havighurst, "Education Among American Indians: Individual and Cultural Aspects," *Annals of the American Academy of Political and Social Science* 311 (May 1958), p. 113.

18. Ruth Strickland, *The Language Arts in the Elementary School* (Boston: D. C. Heath, 1951), p. 3.

19. Edward Sapir, "Language and Environment," *American Anthropologist* 14 (April 1912), p. 242.

20. Robert Lado, *Linguistics across Cultures* (Ann Arbor: University of Michigan Press, 1958), p. v, citing Charles C. Fries.

21. Nancy Ainsworth, "The Cultural Shaping of Oral Discourse," *Theory into Practice* 23 (Spring 1984), p. 135.

22. Terry Tafoya, "Coyote's Eyes: Native Cognitive Styles," *Journal of American Indian Education* 21 (1982), pp. 21–33.

23. Mary C. Cronin, "Cree Children's Knowledge of Story Structure: Some Guidelines for the Classroom," *Canadian Journal of Native Education* 9 (Summer 1982), pp. 12–14.

24. Garth H. Brown, "Children's Sense of Story and Their Reading," *English in Australia* (March 1979), pp. 43–50.

25. Charles C. Fries, *Teaching and Learning English as a Foreign Language* (Ann Arbor: University of Michigan Press, 1952).

26. Ainsworth, "Cultural Shaping," p. 135.

27. William Labov, "Language Characteristics of Specific Groups: Blacks," in Thomas D. Horn, ed., *Reading for the Disadvantaged: Problems of Linguistically Different Learners* (New York: Harcourt, Brace, 1970), p. 139.

28. Ibid., pp. 156–57.

29. William Stewart, "On the Use of Negro Dialect in the Teaching of Reading," Joan Baratz and Roger Shuy, eds., *Teaching Black Children to Read* (New York: Harcourt, Brace, 1970), p. 178.

30. *Ollie* (Experimental Edition), 1970, pp. 5–8, The Black English Version is on the left; the Standard English version is on the right. (The project was supported by funds provided by the National Institute of Mental Health, Project No. MH16078.) Education Study Center, 711 Fourteenth St., N.W., Washington, D.C.

31. Walter A. Wolfram and Ralph W. Fasold, "Toward Reading Materials for Speakers of Black English: Three Linguistically Appropriate Passages," in Joan Baratz and Roger Shuy, eds., *Teaching Black Children to Read* (Washington, D.C.: Center for Applied Linguistics, 1969), pp. 148–49.

32. Linda James Myers, "The Nature of Pluralism and the African American Case," *Theory Into Practice* 20 (Winter 1981), p. 5.

33. Ronald L. Cramer, "Dialectology—A Case for Language Experience," *The Reading Teacher* 25 (October 1971), pp. 33–39.

34. Ibid., pp. 37–38.

35. Kenneth Goodman, "Linguistic Insights Teachers Can Apply," *Education* 88 (May 1968), pp. 313–16.

36. Josephine Piekarz Ives, "Linguistic Principles and Reading Practices in the Elementary School," in J. Allen Figurel, ed., *Reading and Realism* (Newark, Del.: International Reading Association, 1969), pp. 88–93.

37. J. Donald Bowen, "The Structure of Language," in Herman G. Richey, ed., *Linguistics in School Programs,* 69th Yearbook, NSSE (Chicago: University of Chicago Press, 1970), p. 46.

38. William E. Rutherford, "Deep and Surface Structure, and the Language Drill," *TESOL Quarterly* 2 (June 1968), pp. 71–79.

39. Ibid., p. 76.

40. Ben Goldfield, "Semantics: An Aid to Comprehension," *The Journal of Reading* 16 (January 1973), p. 311.

41. Ibid., p. 313.

42. Ibid.

43. Gilliam Brown and George Yule, *Discourse Analysis* (Cambridge: Cambridge University Press, 1983), pp. 1–4.

44. Ibid., p. 27.

45. Ibid., p. 191.

46. Peter Freebody and Richard C. Anderson, "Effects of Vocabulary Difficulty, Text Cohesion, and Schema Availability on Reading Comprehension," *Reading Research Quarterly* 18 (Spring 1983) pp. 280–81.

47. Brown and Yule, *Discourse Analysis,* p. 256.

48. Loyd S. Tireman, "The Bilingual Child and His Reading Vocabulary," *Elementary English* 32 (January 1955), p. 34.

49. Loyd S. Tireman, "School Problems Created by the Homes of Foreign Speaking Children," *California Journal of Elementary Education* 8 (May 1940), pp. 234–38.

50. Ibid., p. 236.

51. Ibid., pp. 236–38.

52. Leona M. Foerster, "Idiomagic," *Elementary English* 51 (January 1974), pp. 125–27.

53. Peter Edwards, "The Effect of Idioms on Children's Reading and Understanding of Prose," in Bonnie Smith Schulwitz, ed., *Teachers, Tangibles, Techniques: Comprehension of Content in Reading* (Newark, Del.: International Reading Association, 1975), pp. 37–46.

54. Ernest Horn, "Language and Meaning," in *The Psychology of Learning,* 41st Yearbook, Part II, NSSE (Chicago: University of Chicago Press, 1942), pp. 298–99.

55. Tireman, "The Bilingual Child," pp. 33–35.

56. William S. Gray et al., *Think and Do Book to Accompany Just Imagine,* Curriculum Foundation Series (Chicago: Scott, Foresman 1954), p. 11.

57. Robert Gallegos, "A Report of a Language Program Designed to Improve Vocabularies of Bilingual and Culturally Deprived Children" (unpublished paper, University of New Mexico, 1963).

58. Ibid., pp. 18–19.

59. Sylvia Ashton-Warner, *Teacher* (New York: Simon and Shuster, 1963).

15
Meeting the Challenge of Severe Reading and Writing Disabilities

Vocabulary

learning disability
neurological impairment
dyslexia
Fernald Kinesthetic Tracing
  Technique
Hegge, Kirk, and Kirk
  "Grapho-Vocal"
  Technique
Gillingham-Stillman
  Remedial Training
Neurological Impress
  Method
repeated readings technique
language experience
hyperactivity
perseveration
perceptual difficulty
operant conditioning
drug therapy
disinhibition
VAK
VAKT

Questions

1. Compare the Fernald; Hegge, Kirk, and Kirk; and Gillingham-Stillman techniques.
2. Describe the techniques that are variants of the neurological impress method.
3. How are the teacher's reading and writing activities related to that of the students?
4. How might hyperactivity, perseveration, and disinhibition be managed in the classroom?
5. What should the teacher know about the use of drugs to manage behavior and support learning?
6. How might a reader's perceptual difficulties be recognized and helped in the classroom?

There are the occasional children that appear in your classroom who look alert, are as vocal as the others, think when you ask for opinions orally, and are warm, creative, imaginative human beings—everything good—until that moment when you ask everyone in the class to read or to write.

School is not particularly well organized to accommodate these youngsters—although the truth is that if we give them their own time schedules about undertaking most of the tasks of the elementary school they will learn to master them.

In an interview about the problem of being a child in our society, Hughes said:

> But do we ask why the children didn't find something intriguing about reading, some time, in some grade? That is the point the public school should be interested in. Why weren't they in a situation, sometime, where someone had a book that they WANTED . . . NEEDED to read . . . the dictionary, the encyclopedia, some resource for something truly meaningful. This just shows us the sterility of the concrete, imposed sequence of skills, the sterility of the experiences we are offering to the children.[1]

Educators must look at not only methods of teaching reading, but also classroom organizational practices that will facilitate learning and minimize feelings of failure and inadequacy.

Michael, a Reluctant Reader

Michael was such a boy when he enrolled in first grade. Fortunately, he was enrolled in an open classroom where many interesting activities went on all the time. There was a skills center, which Michael ignored; a reading center, where he thumbed through pages of books; a games center; a science center where he studied, observed, and asked questions every day about the displays; and a listening center, but Michael was not much interested in that. The teacher had made more space available by having a few tables instead of individual desks; a rug in one corner of the room provided a place where everyone could meet to discuss topics and to plan for the day. There Michael talked well—he talked to all his peers and could explain clearly many things to the adults around him.

Michael's teacher tried to help all the children set their own limits for study; to know what is expected in social behavior and interaction; to be able to perform the skills they accepted as their assignments; and to be sufficiently motivated to want to be successful at whatever they undertook. The teacher knew that discipline used in its negative sense usually means that inadequate planning has been done; bad behavior is caused *by* something and the group could help the teacher decide how to improve on that.

Michael learned that school was a happy, interesting, accepting place, but learned nothing about reading and writing. His experiences were extended so that his vocabulary was growing, his ability to ask questions was improving. His teacher was aware that the skills taught in reading workbooks can, almost all, in some degree, be developed in oral language lessons. For example, students can:

1. Determine the central idea in a discussion as well as they can in a written paragraph.
2. Put ideas in sequential order whether the message is oral or written.
3. Put things in categories; classify, and order by sizes and shapes and colors. These can be done with concrete objects and learning is going on.
4. Detect whether the key idea in simple sentences tells who, where, what, when, or how. These can also be developed orally to some extent.
5. Extend word meanings; choose words that describe more exactly; study word opposites, synonyms, and homonyms.

Michael passed through the second-grade year continuing to feel that he was an important part of his class—extending his interest and curiosity, exercising personal choice, increasing his personal involvement, experiencing some successes other than reading and writing; becoming ever more aware of some of the things he did well, and accepting praise when it was earned.

When Michael came to the third grade, he was beginning to feel the pressures of his peers, his parents, his school principal, and any others who knew that he did not want to face the task of reading. They were becoming alarmed that Michael might never learn to read, which is not surprising. However, the important message here is that he was given two years of positive school attendance without the pressures causing him to devalue his personality, destroy his ego, or make him feel like a failure. By third grade Michael was almost nine years old and he was mature enough to accept the fact that he would have to learn how to overcome the aversion he displayed toward reading— carefully done, it could happen without destroying him.

Michael attempted to write the alphabet when he entered third grade. He wrote all the letters to *T* and they were all in capitals except *i, j, l,* and *r.* The letter *j* was reversed. When asked if he knew any words, he wrote in quite immature manuscript: *no, yes, bed, mom, book, look.*

During that year, he became interested in the *Go-Fish* game and became skilled at winning it. The teacher tried unsuccessfully to get him to dictate stories that could be classified as language-experience stories. Instead, she resorted to sentences, which evolved as little books of three-by-five cards held together by notebook rings. The first was *Michael Can* and included sentences with occasional rebuses. The stories followed this sequence:

Michael Can
Michael can go.
Michael can run and jump
Michael can go to the store.
Michael can go to the store with his mother.
Can Michael see a red car?
Can Michael see a yellow car?

Michael Went

    Michael went to the store.

    Michael went to get some candy.

    Mother said, "Yes, Michael went to get some candy."

    Mother said, "Yes, Michael went to the stupid school."

    (Michael could soon read these stories without help.)

Michael Can

    Look Mother.

    "I can jump up and down," said Michael.

    "Yes, Michael can jump up and down," said mother.

    "Can you look up and down?" said mother.

    "Yes, Mother, I can."

    "I can look up and down."

    "I can jump up and down."

    "I can, I can, I can," said Michael.

Michael Came

    Michael came today.

    Michael came in a yellow car.

    Michael came in the yellow car.

    Mother said, "Michael came with me."

    Michael said, "I came with Mother."

Michael Likes

    Michael likes to chew gum.

    Michael likes to eat candy.

    Michael likes to play.

    Michael likes to play Go-Fish.

    Michael likes television.

    Michael likes to fish.

    Michael likes to go to the store.

Then Michael was asked more directly about reading books and he responded freely. "No! That is a no-no!" However, he was presented with the fairy tales that contain a great deal of repetition, which he had already heard many times. He read all the stories in *I Know a Story* (Harper and Row). All the time, a minimum of writing was required of Michael. He must always put the correct heading on his paper and then write a sentence or two. He was given help with the words so that he would write them correctly. His writing sentences from dictation gradually increased until he was able to do five. Some of his writing practice is included here (figure 15.1).

The next book Michael read from was *Blue Dog and Other Stories* (Lyons and Carnahan). He read other individual stories from other first- and second-grade readers but the teacher often read every other page. Since it was evident that following the lines was difficult, one three-by-five card was used to screen out all lines above the one being read, and another was used to screen out all lines below the one being read. Eventually he advanced to the use of a three-by-five card with a small slot cut out of the middle so that he could move it down the page himself and see only one line at a time (see figure 15.2). His willingness to attempt to read longer passages increased after this.

michael
july 5, 1974

1. I went to see my friend
2. It was the 4th of July.
3. we lit a lot of fire
   works.
4. we played smear the
   queer.
5 David fell down and
   cut his lip.

michael   sept 16, 1974

1. I went on a vacation.
2 We put the toys together
3. the boys sat on the rug.
4. the caw jumped over the
   moon
5. you are my friend.

Figure 15.1. Michael's writing practice

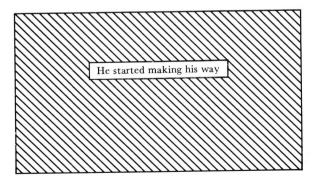

He started making his way

Figure 15.2. The card screens out all but the line being read.

Michael finished the fourth grade. He still found reading done by others fascinating; but he still rejected the idea that he could read what he wanted to learn independently. However, by the end of his fourth-grade year, he was able to read (alternating with his teacher) and with some fluency and complete enjoyment of the story "The Twelve Sillies" in *It Happened One Day,* second grade level (Harper and Row). He had mastered the Dolch Basic Sight Words but did them better in isolation than in a line of print. When he was offered a reward of one dollar for instant recognition of all 220 words, he worked diligently on those in the questionable column for about a week and won his dollar. Knowing the words was not of great importance to him, but he was proud to win in competition with his teacher.

The positive aspects of Michael's program at this point were that he still had a positive image of himself: he knew he could be *all right* even though he rejected reading; he recognized that there are certain school assignments in fourth grade that are just not acceptable to anyone without extensive reading and writing; and he was not overcome with failure or defeated by his lack of this facility. Because of these positive feelings about himself, and the aid he received from helpful teachers, Michael made good growth, albeit a couple of years late. Given the time to overcome his visual, motor, perceptual, neurological, or whatever problems he has, he may be successful in school. If he had encountered negative experiences along the way and developed serious emotional overtones to failure in reading, his remediation might have been more difficult.

Learning Disabilities in Regular and Special Classes

Peggy was a sixteen-year-old who had attended a reading clinic two hours a day for several months. In her developmental skills she had progressed to the reading level where she had learned the rules of syllabication so that she could state them in "figuring out" polysyllabic words. One day her clinician wrote the word *photograph* on the blackboard. Peggy recited:

> There are three separated vowels so there are probably three syllables. *T* goes with the second *o* and *ph* says *f. Gr* stays together and says *grr* and *ph* says *f* at the end. The *o's* are open syllables so they are long. (Pause) *fo-to-graf* (Each syllable pronounced correctly) (Pause) *fo-to-graf.* I don't know what the word is.

Even though she recognized all three of the syllables and pronounced them correctly in isolation, Peggy could not integrate them to produce the word *photograph*. She could not make the association even though the word had appeared in her reading lesson several times the day before and the photographs being read about were some she had taken with her own camera!

Richie, a younger child with severe learning problems, came to a reading clinic at age eight. He had experienced two falls, which doctors said had caused some neurological damage. During Richie's initial evaluation, he was able to write his first name and the first two letters of his last name. He read four Dolch words, *can, is, big,* and *my.* He demonstrated knowledge of all single consonant sounds, but did not appear to be able to use that information to blend words. His attention span was short for writing and reading tasks—two or three minutes at the most.

Richie began a reading program organized around a theme of interest to him—cars. The web that he and his tutor made is shown in figure 15.3. Several activities grew from this web, which was printed on a large sheet of paper for easy reference.

1. Richie and his teacher made a list of the kinds of cars they found in a parking lot near the clinic. From the list they made a picture graph. Then a story was written. The teacher underlined four words for Richie to learn. These were printed on cards that were matched to the words in the story. Richie added these words, *car, pickup, look,* and *I.* These words along with the four words he identified when he was tested formed the beginning of an alphabetized shoe box of words.

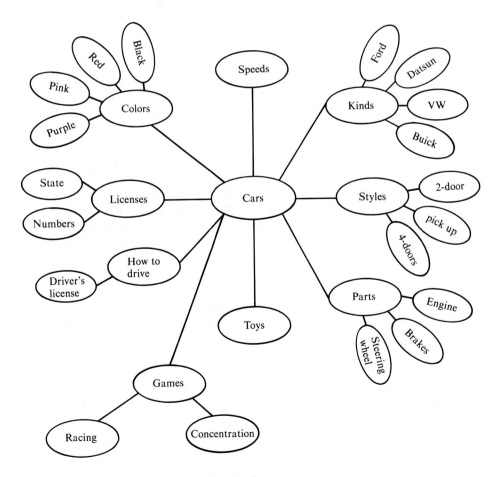

Figure 15.3. Web of ideas related to the theme—cars.

2. Next Richie used a Polaroid camera to photograph several cars he liked in the parking lot. He pasted the pictures in a book he had bound and wrote or dictated brief stories about each. This activity, which lasted over several days, yielded three more words for his shoe box word file.

3. Richie and his tutor took a trip to a nearby car dealership and looked at the new cars on display. They obtained several colorful advertising pamphlets that were read to Richie when they met again. Richie found four words in them he wanted to learn. The tutor found that review of the words he had learned was essential for retention. Part of each session was reserved for rereading stories and working with the word file.

4. Richie wrote a thank you letter to the car dealer. It was one sentence long and required two working sessions. Richie knew few letter forms from memory and reversed any letter that could be reversed. Some of his letters were examples of rotations.

5. The child and his tutor made a concentration-type game of car pictures, pasting matching pairs on 3×5 cards. Richie played this game very well, often beating his tutor. He appeared to have a strong memory for where cards were on the table even though intense practice was required to recall word forms and names consistently.

6. The school year was filled with reading activities similar to the ones described. A variety of topics of interest to the child was selected. When he had about fifty words that he usually recognized, Richie entered a plateau period during which he appeared to have great difficulty adding new words. By the end of the year he had about a hundred words in his reading vocabulary. His writing remained inconsistent from one tutoring session to the next. Occasionally he would write a few reversals, but usually he was generally no longer troubled by letter formation difficulties. His attention span for listening to stories had increased to the point that he would have liked for most of the sessions to have been spent in that way.

One hears more and more today about children who have brain damage or neurological impairment. Teachers must be cautioned that such terms are medical, and they must be very careful not to apply these labels if the pupils' problems have not been diagnosed medically. Also, since it is difficult for parents to accept such a diagnosis when it really exists, the teacher will only create undue anxiety if such terms are applied to specific pupils without medical diagnosis. Nevertheless, if some children have failed to make progress after the teacher has tried a variety of teaching methods, the parents should then be urged to seek medical help.

Many precedents have already been established in this regard. Hypothyroidism and hyperthyroidism have long been treated; their relationship to reading has been reported in the literature, as, for example, by Smith and Carrigan:

> To follow up the possibility of glandular involvement in severe reading disability, a group of young women who exhibited retardation in reading—all freshmen members of a nursing curriculum in a junior college—were given metabolism tests. Among the fifteen tested, the median basal metabolic rate was -19 and, with the exception of one which was $+12$, scores ranged from -6 to -35[2].

The reader is referred also to the case of Betty (see chapter 2).

Learning disability affects boys rather than girls approximately 4:1. The disability is evidenced more often in symbolic written language than in numerical symbolization, as indicated by the frequently higher level of performance in computational areas of arithmetic. Science, too, can be presented graphically rather than verbally and is often a stronger subject for dyslexics than are history and the language arts. Some authorities believe that perception is intact for individual letters but becomes faulty in the Gestalt of words (word wholes). Some believe the symbolic abilities are impaired so that while the child with specific learning disability may have conceptual strengths, he cannot come up with proper symbolic designations (height for tallness; summer for hot weather). Rabinovitch and Ingram[3] interpret this problem of translating perceptions into symbols as conceptual deficiency in orientation. On the other hand, perception may be distorted in certain ways so that faulty concepts arise from faulty percepts. Nevertheless, the children with specific learning disabilities have difficulty with the printed page, whether they read it (receptive) or whether they must perform it in writing (expressive). It is most noticeable in inferior handwriting, with irregularly shaped and poorly spaced characters (see example under the heading "Accommodation in the Classroom" later in this chapter), and in spelling, in which the errors are erratic and bizarre, with frequent reversals of letter shapes and letter order.

The distractible, hyperactive students require a neutral environment, devoid of unnecessary stimuli of sight and sound. If their seats can be placed in the front of the room, a bit separated from others, and/or comfortably confined by a three-panel screen or carrel, they may be able to function more efficiently. There should be no pictures or displays in this corner of the room, to distract their attention. The teachers should avoid such clothing accessories as jingling jewelry or cluttery ornaments. Noise level should be reduced as much as possible. The teachers need to structure their lessons very carefully. They should give short, precise directions, refrain from allowing alternative choices, and speak in well-modulated voices, without overtones of anxiety.

Every new process should be broken down into previously learned components, adding only one new element to be associated with those that are familiar. In other words, learning is a step-by-step process, each new insight building on previously achieved concepts. Memory is not an indication of insight. Insight must be achieved first; then overlearning is desirable until the response by the students becomes automatic. Some children with dyslexia have an amazing rote or "inventory" memory that deceives teachers and parents about their capabilities. But this memory must never be substituted for insight, because the learner cannot make use of what he or she knows without "thinking processes."

Understanding of *numerical* concepts of *more* and *less, bigger* and *smaller,* and so on, can be checked in simple arithmetic problems.

Spatial concepts of *adjacent to, above, under, left* and *right,* can be tested through the directed placement of concrete objects.

Temporal concepts of *before, after, until,* can be observed by having the student follow instructions dependent upon those key words.

Making Connections 15.1: Finding Out about Learning-Disabled Children

Arrange with your instructor to interview a special education teacher of learning-disabled children. When you meet for the conversation, indicate to the teacher you would like to talk about *one* child who has been diagnosed as learning disabled. Take careful notes on the characteristics of the child that the teacher identifies and of the program of instruction that is described.

   After all members of your class have completed their interviews, share the information you have obtained in class. Note the variety of characteristics that teachers identified. Look to see what is common and what is different about their instructional programs.

Working with Learning Disabled Students

Rawson's data demonstrate that dyslexic students, competently diagnosed between the ages of six and twelve, have the *same* chance as do nondyslexic students for success in later educational achievement.[4]

Rawson reported a follow-up study of fifty-six boys with developmental language disability enrolled in the School in Rose Valley, 1930–47. Twenty of these boys were diagnosed as definitely dyslexic.

> A closer look at individual records of the 20 boys adjudged dyslexic in childhood shows two boys who were not college graduates; four who had by 1964–1965 achieved bachelor's degrees only; four who had each added one year of graduate study; one who had a law degree, one a graduate degree in divinity, and three others, already with master's degrees, who were doctoral candidates; five already with doctorates, one of them with two years' post-doctoral study and another with a Ph.D in addition to his M.D. This seems, indeed, an encouragingly good record to have been made by a group of true dyslexics, some of them with severe initial handicaps. Could one conjecture that a disability, when it is not insuperable, may act as a spur to achievement? Some research in motivation and learning points in that direction.[5]

Diagnostic criteria used by Rawson included:

1. The initial failure of the boy to try to read.
2. Ways the boy failed to measure up in language achievement.
3. Persistence of characteristic spelling inadequacies.
4. Many family histories contain reference to other family members with the same or similar symptoms.[6]

Orton defined the problem in 1928:

Our concept of strephosymbolia as a physiological variant rather than a general mental defect naturally gives a decidedly better prognosis, and there is not only good theoretical basis for the belief that the disability can be corrected and the children taught to read, but there is also to be derived from the theory a path of attack for such retraining.[7]

Mrs. Orton reaffirmed the use of her husband's definition in 1966:

Whether or not our theory is right, I do not know, but I do know that the methods of retraining which we have derived from that viewpoint have worked. I do not claim them to be a panacea for reading troubles of all sorts, but I do feel that we understand the blockade which occurs so frequently in children with good minds and which results in the characteristic reading disability of the strephosymbolic type of childhood.[8]

Englebardt reports the difficulty in securing the needed services for children with severe learning problems in school.

Many educators and most parents refuse to recognize the problem. . . . They keep pushing, cajoling, even threatening the youngster, in an attempt to make him pass courses . . . refusing to recognize that maybe he can't do the work.

If the problem is brain damage or emotional disturbance, then special education should be started before the child's self-esteem is completely destroyed.[9]

At the Adams School for Exceptional Children in New York City, Englebardt reports that more than 80 percent of the students who take an academic course go on to college, while 90 percent of those taking occupational courses are able to get and hold productive jobs. These are the youngsters, he says, who would have been classified as "uneducable" ten years ago.

A number of programs planned to help children are available. Fernald,[10] Hegge, Kirk, and Kirk;[11] Ellingson,[12] and de Hirsch, et al.[13] recommend prereading training to develop gross motor skills, eye-hand coordination, laterality, directionality, time-space relationships, and perception of form. Visual perception and discrimination, auditory perception and ability to scrutinize word forms are important prereading activities.

Other programs have been designed to provide exposure to fluent language on a repeated basis. Originally called the Neurological Impress Method,[14] it has been modified and variously labeled.[15]

There has also been an emphasis on exposure to print, on the total development of language, and on the role of the teacher as a language model.

The Fernald Kinesthetic Tracing Technique

This method begins by asking the children what words they would like to learn how to read. Their initial words may build such a sentence as "I live in Albuquerque." They are encouraged to compose their own stories, and the vocabulary is not controlled. They learn to write from memory each word used in their stories. They read their written copies and then within twenty-four hours are presented with a typewritten copy to ensure learning to read print. Either manuscript or cursive writing may be used. The kinesthetic method develops through four stages:

Tracing

The teacher writes the word for the student in large print. The student traces with the middle and index fingers over the teacher's writing *and* pronounces the word in syllables as it is traced, repeating it until he or she can write it without error. The child then attempts to write it in his or her story. If the word is misspelled, the student goes back to tracing. In this stage, finger contact is important, writing from memory to put the word in the story is significant, and the child pronounces the word by syllables as he or she writes it. The teacher writes the words on large uniform strips of paper for filing alphabetically as they are learned. The student then learns alphabetical order through practice from the beginning.

Writing without Tracing

Depending on the individual, after a student has learned about 100 words, he or she looks at the new word, pronounces it in syllables, and writes it from memory without tracing. This is similar to the visual-motor method described by Harris. The child's stock of sight words can be filed alphabetically on three $\times$ five cards.

Recognition in Print

The student becomes able to study the word in print, is told what it says, pronounces it in syllables, and writes it from memory. It is no longer necessary to keep a file of every new word. Book reading can now be introduced. The child knows 150 words and can *begin* to read in a more difficult book than a preprimer.

Word Analysis

Word attack skills are developed through techniques that teach the child to decipher new words through parts of "old" ones and through learning structural analysis skills sequentially.

For the psychoneurologically impaired child learning to read, every device that helps firmly establish a concept or process should be used. These include film strips, tape recorders, tachistoscopes, and slide projectors. All the modalities of learning need to be involved to reinforce new learnings. *Visual, auditory, kinesthetic,* and *tactile (VAKT)* channels should be strengthened. Programmed workbooks are valuable because of their sequential structure and immediate feedback of correct response. New programs that rely minimally on reading can be incorporated into the curriculum, but the reading process should never be discouraged.

The VAKT approach is particularly emphasized in reading. The student sees the word, hears it pronounced, then writes it or traces it as he or she pronounces it slowly. Tactile memory is employed when three-dimensional letters can be traced. These can be made of wood to which sandpaper is applied. Pipecleaner letters are also satisfactory surfaces for tracing.

The Fernald Technique was designed to be used with one learner at a time. Some modifications for working with small groups of children have been proposed, making the technique more practical for teachers.[16] A classroom is known to the authors in which third- to fifth-grade children who had serious reading problems were instructed in how the method would be carried out and how they were to function. The children were then given notebooks for their stories.

Each constructed an alphabetical card file. The teacher provided words on the cards as individuals requested them and typed each child's writing each evening. Time was provided to individuals for reading and rereading their stories and reviewing their card files. Children in the group withdrew from the intensive tracing technique at various times as they felt they could remember the words without that support. The children and their teacher were able to make the method succeed when no more than seven children were working at one time.

The Hegge, Kirk, and Kirk "Grapho-Vocal" Method

This is a method of teaching word recognition in which the students "sound out," pronounce, and write each word. They pronounce words entirely phonetically (synthetically) and later write the words from dictation. As the teacher pronounces words for spelling, the students must sound the parts (analytically). The drills are designed primarily for:

1. Those of primary reader level.
2. Those with whom usual methods of teaching have failed or do not seem to yield results.
3. Those who know the initial consonant sounds or who will be taught these before using the drills.
4. Those needing help in auditory discrimination in word structure.

The drill book is divided into the following four sections:

Section I presents introductory sounds including short vowels, long vowels, double vowels, vowel-consonant teams, and some word endings. The drill is usually presented in these steps:

1. Sound the words letter by letter.
2. Blend the sounds together.
3. Pronounce the words.
4. Write the words as a spelling lesson.

The first of the four parts of Lesson I follows:

s a t	m a t	r a t	b a t	c a t	f a t
c a p	s a p	m a p	t a p	l a p	r a p
a m	r a m	S a m	h a m	d a m	j a m
r a g	b a g	t a g	w a g	h a g	l a g
c a n	m a n	r a n	t a n	f a n	p a n
s a d	m a d	h a d	l a d	p a d	d a d

Section II presents many vowel-consonant combinations of sounds. With some pupils, it may be desirable to discontinue book reading all through Section I of the drills. Book reading at grade two or three level may be started when the pupils are ready for Section II drills. In transferring to story reading, the teacher must pronounce all nonphonetic words for the pupils.

Section III presents advanced sounds including vowel combinations and variants, prefixes and suffixes, and some "family" roots. The manual suggests that when Section III is reached, emphasis should be placed on reading for meaning, evaluation of ideas in print, and developing vocabulary.

Section IV presents supplementary exercises and exceptions to configurations previously taught.

While these drills are designed as a specific reading method for a few pupils with special difficulties, they are often useful with some other students who need extra individual teaching to develop adequate auditory abilities for reading, writing, and spelling.

Gillingham-Stillman Remedial Training for Children with Specific Disabilities

For those students who have a great deal of difficulty in sequencing letters in words, Gillingham and Stillman suggest:

1. When this method is begun, it is to be followed very precisely and no use should be made of reading in any way until after this method is well established.
2. One begins with the names and sounds of the letters and builds words.
3. The learner reads only "phonic" words at first.

Gillingham and Stillman believe that all children would profit from an alphabetic approach; that knowing the names and sounds of the letters facilitates reading and spelling for all children. This method uses visual, tracing, and auditory skills in an integrated fashion. The first task is to teach all the letters.

The first group of letters taught is: *a b h k p i f j m t.*

This makes possible building and teaching the following words:

at	bat	fat	mat	hat	pat
it	bit	fit		hit	pit

am	jam	tam	ham
	map	tap	
	jab		
	hip	tip	
	bib	fib	
	him	Jim	Kim	Tim

The writing procedure follows these five steps:

1. The teacher makes the letter.
2. The student traces the letter.
3. The student copies it.
4. The student writes it without copy.
5. The student writes the word but turns away so he or she cannot see what he is writing.

Gillingham and Stillman describe a four-point process in practicing the writing exercise:

The teacher writes and pronounces the word: for example, *bat*.

The children: 1. Repeat *bat*.
2. Spell "b–a–t."
3. Write the word and spell as they write "b–a–t."
4. Read *bat*.

While learning the letters in Group 1, they read only words and sentences built from the letters taught up to that point. The teacher gradually adds phonemes in this order:

g	o	r	l	n	th (this)
u	ch (chin)	c	e	s	
sh (ship)	d	w	wh	y	
v	z				

Teachers who expect to use the Gillingham-Stillman method would need to study the manual carefully.

The Gillingham-Stillman method was designed to be used with one learner at a time. Therefore, it is suitable for only special learning settings where the focus can be individualized. Slingerland developed a classroom modification of the technique to be used as a preventive or early remedial measure with specific language disability (SLD) or specific developmental dyslexic children in the primary grades. It is a classroom adaptation of the Orton and Gillingham approach to reading, writing, and spelling.[17] The method is supported by extensive testing and detailed teacher's manuals. It continues the visual-auditory-kinesthetic (VAK) methodology of Gillingham-Stillman.

Other Techniques That Have Worked

Ellingson reports an anecdote about a boy who, after deliberate, synthetic teaching, learned all the parts of the word *until*. Yet, he could never recognize the word quickly in print. Ellingson's report follows:

Finally, he said to his teacher, "If I could just *see* an 'until,' I know I could remember it." What was necessary to complete the boy's mastery of the word was an associative method. The boy was instructed to draw, from within himself, his idea of the word—to make a picture to go with a sentence using the word. The boy then carefully drew a picture of a herd of cows, pastureland, a fence with a gate, and a farmhouse in the distance, with the cows going through the gate toward the farmhouse. He then wrote the sentence, "I will wait until the cows come home." For this boy, with this word, "until the cows come home" provided the needed association and visual memory that firmly "set" it in his mind. From then on, whenever he came across the word, no matter how different or complicated the context, he would look at it and say, "Oh, yes, that's until—until the cows come home." This achievement is not inconsequential. The child had used all of his avenues of learning—then added association and was able to read, write, spell, and comprehend the word "until."[18]

If the student is willing, new approaches can be tried, such as one suggested by Harold and Harriett Blau, designed to block the visual channel when learning a new word.[19] The word is pronounced and spelled as it is traced on the pupil's back. The student does not look at the word until he has spelled it (by arranging three-dimensional letters in proper sequence) along with the teacher during the tracing experience. Finally, they look at it, write it on paper or on the blackboard, and then record it on a card to keep in the vocabulary file.

Ravenette, in *Dimensions of Reading Difficulties,* cites the case of a fourteen-year-old boy who was referred to a child guidance center for help with his reading. His reading ability was comparable to that of third graders.

On one occasion . . . he was reading from a book geared to the older backward reader and was confronted with the following sentence: "Tugboat Annie was liked by all the people in the docks." He got as far as the word *was* and then stopped with a puzzled look. The sentence was rewritten, "All the people in the docks liked Tugboat Annie," and this was read unhesitatingly. He was asked about the difficulty and his reply was to the effect that the word "liked" in the original sentence did not seem to make sense, so he did not go on. Using the idea of different linguistic codes, we can say that the sentence in its first form was using elaborate language, expressing an idea using the passive mood. The idea presented in the second form used the active mood, a form which is more common in the restricted code.[20]

For this boy, the linguistic form and therefore the thought it communicated was unusual, and inhibited his ability to read this specific sentence with meaning. Ravenette discusses this example in relation to the sociological and family dimension of poor readers who come from homes in low socioeconomic settings, where the family shows little interest in reading, where many mothers have full-time jobs, and where school gets little encouragement. *However,* this problem of children's ability to understand more *elaborate* as well as *restricted* language needs very badly to be explored for children with psychoneurological learning disabilities.

Neurological Impress Method

The neurological impress method (NIM) was designed to increase reading efficiency, fluency, and comprehension by having the child and the teacher read pages simultaneously. As many pages as possible were to be read so that the child would gain a sense of what fluent discourse should sound like. There are several variations on that method that the reading teacher might wish to study and have available for use. Samuels[21] and Chomsky[22] suggested techniques that are called the *method of repeated readings*. The child reads and rereads short passages until they can be read fluently in Samuel's technique. Then all the short passages can be read as a single, longer unit. Chomsky has children listen to taped stories until they can be read fluently. Holdaway commented on the debate about whether *memorizing* materials is reading:

> Clearly, the extent to which memory for the text contributes to a "reading" varies widely from individual to individual, from stage to stage, and from time to time. To some extent it is dependent on the number of repetitions, the recency of those repetitions, and the place of that particular "story" in the total range of material for which some recall through familiarity is available . . . it is in the area of confirmation and self-correction that memory for text plays the most essential role in early reading. . . . *The most important aspect of memory for text in early reading is not the exact recall of word items learned by heart but the proper assurance of the reader through his own language system that he is operating successfully.*[23]

Kann found that repeated readings resulted in improved fluency, comprehension, attitudes and motivation of disabled readers.[24] Carbo taped entire books for eight elementary school students who had serious reading problems. The students listened to the books and read when they felt they could be successful. Follow-up lessons with games and activities, excluding phonics, were provided for each child.[25]

Other labels for similar methods include "assisted reading,"[26] "echo reading" and impress. The variations among all these methods are in their details, since they are all based on immersion of the reader in fluent discourse. Many researchers and practitioners working with these techniques have shown good results. What seems to be lacking is a neurological explanation of why the methods work.

Language-Based Techniques

Much has been written about reading to children, immersing them in the sound of language and familiarizing them with the literary nature of print as opposed to the informal characteristics of speech.[27] Butler reported a dramatic immersion program in *Cushla and Her Books* that helped transform a severely handicapped child into one performing better than her peers.[28]

Reading is one facet of a total language development, having intimate connections to listening, speaking, and writing with overall umbrellas of experiences and thinking.

Allen provided an extensive guide for carrying out such a unified, or language experience, program.[29] Dionisio described a program for sixth graders in which they wrote, conferenced about their writing, and read not only what they had already written but also materials that provided more opportunities for writing. Eight guidelines were provided for implementing such a program:

1. Develop your own personal background.
2. Assess the students' perceptions of writing.
3. Explore possible topics, audiences, and purposes for writing.
4. Model writing behaviors (for teacher).
5. Choose the first topic.
6. Circulate and respond to the content.
7. Provide materials—books, writing references, writing materials.
8. Adhere to cautions, realizing that writing takes time; writing is controlled by the writer; and technical editing comes after content is developed.[30]

Holt and Vacca remind teachers:

Children learning the written form of language ought to be producing it as well as reading it. They should be reading *and* writing. They should be aware of someone reading their writing, and that what they are reading is someone's writing.[31]

The adult is a powerful model for children. If we want children to read and write, we need to be seen doing those language activities also. If some reading problems that eventually become serious are initially attitudinal and motivational, then teachers and parents need to be faithful to their own reading and writing. It might be worth noting that few youths in our society have to be persuaded to learn to drive cars; the power of the adult model is clearly demonstrated!

A young teacher provided that kind of powerful model for her students when she wrote:[32]

BRUTALITY

Words swim inside
My ink pen,
Happily perfecting
Their backstroke,
Wading through the
Sweet blue-black
And floating contentedly
On their little backs.
But I
(My mind having grown restless)
Selfishly
Pluck out the plug

And watch the bewildered little
Creatures
Be sucked onto
The vast, blank page
Where they
Dry and crystallize
Unable to voice
Their tiny cries
Of protest.

by Opal A. Evans

Besides the model that she provided for taking risks with writing, the author provided some exciting uses of metaphorical language.

One has only to study the titles of articles appearing in various professional publications for teachers to note the emphasis on teacher modeling of reading and writing for children with varied abilities.[33] These models are especially powerful for children with reading problems, for the models can replace much of the nagging that many of these children must endure, provided the children find ways in which they can identify with the teacher.

Techniques to Explore with Younger Reluctant Readers

1. Letters can be cut out of relatively fine sandpaper so that children who have difficulty remembering size, shape, or form of letters can trace them with their fingers—preferably when they are spelling words (see figure 15.4):

Figure 15.4. Sandpaper letter samples

2. Shadow reading is described by Frostig as that situation in which the teacher and child both read aloud. When the child is getting along quite well, the teacher lowers his or her voice so that the child carries the responsibility; when the child does not know the words, the teacher goes on reading, and they get through difficult sections until the child can again read successfully.[34] This is sometimes identified as the "impress method."[35]

3. Auto mechanics, practical arts, and shop classes can be motivation for learning to read. This, of course, involves carpentry, plumbing, and other manual skills. Motivation to read better is likely to be sharpened when students realize the need to read manuals, specifications, directions, and plans. Here the names of tools, how

they are used, for what purposes, how they are maintained in good condition—all of this—is clearly important to the future skilled worker or "man of the house."[36]

The teachers should remember that many of the words used in industrial arts are used in other contexts also, and this understanding can serve as reinforcement to the slow learners; as an example, the word *chisel* is a tool but also is a word used to denote swindling or cheating. There is a relationship, too, between the learning of symbols on drawings, blueprints, and diagrams, and the use of and need for both the understanding of mathematical symbols and of reading maps and charts.[37] For seriously retarded readers, the following is suggested:

An excellent kind of beginning reading material is the description of a process that they have already learned. They can dictate the directions, the teacher writes what they say, has it typed, and returns it to them as part of a shop manual for them to read and study. Being thoroughly familiar with the subject and having expressed it in their own vocabulary and sentence structure, they can read it more easily than the printed material for their grade.[38]

4. Beyond providing the younger children with markers with just one line exposed at a time, teachers may find, though very rarely, older students who in addition to these markers, will adjust to the task easier if the lines are shortened into meaningful phrases. This process makes *short lines,* which is one of its objectives but it also divides the print into *meaningful phrases*—separated on different lines. The following paragraph is taken from *The Mystery of Morgan Castle:*

The man took Gabby
into the basement
of Morgan Castle.
The other two men
were watching them
when they came in.
Gabby saw
Miss Wellington and Bill
on the other side
of the room.
They seemed
to be all right.[39]

5. Associating vowel sounds and letters—as the letter affects the meaning of a word— can be a worthwhile fun game for children in interest centers:

What do you cook in, a *pat* or a *pot?*
What do you sleep on, a *cot* or a *cut?*
Do you ride in a *track* or a *truck?*
Do you put the food in a *dish* or a *dash?*
Do you run a *rice* or a *race?*
Do you bake in an *oven* or an *even?*

Do you write on *piper* or on *paper*?
Do you eat with a *spoon* or a *spin*?
Which can you sleep on, a *cut* or a *cot*?
Which do you eat for breakfast: *ham* or *hum*?
What do you wear on your head, a *hat* or a *hot*?
Do you drink *tea* or *tie*?
Do you sew with a *noodle* or a *needle*?
Do you wear *sacks* or *socks*?
Do you *sing* or *song*?
Can you cook with a *stove* or a *stave*?
Do you put milk in a *glass* or a *gloss*?
Do you *wish* your hands or *wash* your hands?
Which can you write with, a *pin* or a *pen*?
Do you pay the *bill* or the *bell*?
Do you drink *cake* or *coke*?
Do you hear the cow *bowl* or *bawl*?
Do you eat a *bun* or a *bin*?
Do you put *jolly* or *jelly* on your bread?
Can you hear the *dog* or the *dug* barking?
Do you bring water from the *well* or the *wall*?
Is the apple *red* or *rod*?
Did you slip in the *mud* or the *mad*?

This is good practice done *orally* for those needing to improve auditory discriminating ability. For children hearing different dialects of English, different problems arise in hearing vowel sounds. Later, word-recognition exercises can be designed to discriminate the words in print (see figure 15.5):

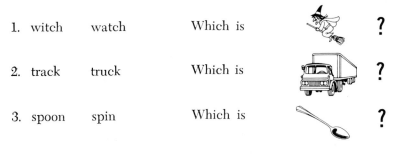

1. witch   watch   Which is

2. track   truck   Which is

3. spoon   spin   Which is

Figure 15.5. Word-recognition exercises

Needs of Older Students

Teenagers who read three or more grades below their grade level need two ingredients in their reading program. They require *practice* with oral and silent reading, and they must experience *success.*

The goals of the secondary reading program are comprehension and independence. These goals are achieved by developing familiarity with our written language. Following are some exercises that have been found to be effective in teaching teenagers who are deficient in skills:

1. Practice: silent reading in materials at individual's independent reading levels.
2. Practice: oral reading in materials at individual's instructional level on a one-to-one basis with the teacher (or another adult).
3. Cloze procedure exercises using short passages at the independent and instructional levels to develop skills in predicting and anticipating.
4. Multiple meanings exercises compiled from various sources to increase vocabulary flexibility (see figures 14.7 and 14.8).
5. Writing articles for the school newspaper where the main idea is summarized in the title and stated in the first sentence of the paragraph.
6. Writing *telegrams:* take a message and reduce it to very basic information.
7. Elaboration: Take a telegraph message and elaborate, using as many descriptive words as you can think of. This can also be nonsensical, but whether it is sense or nonsense, it can be fun.
8. Newspaper and magazine ads. Read them, find the fact and the opinion. Evaluate the propaganda involved. Then write and design your own ads.
9. Reading to follow directions:
   a. Read the auto driver's manual for passing the test to get a driver's license.
   b. Write down the directions for making a macramé purse (or some other project of interest) and then teach this to another student.
10. Commercial games for relaxation—and familiarity with written words:
    a. Spill and Spell.
    b. Dolch Group Word Game (Bingo).
    c. Scrabble.
    d. Word wheels: one smaller circle superimposed on a larger one and fastened with a brad creates word wheels to practice substitutions with initial consonants, blends, prefixes, and suffixes (see figure 15.6).
11. Learning to fill out job applications, driver's license forms, resumes, and other real world writing requirements.
12. Using computer software, including tutorials, simulations, and word processors.
13. Read a story aloud to a small group of teenagers. Of course, the stories have to be carefully chosen; for example, "The Lady or the Tiger." Students may make inferences and draw conclusions in writing or orally.

The remainder of the suggestions never replace numbers one and two. One-to-one instruction is essential. During this time phonics instruction, word analysis, and use of

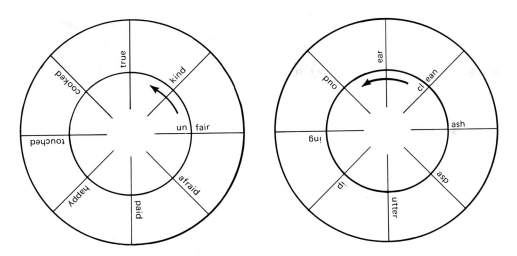

Figure 15.6. Word wheels

context clues are taught as each need arises. Phonics instruction is not very effective if it is isolated or continued over a very long period of time. If these kinds of exercises can be continued and teenagers do experience success, they really can *learn how to learn* and that is what the teacher's job is all about.

Unusual Behaviors That Distress Teachers

The occasional students who (1) distract easily, (2) are hyperactive all day long, (3) are continually interrupting the class, talking about irrelevant topics, or (4) perseverate, are sure to create many difficult classroom situations for their teachers. Professional help, through the services of the school psychologist, is necessary for many of these children. The following suggestions may help the teachers adjust to the children until such help is available.[40]

1. The children who distract easily often need alert redirection and a favorable seating location in the classroom. The teacher's objective is to provide a seating arrangement that minimizes distracting stimuli and puts the child in a good working location without complete isolation. The least distraction may result from seating the children in an "up front" corner near the blackboard, in a side corner partially screened by an easel, a movable blackboard, or a bookcase, or near a shy, quiet child. Greatest distractions come beside the teacher's desk, near the door, or near an obstreperous peer (see figure 15.7).

   The teacher may retain a calm atmosphere in the room by (1) having materials ready on time so the children do not have undirected waiting periods, (2) establishing routines so that the children know what to do next and make these

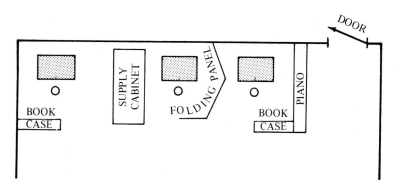

Figure 15.7. Use of carrels in a classroom

transitions with a minimum of interruption, and (3) lending a child support, perhaps by standing in close proximity, putting a hand gently on his or her shoulder, or by speaking quietly after such difficult transitions as seeing a movie or returning from a strenuous game at recess. The teacher's presence may have a quieting effect on overstimulation.

2. The children who are hyperactive need sympathetic understanding rather than censure and punishment. If they *feel* that they cannot sit still, it will not help much to make them do so; if they are constantly playing with a toy, pencil, ruler, eraser, or knife, they may be able to concentrate better on what the teacher is saying with something in their hands than if it is taken away; if ten minutes is as long as they can sit still, they should be permitted a "change" at the end of that time.

The teacher can try (1) giving the hyperactive pupils tasks of short duration, (2) giving them tasks that they are *sure* to do successfully, (3) keeping their frustrations at a minimum by being sure that directions are understood, the work is not too difficult, and the environment has a minimum of distractions.

3. The disinhibited child—the child who interrupts the whole class with irrelevant information—cannot be permitted to continue to talk and, as rapidly as possible, must learn to wait until an appropriate time to express his or her thoughts. The child exhibits this behavior when continually interrupting and asking irrelevant questions in the middle of a class discussion. In the middle of a discussion of a directed reading lesson, the child may ask loudly, "What kind of soup will we have for lunch?" Obviously the group cannot change its activity and permit an endless "sharing period" to go on. The teacher can say firmly, "Not right now, John, in just a few minutes." However, this carries a promise that the teacher will give John his opportunity in a few minutes. By then he may have forgotten. It does seem best to encourage him to wait short periods, and then increasingly longer ones, until he can "share" only when the others do. Luxford suggests for older pupils that they be given a little notebook, and when they interrupt, they are told to make a note of what they wanted to say in the notebook. Then at a later time, they may talk from their notes. This practice has a curing effect because the difficulty of

writing is so great that soon the pupils remember not to interrupt, but do not bother to write anything down and continue quietly with their work.

4. The pupils who persist in continuing a response, a line of activity, or other inappropriate repetition are said to perseverate. If the teacher is getting the wrong response repeatedly to a word-recognition exercise, it would be well to change the subject radically enough to force a new pattern of thought. Dubnoff and others state that perseveration is one of the most common distinguishing symptoms of children with neurological impairments. They recommend that the perseveration may be broken by:

Picture cues, that is, matching a word to the picture it represents; or
color cues, that is, recognizing different *colors* of beginning letters.[41]

Johnson and Myklebust illustrate perseveration in an older child:

A twelve-year-old boy when asked to write the alphabet wrote the letters in proper sequence but with three "e's." When asked why he had written them, he replied, "I got started and couldn't stop." This boy often wrote the words "see" or "three" with either three or four "e's" instead of two.[42]

Accommodation in the Classroom

Classroom organization can help to accommodate children with specific learning disabilities:

1. Each classroom should be planned so that furniture could be rearranged so as to make two or three carrels (individual office space) where children could be seated in relatively isolated, quiet, "protected" places to work. In the traditional classroom this is not difficult to do with bookcases, a piano, if there happens to be one in the room, or folding panels. The diagram in figure 15.7 shows how one teacher made three carrels along one side of the classroom.

   In the modular style buildings being built today, it will be necessary to organize "quiet" areas in other ways. But the hyperactive, distractible child needs help in order to concentrate and make progress.

   The carrels are useful for other children, too, and should be available to them, of course. Not only the inattentive children but also the ambitious children who write scholarly reports can profitably work there occasionally. Work that distracts others, reading aloud or telling stories to record them on a tape recorder, or other kinds of language activities that require "office space" or "conference room" space to best carry on the activity can be done in these cloistered areas.

2. Admitting children to the regular classroom for short periods of time each day is an important step in helping them to adjust to staying for longer periods. If a child can conform for half an hour in a large group of children, he or she should be accommodated for that period of time. Normally, the child will want to stay with peers. Normally, too, he or she wants to lengthen the attention span. If this does

not happen, the help of a counselor, psychologist, or resource teacher is needed. Hopefully, the half hour can be extended to an hour, and progressively the child learns to adjust to a full half day in the room. The important point is that if the child is excluded altogether from the classroom, no opportunity to begin making this adjustment gradually is provided.

3. Encourage parents to discuss the use of drug therapy with their family physician for the child who is hyperactive, disinhibited, a constant talker in the classroom, or who in other ways continually interrupts classroom routine. The administration of drugs is strictly a medical problem. There are numbers of both physicians and parents who do not look favorably upon this practice, yet it is the teacher's responsibility to try to accommodate the child in the classroom. For some children the behavior is so marked that after half an hour of a tutoring session, competent clinicians can safely record in their log, "Bruce must not have had his medicine today; his behavior was just like it always is when his mother forgets."

Sally Williams, California School Nurses Association, testifying before the Government Operations Subcommittee of the U.S. House of Representatives on the Right to Private Inquiry on the Use of Various Behavior Modification Drugs on Elementary School Pupils said that:

. . . about two percent of the pupils with normal or above normal intelligence were unable to achieve acceptably in reading, spelling, and mathematics. Parents, teachers, and school nurses agreed that this pupil tended to have these characteristics. "The child was extremely hyperactive, as though he had 'springs inside,' had a very short attention span, could not write his full name, was excessively distractible, and had no impulse control."

Mrs. Williams noted that the literature is filled with documented case studies showing that such pupils, carefully identified by psychological and medical evaluation have been significantly helped by amphetamines and Ritalin.[43]

Carpenter writes:

Learning disabilities vary greatly among students. What helps one child will not necessarily help another, even though the problems are similar. . . .

proper medication can calm the overactive child and cause a dramatic improvement in behavior and learning ability.

But . . . medication can also properly make more alert a listless daydreamer by increasing his attention span and improving his ability to concentrate.

. . . medication can also be used to improve significantly short attention span, poor concentration, distractibility, handwriting and printing, visual perception and fidgetiness.

. . . medication can also reduce tempers, mood swings, hostility, and certain types of headaches, stomach aches and sleep problems.[44]

However, Divoky presents another side to the argument.[45] She states that the widespread habit of grossly labeling children is sure to be more harmful than helpful. Creating misleading expectations is sure to lead to an inadequate prognosis of behavior.

Unfortunately, there is little agreement either in medicine or in education as to the criteria which would be used to identify children with minimal brain dysfunction or learning disabilities. The disabilities presented by these children are extremely heterogeneous and the search for commonality in symptoms, pathology or etiology has, so far, been fruitless. . . . General terms such as minimal brain dysfunction and undefined learning disabilities have no consistent meaning and no value as a basis either for the development or application of effective methods.[46]

Classroom teachers have to make sure that labeling boys and girls as learning disabilities does not become an "easy cop-out" for not teaching these children.

4. Teachers must be constantly alert to specific methodologies that help children overcome whatever specific problem they face presently. Westeen reports that a fourth-grade boy had great difficulty separating his letters in cursive writing. It was hardly readable, as is illustrated in figure 15.8.

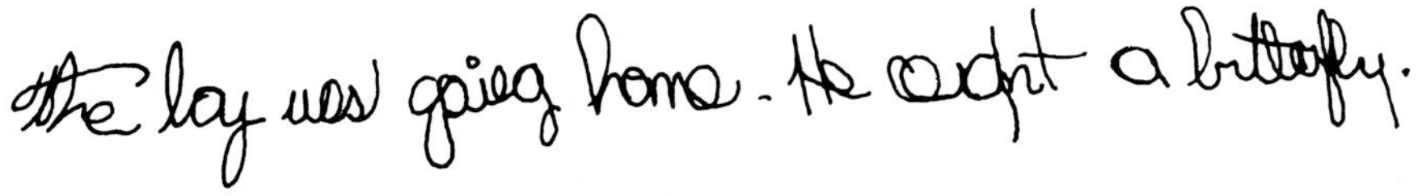

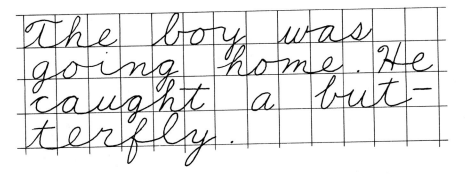

Figure 15.8. Cursive writing before letter separation

One day she gave him paper ruled in one-half inch squares and instructed him that only one letter went into each square (see figure 15.9). She demonstrated carefully and worked with Tom while he started. Amazingly, his first paper written on this lined paper was very well done and, after using the lined paper for a period of time, he separated his letters very satisfactorily in cursive writing.[47]

Figure 15.9. Cursive writing with letter separation

5. *Operant Conditioning*. Bandura reported a remedial reading case treated by operant conditioning. The three elements in operant conditioning in psychotherapy were: (1) reinforcing through the use of tangible rewards, in enjoyable activities, in praise, and in special attention; (2) making reinforcement conditional on achieving desired behavior correctly timed, and behavior that is predictable; and (3) being able later to elicit the desired behavior.[48]

These principles were applied to a fourteen-year-old delinquent boy who, in addition to a history of aggressive, destructive behavior, always received failing school grades and read at second-grade level. He was judged at school to be uneducable, incorrigible, and mentally retarded.

In remedial reading therapy, he received points for each new word mastered; these points could be exchanged for tangible rewards, such as phonograph records, for small sums of money, or for other requests. In four and one-half months, his reading level progressed from second to fourth grade, he received passing grades in all subjects, and his aggressive, destructive behavior stopped. The tangible rewards that helped obtain these desirable results had cost a total of $20.31 for all the items received in exchange for points.

Behavior modification became a very popular technique for discussion in educational circles a decade ago. While it is less discussed as a "new" or unusual methodology for changing behavior today, it is certainly being used by many teachers. Certain modification techniques are more appropriate than others, but many of the expected ends of behavior modification have been in vogue for some time. A few of these are:

a. Praise. Generally speaking, praise is given easily enough by some people, but not nearly often enough. Both children and teachers should be given much more praise than they get. Ignoring people's undesirable behavior and commenting only on the good behavior that one sees pays dividends.

b. Modeling. Children need models to imitate. And they do modify their behaviors to try to conform to the model of someone they respect or might want to emulate. Young children can model behaviors of older children, their teachers, or other adults.

c. Token reinforcement. Technically, this behavior involves the systematic giving of rewards for desired behavior. Tangible rewards with which we are familiar, or social rewards such as earning extra playtime or an opportunity to spend a dinner hour with the teacher, have both worked in appropriate circumstances.

If they are to use behavior modification as a technique of behavior control, then teachers need adequate preparation and discipline in the technique they are using. Under proper circumstances this technique can strengthen students' self-control and expand their skills.[49]

6. *Amplifying Sound*. Johnson, in an article entitled "Treatment Approaches to Dyslexia," discusses the possibility of amplifying the sound for some children that have auditory perceptual problems:

Occasionally, we give children portable, binaural amplifiers to use during brief periods of instruction. When the sound is amplified through the headsets, many can perceive units within words that they cannot detect under ordinary listening conditions. A seventh grade boy improved substantially in spelling when he decided to wear the amplifier while the teacher dictated words in class.[50] Teachers and parents need to keep alert to breakthroughs in technology for improvement of aids for the hearing impaired.

7. *Restating instructions before starting work.* Zedler worked with a group of children diagnosed as neurologically impaired.[51] The teachers tried to improve the auditory comprehension of these children by requiring them to repeat their oral instructions before responding. This helped the teacher to "see whether or not the child understood what was said to him, it reinforced auditory retention and recall, and it provided feedback for constructing a response."

8. *Suggestions for materials preparation.* The children in Miss Zedler's classes made the following evaluations about the books they used.[52]
   (a) Pictures should not be on the pages with the print. Pictures distract.
   (b) Put only one column of print on one page. It is difficult to interrupt left-to-right progression at midpage.
   (c) Avoid pronouns; it is difficult to remember their referents.
   (d) Avoid expressions that have other than their literal meanings.
   (e) Print consistently in lowercase type letters so they will be easier to follow.
   (f) Use simple sentences that are easily decoded.
   (g) Keep punctuation as simple as possible.

9. *Managing diet.* Many studies have been conducted concerning diets, allergies, food additives and "junk foods" for children.[53] The results of the studies frequently offer conflicting advice. Teachers and parents should look at children's responses to foods individually and base their decisions on the actual behaviors of children. Some children do respond better to instruction if sugar intake is limited, if foods with specific additives are eliminated, or if "junk foods" are denied or severely limited. If teachers and parents keep careful records and communicate about what each is doing in experimenting with foods and instruction, the best learning situation for the child will be identified.

Making Connections 15.2: Examining Perceptual Handicaps

For this activity you can use Figure 15.12 in this chapter, or you can select any other picture that contains hidden pictures.

Hunt the hidden pictures with as many children as you can find to work with. Complete the task with each child individually. Keep notes about each child's performance. Plan to share with your class what you learned about the variety of perceptual abilities among children you worked with. Note especially any comments children made and the nonverbal messages they were sending during the task.

Visual Motor Exercises

Perceptual disabilities in reading may be improved by having the students pay attention to letter details. This can be accomplished by supplying missing letters or filling in disconnected letters. Exercises in left to right direction can be devised. Outlining, stenciling, finding hidden pictures, and coloring first letters or difficult letters in heavy crayon are all beneficial activities. Sequencing can be practiced in copying and reproducing from memory.

Exercises in figures 15.10, 15.11, and 15.12 illustrate:

1. Finding the missing parts in pictures.
2. Finding the right "other half" of the picture.
3. Finding many hidden pictures of objects in the large picture.

A "hidden pictures" page (see figure 15.12) appears in each month's issue of *Highlights for Children*. "Hidden pictures" are also available in a handbook entitled *Hidden Pictures and Other Thinking Activities* or as one of the items of *Highlights Learning Pack*. The handbook contains an acetate sheet that the child can place over the "hidden pictures" for marking purposes.

In Conclusion

The text has presented a need for the teacher to understand both the individual student and the procedures for assessing his or her abilities and skill deficiencies, and planning for his or her growth in reading. Understanding the student as a person requires some knowledge of the student's language background and language ability, learning difficulties if they exist, and home and adults who most influence his or her learning. Teachers must be competent to use the informal reading inventory, informal tests of word recognition, and tests of comprehension. They must know where to look beyond the classroom when they need special help. Finally, the teacher must be able to plan the range of skills that students are not using so they will be able to complete the range of school work expected of them. This concluding statement asks the reader to think philosophically about the student and his or her reading.

The brief case studies of Lester and John that follow represent two very different but fairly common types of readers found in regular classes. They need teachers who can respond to them first in affective ways and then program for them the needed cognitive skills.

Lester was referred to the reading center because he made many mistakes in his oral reading, and his writing was so badly spelled that his teacher could not read it. He was eight years old and finishing the second grade. His clever, well-thought-out story (figure 15.13) is fine but his spelling is hardly the expected Standard English spelling! For example: *eche* for *each; siad* for *said; are* for *our; how* for *who; bos* for *does; lost* for *lots; jumt* with the *j* backwards, for *jumped; win* for *when; thow* for

Figure 15.10. What important part is missing?

Figure 15.11. Draw a line from half of the picture in the first column to the half of the picture in the second column.

Hidden Pictures

In this large picture find the scissors, cup, book, turkey's head, banana, butterfly, sea gull, paintbrush, ice-cream cone, sea horse, pencil, apple, fish.

★ Practice in perception for all ages.

Figure 15.12. Hidden pictures (Copyright 1970 Highlights for Children, Inc., Columbus Ohio. The "Hidden Pictures" page appears in each month's issue of *Highlights for Children.* Reprinted by permission. [The bold lines have been added by the author.])

Lester
May 17
once upon a time There Livd
A Frog And A Mouse.
une dAY ThAY ARt.

Ahd ThAY HAd A FiGHT.
eche Siad IM BeTTer.

"The Mouse Siad WiFH
doNT WeA do ARe
BRST AT Thing Ahd Thin
See How bos BesT
Ahd He is The Winnen"

So The Mouse WMT
And The Frog WmT
Ahd LOST oF Thing.

Wir ThAY wer Thow
iT WAS A Tiy.

Figure 15.13. Lester's story

through; and *tiy* for *tie* suggest that he is listening carefully to what he thinks the word sounds like and then is trying to record that. Of course, reversals are giving him problems, too. Hopefully he can have some help with the directional difficulty before he becomes discouraged and loses his creative imagination for writing his own stories.

A translation may help for parts of Lester's story:

> Once upon a time there lived a frog
> and a mouse. One day they met. And
> they had a fight. Each said, "I'm
> better."
> The mouse said, "Why don't we do our
> best at things and then see who does
> best and he is the winner."
> So the mouse jumped and the frog
> jumped and lots of things.
> When they were through, it was
> a tie.

John was in a special seventh-grade language arts class. He had no independent skills in reading and writing. However, as the story in figure 15.14 will make quite clear, he was informed about many of the activities going on in his neighborhood. The story was dictated to a seventh-grade peer who possessed grade-level skills, but the story is entirely John's. Also, he could read it amazingly accurately when he saw it in typewritten form. And he was delighted and motivated to prepare another one when his teacher had copies multilithed for his entire class (figure 15.14). Not only had he "written" a story, but also it was "published."

Numerous writers have conveyed to teachers the need to reflect objectively on their responsibilities in teaching all of the students and accept the range of results in achievement. McCullough asks her readers to take an *eclectic* position in teaching reading

---

A Junkie on the Loose

The junkie was a heroin addict. He had escaped from prison and he did not have any money to buy heroin. He broke into a house and stole a television, stereo, and some money that was hidden. He sold the television and the stereo and got $200.00. He bought $200.00 worth of heroin and it would last him for three days. After three days passed, he broke into a grocery store and stole the money and some food because he was very hungry. He got $12,000.00 from the store. He bought himself a car, and rented an apartment and he bought more heroin. He still had some money left so he went to a concert and he almost got busted. One day, he was driving real fast, the pig stopped him and found some heroin on him. They took him to city hall. Then they found out that he had robbed the store and broke into the house. Then they took him back to prison and he was sentenced for 25 years.

John
2/16
4th period

Figure 15.14. John's story, as dictated

and utilize all the suggestions that they find to be helpful. She seeks a balance of silent reading, oral reading, word recognition practice, and comprehension. Meier writes of four myths that cause some people to expect the impossible of the classroom teachers. These myths themselves defy all that is known about the normal growth and development of children. Individual differences, readiness to master a task, motivation, and the psychological and physical well being of the students in any given classroom have predetermined a wide range in achievement. All members of a given class will not read meaningfully at the *same level;* some are "ready" for the tasks of formal reading long before others; and it is not possible to master the skills of reading in isolation from thinking, problem-solving activities in subject matter fields. Further, Meier reminds us that "the good old days" were not really as good as they seem in retrospect. Vickery offers some excellent suggestions about the conditions under which students will learn best. And finally, Johnson chides us about the apathy we nurture when we are willing to be passive observers in front of the television set.

> Much of the knowledge we now have about the teaching of reading has been developed by a curious and—in terms of the lives of children—wasteful pattern of extremes. We learned a great deal about oral reading by having too much of it, about silent reading by neglecting oral, about extensive reading by neglecting intensive, about sight vocabulary by neglecting phonics, about phonics and speed by neglecting comprehension. We are now involved in a great controversy over the relative virtues of a developmental program with systematic instruction and an individualized program with incidental instruction.
>
> One would think that it should finally have dawned on us that all of these practices have value and that the sensible, most efficient program encompasses them all.[54]

Brighton has said that today's teachers are expected to be all things to all people, at all times, for all reasons, on all occasions that appear to be even remotely related to the school.[55]

Meier explains that the public-at-large generally still accepts four myths about reading instruction in school, and because they believe these myths they do not understand why we need new approaches to school organization to meet all of the needs of all the children.[56]

1. Schools used to teach children how to read in the "good old days."
2. The success of the schools can be measured by their capacity to bring everyone up to "grade level" in reading.
3. The best way to have everyone read at grade level is to start teaching reading as early as possible.
4. Schools should concentrate on nothing but reading skills until they are mastered.

Meier urges teachers to try to dispel these myths and try to demonstrate for parents any new innovations that work in their classrooms. She explains that children have to read about *something.* If they do not *know* about anything, if they do not *care* about anything, if they do not *think* problems through, and if they do not relate knowing, caring, thinking, and *reading,* then what will they ever do with all the discrete little reading skills teachers work so hard to teach.[57]

And Vickery reminds us that:

1. The child learns best in an environment where he is rewarded, his differences accepted, and his humanness respected.
2. The child will learn best if the teacher knows that word recognition is much more than phoneme-grapheme relationships.
3. The child will learn best if the teacher carefully analyzes the prerequisite skills with the child that he needs for that lesson.
4. The child will learn best when the teacher uses language cues in both word recognition and achieving meaning.
5. The child will learn best when the teacher utilizes and develops the auditory-perceptual base for language.
6. The child will learn best when the teacher asks worthwhile questions.
7. The child will learn best when the teacher focuses positively on helping the child to organize and use culturally-appropriate experiences or those experiences common to all human existence.
8. The child will learn best when the teacher does diagnostic teaching.
9. Finally, the child learns best how to read when he reads.[58]

Nicholas Johnson expresses his apprehension about the use of the television media causing the viewer to be mentally unresponsive and to develop vacuous attitudes and behaviors:

Very few of the American people are performing at more than five per cent of their capacity—their capacity to perceive, to produce, to understand, to create, to relate to others, to experience joy. Of all the tragedies confronting an American of the 1970s; this one may well be the most sad. I believe that television—which provides most of the people of this country with their principal source of education, entertainment, information and opinion—bears perhaps more responsibility for this state of the nation than any other single institution.[59]

Summary

The primary task of the corrective reading teacher is the teaching that meaning is the first requisite in the process. The readers must find the sentences and the paragraphs they are reading interesting and meaningful. Any teaching of phonic or structural skills as a word analysis process must be subordinated to a reading experience that is important to the students. Short, motivated phonics lessons can be interesting if they are making worthwhile reading material easier to decode and understand.

Too many students have cracked the symbol-sound code and yet remained reading cripples. Although they read so someone else could understand the message, they themselves fail to understand what they read either orally or silently. For instance, after pronouncing, "The cat sat on a mat," a first grader drew a picture of the cat and the mat widely separated. Certainly the words had meaning for him or he could not have pictured the cat or the mat; but the sentence had no meaning. A fifth grader read a paragraph correctly and answered the question, "What did you read?" with "I don't know." A seventh grader answered the question, "How fast did the boat go?" with "It didn't say," although it plainly did. Obviously, cracking the code had not allowed these children to attach meaning to what they read aloud.[60]

Rather than intensifying remedial effort to develop prescribed reading ability in primary school children who have learning disabilities or demonstrate no interest in learning to read, responding to their interests and extending their intellects in many areas orally may be more productive in the long run. This is not to say that all reading activities will be delayed; but rather that those reading activities needed with all the work the children are doing will be continued and utilized to try to develop a need for and encourage an interest in reading.

Older students must keep meaning as the primary focus of their remedial work. They need to see any special instruction as directed to their interests, present activities, and even future career goals.

The classroom teachers can organize the school day into flexibly arranged blocks of time during which students complete tasks for which they have a purpose and sufficient reading power. The teachers should remember:

1. Start where the student is.
2. Respect the individual.
3. Success may be its own motivation.
4. Specific lessons need to be related to a unified whole so that learning is cumulative, integrated, and purposeful.
5. A few children have special problems and need continued observation and planning.
6. The environment must be restructured for those who have experienced serious disapproval, rejection, or failure.
7. No one method works for all students—what awakens interest in some, or convinces them that they can learn, may not elicit such a response in others.
8. As long as the pupils are enrolled, a search for the best ways to "reach" them must continue.

For Further Reading

Bond, Guy L.; Tinker, Miles A.; Wasson, Barbara B.; and Wasson, John B. *Reading Difficulties: Their Diagnosis and Correction,* 5th ed. Englewood Cliffs, N.J.: Prentice-Hall, 1984: Chapter 12, "Treating the Extremely Disabled Reader," pp. 225–41.

Butler, Dorothy. *Cushla and Her Books.* Boston: The Horn Book, 1979.

Ekwall, Eldon E., and Shanker, James L. *Diagnosis and Remediation of the Disabled Reader,* 2d. ed. Boston: Allyn and Bacon, 1985: Chapter 9, "Diagnosis and Remediation of the Severe Reading Disabilities," pp. 313–41.

Fernald, Grace. *Remedial Techniques in Basic School Subjects.* New York: McGraw-Hill, 1971.

Gillingham, Anna, and Stillman, Bessie W. *Remedial Training for Children with Specific Disability in Reading, Spelling and Penmanship.* Cambridge, Mass.: Educators Publishing Service, 1966.

Harris, Albert, and Sipay, Edward R. *How to Increase Reading Ability,* 7th ed. New York: Longman, 1980: Chapter 11, "Correlates of Reading Disability: Physical and Physiological Factors," pp. 280–307.

Loughlin, Catherine, and Suina, Joseph. *The Learning Environment: An Instructional Strategy.* New York: Teachers College Press, 1982.

Notes

1. Mavis Martin, "A Talk with Marie Hughes," *Insights Into Open Education* 11 (March 1979), p. 8.
2. Donald E. P. Smith and Patricia M. Carrigan, *The Nature of Reading Disability* (New York: Harcourt, Brace, 1959), p. 22.
3. R. D. Rabinovitch and W. Ingram, "Neuropsychiatric Considerations in Reading Retardation," *The Reading Teacher* 15 (May 1962), pp. 433–38.
4. Margaret B. Rawson, *Developmental Language Disability: Adult Accomplishments of Dyslexic Boys* (Baltimore: Johns Hopkins Press, 1968), p. 81.
5. Ibid., p. 76.
6. Ibid.
7. S. T. Orton, "Specific Reading Disability—Strephosymbolia," *Journal of the American Medical Association* 90 (1928), 1095–1099.
8. J. L. Orton, "Word-Blindness in School Children and Other Papers on Strephosymbolia" (Specific Language Disability, Dyslexia), 1925–1946, Monograph no. 2 (Pomfret, Conn.: The Orton Society, 1966).
9. Stanley L. Englebardt, "Disturbed Children: Reaching the Unreachables" *Think* 36 (July/August 1970), pp. 24–26.
10. Grace Fernald, *Remedial Techniques in Basic School Subjects* (New York: McGraw-Hill, 1943, 1971).
11. Thorlief Hegge, Samuel Kirk, and Winifred Kirk, *Remedial Reading Drills* (Ann Arbor, Mich.: George Wahr, 1940).
12. Careth Ellingson, *The Shadow Children: A Book About Children's Disorders* (Chicago: Topaz Books, 1967); *Winter Haven Testing and Training Materials* (Winter Haven, Fla.: Winter Haven Lions Research Foundation, 1963).
13. Katrina de Hirsch et al., *Predicting Reading Failure* (New York: Harper and Row, 1966).
14. R. G. Heckelman, "Using the Neurological Impress Remedial Technique," *Academic Therapy Quarterly* 1 (1966), pp. 235–39.
15. Albert J. Harris and Edward R. Sipay, *How to Increase Reading Ability,* 7th ed. (New York: Longman, 1980), pp. 416–17; Dorothy J. McGinnis and Dorothy E. Smith, *Analyzing and Treating Reading Problems* (New York: Macmillan, 1982), pp. 307–8; Robert Kann, "The

Method of Repeated Readings: Expanding the Neurological Impress Method for Use with Disabled Readers," *Journal of Learning Disabilities* 16 (February 1983), pp. 90–92.

16. Serena Niensted, "A Group Use of the Fernald Technique," *Education Digest* 33 (May 1968), pp. 52–54.

17. Beth H. Slingerland, *A Multi-Sensory Approach to Language Arts for Specific Language Disability Children, A Guide for Primary Teachers* (Cambridge, Mass.: Educators Publishing Service, 1971), p. xv.

18. Ellingson, *The Shadow Children,* pp. 88–90.

19. Harold Blau and Harriett Blau, "A Theory of Learning to Read," *The Reading Teacher* 22 (November 1968), pp. 126–29, 144.

20. A. T. Ravenette, *Dimensions of Reading Difficulties* (Elmsford, New York: Pergamon Press, 1968), pp. 42–43.

21. S. J. Samuels, "The Method of Repeated Readings," *The Reading Teacher* 32 (1979), pp. 403–8.

22. C. Chomsky, "When You Still Can't Read in Third Grade: After Decoding, What?" in S. J. Samuels, ed., *What Research Has to Say About Reading Instruction* (Newark, Del.: International Reading Association, 1978).

23. Don Holdaway, *The Foundations of Literacy* (Sydney, Australia: Ashton, Scholastic, 1979), pp. 126–27.

24. Kann, "Method of Repeated Readings," pp. 90–92.

25. Marie Carbo, "Teaching Reading with Talking Books," *The Reading Teacher* 32 (December 1978), pp. 267–73.

26. Kenneth Hoskisson, "The Many Facets of Assisted Reading," *Elementary English* 52 (March 1975), pp. 312–15.

27. Andee Rubin, "A Theoretical Taxonomy of the Differences between Oral and Written Language," in Rand J. Spiro, Bertram C. Bruce, and Wm. F. Brewer, eds., *Theoretical Issues in Reading Comprehension* (Hillsdale, N.J.: Lawrence Erlbaum Associates, 1980), pp. 411–38.

28. Dorothy Butler, *Cushla and Her Books* (Boston: The Horn Book, 1979).

29. Roach Van Allen, *Language Experiences in Communication* (Boston: Houghton Mifflin, 1976).

30. Marie Dionisio, "Write? Isn't This Reading Class?" *The Reading Teacher* 36 (April 1983), p. 749.

31. Suzanne L. Holt and JoAnne L. Vacca, "Reading with a Sense of Writer: Writing with a Sense of Reader," *Language Arts* 58 (November/December 1981), p. 939.

32. O. A. Evans, prepared December 1984 as part of a student teaching assignment, University of New Mexico, Albuquerque, N. Mex.

33. Dianne W. Hampton, "Hey, Teacher, What Did You Write!" *Language Arts* 60 (March 1983), pp. 341–43; Kathleen Matthews, "Are You Willing to Be the Kind of Writer You Want Your Students to Be," *Learning* 12 (April/May 1984), pp. 42–45; Nina Middelsen, "Teacher as Partner in the Writing Process," *Language Arts* 61 (November 1984), pp. 704–11.

34. Marianne Frostig, *Selection and Adaptation of Reading Methods* (San Rafael, Calif.: Academic Therapy Publications, 1973), p. 69.

35. Kenneth Langford, Kenneth Slade, and Allyson Barnett, "An Examination of Impress Techniques in Remedial Reading," *Academic Therapy* 9 (Spring 1974), pp. 309–19.

36. Ruth Strang and Donald Lindquist, *The Administrator and the Improvement of Reading* (New York: Appleton-Century Crofts, 1960), p. 81.

37. Ibid.

38. Ibid., pp. 81–82.

39. John Rambeau and Nancy Rambeau, *The Mystery of Morgan Castle* (San Francisco: Field Education Publications, 1962), p. 54.

40. Jane Luxford, *Behavioral Changes in Children with Learning Disabilities Resulting from Specific Suggestions for Restructuring the Child's Environment* (unpublished Doctoral Dissertation, The University of New Mexico, 1965), pp. 35–43.

41. Belle Dubnoff, George Fargo, and Donald Weiss, "Aspects of Perceptual Training with Brain Injured and Emotionally Disturbed Children as Related to Reading," in *Twenty-Fifth Yearbook*, Claremont College Reading Conference, 1961 (Claremont, Calif.: Claremont University College, 1961).

42. Doris J. Johnson and Helmer R. Myklebust, *Learning Disabilities* (New York: Grune and Stratton, 1967), p. 302.

43. "School Nurses Back Medicine for Pupil Control," *The NEA Reporter* 9, no. 8 (October 23, 1970).

44. Robert D. Carpenter, M.D., *Why Can't I Learn?* (Glendale, Calif.: Regal Books Division, G/L Publications, 1972), p. 2 of the author's preface.

45. Diane Divoky, "Education's Latest Victim: the LD Kid," *Learning* 3 (October 1974), pp. 20–25.

46. Ibid., p. 25.

47. Miriam Westeen, fourth-grade teacher, Gallup-McKinley County Public Schools, Gallup, New Mexico, 1970.

48. Albert Bandura, "Behavior Psychotherapy," *Scientific American* 216 (March 1967), p. 81, reporting on a study by A. W. Staats and W. Butterfield, "Treatment of Non-Reading in a Culturally Deprived Juvenile Delinquent: An Application of Reinforcement Principles," *Child Development* 36 (1963), pp. 925–42.

49. Bertram S. Brown, MD, "Behavior Modification: What It Is and Isn't," *Today's Education* 65 (January/February 1976), pp. 67–69.

50. Doris J. Johnson, "Treatment Approaches to Dyslexia," in *Reading Disability and Perception*, George D. Spache, ed. (Newark, Del.: International Reading Association, 1969), p. 100.

51. Empress Y. Zedler, "Management of Reading in the Educational Program of Pupils with Neurologically Based Learning Problems," George D. Spache, ed., *Reading Disability and Perception* (Newark, Del.: International Reading Association, 1969), p. 106.

52. Ibid.

53. Jeffrey A. Mattes, "The Feingold Diet: A Current Reappraisal," *Journal of Learning Disabilities* 16 (June/July 1983), pp. 319–23; D. J. Rapp, "Does Diet Affect Hyperactivity?" *Journal of Learning Disabilities* 11 (1978), pp. 56–62; F. J. Stare, E. M. Whalen, and M. Sheridon, "Diet and Hyperactivity: Is There a Relationship?" *Pediatrics* 66 (1980), pp. 521–25.

54. Constance M. McCullough, "Individualized Reading," *NEA Journal* 47 (March 1958), p. 163.

55. Howard Brighton, *Utilizing Teacher Aides in Differentiated Staffing* (Midland, Mich.: Pendleton Publishing Co., 1972), p. 17.

56. Deborah M. Meier, "Poor Readers—I: Children with Problems," *Today's Education* 63 (October 1974), pp. 32–36.

57. Ibid., p. 36.

58. Verna Vickery, "A Note of Encouragement: Can We Teach Reading?" *New Mexico School Review* 50, no. 4 (Fall 1974), p. 43.

59. *How to Talk Back to Your Television Set* (New York: Bantam Books, 1970), p. 7.

60. Serena Niensted, "Meaninglessness for Beginning Readers," *The Reading Teacher* 23 (November 1969), p. 112.

APPENDIX A

Books for Teachers
of Corrective Reading

Allen, Roach Van. *Language Experiences in Communication.* Boston: Houghton Mifflin, 1976.

Bond, Guy L.; Tinker, Miles A.; Wasson, Barbara; and Wasson, John B. *Reading Difficulties: Their Diagnosis and Correction,* 5th ed. (Englewood Cliffs, N.J.: Prentice-Hall, 1984).

Bowren, Fay F., and Zintz, Miles V. *Teaching Reading in Adult Basic Education.* Dubuque, Ia.: Wm. C. Brown, 1977.

Burmeister, Lou E. *Reading Strategies for Secondary School Teachers,* 2d ed. Reading, Mass.: Addison Wesley, 1978.

Burmeister, Lou E. *Words—From Print to Meaning, Classroom Activities for Building Sight Vocabulary, for Using Context Clues, Morphology and Phonics.* Reading, Mass.: Addison Wesley, 1975.

Carroll, John B., and Chall, Jeanne S. *Toward a Literate Society.* New York: McGraw-Hill, 1975.

Cazden, Courtney; John, Vera; and Hymes, Dell, ed. *Functions of Language in the Classroom.* New York: Teachers College Press, Columbia University, 1972.

Clay, Marie M. *The Early Detection of Reading Difficulties: A Diagnostic Survey with Recovery Procedures,* 2d ed. (Auckland, New Zealand: Heinemann, 1979).

DeStefano, Johanna, ed. *Language, Society, and Education: A Profile of Black English.* Worthington, Ohio: Charles A. Jones, 1973.

Ekwall, Eldon E., and Shanker, James L. *Diagnosis and Remediation of the Disabled Reader,* 2d ed. Boston: Allyn and Bacon, 1985.

Ekwall, Eldon E. *Locating and Correcting Reading Difficulties,* 4th ed. Columbus: Merrill, 1985.

Fernald, Grace. *Remedial Techniques in Basic School Subjects.* New York: McGraw-Hill, 1971.

Frostig, Marianne. *Selection and Adaptation of Reading Methods.* San Rafael, Calif.: Academic Therapy Publications, 1973.

Gallant, Ruth. *Handbook in Corrective Reading,* 2d ed. Columbus, Ohio: Charles E. Merrill, 1977.

Gearheart, B. R. *Learning Disabilities: Educational Strategies,* 2d ed. St. Louis: C. V. Mosby, 1977.

Goodman, Kenneth; Smith, E. Brooks; and Meredith, Robert. *Language and Thinking in the Elementary School,* 2d ed. New York: Holt, Rinehart and Winston, 1976.

Guszak, Frank. *Diagnostic Reading Instruction in the Elementary School,* 2d ed. New York: Harper and Row, 1978.

Hall, Mary Anne. *Teaching Reading as a Language Experience,* 2d ed. Columbus, Ohio: Merrill, 1976.

Harris, Albert J., and Sipay, E. R. *How to Increase Reading Ability,* 7th ed. New York: Longman, 1980.

Herr, Selma. *Learning Activities for Reading,* 4th ed. Dubuque, Iowa: Wm. C. Brown, 1982.

Jansky, Jeannette, and DeHirsch, Katrina. *Preventing Reading Failure.* New York: Harper and Row, 1972.

Kennedy, Eddie C. *Classroom Approaches to Remedial Reading,* 2d ed. Itasca, Ill.: F. E. Peacock, 1977.

Kroth, Roger L. *Communicating with Parents of Exceptional Children: Improving Parent-Teacher Relationships.* Denver: Love Publishing Co., 1975.

LaPray, Margaret. *Teaching Children to Become Independent Readers.* New York: Center for Applied Research in Education, 1972.

Leibert, Robert, ed. *Diagnostic Viewpoints in Reading.* Newark, Del: International Reading Association, 1971.

McGinnis, Dorothy J., and Smith, Dorothy E. *Analyzing and Treating Reading Problems.* New York: Macmillan, 1982.

O'Brien, Carmen A. *Teaching the Language-Different Child to Read.* Columbus: Merrill, 1973.

Piercey, Dorothy. *Reading Activities in Content Areas: An Ideabook for Middle and Secondary Schools.* Boston: Allyn and Bacon, 1976.

Roswell, Florence, and Natchez, Gladys. *Reading Disability: Diagnosis and Treatment,* 2d ed. New York: Basic Books, 1971.

Rubin, Dorothy. *Diagnosis and Correction in Reading Instruction.* New York: Holt, Rinehart and Winston, 1982.

Rupley, William H., and Blair, Timothy R. *Reading Diagnosis and Remediation,* 2d ed. Chicago: Rand McNally, 1983.

Savage, John F., and Mooney, Jean F. *Teaching Reading to Children with Special Needs.* Boston: Allyn and Bacon, 1979.

Schubert, Delwyn G., and Torgerson, Theodore. *Improving the Reading Program,* 4th ed. Dubuque, Ia.: Wm. C. Brown, 1976.

Silvaroli, Nicholas. *Classroom Reading Inventory,* 4th ed. Dubuque, Ia.: Wm. C. Brown, 1982.

Spache, Evelyn. *Reading Activities for Child Involvement,* 3d. ed. Boston: Allyn and Bacon, 1981.

Spache, George D. *Diagnosing and Correcting Reading Disabilities.* Boston: Allyn and Bacon, 1976.

Spache, George D. *Investigating the Issues of Reading Disabilities.* Boston: Allyn and Bacon, 1976.

Tonjes, Marian J., and Zintz, Miles V. *Teaching Reading/Thinking/Study Skills in Content Classrooms.* Dubuque, Iowa: Wm. C. Brown, 1981.

Turnbull, Ann P., and Schulz, Jane B. *Mainstreaming Handicapped Students: A Guide for the Classroom Teacher.* Boston: Allyn and Bacon, 1979.

Veatch, Jeannette, et. al. *Key Words to Reading: The Language Experience Approach Begins,* 2d ed. Columbus, Ohio: Merrill, 1979.

Wallen, Carl J. *Word Attack Skills in Reading.* Columbus, Ohio: Merrill, 1969.

Wilson, Robert M. *Diagnostic and Remedial Reading for Classroom and Clinic,* 3d ed. Columbus, Ohio: Merrill, 1977.

Wilson, Robert, and Hall, Maryanne. *Programmed Word Attack for Teachers,* 3d ed. Columbus, Ohio: Merrill, 1979.

A Bibliography of Books for Corrective Reading

Books recommended for pupils who read below their assigned grade level that combine *high interest level* and *low vocabulary load*.

1. **Action**

   Scholastic Book Services, 904 Sylvan Ave., Englewood Cliffs, N.J. 07632. For severely retarded readers in secondary schools. Reading levels 2.0–4.0. They are available in kits: each kit contains four copies of five titles. Ditto masters and cassettes are also available.

   Action Libraries I and IA—reading levels 2.0–2.4;
   Action Libraries II and IIA—reading levels 2.5–2.9;
   Action Libraries III and IIIA—reading levels 3.0–3.4;
   Action Libraries IV and IVA—reading levels 3.5–3.9;
   Double Action Library I—reading levels 3.0–3.4;
   Double Action Library II—reading levels 3.5–3.9.

2. **Adapted Classics**

   Globe Book Company, Inc., 175 Fifth Ave., New York, N.Y. 10010. There are many titles in the series—clothbound and well illustrated. Teaching aids and testing materials are provided in the books. The following are representative of the entire list:

TITLE	READING LEVEL
Prince and the Pauper	4–5
Robin Hood	4–5
Swiss Family Robinson	4–5
Tom Sawyer	4–5
20,000 Leagues Under the Sea	4–5

3. **Animal Adventure Series**

   Benefic Press, 10300 W. Roosevelt Road, Westchester, Ill. 60153. Preprimary to grade 3. Record or cassette available for each book.

TITLE	READING LEVEL	INTEREST LEVEL
Becky, the Rabbit	PP	1–3
Squeaky, the Squirrel	PP	1–3
Doc, the Dog	PP	1–3
Pat, the Parakeet	PP	1–3
Kate, the Cat	PP	1–3

Gomer, the Gosling	P	1–3
Skippy, the Skunk	P	1–3
Sandy, the Swallow	P	1–3
Sally, the Screech Owl	1	1–4
Pudgy, the Beaver	1	1–4
Hamilton, the Hamster	1	1–4
Horace, the Horse	1	1–4

4. **Beginner Books**

Random House, Inc., 201 E. 50th St., New York, N.Y. 10022. Regular and special library bindings are available. Reader level is based on the Spache Readability Formula.

TITLE	GRADE READING LEVEL	NUMBER OF DIFFERENT WORDS
The Cat in the Hat	2.1	223
The Cat in the Hat Comes Back	2.0	253
A Fly Went By	2.1	180
The Big Jump and Other Stories	2.4	216
A Big Ball of String	2.5	215
Sam and the Firefly	2.0	200
You Will Go to the Moon	1.8	181
Cowboy Andy	1.8	226
The Whales Go By	1.8	183
Stop That Ball!	1.9	201
Bennett Cerf's Book of Laughs	2.1	237
Ann Can Fly	2.0	210
One Fish, Two Fish, Red Fish, Blue Fish	1.7	276
The King's Wish and Other Stories	2.0	198
Bennett Cerf's Book of Riddles	2.2	194
Green Eggs and Ham	1.9	50
Put Me in the Zoo	1.5	100
Are You My Mother?	1.7	100
Go, Dog, Go!	1.5	75

5. **Better Reading Series**

By John F. Rambeau and Nancy Rambeau. Educational Guidelines Co., A Division of The Economy Co., Oklahoma City, Okla.

TITLE	GRADE READING LEVEL
The Jinx Boat	2
Explore	3
Venture	4
Quest	5
Las Caras de Chico	3

On Polecat Mountain	5
Moneywise	5
Teacher's Guide	

6. Blue Bug Books

By Virginia Poulet. Children's Press, 1224 W. Van Buren St., Chicago, Ill. 60607. Talking-picture books for pre-school to grade 3. Thirty-two pages.

Blue Bug's Circus
Blue Bug's Surprise
Blue Bug Finds a Friend
Blue Bug's Vegetable Garden

7. Box Car Children Books, The, *See Pilot Books* (listing no. 41)

By Gertrude Warner. Pilot Books, Albert Whitman, 506 West Lake Street, Chicago, Ill. 60637. Mystery stories about the four Alden children—Jessie, Henry, Violet, and Benny.

8. Butternut Bill Series

By Edith McCall. Benefic Press, 10300 W. Roosevelt Road, Westchester, Ill. 60153. Carefully controlled vocabularies. An LP record (33⅓-rpm) is available with each book in the series. Sight Sound Sets (five books and one record) are also available.

TITLE	READING LEVEL	WORD COUNT	PAGES
Butternut Bill	PP	35	48
Butternut Bill and the Bee Tree	PP	58	48
Butternut Bill and the Big Catfish	PP	51	48
Butternut Bill and the Bear	P	43	64
Butternut Bill and the Little River	P	64	64
Butternut Bill and the Big Pumpkin	P	64	64
Butternut Bill and his Friends	1	158	64
Butternut Bill and the Train	1		64

9. Button Family Adventure Series

By Edith McCall. Benefic Press, 10300 W. Roosevelt Road, Westchester, Ill. 60153.

TITLE	READING LEVEL	INTEREST LEVEL	WORD COUNT
Buttons at the Zoo	PP	PP–2	30
Buttons Takes a Boat Ride	P	P–2	75
Buttons and the Pet Parade	P	P–2	80
Buttons and the Boy Scouts	2	2–4	281
Buttons and the Little League	3	3–5	340
Teacher's Manual for the Series			

10. **Checkered Flag Series, The**

By Henry A. Bamman and Robert J. Whitehead. San Francisco: Field Educational Publications, Inc. Study exercises in each book teach: reading for specific details, recall of a main idea, character identification, word usage, discussion and critical thinking, and word meanings. Audio-Visual Kit with each title includes color filmstrip, LP record, and magnetic tape.

Title	Grade Level
Wheels	2.4
Riddler	2.5
Bearcat	2.5
Smashup	2.6
Scramble	3.0
Flea	3.5
Grand Prix	4.0
500	4.5
Teacher's Guide for the Series	

11. **Childhood of Famous American Series, The**

Bobbs-Merrill Co., Inc., 4300 W. 62nd St., Indianapolis, Ind. 46268. The reader level of all the books in this series is about fourth grade. The 1974 Publishers Trade List Annual showed 216 books available in this series. Newer titles include:

Dwight D. Eisenhower: Young Military Leader, by Wilma Hudson
Carl Sandburg: Young Singing Poet, by Grace Hathaway Melin
David Sarnoff: Radio and TV Boy, by Elisabeth P. Myers
Frederick Douglass: Boy Champion of Human Rights, by Elisabeth P. Myers
Harry S. Truman: Missouri Farm Boy, by Wilma J. Hudson
J. C. Penney: Golden Rule Boy, by Wilma J. Hudson
Langston Hughes: Young Black Poet, by Montrew Dunham
Louis Armstrong: Young Music Maker, by Dharathula H. Millender
Lyndon B. Johnson: Young Texan, by Thomas F. Barton
Mahalia Jackson: Young Gospel Singer, by Montrew Dunham
Pearl S. Buck: Literary Girl, by Elisabeth P. Myers
Older titles in the series include: *Abe Lincoln, Booker T. Washington, Sacagawea, Clara Barton, John F. Kennedy, Henry Ford, Babe Ruth,* and *Davy Crockett.*

12. **Contact**

Prepared by the editors of Scholastic Scope. Scholastic Book Services, 904 Sylvan Ave., Englewood Cliffs, N.J. 07632. Interest level for the secondary school student; reading level *third* to *sixth* grade. Units are organized around *themes* with the general objective of all units to teach better communication skills.

Title	Recommended for Grade Levels
Drugs: Insights and Illusions	9–12
Environment: Earth in Crisis	9–12
The Future: Can We Shape It?	9–12
Getting Together: Problems We Face	8–10

Imagination: World of Inner Space   7–8
Law: You, The Police and Justice   9–12
Loyalties: Whose Side Are You On?   9–12
Maturity: Growing Up Strong   8–10
Prejudice: The Invisible Wall   9–12
Materials for *Contact* include log books for writing, long-playing records of teenage interviews, posters for stimulating discussion, and teachers' guides.

13. **Cowboy Sam Series**
    By Edna Walker Chandler. Benefic Press, 10300 W. Roosevelt Road, Westchester, Ill. 60153.

TITLE	READING LEVEL	INTEREST LEVEL	WORD COUNT
Cowboy Sam and Flop	1	1–4	149
*Cowboy Sam and Shorty**	1	1–4	158
Cowboy Sam and Freddy	1	1–4	237
Cowboy Sam and Sally	2	2–5	356
*Cowboy Sam and the Fair**	2	2–5	278
Cowboy Sam and the Rodeo	2	2–5	333
Cowboy Sam and the Airplane	3	3–6	431
*Cowboy Sam and the Indians**	3	3–6	421
Cowboy Sam and the Rustlers	3	3–6	485

Teacher's Manual for Series
*Workbooks available

14. **Crossroads**
    By James Olson and Lawrence Swinburne, Eds. Noble and Noble Publishers, 1 Dag Hammerskjold Plaza, 245 E. 47th St., New York, N.Y. 10017. Level of difficulty—grades 4–9.

    LEVEL ONE: Four student paperbacks, four 12-inch 33⅓-rpm records, a student activity book, a teacher's manual, and a library of twelve additional paperbacks. The four student books are: *With It, Solo, Against All Odds,* and *Beyond Tomorrow.*
    LEVEL TWO: Four student paperbacks, four twelve-inch 33⅓-rpm records, a student activity book, a teacher's manual, and a library of twelve additional paperbacks. The four student books are: *Love's Blues, Me, Myself, and I, Dreamer of Dreams,* and *He Who Dares.*
    LEVEL THREE: Four student paperbacks, four twelve-inch 33⅓-rpm records, a student activity book, a teacher's guide, and a library of twelve additional paperbacks. The four student books are: *Tomorrow Won't Wait, Breaking Loose, In Other's Eyes,* and *Playing It Cool.* This was designed to be a highly motivating, nongraded program for junior and senior high school use; readability levels fourth to ninth grades. It is an attempt to be *relevant* to teenagers. The workbooks provide opportunity for critical thinking and for composition and writing practice.

15. Dan Frontier Series

By William J. Hurley. Benefic Press, 10300 West Roosevelt Road, Westchester, Ill. 60153.

Title	Reading Level	Interest Level	Word Count
Dan Frontier	PP	PP–2	57
Dan Frontier and the New House	PP	PP–2	44
Dan Frontier and the Big Cat	P	P–3	86
Dan Frontier Goes Hunting	P	P–3	86
Dan Frontier, Trapper	1	1–4	142
Dan Frontier with the Indians	1	1–4	131
Dan Frontier and the Wagon Train	2	2–5	278
Dan Frontier Scouts with the Army	2	2–5	227
Dan Frontier, Sheriff	3	3–6	323
Dan Frontier Goes Exploring	3	3–6	276
Dan Frontier Goes to Congress	4	4–7	
Teacher's Manual for Series			

16. Discovery, Short Introductory Biographies

Mary C. Austin, Consultant. Garrard Publishing Co., Champaign, Ill. 61820. 65 titles in series. Reading level, grade 3; interest level, grades 2–5. Selected titles of recent books include:

Rachel Carson, Who Loved the Sea
Martha Washington, First Lady of the Land
Jim Beckwourth, Black Trapper and Indian Chief
Robert H. Goddard, Space Pioneer

17. Dolch Four-Step Program

Garrard Publishing Company, Champaign, Ill. 61820.

First Reading Books: Reading level, grade 1; interest level, grades 1–4. Vocabulary: Easier half of the 220 Basic Sight Words, the 95 commonest nouns. Set of sixteen books includes:
Dog Pals
I Like Cats
Once There Was A Bear
Some Are Small
Basic Vocabulary Books: Reading level, grade 2; interest level, grades 1–6. Vocabulary: 220 Basic Sight Words, the 95 commonest nouns. Set of sixteen books includes:
Bear Stories
Circus Stories
Folk Stories
Navajo Stories

Folklore of the World Books: Reading level, grade 3; interest level, grades 2–8. Vocabulary: The Storytellers' vocabulary, 684 words. Set of twelve books includes:

Stories from Alaska
Stories from France
Stories from Japan
Stories from Russia

Pleasure Reading Books: Reading level, grade 4; interest level, grades 3–8. Vocabulary: First 1,000 words for children's reading.

There are thirteen books in this set, all good for remedial reading. Among them are:

Aesop's Stories
Andersen Stories
Far East Stories
Robinson Crusoe

18. **Doubleday Signal Books**

Doubleday & Company, School and Library Division, Garden City, N.Y. 11530. There are more than 70 books in this series. The stories have high interest for teenagers; written in vocabulary and style suited to fourth grade reading level. Prepared especially for reluctant readers in junior and senior high school. Newer titles include:

The Day the World Went Away, by Anne Schraff
High School Dropout, by John Clarke
I Was a Black Panther, by Chuck Moore
Loner, by Constance Kwolek
Mighty Hard Road: The Story of Cesar Chavez, by James Terzian and Kathryn Cramer
Motorcycle Racer, by John P. Covington
Nat Dunlap: Junior "Medic", by Evelyn Fiore
The Otis Redding Story, by Jane Schiesel
Shirley Chisholm, by Susan Brownmiller

19. **Easy Reading Books**

Children's Press, 1224 W. Van Buren St., Chicago, Ill. 60607. Available in multiple copy sets with cassette and resource cards.

Benje
Birds in the Sky
Chicken Little Count to Ten
Lucky and the Giant
Martin Luther King, Jr.
Mystery of the Roll Top Desk
Seven Diving Ducks
We're Very Good Friends, My Brother and I

20. **Fast Mystery Series, 1984**

Pitman Learning, Inc., 6 Davis Drive, Belmont, Calif. 94002. Contains twelve books by various authors. Intended for middle schoolers and beyond, but at elementary reading levels.

21. **Fastback Romance Series, 1984**
Pitman Learning, Inc., 6 Davis Drive, Belmont, Calif. 94002. Contains twelve books by various authors. Intended for middle schoolers and beyond. Reading levels are elementary.

22. **Field Literature Program, K–6**
Henry Bamman, Helen Huus, and Robert Whitehead. Field Educational Publications, Inc., 2400 Hanover St., Palo Alto, Calif. 94304. Excellent selection of children's literature, beautifully illustrated.

TITLE	GRADE LEVEL
Apple Trees	PP
Gingerbread	P
Toadstools	1
Roller Skates	2
Sailboats	3
Windowpanes	4
Fox Eyes	5
Seabirds	6

23. **Follett Just Beginning-to-Read Books**
By Margaret Hillert. Follett Publishing Company, 1010 W. Washington Blvd., Chicago, Ill. 60607.

PREPRIMER LEVEL:
The Birthday Car
Circus Fun
The Funny Baby
The Little Runaway
The Magic Beans
Snow Baby
The Three Bears
The Three Goats
The Three Little Pigs
The Yellow Boat
Cinderella at the Ball
A House for Little Red

24. **Follett Beginning-to-Read Books**
Follett Publishing Co., 1010 W. Washington Blvd., Chicago, Ill. 60607.

END OF GRADE ONE LEVEL:
Big Bug, Little Bug
Big New School
The Elf in the Singing Tree
Gertie the Duck
Have You Seen My Brother?
Jiffy, Miss Boo and Mr. Roo
Just Follow Me
Little Quack

Nobody Listens to Andrew
Sad Mrs. Sam Sack
Too Many Dogs
The Wee, Little Man
MIDDLE GRADE TWO LEVEL:
Barefoot Boy
Big Bad Bear
The Boy Who Wouldn't Say His Name
The Dog Who Came to Dinner
The Dog Who Took the Train
Linda's Air Mail Letter
Mabel, the Whale
The No Bark Dog
When the Wild Ducks Came
Crocodiles Have Big Teeth All Day
END OF GRADE TWO LEVEL:
Beginning to Read Riddles and Jokes
Benny and the Bear
A Day on the Big O
A Frog Sandwich: Riddles and Jokes
Gingerbread Children
The Ice Cream Cone
Sparky's Fireman
A Uniform for Harry
Ride, Willy, Ride

25. **The Galaxy 5 Series, 1979**
Pitman Learning, Inc., 6 Davis Drive, Belmont, Calif., 94002. Reading difficulty is third reader; skill builders included.

Goodbye to Earth
On the Red World
Vacation in Space
Dead Man
Where No Star Shines
King of the Stars

26. **Helicopter Adventure Series**
By Selma Wassermann and Jack Wassermann. Westchester, Ill.: Benefic Press. Any grade level 1–6.

TITLE	READING LEVEL
Chopper Malone and the New Pilot	Primer
Chopper Malone and Susie	Primer
Chopper Malone and the Big Snow	Grade 1
Chopper Malone and Trouble at Sea	Grade 1
Chopper Malone and the Mountain Rescue	Grade 2
Chopper Malone and the Skylarks	Grade 3
Teacher's Guide	

27. **Hip Pocket Stories**
    Biographies of celebrities. Developmental levels: 4–12; remedial levels: 7–12. Cassettes, workbooks, teacher's guide. About third grade level on the Spache formula. (Mankato, Minnesota: Creative Education, Inc.)

    Diana Ross
    Bill Cosby
    Shirley Chisholm
    Geraldo Rivera
    Johnny Bench

28. **Impact** For reluctant readers, grades 7–9
    Charlotte Brooks, Gen. ed. Holt, Rinehart and Winston, Inc., 383 Madison Ave., New York, N.Y. 10017. Teacher's guides and twelve-inch LP records.

    Level I:
    I've Got a Name
    At Your Own Risk
    Cities
    Larger than Life
    Level II:
    Unknown Worlds
    Conflict
    Sight Lines
    Search for America
    Level III:
    Turning Point
    I (Me)
    Nobody but Yourself
    On Edge

29. **Instant Readers, The**
    By Bill Martin and Peggy Brogan. Holt, Rinehart and Winston, Inc., 383 Madison Ave., New York, N.Y. 10017. Three levels, primary grades. Listening, reading and listening, reading. Books and cassettes. Guitar accompaniment on cassettes by Al Caiola.

30. **Jim Forest Readers, The**
    By John F. Rambeau and Nancy Rambeau. San Francisco: Field Educational Publications, Inc. Teacher's manual provides suggestions for skill development and the first four books have accompanying workbooks for remedial reading use.

Title	Reading Level
Jim Forest and Ranger Don	1.7
Jim Forest and the Trapper	1.7
Jim Forest and the Ghost Town	1.8
Jim Forest and the Bandits	1.9
Jim Forest and the Lightning	1.9

Jim Forest and the Phantom Crater	2.0
Jim Forest and the Mystery Hunter	2.2
Jim Forest and the Plane Crash	2.4
Jim Forest and Dead Man's Peak	2.6
Jim Forest and the Flood	2.8
Jim Forest and Lone Wolf Gulch	3.1
Jim Forest and Woodman's Ridge	3.2
Teacher's Manual	

31. **Jim Hunter Books**

Ben Butterworth and Bill Stockdale. A 12-book series. Increase in length (32 to 80 pages) and in reading level (grade 1 to grade 3): Belmont, Calif.: Pitman Learning.

Danger in the Mountains
Jim and the Sun Goddess
The Sniper at Zimba
The Temple of Mantos
Teacher's guide

32. **Keytext**

The Economy Company, 1901 West Walnut St., Oklahoma City, Okla. 73125. This is a basal reading program for students reading below grade level:

Puddlejumpers and *Castlebuilders*, Level 1 for use in grade 2
Summerdaze and *Streetsongs*, Level 2 for use in grade 3
Thundercover and *Turnstyles*, Level 3 for use in grade 4
Daystreaming and *Bootstraps*, Level 4 for use in grade 5
Worldwind and *Forerunners*, Level 5 for use in grade 6

33. **Learning to Read While Reading to Learn Series**

By Jo Stanchfield, S. I. Hayakawa, Ralph Kellogg, and Frank Hutchinson. San Rafael, Calif.: Leswing Press.

TITLE	READING LEVEL
A Peculiar Lawnmower	Grades 4–6
Pedro's Secret	Grades 4–6
Dognappers	Grades 4–6
Loud and Clear	Grades 4–6
Operation Phoenix	Grades 4–6
Hundred Milers	Grades 7–8
Deadline for Tim	Grades 7–8
The Vanishing Pirate	Grades 7–8

34. **Monster Books**

Bowman, 4563 Colorado Boulevard, Los Angeles, Calif. 90039. Easy to read. Relevant interest for middle grades and junior high. Presently twenty-four titles, including:

Monster Looks for a Friend
Monster Gets a Job
Lady Monster Has a Plan

35. **Morgan Bay Mystery Series**

By John F. Rambeau and Nancy Rambeau. San Francisco: Field Educational Publications, Inc.

TITLE	READING LEVEL
The Mystery of Morgan Castle	2.3
The Mystery of Marble Angel	2.6
The Mystery of Midnight Visitor	3.2
The Mystery of the Missing Marlin	3.5
The Mystery of the Musical Ghost	3.5
The Mystery of the Monks' Island	3.7
The Mystery of the Marauder's Gold	3.9
The Mystery of the Myrmidon's Journey	4.1
Teacher's Manual	

36. **Mystery Adventure Series**

Henry A. Bamman, Benefic Press, 10300 W. Roosevelt Road, Westchester, Ill. 60153. Written at fourth to ninth grade interest level.

TITLE	READING LEVEL
Mystery Adventure at Cave Four	3
Mystery Adventure at Longcliff Inn	5
Mystery Adventure of the Indian Burial Ground	4
Mystery Adventure of the Jeweled Bell	2
Mystery Adventure of the Smuggled Treasure	6
Mystery Adventure of the Talking Statues	2

37. **Owl Books, The**

Bill Martin, ed. Holt, Rinehart and Winston, Inc., 383 Madison Ave., New York 10017.

Kin/Der Owl Books (Preschool-grade 1)
Little Owl Books (K–2)
Young Owl Books (Grades 2–4)
Wise Owl Books (Grades 4–6)

38. **Pacemakers—Bestellers**

Bestellers I (ten titles), Bestellers II (ten titles), and Bestellers III (ten titles) are written at third grade level or below using the Pacemaker Core Vocabulary of 1,821 words. They have an adult format and are stories of adventure, science fiction and mystery. Available in sets (four copies of each of ten titles) with teacher's guides. Selected titles are:

Bestellers I:	*The Candy Man*
	Diamonds in the Dirt
	Night of the Kachina
	The Time Trap
Bestellers II:	*Escape from Tomorrow*
	Tiger, Lion, Hawk
	Wind over Stonehenge
	Wet Fire
Bestellers III:	*Counterfeit*
	Secret Spy
	Star Gold
	Village of Vampires

39. Pacemaker—True Adventure

An eleven book series; reading level 2.0–2.5; interest level grade 5–adult basic

Tales of Escape
Tales of Flying
Tales of Rescue
Tales of Speed
Teacher's Guide

40. Pacemaker—Vocational Readers

A ten-book series; reading level about second grade; interest level grades 7–12. Each book has 64 pages. Tape cassettes of the stories are available.

I'll Try Tomorrow (Gardener)
The Other Side of the Counter (Short Order Cook)
Ready to Go (Auto Mechanic)
Until Joe Comes Back (Supermarket)
Teacher's Guide

41. Pilot Books

Albert Whitman, 506 West Lake Street, Chicago, Ill. 60637. The Box Car Children Books, by Gertrude Warner. Mystery stories about the four Alden children—Jessie, Henry, Violet, and Benny—are about third grade reader level, with third grade to sixth grade interest.

Bus Station Mystery	*Mike's Mystery*
Mystery in the Sand	*Blue Bay Mystery*
Bicycle Mystery	*The Woodshed Mystery*
Tree House Mystery	*The Lighthouse Mystery*
Snowbound Mystery	*Mystery Behind the Wall*
Houseboat Mystery	*Caboose Mystery*
Schoolhouse Mystery	*Mountain Top Mystery*
Mystery Ranch	*The Yellow House Mystery*
Surprise Island	*The Box Car Children*

42. Racing Wheels Readers

By Anabel Dean. Benefic Press, 10300 W. Roosevelt Road, Westchester, Ill. 60153. Each book is fourth to twelfth grade interest level. All books are 80 pages in length.

Title	Reading Level
Hot Rod	2
Destruction Derby	2
Drag Race	3
Stock Car Race	3
Road Race	4
Indy 500	4

43. Ranger Don Series

Written by Robert Whitehead. Level of difficulty: grades 1–3; interest level: grades 1–6. Sold in learning kits, there are five copies of a book, 1 cassette, 1 filmstrip, 1 teacher's guide, 5 pupil activity cards, 5 evaluation cards, and 5 answer cards.

Ranger Don
Ranger Don and the Forest Fire
Ranger Don and the Ghost Town
Ranger Don and the Mountain Trail
Ranger Don and the Wolverine

44. Reading Incentive Program

Bowmar Publishing Co., 622 Rodier Drive, Glendale, Calif. 91201. The books listed below are written by Ed Radlauer and are available in single copy or in *sets*. A set includes ten copies (paper-bound) of a reader, one seven-inch long playing recorded narration, and one full color filmstrip. There is also a teacher's manual. The level of difficulty of the reading material in all of these books is about fourth grade.

Slot Car Racing
Drag Racing
The Mighty Midgets
Motorcycles
Karting
Teen Fair
Horses
Surfing
Drag Racing Funny Cars
Dune Buggies
Dune Buggy Racing
Custom Cars
Teacher's Manual

45. Science Research Associates Pilot Libraries

Science Research Associates, 259 E. Erie St., Chicago, Ill. 60611. Pilot Library selections are unaltered excerpts from carefully chosen juvenile books. Each *Library* contains 72 selections (each 24–32 pages in length), of graded levels of difficulty. With each *Library,* the teacher is furnished a handbook that provides a synopsis of each selection and questions for discussion. A student record book provides exercises for testing the student's comprehension.

Pilot Library IIa, Fourth grade
Pilot Library IIb, Fifth grade
Pilot Library IIc, Sixth grade
Pilot Library IIIa, Seventh grade
Pilot Library IIIb, Eighth grade

46. **Sailor Jack Series**
By Selma Wassermann and Jack Wassermann. Benefic Press, 10300 W. Roosevelt Road, Westchester, Ill. 60153.

TITLE	READING LEVEL	INTEREST LEVEL	WORD COUNT
Sailor Jack	PP	PP–2	62
Sailor Jack and Bluebell's Dive	P	P–3	73
Sailor Jack and Bluebell	P	P–3	73
Sailor Jack and the Jet Plane	P	P–3	96
Teacher's Guide			

47. **Scope**
Prepared by the editors of Scholastic Scope, Scholastic Book Services, 904 Sylvan Ave., Englewood Cliffs, N.J. 07632. For grades 7–12 language arts classes. Readability level fourth to sixth grade.

SCOPE I:
Seven Plays, edited to a fourth to sixth grade reader level, extensively illustrated, selected to motivate discussion and role-playing.
Twelve Angry Men and Other Plays
Appalachian Autumn and Other Plays
Requiem for a Heavyweight and Other Plays
No Time for Sergeants and Other Plays
Dino and Other Plays
Teacher, Teacher and Other Plays
The Winner and Other Plays
SCOPE II:
Visuals (visual masters and transparencies)
Reading Skills
Vocabulary Building
Observation Skills
Determining Sequence
Reasoning Skills
Vowel Crossroads
Consonant Crosswords
Language Usage Crosswords
Word Attack
Word Power

Word Meaning Through Context
Puzzle Crostics
Getting Applications Right (filling in forms)
Building Reading Skills
Figurative Language
Career Crosswords
SCOPE III:
Wide World
Dimensions
Spotlight
Across and Down
Word Puzzles and Mysteries
Jobs in your Future (Job Skills)
Countdown (Study Skills)
Trackdown (Language Skills)
Sprint (Speed-Reading Skills)

48. **See How I Read Books, 1981**
Modern Curriculum Press, 13900 Prospect Rd., Cleveland 44136. Six books at first- and second-reader levels.

Blossom Bird Finds a Family
Blossom Bird Goes South
Blossom Bird Falls in Love
2-B and the Rock 'N Roll Band
2-B and the Space Visitor
Finn the Foolish Fish

49. **See How It Grows Series, 1983**
Modern Curriculum Press, 13900 Prospect Rd., Cleveland 44136. Includes twelve books at the first-reader level.

50. **See How It's Made Series, 1983**
Modern Curriculum Press, 13900 Prospect Rd., Cleveland 44136. First-reader level difficulty.

Titles include:
The Bar of Chocolate
The Knife and Fork
The Glass Jug
Rubber

51. **Shapes Around Us Reading Series**
By Frances Fox and Penrod Moss. Century Communications, Inc., San Francisco, Calif. Designed for primary reading levels. Most words are first grade words and the pictures and context should help with all others.

What Is Round?
What Has Four Sides?

What Has Three Sides?
What Comes In A Can?
What Comes In A Box?
What Shape Is It?

52. **Signal Books, see Doubleday Signal Books** (listing no. 18)

53. **Sounds of Language Readers, The**
Revised, 1974. Grades K–8. By Bill Martin and Peggy Brogan. Holt, Rinehart and Winston, Inc., 383 Madison Ave., New York, N.Y. 10017.

Listening and observing pictures
Reading and listening to the voice on the cassette
Reading the book alone

54. **The Specter Series, 1979**
Pitman Learning, Inc., 6 Davis Drive, Belmont, Calif. 94002. Reading difficulty is third reader; skill builders included.

Dreams
'57 T-Bird
A Deadly Game
The Actor
No Rent to Pay
Homecoming
The Ear
ZB4

55. **Space Science Fiction Series**
By Henry A. Bamman, et al., Benefic Press, 10300 W. Roosevelt Road, Westchester, Ill. 60153. Each book is fourth to twelfth grade interest level. All books are 72 pages in length.

TITLE	GRADE LEVEL
Space Pirate	2
Milky Way	2
Bone People	3
Planet of the Whistlers	4
Ice-Men of Rime	5
Inviso Man	6

56. **Sports Mystery Series**
By Evelyn Lunemann. Benefic Press, 10300 W. Roosevelt Road, Westchester, Ill. 60153. Each book is fourth to twelfth grade interest level. All books are 72 pages in length.

TITLE	READING LEVEL
Ten Feet Tall	2
No Turning Back	2
Fairway Danger	3

Tip Off	3
Pitcher's Choice	3
Face Off	4
Swimmer's Mark	4
Tennis Champ	4

57. **Sprint Libraries**

Scholastic Book Services, 904 Sylvan Ave., Englewood Cliffs, N.J. 07632. For severely retarded readers in secondary schools. Reading levels 1.5–4.0. Available in kits containing four copies each of five titles. Ditto masters and teacher's guide are also provided.

Sprint Starter: Libraries A and B (ten titles)
   The Haunted House—32 pp., reading level 1.5
   Kitchen Caper—32 pp., reading level 1.6
Sprint, Libraries I, IA, and IB
   The Prize—32 pp., reading level 2.0
   Karate Ace—32 pp., reading level 2.2
Sprint, Libraries II, IIA, and IIB
   Mystery on Elm Street—64 pp., reading level 2.6
   The Liquid Trap—64 pp., reading level 2.7
   The Homesteaders—64 pp., reading level 2.9
Sprint, Libraries III, IIIA, and IIIB
   The Mystery of the Jade Princess—96 pp., level 3.0
   Sabotage Rock—96 pp., reading level 3.1
   Sea Lab 2020—96 pp., reading level 3.4
Sprint, Libraries IV, IVA, and IVB
   Ghost Town—96 pp., reading level 3.5
   Cartwheels—96 pp., reading level 3.9
   Skyhawks—96 pp., reading level 3.8

58. **Superstars, Creative Education Books**

By James T. Olsen. Children's Press, 1224 W. Van Buren St., Chicago 60607. Grade level: 3–8. More than 60 books in this series.

Evone Goolagong: Superstar
Jackie Robinson: Superstar
Joe Namath: Superstar
Lee Trevino: Superstar
Muhammed Ali: Superstar
Roberto Clemente: Superstar
Vince Lombardi: Superstar

59. **Target Books**

Garrard Publishing Company, Champaign, Ill. 61820. Easy reading, high interest, mature format. Reading level, grades 3–4: interest level 5 and up. Some titles are:

Adventures in Buckskin
Heroes of the Homerun
Jazz Greats
Women Who Dared to be Different

60. **Teen-Age Tales**
Edited by Ruth Strang et al., eds. D. C. Heath & Company, 125 Spring St., Lexington, Mass. 02173. The level of reading difficulty is about fifth or sixth grade. The interest appeal is very good for adolescents. There are eight books in the series.

Teen-Age Tales: Books A, B, I, II, III, IV, V, and VI.

61. **Tom Logan Series**
By Edna Walker Chandler. Benefic Press, 10300 W. Roosevelt Road, Westchester, Ill. 60153.

TITLE	READING LEVEL	INTEREST LEVEL	PAGES
Pony Rider	PP	PP–2	48
Talking Wire	PP	PP–2	48
Track Boss	P	P–3	64
Cattle Drive	P	P–3	64
Secret Tunnel	1	1–4	64
Gold Train	1	1–4	64
Gold Nugget	2	2–5	96
Stage Coach Driver	3	3–6	96

62. **Treat Truck Series**
By Genevieve Gray, Sylvajean Harrington, Lee Harrington, and Sandra Altheide. Benefic Press, 10300 W. Roosevelt Road, Westchester, Ill. 60153. Each book in the series is 48 pages in length.

TITLE	READING LEVEL	INTEREST LEVEL
Mike and the Treat Truck	PP	PP–2
Treat Truck and the Fire	PP	PP–2
Treat Truck and the Dog Show	P	P–2
Treat Truck and the Big Rain	P	P–2
Treat Truck and the Parade	1	1–2
Treat Truck and the Lucky Lion	1	1–2
Treat Truck and the Storm	2	2–4
Treat Truck and the Bank Robbery	3	3–5

63. **True Books**
Children's Press, 1224 W. Van Buren St., Chicago 60607. Each book contains 48 pages; interest level, grades 2–5.

True Book of Dinosaurs, by Mary Clark
True Book of the Mars Landing, by Leila Gemme
True Book of Metric Measurement, by June Behrens
True Book of Moonwalk Adventure, by Margaret Friskey

64. **Venture Books**

Leland Jacobs and John McInnes, Consultants. Garrard Publishing Co., Champaign, Ill. 61820. For first grade, there are 32 books of 40 pages each, on four levels of difficulty. Illustrative titles are given.

Level 1 (yellow cloth with green titles):
Bedtime for Bears
Count on Leo Lion
Dance to a Happy Song
Level 2 (yellow cloth, black titles):
The Sleep-leaping Kangaroo
Pink, Pink
April Fool!
Level 3 (yellow cloth, blue titles):
Too Fat to Fly
On With the Circus
No, No, No, and Yes
Level 4 (blue cloth, red titles):
Willie's Whizmobile
Drat the Dragon
A Dog for Danny
For second grade, there are twenty books of 64 pages each, on four levels of difficulty.
Level 1 (blue cloth, green titles):
That's How the Ball Bounces
Mrs. Twitter, the Animal Sitter
Level 2 (blue cloth, black titles):
The Jelly Bean Contest
Hello, People
Level 3 (blue cloth, blue titles):
Percy the Parrot Passes the Puck
The Chocolate Chip Mystery
Level 4 (blue cloth, red titles):
Here Comes Mirium the Mixed-up Witch
You're Sure Silly, Billy

65. **Wonder Story Books**

By Miriam Huber and Mabel O'Donnell. Harper & Row, Publishers, 10 E. 53rd St., New York 10022. Although written for children in the primary grades, these books of old fairy tales are good reading in the intermediate grades also.

Title	Reading Level
Once Upon a Time	Primer
I Know a Story	First Reader
It Happened One Day	Second Reader
After the Sun Sets	Third Reader

66. **World of Adventure Series**

By Henry A. Bamman and Robert Whitehead. Benefic Press, 10300 W. Roosevelt Road, Westchester, Ill. 60153. All of the following are fourth to ninth grade interest level.

Title	Reading Level
City Beneath the Sea	4
Fire on the Mountain	3
Flight to the South Pole	2
Hunting Grizzly Bears	3
Lost Uranium Mine	2
Sacred Well of Sacrifice	5
Search for Piranha	4
Viking Treasure	6

67. **Yearling Individualized Reading Program**

Noble and Noble, 1 Dag Hammerskjold Plaza, 245 E. 47th St., New York, N.Y. 10017.

LEVEL 3—for third grade—contains 75 books, two or three copies of each of thirty titles, and 36 teacher reference cards. Selected titles are:
Amelia Earhart, level 3.3
A Bear Called Paddington, level 4.1
Helen Keller, level 2.8
Charlotte's Web, level 3.5
LEVEL 4—for fourth grade—contains 65 books, two or three copies of each of twenty-five titles, and 31 teacher reference cards. Selected titles are:
All-of-a-Kind Family, level 4.0
Call Me Charley, level 3.3
Mystery of the Fat Cat, level 3.7
Story of Dr. Doolittle, level 3.8
LEVEL 5—for fifth grade—contains 65 books, two or three copies of each of twenty-five titles, and 32 teacher reference cards. Selected titles are:
Blue Ridge Bill, level 3.4
The Four Story Mistake, level 5.8
Roller Skates, level 4.7
The Secret Garden, level 5.5
LEVEL 6—for sixth grade—contains 65 books, two or three copies of each of twenty-five titles, and 31 teacher reference cards. Selected titles are:
The Black Cauldron, level 6.4
Edge of Two Worlds, level 3.7
The Singing Tree, level 4.6
The Wolves of Willoughby Chase, level 6.6

APPENDIX C

Selected Tests for Classroom Teachers

1. *Basic Achievement Skills Individual Screener,* 1983
   For all elementary reading levels. Tests reading, spelling, and mathematics. Psychological Corp.

2. *California Reading Tests,* 1970–1971 editions
   Level I for grades 1 and 2 requires 46 minutes working time; Level II for grades 2–4 requires 40 minutes working time; Level III for grades 4–6 requires 45 minutes working time; Level 4 for grades 7–9 and Level 5 for grades 9–14 each require about 50 minutes of working time. Tests give vocabulary, comprehension, and total scores. Levels I and II include a word attack test. McGraw-Hill. Two forms.

3. *Doren Diagnostic Reading Test,* 1973 edition
   Diagnoses weaknesses in primary and intermediate grade word recognition skills: letter recognition, beginning sounds, whole word recognition, words within words, speech consonants, ending sounds, blending, rhyming, vowels, discriminate guessing, spelling sight words. A group test requires one to three hours depending upon group size and reading level. American Guidance Service. One form.

4. *Durrell Analysis of Reading Difficulty,* 1980 edition
   Tests oral and silent reading, listening comprehension, word analysis and word recognition, visual and auditory memory of words, spelling and handwriting. Individually administered. Requires 40 to 50 minutes to administer but yields a valuable profile. Psychological Corp.

5. *Gates-MacGinitie Reading Tests,* 1978 edition
   Level A, grade 1; Level B, grade 2; Level C, grade 3; Level D, survey, grades 4–6; Level E, survey, grades 7–9; Level F, survey, grades 10–12. Two forms. Tests vocabulary and comprehension. Houghton Mifflin.

6. *Nelson Reading Skills Tests,* 1977 edition
   Level A, grades 3.0–4.5, requires 60 minutes working time; Level B, grades 4.5–6.0, requires 36 minutes working time; Level C, grades 7–9, requires 36 minutes working time. Two forms. Vocabulary and Comprehension. Houghton Mifflin.

7. *Nelson Reading Test,* 1962 edition

   Forms A and B, grades 3–9. Tests vocabulary and comprehension. Requires 30 minutes working time. Houghton Mifflin.

8. *Silent Reading Diagnostic Tests,* 1970 edition

   For students having difficulties in grades 2–6. Tests word recognition, words in context, syllabication, synthesis, beginning sounds, ending sounds. A group test. Rand McNally.

9. *Stanford Diagnostic Reading Test,* 1976 edition

   Red level, grades 1.6–3.5, working time 110 minutes; Green level, grades 2.6–5.5, working time 125 minutes; Blue level, grades 4.5–8.5, working time 91 minutes; Brown level, grades 9–13, working time 103 minutes. A group test. Psychological Corp.

10. *Stanford Reading Test,* 1973 edition

    Level Primary I, grades 1.5–2.4, working time 40 minutes; Level Primary II, grades 2.5–3.4, working time 90 minutes; Level Primary III, grades 3.5–4.4, working time 90 minutes; Level Intermediate I, grades 4.5–5.4, working time 85 minutes; Level Intermediate II, grades 5.5–6.9, working time 80 minutes; Level Advanced, grades 7.0–9.5. Three forms. Vocabulary and Comprehension. Psychological Corp.

Teaching the Directed Reading Lesson

A guided reading lesson usually follows five sequential steps. These are:

1. Motivating an interest in the lesson by:
   a. Studying the pictures that illustrate the story;
   b. Talking about new or unusual words in the story;
   c. Relating the ideas in the story to the background of experience of the class;
   d. Setting up a purpose for reading, that is, reading to find out something.

2. Teaching new vocabulary and reviewing words "that cause trouble" by:
   a. Presenting new words in meaningful ways;
   b. Practicing flash card drills;
   c. Playing games that teach or give practice matching, comparing, arranging, and so on, the basic vocabulary.

3. Guiding the silent reading of the lesson by:
   a. Asking guide questions so that pupils read to find specific information;
   b. Completing the story section by section with attention to understanding the plot of the story;
   c. Checking pupils' understanding as indicated throughout the story.

4. Interpreting the story by:
   a. Reading orally conversation parts;
   b. Reading orally favorite parts;
   c. Retelling the ideas in the story in proper sequence;
   d. Reading sentences or paragraphs to answer specific questions or to evaluate pupils' opinions;
   e. Evaluating the happenings in the story with such questions as:
      (1) Would you have done what Bob did? or
      (2) Is this true or only imaginary?

5. Providing related activities (follow-up) by:
   a. Using seatwork exercises to give:
      (1) Further practice on vocabulary;
      (2) Attention to phonic and structural skills;
      (3) Comprehension checks.
   b. Extending the lesson through:
      (1) Free reading at the book table;
      (2) Searching encyclopedias for additional information;
      (3) Art work, writing, dramatization as related to the lesson;
      (4) Shared oral reading in small groups.

These steps are amplified in the following outline only for clarification. The story "The Five Brothers" in the second reader *Come Along*[1] has been selected for this purpose. This story of the five Chinese brothers has been divided into four teaching units. The first of these units is summarized as it might be taught to a reading group in second grade.

1. Motivation

    It is suggested that teachers and pupils study three pictures: the mother with her five grown sons; one man gathering fish from the bottom of the sea; and one man with his arm in the mouth of a ferocious crocodile. The teacher may elicit the responses that the family lives in China, that the brothers may be fishermen, and that each brother can do something remarkable.

2. New vocabulary[2]

    The new words are introduced in context by use of the chalkboard with class discussion:

    a. Mrs. Brown is Jack's mother.
       She is Bill's mother too.
       Bill and Jack are *brothers*.
    b. We catch fish in the *sea*. (If the group does not pronounce "sea" quickly, the teacher may ask what word that begins with the sound "s" would make the sentence clear.)
    c. A crocodile has a very big *mouth*.
    d. Any box has a top.
       Does it have a *bottom* too?
    e. Bill got the first prize.
       Jack got the *second* prize.
    f. The ball hit Freddy, but it didn't *hurt* him.

    Six other words are similarly presented.

3. Guided silent reading

    Now we are ready to begin reading the story about the five brothers. . . . Read these three pages to yourself. Find out what the remarkable things were about the first two brothers. If you come to a word you do not know, use the beginning sound of that word and the meaning of what you are reading to help you decide what the word is. If you need more help, use the sound of any other part you know in the word.[3]

4. Interpreting the story[4]

    What was the remarkable thing about the first brother?
    How did this help him?
    Did the people know what the first brother could do?
    What was the remarkable thing about the second brother?
    Why did the second brother work at the zoo?
    Could anyone tell the brothers apart?
    Is this a true story? (It is really a Chinese fairy tale.)
    Read aloud the lines on page 154 that tell what the brothers could do and whether they told people about these things.
    Read the lines on page 155 that tell what the first brother did while he held the sea in his mouth and how he did it.
    Read the lines on page 156 that tell what was remarkable about the second brother.

5. Related activities[5]
  a. Word analysis and reading skills
    (1) Word recognition

brother	second	stretch
sea	fourth	burn
bottom	mouth	third

    (2) Initial consonant substitution
        Take *s* from *sea*, substitute *t* and make *tea*.
        Take *s* from *sea*, substitute *p* and make *pea*.
        Take *m* from *mouth*, substitute *s* and make *south*.
        Take *b* from *burn*, substitute *ch* and make *churn*.
    (3) Recognizing antecedents in sentences.
        Go upstairs and get the *shoes. They* have already been wrapped.
    (4) Reading new sentences using new words.
    (5) Associating letters and sounds:

whine	when	whistle	whit
thine	that	the	
thin	thing	thick	
shine	shoe	she	shin

    (6) Choosing and writing the correct word:
        He is my _____ .
            mother   brother   brown
        There is water in the _____ of the well.
            bounce   balloon   bottom
    (7) Choosing the correct word:

learn	to find out about something
	to go to sleep
follow	to go before
	to come after

    (8) Using beginning sounds:
        Which of these could you put on your head?
            good   hood   stood
        Which one of these do you have on your feet?
            toes   foes   goes

  b. Extending the lesson[6]
    (1) The lesson for Part One of "The Five Brothers" does not suggest any activity for this part. However, at the end of Part Two, it is suggested that the class may draw pictures to illustrate sentences:
        No. 3: It is brown.
               It is up in a tree.
               A bird made it.
               It has three babies in it.
    (2) At the end of the story of "The Five Brothers," it is suggested that individual pupils may wish to read *The True Book of Birds We Know* by Margaret Friskey.[7]

Notes

1. Paul McKee, et al., *Come Along,* revised, Teacher's Edition (Boston: Houghton Mifflin, 1957), pp. 327–37.
2. Ibid., pp. 328–29.
3. Ibid., p. 330.
4. Ibid., pp. 330–31.
5. Ibid., pp. 333–35.
6. Ibid., p. 348 and p. 367.
7. Margaret Friskey, *The True Book of Birds We Know* (Chicago: Children's Press, 1954).

APPENDIX E

The Informal Reading Inventory

Making an informal reading inventory (IRI) is a task each teacher should accomplish. The material for the stories may come from the children's readers, from trade books, from stories they write, or from stories made by the teacher. After stories are selected, they will need to be assigned reading levels. Levels can be estimated by using Fry's Readability Graph. Then, questions must be prepared. The questions should be written at different levels of thinking. Questions about word meanings may also be asked. Finally, the IRI needs to be tried out on several children to see if the assigned reading levels and the questions are appropriate.

Passages from a teacher-made IRI are shown here to be used as a guide for constructing one for classroom use. In practice, the teacher would need one with several more levels than are provided in this sample.

Informal Reading Inventory

First-Reader Level (Oral)

Motivating Statement: This story is about a child whose father went away on a trip. Let's find out what happens.

THE JET AIRPLANE TRIP

My father went on a jet airplane.
He went to a city far away.
He flew for three hours.
He had work to do in the city.
The work took one week.
It was very hard.
He had to talk to people and write what they said.
I was glad when he came home.
He came down the steps and hugged my mom and me.
He brought us both presents.

Questions:

1. What did the child tell that shows the city was far away?
2. What were the two kinds of work the father had to do?
3. How do we know that the family was glad to be together again?
4. How many days was the father gone?
5. Where was the father just before he came down the steps and hugged the family?

		Summary:	
No. of words	70	Word recognition:	
No. of syllables	77	No. of miscues	_____
No. of sentences	10	% accuracy	_____
		Level	_____
		Comprehension	
		No. of errors	_____
		% accuracy	_____
		Level	_____
		Overall Level	_____

Informal Reading Inventory

First-Reader Level (Silent)

Motivating Statement: This story is about two children who went to play. Let's see what happened during the play time.

PLAYING ON THE MESA

My friend and I went to the mesa to play.
Our moms knew we were going.
We didn't go far.
We could still see our houses.
First, we made a road for our toy cars.
A lizard ran on it.
We thought it was funny that a lizard ran on our road.
We made our cars go on the road, too.
Then we made a parking lot.
We parked our cars in it.
All at once we stopped!
There was a noise—a buzz!
Then we saw the snake.
We took our cars and ran home as fast as we could.

Questions:

1. Who knew the children were going to play on the mesa?
2. How did the children know they were not far from home?
3. Why do you think the children thought it was funny that the lizard ran on the road?
4. What made the children stop playing?
5. Why did the children run home as fast as they could?

No. of words	101	Summary:
No. of syllables	107	Comprehension
No. of sentences	14	No. of errors _____
		% accuracy _____
		Level _____

Informal Reading Inventory

Second-Reader Level (Oral)

Motivating Statement: This is a story of a child whose big brother bought a snow-mobile. Let's see how he felt about it.

STEVE'S SNOWMOBILE

My big brother's name is Steve.
Last year he decided to buy a snowmobile.
He saved his money until he had enough to buy it.
He went to some stores.
He found the one he wanted.
When it began to snow, he took it up in the mountains.
He rode it along the roads.
He didn't want to hurt the trees in the forest.
He didn't want to scare the animals, either.
Once the snowmobile went into a snow bank.
Steve was covered with snow.
When he got home, he told me about the fun he had.
Someday I want a snowmobile, too.

Questions:

1. How did Steve get the money to pay for the snowmobile?
2. Where did Steve ride the snowmobile?
3. How do you know that Steve cared about the plants and animals in the forest?
4. What do you think a snow bank looks like?
5. What did the person who wrote the story decide about snowmobiles?

		Summary:
No. of words	108	Word Recognition
No. of syllables	126	No. of miscues _____
No. of sentences	14	% accuracy _____
		Level _____
		Comprehension
		No. of errors _____
		% accuracy _____
		Level _____
		Overall level _____

Informal Reading Inventory

Second-Reader Level (Silent)

Motivating Statement: This is a story about a girl who visited her friend and learned about other families.

ANN'S FAMILY

I went to visit my friend.
Her name is Ann, and she lives across the city.
Her grandfather and grandmother live with them.
Her family is different than mine.
Grandmother stays at home and takes care of the children.
They all live in an apartment.
Other families live in the building, too.
You can hear them laugh and talk.
All the families like each other.

At night Ann's family comes home.
They eat in the kitchen.
When I was there, they didn't have enough chairs.
So Ann and I watched TV and ate.
At bedtime, Ann and I slept on the sofa.
She doesn't have her own room.
When I got home I told my mother that families live in all sorts of ways.

Questions:

1. Who looked after Ann and the other children in the family?
2. Where did Ann's family live?
3. Why did Ann and her guest eat in front of the TV?
4. What is a sofa?
5. What did the writer mean when she told her mother that families live in all sorts of ways?

No. of words	124	Summary:	
No. of syllables	134	Comprehension:	
No. of sentences	16	No. of errors	_____
		% accuracy	_____
		Level	_____

Informal Reading Inventory

Third-Reader Level (Oral)

Motivating Statement: Have you ever lost a book? This is about a child who did. Let's see if it was found.

THE DAY I LOST MY LIBRARY BOOK

I love to read books. I am lucky because our school has a good library, and we can check out three books each week. Ever since I was little, my mother has warned me to take good care of books, especially borrowed ones.

That Monday I checked out two mysteries and a thin joke book. By Friday I had read them and told the jokes to my friends.

When it was library time on Monday, I got the two mysteries out of my desk. But the joke book was missing. I thought my friends had taken it. They got mad when I accused them. I looked everywhere, but I couldn't find it. The teacher said we had to go to the library. She said I just wouldn't be able to check out more books until the joke book was found. I was so upset!

Then my spelling workbook fell out on the floor and the joke book fell out of the spelling workbook. I was very happy and I told my friends I was sorry I had accused them of taking it. So I got to check out more books after all.

Questions:

1. Why do you think losing a book was so upsetting to the writer?
2. What did the writer do when the book couldn't be found?
3. What did the teacher say would happen because the book was missing?
4. Why do you think the child missed the joke book in the desk?
5. What does *warned* mean?

		Summary:	
No. of words	192	Word recognition:	
No. of syllables	235	No. of miscues	_____
No. of sentences	16	% accuracy	_____
		Level	_____
		Comprehension	
		No. of errors	_____
		% accuracy	_____
		Level	_____
		Overall Level	_____

Informal Reading Inventory

Third-Reader Level (Silent)

Motivating Statement: This story is about some neighbors who had a problem. Let's see what it was.

NEIGHBOR DOGS

We have a little black poodle. He stays in the house most of the time. He loves to watch TV and sleep in my dad's special chair. When Dad arrives home, Teddy has to get out of the chair.

Our neighbors have a big, black German shepherd dog. He barks a lot and will try to attack anyone who goes in his yard. He is a good guard dog, and the neighbors are all glad he guards our houses.

One day Teddy got in the yard with the German shepherd and was attacked by the big dog. My mother and I couldn't help Teddy. The big dog's owner came out and got Teddy away.

Poor Teddy had a torn ear and a cut on his shoulder. We took him to the vet and got stitches in the cuts. Teddy cried a lot, but he got well. He still sleeps in my dad's chair. He knows not to go in the German shepherd's yard.

Questions:

1. Compare how the two dogs lived.
2. Why did the neighbors like the German shepherd?
3. What mistake did Teddy make?
4. Why do you think the writer and the mother couldn't help Teddy?
5. Why did Teddy cry after his trip to the vet?

No. of words	165	Summary:	
No. of syllables	193	Comprehension:	
No. of sentences	15	No. of errors	_____
		% accuracy	_____
		Level	_____

APPENDIX F

Home Information Questionnaire

THE UNIVERSITY OF NEW MEXICO

MANZANITA CENTER

HOME INFORMATION QUESTIONNAIRE   Remedial Reading Program

_____   _____
Name of student   Date

The staff at Manzanita Center wants to provide the best possible reading program for your son/ daughter. The information asked for below will be helpful in achieving that goal.

1. We are interested in your observations of your child's reading performance. Does your he/ she:

   a. Read orally? _____ Read silently? _____

   b. Move his/her lips when reading silently? _____

   c. Follow the line with finger or pointer? _____

   d. Hold book about 16 inches from the eyes? _____

   e. Appear relaxed when reading? _____

   f. Choose to read on his/her own? _____

   g. Talk to you about what he/she has read? _____

   h. Ask you to pronounce words? _____

   j. Become easily distracted when reading? _____

   Please attach any additional comments about your child's reading performance.

2. Good vision and hearing are important in learning to read.

   Has your child had a vision test? _____ When? _____

   Results? _____

   Has your child had a hearing test? _____ When? _____

   Results? _____

   Does your child: blink constantly _____ ; rub the eyes _____ ; squint? _____ ;

   complain about not being able to see _____ ; complain of headaches after reading?

   _____ ; have red eyes frequently? _____ ; wear his/her glasses when reading

   _____ ?

Does your child: Turn up the TV or radio abnormally loud? _____ : talk loudly? _____ ; ask you to repeat statements? _____ ; have problems following directions? _____ ; fail to respond to what you say occasionally _____

3. A student's health, both past and present, may be important to present reading performance. It may also be a factor in future achievement. Please give information about the items below: Please give approximate date each occurred.

Childhood diseases	Surgery	Accidents	Allergies

4. Reading is closely related to general speech and language development. It would be helpful to know the following:

   a. At about what age did your child begin to talk? _____

   b. At about what age did your child talk in sentences? _____

   c. Were there problems with making specific sounds? _____
      If so, which ones? _____

   d. What language or languages did your child learn to speak? _____
      _____

   e. At about what age did your child start noticing signs and asking to have them read?
      _____

   f. At about what age did your child start having books and stories read to him/her?
      _____

5. Emotions also seem to influence reading achievement.

   Does your child: seem to worry about little things? _____ get nervous? _____ ; show nervous mannerisms? (nail biting, complain of stomachache, twisting hair, picking nose) _____ ; cry easily? _____ ; make friends easily? _____ ; prefer to play alone? _____ ; prefer to play in a group? _____ ; act tolerant of others? _____ ; adjust to new situations easily? _____ .

6. Your child's attitude toward reading and school are important factors in his/her future reading success.

   Does your child: like school? _____ ; like to read? _____ ; tell you what happens at school? _____ ; like the teacher (s)? _____ ; have a good attendance record? _____ .

7. Has anyone in the family tried to help your child with his/her reading? What kind of things were done to help? Do you feel the family efforts were helpful? (Please write comments on the back of this form.)

8. Why do you think your student is having reading problems?

   _____

9. Have you talked with the school teacher(s) about the reading situation? What were the teacher's suggestions? Did the school suggest remedial help? _____

   _____

10. Please add any other comments which could be helpful in planning a program for your child. (Use the back side of this form or attach your response.)

Instructional Materials for Word Identification and Comprehension

1. Anderson, Donald, *New Practice Readers,* 2d. ed., (New York: McGraw-Hill Book Co., 1978). Each book contains a series of short stories with accompanying vocabulary words and comprehension questions. The entire books are taped so that children may use them independently.

Book A	Grade 2	Book E	Grade 6
Book B	Grade 3	Book F	Grade 7
Book C	Grade 4	Book G	Grade 8
Book D	Grade 5		

2. Anderson, Murray, George Turner, Millard Black, and Evelyn Taylor, *Reading Skills Texts* (Workbooks). (Columbus, Ohio: Merrill, 1970).

Pre-Primer:	We Can Read	Grade 4:	Ben, the Traveler
Grade 1:	Bibs	Grade 5:	Tom, the Reporter
Grade 2:	Nicky	Grade 6:	Pat, the Pilot
Grade 3:	Uncle Benny		

3. *Barnell Loft Multiple Skills Series,* (Baldwin, New York: Barnell Loft, 1982). This series is designed for primary, intermediate, and mid-school levels.

4. Benner, Patricia Ann, and Virginia Law, *Troubleshooters I.* (Boston: Houghton Mifflin, 1975). This program includes eight consumable workbooks to teach English language communication skills in junior and senior high school, and it is self-teaching, self-correcting, and self-directing. Titles: *Sound Out, Sound Off, Spelling Action, Word Attack, Word Mastery, Sentence Strength, Punctuation Power,* and *English Achievement.* Teacher's guides are included. Spirit Masters are also available.

5. Boning, Richard A., *Cloze Connections.* (Baldwin, New York: Barnell Loft, 1980). Materials are written at grade levels third through ninth.

6. Boning, Richard A., *Specific Skills Series Skills.* (Baldwin, New York: Barnell Loft).
   Detecting the Sequence, Levels 1–6 and Adv, 1982
   Using the Context, Levels 1–6 and Adv, 1982
   Getting the Facts, Levels 1–6, 1982
   Working with Sounds, Levels 1–6 and Adv, 1982
   Drawing Conclusions, Levels 1–6, 1982
   Getting the Main Idea, Levels 1–6, 1982
   Locating the Answer, Levels 1–6 and Adv, 1982
   Following Directions, Levels 1–6 and Adv, 1982
   Using Guide Words, Levels 4–6 and Adv, 1974

Using an Index, Levels 3–6 and Adv, 1975
Syllabication, Levels 2–6 and Adv, 1975
Using a Table of Contents, Levels 1–6 and Adv, 1975
Understanding Questions, Levels 1–6 and Adv, 1975
These skills books provide exercises that focus on necessary subskills to improve reading with understanding. Pretests and posttests are provided. Many new exercise booklets are added to the list each year.

7. *Bracken Specific Reading Skills Program.* (Dallas: Jones-Kenilworth Co., Inc., 1973). Exercises are graduated in levels of difficulty from first to eighth grade.

8. *Building Reading Competencies.* (Dobbs Ferry, New York: Oceana Educational Communications, Inc., 1981). *Structural Analysis* was prepared for levels A through E, as was *Antonyms, Synonyms,* and *Analogies.*

9. Cohen, Lawrence H., *Neighborhood Stories.* (Providence, R.I.: Jamestown Publishers, 1982). These materials are designed for the intermediate grades.

10. *Developing a Sight Vocabulary.* (Baldwin, New York: Barnell Loft, 1983). This same company developed *A Word Recognition Program,* 1982. The levels are: A1, first grade; A2, first grade; B, second grade; C, third grade; and D, fourth grade.

11. Durham, John, Lorenz Graham, Kirstin Hunter, Jean Merrill, and Elsa Grasser, *Directions.* (Boston: Houghton Mifflin). Readability: Fourth grade level measured by the Dale-Chall readability formula. There are two reading levels: Levels I and II. Each level contains two anthologies, six novelettes, teacher's guides, and two workbooks.

12. *Hits Pak.* (San Juan Capistrano, California: Modu Learn, Inc., 1976). This program designed by Matt Glavach uses popular songs to help upper elementary grade students to adults who need primary grade reading abilities.

13. Kelley, Sandra, Project manager. *Spotlight on Reading.* (New York: Random House, 1984). Each level contains stories followed by questions and covers eight skills: main idea, sequence, critical reading, story elements, inference, vocabulary, details, and charts, maps and globes. Level 2, 1.5–2.5; Level 3, 2.5–3.5; Level 4, 3.5–4.5; Level 5, 4.5–5.5; Level 6, 5.5–6.5; Level 7, 6.5–7.5; Level 8, 7.5–8.5.

14. Lapp, Diane and James Flood, *Clues for Better Reading.* (North Billerica, Mass.: Curriculum Associates, 1982). The kits are designed for grades 2–3, 4–6, and 7–9.

15. Liddle, William, *Reading for Concepts.* (Manchester, Mo.: Webster Division, McGraw-Hill, 1977). A series of graded workbooks which includes factual articles and worthwhile information, drawn from many academic disciplines. Test exercises cause students to think evaluatively about factual details, using context, drawing inferences, recognizing antecedents, finding key ideas, verifying information, and recognizing cause and effect. The readability levels of the books are roughly: Book A, 1.9; B, 2.5; C, 3.2; D, 3.9; E, 4.6; F, 5.2; G, 5.8, and H, 6.4. They are available in either hard or soft cover. Informal tests for placement at each level are available.

16. Potter, Dan, *Little Trolley Books.* (Oklahoma City: The Economy Co., 1977). The collection of books is meant for readers at the primary levels. Examples of titles are *Water, Water Everywhere; Columbus;* and *A Workday in the City.*

17. *Reader's Digest Reading Skill Builders.* (Pleasantville, N.Y.: Educational Division, Reader's Digest Services, Inc.). The format is similar to Reader's Digest. There are two books for each reading level, grades 1–6. Levels A and B are for adult reading level and are somewhat easier than grade 3, but with the same format.

18. *Reading Comprehension Series, The,* Levels A–H. (Bingham, Mass.: Teaching Resources Corp., 1983). This series is for elementary students.

19. Ribisl, Jean and Paul Ribisl, *Consonant Capers.* (Boston: Houghton Mifflin, 1975). This includes finger plays, stories, tongue twisters, riddles, activities and games.

20. Smith, Nila B., *Be A Better Reader Series,* 5th ed., (Englewood Cliffs, N.J.: Prentice-Hall, Inc., 1984). The levels are planned for the middle grades through high school.

21. Weinberg, Joel, *Troubleshooters II.* (Boston: Houghton Mifflin, 1975). This program includes six consumable workbooks that teach structural analysis, vocabulary, and comprehension in junior and senior high school. Titles: *Word Recognition, Vocabulary, Spelling and Parts of Speech, Reading Rate and Comprehension, Reading in Specific Subjects,* and *Reading and Study Skills.* Teacher's guides are included. Spirit Masters are also available.

22. Wolfe, Josephine B., *Merrill Phonics Skilltext Series: The Sound and Structure of Words.* (Columbus, Ohio: Charles E. Merrill, 1973).

Glossary

Ability grouping A process by which classroom teachers subdivide their classes into small groups for efficient teaching. Many teachers provide several reading groups in their classes based on general reading ability.

Accountability The responsibility of educators to do their job—and to provide measurable results to show success of the educational endeavor.

Advance organizer A passage written as a clarifying structure to introduce material to be read later.

Advocacy Support and encouragement given by parents and teachers for the best possible education of children.

Affect A measure of a person's emotional response to any situation (feelings, interests, attitudes already learned.) As contrasted with cognition (knowing and understanding), affect measures personal responses to whatever is read.

Affixes Prefixes and suffixes.

Ambidexterity Ability to use either hand for many activities usually done only with the right hand.

Ancillary services Related, or auxiliary services provided to insure that children's programs are most successfully augmented.

Anomaly Deviation from the common rule, or type or form; an abnormality.

Audiometer A device for testing hearing.

Auditory discrimination Ability to differentiate between different sounds, for example, *big* and *pig*.

Basal readers Carefully graded (sequenced) series of texts with workbooks. The detailed teacher's manual provides for teaching word recognition and comprehension skills.

Basic sight vocabulary Those high frequency words (*the, in, is, for, to*) that constitute about 65 percent of the words in primary reading and 50 percent of the words in the upper elementary grades.

Behavior modification A highly structured program in a planned environment in which the desired behavior (either social or academic) is immediately rewarded (reinforced). The concept of immediate feedback is to praise, reward, or reinforce desirable behavior and to ignore or not reward undesirable behavior.

Bibliotherapy Literally, "treatment with books." It is a strategy of asking clients to read books in which characters have kinds of problems or handicaps that may enable them to better understand their own and make a better adjustment by finding out how others have managed.

Bilingualism The ability to use two languages. Some people hope this means literacy skills in two languages; there are many levels of bilingualism.

Blend Two or three consonant letters that retain the sound of each consonant when pronounced; *tr*ap; *spr*ing; *spl*endid.

Breve The arc placed over a vowel (ă) to indicate the short sound.

Capacity reading level The highest grade level at which the students understand at least 75 percent of the ideas in material read aloud by an examiner.

Chapter I Classes that are federally funded for students who read below grade level and come from lower socio-economic groups.

Cloze technique A strategy of deleting every nth word in a passage (n may be any number from 5 to 12). Students develop the ability to anticipate meaning in print by being forced to make closure wherever words are deleted. Cloze can also be used in practice exercises to delete only nouns, prepositions, or other classes of words.

Cognition The process of perceiving or knowing.

Cohesion The linguistics elements speakers use to connect parts of text. The meaning of one element of text depends on another element.

Configuration The general form or shape of a word.

Congenital From birth (existing at birth).

Content fields Organized bodies of knowledge commonly called mathematics, social science, and so forth. Reading is *one tool* for learning in content fields.

Context The linguistic, social, emotional and physical settings in which language, written and spoken, is produced.

Context clue Identification of a new word in context by anticipation of its meaning from the other words and ideas.

Criterion A standard by which a test may be judged; a set of scores, ratings.

Criterion referenced test A test that measures students' performances on criteria specifically set by the examiner. The criteria detail what will be mastered and the level of performance required on that specific test. Criterion referenced tests may be contrasted with norm-referenced tests in which students' performances are compared to the general ability of large numbers of others who took the same test.

Decoding Changing the written message into a spoken message; understanding the relationship between the writing system and the more familiar sound system; the process of rendering written or printed symbols into speech.

Deep structure The underlying meaning or the semantic interpretation of the sentence—what the sentence really means. "I had Mary for lunch" means "I invited Mary to eat with me."

Diacritical marks Symbols that designate particular sounds of letters: ă, a, ä.

Diagnostic test A test designed to determine specific areas of weakness or strength; to determine the nature of weakness by finding, for example, some sub-tests in a given battery on which the client is unable to perform.

Dialect Any form of the language spoken by a large number, or a specific group, of people. Dialect differs from the standard form of the language.

Dialectology The study of variations in language production as they are influenced by social, regional, and temporal conditions.

Differential diagnosis The process of analyzing the nature of a given student's learning or behavior problem.

Digraph Two letters of the alphabet that form a single phoneme. There are consonant digraphs; sh, th, ch, wh, ng, ph. There are vowel digraphs: ea, ai, oa.

Diphthong Two vowels together which are glided to form a sound to which both contribute, as in *oi*l and b*oy*. A glide from one vowel sound to another in the syllable as in c*ow* and f*ou*l.

Directed reading A reading lesson, usually with a basal reader, including building motivation, teaching new words, guiding silent reading, discussing the story, and rereading parts orally or doing other follow-up work.

Discourse analysis The study of units of language, oral or written, that are larger than sentences and the settings in which the language samples are produced.

Dyslexia A label for the disorder in which students do not attain the communication skills of reading, writing and spelling commensurate with their general learning (intellectual) abilities.

Environmental print Print found apart from the usual sources in schools—books and related materials. May be in the classroom environment (announcements or assignments) or in the non-school environment (street signs, store names, labels on products).

Etiology Pertaining to the causes of a disorder.

Expository text Discourse that is arranged logically or chronologically; usually found in subject area texts or reference materials.

Eyedness The preference or dominance of one eye in perceptual motor tasks.

Feedback Information individuals receive from intrinsic or extrinsic sources supporting their decisions about the accuracy of their responses or understandings.

Free reading Independent reading for one's own pleasure or to obtain information.

Frustration level The lowest level at which the student fails to recognize more than five words in 100 words in context or comprehends less than 70 percent of the ideas read.

Gloss Notes written in the margins of texts that help a reader focus on the content of what is being read or on the reading process. The notes may be written on strips of paper and laid along side the text.

Grade Equivalent The grade level for which a given score is the estimated value: a 5.7 is the seventh month of fifth grade.

Grapheme A minimum unit of the writing system as in the letter "b" or the digraph "ch."

Grapheme-phoneme correspondence The relationship between the grapheme of writing and the phoneme of speech.

Hyperactivity A higher than normal level of activity that is chronic in nature and is often characterized by distractability, emotional instability, poor social skills and inability to adjust to environmental changes.

Idiom A phrase whose meaning is derived from sources other than the common definitions of its words. An idiom is based on connotative, rather than denotative, meanings.

Independent reading level On the IRI, the students score no less than 99 percent in word recognition and have no difficulties in understanding the context.

Individualized educational program (IEP) A curriculum plan for any child which includes objectives, methodology, specific curriculum changes, and any classroom adjustments. IEPs are required by PL 94–142 for all exceptional children.

Individualized reading A method of teaching reading based on self-seeking, self-selecting, and self-pacing in which the teacher plans individual conferences with students. The teacher keeps individual progress reports for students on the basis of these conferences.

Inference The process of obtaining the intended meanings in discourse. Requires deriving implied, rather than directly stated, ideas.

Informal reading inventory (IRI) A test in which the student reads from a series of passages, easy to more difficult, until he or she reaches the frustration level. By recording all errors in word recognition and measuring comprehension, the teacher can determine independent, instructional, and frustration levels of reading. If the teacher uses the same series of paragraphs and reads to the student beyond the frustration level of reading, the highest level of hearing comprehension, or capacity level for reading, can also be estimated.

Instructional reading level On an IRI, the highest level at which the student scores 95 percent in word recognition and at least 75 percent in comprehension; the level at which the student can make progress in reading growth.

Intelligence quotient A ratio of mental ability (I.Q.) of an individual based on performance on an intelligence test and the chronological age.

Kinesics The term applied to what people do when they communicate through body movement or gesture such as a frown, a stern look, or a defiant posture.

Language A system of communication by means of spoken or written symbols.

Language experience approach (LEA) A method of reading instruction in which learners dictate stories from their own experience. The stories are written by the teacher and used as the content of reading lessons.

Limited English proficiency (LEP) child The child with less than an adequate command of English for basic interpersonal communicative needs and/or cognitive academic language demands.

Look-say approach A method of beginning reading instruction in which teachers stress word recognition without intensive work in phonics in teaching an initial sight vocabulary.

Macron A diacritical mark (ā) to indicate, for example, that the long vowel sound is found in the word "māte."

Mainstreaming The process by which many exceptional children are integrated into the regular classroom setting for some part of, or for all of, the school day.

Miscue The unexpected response to written language so that the reader's pronunciation is at variance with the writer's words.

Morpheme The smallest unit of meaning in a language. *Girls* has two morphemes, *girl* which has meaning by itself and *s* which is a bound morpheme which does not have meaning by itself.

Morphology The study of the structure of words, derivations, inflections, and the addition of prefixes and suffixes.

Myopia Nearsightedness.

Narrative A discourse form in which a story is told.

Non-reader The individual who cannot read even after considerable instruction.

Normal curve The symmetrical, bell-shaped curve of the normal distribution.

Norm-referenced test Any standardized test in which a given student's performance is compared with the performance of many others of similar age and educational achievement.

Ophthalmograph A device for photographing eye movements during reading.

Pacing Controlling the rate of reading; also assigning materials to students at a rate that insures success at a given stage of reading development.

Percentile A point on a scale of scores in a distribution below which a given per cent of scores occur. Thirty-eight percent of the scores fall below the 38th percentile.

Perseveration The persistence of an activity or a response after the stimulus or need is past.

Phoneme The smallest speech sound unit; the *f, a,* and *t* in *fat* are each phonemes.

Phonemics The study of language in terms of its sound elements: the phonemes.

Phonetics The study and classification of all the sounds in human communication.

Phonic analysis A process of "sounding out" words according to the letter-sound relationships.

Phonics The study of sound-letter relationships in reading and spelling.

Phonogram The consonant and vowel of a word ending such as "ill" or "ent" to which single consonants can be added to form words, as in *bill* and *sent*. Sometimes referred to as word families, *as, at, ap, an.*

Phonology The study of the sounds of the language.

Predictable book A book that is written so that the text is likely to be identified from the repetitive patterns, sentence meanings, and the pictures.

Prefix A syllable before the root word that usually changes the meaning, as in *im*possible.

Profile A chart, or diagram, that shows an individual's relative position in the performance of several traits or tests—performances vary from trait to trait or test to test.

Random sample A scientific selection of a total population—operating on the principle that each one had equal chance of selection—without bias.

Range The distance between the highest and lowest measures of a distribution.

Rapport Mutually harmonious working relationships.

Readability The level of difficulty of a book or article as measured by any one of several readability formulas.

Reading expectancy The level at which given students would be expected to read as judged by their intellectual maturity.

Realia Real things as opposed to representations, or abstractions, from a time in history or from a geographical area.

Redundancy The duplication of information in a sentence. The duplication is provided by the syntax, number, gender, or verb forms.

Reinforcement The strengthening of a response by reward or satisfaction.

Retention Learning that permits later recall or recognition.

Reversals Producing symbols backwards: *b* for *d; n* for *u; how* for *who;* or one may reverse Arabic numbers: ɘ for 6; ɘ for 9. the word *strephosymbolia* is sometimes used in referring to reversals.

Root A basic word form from which new words are developed by the addition of suffixes or prefixes.

Scaffolding The strategies skilled persons use to help novices learn what *they* want to learn. Reading scaffolding might include pointing to the place to begin reading or helping break a word into parts so it can be pronounced.

Schema A dynamic data structure, in the mind, for representing the generalized concepts for understanding the environment; a building block of cognition.

Schwa An unaccented vowel. Written as an upside down *e,* it has the sound of *uh* as in *a*bout.

Self-concept The status of one's ego; the ability to accept oneself as one is. Also requires an understanding of oneself in relation to other people.

Semantics The study of meaning in words, phrases, thought units.

Sight word A word that is memorized and recognized as a unit.

Sinistral Innately left-handed. Opposed to dextral.

Skimming Very rapid reading through a selection for a specific purpose.

Standard deviation A measure of variability of scores around an average. The closer the scores cluster around the average, the smaller the standard deviation.

Standard score Statistically manipulated scores converted from raw scores for ease of interpretation.

Standardized test A systematic sample of performance obtained under prescribed conditions, scored according to definite rules, and capable of evaluation by reference to normative information. Validity and realiability are established for standardized tests.

Stanine One of the steps in a nine-point scale of normalized standard scores with a mean of 5 and a standard deviation of 2.

Strabismus Squint or cross-eye.

Strephosymbolia Literally, twisted symbols, as in the reversing of *was* and *saw* or *left* and *felt.*

Structural analysis Analysis of words by affixes, roots, syllabication, or their compound parts.

Structured overview A diagram or outline prepared with the learners to show the relationships existing between related ideas; a cognitive map.

Study skills Techniques and strategies readers apply to the acquisition, retention, and application of information and concepts.

Suffixes Affixes at the ends of words: *ing, ful, ness, ment*. Derivational suffixes change the part of speech and the meaning: *ment, ism;* inflectional suffixes do not change the part of speech or the meaning: *ing, ed*.

Supplementary reading Reading assigned to reinforce, or add to, some learned ability in reading or any other subject.

Surface structure The observed-phoneme-grapheme representation of the sentence.

Survey test A standardized test that measures general achievement in a subject or area.

Syllabication Division of words into syllables, as *com for ta ble*.

Syndrome A constellation of symptoms of a given condition.

Synonym A word that has the same, or nearly the same, meaning as another word, as happy—pleased.

Syntax The grammar of the language, that is, the rules by which sentence structure is regulated.

Tachistoscope A device in which exposure time is controlled to permit flashing words, letters, numbers, or figures on a screen.

Tactile Pertaining to the sense of touch.

Taxonomy A classification for systematically labeling, and organizing characteristics in a given field; Bloom's taxonomy for cognition: knowledge, comprehension, application, analysis, synthesis, and evaluation.

Text A verbal record of communication; written material; the theme of a discourse.

Trade books The books provided in the school library for general information, research, and pleasure. Not part of any basal reading series.

Validity The extent to which a test serves the purpose for which it is used.

Visual discrimination Recognizing likenesses and differences in symbols, words, and phrases. One discriminates *b* from *d; horse* from *house*.

Visual memory span The number of items that can be recalled after seeing them presented.

Visual perception Receiving images and interpreting them through the sense of sight.

Vowel In the alphabet, *a, e, i, o, u,* and sometimes *w* and *y*.

Vowel digraph Two vowels together with only one vowel sound, as in cr*ea*m.

Webbing The process of representing schematically ideas that relate to a central concept and the relationships between those ideas.

Word analysis Analyzing a new word into known elements for the purpose of identification.

Word blindness A label indicating the inability to read words owing to pathological causes, either congenital or acquired.

Word calling Generally refers to the students who pronounce the words correctly but do not demand meaning from the passage. One can "word call" all the words in a sentence correctly but the sentence will make no sense.

Author Index

Subject Index